FINANCIAL ACCOUNTING THEORY

Third Edition

WILLIAM R. SCOTT
University of Waterloo

Toronto

To Mary Ann, Julie, Martha,
Kathy, Paul and Cary

Canadian Cataloguing in Publication Data

Scott, William R. (William Robert), 1931-
Financial accounting theory

3rd ed.
Includes bibliographical references and index.
ISBN 0-13-065577-5

Accounting. I. Title.

HF5635.S36 2003   657'.044   C2002-900587-6

ISBN: 0-13-065577-5

Vice President, Editorial Director: Michael J. Young
Senior Acquisitions Editor: Samantha Scully
Executive Marketing Manager: Cas Shields
Developmental Editor: Laurie Goebel
Production Editor: Judith Scott
Copy Editor: Karen Hunter
Production Coordinator: Andrea Falkenberg
Page Layout: Heidi Palfrey
Art Director: Mary Opper
Interior Design: Julia Hall
Cover Design: Jennifer Federico
Cover Image: Photodisc

6 7 8 9 10   07 06 05 04

Printed and bound in the United States of America.

The articles "Study of CEO Compensation Finds Surprises," "Taking Stock – Big Firms Rely More on Options But Fail to End Pay Criticism," "Natural-Gas Producers Bristle at 'Snapshot' Accounting," "Presidential Life is Accused by SEC of Overstatement," "Former Critic of Big Stock Plans for CEOs Now Supports Them," "Wrongheaded Hit at Retiree Benefit," "GE Posts 6.2% Rise in 4th-Quarter Net, Record 1992 Profit," "The Pros Get Trounced in Stock Contest," "RJR Nabisco's Use of Accounting Technique Dealing with Goodwill Is Getting a Hard Look," "Firms Get Around Big One-Time Earnings Hits to Save Executive Bonuses," "SEC Rule Forces More Disclosure," "Accounting Rule-Making Board's Proposal Draws Fire," "U.S. Deloitte Said to Be Close to Thrift Pact," "Exxon Told to Pay $5 Billion for Valdez Spill," "Bank Regulators Drop Plan Pegged to Market Value of Securities," "Few Support Any New Rules on Derivatives," "Compaq Posts Record Results but Stock Falls," "Bausch and Lomb Posts 4th-Quarter Loss, Says SEC Has Begun Accounting Probe," "Royal Dutch/Shell Net Rises 31%; Shares Fall on Cautious Outlook," "Bill Curbing Investors' Lawsuits Wins SEC Support of 'Safe-Harbor' Provision," "Investors Thirst for Liquid Stocks" paraphrased by permission of *The Wall Street Journal*, © Dow Jones & Company, Inc.

CONTENTS

PREFACE

This book began as a series of lesson notes for a financial accounting theory course of the Certified General Accountants' Association of Canada. The lesson notes grew out of a conviction that we have learned a great deal about the role of financial accounting and reporting in our society from securities markets and information economics-based research conducted over many years, and that financial accounting theory comes into its own when we formally recognize the information asymmetries that pervade business relationships.

The challenge was to organize this large body of research into a unifying framework and to explain it in such a manner that professionally oriented students would both understand and accept it as relevant to the financial accounting environment and ultimately to their own professional careers.

This book seems to have achieved its goals. In addition to being part of the CGA program of professional studies for a number of years, it has been extensively class-tested in financial accounting theory courses at the University of Waterloo, Queen's University, and several other universities, both at the senior undergraduate and professional Master's levels. I am encouraged by the fact that, by and large, the students comprehend the material and, indeed, are likely to object if the instructor follows it too closely in class. This frees up class time to expand coverage of areas of interest to individual instructors and/or to motivate particular topics by means of articles from the financial press and professional and academic literature.

Despite its theoretical orientation, the book does not ignore the institutional structure of financial accounting and standard setting. It features considerable coverage of financial accounting standards. Many important standards, such as reserve recognition accounting, management discussion and analysis, employee stock options, postretirement benefits, financial instruments, marking-to-market and ceiling tests, and hedge accounting are described and critically evaluated. The structure of standard-setting bodies is also described, and the role of structure in helping to engineer the consent necessary for a successful standard is evaluated. While the text discussion concentrates on relating standards to the theoretical framework of the book, the coverage provides students with the occasion to learn the contents of the standards themselves.

I have also used this material in Ph.D. seminars. Here, I concentrate on the research articles that underlie the text discussion. Nevertheless, the students appreciate the framework of the book as a way of putting specific research papers into perspective. Indeed, the book proceeds in large part by selecting important research papers for description and commentary, and provides extensive references to other research papers underlying the text discussion. Assignment of the research papers themselves could be especially useful for instructors who wish to dig into methodological issues that, with some exceptions, are downplayed in the book itself.

In this third Canadian edition, I have added references and discussion of recent research articles, updated the coverage of financial accounting standards of Canada and the United States, and generally revised the exposition as a result of experience in teaching from earlier editions. Major changes include a brief outline of the historical development of financial accounting in Chapter 1, an expanded discussion of the possibility of securities market inefficiency in Chapter 6 including behavioural underpinnings and recent analytical modelling, further expansion of the discussion of clean surplus accounting in Chapter 6, and updating of the structure of international accounting standard setting in Chapter 13. In addition, I have changed the tone somewhat of the coverage of earnings management in Chapter 11. In previous editions, it was argued that earnings management is primarily "good," since it can reveal management's inside information about future earning power. This point of view is retained, but modified to give greater recognition to the possibility that earnings management can be "bad," that is, intended to manipulate investors' perceptions of the firm so as to possibly increase share price. This latter possibility becomes of greater concern once it is recognized that securities markets may not be as fully efficient as previously believed.

Despite these changes, the book largely retains the structure, organization and markets-oriented outlook of the earlier editions. In particular, it retains the view that investor rationality and efficient securities market theory are still the most useful theories to guide accountants in their disclosure decisions, and that the motivation of responsible managerial performance is an equally important role of financial reporting as the providing of useful information to investors.

Supplements

The Instructor's Manual includes suggested solutions to the end-of-chapter Questions and Problems, including a number of new problems added in this edition. It also discusses the Learning Objectives for each chapter and suggests teaching approaches that could be used. In addition, it comments on other issues for consideration, suggests supplementary references, and contains some additional problem material. In addition to this material, the third edition Instructor's Manual adds PowerPoint slides to the Instructor's Manual.

The Instructor's Manual for the third edition is available in hard copy with all the solutions and PowerPoint Presentations also included on a CD ROM. electronic format. I intend to use this flexibility to add discussions of relevant new topics and interesting new problem material as they arise.

For students who wish to explore the Internet as a dynamic source for up-to-the-minute information, Pearson Education Canada is proud to present Accounting Central. This site contains numerous features designed to help students and instructors with all their accounting courses. You will find Accounting Central at www.pearsoned.ca/accounting. The features on the site include links to Pearson Education Canada's accounting catalogue, drop-down menus for all Canadian accounting, Companion Websites and text-resource sites where you can find text-specific information, the Accountant's Toolbox containing descriptions of and links to resources sites for accounting, Virtual Tours of new and revised titles in accounting and much more!

We are constantly updating and adding to this site, so check back often!

Acknowledgments

I have received a lot of assistance in writing this book. First, I thank CGA Canada for their encouragement and support over a number of years. Much of the material in the questions and problems has been reprinted or adapted from the *Accounting Theory I* course and examinations of the Certified General Accountants' Association of Canada. These are acknowledged where used.

At Pearson Education Canada I would like to thank Samantha Scully, Judith Scott, Laurie Goebel, and Karen Hunter. I extend my thanks and appreciation to the following reviewers as well: Joel Amernic, University of Toronto; Bert Dartnell, Certified General Accountants' Association of Canada; Johan de Rooy, University of British Columbia; Steve Fortin, McGill University; Maureen Gowing, Concordia University; George Lan, University of Windsor; A. William Richardson, Brock University; Pamela Ritchie, University of New Brunswick; David Senkow, University of Regina. I acknowledge the financial assistance of the Ontario Chartered Accountants' Chair in Accounting at the University of Waterloo, which has enabled teaching relief and other support in the preparation of the original manuscript. Financial support of the School of Business of Queen's University is also gratefully acknowledged.

I also thank numerous colleagues and students for advice and feedback. These include Sati Bandyopadhyay, Phelim Boyle, Dennis Chung, Len Eckel, Haim Falk, Steve Fortin, Jennifer Kao, David Manry, Patricia O'Brien, Bill Richardson, Gordon Richardson, Dean Smith, and Dan Thornton.

I thank the large number of researchers whose work underlies this book. As previously mentioned, numerous research papers are described and referenced. However, there are many other worthy papers that I have not referenced. This implies no disrespect or lack of appreciation for the contributions of these authors to financial accounting theory. Rather, it has been simply impossible to include them all, both for reasons of space, and the boundaries of my own knowledge.

I am grateful to Carolyn Holden for skillful, timely, and cheerful typing of the original manuscript in the face of numerous revisions, and to Jill Nucci for research assistance.

Finally, I thank my wife and family who, in many ways, have been involved in the learning process leading to this book.

William Scott

1

Introduction

1.1 *The Objective of This Book*

This book is about accounting, not how to account. It argues that accounting students, having been exposed to the methodology and practice of accounting, need at least one course that critically examines the broader implications of financial accounting for the fair and efficient operation of our economy. Its objective is to give the reader an understanding of the current financial accounting and reporting environment, taking into account the diverse interests of external users and management.

1.2 *Some Historical Perspective*

Accounting has a long history. The first complete description of the double entry bookkeeping system appeared in 1494, authored by Luca Paciolo, an Italian monk/mathematician.[1] Paciolo did not invent this system—it had developed over a long period of time. Segments that developed first included, for example, the collection of an account receivable. "Both sides" of such a transaction were easy to see, since cash and accounts receivable have a physical and/or legal existence, and the amount of the increase in cash was equal to the decrease in accounts receivable. The recording of other types of transactions, such as sale of goods or the incurring of expenses, however, took longer to develop. In the case of a sale, it was obvious that cash or accounts receivable increased, and that goods on hand decreased. But, what about the difference between the selling price and the cost of the goods sold? There is no physical or legal representation of the profit on the sale. For the double entry system to handle transactions such as this, it was necessary to create *abstract* concepts of income and capital. By Paciolo's time, a complete double entry system quite similar to the one in use today was in place. Indeed, it was the abstract nature of the system, including the properties of capital as the accumulation of income and income as the rate of change of capital[2] that attracted the attention of mathematicians of the time. The "method of Venice," as Paciolo's system was called, was frequently included in mathematics texts in subsequent years.

Following 1494, the double entry system spread throughout Europe, and Paciolio's work was translated into English in 1543. It was in England that another sequence of important accounting developments took place.

By the early eighteenth century, the concept of a joint stock company had developed in England to include permanent existence, limited liability of shareholders, and transferability of shares. Transferability of shares led in turn to the development of a stock market where shares could be bought and sold. Obviously, investors needed financial information about the firms whose shares they were trading. Thus began a long transition for financial accounting, from a system to enable a merchant to control his/her own operations to a system to inform investors who were not involved in the day-to-day operations of the firm. It was in the joint interests of the firm and investors that financial information provided by the firm was trustworthy, thereby laying the groundwork for the development of an auditing profession and government regulation. In this regard, the 1844 Companies Act was notable. It was in this act that the concept of providing an audited balance sheet to shareholders first appeared in the law, although this requirement was dropped in subsequent years[3] and not reinstated until the early 1900s. During the interval, voluntary provision of information was common, but its effectiveness was hampered by a lack of accounting principles. This was demonstrated, for example, in the controversy of whether amortization of capital assets had to be deducted in determining income available for dividends (the courts ruled it did not).

In the twentieth century, major developments in financial accounting shifted to the United States, which was growing rapidly in economic power. The introduction of a corporate income tax in the United States in 1909 provided a major impetus to income measurement, and, as noted by Hatfield (1927, p. 140), was influential in persuading business managers to accept amortization as a deduction from income.

Nevertheless, accounting in the United States continued to be relatively unregulated, with financial reporting and auditing largely voluntary. However, the stock market crash of 1929 and resulting Great Depression led to major changes. The most noteworthy was the creation of the Securities and Exchange Commission (SEC) by the Securities Act of 1934, with a focus on protecting investors by means of a disclosure-based regulatory structure.

Merino and Neimark (1982) (MN) examined the conditions leading up to the creation of the SEC. In the process, they reported on some of the securities market practices of the 1920s and prior. Apparently, voluntary disclosure was widespread, as also noted by Benston (1973). However, MN claim that such disclosure was motivated by big business's desire to avoid regulations to enhance "potential competition," that is, to avoid regulations to encourage competition.

Full disclosure regulations would encourage competition by enabling potential entrants to identify high-profit industries. Presumably, if voluntary disclosure was adequate, the government would not feel regulated disclosure was necessary. Thus, informing investors was not the main motivation of disclosure. Instead, investors were "protected" by a "2-tiered" market structure whereby prices were set by knowledgeable insiders, subject to a self-imposed "moral regulation" to control misleading reporting. Unfortunately, moral regulation was not always effective, and MN refer to numerous instances of manipulative financial reporting and other abuses, which were widely believed to be the immediate causes of the 1929 crash.

The 1934 securities legislation can then be regarded as a movement away from a potential competition rationale for disclosure towards the supplying of better-quality information to investors as a way to control manipulative financial practices.[4]

One of the practices of the 1920s that received criticism was the frequent appraisal of capital assets, the values of which came crashing down in 1929. A major lesson learned by accountants as a result of the Great Depression was that values were fleeting. The outcome was a strengthening of the historical cost basis of accounting. This basis received its highest expression in the famous Paton and Littleton monograph, *An Introduction to Corporate Accounting Standards*, of 1940. This document elegantly and persuasively set forth the case for historical cost accounting, based on the concept of the firm as a going concern. This concept justifies important attributes of historical cost accounting such as waiting to recognize revenue until objective evidence of realization is available, the matching against realized revenues of the allocated costs of earning those revenues, and the deferral of unrealized gains and losses on the balance sheet until the time came to match them with revenues. As a result, the income statement reliably shows the current "installment" of the firm's earning power. The income statement replaced the balance sheet as the primary focus of financial reporting.

It is sometimes claimed that the Paton and Littleton monograph was "too" persuasive, in that it shut out exploration of alternative bases of accounting. As we shall see in this book, historical cost is still the primary basis of accounting and it has only recently begun to yield to **fair value** accounting and the renewed importance of the balance sheet. The term "fair value" is a general expression for the valuation of any asset or liability on the basis of its market value, the discounted present value of its future receipts, or in some cases by means of a mathematical model.[5]

Another lesson learned by accountants was how to survive in the new SEC-regulated environment. The SEC has the power to establish the accounting standards and procedures used by firms under its jurisdiction. If the SEC chose to use this power, the prestige and influence of the accounting profession would be greatly eroded, possibly to the point where financial reporting becomes a process of "manual thumbing" with little basis for professional judgement and little influence on the setting of accounting standards. However, the SEC chose (and still chooses) to delegate most standard setting to the profession.[6] To retain this delegated authority, however, the accounting profession must retain the SEC's confidence that it is doing a satisfactory job of creating and maintaining a financial reporting environment that protects and informs investors and encourages the proper operation of capital markets. Thus began the search for accounting principles, those underlying truths on which the practice of accounting is, or should be, based. This was seen as a way to improve practice by reducing inconsistencies in choice of accounting policies across firms and enabling the accounting for new reporting challenges[7] to be deduced from basic principles rather than developing in an ad hoc and inconsistent way.

Accountants have laboured long and hard to find these basic principles, but with relatively little success.[8] Indeed, they have never agreed on a definition of what accounting principles are, let alone a list of them.

As a result, accounting theory and research up to the late 1960s consisted largely of a priori reasoning as to which accounting principles and practices were "best." For example, should the effects of changing prices and inflation on financial statements be taken into account, and, if so, how? This debate can be traced back at least as far as the 1920s. Some accountants argued that the fair values of specific assets and liabilities held by the firm should be recognized, with the resulting unrealized holding gains and losses included in net income. Other accountants argued that inflation-induced changes in the purchasing power of money should be recognized. During a period of inflation, the firm suffers a purchasing power loss on assets such as cash and accounts receivable, since the amounts of goods and services that can be obtained when they are collected and spent is less than the amounts that could have been obtained when they were created. Conversely, the firm enjoys a purchasing power gain on liabilities such as accounts payable and long-term debt. Separate reporting of these gains and losses would better reflect real firm performance, it was argued. Still other accountants argued that the effects of *both* specific and inflation-induced changes in prices should be taken into account. Others, however, often including firm management, resisted these suggestions. One argument, based in part on experience from the Great Depression, was that estimates of fair values and measurements of inflation were unreliable, so that taking them into account would not necessarily improve the measurement of the firm's performance.

Nevertheless, standard setters in numerous countries did require some disclosures of the effects of changing prices. In Canada, for example, Section 4510 of the *CICA Handbook* required disclosure in the notes to the financial statements of the fair values of inventories and capital assets, and of purchasing power gains and losses resulting from inflation. Section 4510 was subsequently withdrawn. However, this withdrawal was due more to the decline in inflation in the years following introduction of the section rather than to the debate having been settled.

The basic problem with debates such as the accounting for changing prices was that there was little theoretical basis for choosing among the various alternatives, particularly since, as mentioned, accountants were unable to agree on a set of basic accounting principles.

During this period, however, major developments were taking place in other disciplines. In particular, a theory of rational decision making under uncertainty developed as a branch of statistics. The theory of efficient securities markets developed in economics and finance. The Possibility Theorem of Arrow (1963) led to the realization that there was no such thing as "true" net income, implying that the search for the best accounting principles and practices was a "will-o'-the-wisp." These theories, which began to show up in accounting theory in the latter half of the 1960s, generated the concept of decision—useful (in place of "true") financial statement information. This concept first appeared in the American Accounting Association (AAA)[9] monograph, *A Statement of Basic Accounting Theory*, in 1966. Current statements of basic accounting principles, most notably the Conceptual Framework of the Financial Accounting Standards Board (FASB), are based on decision usefulness.

Equally important was the development of the economics of imperfect information, a branch of economics that formally recognizes that some individuals have an information advantage over others. This led to the development of the theory of agency, which has greatly increased our understanding of the legitimate interests of business management in financial reporting and standard setting.

These theories suggest that the answer to which way to account, if any, for changing prices outlined above will be found in the extent to which they lead to good investment decisions. Furthermore, any resolution will have to take the concerns of management into account.

In Canada, the development of financial accounting and reporting has proceeded differently, although the end result is basically similar to that of the United States. Financial reporting requirements in Canada were laid down in federal and provincial corporations acts, along the lines of the English corporations acts referred to above. The ultimate power to regulate financial reporting rests with the legislatures concerned. However, in 1946, the Committee on Accounting and Auditing Research, now the Accounting Standards Board (AcSB), of The Canadian Institute of Chartered Accountants (CICA) began to issue bulletins on financial accounting issues. These were intended to guide Canadian accountants as to best practices, and did not have force of law. In 1968, these were formalized into the *CICA Handbook*. At first, adherence to these provisions was voluntary but, given their prestigious source, were difficult to ignore. Over time, the *Handbook* gained recognition as the authoritative statement of Generally Accepted Accounting Principles (GAAP) in Canada. Ultimately, provincial securities commissions and the corporations acts formally recognized this authority. For example, in 1975 the Canada Business Corporations Act required adherence to the *CICA Handbook* to satisfy reporting requirements under the act. The end result, then, is similar to that in the United States in that the body with ultimate authority to set accounting standards has delegated this function to a private professional body.[10]

These various developments set the stage for the current financial accounting and reporting environment that is the subject of this book.

1.3   *The Complexity of Information in Financial Accounting and Reporting*

The environment of accounting is both very complex and very challenging. It is complex because the product of accounting is **information**—a powerful and important commodity. One reason for the complexity of information is that individuals are not unanimous in their reaction to it. For example, a sophisticated investor may react positively to the valuation of certain firm assets at fair value on the grounds that this will help to predict future firm performance.[11] Other investors may be less positive, perhaps because they feel that fair value information is unreliable, or simply because they are used to historical cost information. Furthermore, managers, who will have to report the fair values, might react quite negatively. While ultimately part of management's job is to anticipate changes in fair values, such changes are typically perceived by managers as beyond their control. Thus, they argue, unrealized gains and losses resulting from changes in fair value do not reflect their performance and should not be included in income. As a result, accountants quickly get caught up in whether reported net income should fulfill a role of facilitating the prediction of firm performance, or a role of reporting on management's stewardship of the firm's resources.

Another reason for the complexity of information is that it does more than affect individual decisions. In affecting decisions it also affects the operation of markets, such as securities markets and managerial labour markets. The proper operation of such markets is important to the efficiency and fairness of the economy itself.

The challenge for financial accountants, then, is to survive and prosper in a complex environment characterized by conflicting pressures from different groups with an interest in financial reporting. This book argues that the prospects for survival and prosperity will be enhanced if accountants have a critical awareness of the impact of financial reporting on investors, managers, and the economy. The alternative to awareness is simply to accept the reporting environment as given. However, this is a very short-term strategy, since environments are constantly changing and evolving.

1.4   *The Role of Accounting Research*

A book about accounting theory must inevitably draw on accounting research, much of which is contained in academic journals. There are two complementary ways that we can view the role of research. The first is to consider its effects on accounting practice. For example, a decision usefulness approach underlies Section 1000 of the *CICA Handbook*, and the Conceptual Framework of the FASB in the United States. The essence of this approach is that investors should be supplied with information to help them make good investment decisions. One has only to compare the current annual report of a public company with those issued in the 1960s and prior to see the tremendous increase in disclosure over the 25 years or so since decision usefulness formally became an important concept in accounting theory.

Yet, this increase in disclosure did not "just happen." It, as outlined in Section 1.2, is based on fundamental research into the theory of investor decision-making and the theory of capital markets, which have guided the accountant in what information is useful. Furthermore, the theory has been subjected to extensive empirical testing, which has established that, on average, investors use financial accounting information much as the theory predicts.

Independently of whether it affects current practice, however, there is a second important view of the role of research. This is to improve our *understanding* of the accounting environment, which we argued above should not be taken for granted. For example, fundamental research into models of conflict resolution, in particular agency theory models, has improved our understanding of managers' interests in financial reporting, of the role of executive compensation plans in motivating and controlling management's operation of the firm, and of the ways in which such plans use accounting information. This in turn leads to an improved understanding of managers' interests in accounting policy choice and why they may want to bias or otherwise manipulate reported net income, or, at least, to have some ability to manage the "bottom line." Research such as this enables us to understand the boundaries of management's legitimate role in financial reporting, and why the accountant is frequently caught between the interests of investors and managers. In this book, we use both of the above views. Our approach to research is twofold. In some cases, we choose important research papers, describe them intuitively, and explain how they fit into our overall framework of financial accounting theory and practice. In other cases, we simply refer to research papers on which our discussion is based. The interested reader can pursue the discussion in greater depth if desired.

1.5   *The Importance of Information Asymmetry*

This book is based on information economics. This is a unifying theme that formally recognizes that some parties to business transactions may have an information advantage over others. When this happens, the economy is said to be characterized by **information asymmetry**. We shall consider two major types of information asymmetry.

The first is **adverse selection**. For our purposes, adverse selection occurs because some persons, such as firm managers and other insiders, will know more about the current condition and future prospects of the firm than outside investors. There are various ways that managers and other insiders can exploit their information advantage at the expense of outsiders, for example, by biasing or otherwise managing the information released to investors. This may affect the ability of investors to make good investment decisions. In addition, if investors are concerned about the possibility of biased information release, they will be wary of buying firms' securities, with the result that capital and managerial labour markets will not function as well as they should. We can then think of financial accounting and reporting as a mechanism to control the adverse selection problem by credibly converting inside information into outside information.

> *Adverse selection* is a type of information asymmetry whereby one or more parties to a business transaction, or potential transaction, have an information advantage over other parties.

The second type of information asymmetry is **moral hazard**. In our context, this problem occurs because of the separation of ownership and control that characterizes most large business entities. It is effectively impossible for shareholders and creditors to observe directly the extent and quality of top manager effort on their behalf. Then, the manager may be tempted to shirk on effort, blaming any deterioration of firm performance on factors beyond his or her control. Obviously, if this happens, there are serious implications both for investors and for the efficient operation of the economy.

We can then view accounting net income as a measure of managerial performance, or stewardship. This helps to control the moral hazard problem in two complementary ways. First, net income can serve as an input into executive compensation contracts to motivate manager performance. Second, net income can inform the securities and managerial labour markets, so that a manager who shirks will suffer a decline in income, reputation, and market value over time.

> *Moral hazard* is a type of information asymmetry whereby one or more parties to a business transaction, or potential transaction, can observe their actions in fulfillment of the transaction but other parties cannot.

1.6 The Fundamental Problem of Financial Accounting Theory

It turns out that the most useful measure of net income to inform investors, that is, to control adverse selection, need not be the same as the best measure to motivate manager performance, that is, to control moral hazard. Investors' interests are best served by information that provides a useful tradeoff between relevance and reliability, where relevant information is that which enables investors to assess the firm's future economic prospects, and reliable information is that which is precise and free of bias or other management manipulation.

Managers' interests are best served by "hard" information,[12] that is, information that is highly correlated with their effort in running the firm. But information that is relevant for investors, such as fair values of assets and liabilities, may be very volatile in its impact on reported net income. Also, to the extent that reliable market values are not available, fair value-oriented information may be more subject to bias and manipulation than historical-cost-based information. Both of these effects reduce correlation with managers' efforts. Given that there is only one bottom line, the fundamental problem of financial accounting theory is how to reconcile these different roles for accounting information.

1.7   Regulation as a Reaction to the Fundamental Problem

There are two basic reactions to the fundamental problem. One is, in effect, to ask, "What problem?" That is, why not let market forces determine how much and what kinds of information firms should produce? We can think of investors and other financial statement users as demanders of information and of managers as suppliers. Then, just as in markets for apples and automobiles, the forces of demand and supply can determine the quantity produced.

This view argues, in effect, that market forces can sufficiently control the adverse selection and moral hazard problems so that investors are protected, and managerial labour markets and securities markets will work reasonably well. Indeed, as we shall see, there are a surprising number of ways whereby managers can credibly supply information, including accounting information. Furthermore, investors as a group are surprisingly sophisticated in ferreting out the implications of information for future firm performance.

The second reaction is to turn to **regulation** to protect investors, on the grounds that information is such a complex and important commodity that market forces alone fail to adequately control the problems of moral hazard and adverse selection. This leads directly to the role of standard setting, which is viewed in this book as a form of regulation that lays down generally accepted accounting principles.

The rigorous determination of the "right" amount of regulation is an extremely complex issue of social choice. At the present time we simply do not know which of the above two reactions to the fundamental problem is on the right track. Certainly, we witness lots of regulation in accounting, and there appears to be no slowing down in the rate at which new standards are coming on line. Consequently, it may seem that society has resolved the question of extent of regulation for us.

Yet, we live in a time of deregulation. Recent years have witnessed substantial deregulation of major industries such as transportation, telecommunications, financial services, and electric power generation, where deregulation was once thought unthinkable. The reason it is important to ask whether similar deregulation should take place in the information "industry" is because regulation has a cost—a fact often ignored by standard setters. Again, the answer to the question of whether the benefits of regulation outweigh the costs is not known. However, we shall pursue this issue later in the book.

1.8   *The Organization of This Book*

Figure 1.1 summarizes how this book operationalizes the framework for the study of financial accounting theory outlined above. There are four main components of the figure, and we will outline each in turn.

1.8.1   *IDEAL CONDITIONS*

Before considering the problems introduced into accounting by information asymmetry, it is worthwhile to consider what accounting would be like under ideal conditions. This is depicted by the leftmost box of Figure 1.1 shown above. By ideal conditions we mean an economy characterized by perfect and complete markets or, equivalently, by a lack of information asymmetry and other barriers to fair and efficient market operation. Such conditions are also called "first best." Then, asset and liability valuation is on the basis of expected present values of future cash flows. Arbitrage ensures that present values and market values are equal. Financial statements are both completely relevant and completely reliable, and investors and managers would have no scope for disagreement over accounting policy choice and no incentives to call for regulation.

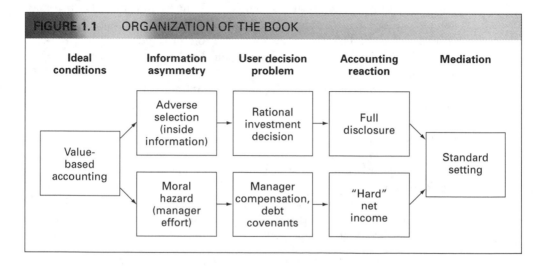

FIGURE 1.1   ORGANIZATION OF THE BOOK

Unfortunately, or perhaps fortunately, ideal conditions do not prevail in practice. Nevertheless, they provide a useful benchmark against which more realistic, "second best" accounting conditions can be compared. For example, we will see that there are numerous instances of the actual use of fair value-based accounting techniques in financial reporting. Reserve recognition accounting for oil and gas companies is an example. Furthermore, the use of such techniques is increasing, as in recent standards requiring fair value accounting for financial instruments. A study of accounting under ideal conditions is useful not only because practice is moving to increased use of fair values, but more importantly, it helps us to see what the real problems and challenges of fair value accounting are when the ideal conditions that they require do not hold.

1.8.2 ADVERSE SELECTION

The top three boxes of Figure 1.1 represent the second component of the framework. This introduces the adverse selection problem, that is, the problem of communication from the firm to outside investors. Here, the accounting role is to provide a "level playing field" through full disclosure of relevant, reliable, timely, and cost-effective information to investors and other financial statement users.

To understand how financial accounting can help to control the adverse selection problem, it is desirable to have an appreciation of how investors make decisions. This is because knowledge of investor decision processes is essential if the accountant is to know what information they need. The study of investment decision-making is a large topic, since investors undoubtedly make decisions in a variety of ways, ranging from intuition to "hot tips" to random occurrences such as a sudden need for cash to sophisticated computer-based models.

The approach we will take in this book is to assume that most investors are **rational**, that is, they make decisions so as to maximize their expected utility, or satisfaction, from wealth. This theory of rational investment decision has been widely studied. In making the rationality assumption we do not imply that all investors make decisions this way. Indeed, there is increasing recognition that many investors do not behave rationally in the sense of maximizing their expected utility of wealth. We do claim, however, that the theory captures the average behaviour of those investors who want to make informed investment decisions, and this claim is backed up by substantial empirical evidence.

The reporting of information that is useful to rational investors is called the **decision usefulness** approach. As suggested in Section 1.2, this approach underlies the pronouncements of major standard setting bodies, such as the Conceptual Framework of the FASB.

When a large number of rational investors interact in a properly working securities market, the market becomes **efficient**. The accounting reaction to securities market efficiency has been **full disclosure**, that is, the supplying of large amounts of information to help investors make their own predictions of future firm performance. This is depicted in the third box in the top row of Figure 1. This reaction is called the **information perspective** on decision usefulness. An implication is that the form of disclosure does not matter—it can be in notes, or in supplementary disclosures such as reserve recognition accounting and management discussion and analysis, in addition to the financial statements proper.[13] The market is regarded as sufficiently sophisticated that it can digest the implications of public information from any source.

Recent years, however, have seen a considerable increase in the use of fair values in financial statements proper, including for leases, pensions, other post-retirement benefits, and financial instruments. This is called the **measurement perspective** on decision usefulness. It seems that accountants are expanding their approach to decision usefulness by taking more responsibility for incorporating measurements of fair values into the accounts. In Section 1.2 we noted that abuses of fair value accounting were widely viewed as contributing to the 1929 stock market crash, and that the result was a strengthening of historical cost-based accounting. It is interesting that accountants are finally moving back to increased use of fair values, with its implication that the balance sheet is the primary financial statement. Whether this means that accountants have forgotten the lessons of the 1920s and 1930s, or whether improvements in measurement tools, such as statistical analysis of large data bases and the use of mathematical models to estimate fair values will help to avoid the documented abuses of fair values during the earlier period, is difficult to say. Only time will tell if the recent collapse of share values of "high-tech" firms and resulting economic downturn will slow down or reverse the measurement perspective.

1.8.3   MORAL HAZARD

The bottom three boxes of Figure 1.1 represent the third component of the book. Here, the information asymmetry problem is moral hazard, arising from the unobservability of the manager's effort in running the firm. That is, the manager's decision problem is to decide on how much effort to devote to running the firm on behalf of the shareholders. Since effort is unobservable, the manager may be tempted to shirk on effort. However, since net income reflects manager performance, it operates as an indirect measure of the manager's effort decision. Consequently, management compensation and reputation depends, directly and indirectly, on reported net income. Long-term debt usually is accompanied by debt covenants that depend on maintenance of certain accounting ratios, such as debt-to-equity. This role of financial reporting to motivate and monitor manager performance, including adherence to debt covenants, is depicted by the middle box of the bottom row of Figure 1.1.

Given the importance of reported net income to the manager, it is natural that he or she is concerned about the accounting policies that are used to determine net income. This concern leads to the concept of **economic consequences**, that is, accounting policies matter to managers. As a result, managers will object to accounting policies that decrease the ability of net income to reflect their efforts (for example, if unrealized gains and losses resulting from adjusting assets and liabilities to fair value are included in net income, managers may object on the grounds that changes in fair values result from market forces beyond their control, hence do not reflect their efforts in running the firm). Futhermore, the manager may be tempted to bias or manipulate reported net income so as to improve compensation, reputation, and covenant ratios. To control these concerns and tendencies, net income should be hard, that is, highly correlated with manager effort.

1.8.4 STANDARD SETTING

We can now see the source of the fundamental problem of financial accounting theory more clearly. Fair values of assets and liabilities are of greater interest to investors than their historical costs, since fair values provide the best available indication of future firm performance. However, as mentioned, managers may feel that gains and losses from adjusting the carrying values of assets and liabilities do not reflect their own performance. Accounting standard setters quickly get caught up in mediation between the conflicting interests of investors and managers. This is depicted by the rightmost box in Figure 1.

1.9 Relevance of Financial Accounting Theory to Accounting Practice

The framework just described provides a way of organizing our study of financial accounting theory. However, this book also recognizes an obligation to convince you that the theory is relevant to accounting practice. This is accomplished in two main ways. First, the various theories and research underlying financial accounting are described and explained in plain language, and their relevance is demonstrated by means of numerous references to accounting practice. For example, Chapter 3 describes how investors may make rational investment decisions, and then goes on to demonstrate that this decision theory underlies the Conceptual Framework of the FASB. Also, the book contains numerous instances where accounting standards are described and critically evaluated. In addition to enabling you to learn the contents of these standards, you can better understand and apply them when you have a grounding in the underlying reasoning on which they are based. The second approach to demonstrating relevance is through assignment problems. A real attempt has been made to select relevant problem material to illustrate and motivate the concepts.

Recent years have been challenging, even exciting, times for financial accounting theory. We have learned a tremendous amount about the important role of financial accounting in our economy from the information economics research outlined above. If this book enables you to better understand and appreciate this role, it will have attained its objective.

Notes

1. For some information about Paciolo, a translation of his bookkeeping treatise, and a copy of an Italian version, see *Paciolo on Accounting*, by R. Gene Brown and Kenneth S. Johnston (1963).

2. Readers with a mathematical background will recognize these relationships as related to the fundamental theorem of calculus.

3. The dropping of these requirements did not mean that firms should not supply information to shareholders, but that the amount and nature of information supplied was a matter between the firm and its shareholders. In effect, it was felt that market forces, rather than legal requirement, were sufficient to motivate information production.

4. Actually, MN pose a much deeper question. Widespread share ownership had long been seen as a way of reconciling increasingly large and powerful corporations with the popular belief in individualism, property rights, and democracy, whereby the "little guy" could take part in the corporate governance process. With the 1929 crash and subsequent revelation of manipulative abuses, a new approach was required that would both restore public confidence in securities markets and be acceptable to powerful corporate interest groups. MN suggest that the creation of the SEC was an embodiment of such a new approach.

5. Fair value is defined in *CICA Handbook* Section 3860.05, with respect to financial instruments as the amount of the consideration that would be agreed upon in an arm's-length transaction between knowledgeable, willing parties who are under no compulsion to act. The term originated with the Financial Accounting Standards Board, the current U.S. accounting standard setter, as, for example, in SFAS 87 (1986) with respect to pension assets and in SFAS 107 (1992) with respect to financial instruments.

6. This is not to say that the SEC stands aloof from accounting standards. If it perceives that standards as set by the profession are straying too far from what it wants, the SEC can bring considerable pressure to bear short of taking over the process. In this regard, see Note 7.

7. The controversy over the investment tax credit in the United States provides an excellent example. The 1962 Revenue Act provided firms with a credit against taxes payable of 7 percent of current investment in capital assets. The controversy was whether to account for the credit as a reduction in current income tax

expense or to bring all or part of it into income over the life of the capital assets to which the credit applied. The Accounting Principles Board (the predecessor body to the FASB) issued APB2, requiring the latter alternative. The SEC, however, objected and issued its own standard, allowing greater flexibility in accounting for the credit. The Accounting Principles Board backed down and issued APB4 in 1964 allowing either alternative. The basic problem, as seen by the standard setters, was the lack of a set of basic accounting principles from which the "correct" accounting for the credit could be deduced.

8. For a detailed description of the search for accounting principles in the United States from the inception of the SEC to the present, see Storey and Storey (1998).

9. The American Accounting Association is an association of academic accountants. It does not have standard setting authority like the FASB. Nevertheless, professional accountants later picked up on the decision usefulness concept. See *Study Group on the Objectives of Financial Statements* (1973), also called the Trueblood committee report.

10. Strictly speaking, the AcSB is sponsored by the CICA, whereas the FASB is a privately funded body separate from The American Institute of Certified Public Accountants, the professional accounting body analogous to the CICA in Canada.

11. If markets work properly, market value is equally likely to rise or fall. Thus current market price is the best predictor of future price, hence of future firm performance.

12. The term "hardness" was introduced by Ijiri (1975), who defined it as difficulty of manipulation of financial reports by persons with a vested interest in those reports.

13. Strictly speaking, the term "financial statements" includes the notes to the statements. When we refer to disclosure within the financial statements themselves, we will use the term "financial statements proper." Thus, if a firm values an asset at fair value in its accounts and reports the resulting number on the balance sheet, it reports fair value in the financial statements proper. If it discloses the fair value only in a note, this would be reported in the financial statements but not in the financial statements proper.

2

Accounting Under Ideal Conditions

2.1   Overview

We will begin our study of financial accounting theory by considering the present value model. This model provides the utmost in relevant information to financial statement users. In this context we define relevant information as information about the firm's future economic prospects, that is, its dividends, cash flows, and profitability.

Our concern is with the conditions under which relevant financial statements will also be reliable, where we define reliable information as information that is precise and free from bias. We will also explore the conditions under which market values of assets and liabilities can serve as indirect measures of value. This will be the case under ideal conditions (to be defined later). If conditions are not ideal (which is usually the case), fundamental problems are created for asset valuation and income measurement.

2.2   The Present Value Model Under Certainty

The present value model is widely used in economics and finance and has had considerable impact on accounting over the years. We first consider a simple version of the model under conditions of certainty. By "certainty" we mean that the future cash flows of the firm and the interest rate in the economy are publicly known with certainty. We denote these as **ideal conditions**.

EXAMPLE 2.1 THEORETICAL ILLUSTRATION OF THE PRESENT VALUE MODEL UNDER CERTAINTY

Consider P.V. Ltd., a one-asset firm with no liabilities. Assume that the asset will generate end-of-year cash flows of $100 each year for two years and then will have zero value. Assume also that the risk-free interest rate in the economy is 10%. Then, at time 0 (the beginning of the first year of the asset's life), the present value of the firm's future cash flows, denoted by PA_0, is:

$$PA_0 = \$100 \div 1.10 + \$100 \div (1.10)^2$$
$$= \$90.91 + \$82.64$$
$$= \$173.55$$

We can then prepare a present value opening balance sheet as follows:

P.V. LTD.
BALANCE SHEET
As at Time 0

Capital asset, at present value $173.55   Shareholders' equity $173.55

Now, move on to time 1, one year later. At that time, the present value of the remaining cash flows from the firm's asset is:

$$PA_1 = \$100 \div 1.10$$
$$= \$90.91$$

The firm's income statement for year 1 is:

P.V. LTD.
INCOME STATEMENT
For Year 1

Sales (cash received)	$100.00
Amortization expense	82.64
Net income	$ 17.36

Amortization expense is calculated as $173.55 − $90.91 = $82.64—that is, the decline in the present value of the future receipts from the asset over the year. This way of calculating amortization differs from the way that accountants usually calculate it. Nevertheless, it is the appropriate approach under the ideal conditions of this example, namely, future cash flows known with certainty and a fixed risk-free interest rate.

Then, the end-of-year-1 balance sheet is:

P.V. LTD.
BALANCE SHEET
As at End of Year

Financial Asset			**Shareholders' Equity**	
Cash		$100.00	Opening value	$173.55
Capital Asset			Net income	17.36
Opening value	$173.55			
Accumulated				
amortization	82.64	90.91		
		$190.91		$190.91

This assumes that the firm pays no dividend. A dividend can be easily incorporated by reducing cash and shareholders' equity by the amount of the dividend.

Note the following points about Example 2.1:

1. The net book value of the capital asset at any year-end is equal to its fair value (see the definition of fair value in Section 1.2), where fair value is here determined as the present value of the future cash flows from that asset, discounted at 10%. Amortization expense is the change in present value over the year.

2. Net income for the year is equal to the year's cash flow of $100 less the $82.64 decline in the present value of the asset. Note that it is also equal to $PA_0 \times 10\% = \$173.55 \times 10\% = \$17.36$. This amount is called **accretion of discount**. It is the opening present value multiplied by the interest rate. The term arises because the stream of cash receipts is one year closer at the end of the year than it was at the beginning. The $17.36 is also referred to as *ex ante* or **expected** net income since, at time 0, the firm expects to earn $17.36. Of course, because all conditions are known with certainty, the expected net income will equal the *ex post* or **realized** net income.

3. **Relevant** financial statements are defined as those that give information to investors about the firm's future economic prospects. The information in Example 2.1 is entirely relevant. To see this, note first that, fundamentally, economic prospects are defined by the firm's stream of future dividends—it is dividends that provide a payoff to investors, the present value of which serves to establish firm value.

Then, it might seem that the firm's dividend policy will affect its value, since the timing of dividends will affect their present value. However, under ideal conditions, this would not be the case, and is called **dividend irrelevancy**.

To see why dividend policy does not matter under ideal conditions, note that as long as investors can invest any dividends they receive at the *same rate* of return as the firm earns on cash flows *not* paid in dividends, the present value of an investor's overall interest in the firm is independent of the timing of dividends. This holds in our example since there is only one interest rate in the economy. In effect, the firm's cash flows establish the size of the "pot" that is ultimately available to investors and it does not matter if this pot is distributed sooner or later. If it is distributed during the current year, investors can earn 10% on the distributions. If it is distributed in a subsequent year, the firm earns 10% on amounts not distributed, but this accrues to investors through an increase in the value of their investment. The present value to the investor is the same either way.

Under dividend irrelevancy, cash flows are just as relevant as dividends, because cash flows establish the firm's dividend-paying ability. As a result, the financial statements under Example 2.1 are entirely relevant.

4. As an accountant, you might be wondering why the firm's **net income** seems to play no role in firm valuation. This is quite true—it doesn't, under ideal conditions of certainty. The reason is that future cash flows are known and hence can be discounted to provide balance sheet valuations. Net income is then quite trivial, being simply accretion of discount as pointed out above. In effect, under ideal conditions, the balance sheet contains all the relevant information and the income statement contains none.[1] Even though net income is "true and correct," it conveys no information because investors can always figure it out by multiplying the opening balance sheet value by the interest rate. To put this another way, there is no information in the current net income that helps investors predict future economic prospects of the firm. These are already known to investors by assumption. This is an important point and we shall return to it later. For now, suffice it to say that when ideal conditions do not hold, the income statement assumes a much more significant role.

5. Define **reliable** financial statements as being precise and free from bias. The information in Example 2.1 is entirely reliable, since we have assumed that future cash flows and the interest rate are known with certainty. Note that there are *two components* of reliability. One is precision, the extent to which the financial statements are free of random error, or noise. Noise can arise from errors in the firm's accounting system, and from errors in estimates. Noise can also be present even in the absence of errors. This can occur if the quantity being estimated is subject to wide variation. For example, suppose that present value, or current market

value, is used in the financial statements as a measure of the fair value of an asset. Even if they are not biased, these volatile measures of value may be proved wrong by subsequent events, such as changing market prices, if conditions are not ideal. Of course, under ideal conditions of certainty, this would not occur.

The second component of reliability is freedom from bias or manipulation, also called "hardness." Lack of reliability harms investors in two related ways. First, information that is imprecise will need revision later. This can adversely affect investors' current decision calculations. Second, managers may bias or otherwise manipulate financial statement information, which can also adversely affect investor decisions. When information is perfectly reliable, neither of these problems can arise.

In sum, noise is absent under ideal conditions of certainty, since future cash flows and the interest rate are publicly known. As a result, present value and market value cannot be proven wrong by later events. Also, any errors, or attempts by management to bias the financial statements, would be immediately detected.

6. Under the ideal conditions of future cash flows known with certainty and the economy's risk-free interest rate given, the market value of the asset will be equal to its present value. To see this, consider the following argument: Given an interest rate of 10%, no one would be willing to pay more than $173.55 for the asset at time 0—if they did, they would be earning less than 10%. Also, the owners of the asset would not sell it for less than $173.55—if offered less than $173.55, they would be better off to retain it and earn 10%. If they needed the money they could borrow at 10% against the asset as security. Thus, the only possible equilibrium market price is $173.55. This argument is a simple example of the principle of **arbitrage**. If market prices for identical goods and services are such that it is possible to make a profit by simply buying in one market and selling in another, these are called arbitrage profits. However, it seems reasonable to expect that, if future cash flows and the risk-free rate are publicly known, the scramble of self-interested individuals to make these quick profits would eliminate any price discrepancies.

7. Arbitrage means that there are two ways to determine asset fair value. We can calculate the discounted present value of future cash flows, as in Example 2.1. We will call this the **direct** approach. Alternatively, we can use market value. We will call this the **indirect** approach. Under ideal conditions, the two approaches yield identical results.

As P.V. Ltd. owns only one asset and has no liabilities, the firm's market value would also be $173.55 at time 0, being the sum of the financial assets[2] and the present value of future cash receipts from the capital asset. Thus, the total market value of P.V.'s shares outstanding would be $173.55. In more general terms, if a firm owns more than one asset, the market value of the firm would be the sum of the value of its financial assets plus the value of the joint future receipts from its capital assets, less the present value of any liabilities. At points in time after time 0, the firm's market value continues to equal the sum of its financial assets plus capital assets, net of liabilities. Note, however, that dividend policy affects the amount of financial assets. To the extent that the firm does not pay out all of its profits in dividends, it will earn a return on reinvested assets. Question 2, at the end of this chapter, illustrates this point. See also the discussion of dividend irrelevancy above.

SUMMARY

The purpose of Example 2.1 is to demonstrate that under the ideal conditions of future cash flows known with certainty and a fixed risk-free interest rate in the economy, it is possible to prepare relevant financial statements that are also reliable. The process of arbitrage ensures that the market value of an asset equals the present value of its future cash flows. The market value of the firm is then the value of its financial assets plus the value of its capital assets (less any liabilities).

Net income for the period equals cash flow plus or minus the change in the value of its financial and capital assets during the period or, equivalently, the firm's opening market value multiplied by the interest rate. However, even though net income can be perfectly calculated, it has no information content, because investors can easily calculate it for themselves. All of the "action" is on the balance sheet, which shows the value of the firm.

Because of dividend irrelevancy, all of these conclusions are independent of the firm's dividend policy.

2.3   *The Present Value Model Under Uncertainty*

It is instructive to extend the present value model to the presence of uncertainty. With one major exception, most of the concepts carry over from Example 2.1. Again, we will proceed by means of an example.

EXAMPLE 2.2   THEORETICAL ILLUSTRATION OF THE PRESENT VALUE MODEL UNDER UNCERTAINTY

Let us continue Example 2.1 taking into account that the economy can be in a "bad" state or a "good" state during each year. If it is in the bad state, cash flows will be $100 for the year. If it is in the good state, however, cash flows will be $200 for the year. Assume that during each year the bad state and the good state each occur with probability 0.5. This assumption implies that the state realizations are independent over the two years of the example. That is, the state realization in year 1 does not affect the probabilities[3] of state realization in year 2.

Uncertain future events such as the state of the economy are called **states of nature**, or **states** for short. Thus the states in this example are, for each year:

State 1: Economy is bad.

State 2: Economy is good.

Note that no one can control which of the states is realized—this is why they are called states of *nature*. Other examples of states that affect cash flows are weather, government policies, strikes by suppliers, equipment breakdowns, etc. In any realistic situation there will be a large number of possible states. However, our two-state example is sufficient to convey the idea— states of nature are a conceptual device to model those uncertain, uncontrollable future events whose realization affects the cash flows of the firm.

While at time 0 no one knows which state will occur, we assume that the *set* of possible states is publicly known and complete. That is, every possible future event that can affect cash flows is known to everyone. Thus, while no one knows for sure which state will occur, it is known that whatever state does happen must be an element of the set. Furthermore, we assume that the state realization is publicly observable—everyone will know which state actually happens. Finally, we assume that the state probabilities are **objective**, and publicly known. By objective we mean that if we imagine a long-run sequence of repetitions of our economy, the bad state will occur with relative frequency 0.5 (or whatever other state probability we were to assume). Think by analogy with rolling a pair of fair dice. We know that the probability of a seven, say, is 1/6, and that if we were to roll the dice a large number of times a seven will appear with relative frequency 1/6. Note that an implication of objective probabilities here is that the outcome of any particular roll tells us nothing about the true state of the dice—we already know that the true state is that they are fair. Thus, the probability of a seven on the next roll remains at 1/6, and similarly for the probability of any other outcome.

These assumptions extend the concept of ideal conditions, also called "first-best" conditions, to take uncertainty into account. To summarize[4]

> ***Ideal conditions*** *under uncertainty are characterized by: (1) a given, fixed interest rate at which the firm's future cash flows are discounted, (2) a complete and publicly known set of states of nature, (3) state probabilities objective and publicly known, and (4) state realization publicly observable.*

Another way to think about ideal conditions here is that they are similar to conditions of certainty except that future cash flows are known *conditionally* on the states of nature. That is, *if* state 1 happens, *then* cash flows will be $200, etc. We will assume that P.V. Ltd.'s future cash flows are discounted at 10%.

Given these ideal conditions, we can now calculate the **expected present value** of P.V.'s future cash flows at time 0:

$$PA_0 = 0.5\left(\frac{\$100}{1.10} + \frac{\$200}{1.10}\right) + 0.5\left(\frac{\$100}{1.10^2} + \frac{\$200}{1.10^2}\right)$$
$$= 0.5 \times \$272.73 + 0.5 \times \$247.93$$
$$= \$136.36 + \$123.97$$
$$= \$260.33$$

We can then prepare P.V.'s opening balance sheet as:

P.V. LTD.
BALANCE SHEET
As at Time 0

Capital asset, at expected present value	$260.33	Shareholders' equity	$260.33

It is worthwhile to ask whether the time 0 market value of the asset, and hence of the firm, would be $260.33, as per the balance sheet. It is tempting to answer yes, since this is the firm's expected value given dividend irrelevance. But, uncertainty introduces an additional consideration not present in the certainty model of Section 2.2. This is that investors may be averse to risk. While the *expected* value of the firm is $260.33 at time 0, it is shown below that the expected value of the firm at the *end* of year 1 will be $236.36 or $336.36 depending on whether the bad state or the good state happens in that year. Ask yourself whether you would be indifferent between having $260.33 in your pocket today or a 50/50 gamble of $236.36 or $336.36 a year from now. The present value of the 50/50 gamble is:

$$PA_0 = 0.5 \times \frac{\$236.36}{1.10} + 0.5 \times \frac{\$336.36}{1.10}$$
$$= 0.5 \times \$214.87 + 0.5 \times \$305.78$$
$$= \$107.44 + \$152.89$$
$$= \$260.33$$

the same as the sure thing. But, most people would prefer the sure thing, because it is less risky. Then, the market value of the firm will be less than $260.33, since to the extent that investors are collectively risk-averse they will value the risky firm at less than its present value.

In this chapter, we will ignore this complication, by assuming that investors are risk-neutral. That is, they are indifferent between the sure thing and the 50/50 gamble above. Then, the firm's market value will be $260.33 at time 0. This assumption of risk-neutral investors will be relaxed later, since accountants have a role to play in informing investors about the firm's riskiness as well as its expected value. The concept of a risk-averse investor is introduced in Section 3.4 and the impact of risk on firm valuation is shown in

Section 4.5. For now, suffice it to say that the expected value of future cash flows is relevant for investors irrespective of their attitudes to risk.

Given risk-neutral valuation, the arbitrage principle will ensure that the market value of the firm's asset, and of the firm itself, is $260.33. The arbitrage principle would still hold if investors were averse to risk but the market value would be driven to an amount less than $260.33.

To return to the example, you should verify that *expected* net income for year 1—also called accretion of discount—is 0.10 × $260.33 = $26.03, analogous to the certainty case (see question 3).

Now, at the end of year 1 the expected present value of the remaining cash flows from the asset is:

$$PA_1 = 0.5 \left(\frac{\$100}{1.10} + \frac{\$200}{1.10} \right) = \$136.36$$

Assuming that the year 1 state realization is bad economy, P.V.'s year 1 *realized* income statement is:

P.V. LTD.
INCOME STATEMENT
(bad economy)
For Year 1

Sales (cash received)	$100.00
Amortization expense ($260.33 − $136.36)	123.97
Net loss	$ 23.97

The year-end balance sheet is:

P.V. LTD.
BALANCE SHEET
(bad economy)
As at End of Year 1

Financial Asset			**Shareholders' Equity**	
Cash		$100.00	Opening value	$260.33
Capital Asset			Net loss	23.97
Opening value	$260.33			
Accumulated				
amortization	123.97	136.36		
		$236.36		$236.36

Again, arbitrage ensures that the market value of the asset is $136.36 and of the firm is $236.36 at time 1. We continue the assumption that the firm pays no dividend. Ideal conditions ensure that it makes no difference whether the firm pays a dividend or not, as in the certainty case. In other words, dividend irrelevancy continues to hold. Question 4 pursues this point.

The major difference between the uncertainty and certainty cases is that *expected net income and realized net income need not be the same under uncertainty*. To analyze this further, consider the following alternative calculation of net income given state 1:

P.V. LTD. ALTERNATIVE INCOME STATEMENT (bad economy) For Year 1		
Accretion of discount (0.10 × $260.33)		$26.03
Less: Abnormal earnings, as a result of bad-state realization:		
Expected cash flows (0.5 × $100 + 0.5 × $200)	$150	
Actual cash flows	100	50.00
Net loss		$23.97

Note that the negative $50 of unexpected cash flows results in a $50 "shock" to earnings for the year. The negative $50 earnings shock is called **abnormal earnings**, or, equivalently, **unexpected earnings**, since it reduces expected earnings of $26.03 to a loss of $23.97. Under this calculation, net income consists of *expected* net income less the abnormal earnings for year 1 resulting from the bad-state realization of $50.

It should be noted that in our example abnormal earnings do not **persist**. That is, their effect dissipates completely in the year in which they occur. In general, this need not be the case. For example, if the bad-state realization was due to, say, a tax increase that affected economic activity, the abnormal effect on earnings may persist for several periods. We ignore this possibility here to keep the example simple. However, we will return to the concept of persistence in Chapters 5 and 6.

Yet another way to calculate income, familiar from introductory accounting, is to calculate the change in balance sheet net assets for the year, adjusted for capital transactions. In this example, we have:

Net income = $236.36 − $260.33 − $0 = −$23.97

where capital transactions are zero. Thus, knowing the present values of all assets and liabilities enables one to calculate present-value-based net income.

Now, let's consider the accounting if the state realization is a good economy. At the end of year 1, the present value of the remaining cash flows is still $136.36, and the year 1 income statement is:

P.V. LTD.
INCOME STATEMENT
(good economy)
For Year 1

Sales (cash received)	$200.00
Amortization expense ($260.33 − $136.36)	123.97
Net income	$ 76.03

Under the alternative calculation of net income, we have:

P.V. LTD.
ALTERNATIVE INCOME STATEMENT
(good economy)
For Year 1

Accretion of discount	$26.03
Add: Abnormal earnings, as a result of good-state realization ($200 − $150)	50.00
Net income	$76.03

The abnormal earnings of $50 is the difference between actual and expected cash flows for year 1, and these abnormal earnings increase expected earnings up to a profit of $76.03.

The year-end balance sheet is:

P.V. LTD.
BALANCE SHEET
(good economy)
As at End of Year 1

Financial Asset			**Shareholders' Equity**	
Cash		$200.00	Opening value	$260.33
Capital Asset			Net income	76.03
Opening value	$260.33			
Accumulated				
amortization	123.97	136.36		
		$336.36		$336.36

Again, arbitrage ensures that the firm's market value at time 1 will be $336.36, given risk-neutral investors.

Note the following points about Example 2.2:

1. It continues to be the case that financial statements are both completely relevant and completely reliable. They are relevant because balance sheet values are based on expected future cash flows, and dividend irrelevancy holds. They are reliable because ideal conditions ensure that present value calculations are precise and free of bias—a complete set of states of nature plus objective state probabilities, together with a given, fixed interest rate, enable a present value calculation that is incapable of error, or of being manipulated by management. All relevant future states are anticipated and since state probabilities are objective and publicly known, the expected present value cannot be proven wrong by subsequent events. Of course, reliability here is in an *ex ante* sense. Expected time 1 value calculated at time 0 will generally not equal actual value at time 1, depending on which state is realized. Nevertheless, for investor decision-making purposes, beginning-of-period present value is what is needed, and this is completely reliable in our example.

2. Like the certainty case, there are still two ways of calculating balance sheet fair values: we can calculate expected present values directly or we can use market values. Under ideal conditions, arbitrage forces the two ways to yield identical results.

3. Despite the fact that expected and realized net income need not be equal, the income statement still has no information content when abnormal earnings do not persist. Investors have sufficient information to calculate for themselves what realized net income will be, once they know the current year's state realization. This calculation is programmable and no accounting policy decisions are needed.

4. At the risk of getting ahead of ourselves, let us see how the income statement *can* be informative. For this, we need only relax the assumption that state probabilities are objective. This puts us into the realm of **subjective** probabilities, which are formally introduced in Chapter 3. Then, investors no longer have "ready-made" state probabilities available to them for purposes of calculating expected future cash flows and income. Rather, they must assess these probabilities themselves, using whatever information is available. There is no longer any guarantee that in a long-run sequence of repetitions of the economy, the bad and good states will occur with the same relative frequencies as the probabilities assigned by the investor. The reason, of course, is that individuals are limited in their knowledge and forecasting ability. Note that if state probabilities are subjective, so are the resulting expected values. That is, the value of the firm is also subjective.

    Subjective probabilities are a more reasonable assumption than objective probabilities, because the future performance of a business entity is much more complex and difficult to predict than a simple roll of fair dice. Since investors know that their predictions are subject to error, they will be alert for information sources that enable them to revise their probability assessments. The income statement is one such source. When state probabilities are subjective, the income statement can provide information about what these probabilities are. For example, observing a net income of $76.03 this year in Example 2.2 may cause you to increase your probability of the high state in future years. This would improve your ability to predict firm cash flows and profitability.

If this argument is unclear to you, return to the analogy of rolling dice, but now assume that you do not know whether the dice are fair. What is your probability of rolling a seven? Obviously, this probability is no longer objective, and you must assess it on the basis of whatever information and prior experience you have. However, rolling the dice (analogous to observing the income statement) provides information, and after a few rolls you should have a better idea whether their true state is fair or not fair. For example, if you rolled five times and a seven came up each time, you would probably want to increase from 1/6 your subjective probability of rolling a seven. Just as improved knowledge of the true state of the dice will help you to predict future rolls, improved knowledge of the true state of the firm will help you to predict future profitability and investment returns. In Chapter 3 we will show how investors can use financial statement information to revise their subjective probabilities of future firm performance.

SUMMARY

The purpose of Example 2.2 is to extend the present value model to formally incorporate uncertainty, using the concepts of states of nature and objective probabilities. The definition of ideal conditions must be extended to include a complete and publicly known set of states of nature, with future cash flows known *conditionally* on state realization. Also, ideal conditions now specify objective state probabilities and that the state realization be publicly observable. The logic of the present value model under certainty then carries over, except that market values are based on *expected* cash flows, assuming investors are risk-neutral.

The major difference between the certainty and uncertainty cases is that *expected* and *realized* net income need no longer be the same under uncertainty, and the difference is called abnormal earnings. Nevertheless, financial statements based on expected present values continue to be both relevant and reliable. They are relevant because they are based on expected future cash flows. They are reliable because financial statement values objectively reflect these expected future cash flows and, as in the certainty case, management manipulation is not possible.

All of these conclusions are independent of the firm's dividend policy, since dividend irrelevancy continues to hold.

2.4 Reserve Recognition Accounting (RRA)

2.4.1 AN EXAMPLE OF RRA

By now, you probably want to point out that the real world is *not* characterized by ideal conditions. This is quite true. Nevertheless, accounting practice is moving strongly towards increased use of fair values for major classes of assets and liabilities. For example, defined postemployment benefits to retirees, such as pensions, health-care, and disability are accounted for on the basis of expected future benefit payments under the FASB's Statement of Financial Accounting Standards (SFAS) 87 and 106 in the United States, and Section 3461 of *CICA Handbook* in Canada. Also, SFAS 133 requires that all derivative financial instruments be measured at fair value. These and other examples of the measurement perspective are reviewed in Chapter 7.

Despite the moves towards fair value, the present value model encounters serious reliability problems when we try to apply it without ideal conditions. To illustrate these problems, we now consider reserve recognition accounting for oil and gas companies.

In 1982, the FASB issued SFAS 69, which requires supplemental disclosure of certain information about the operations of publicly traded oil and gas companies. An interesting aspect of SFAS 69 is that disclosure of the estimated present value of future receipts from a company's proved oil and gas reserves is required. The estimate is known as the "standardized measure." The intent, presumably, is to provide investors with more relevant information about future cash flows than that contained in the conventional, historical cost-based financial statements. Oil and gas companies, it can be argued, particularly need to give this type of supplementary disclosure because the historical cost of oil and gas properties may bear little relationship to their value.

It can hardly be said that oil and gas companies operate under conditions of certainty. Consequently, we shall consider SFAS 69 in relation to our present value model under uncertainty, which was illustrated in Example 2.2. Present value accounting applied to oil and gas reserves is known as **reserve recognition accounting (RRA)**.

Consider first Table 2.1, adapted from the 2000 annual report of Chieftain International, Inc., a Canadian corporation with shares traded on the Toronto Stock Exchange and on the American Stock Exchange in the United States. Note that the undiscounted future net cash flows are shown, and also the present value of these cash flows, discounted at 10%. No information is given about the riskiness of the estimates. That is, no states of nature and probabilities are given, only the end results of the expectation calculation.

TABLE 2.1   CHIEFTAIN INTERNATIONAL, INC.
PRESENT VALUE OF ESTIMATED FUTURE NET CASH FLOWS (millions)

December 31	2000	1999	1998
Future cash inflows	$2,096	$677	$402
Future production and development costs	(329)	(274)	(186)
Future income taxes	(544)	(63)	–
Future net cash flows	1,223	340	216
10% discount factor	(374)	(115)	(63)
Standardized measure	$ 849	$225	$153

SOURCE: 2000 annual report of Chieftain International, Inc. Reprinted by permission.

This disclosure seems to conform fairly well to our theoretical Example 2.2. The $849 is the amount that would appear on Chieftain's December 31, 2000 present value-based balance sheet for the asset "proved oil and gas reserves" if one was prepared. It corresponds to the $136.36 valuation of the capital asset at time 1 in Example 2.2. It should be noted, however, that the 10% discount rate used by Chieftain is not the single known rate in the economy. Rather, this rate is mandated by SFAS 69, presumably for comparability across firms. Also, as mentioned, the figures apply only to proved reserves and not all of Chieftain's assets.

Table 2.2 gives changes in the standardized measure.

TABLE 2.2   CHIEFTAIN INTERNATIONAL, INC.
CHANGES IN THE STANDARDIZED MEASURE OF DISCOUNTED FUTURE NET
CASH FLOWS (thousands of dollars)

	2000	1999	1998
Standardized measure, beginning of year	$225	$153	$200
Changes result from:			
Sales, net of production costs	(103)	(61)	(45)
Net change in prices and production costs	710	83	(80)
Extensions and discoveries, net of costs	224	83	30
Change in estimated future development costs	(39)	(23)	(16)
Development costs incurred during the year	28	10	23
Revisions to quantity estimates	88	(8)	(17)
Accretion of discount	22	15	20
Purchase of reserves in place	11	–	3
Changes in timing and other	14	15	(4)
Net change in income taxes	(331)	(42)	39
Standardized measure, end of year	$849	$225	$153

SOURCE: 2000 annual report of Chieftain International, Inc. Reprinted by permission.

To understand this statement, we rework Example 2.2 in Table 2.3 to show the changes in the book value of the capital asset during the year, assuming state 2 (good economy) is realized (a similar analysis applies to state 1).

TABLE 2.3 EXAMPLE 2.2: CHANGE IN BOOK VALUE OF CAPITAL ASSET DURING THE YEAR (state 2 realized)		
Present value of capital asset, beginning of year (time 0)		$260.33
Less: Sales in year 1		200.00
		60.33
Add:		
Accretion of discount	$26.03	
Unexpected cash flows	50.00	76.03
BV of capital asset, end of year (time 1)		$136.36

Now, we rework Chieftain's Changes in the Standardized Measure in Table 2.2 into a format consistent with Table 2.3, as shown in Table 2.4.

TABLE 2.4 CHIEFTAIN INTERNATIONAL, INC. REWORKED STANDARDIZED MEASURE FOR THE YEAR ENDED DECEMBER 31, 2000 (thousands of dollars)			
Present value of standardized measure at beginning of year			$225
Less: Sales in year			103
			122
Add:			
Accretion of discount		$ 22	
Present value of additional reserves added during year (224 + 11)		235	
Development costs incurred during year		28	
Unexpected items—changes in value of previous-year reserves:			
Net change in prices and production costs	$710		
Revisions to quantity estimates	88		
Change in future development costs	(39)		
Changes in timing and other	14		
Net change in income taxes	(331)	442	727
Present value of standardized measure at end of year			$849

Check each of these numbers from the original Chieftain International statement in Tables 2.1 and 2.2. The $28 of development costs incurred during the year represents the increase in present value resulting from the expenditure of some of the development costs allowed for in the beginning-of-year present value.

The changes in estimates of $442 should be considered carefully. Note, in particular, that there are a number of changes, including revisions of quantities, prices, and costs as well as income taxes. Note also that the amounts are quite material. For example, the net change in prices and production costs of $710 is 3.16 times the present value at the beginning of 2000. The number and magnitude of these changes are the main differences between our Example 2.2, which assumed ideal conditions, and the "real world" environment in which Chieftain operates. We shall return to this point shortly.

Note that the accretion of discount is 10% of beginning-of-year present value, as it was in Example 2.2.

Finally, what would Chieftain's 2000 present value-based net income from proved oil and gas reserves be? This can be quite simply calculated as in Table 2.5.

TABLE 2.5   CHIEFTAIN INTERNATIONAL, INC.
INCOME STATEMENT FOR 2000 FROM PROVED OIL AND GAS RESERVES
(thousands of dollars)

Sales in year	$103
Development costs incurred in year	(28)
Amortization "expense" (increase in present value of reserves during the year (849 − 225)	624
Net income from proved oil and gas reserves	$699

Or, in the alternative format:

Expected net income—accretion of discount		$ 22
Abnormal Earnings:		
Present value of additional reserves added during year	235	
Unexpected items—changes in value of previous-year reserves	442	677
Net income from proved oil and gas reserves		$699

Again, the material impact on net income of changes in estimates is apparent. These amount to almost 31 times expected net income. Note also that amortization expense is negative for the year. This can happen under present value accounting, and simply means that present value increased over the year.

Summary

The procedures used by Chieftain International to account for the results of its oil and gas operations under RRA seem to conform to the theoretical present value model under uncertainty, except that it is necessary to make material changes to the estimates.

2.4.2   CRITIQUE OF RRA

Management's Reaction

This necessity to make changes in estimates seems to be the Achilles' heel of RRA. Oil company managers, in particular, tend to regard RRA with reservation and suspicion. As an example, the following statement appears in Chieftain's 2000 RRA disclosure:

> *The inexactness associated with estimating reserve quantities, future production streams, and future development and production expenditures, together with the assumptions applied in valuing future production, substantially diminish the reliability of this data. The values so derived are not considered to be estimates of fair market value. We therefore caution against simplistic use of this information.*

One might ask why Chieftain reports RRA information at all, since SFAS 69 is a U.S. accounting standard. However, since its shares are traded on the American Stock Exchange, it must meet U.S. reporting requirements. Also, it may want to report information with which U.S. investors are familiar. Since the RRA information has been prepared, it can also be reported to Canadian shareholders at little additional cost.

Usefulness to Investors

While it is clear that management is cautious about RRA, this does not necessarily mean that it does not provide useful information to investors. Certainly, RRA is more relevant than historical cost information, so it has the potential to be useful. To see the potential for relevance, compare the present value-based 2000 net income from Table 2.5 with Chieftain's historical cost-based earnings from oil and gas[5] summarized in Table 2.6.

TABLE 2.6   CHIEFTAIN INTERNATIONAL, INC.
EARNINGS FROM OIL AND GAS PRODUCING ACTIVITIES FOR THE YEAR ENDED
DECEMBER 31, 2000 (thousands of dollars)

RESULTS OF OPERATIONS

December 31	2000	1999	1998
Total sales to customers	$117	$75	$62
Production expenses	(17)	(19)	(18)
Depletion and depreciation	(44)	(68)	(48)
Income taxes	(20)	6	2
Results of operations	36	$ (6)	$ (2)

SOURCE: 2000 annual report of Chieftain International, Inc. Reprinted by permission.

Comparison of net income under the two bases is complicated by the fact that the present value calculations relate only to proved reserves. However, let us take the $36 thousand total results of operations for 2000 in Table 2.6 as the historical cost analogue of the $699 thousand present value-based income in Table 2.5. We see that the present value-based earnings are *much* higher than their historical cost-based counterpart. This seems reasonable, since Table 2.2 tells us that the present value of proved reserves increased by $624,000 during the year. The reason for the increase is primarily the major rise in oil and gas prices during the year. From Table 2.2, this rise in prices increased the present value of proved reserves by $710 (less income taxes of $331). Under historical cost accounting, as you know, this increase in the value of the proved reserves would not show up in the income statement until the proved reserves were produced and sold. In effect, the present value-based income statement recognizes the increase "sooner." Thus, present value information has the potential for usefulness because of this greater relevance.

If RRA is in fact useful, we should observe some reaction in the price of Chieftain's shares to the release of RRA information. Empirical evidence on the usefulness of RRA is reviewed in Chapter 5. For now, suffice it to say that it has been difficult to find evidence of usefulness.

Discussion

Management's concerns, as quoted above, suggest that something is amiss. Why would management be concerned about information that has considerable relevance for investors? The main point to realize is that Chieftain does not operate under the ideal conditions of Examples 2.1 and 2.2. Consider the difficulties that Chieftain's accountants face in applying ideal conditions. First, interest rates in the economy are not fixed, although SFAS 69 deals with this by requiring a fixed, given rate of 10% for the discounting. Second, the set of states of nature affecting the amounts, prices, and timing of future production is much larger than the simple two-state set in Example 2.2, due to the complex environment in which oil and gas companies operate. However, in principle, it should be possible to come up with a reasonable list of future possibilities. For example, management could list the possible future events that it is "worried about." Third, it is unlikely that the state realization would be publicly observable. Events like equipment breakdowns, production problems, and minor oil spills would most likely be inside information of the firm. As a result, outsiders have no way of knowing whether the changes in estimates are precise and unbiased, particularly since RRA is unaudited.[6]

While these difficulties could probably be dealt with, a fourth problem is more fundamental. Objective state probabilities are not available. Consequently, subjective state probabilities need to be assessed by Chieftain's engineers and accountants, with the result that the standardized measure is itself a subjective estimate.

Because of these difficulties in applying ideal conditions, the reliability of RRA information is severely compromised. This shows up in the number and materiality of revisions to estimates that need to be made, as shown in Table 2.4. It is not that estimates of expected future cash flows cannot be made. After all, RRA is "on line." Rather, lacking objective probabilities, these estimates become subject to revisions that threaten reliability to the point where the benefit of increased relevance is compromised, at least in management's opinion. The important point is that, without ideal conditions, complete relevance and reliability are no longer jointly attainable. One must be traded off against the other.

2.4.3 SUMMARY

RRA represents a valiant attempt to convey relevant information to investors. On the surface, the present value information conforms quite closely to the theoretical present value model under uncertainty. If one digs deeper, however, serious problems of estimation are revealed. This is because oil and gas companies do not operate under the ideal conditions assumed by the theoretical model. As a result, reserve information loses reliability, as evidenced by the need for substantial annual revisions, as it gains relevance. It seems necessary to trade off these two desirable information qualities.

2.5 *Historical Cost Accounting Revisited*

As our discussion of RRA in Section 2.4 points out, as a practical matter it seems impossible to prepare financial statements that are both completely relevant and completely reliable. Consequently, relevance and reliability must be traded off. The historical cost basis of accounting can be thought of as one such tradeoff. Recall that under historical cost accounting the primary basis of valuation for several major asset categories, such as inventories, long-term portfolio investments, and capital assets including intangibles, is *cost*, or cost less amounts written off as amortization. On the liability side, long-term debt is also valued at cost, in the sense that the carrying value of such debt is based on interest rates in effect when the debt was issued—carrying value is not adjusted for subsequent interest rate changes.

Historical cost accounting is relatively reliable because the cost of an asset or liability to a firm is usually an objective number that is less subject to errors of estimation and bias than are present value calculations. Unfortunately, however, historical costs may lack relevance. While historical cost, market value, and present value may be similar as at the date of acquisition, market values and present values will change over time as market conditions change. Nevertheless, accountants continue to use the historical cost basis of accounting for major asset types because they are willing to trade off a considerable amount of relevance to obtain reasonable reliability. Consequently, historical cost accounting represents a particular tradeoff between the two.

2.5.1   THE CHALLENGE OF HISTORICAL COST ACCOUNTING

The essential difference between present value-based accounting such as RRA and historical cost-based accounting (or any other basis of accounting, for that matter) is one of *timing* of recognition of changes in asset value (on this point, see Chapter 3, Question 19). Present value accounting is a balance sheet approach to accounting, also called a **measurement perspective**. That is, increases (or decreases) in asset and liability values are recognized (measured) as they occur, by discounting future cash flows (the essence of value) and capitalizing them on the balance sheet. Income is then essentially the net change in present values for the period.

Historical cost accounting, however, is an income statement approach, also called an **information perspective**. Under this perspective, unrealized increases in value are not recognized on the balance sheet, and net income lags behind real economic performance. That is, the accountant "waits" until increases in value are validated through realization as increased sales or cash flows. Income is then a process of matching of revenues with the costs of earning those revenues. The income statement assumes a more important role, since it provides information on the current "installment" of the value created by the firm.[7]

When conditions are not ideal, the question then is, does historical cost-based accounting provide better information about the firm's *future* economic prospects (the primary interest of investors) than present value-based accounting? Accountants have debated this question for many years, and we return to it in Chapter 6. For now, suffice it to say that arguments can be made in favour of the income statement approach. One argument is the relative reliability of historical cost, as mentioned above. More fundamentally, historical cost accounting is a way to "smooth out" current period cash flows into a measure of the longer-run or persistent earning power that is implied by those cash flows. Persistent earning power then provides the basis for an assessment of future economic prospects.

To smooth out current period cash flows, the accountant has to calculate **accruals**, that is, to match costs and revenues. However, at this point, historical cost accounting faces a major challenge. There is usually no unique way to match costs with revenues. This complicates the ability of historical cost-based earnings to reveal persistent earning power. To illustrate, we now consider three examples.

Amortization of Capital Assets

A major problem with matching is the amortization of capital assets. The matching principle deems it necessary to deduct amortization of capital assets from revenue for the period to arrive at net income. Yet, it does not state *how much* amortization should be accrued except for a vague indication that it should be systematic and rational. For example, paragraph 3060.31 of the *CICA Handbook* states that amortization should be recognized in a rational and systematic manner appropriate to the nature of a capital asset with a limited life and its use by the firm.

As a result of this vagueness, a variety of amortization methods are acceptable for use in practice, such as straight-line, declining-balance, and so on.

If it were possible to value capital assets on a present value basis for the financial statements, we would need only *one* amortization method—the change in the present value of the future receipts from the assets during the period, as illustrated in Examples 2.1 and 2.2. As it is not usually possible to reliably value capital assets this way, the door is opened to a variety of amortization methods. This complicates the comparison of profitability across firms, because we must ascertain the amortization methods firms are using before making comparisons. It also means that firm managers have some room to manage their reported profitability through choice of amortization method or through changes to the method used. Thus, while one can argue, as we have above, that historical cost financial statements may be more reliable than those prepared on a present value or market value basis, this reliability may be eroded to the extent that managers can choose between alternative historical-cost-based accounting policies to manage reported net income for their own purposes. In other words, while historical cost accounting may be more reliable than value-based methods, it is by no means completely reliable.

Future Income Tax Liability

A major accounting controversy in Canada arose in 1953 when the *Income Tax Act* was amended to allow firms to choose the method of amortization they wanted for their reported financial statements, while claiming maximum capital cost allowance on their tax returns. Prior to this, firms could not claim more capital cost allowance than the amortization they recorded in their financial statements. Most firms responded to the 1953 amendment by using straight-line amortization for financial reporting while claiming maximum capital cost allowance for tax purposes. Since capital cost allowance is a form of declining balance amortization, this created an income tax accounting problem. Taxes saved by claiming maximum capital cost allowance in the early years of an asset's life did not necessarily represent a permanent saving but instead created a liability to repay the taxes in later years, when maximum capital cost allowance was less than straight-line amortization for capital assets.

The controversy was whether to record the tax liability (and resulting higher income tax expense) on the firm's financial statements. Some argued that these should be recorded, because the matching principle of historical cost accounting required that income tax expense should be matched with the amount of amortization actually recorded on the financial statements. Others, however, felt that the recording of a liability was not required by the matching principle. In most cases (for example, if a firm was growing, in which case capital cost allowance would tend to remain greater than straight line amortization), the possibility that the taxes saved would have to be repaid in some future year was remote. It does not make sense, they argued, to match costs that are unlikely to be paid with revenue. The controversy continued until 1963, when the *CICA Handbook* required recording of the liability.

Currently, paragraph 3465.10 of *CICA Handbook* states that the firm shall recognize a future income tax liability whenever recovery or settlement of the carrying amount of an asset or liability would result in future income tax payments.

Note that the essential source of the future tax liability question is the multiplicity of acceptable amortization methods under historical cost accounting. The problem arises because the method firms use on their financial statements usually differs from the method allowed for tax purposes. If there was only one amortization method, as under present value accounting with ideal conditions, firms' book and tax figures would be the same and the tax liability problem for amortization would not arise.

Full-Cost Versus Successful-Efforts in Oil and Gas Accounting

Under historical cost accounting, we need to know the *cost* of assets, so that they can be amortized (matched) against revenues over their useful lives. We suggested earlier in this section that the cost of assets is usually reliably determinable. However, in some cases, even the cost of assets is not clear. Oil and gas accounting provides an interesting and important example.

There are two basic methods of determining the cost of oil and gas reserves. The **full-cost** method capitalizes all costs of discovering reserves (subject to certain exceptions), including the costs of unsuccessful drilling. The argument is that the cost of successful wells includes the costs of dry holes drilled in the search for the successful ones. The **successful-efforts** method capitalizes only the costs of successful wells and expenses dry holes, the rationale being that it is difficult to regard a dry hole in the ground as an asset.

Clearly, these two approaches can produce materially different recorded costs for oil and gas reserves, with the result that amortization expense can also be materially different. In turn, this complicates the comparison of the reported net incomes of oil and gas firms, because different firms may use different methods for determining the cost of their reserves. For our purposes, however, simply note that the historical cost basis of accounting cannot settle the question of which method is preferable. The historical cost basis requires only that a cost of oil and gas reserves be established. It does not require a particular method for establishing what the cost should be. In fact, the *CICA Handbook* (paragraph 3060.25) allows both methods to be used in Canada (subject to certain exceptions).

Notice that use of RRA in the firm's accounts would eliminate the full-cost versus successful-efforts controversy. RRA values oil and gas reserves at their present values. It is *not* a cost-based approach, so the question of how to determine cost does not arise. Under RRA, amortization expense is the change in the present value of oil and gas reserves during the period.

2.5.2   ACCOUNTANTS' REACTION TO THE CHALLENGE

Since it seems impossible to prepare a complete set of present value-based financial statements with sufficient reliability, the historical cost accounting framework will likely be with us for a long time to come. Consequently, the major accounting bodies have reacted to the challenge of historical cost-based accounting by retaining its framework, but turning their attention to making financial statements more *useful*, within that framework. This is not to say that certain assets and liabilities cannot be reported on a present value or market value basis. Indeed, use of fair values in the financial statements is increasing, as will be discussed in Chapters 6 and 7. Nevertheless, since major asset and liability categories, such as capital assets and long-term debt, continue to be accounted for primarily on the historical cost basis, we can still say that this is the basic framework of accounting.

To increase the usefulness of historical cost accounting, accountants have tended to adopt a strategy of *full disclosure*. Disclosure of accounting policies used enables investors to at least be aware of the particular policies the firm has chosen out of the multiplicity of policies that are available for most assets and liabilities. Also, **supplementary information** is given to help investors project current performance into the future. The RRA disclosure discussed in Section 2.4 is an example of such supplementary information.

2.5.3   SUMMARY

The continued use of historical cost accounting in financial reporting can be thought of as a consequence of the impossibility of preparing reliable financial statements on a present value basis. The use of historical cost accounting represents a particular tradeoff between relevance and reliability. Complete relevance is not attained, because historical cost-based asset values need bear little resemblance to discounted present values. However, complete reliability is not attained either, since the possibility of imprecision and bias remains. The measurement of net income becomes a process of matching, rather than a simple calculation of accretion of discount, and the matching principle usually allows different ways of accounting for the same item. Frequently, accounting standard setting bodies step in to impose uniform accounting policies to reduce the multiplicity of policy choices.

Given the continuing use of historical cost-based accounting in practice, accountants have tried to make the historical cost framework more useful. One way of increasing usefulness is to retain the historical cost framework but expand disclosure in the annual report, so as to help investors to make their own estimates of future economic prospects.

2.6 The Non-Existence of True Net Income

To prepare a complete set of financial statements on a present value basis, recall that it is necessary to value *all* of the firm's assets and liabilities this way, with net income being the change in the firm's present value during the period (adjusted for capital transactions such as dividends). Yet, we saw with RRA that severe problems arise when we try to apply the present value approach to even a single type of asset. These problems would be compounded if the approach was extended to all other assets and liabilities.

This leads to an important and interesting conclusion, namely that under the real-world conditions in which accounting operates, *net income does not exist as a well-defined economic construct*. As evidence, simply consider Chieftain International's 2000 RRA net income of $699,000 in Table 2.5. How can we take this as well-defined, or "true," income when we know that next year there will be another flock of unanticipated changes to the estimates that underlie the 2000 income calculation?

A fundamental problem is the lack of objective state probabilities. With objective probabilities, present values of assets and liabilities correctly reflect the uncertainty facing the firm, since present values then take into account all possible future events and their probabilities. In this case, accounting information is completely relevant as well as completely reliable and true economic income exists.

An indirect approach to true economic income of basing the income calculation on changes in market values rather than present values runs into the problem that market values need not exist for all firm assets and liabilities, a condition known as **incomplete markets**. For example, while there may be a market price for a barrel of crude oil, what is the market value of Chieftain's reserves? In the face of uncertainties over quantities, prices, and lifting costs, an attempt to establish their market value runs into the same estimation problems as RRA. As a result, a ready market value is not available. If market values are not available for all firm assets and liabilities, an income measure based on market values is not possible. Beaver and Demski (1979) give formal arguments to show that income is not well defined when markets are incomplete.[8]

Lacking objective probabilities, the door is opened for subjective estimates of future firm performance. These estimates can be subject to both lack of precision and possible bias. As a result, accounting estimates based on present value lose reliability as they strive to maintain relevance.

Thus, a second conclusion is that accountants feel that historical cost-based accounting for major classes of operating assets and liabilities represents a more useful way to account, since we observe historical cost accounting for these classes strongly rooted in practice. Some relevance is lost, but hopefully this is more than made up for by increased reliability.

You may be bothered by the claim that true net income does not exist. Should we devote our careers to measuring something that doesn't exist? However, we should be glad of the impossibility of ideal conditions. If they existed, no one would need accountants! As discussed in Examples 2.1 and 2.2, net income has no information content when conditions are ideal. The present value calculations and related income measurement could then be programmed in advance. All that is needed is the set of states, their probabilities, and knowledge of which state is realized, and accountants would not be needed for this. Thus, we can say of income measurement, "If we can solve it, we don't need it."

This lack of a theoretically correct concept of income is what makes accounting both frustrating and fascinating at the same time. It is frustrating because of the difficulty of agreeing on accounting policies. Different users will typically want different tradeoffs between relevance and reliability. As a result, there are often several ways of accounting for the same thing. It is fascinating because the lack of a well-defined concept of net income means that a great deal of *judgement* must go into the process of asset valuation and income measurement. It is judgement that makes accounting valuable and, indeed, provides the very basis of a profession.

2.7   Conclusion

Instead of dwelling on questions of existence of net income, accountants turned their efforts to making historical cost-based financial statements more useful. We will now proceed to study decision usefulness.

Questions and Problems

1. Prepare the income statement for year 2 and the balance sheet at the end of year 2 for P.V. Ltd. in Example 2.1 under the assumption that P.V. Ltd. pays no dividends.
   (CGA-Canada)

2. Show that an owner of P.V. Ltd. in Example 2.1 would not care whether P.V. Ltd. paid any dividend at the end of year 1. State precisely why this is the case.
   (CGA-Canada)

3. Calculate the expected net income for P.V. Ltd. for years 1 and 2 in Example 2.2. Explain why expected net income is also called "accretion of discount."
   (CGA-Canada)

4. Show that an owner of P.V. Ltd. in Example 2.2 would not care whether P.V. Ltd. paid any dividend at the end of year 1. Assume that the good-economy state was realized in year 1.
   (CGA-Canada)

5. In Example 2.2, assume that P.V. Ltd. pays no dividends over its life, until a liquidating dividend is paid at the end of year 2 consisting of its cash on hand at that time.

   Required

   Verify that the market value of P.V. Ltd. at time 0 based on the present value of dividends equals $260.33, equal to P.V.'s market value based on expected future cash flows.

6. A simple example of the difference between ideal and non-ideal conditions is the rolling of a die.

   Required

   a. Calculate the expected value of a single roll of a fair die.
   b. Now suppose that you are unsure whether the die is fair. How would you then calculate the expected value of a single roll?
   c. Now roll the die four times. You obtain 6, 4, 1, 3. Does this information affect your belief that the die is fair? Explain.

7. Explain why, under ideal conditions, there is no need to make estimates when calculating expected present value.

8. Explain why estimates are required to calculate expected present value when conditions are *not* ideal.
   (CGA-Canada)

9. Do you think that the market value of an oil and gas firm will be affected when RRA information is presented in addition to historical cost-based earnings from oil and gas producing activities? Explain why or why not.

10. Explain why, under non-ideal conditions, it is necessary to trade off relevance and reliability. Define these two terms as part of your answer.   (CGA-Canada)

11. Why do you think Chieftain International's management expresses severe reservations about RRA?

12. The text discussion of RRA is in terms of the relevance and reliability of the asset valuation of oil and gas reserves. RRA can also be evaluated in terms of the criteria for revenue recognition. *CICA Handbook*, Section 3400, states that revenue involving the sale of goods and services should be recognized when the seller has transferred to the buyer the significant risks and rewards of ownership, and reasonable assurance exists regarding the measurement of the consideration that will be received.

    Required
    a. At what point in their operating cycle do most industrial and retail firms regard revenue as having been earned (i.e., realized)? Use the two *CICA Handbook* criteria above to explain why.
    b. Suppose that X Ltd. is an oil and gas producer. X Ltd. uses RRA on its books and prepares its financial statements on this basis. When (i.e., at what point in the operating cycle) is revenue recognized under RRA? Does this point meet the criteria for revenue recognition under GAAP as given in the *CICA Handbook* above? Explain why or why not.

13. Inventory is another asset for which there is a variety of ways to account under historical cost accounting, including first-in, first-out; last-in, first-out; average cost; etc.

    a. How would inventory be accounted for under ideal conditions?
    b. Give reasons why inventory is usually accounted for on a historical cost basis. Is accounting on this basis completely reliable? Why?

14. P Ltd. operates under ideal conditions. It has just bought a fixed asset for $3,100, which will generate $1,210 cash flow at the end of one year and $2,000 at the end of the second year. At that time, the asset will be useless in operations and P Ltd. plans to go out of business. The asset will have a known salvage value of $420 at the end of the second year. The interest rate in the economy is constant at 10% per annum.

    P Ltd. finances the asset by issuing $605 par value of 12% coupon bonds to yield 10%. Interest is payable at the end of the first and second year, at which time the bonds mature. The balance of the cost of the asset is financed by the issuance of common shares.

    Required
    a. Prepare the present value-based balance sheet as at the end of the first year. P Ltd. plans to pay no dividends in this year.

b. Give two reasons why ideal conditions are unlikely to hold.

c. If ideal conditions do not hold, but present-value-based financial statements are prepared anyway, is net income likely to be the same as you calculated in part **a**? Explain why or why not.   (CGA-Canada)

15. Relevant Ltd. operates under ideal conditions of uncertainty. Its operations are highly dependent on the weather. For any given year, the probabilities are 0.3 that the weather will be bad and 0.7 that it will be good. These state probabilities are independent over time. That is, the state probabilities for a given year are not affected by the actual weather in previous years.

Relevant Ltd. produces a single product for which the demand will fall to zero at the end of 2 years. It produces this product using specialized machinery, which will have no value at the end of 2 years. The machinery was purchased on 1 January, 2001. It was financed in part by means of a bank loan of $2,000 repayable at the end of 2002, with the balance financed by capital stock. No dividends will be paid until the end 2002. Interest on the bank loan is payable at the end of each year. The interest rate in the economy is 6%.

Cash flows are not received until the end of each year. Amounts of cash flows for each year are given in the following payoff table:

STATE	PROBABILITY	CASH FLOW YEAR 1	CASH FLOW YEAR 2
Bad weather	0.3	$600	$400
Good weather	0.7	$6000	$3000

State realization for 2001 is good weather.

Required

a. Prepare, in good form, a balance sheet for Relevant Ltd. as at the end of 2001 and an income statement for 2001.

b. As at January 1, 2002, how much is expected net income for 2002?

c. Explain why the financial statements you have prepared in part **a** are both completely relevant and completely reliable.

Note: In the following two problems, state probabilities are not independent over time.

16. XYZ Ltd. purchased an asset on January 1, 2000 with a useful life of two years at the end of which it has no residual value. The cash flows from the asset are uncertain. If the economy turns out to be "normal," the asset will generate $4,000 in cash flow each year; if the economy is "bad," it will generate $3,000 in cash flow per year; and if the economy is "good," the cash flow generated will be $5,000 per year. Cash flows are received at year-end. The chances of a "normal" economy being realized are 30%, the chances of a "bad" economy are

50%, and the chances of a "good" economy are 20%. State realization for both years becomes publicly known at the end of 2000, that is, if the normal state happens for year 1, it will also happen for year 2, etc.

Assumptions

- Ideal conditions hold under uncertainty.
- The economy-wide interest rate is 10%.
- XYZ Ltd. finances the asset purchase partly by a bond issue and partly by a common share issue. The bond has a $3,000 face value and a 10% coupon rate and matures on December 31, 2001.
- XYZ Ltd. has adopted the policy of paying out 50% of its net income as dividends to its shareholders.
- The economy turns out to be "good."

Required

a. Calculate the present values of the asset at January 1, 2000, and December 31, 2000.

b. Prepare the present value-based income statement of XYZ Ltd. for the year ended December 31, 2000.

c. Prepare the present value-based balance sheet of XYZ Ltd. as at December 31, 2000.

d. Explain why, even under uncertainty, present value-based financial statements are relevant and reliable provided ideal conditions hold.

e. Explain why shareholders of XYZ Ltd. are indifferent to whether they receive any dividend from the company.

17. Conditional Ltd. operates under ideal conditions of uncertainty. It has just purchased a new machine, at a cost of $3,575.10, paid for entirely from the proceeds of a stock issue. The interest rate in the economy is 8%. The machine is expected to last for 2 years, after which time it will have zero salvage value.

The new machine is an experimental model, and its suitability for use in Conditional's operations is not completely known. Conditional assesses a 0.75 probability that there will be a major machine failure during the first year of operation, and a 0.25 probability that the machine will operate as planned. If there is a major failure, cash flow for the year will be $1,000. If the machine operates as planned, cash flow will be $3,000 for the year. If there is no major failure in the first year, the probability of a major failure in the second year, and resulting cash flows of $1,000, falls to 0.60. If there is no major failure in the second year, cash flows for that year will again be $3,000. However, if there is a major failure in the first year, the lessons learned from correcting it will result in only a 0.10 probability of failure in the second year.

It turns out that there is no major failure in the first year.

Required

a. Verify that the cost of $3,575.10 for the machine is correct.

b. Prepare the income statement for year 1 under the "sales less amortization" format.

c. Prepare the income statement for year 1 under the "alternative" format.

d. Prepare a balance sheet as at the end of the first year.

18. An area where discounting could possibly be applied is for income tax liability resulting from timing differences. Consider a firm that purchases an asset costing $100,000 on January 1 of year 1. It is amortized on a straight-line basis at 20% per year on the firm's books. Tax amortization is 40% on a declining-balance basis. The income tax rate is 45%.

The following schedule shows a simplified calculation of the income tax liability balance for this asset over its life, assuming zero salvage value. This is the firm's only capital asset.

Year	Opening Tax B.V.	Additions	Tax Amortization	Straight-Line Amortization	Difference
1	—	100,000	40,000	20,000	20,000
2	60,000		24,000	20,000	4,000
3	36,000		14,400	20,000	(5,600)
4	21,600		8,640	20,000	(11,360)
5	12,960		12,960*	20,000	(7,040)

Year	Tax on Difference	Income Tax Liability
1	9,000	9,000
2	1,800	10,800
3	(2,520)	8,280
4	(5,112)	3,168
5	(3,168)	0

*It is assumed that all of the remaining tax book value is claimed in year 5.

Required

a. Calculate the discounted present value of the income tax liability at the end of each of years 1 to 5. Use a discount rate of 12%.

b. Why are the balances calculated in part a. different from the undiscounted income tax liabilities?

c. What problems would there be if the discounting approach was applied to the tax liability of a large, growing firm with many capital assets?

19. On January 1, 2000, ABC Ltd. started its business by purchasing a productive oil well. The proved oil reserves from the well are expected to generate $7,000 cash flow at the end of 2000, $6,000 at the end of 2001, and $5,000 at the end of 2002. Net sales is gross revenues less production costs. Net sales equals cash flows. On January 1, 2003, the oil well is expected to be dry. The management of ABC Ltd. wishes to prepare financial statements based on RRA in accordance with SFAS 69. The following information is known about the well at the end of 2000.

   - Actual cash flows in 2000 amounted to $6,500.

   - Changes in estimates: Due to improved recovery (of oil from the well), cash flows in 2001 and 2002 are estimated to be $6,500 and $6,000 respectively.

Required

a. Prepare the income statement of ABC Ltd. for 2000 from its proved oil reserves.

b. Management of some firms have expressed serious concerns about the reliability of the RRA information. Outline two of these concerns. (CGA-Canada)

20. On January 1, 2000, GAZ Ltd. purchased a producing oil well, with an estimated life of 15 years, and started operating it immediately. The management of GAZ Ltd. calculated the present value of future net cash flows from the well as $1,500,000. The discount rate used was 10%, which is the company's expected return on investment. During 2000, GAZ Ltd. recorded cash sales (net of production costs) of $600,000. GAZ Ltd. also paid $50,000 cash dividends during 2000.

Required

a. Prepare the income statement of GAZ Ltd. for the year ended December 31, 2000, using RRA.

b. Prepare the balance sheet of GAZ Ltd. as at December 31, 2000, using RRA.

c. Summarize the perceived weaknesses of RRA accounting.

d. Why does SFAS 69 require that a 10% discount rate should be used by all oil and gas firms rather than allowing each firm to select its own discount rate?

(CGA-Canada)

21. The following RRA information is taken from the December 31, 2000, annual report of FX Energy, Inc.

FX ENERGY, INC. CHANGES IN THE STANDARDIZED MEASURE OF DISCOUNTED FUTURE CASH FLOWS For the year ended December 31, 2000 ($ thousands)	
Present value at January 1, 2000	$5,460
Sales of oil produced, net of production costs	(1,172)
Net changes in prices and production costs	(159)
Extensions and discoveries, net of future costs	2,511
Changes in estimated future development costs	(53)
Previously estimated development costs incurred during the year	202
Revisions in previous quantity estimates	(31)
Accretion of discount	546
Changes in rates of production and other	116
Present value at December 31, 2000	$7,420

Required

a. Prepare income statements, similar to Table 2.5, in both the "sales less amortization" format and the "alternative" format.

b. Explain why amortization expense for 2000 is negative. FX Energy reports elsewhere in its annual report an (historical cost-based) operating loss from exploration and production for 2000 of $7,245. While all of this amount may not derive from proved reserves, take this operating loss as a reasonable historical cost-based analogue of the RRA income you calculated in part **a**. Also explain why RRA income for 2000 is different from the $7,245 loss under historical cost.

c. Explain why the standardized measure is applied only to proved reserves under SFAS 69.

d. SFAS 69 mandates a discount rate of 10% for the RRA present value calculations, rather than allowing each firm to choose its own rate. Why? Can you see any disadvantages to mandating a common discount rate?

Note: The item "extensions and discoveries, net of future costs" represents additional reserves proved during the year. Treat it as a separate abnormal earnings item in the alternative income statement. The item "changes in rates of production and other" represents changes in timing of extraction from the timing that was expected at the beginning of 2000.

22. The text states that matching of costs and revenues is a major challenge of historical cost accounting. Another challenge is **revenue recognition**, that is, when to recognize revenue as realized, or earned. Most firms recognize revenue as earned at the

point of sale. More generally, revenue from sale of goods should be recognized when the significant risks and rewards of ownership are transferred to the buyer, and reasonable assurance exists with respect to the amount of consideration to be received. For services and long-term contracts, revenue should be recognized as the work is performed, providing there is reasonable assurance of the amount of consideration that will be received from the service or contract (see *CICA Handbook*, Section 3400).

It is often not clear just when these general criteria are met. Furthermore, firms with no earnings history (e.g., startup firms) and firms that are incurring significant losses or declines in earnings have an incentive to record revenue as early as possible, so as to improve the appearance of their financial statements. Consider the case of Lucent Technologies Inc. In December 2000, Lucent restated its revenue for its fiscal year ended September 30, 2000, reducing the amounts originally reported as follows:

Vendor financing	$199 (millions)
Partial shipments	28
Distribution partners	452
Total	$679

The vendor financing component of the restatement represents previously unrecorded credits granted by Lucent to customers, to help them finance purchases of Lucent products. That is, the customer sales were originally recorded gross, rather than net, of the credits. The distribution partners component represents product shipped to firms with which Lucent did not deal at arms length, but which was not resold by these firms at year end. These firms included certain distributors in which Lucent had an ownership interest. The practice of over-shipping to distributors is called "stuffing the channels."

On February 9, 2001, *The Wall Street Journal* reported that the SEC was launching an investigation into possible fraudulent accounting practices at Lucent Technologies, arising from the original recording of the above revenue items.

In its 2000 Annual Report, Lucent reported net income of $1,219 (millions), compared to $4,789 millions for 1999 and $1,065 millions for 1998.

Required

a. What is the most relevant point of revenue recognition? The most reliable? Explain.

b. Do you feel that Lucent's original recognition of the above components as revenue was consistent with the general revenue recognition criteria given above? Explain why or why not. In your answer, consider the tradeoff between relevance and reliability.

c. What additional revenue recognition questions arise when the vendor has an ownership interest in the customer?

Notes

1. This argument can be turned around. We could argue that if the firm's future income statements were known with certainty, in conjunction with the interest rate, then they would contain all relevant information and the balance sheet could be easily deduced. In effect, each statement contains all the information needed for the other. We view the balance sheet as more fundamental under ideal conditions of certainty, however.

2. Here, the only financial item is cash. Generally, financial assets are assets whose values are fixed in terms of money, such as accounts receivable and investments with a fixed face value, such as bonds. Certain other assets, such as investments in shares, are also regarded as financial assets if a ready market value is available. Financial liabilities, such as accounts payable, bank loans, bonds issued, are defined similarly.

3. The independence assumption is not crucial to the example. With slight added complexity we could allow for conditional probabilities, where the probability of state realization in year 2 depends on the state realization in year 1. For example, if the high state happened in year 1, this might increase the probability that the high state would also happen in year 2. See problems 16 and 17.

4. Somewhat weaker conditions than these would be sufficient to give a first-best economy. Our purpose here, however, is only to give a set of conditions sufficient to ensure that net income is well defined and without information content.

5. SFAS 69 also requires the reporting of historical cost-based results of operations for oil and gas producing activities.

6. Note, however, from Table 2.2, that changes to estimates are separately reported under RRA. A manager who may be tempted to prepare careless or biased estimates knows that resulting errors will be brought out in the following year.

7. For an extensive discussion of the balance sheet versus income statement approaches, and the inability of the income statement approach to resolve the question of how to match costs and revenues, see Storey and Storey (1998)

8. For a counterargument, see Ohlson (1987).

3

The Decision Usefulness Approach to Financial Reporting

3.1 Overview

In Chapter 2 we concluded that the present value model faces some severe problems in practice. It is doubtful that a complete set of financial statements on this basis is feasible. This inability to value the whole firm on a present value basis means that a theoretically well-defined concept of net income does not exist in the complex, real world in which accountants operate.

In this chapter we will begin our study of how to tackle this problem. In Chapter 2 we suggested that historical cost accounting makes more sense perhaps than many give it credit for, particularly when we recognize that it produces reliable information, even though historical cost information is not as relevant as market or present value-based approaches to fair value.

Given that historical cost accounting for major classes of assets and liabilities is firmly fixed in practice, the next question is: How can financial statements based on historical costs be made more *useful?* This leads to an important concept in accounting—the concept of **decision usefulness.** To properly understand this concept, we need to consider other theories (that is, other than the present value model) from economics and finance. We, as accountants, cannot proceed to make financial statements more useful until we know just what usefulness means. We also need a precise definition of information. As it turns out, decision theories and capital market theories assist in conceptualizing the meaning of useful financial statement information.

The main purpose of this chapter is to introduce you to some of these theories and to discuss their relevance to accounting. As we shall see, major accounting standard setting bodies have picked up on these theories, to such an extent that they underlie many of the accounting standards and pronouncements issued by these bodies.

3.2   *The Decision Usefulness Approach*

As we can infer from Section 2.5, the decision usefulness approach to accounting theory takes the view that "if we can't prepare theoretically correct financial statements, at least we can try to make historical cost-based statements more useful." First enunciated in 1966,[1] and reinforced by the influential 1973 report of the Trueblood Commission,[2] this simple observation has had major implications for accounting theory and practice. In particular, we must now pay much closer attention than we did in Chapter 2 to financial statement users and their decision needs, since under non-ideal conditions it is not possible to read the value of the firm directly from the financial statements.

Decision usefulness is contrasted with another view of the role of financial reporting, namely stewardship, whereby the role is to report on management's success, or lack thereof, in managing the firm's resources. As stated in Chapter 1, we regard each role as equally important. In this chapter, we begin our discussion of decision usefulness. Discussion of the second role begins in Chapter 8.

In adopting the decision usefulness approach, two major questions must be addressed. First, who are the users of financial statements? Clearly, there are many users. It is helpful to categorize them into broad groups, such as investors, lenders, managers, unions, standard setters, and governments. These groups are called **constituencies** of accounting.

Second, what are the decision problems of financial statement users? By understanding these decision problems, accountants will be better prepared to meet the information needs of the various constituencies. Financial statements can then be prepared with these information needs in mind. In other words, tailoring financial statement information to the specific needs of the users of those statements will lead to improved decision-making. In this way, the financial statements are made more *useful*.

Of course, determining the specific decision needs of users is by no means an obvious process. For example, what information does a holder of the firm's long-term debt need to make a rational decision about whether to sell certain holdings? Would this decision be helped or hindered by including future income tax liabilities on the balance sheet?

In the face of difficult questions like these, accountants have turned to various theories in economics and finance for assistance. In this chapter we consider the single-person **theory of decision**. This theory is a good place to begin to understand how individuals may make rational decisions under uncertainty. The theory enables us to appreciate the concept of information, which enables decision-makers to sharpen up their subjective beliefs about future payoffs from their decisions.

We also consider the **theory of investment,** a specialization of decision theory to model the decision processes of a rational investor. In particular, the theory of investment helps us to understand the nature of *risk* in a portfolio investment context.

These theories are important to accountants because they have been adopted by major professional accounting standard setting bodies. An examination of some of the pronouncements of the Conceptual Framework project of the FASB (Section 3.8) shows that the above theories lurk just under the surface. Consequently, an understanding of the theories enables a deeper understanding of the pronouncements themselves.

SUMMARY

Accountants have adopted a decision usefulness approach to financial reporting as a reaction to the impossibility of preparing theoretically correct financial statements. However, the decision usefulness approach leads to the problems of identifying the users of financial statements and selecting the information they need to make good decisions. Accountants have decided that investors are a major constituency of users and have turned to various theories in economics and finance—in particular, to theories of decision and investment—to understand the type of financial statement information investors need.

3.3   Single-Person Decision Theory

Single-person decision theory takes the viewpoint of an individual who must make a decision under conditions of uncertainty.[3] It recognizes that state probabilities are no longer objective, as they are under ideal conditions, and sets out a formal procedure whereby the individual can make the best decision, by selecting from a set of alternatives. This procedure allows additional information to be obtained to revise the decision-maker's subjective assessment of the probabilities of what might happen after the decision is made (i.e., the probabilities of states of nature). Decision theory is relevant to accounting because financial statements provide additional information that is useful for many decisions, as illustrated in Example 3.1.

3.3.1   DECISION THEORY APPLIED

EXAMPLE 3.1 A TYPICAL INVESTMENT DECISION

Bill Cautious has $10,000 to invest for one period. He has narrowed down his choice to two investments: shares of X Ltd. or risk-free government bonds yielding 2 1/4%. We will denote the act of buying the shares by a_1, and the bonds by a_2.

If he buys the shares, Bill faces risk. That is, the next-period return on the share investment is not known when Bill makes his decision. Bill feels that this return depends primarily on the long-run, or persistent, earning power of X Ltd. Consequently, he defines two states of nature:

State 1: High earning power

State 2: Low earning power

If X Ltd. is in state 1, the next-period net return will be $1,600, where net return is calculated as:

Net return = End-of-period market value + Dividends in period − Original investment

If X Ltd. is in state 2, next-period net return will be zero. The reason that net return varies with earning power, of course, is that market value will respond positively to earning power. Also, the higher earning power is the higher dividends will be, other things being equal.

Note that if Bill buys the bonds, he receives interest of $225 next period, regardless of the state of nature. That is, the bond investment is treated as riskless.

The amounts to be received from a decision are called **payoffs**, which we can summarize by a **payoff table** as shown in Table 3.1. Note that in this decision problem the payoffs are in the form of net returns from an investment. We will use payoffs and (net) investment returns interchangeably throughout our discussion.

TABLE 3.1 PAYOFF TABLE FOR DECISION THEORY EXAMPLE 3.1		
Act	State	
	HIGH	**LOW**
a_1 (buy shares)	$1,600	0
a_2 (buy bonds)	$225	$225

Now consider the state probabilities. Bill subjectively assesses the probability of state 1 (the high earning power state) as P(H) = 0.30. The probability of state 2 is then P(L) = 0.70. These probabilities incorporate all that Bill knows about X Ltd. to this point in time. These are called **prior probabilities**. He could base these probabilities, for example, on an analysis of X Ltd.'s past financial statements. Instead, or in addition, he could study the current market price of X Ltd. shares. If share price is low, it would indicate an unfavourable market evaluation of X's prospects, and Bill might also take this into account when assessing his state probabilities.

Bill is risk-averse. Let us assume that the amount of utility, or satisfaction, he derives from a payoff is equal to the square root of the amount of the payoff.[4] Thus, if he receives $1,600, his utility is 40. This assumption of risk aversion is not necessary to our example. We could just as easily assume Bill was risk-neutral and evaluate the expected *dollar* amounts of the various payoffs. However, investors are generally risk-averse, so we will work in utilities rather than dollars. Section 3.4 considers risk aversion in greater detail.

Figure 3.1 gives a decision tree diagram for this decision problem. The leftmost numbers in parentheses are the probabilities of the states, the second column from the right shows the dollar amounts of the payoffs, and the rightmost column gives Bill's utility for each amount.

The decision theory tells us that, if he must decide now, Bill should choose the act with the highest **expected utility**. We will denote the expected utility of act a_1 by $EU(a_1)$, and so on.

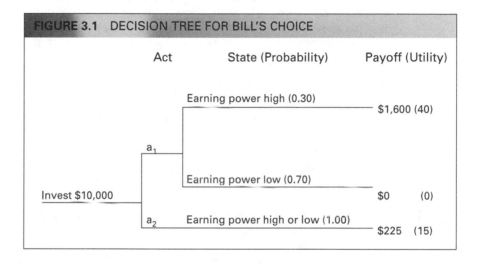

FIGURE 3.1   DECISION TREE FOR BILL'S CHOICE

Act	State (Probability)	Payoff (Utility)

Earning power high (0.30) — $1,600 (40)

a_1

Earning power low (0.70) — $0   (0)

Invest $10,000

a_2 Earning power high or low (1.00) — $225   (15)

$$EU(a_1) = 0.30 \times 40 + 0.70 \times 0 = 12$$
$$EU(a_2) = 1.00 \times 15 = 15$$

Therefore, it appears that Bill should choose a_2 and buy the bonds. (A possible alternative would be to diversify, that is, buy some of each type of security. We will rule this out for now by assuming that the brokerage fees for buying small amounts are prohibitive.)

However, Bill has another alternative: to obtain *more information* before deciding. Accordingly, let's assume that he decides to become more informed. The current year's annual report of X Ltd. is to be released within the next few days and Bill decides to wait for it, since it provides readily available and cost-effective evidence about the state of the firm. When the annual report comes, Bill notes that net income is quite high. In effect, the current financial statements show "good news" (GN).

On the basis of extensive experience in financial statement preparation and analysis, Bill knows that if X Ltd. really is a high-earning-power firm, there is an 80% probability that the current year's financial statements will show GN and 20% probability that they will show bad news (BN). Denote these conditional probabilities by $P(GN/H) = 0.80$ and $P(BN/H) = 0.20$ respectively.

Bill also knows that if X Ltd. is a low-earning-power firm, it is still possible that the financial statements show GN, since historical-cost-based net income is not completely relevant and reliable. Assume that if X Ltd. really is a low-earning-power firm, the probability that the current year's financial statements will show GN is 10%, giving a 90% probability that they will show BN. Denote these conditional probabilities by $P(GN/L) = 0.10$ and $P(BN/L) = 0.90$ respectively.

Now, armed with the GN evidence from the current financial statements and the above conditional probabilities, Bill can use Bayes' theorem to calculate his **posterior** state probabilities (that is, posterior to the financial statement evidence). The posterior probability of the high-earning-power state is:

$$P(H/GN) = \frac{P(H)\,P(GN/H)}{P(H)\,P(GN/H) + P(L)\,P(GN/L)}$$

$$= \frac{0.30 \times 0.80}{(0.30 \times 0.80) + (0.70 \times 0.10)}$$

$$= 0.77$$

where:

P(H/GN) is the (posterior) probability of the high state given the good-news financial statement
P(H) is the prior probability of the high state
P(GN/H) is the probability that the financial statements show good news given that the firm is in the high state
P(GN/L) is the probability that the financial statements show good news given that the firm is in the low state

Then, the posterior probability $P(L/GN)$ of X Ltd. being in a low-earning-power state is $1.00 - 0.77 = 0.23$. Recall that if earning power is high, the payoff from Bill's share investment will be high ($1,600), and if it is low, the payoff will be low ($0).

Bill can now calculate the expected utility of each act on the basis of his posterior probabilities:

$$EU(a_1/GN) = 0.77 \times 40 + 0.23 \times 0 = 30.8$$
$$EU(a_2/GN) = 1.00 \times 15 = 15$$

Thus, the GN current financial statement information has caused Bill's optimal decision to change to a_1—he should buy the shares of X Ltd.

3.3.2 THE INFORMATION SYSTEM

It is important to understand why financial statement information is useful here. To be useful, it must help predict future investment returns. Under historical cost accounting, the financial statements do not show expected future values directly (as they did under the ideal conditions of Examples 2.1 and 2.2). Nevertheless, financial statements will still be useful to investors to the extent that they enable a prediction that the good or bad news they contain will persist into the future. Think of a progression, from current good or bad news to future earning power to future expected investment returns.

Notice that we develop the decision process in terms of the investor using *current* financial statement information (here, the good or bad news in net income) to predict future earning power. Then, the prediction of earning power is used to predict future investment return, which is the investor's ultimate interest.

Recall, however, that in Examples 2.1 and 2.2 we worked with predicted future cash flows, rather than predicted earning power. In the long run, as will be shown in Section 6.5.1, the two approaches yield the same predictions since, over time, cash flows and earnings will average out to be the same. That is, accruals, the timing differences between cash flows and net income, will net out to zero over time since accruals reverse.

In the short run, though, one can argue that earning power has certain advantages in predicting future investment return. Because of accruals, earnings are less "lumpy" than cash flows, which are affected, for example, by capital asset acquisitions and disposals. Consequently, it can be difficult and time-consuming to back out projections of operating cash flows from accrual-based financial statements. Projecting future earnings is conceptually equivalent, and often much easier.[5] In addition, as we will see in Section 11.6, the amounts and timing of accruals can themselves have information content.

In this book, we will usually think of the investor as using the first approach, that is, using current financial statement information to predict future earning power. However, it will occasionally be convenient to predict future cash flows, one reason being that it is quite common in practice.

To return to our example, the good news was that current earnings were high. This information enabled Bill to predict high future earning power with probability 0.77, and this is also the probability of the high future investment return. Of course, such information is a double-edged sword. Had the financial statements contained bad news, Bill's probability of high future earning power would have been lowered just as surely as it was raised by good news.

We may conclude that financial statements can still be useful to investors even though they do not report directly on future cash flows by means of present-value-based calculations. Here, it is the lack of ideal conditions that gives the income statement its information content—recall that there was really no information in net income in Examples 2.1 and 2.2.

The heart of the linkage between current and future financial statement information is the conditional probabilities P(GN/H) and P(BN/L). These probabilities are called an **information system**, which can be summarized by a table such as Table 3.2. Recall that, in our example, the probability that the current financial statements of X Ltd. show good news, conditional on the firm being in the high-earning-power state, is 0.80 etc. The 0.80 and 0.90 probabilities are called **main diagonal**; the others are called **off-main diagonal**.

An information system is a table giving, conditional on each state of nature, the objective[6] probability of each possible financial statement evidence item.

TABLE 3.2 INFORMATION SYSTEM FOR DECISION THEORY EXAMPLE 3.1		
	Current Financial Statement Evidence	
	GN	**BN**
High	0.80	0.20
State		
Low	0.10	0.90

Note that financial statements are not perfect—this would be true only under ideal conditions. Thus, there is a 20% probability that even if the firm is in the high state the financial statements would show BN. This weakening of the contemporaneous relationship between current financial statement information and future firm performance is sometimes described as **noise** or as low earnings **quality** in the financial statements. Nevertheless, the information system is **informative**, since it enables Bill to sharpen up or, more precisely, to update his prior probabilities based on new information. For cases of fully informative and non-informative information systems, see question 1 at the end of this chapter.

Note also that the extent of informativeness depends on the relevance and reliability of the financial statements. For example, suppose X Ltd. was to switch to fair value from historical cost for its capital assets. The resulting increase in relevance would tend to increase the main diagonal probabilities of the information system and lower the off-main diagonal ones. This is because fair values, for example, current market values, of assets are better predictors of their future values (and hence of firm earning power) than are historical costs of capital assets. However, the use of fair values would also decrease reliability, because market values are volatile and, if current market values are not readily available, subject to possible managerial bias. This would have the opposite effect on the main diagonal probabilities. Thus, it is difficult to say whether such an accounting policy change would increase or decrease the informativeness of the information system.

However, if it were possible to increase relevance without sacrificing reliability or vice versa, the result would be to increase financial statement usefulness. One way to accomplish this would be to present **supplementary** present value information, as in RRA. This would increase relevance for those who wanted to use supplemental information. However, the historical cost-based primary statements are still available for those who are concerned about the reliability of RRA.

The concept of informativeness of an information system is useful in understanding the role of information in decision-making. The higher the main diagonal probabilities relative to the off-main diagonal ones, the more informative the system—or, equivalently, the higher its quality. Consequently, the more informative an information system, the more decision useful it is. It enables better predictions of relevant states of nature and payoffs. In an investment context, these payoffs are returns on investments.

While thinking of financial statements as a table of conditional probabilities may take some getting used to, the concept of an information system is one of the most powerful and useful concepts in financial accounting theory. It is a powerful concept because it captures the information content of financial statements, thereby determining their value for investor decision making. It is a useful concept because many practical accounting problems can be framed in terms of their impact on the information system. We pointed out above that if a move to fair value accounting for capital assets is to be decision useful, the increase in relevance (which increases the main diagonal probabilities) must outweigh the decrease in reliability (which decreases them). Similar reasoning can be applied to new or proposed accounting standards. Recent standards requiring fair value accounting for financial instruments, as in SFAS 133 for derivatives, will be decision useful only if the increased relevance of reporting is not outweighed by decreased reliability. Since most financial accounting debates can be cast in terms of relevance versus reliability, the information system provides a useful framework for evaluation.

The quality of an information system can be estimated empirically. For example, Easton and Zmijewski (1989) (EZ) examined Value Line analysts' revisions of future quarterly earnings forecasts following the GN or BN in firms' current quarterly earnings. Future quarterly earnings are analogous to the states of nature in Table 3.2 and the GN or BN in current quarterly earnings constitutes the financial statement evidence in that Table. Value Line provides forecasts for a large number of firms, and these forecasts are revised quarterly.

For a sample of 150 large U.S. corporations followed by Value Line over the period 1975–1980, EZ found that for every $1 of GN or BN in reported earnings, the Value Line analysts increased or decreased next quarter's earnings forecast by about 34 cents on average. This implies that the information systems underlying the sample firms' financial statements are informative, that is, analysts use current financial statement information to revise their beliefs about future earnings. EZ called the effect of current financial statement information on analysts' next quarter earnings forecast a "revision coefficient." This coefficient is a proxy for earnings quality.

EZ also found that the higher a firm's revision coefficient is (recall that the 34 cents above is an average), the stronger was the effect of the GN or BN in current earnings on the market price of the firm's shares. This is consistent with investors accepting the analysts' evaluation of the information system, bidding share price up or down more strongly the higher the quality of the system.

EZ's results are consistent with the decision theory model of Example 3.1. Empirical studies of the response of share price to financial statement information are considered in greater detail in Chapter 5.

3.3.3   INFORMATION DEFINED

Decision theory and the concept of informativeness give us a precise way to define information:

> **Information** *is evidence that has the potential to affect an individual's decision.*

Notice that this is an *ex ante* definition. We would hardly expect an individual to gather evidence if he or she didn't expect to learn enough so as to possibly affect a decision. Bayes' theorem is simply a device to process what has been learned. The crucial requirement for evidence to constitute information is that for at least some evidence that might be received, beliefs will be sufficiently affected that the optimal decision will change.

Also, the definition is individual-specific. As pointed out in Chapter 1, individuals may differ in their reaction to the same information source. For example, their prior probabilities may differ, so that posterior probabilities, and hence their decisions, may differ even when confronted with the same evidence.

The definition should really be interpreted net of cost. An information source may have the potential to affect an individual's decision but, if it is too costly, it is not information because it will not be used. It can be argued, however, that financial statements are a cost-effective information source because of the large number of potential users.

Finally, it should be emphasized that an individual's receipt of information and subsequent belief revision is really a continuous process. We can think of the individual as using Bayes' theorem every time a new information item comes along. Example 3.1 concentrated on belief revision following receipt of the annual report, but obviously there are many other information sources, such as newspapers, speeches and announcements, statistical reports, etc. that can also affect decisions. Hopefully, by supplying relevant and reliable information, financial statements will continue their role as an important source of information.

3.3.4   CONCLUSION

Decision theory is important because it helps us to understand why information is such a powerful commodity—it can affect the actions taken by investors.

Accountants, who prepare much of the information required by investors, need to understand this powerful role.

3.4   *The Rational, Risk-Averse Investor*

In decision theory, the concept of a rational individual simply means that in making decisions, the chosen act is the one that yields the highest expected utility.[7] Note that this implies that the individual may search for additional information relevant to the decision, using it to revise state probabilities by means of Bayes' theorem.

Of course, whether individuals actually make decisions this way is difficult to say. Nevertheless, in thinking about questions of decision usefulness, it is helpful to assume that they do. As we will discuss in Section 6.2, we do not mean to imply that all individuals make decisions as the theory suggests, but only that the theory captures the average behaviour of investors who want to make good investment decisions. Alternatively, we can argue that if investors want to make good decisions this is how they *should* proceed. If individuals do not make decisions in some rational, predictable manner it is difficult for accountants, or anyone else, to know what information they find useful. At any rate, implications of the theory have been subjected to much empirical testing, as we shall see in Chapter 5. To the extent that predictions of the theory are confirmed empirically, our confidence that the decision theory model is a reasonable one is strengthened.

It is also usually assumed that rational investors are **risk-averse**.[8] To see the intuition underlying this concept, think of yourself as an investor who is asked to flip a fair coin with your university instructor—suppose the coin is a penny. You would probably be willing to flip for pennies, if for no other reason than to humour the instructor. If the ante were raised, you would probably be willing to flip for dimes, quarters, even dollars. However, there would come a point where you would refuse—say, flipping for $100,000 (if you didn't refuse, the instructor would).

Remind yourself that the expected payoff of flipping a fair coin is zero, regardless of the amount at stake, since you have a 50% chance of winning and a 50% chance of losing in all cases. Thus, your increasing nervousness as the stakes are raised means that another effect, beyond the expected value of the gamble, is operating. This is risk aversion.

Note also that risk-averse individuals trade off expected return and risk. For example, if the coin was biased in your favour—say you have a 75% chance of winning—you would probably be willing to flip for higher stakes than if the coin was fair. In effect, you are now willing to bear more risk in exchange for a higher expected value—the expected value of your gamble is now $0.50 per dollar rather than 0.

To model risk aversion, decision theorists use the device of a **utility function**, which relates payoff amounts to the decision-maker's utility for those amounts.

To portray a utility function, consider Figure 3.2. The solid line shows the utility function of Bill Cautious in Example 3.1. Bill's utility function is:

$$U(x) = \sqrt{x}, \; x \geq 0$$

where is the amount of the payoff.

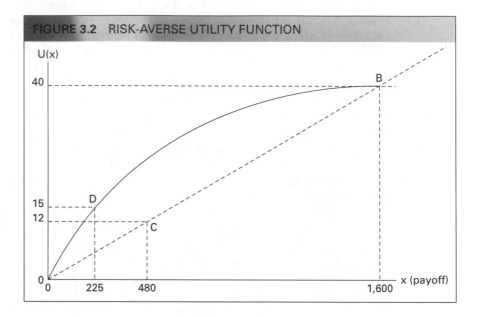

FIGURE 3.2 RISK-AVERSE UTILITY FUNCTION

Based on his prior probabilities, Bill's expected payoff is (0.3 × $1,600 + 0.7 × 0) = $480. The expected *utility* of the payoff is at point C on the dotted line joining A and B. This expected utility of (0.3 × 40 + 0.7 × 0) = 12 is less than the utility of 15 for the risk-free investment at point D on Figure 3.2. Consequently, Bill's rational decision is to choose the risk-free investment, if he were to act on the basis of his prior probabilities. This is the case even though the expected payoff of the risky investment ($480) is greater than the risk-free payoff ($225). This demonstrates that Bill is averse to risk.

To see how Bill's decision may change if the risky investment were less risky, assume that the possible payoffs are now $200 (with probability 0.7) and $1,133.33 (with probability 0.3) instead of the earlier $0 and $1,600. You should verify that the expected payoff is still $480 but the expected utility rises to 20.[9] Then, Bill's rational decision, a priori, is to buy the risky investment. The reduction in risk raises expected utility, even though the expected payoff has not changed.

Despite the intuitive appeal of risk aversion, it is sometimes assumed that decision-makers are **risk-neutral**. This means that they evaluate risky investments strictly in terms of expected payoff—risk itself does not matter per se. We made this assumption in Example 2.2. Figure 3.3 shows the utility function of a risk-neutral decision-maker. A typical risk-neutral utility function is $U(x) = bx$, where b is the slope of the line. Here, utility is simply a linear function of the payoff.

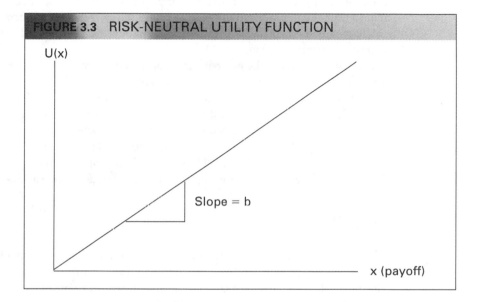

FIGURE 3.3 RISK-NEUTRAL UTILITY FUNCTION

Risk neutrality may be a reasonable assumption when the payoffs are small. However, risk aversion is the more realistic assumption in most cases. The concept of risk aversion is important to accountants, because it means that investors need information concerning the risk, as well as the expected value, of future returns.

3.5 *The Principle of Portfolio Diversification**

In Section 3.4, we stated that individual investors were typically assumed to be risk-averse. Consequently, for a given expected payoff from investments the rational investor wants the lowest possible risk or, equivalently, for a given risk, will want the highest possible expected payoff. In effect, the investor adopts a tradeoff between risk and return; greater risk will be borne only if expected return is higher and vice versa.

*Note: Sections 3.5, 3.6, and 3.7 can be ignored with little loss of continuity. However, diversification and beta are referred to frequently in subsequent chapters. Readers with no previous exposure to these concepts should read at least Sections 3.5 and 3.7.1.

One way investors can lower risk for a given expected return is to adopt a strategy of diversification, that is, to invest in a portfolio of securities. The principle of portfolio diversification shows us that some, but not all, risk can be eliminated by appropriate investment strategy. This principle has important implications for the nature of the risk information that investors need. The risk reported on by many common accounting-based risk measures, such as times interest earned or the current ratio, can be reduced or eliminated a priori by appropriate diversification.

Before illustrating the diversification principle, we return briefly to our risk-averse investor. Note that before we can calculate an individual's expected utility for different investment acts, we need to know what that individual's utility function looks like. For example, Bill Cautious' utility function in Example 3.1 was $U(x) = \sqrt{x}$, $x \geq 0$. With this utility function and payoff probabilities, Bill's expected utilities for different acts were calculated and compared.

One might reasonably ask, "How do we know what an individual's utility function is?" To avoid this question, we shall now assume **mean-variance utility**:

$$U_i(a) = f_i(\bar{x}_a, \sigma_a^2)$$

where symbol a represents an investment act. For example, investment act a could be an investment in a riskless government bond, or in a firm's shares, as in Example 3.1. Alternatively, it could be an investment in a portfolio of securities.

The equation states that the utility of an investment act a to investor i is a function f_i of the expected rate of return from that act $\bar{x}_a$ and the risk as measured by its variance σ_a^2. We assume that f_i is increasing in $\bar{x}_a$ and decreasing in σ_a^2. A specific example of a mean variance utility function is:

$$U_i(a) = 2\bar{x}_a - \sigma_a^2$$

which can be seen to increase in $\bar{x}_a$ and decrease in σ_a^2. Individuals will have different tradeoffs between expected rate of return and risk—for example, a more risk-averse investor might have $-2\sigma_a^2$ rather than $-\sigma_a^2$ as shown above. It is not true in general that the utility of an act depends only on its mean and variance. However, investigation of this is beyond our scope.

The significance of mean-variance utility to accountants is that it makes investors' decision needs more explicit—all investors need information about the expected values and riskiness of returns from investments, regardless of the specific forms of their utility functions. Without such an assumption, specific knowledge of investors' utility functions would be needed to fully deduce their information requirements.

With this background in mind, we now illustrate the principle of portfolio diversification by means of two examples.

EXAMPLE 3.2 THE PRINCIPLE OF PORTFOLIO DIVERSIFICATION (PART 1)

Suppose that a risk-averse investor (Toni Difelice) has $200 to invest and is considering investing all of it in the shares of firm A, currently trading for $20. Assume that Toni assesses a 0.74 probability [10] that the shares will increase in market value to $22 over the coming period and a 0.26 probability that they will decrease to $17. Assume also that A will pay a dividend of $1 per share at the end of the period (we could also make the dividend uncertain, but this would just add complexity without affecting the point to be made).

As in our decision theory Example 3.1, Toni's subjective probabilities could be posterior to her analysis of firm A's financial statements and the resulting application of Bayes' theorem. Alternatively, they could be her prior probabilities based on whatever other information is at her disposal. For present purposes, the extent to which Toni may have become informed does not matter. The important point is that she has assessed probabilities.

The payoffs from Toni's proposed investment are as follows:

If shares increase: 22×10 shares + $10 dividend = $230

If shares decrease: 17×10 shares + $10 dividend = $180

TABLE 3.3 CALCULATING EXPECTED RATE OF RETURN AND VARIANCE

Payoff	Rate of Return	Probability	Expected Rate of Return	Variance
$230	$\frac{230-200}{200} = 0.15$	0.74	0.1110	$(0.15 - 0.0850)^2 \times 0.74 = 0.0031$
$180	$\frac{180-200}{200} = -0.10$	0.26	−0.0260	$(-0.10 - 0.0850)^2 \times 0.26 = \underline{0.0089}$
			$\overline{x}_a = \underline{0.0850}$	$\sigma_a^2 = \underline{0.0120}$

Table 3.3 shows the calculation of the expected rate of return and variance of this investment. Henceforth, we will work with the *rate* of return. As can be seen from Table 3.3, this just involves dividing net returns by the amount of investment ($200). Note that the rate of return for a period depends on the closing share price and any dividends paid during the period. The division by opening price is a standardization device—rates of return can be directly compared across securities while returns cannot. Also, rate of return fits in nicely with the assumption of mean-variance utility, which is in terms of the expected value and variance of rate of return.

The variance of return is 0.0120. The variance of an investment return serves as a measure of its riskiness. Since Toni is risk-averse, increasing riskiness will lower her utility, other things equal.

Assume that Toni's utility function is:

$$U_i(a) = 2\bar{x}_a - \sigma_a^2$$

as given above. Then, her utility for this investment is:

$$2 \times 0.0850 - 0.0120 = 0.1580$$

Toni now has to decide whether to take this investment act. If she feels that this utility is not sufficiently high, further search would be necessary to find a more attractive investment, or some other use for the $200 of capital.

EXAMPLE 3.3   THE PRINCIPLE OF PORTFOLIO DIVERSIFICATION (PART 2)

It turns out that Toni would not be rational to accept the above investment— a more attractive investment can be found. It is possible to find another investment decision that has the same expected return but lower risk. This is because of the **principle of portfolio diversification.**

To illustrate, assume that shares of firm B are also traded on the market, with a current market value of $10. These shares also pay a dividend of $1. Assume there is a 0.6750 probability that firm B's shares will increase in market value to $10.50 at the end of the period, and a 0.3250 probability that they will decrease to $8.50.

Now suppose that Toni decides to invest $200 in six shares of firm A at $20 and eight shares of firm B at $10. We must calculate Toni's expected utility for the portfolio consisting of six shares of firm A and eight shares of firm B. Notice that the same amount ($200) is invested, but that it is now spread over two different securities.

Four possible payoffs now exist from the portfolio: both shares increase in market value, one share increases and the other decreases, or both shares decrease. The amounts of the payoffs and their assumed probabilities are as follows:

TABLE 3.4   PAYOFFS AND THEIR PROBABILITIES

A		B		Dividends		Total Payoff	Probability
132	+	84	+	14	=	$230	0.5742
132	+	68	+	14	=	$214	0.1658
102	+	84	+	14	=	$200	0.1008
102	+	68	+	14	=	$184	0.1592
							1.0000

Recall that six shares of firm A and eight shares of firm B are held, and that the high payoff is $22 per share for firm A and $10.50 for firm B, plus a

$1 dividend from each share. This gives the $230 payoff on the first line of the table. The other payoffs are similarly calculated.

Now let us consider more closely the probabilities we have assumed for the four possible payoffs. The returns from shares of firm A and firm B are correlated in our example. To see this, consider the first row in Table 3.4 with a total payoff of $230. This payoff will be realized if both shares A and B realize their high-payoff values. On the basis of our assumption about the probabilities of the individual payoffs of shares A and B, the probabilities of these two payoffs, when each share is considered separately, are 0.74 for A and 0.6750 for B. If the payoffs of shares A and B were independent, the probability of both shares realizing their high payoffs would be 0.74 × 0.6750 = 0.4995.

However, in any economy, there are states of nature, also called factors, which affect the returns of *all* shares, such as levels of interest rates, foreign exchange rates, the level of economic activity, and so on. These are called **market-wide** or **economy-wide** factors. Their presence means that if the return on one share is high, it is more likely that the returns on most other shares in the economy will also be high—more likely, that is, than would be the case if the returns on shares were independent. Thus, we have assumed that the probability that both shares A and B realize their high payoffs is 0.5742, greater than the 0.4995 that we would obtain under independence, to reflect these underlying common factors.

Similar reasoning applies to the last row of Table 3.4 with a payoff of $184. Here we have assumed that the joint probability of both firm A and firm B realizing their low payoffs is 0.1592, greater than the (0.26 × 0.3250 = 0.0845) probability under independence. If market-wide state realizations are such that they work against high returns (that is, if the economy is performing poorly), then the probability that both shares realize low payoffs is greater than what would be expected under independence.

Of course, while share returns may be correlated because of common factors, they will not be perfectly correlated. It is still possible that one firm realizes a high return and another a low return—witness the two middle rows of Table 3.4. This is because, in addition to economy-wide factors, there are also **firm-specific** factors that affect the return of one firm only. Examples include the quality of a firm's management, new patents, strikes, machine breakdowns, and so on. Thus, the second row of the table represents a situation where firm A realizes a high return (say, because of a new invention it has just patented) and firm B realizes a low return (say, because of a critical machine failure in its assembly line). However, because of the presence of economy-wide factors, the probabilities for these high/low payoff realizations will also be different than under independence. This is true of Example 3.3.

It should be pointed out that the preceding argument assumes that the *only* source of correlation between returns on firms' shares is market-wide factors. In effect, we have partitioned states of nature that can affect share returns into two components—economy-wide and firm-specific. This is a simplification, since, for example, industry-wide factors could introduce additional returns correlation. However, the simplification is a widely used one and is sufficient for our purposes. It leads to an important measure of share riskiness (beta), which we will discuss shortly. For now, you should realize that the assumption implies that if *all* factors were economy-wide, returns on firms' shares would be perfectly correlated. If *all* factors were firm-specific, returns would be independent. As is usually the case, the truth lies somewhere in between. Consequently, the probabilities given in Table 3.4 assume that both types of factors are present.

The expected rate of return and variance of Toni's portfolio of A and B shares are calculated in Table 3.5 using the correlated probabilities. Thus, the expected rate of return of the portfolio is 0.0850, as before (we have forced this result by appropriate choice of the probabilities, to facilitate comparison), but the variance has decreased to 0.0074, from 0.0120. Since Toni is risk-averse, she would be better off buying the portfolio of A and B shares rather than just A, because the expected return is the same, but the risk is lower.

TABLE 3.5   CALCULATING EXPECTED RATE OF RETURN AND VARIANCE

Payoff	Rate of Return		Probability	Expected Rate of Return	Variance
$230	$\dfrac{230 - 200}{200} =$	0.15	0.5742	0.0861	$(0.15 - 0.0850)^2 \times 0.5742 = 0.0024$
$214	$\dfrac{214 - 200}{200} =$	0.07	0.1658	0.0116	$(0.07 - 0.0850)^2 \times 0.1658 = 0.0000$
$200	$\dfrac{200 - 200}{200} =$	0.00	0.1008	0.0000	$(0.00 - 0.0850)^2 \times 0.1008 = 0.0007$
$184	$\dfrac{184 - 200}{200} =$	−0.08	0.1592	− 0.0127	$(-0.08 - 0.0850)^2 \times 0.1592 = 0.0043$
				$\overline{x}_a = 0.0850$	$\sigma_a^2 = 0.0074$

In fact, her utility now is:

$$U_i(a) = 2 \times 0.0850 - 0.0074$$
$$= 0.1626$$

up from 0.1580 for the single-share investment.

SUMMARY

Risk-averse investors can take advantage of the principle of portfolio diversification to reduce their risk, by investing in a portfolio of securities. This is because realizations of firm-specific states of nature tend to cancel out across securities, leaving economy-wide factors as the main contributors to portfolio risk.

While individual attitudes to risk may differ, we can see investors' decision needs with particular clarity if we assume mean-variance utility. Then, regardless of the degree of risk aversion, we know that utility increases in expected rate of return and decreases in variance of the portfolio.

3.6   The Optimal Investment Decision

If a portfolio of two shares is better than one, then a three-share portfolio should be better than two, and so on. Indeed, this is the case and, assuming there are no transaction costs such as brokerage fees, Toni should continue buying until the portfolio includes some of every security traded on the market. This is called "holding the market portfolio." Note again that the total amount invested remains at $200, but is spread over a greater number of securities.

Be sure you understand *why* the same amount invested in a portfolio can yield lower risk than if it were invested in a single firm for the same expected rate of return. The reason is simply that when more than one risky investment is held, *the firm-specific risks tend to cancel out*. If one share realizes a low return, there is always the chance that another share will realize a high return. The larger the number of different firms' shares in the portfolio, the more this effect can operate. As a result, the riskiness of returns is reduced, which we have illustrated above by means of our variance calculations. Of course, in the presence of economy-wide risk, there is not a complete cancelling out. At a minimum, that is, when the market portfolio is held, the economy-wide factors will remain to contribute to portfolio risk, and this risk cannot be diversified away. Such non-diversifiable risk is called **systematic risk.**

Conceptually, the market portfolio includes all assets available for investment in the economy. As a practical matter, the market portfolio is usually taken as all the securities traded on a major stock exchange. The return on the market portfolio can then be proxied by the return on a market index for that exchange, such as the Dow Jones Index of the New York Stock Exchange, the Toronto Stock Exchange 300 Index, etc.

Now return to our investor, Toni Difelice. Toni decides to buy the market portfolio after hearing about the benefits of diversification. Her first task is to assess the expected return and variance of the market portfolio. She subjectively assesses a 0.8 probability that the Toronto Stock Exchange 300 Index will increase by 10% for the coming period and a 0.2 probability that it will increase by 2 1/2%. Then, denoting the expected return and variance of the market portfolio by $\bar{x}_M$ and σ_M^2 respectively:

$$\overline{x}_M = 0.10 \times 0.8 + 0.0250 \times 0.2 = 0.0850$$
$$\sigma_M{}^2 = (0.10 - 0.0850)^2 \times 0.8 + (0.0250 - 0.0850)^2 \times 0.2$$
$$= 0.0002 + 0.0007$$
$$= 0.0009$$

This gives Toni a utility of:

$$2\overline{x}_M - \sigma_M{}^2 = 0.1700 - 0.0009$$
$$= 0.1691$$

which is greater than the 0.1626 utility of the two-share portfolio in Example 3.3.

The question now is: Is this Toni's optimal investment decision? The answer is probably not. If Toni were quite risk-averse, she might prefer a portfolio with lower risk than 0.0009, and would be willing to have a lower expected return as a result.

One strategy she might follow would be to sell some of the high-risk stocks in her portfolio. But, if she does this, she is no longer holding the market portfolio, so some of the benefits of diversification are lost. How can Toni adjust portfolio risk to her desired level without losing the benefits of diversification?

The answer lies in the **risk-free asset.** If a risk-free asset, such as treasury bills yielding, say, 4%, is available, an investor could sell some of the market portfolio (that is, sell some of each security, so that the market portfolio is still held but total investment in it is lower) and use the proceeds to buy the risk-free asset. This strategy is depicted in Figure 3.4 as a move from M, where only the market portfolio is held, to Y. Risk is lower at Y, but so is expected return, compared to M. However, if the investor is quite risk-averse this could raise utility.

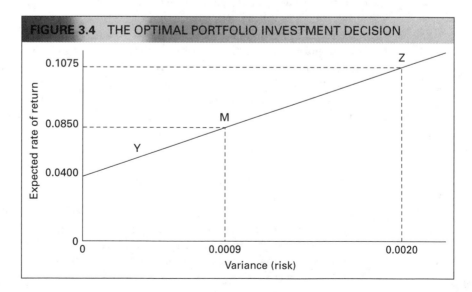

FIGURE 3.4   THE OPTIMAL PORTFOLIO INVESTMENT DECISION

Conversely, if Toni were less risk-averse, she may prefer to borrow at the risk-free rate and buy more of the market portfolio, thereby moving to Z, with higher expected return and risk.

In this way, each investor can secure a desired risk-return tradeoff while continuing to enjoy the maximum risk-reduction effects of diversification.

To illustrate, suppose that Toni borrows $100 at a rate of 0.04 and buys an additional $100 of the market portfolio. Toni now has $300 of market portfolio, on which she expects to earn 0.0850, and owes $100 at 4% interest. But her own investment is still $200. Consequently, her expected return is now:

$$\bar{x}_a = \left(\frac{300}{200} \times 0.0850 - \frac{100}{200} \times 0.0400 \right)$$

$$= (0.1275 - 0.0200)$$

$$= 0.1075$$

The variance of her return also increases, since she now has $300 at risk on an investment of $200. There is no variance attached to the $100 borrowed, of course, since interest and principal payments are fixed. The variance of her return is now:

$$\sigma_a^2 = (300/200)^2 \times 0.0009$$

$$= 0.0020$$

yielding utility of $2 \times 0.1075 - 0.0020 = 0.2130$. This yields Toni a higher utility than simply holding the market portfolio (0.1691). Toni will continue to borrow until the amount borrowed and reinvested yields an $\bar{x}_a$ and σ_a^2 that maximizes her utility. In fact, if she can borrow all she wants at 4%, she would borrow $9,800, which would yield her utility of 2.33.

SUMMARY

When transaction costs are ignored, a risk-averse investor's optimal investment decision is to buy that combination of market portfolio and risk-free asset that yields the best tradeoff between expected return and risk. This tradeoff is individual-specific—it depends on the investor's utility function. Some investors may wish to reduce their investment in the market portfolio and buy the risk-free asset with the proceeds. Others may wish to borrow at the risk-free rate and increase their investment. Either way, all investors can enjoy the full benefits of diversification while at the same time attaining their optimal risk-return tradeoff.

3.7   *Portfolio Risk*

3.7.1   *CALCULATING AND INTERPRETING BETA*

The principle of diversification leads to an important risk measure of a security in the theory of investment. This is **beta**, which measures the co-movement between changes in the price of a security and changes in the market value of the market portfolio. To illustrate, we will calculate the betas of shares of firms A and B in Example 3.3, in relation to the market portfolio M given in Section 3.6.

Beta is an important and useful concept in financial accounting. As we shall see in Chapter 5, a stock's beta is a crucial component of empirical studies of the usefulness to investors of financial accounting information. Also, it is a "launching pad" for reporting on firm risk. Reporting on risk is discussed in Section 7.6. Consequently, an understanding of what a stock's beta is and what it tells us about firm risk is an important part of an accountant's knowledge base.

EXAMPLE 3.4   CALCULATING BETA

The beta of A shares, denoted by β_A, is given by:

$$\beta_A = \frac{Cov(A,M)}{Var(M)}$$

where $Cov(A,M)$ is the covariance of the returns on A with the returns on the market portfolio M. In effect, β_A measures how strongly the return on A varies as the market varies. For example, a high-beta security would undergo wide swings in rate of return as market conditions change. Shares of airlines and aircraft manufacturers are examples, since these industries are sensitive to economic conditions. Shares of electric utilities and fast food firms would be low-beta, since the returns of such firms are less subject to the state of the economy.

Division by $Var(M)$ is simply a standardization device, to express $Cov(A,M)$ in units of market variance. For example, if the returns on the Toronto and New York Stock Exchanges have different variances, standardization by the variance of returns on the respective exchanges enables betas of Canadian and U.S. firms to be compared.

To calculate the beta of security A, assume that the conditional payoff probabilities of A are as follows:

- When return on M is high:

  Probability that return on A is high = 0.90
  Probability that return on A is low = 0.10

- When return on M is low:

Probability that return on A is high = 0.10

Probability that return on A is low = 0.90

These probabilities could be estimated by examining past data on the returns on A shares in relation to the returns on M. Cov(A,M) is calculated in Table 3.6.

TABLE 3.6	CALCULATION OF COVARIANCE	

Returns A	M	Joint Probabilities			
High	High	(0.15 − 0.0850)(0.10 − 0.0850) × 0.72	=	0.0007
High	Low	(0.15 − 0.0850)(0.0250 − 0.0850) × 0.02	=	−0.0001
Low	High	(−0.10 − 0.0850)(0.10 − 0.0850) × 0.08	=	−0.0002
Low	Low	(−0.10 − 0.0850)(0.0250 − 0.0850) × 0.18	=	0.0020
		Cov(A,M)	=	0.0024

In the first row of the table, the values 0.15 and 0.0850 are the high return and the expected return respectively of A (see Table 3.3). Similarly 0.10 and 0.0850 are the high return and the expected return of M (see Section 3.6). The joint probability that both A and M pay off high is:

Prob(A high and M high) = Prob(M high) Prob(A high/M high)
                        = 0.8 × 0.9
                        = 0.72

You should verify the remaining rows in the table.

Then, recalling from Section 3.6 that $\sigma_M^2 = $ Var(M) = 0.0009, we obtain:

$$\beta_A = \frac{0.0024}{0.0009} = 2.6667$$

For security B in Example 3.3, assume that the conditional payoff probabilities are:

- When return on M is high:

Probability that return on B is high = 0.7917

Probability that return on B is low = 0.2083

- When return on M is low:

Probability that return on B is high = 0.2083

Probability that return on B is low = 0.7917

Then, similar calculations give:

$$\beta_B = \frac{0.0014}{0.0009} = 1.5556$$

You should verify this calculation.[11]

Because β_B is lower than β_A, an investor who buys B shares is more insulated from the ups and downs of the stock market. This is the sense in which a low-beta security has low risk.[12]

3.7.2   *PORTFOLIO EXPECTED VALUE AND VARIANCE*

Since risk-averse investors with mean-variance utility functions need to know the expected value and variance of their investment portfolios, we give here formulae for their calculation. In the process, we shall see that beta measures the amount of systematic risk contributed by a security to a portfolio.

The expected value of return on a portfolio P is calculated as a weighted average of the expected returns on the securities in the portfolio:

$$\bar{x}_P = k_1\bar{x}_1 + k_2\bar{x}_2 + \dots + k_n\bar{x}_n$$

where $\bar{x}_P$ is the expected return on P, $\bar{x}_1$ is the expected return on security 1, etc., k_1 is the proportion of total portfolio investment in security 1, etc., and there are n securities in the portfolio.

In Example 3.3, $n = 2$, $k_1 = \$120/\$200 = 0.6$, $k_2 = (1 - k_1) = 0.4$, and the expected returns on the two securities A and B in Toni's portfolio were both 0.0850. Then, the formula gives:

$$\bar{x}_{A + B} = 0.6 \times 0.0850 + 0.4 \times 0.0850 = 0.0850$$

which, of course, agrees with the direct calculation in Table 3.5.

For the variance of portfolio return, we have the following standard formula for the variance of a sum of random variables:

$$Var(P) = \sigma_P^2 = k_1^2\sigma_1^2 + k_2^2\sigma_2^2 + \dots + k_n^2\sigma_n^2 + 2k_1k_2\,Cov(x_1,x_2) + 2k_1k_3\,Cov(x_1,x_3)$$
$$+ \dots + 2k_{n-1}k_n\,Cov(x_{n-1},x_n)$$

That is, the variance of P is the weighted sum of the variances of the individual securities in P plus the weighted sum of covariances of all the pairs of securities in P.

In Example 3.3, the formula reduces to:

$$Var(A + B) = k_1^2\,Var(A) + (1 - k_1)^2\,Var(B) + 2k_1(1 - k_1)\,Cov(A,B)$$

The main point here is that portfolio variance depends not only on the variances of the component securities, but also, if the security returns are correlated, on the covariance between them (if the returns on A and B are uncorrelated, $Cov(A,B) = 0$).

In an investment context, the returns on A and B are most definitely correlated because of economy-wide factors. In fact, we have assumed that economy-wide factors are the *only* source of correlation between security returns. Then, we can write the covariance between A and B in terms of their covariances with the market portfolio M:

$$Cov(A,B) = \frac{Cov(A,M)\ Cov(B,M)}{Var(M)}$$

$$= Var(M)\beta_A\beta_B$$

The portfolio variance becomes:[13]

$$\begin{aligned}
Var(A + B) &= 0.6^2\,Var(A) + 0.4^2\,Var(B) + 2 \times 0.6 \times 0.4\,Var(M)\beta_A\beta_B \\
&= 0.36 \times 0.0120 + 0.16 \times 0.0088 + 0.48 \times 0.0009 \times 2.6667 \times 1.5556 \\
&= 0.0043 + 0.0014 + 0.0017 \\
&= 0.0074
\end{aligned}$$

which agrees with the direct calculation in Table 3.5. Thus, we see that securities A and B contribute systematic risk of 0.0017 to the portfolio variance of 0.0074, or about 23%.

3.7.3 PORTFOLIO RISK AS THE NUMBER OF SECURITIES INCREASES

A contribution of 23% may not seem like much, but this results from the presence of only two securities in the portfolio. Consider what happens as the number of securities in the portfolio increases. Let there now be n securities in portfolio P. To simplify a bit, we will assume that an equal amount is invested in each security, so that the proportion of each security in P is $1/n$ of the total amount invested. Then:

$$\begin{aligned}
Var(P) &= \frac{1}{n^2}\sigma_1^2 + \frac{1}{n^2}\sigma_2^2 + ... + \frac{1}{n^2}\sigma_n^2 + \frac{2}{n^2}Cov(x_1,x_2) + \frac{2}{n^2}Cov(x_1,x_3) + ... + \frac{2}{n^2}Cov(x_{n-1},x_n) \\
&= \frac{1}{n^2}\left[\sigma_1^2 + \sigma_2^2 + ... + \sigma_n^2\right] + \frac{2}{n^2}Var(M)\left[\beta_1\beta_2 + \beta_1\beta_3 + ... + \beta_{n-1}\beta_n\right]
\end{aligned}$$

There are n variance terms in the formula. However, the number of covariance terms goes up quite quickly relative to n. In fact, there are $n(n-1) \div 2$

covariance terms. For example, if n = 10, there are 10 variance terms but 45 covariance terms.

This means that, even for portfolios that contain a modest number of securities, *most of the risk is systematic risk*, from the covariance terms. For example, for n = 10, the coefficient of the variance terms is only 1/100, so that the variances of the 10 securities contribute only 10% of their average variance to the portfolio variance. However, while the coefficient of the systematic risk terms is only 2/100, there are 45 terms, so the covariances contribute fully 90% of their average covariance to the portfolio variance. In other words, *most of the benefits of diversification can be attained with only a few securities in the portfolio*. This is fortunate, since brokerage and other transactions costs would prevent most investors from buying the market portfolio.[14] From an accounting standpoint, this means that for most investors, useful information is that which helps them assess securities' expected returns and betas.

3.7.4   SUMMARY

When transactions costs are not ignored, a risk-averse investor's optimal investment decision is to buy relatively few securities, rather than the market portfolio. In this way, most of the benefits of diversification can be attained, at reasonable cost.

Information about securities' expected returns and betas is useful to such investors. This enables them to estimate the expected return and riskiness of various portfolios that they may be considering. They can then choose the portfolio that gives them their most preferred risk-return tradeoff, subject to the level of transactions costs that they are willing to bear.

3.8   *The Reaction of Professional Accounting Bodies to the Decision Usefulness Approach*

It is interesting to note that major professional accounting bodies have adopted the decision usefulness approach. For example, Section 1000 of the *CICA Handbook* states (paragraph 1000.15), in part:

> *The objective of financial statements is to communicate information that is useful to investors, members, contributors, creditors and other users ... in making their resource allocation decisions and/or assessing management stewardship.*

However, the earliest and most complete statement of this adoption comes from the FASB in its Conceptual Framework project. The Conceptual Framework specifically mentions investors' needs for information about the uncertainty of future investment returns as well as their expected values. While Section 1508 of the *CICA Handbook* lays down conditions for disclosure of measurement uncertainty,

Section 1000 per se does not mention risk. In view of our demonstration above that rational investors need information about risk as well as expected value of returns, we shall concentrate here on the Conceptual Framework.

According to *Statement of Financial Accounting Concepts* (1978) (SFAC 1), the purpose of the concepts project is "to set forth fundamentals on which financial accounting and reporting standards will be based." SFAC 1 gives a series of objectives of financial reporting. Its first objective of financial reporting is to:

> *provide information that is useful to present and potential investors and creditors and other users in making rational investment, credit, and similar decisions.*

Note particularly the use of the word "rational" in this objective. This is the tie-in to the economic decision theory. As pointed out in Section 3.4, decision-makers who proceed in accordance with the theory, that is, those who make decisions so as to maximize their expected utility, are referred to as rational.

Note also that a variety of constituencies are included in this most general objective (present and potential investors and creditors and other users) and also that a wide variety of decisions are contemplated (investment, credit, and similar decisions). This immediately raises the question of what particular decision-makers and decisions are involved. Thus, SFAC 1 states that the second objective of financial reporting is to:

> *provide information to help present and potential investors and creditors and other users in assessing the amounts, timing and uncertainty of prospective cash receipts from dividends or interest and the proceeds from the sale, redemption, or maturity of securities or loans.*

Thus, we can see that the primary decision addressed in SFAC 1 is the investment decision in firms' shares or debt. Specifically, cash receipts from dividends or interest are *payoffs*, similar to those in the payoff table (Table 3.1) of Example 3.1. Note that these investment decisions apply to potential investors as well as present ones. This means that financial statements must communicate useful information to the market, not just to existing investors in the firm.

Note also that the second objective is future-oriented—it calls for information about "prospective" cash receipts from dividends or interest. There is a clear recognition that investors need information to help them estimate *future* payoffs from their investments. In particular, the second objective states that investors need to assess "the amounts, timing and uncertainty" of prospective returns. While the terms used are somewhat different, these will be recognized as relating to the expected value and risk of future returns. Thus, the second objective also contains a clear recognition that (risk-averse) investors will want information about risk of returns as well as their expected amounts, just as the theory of investment predicts.

The question now arises: How can historical-cost-based financial statements be useful in predicting future returns? This is probably the major difficulty that the FASB's Conceptual Framework has faced. Given that historical cost accounting is firmly fixed in practice, it is necessary to establish some linkage between past firm performance and future prospects. Without such linkage, the decision-oriented objectives of SFAC 1 would not be attainable.

We can see the linkage clearly, however, by drawing on the decision theory model. In particular, refer to the information system (Table 3.2) for Example 3.1. The table provides a probabilistic relationship between current financial statement information (GN or BN) and the future-oriented states of nature (high or low earning power), that will determine future investment payoffs. In effect, current financial statement information and future returns are linked via the conditional probabilities of the information system.

Consistent with the information system linkage, SFAC 1 states:

Although investment and credit decisions reflect investors' and creditors' expectations about future enterprise performance, those expectations are commonly based at least partly on evaluations of past enterprise performance.

This is the crucial argument that enables the Conceptual Framework to maintain that past-oriented, historical cost-based financial statement information can be useful to forward-looking investors. It is consistent with the decision usefulness approach, which purports that information is useful if it helps investors make their own estimates of future returns.

In SFAC 2, the FASB goes on to consider the characteristics that are necessary if financial statement information is to be useful for investor decision-making. This is another crucial and delicate aspect of the whole conceptual framework—how can financial statement information be presented so as to be of maximum use to investors in predicting future returns? Once again, the answer lies in the concepts of **relevance** and **reliability**.

In Chapter 2, we defined relevant financial statements as ones that showed the discounted present values of the cash flows from the firm's assets and liabilities. The SFAC 2 definition is somewhat broader:

Relevant accounting information is capable of making a difference in a decision by helping users to form predictions about the outcomes of past, present, and future events or to confirm or correct prior expectations. Information can make a difference to decisions by improving decision makers' capacities to predict or by providing feedback on earlier expectations. Usually, information does both at once, because knowledge about the outcomes of actions already taken will generally improve decision makers' abilities to predict the results of similar future actions. Without a knowledge of the past, the basis for a prediction will usually be lacking. Without an interest in the future, knowledge of the past is sterile.

The essence of the SFAC 2 definition is that information is relevant if it helps financial statement users to form their own predictions of events (such as future profitability). Again, this is consistent with the decision usefulness approach. Thus, we can say that under the ideal conditions of Chapter 2, relevant financial statement information consists of (the discounted present values of) future payoffs, or expected future payoffs. Under less-than-ideal conditions, relevant financial statement information consists of information that helps investors form *their own* expectations of future payoffs. By extending the definition of relevance to include information that can help investors form their own payoff estimates, the scope for information to be relevant is greatly enlarged.

It is also worth noting that the FASB notion of relevance is consistent with the definition of information in decision theory. Recall that information is that which has the potential to change individual decisions, that is, it can "make a difference." In effect, evidence is not really information unless it is capable of affecting user decisions. This role of information comes across with particular clarity in Bayes' theorem. Recall that Bayes' theorem provides a vehicle for investors to update their prior beliefs about relevant states of nature on the basis of new information, as illustrated in Example 3.1.

Another desirable information characteristic in SFAC 2 is reliability. In Chapter 2 we defined reliable information as information that is *precise and free from bias*. According to SFAC 2:

> *To be reliable, information must have representational faithfulness and it must be verifiable and neutral.*

This characteristic can be reconciled with our definition. We can equate representational faithfulness and neutrality with freedom from bias. For example, if financial statement information is biased due to managerial misrepresentation towards a predetermined result, that information would be neither representationally faithful nor neutral.

Also, the precision of financial statement information can be equated with representational faithfulness and verifiability. We saw in Section 2.4 that a major problem with RRA was the imprecision of the discounted reserves' valuation, with the consequence that major adjustments of prior years' valuations were frequently required. In effect, the estimates were not sufficiently precise for purposes of estimating an oil company's future cash flows; hence, they were not representationally faithful to the resources or events those numbers purport to represent. In addition, they would lack verifiability in the sense that independent measurers would be likely to achieve different RRA estimates under similar circumstances.

SFAC 2 continues on to explore other desirable characteristics of useful financial statement information. One of these is **timeliness**, which is best thought of as a constraint on relevance. That is, if a manager delays the release of information, it loses any relevance it may have had if it had been released promptly.

As previously mentioned, the main point to realize is that, to be useful for investment decision purposes, financial statement information need not necessarily involve a direct prediction of future firm payoffs. Rather, if the information has certain desirable characteristics, such as relevance, reliability, and timeliness, it can be an informative input to help investors form their own predictions of these payoffs.

SUMMARY

The FASB's SFAC 1 represents an important adaptation of decision theory to financial accounting and reporting. Furthermore, this theory is oriented in SFAC 1 to the theory of decision-making for investors, which has been much studied in economics and finance.

SFAC 2 operationalizes the decision usefulness approach by developing the characteristics that accounting information should have in order to be useful. In essence, accounting information should provide an informative information system that links current financial statements with future state realizations and payoffs. Two major informative characteristics are *relevance* and *reliability*. Relevant information is information that has the capacity to affect investors' beliefs about future returns, and it should be released in a timely manner. Reliable information faithfully represents what it purports to measure. It should be precise and free from bias.

3.9   *Conclusions on Decision Usefulness*

Following from the pioneering *ASOBAT* and Trueblood Committee reports, the decision usefulness approach to financial reporting implies that accountants need to understand the decision problems of financial statement users. Single-person decision theory and its specialization to the portfolio investment decision provides an understanding of the needs of rational, risk-averse investors. This theory tells us that such investors need information to help them assess securities' expected returns and the riskiness of these returns. In the theory of investment, beta is an important risk measure, being the standardized covariance of a security's return with the return on the market portfolio. This covariance risk is the main component of the riskiness of a diversified portfolio, even if the portfolio contains only a relatively few securities.

Historical cost-based financial statements are an important and cost-effective source of information for investors, even though they do not report directly on future investment payoffs. They provide an information system that can help investors to predict future firm profitability or cash flows, which, in turn, predict future returns. This predictive role is enhanced to the extent that financial statements are relevant and reliable.

Major accounting standard setting bodies such as the CICA and the FASB have adopted the decision usefulness approach. This is evidenced by their conceptual frameworks, which show a clear recognition of the role of financial reporting in providing relevant and reliable information for investors.

Questions and Problems

1. Refer to Table 3.2, the information system table for Example 3.1. Prepare a similar table for a **perfect**, or **fully informative**, information system, that is, an information system that perfectly reveals the true state of nature. Do the same for a **non-informative** information system, that is, one that reveals nothing about the true state.

    Use the probabilities from the two tables you have prepared to revise state probabilities by means of Bayes' theorem, using the prior probabilities and GN message given in Example 3.1. Comment on the results.   (CGA-Canada)

2. What would the utility function of a **risk-taking** investor look like? What sort of portfolio would such an individual be likely to invest in? What information would the investor need?   (CGA-Canada)

3. An investor's utility function is:

    $$U_i(a) = 3\bar{x} - \frac{1}{2}\sigma_x^2$$

    Act a_1 has $\bar{x} = 0.88$, $\sigma_x^2 = 0.512$, yielding $U_i(a_1) = 2.384$. Act a_2 has $\bar{x} = 0.80$.

    What σ_x^2 would this act require to yield the same utility as a_1? Comment on the result with regard to risk and expected return.   (CGA-Canada)

4. Refer to Figure 3.4. Suppose Toni's utility function is:

    $$U_i(a) = \frac{1}{2}\bar{x} - 16\sigma_x^2$$

    Calculate Toni's utility at point Z on Figure 3.4 and compare it with her utility at point M. Which act does Toni prefer? Explain.   (CGA-Canada)

5. What is the beta of:

    a. The market portfolio
    b. The risk-free asset
    c. Portfolio A + B in Example 3.3 and Section 3.7   (CGA-Canada)

6. Explain why most of the benefits of diversification can be attained with only a relatively few securities in the portfolio. Assume that an equal amount is invested in each security. Does the riskiness of the return on a diversified portfolio approach zero as the number of securities in the portfolio gets larger? Explain.
                                                                     (CGA-Canada)

7. The FASB states in SFAC 1:

   > Information about enterprise earnings based on accrual accounting generally provides a better indicator of an enterprise's present and continuing ability to generate favourable cash flows than information limited to the financial effects of cash receipts and payments.

   In other words, the FASB is arguing that net income is a better predictor of future cash flows than cash flows themselves. This may seem surprising.

   Why do you think the FASB makes this argument?   (CGA-Canada)

8. Verify the statement made at the end of Section 3.6 that if Toni Difelice can borrow all she wants at 4% she would borrow $9,800, yielding utility of 2.33.

9. Give some reasons why the off-main diagonal probabilities of an information system such as that depicted in Table 3.2 are non-zero. Use the concepts of relevance and reliability in your answer. Explain why an information system is more useful the lower the off-main diagonal probabilities are.

10. a. State the decision usefulness approach to accounting theory.

    b. What two questions arise once the decision usefulness approach is adopted?

    c. What primary constituency of financial statement users has been adopted by the major professional accounting bodies as a guide to the reporting of decision-useful financial information?

    d. According to the FASB Conceptual Framework's second objective of financial reporting, what information is needed by the constituency of users that you have identified in part **c**?

    e. Explain why information about the riskiness of securities is useful to investors.   (CGA-Canada)

11. Mr. Smart is an investor with $15,000 to invest. He has narrowed his choice down to two possible investments:

    - Mutual fund
    - Common shares in Buyme Corporation

    Mr. Smart is risk-averse. The amount of utility he derives from a payoff is:

    Utility = 2ln(payoff)

    where ln denotes natural logarithm. The decision tree for Mr. Smart's problem appears as in Figure 3.5.

    Because of a planned major purchase, Mr. Smart intends to sell his investment one year later. The payoffs represent the proceeds from the sale of the investment and receipt of any dividends, net of initial investment. The probabilities represent Mr. Smart's prior probabilities about the state of the economy (good or bad) over the coming year.

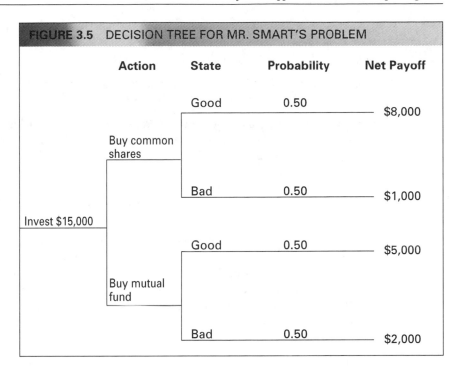

FIGURE 3.5   DECISION TREE FOR MR. SMART'S PROBLEM

Action	State	Probability	Net Payoff
Buy common shares	Good	0.50	$8,000
	Bad	0.50	$1,000
Buy mutual fund	Good	0.50	$5,000
	Bad	0.50	$2,000

(Invest $15,000)

Required

a. Calculate Mr. Smart's expected utility for each action and indicate which action he would choose if he acted on the basis of his prior information.

b. Now, suppose Mr. Smart decides that he would like to obtain more information about the state of the economy rather than simply accepting that it is just as likely to be good as bad. He decides to take a sample of current annual reports of major corporations. Every annual report shows that its firm is doing well, with increased profits over the previous year. The probability that there would be such healthy profits if the state of the economy actually was good is 0.75. The probability of such healthy profits is only 0.10 if the state of the economy actually was bad.

Use Bayes' theorem to calculate Mr. Smart's posterior probabilities of the high and low states of the economy. Will he change his decision?

Note: Round your calculations to two decimal places.

12. John Save plans to invest $5,000 in one of the following instruments:

- Bonds of J Ltd., yielding 12%
- Canada Savings Bonds, yielding 8%

On the basis of his knowledge of current economic conditions and the outlook for the industry of J Ltd., John assesses the prior probability that J Ltd. will go bankrupt as 0.05. If this happens, John will lose both principal and interest and receive no money at the end of the year. If J Ltd. does not go bankrupt, John plans to sell the bonds, plus interest, at the end of one year.

Of course, the probability that the Canada Savings Bonds will fail to pay off is zero. John also plans to sell these, plus interest, one year later.

John is risk-averse, and decides to choose that investment that yields the highest expected utility. Assume that John's utility for an amount of $x is given by $\sqrt{x}$, where x is the gross payoff.

Required

a. On the basis of his prior probabilities, which investment should John choose?

b. Rather than choosing on the basis of his prior probabilities, assume that John decides to analyze the current financial statements of J Ltd. These financial statements can look "good" (G) or "bad" (B). After his analysis, John realizes that the statements look good. On the basis of his extensive understanding of financial statement analysis, he knows that the probability that the financial statements would look good given that the firm was actually heading for bankruptcy is 0.10, that is:

$$P(G/S_1) = 0.10$$

where S_1 denotes the state of heading for bankruptcy.

Similarly, John knows that:

$$P(G/S_2) = 0.80$$

where S_2 denotes the state of not heading for bankruptcy.

Advise John as to which investment he should now take. Use Bayes' theorem.

Note: Round your calculations to four decimal places.   (CGA-Canada)

13. "A theoretically correct measure of income does not exist in the real world in which accountants must operate."

Required

a. What is meant by the phrase "a theoretically correct measure of income"?

b. Why does a theoretically correct measure of income not exist in the real world? Discuss.

c. Discuss how the historical cost basis of accounting trades off relevance against reliability.

d. Give two examples of problems or weaknesses associated with historical cost accounting.   (CGA-Canada)

14. Consider the common stock of A Ltd. and the common stock of B Ltd. These two common stocks have the same expected return and the same variance of return.

You are a risk-averse investor and have a fixed sum of money to invest. You are considering the following two choices:

a. Investing the entire sum of money in common stock of A Ltd.

b. Investing in a portfolio with the investment equally distributed between common stock of A Ltd. and common stock of B Ltd.

Required

Discuss whether you would choose alternative **a** or **b** or whether you are indifferent between them. Explain your choice. (CGA-Canada)

15. "It is possible to reduce risk in a portfolio by diversification."

Required

a. Do you agree with this statement? If so, why? Discuss.

b. Can the risk of a portfolio be reduced to zero by diversification? Discuss.

c. Why is beta the most relevant measure of risk in a diversified portfolio?

(CGA-Canada)

16. Marie has $1,000 that she wishes to invest for one year. She has narrowed her choices down to one of the following two actions:

a_1: Buy bonds of Risky Mining Ltd. These pay 14.4% interest, unless Risky goes bankrupt, in which case Marie will lose her principal and interest.

a_2: Buy Canada Savings bonds, paying 6.4% interest.

Marie assesses her prior probability of Risky Mining Ltd. going bankrupt as .40. Marie's utility for money is given by the square root of the amount of her gross payoff. That is, if she buys the Canada Savings Bonds her payoff is $1,064, etc. Marie is a rational decision-maker.

Required

a. Based on her prior probabilities, which action should Marie take? Show your calculations.

b. Before making a final decision, Marie decides she needs more information. She obtains Risky Mining's current financial statements and examines its debt-to-equity ratio. This ratio can be either "HI" or "LO." Upon calculating the ratio, Marie observes that it is LO. On the basis of her prior experience in bond investments, Marie knows the following conditional probabilities:

	DEBT-TO-EQUITY RATIO	
FUTURE STATE	LO	HI
NB Not Bankrupt	0.50	0.50
B Bankrupt	0.05	0.95

Which action should Marie now take? Show your calculations, taken to two decimal places.

c. The Accounting Standards Board adopts a major new standard affecting Risky Mining Ltd.'s financial statements. Pension liabilities and other post-retirement benefits must now be measured in the financial statements at their expected discounted present values, instead of the previous pay-as-you-go accounting.

Evaluate the likely impact of the new standard on the main diagonal probabilities of the information system in part **b**.

17. The owner of a building approaches a banker for a loan to improve the property, to be secured by the rental proceeds. After reviewing the application, the banker assesses that, if the loan is granted, there is a 70% probability the rental proceeds will be $100 and a 30% probability the rental proceeds will be $30.

Required

a. Assume that the banker is risk neutral. How much would the banker be willing to lend on the security of the rental proceeds?

b. If the banker is risk averse, explain why he/she would only be willing to lend a lesser amount than in part **a**.

c. Now assume that if the rent is only $30, the banker assesses a 90% probability that the building owner will be "bailed out" by the government, in which case the rent would be restored to $100. How much would the risk neutral banker be willing to lend now? If every banker felt this way, what implications do you see for the banking system and the economy?

18. The following problem is designed to encourage your consideration of Bayes' theorem. It shows how unaided judgement about probabilities can often be far off the mark. The problem is adapted from one appearing in an article in *The Economist*, "Getting the goat," February 20, 1999, p. 72. This article discusses how people who guess at probabilities can frequently be wrong:

> *A disease is present in the population at the rate of one person per thousand. A test for the disease becomes available. The drug company that is marketing the test randomly selects you to take the test. You agree, and the test results are positive. However, the test has a 5% probability of showing a positive result when in fact the disease is not present. What is the probability that you have the disease?*

19. Over its life, a firm "earns what it earns." That is, its *total* cash flows and reported net incomes will be equal, regardless of the accounting policies used to report net income year-by-year.

Refer to Example 2.1, where P.V. Ltd. has purchased a capital asset for $173.55. Assume, contrary to the example, that P.V. does *not* operate under ideal conditions. Assume further that its cash sales for each year are $100, as in the example, but that it uses straight line amortization for the capital asset.

Required

a. Verify that over its 2-year life P.V.'s *total* cash flows, historical cost accounting-based earnings, and present value-based earnings are equal.

b. On realizing this equality, an investor suggests that P.V. drop annual reporting of net income and simply report annual cash flows. This, he says, will avoid the problems of matching costs and revenues, and will be just as useful since "it all comes out the same in the end." Do you agree with this suggestion? Explain why or why not.

20. A problem that complicates the relationship between current reported earnings and future earning power is when to recognize revenue as earned. Section 1000.47 of *CICA Handbook* states that revenue is usually recognized when the vendor has performed its obligations and there is reasonable assurance of the amount and collectibility of the sales consideration. For many firms, the point of sale is regarded as the point in the operating cycle at which these criteria are met. Under some conditions, however, it is debatable if the point of sale does satisfy these criteria. If it does not, this can reduce the ability of the information system to capture the relationship between current and future performance. Greater relevance from recognizing revenue early in the operating cycle will increase the main diagonal probabilities of the information system. However, if revenue is recognized too early, problems of reliability will decrease them even more.

A case in point is Nortel Networks Corporation. In its 2000 annual report, Nortel states:

> *The competitive environment in which we operate requires that we, and many of our principal competitors, provide significant amounts of medium-term and long-term customer financing....At December 31, 2000, we had entered into certain financing agreements of...up to $4,100 (millions of U.S. dollars), not all of which is expected to be drawn upon....We may be required to hold certain customer financing obligations for longer periods prior to placement with third party lenders, due to recent economic uncertainty... and reduced demand for financings in capital and bank markets....As well, certain competitive local exchange carriers have experienced financial difficulties....we have various programs in place to monitor and mitigate customer credit risk. However, there can be no assurance that such measures will reduce or eliminate our exposure to customer credit risk. Any unexpected developments in our customer financing arrangements could have a material adverse effect on our business, results of operations, and financial condition.*

Despite these reservations, Nortel includes sales under extended-term customer financing in current revenue. Note 1. (c) to its 2000 financial statements states, in part:

Nortel Networks provides extended payment terms on certain software con-tracts....The fees on these contracts are considered fixed or determinable based on Nortel Networks' standard business practice of using these types of contracts as well as Nortel Networks' history of successfully collecting under the original payment terms without making concessions.

Required

a. Discuss the extent to which Nortel's revenue recognition policy on contracts for which extended-term customer financing is provided meet the revenue recognition criteria of *CICA Handbook.*

b. Which revenue recognition policy—Nortel's policy, or a policy of recogniz-ing revenue only as payments are received under extended-term customer financing contracts—results in the highest main diagonal probabilities of the information system? In your answer, consider both the relevance and reliability of the information.

c. On April 11, 2001, *The Globe and Mail* reported that Savis Communications Corp. is in default on a $235 millions (U.S.) extended term loan facility advanced by Nortel. As a rational investor, does this new information affect your evaluation of Nortel's future earning power? Draw on decision theory concepts in your answer (no calculations required).

Notes

1. As mentioned in Section 1.2, decision usefulness was the focus of the 1966 AAA monograph, *A Statement of Basic Accounting Theory (ASOBAT).*

2. The Trueblood Commission was a study group of the American Institute of Certified Public Accountants, which, in its 1973 report, *Objectives of Financial Statements,* accepted the decision usefulness approach of *ASOBAT.* The signifi-cance of this acceptance is that the AICPA is a professional accounting body, whereas the AAA is an association of academics.

3. For a formal development of the concepts of decision theory, including utility theory, the information system, and the value of information, see Laffont (1989), especially Chapters 1, 2, and 4. See also Demski (1972), especially Chapters 1 to 3. For an excellent intuitive development of the theory, see Raiffa (1968).

4. We define the utility function here in terms of the net payoff. Conceptually, the utility function should be defined in terms of the investor's total wealth. However, we opt for the simplest presentation in this example.

5. I am indebted to Professor Charles Lee for this point.

6. While the decision-maker's prior and posterior probabilities are subjective, the information system probabilities are objective. As explained below, these objective probabilities are determined by the quality of the financial statements. For the distinction between objective and subjective probabilities, see Example 2.2.

7. Strictly speaking, choosing the act that maximizes expected utility is a *consequence* of rationality, not rationality itself. Savage (1954) defines a set of axioms of rational behaviour under uncertainty. If an individual behaves according to these axioms, it can be shown that that individual will prefer one act to another if and only if its expected utility is higher than the other, where the expectation is with respect to the individual's subjective state probabilities. See, for example, Laffont (1989) for a discussion.

8. For a formal development and analysis of risk aversion, see Pratt (1964), or Laffont (1989), Chapter 2.

9. The expected payoff is:

$$0.7 \times \$200 + 0.3 \times \$1{,}133.33 = \$480$$

Expected utility is:

$$\begin{aligned}
0.7 \times \sqrt{200} + 0.3 \times \sqrt{1{,}133.33} &= 0.7 \times 14.14 + 0.3 \times 33.66 \\
&= 9.90 + 10.10 \\
&= 20
\end{aligned}$$

10. Note that we have suppressed the set of states of nature in this example. That is, Toni assesses payoff probabilities directly, rather than routing them through states. Thus, instead of saying "The probability that firm A is in high earning power state is 0.74 and if A really is in this state the payoff will be \$230," we simply say "The probability of the \$230 payoff is 0.74." This simplification has certain analytical advantages and is frequently used.

11. The expected return of B is:

$$0.6750 \times \frac{92 - 80}{80} + 0.3250 \times \frac{76 - 80}{80}$$

$$= 0.6750 \times 0.15 + 0.3250 \times -0.05 = 0.0850$$

(See Example 3.3.)

Cov(B,M) is calculated as:

Returns		Joint Probabilities		
B	**M**			
High	High	$(0.15 - 0.085)(0.10 \ - 0.085) \times 0.6333 =$	0.0006
High	Low	$(0.15 - 0.085)(0.025 - 0.085) \times 0.0417 =$	-0.0002
Low	High	$(-0.05 - 0.085)(0.10 \ - 0.085) \times 0.1667 =$	-0.0003
Low	Low	$(-0.05 - 0.085)(0.025 - 0.085) \times 0.1583 =$	0.0013
		Cov(B,M) $=$	0.0014

The joint probability of B high and M high is given by $0.8 \times 0.7917 = 0.6333$. You should now verify the remaining lines.

12. This raises the question: Who would buy A shares if B shares were available? Both securities have an expected rate of return of 0.0850, but the risk of A, as measured by its beta, is 2.6667, which is higher than B's of 1.5556. However, we do not claim that portfolio A + B is an optimal investment decision. These securities are used only to illustrate portfolio diversification.

    What would probably happen, should this situation actually occur, is that the market price of A would fall until its expected return rose sufficiently to overcome its greater riskiness.

13. $\text{Var(B)} = \sigma_B^2 = 0.6750 \times (0.15 - 0.0850)^2 + 0.3250 \times (-0.05 - 0.0850)^2$
    $= 0.0029 + 0.0059$
    $= 0.0088$

14. An alternative to buying the market portfolio is to invest in an index fund. This is a fund that tracks the rate of return on a stock market index. This attains the benefits of full diversification, but with lower transactions costs. However, the manager of such a fund would be crucially interested in stocks' expected returns and betas.

4

Efficient Securities Markets

4.1   Overview

In this chapter, we consider the interaction of investors in a securities market. The theory of efficient securities markets predicts that the security prices that result from this interaction have some appealing properties. In essence, these prices "properly reflect" the collective knowledge and information-processing ability of investors. The process by which prices do this is quite complex and not fully understood. Nevertheless, the general outlines of the process are easy to see, and we shall concentrate on these.

Securities market efficiency has important implications for financial accounting. One implication is that it leads directly to the concept of *full disclosure*. Efficiency implies that it is the information content of disclosure, not the form of disclosure itself, that is valued by the market. Thus, information can be released as easily in notes and supplementary disclosures as in the financial statements proper. The theory also affects how the accountant should think about reporting on firm risk.

In efficient markets theory, accounting is viewed as being in competition with other information sources such as news media, financial analysts, and even market price itself. As a vehicle for informing investors, accounting will survive only if it is relevant, reliable, timely, and cost-effective, relative to other sources.

Efficient securities market theory also alerts us to what is the primary theoretical reason for the existence of accounting, namely information asymmetry. When some market participants know more than others, pressure arises to find mechanisms whereby the better informed, who wish to do so, can credibly communicate their information to others, and whereby those with information disadvantage can protect themselves from possible exploitation by the better informed. Insider trading is an example of such exploitation.

We can then think of accounting as a mechanism to enable communication of relevant information from inside the firm to outside. In addition to enabling better investor decisions, this has social benefits through improving the operation of securities markets.

As mentioned in Section 1.2, accounting theorists began to realize the importance of securities market efficiency in the late 1960s. Since that time, the theory has guided much accounting research and has had major implications for accounting practice. By and large, financial accounting standard-setting bodies have accepted the full disclosure and decision usefulness implications of securities market efficiency. To illustrate this, we will examine two important standards from an informational perspective.

Finally, it should be emphasized that efficiency is a *model* of how a securities market operates. Like any model, it does not capture the full complexity of such a market. Indeed, recent years have seen an increasing number of questions about whether investors are as rational as the model assumes. We will explain some of these questions in Chapter 6, and evaluate their implications for financial accounting. The real question, however, is whether the efficient securities market model captures *enough* of the real market that accountants can be guided by its predictions. In Chapter 6 we conclude that it does. We also conclude that to the extent securities markets are not fully efficient, this increases the importance of financial reporting.

4.2   *Efficient Securities Markets*

4.2.1   *THE MEANING OF EFFICIENCY*

In Chapter 3 we studied the optimal investment decisions of rational investors. Now consider what happens when a large number of rational individuals interact in a securities market. Our interest is in the characteristics of the market prices of securities traded in the market, and how these prices are affected by new information.

If information was free, it is apparent that investors would want to take advantage of it. For instance, under the ideal conditions of Example 2.2, investors would want to know which state of nature was realized, since this affects the future cash flows and dividends of the firm. By assumption, information is free under ideal conditions since state realization is publicly observable. Thus, all investors would use this information, and the process of arbitrage ensures that the market value of the firm then adjusts to reflect the revised cash flow expectations that result, as illustrated in Example 2.2.

Unfortunately, information is not free under non-ideal conditions. Investors have to form their own subjective estimates of firms' future profitability, cash flows, or dividends. Furthermore, these estimates will need revision as new information comes along. Each investor then faces a cost-benefit tradeoff with respect to how much information to acquire. There is a variety of relevant information sources—the financial press, tips from friends and associates, changes in economic conditions, advice from analysts and brokers, etc. We can think of investors as continuously revising their subjective state probabilities as such information is received. From our standpoint, of course, a major source of cost-effective information is firms' annual reports. Probability revision arising from financial statement information was illustrated in Example 3.1.

At least some investors spend considerable time and money to use these information sources to guide their investment decisions. Such investors are called **informed**. Bill Cautious, in Example 3.1, is an example of such an investor.

It should be apparent that informed investors will want to move *quickly* upon receipt of new information. If they do not, other investors will get there first and the market value of the security in question will adjust so as to reduce or eliminate the benefit of the new information.

When a sufficient number of investors behave this way, the market becomes **efficient**. There are several definitions of an efficient securities market. The definition that we shall use here is the **semi-strong form**.

> *An **efficient securities market** is one where the prices of securities traded on that market at all times "properly reflect" all information that is publicly known about those securities.*

Three points are particularly noteworthy. First, market prices are efficient with respect to *publicly known* information. Thus, the definition does not rule out the possibility of inside information. Persons who possess inside information, in effect, know more than the market. If they wish to take advantage of their inside information, insiders may be able to earn excess profits on their investments. This is because the market prices of these investments, reflecting only outside or publicly available information, do not incorporate the knowledge that insiders possess.

A second, related, point is that market efficiency is a *relative* concept. The market is efficient relative to a stock of publicly available information. There is nothing in the definition to suggest that the market is omniscient and that market prices always reflect real underlying firm value. Market prices can certainly be wrong in the presence of inside information, for example.

The definition does imply, however, that once new or corrected information becomes publicly available, the market price will quickly adjust to this new information. This adjustment occurs because rational investors will scramble to revise their beliefs about future returns as soon as new information, from whatever source, becomes known. As a result, the expected returns and risk of their existing portfolios will change and they will enter the market to restore their optimal risk/return tradeoffs. The resulting buy-and-sell decisions will quickly change security prices to reflect the new information.

Third, investing is **fair game** if the market is efficient. This means that investors cannot expect to earn excess returns on a security, or portfolio of securities, over and above the normal expected return on that security or portfolio, where the normal expected return allows for risk. One way to establish a normal return benchmark is by means of a capital asset pricing model, as will be illustrated in Section 4.5.

An implication of securities market efficiency is that a security's market price should fluctuate randomly over time. That is, there should be no serial correlation of share returns. Thus, if a firm reports GN today, its share price should rise to reflect this news the same day. If, in the absence of any further news, its price continues to rise during succeeding days, this is evidence of inefficiency. The reason for random fluctuation of market price is that anything about a firm that can be *expected*, such as the seasonal nature of its business, the retirement of its chief executive, or the expected profit on a major new contract, will be properly reflected in its security price by the efficient market as soon as the expectation is formed. That is, the market's expectation of the effect of such events on the value of the firm is on average *unbiased*. The only reason that prices will change is if some relevant, but *unexpected*, information comes along. By definition, unexpected events occur randomly. For example, an accident may change the expected profit on a contract, and share price will quickly respond to reflect this random event. Thus, if we examine the time series formed by the sequence of price changes for a particular security, this series should fluctuate randomly over time according to market efficiency theory. A time series that exhibits such serially uncorrelated behaviour is sometimes called a **random walk**.[1]

4.2.2   HOW DO MARKET PRICES PROPERLY REFLECT ALL AVAILABLE INFORMATION?

We now consider *how* market prices properly reflect all available information. This process is by no means obvious or transparent. As described previously, rational, informed investors will demand information about securities. However, there is no guarantee that all individuals will react identically to the same information. For example, they may have different prior beliefs. Some may have superior ability to analyze financial statement information. In a sense, the decision theory model is like an automobile. It provides a vehicle to process information, but nothing guarantees that everyone's driving habits are identical or that they all take the same route to a destination.

As a result, it is quite likely that different investors will react to the same information differently, even though they all proceed rationally. Yet, investors interact in a market, each making buy/sell decisions about various securities. Since the market price of a security is the result of the demand for and supply of the security by investors, how can the market price properly reflect all available information when the individuals making the demand and supply decisions are different?

An interesting insight into this question can be gained from an example in Beaver (1989, p. 150, Table 6-1). The example relates to forecasting the results of football games. The *Chicago Daily News*, during 1966–68, printed weekly the predictions of each of its sports staff as to who would win that weekend's college football games. Table 4.1, taken from Beaver, summarizes the outcomes of these predictions.

Note the following points from Table 4.1. First, there were a number of different forecasters (15–16) and a large number of forecasts were made (619 over the three years). Second, no one individual forecaster dominated in terms of forecasting ability. The best forecasters in 1966 were well down the list in subsequent years, and vice versa. Third, note the consistent performance of the consensus forecast. The consensus forecast was also published weekly by the *Chicago Daily News* and, for each game, consisted of the team favoured to win by the majority of those forecasting. It is clear that the consensus forecast has a quality that transcends the forecasting ability of the individual forecasters from which the consensus is derived.

TABLE 4.1 FORECASTING OUTCOMES OF FOOTBALL GAMES

	1966	1967	1968
Total forecasters (including consensus)	15	15	16
Total forecasts made per forecaster	180	220	219
Rank of consensus*	1 (tie)	2	2
Median rank of forecasters	8	8	8.5
Rank of best forecasters:			
J. Carmichael (1966)	1 (tie)	8	16
D. Nightingale (1966)	1 (tie)	11	5
A. Biondo (1967)	7	1	6
H. Duck (1968)	8	10	1

*When all three years are combined, the consensus outperforms every one of the forecasters (that is, ranks first).

SOURCE: William H. Beaver, *Financial Reporting: An Accounting Revolution* ® 1981, p. 162, Table 6-1. Reprinted by permission of Prentice-Hall Inc., Upper Saddle River, New Jersey. Data are from "Here's How Our Staff Picks 'Em," *Chicago Daily News*, November 25, 1966 (p. 43), November 24, 1967 (p. 38), and November 29, 1968 (p. 43). Reprinted with special permission from the *Chicago Sun-Times* © 1999.

To translate the example into a securities market context, we can think of the forecasters as investors in a security and the forecasts as their various buy/sell decisions. The consensus forecast is analogous to the market price, since it is a type of average of the various individual forecasting decisions.

The rationale behind the example is not hard to see. It appears that the differences in forecasting ability of individual forecasters tend to cancel out when the consensus is formed, leaving a "market price" that outperforms the ability of any of the market participants.

Of course, just because a consensus forecast outperforms individual forecasters of football games does not by itself mean that the same phenomenon carries over to security prices. Essentially, what is required is that investors' estimates of security values must on average be unbiased. That is, the market does not systematically misinterpret the valuation implications of a stock of information, but rather puts a valuation on securities that is *on average* correct or unbiased. As mentioned, this does not mean that any individual investor will necessarily be correct, but it does mean that *on average* the market uses all available information.

To see how the market may behave this way, recall our argument above, which comes from Fama (1970), that when a "sufficient number" of investors can fully exploit available information, this is enough to generate efficiency. For example, financial analysts and institutional investors may be sufficiently adept at evaluating security value that, when other investors follow their recommendations, the resulting prices properly reflect available information about these securities.

It should be emphasized that the above argument assumes that individual decisions are independent, so that individual differences cancel out in their effect on price. If this is not the case, efficiency arguments break down. Thus, if our football forecasters got together to work out and agree on a consensus forecast, their forecasts would not be independent if they reflected the views of, say, a dominant and persuasive member of the group. Similarly, if investors display a collective bias in their reaction to new information about a firm, the resulting share price will be biased. For example, a firm may have reported a pattern of increasing earnings. If investors expect future earnings growth to continue simply because of growth in the past, share price momentum may develop. Then, share prices may be " too high," driven by past price increases rather than by rational evaluation of information by independent investors. We will return to this point in Chapter 6, where we discuss whether securities markets are fully efficient.

4.2.3   SUMMARY

In an efficient securities market, prices properly reflect all available information, and the price changes on such a market will behave randomly over time. Efficiency is defined relative to a stock of information. If this stock of information is incomplete, say because of inside information, or wrong, security prices will be wrong. Thus, market efficiency does not guarantee that security prices accurately reflect underlying firm value. It does suggest, however, that prices are unbiased relative to publicly available information and will react quickly to new or revised information.

The quantity and quality of publicly available information will be enhanced by prompt and full reporting. However, individual investors may have different prior beliefs and/or may interpret the same information differently. Nevertheless, roughly speaking, we can think of these differences as "averaging out," so that the market price has superior quality to the quality of the information processing of the individuals trading on the market. This argument assumes, however, that investors, or at least a major subset of investors, evaluate new information independently.

4.3 *Implications of Efficient Securities Markets for Financial Reporting*

4.3.1 IMPLICATIONS

An early examination of the reporting implications of efficient securities markets appeared in an article by W. H. Beaver, "What Should Be the FASB's Objectives?" (1973). Here, we will outline Beaver's arguments.

According to Beaver, the first major implication is that accounting policies adopted by firms do not affect their security prices, as long as these policies have no differential cash flow effects, the particular policies used are disclosed, and sufficient information is given so that the reader can convert across different policies. Thus, Beaver would regard accounting disputes such as a firm's choice of amortization method, the accounting for future tax liabilities, and the full-cost versus successful-efforts approach for oil and gas firms as, essentially, "tempests in a teapot." Notice that a firm's choice between different accounting policies in each of these disputes involves only "paper" effects. The policy chosen will affect reported net income, but will not directly affect future cash flows and dividends. For example, an oil and gas firm's proceeds from sale of crude and refined products will not depend directly on whether it uses full-cost or successful-efforts accounting. In particular, the amount of income tax the firm must pay will not be affected by its accounting policy choice in any of these three disputed areas since the tax department has its own way of calculating expenses and income in each area, independent of how the firm accounts for them on its books. If investors are interested in future cash flows and dividends and their impact on security values, and if choosing between accounting policies does not directly influence these variables, the firm's choice between accounting policies should not matter.

Thus, the efficient market argument is that as long as firms disclose their selected policy, and any additional information needed to convert from one method to another, investors are able to make the necessary calculations to see through to the resulting differences in reported net income. That is, the market can see through to the ultimate cash flow and dividend implications regardless of which accounting policy is actually used for reporting. Thus, the efficient market is not "fooled" by differing accounting policies when comparing different firms' securities. This suggests that management should not care about which particular accounting policies they use as long as those policies have no direct cash flow effects.

We thus see that full disclosure extends to disclosure of the firm's accounting policies. This is recognized by standard setters. For example, the *CICA Handbook*, paragraph 1505.04, states:

> *A clear and concise description of the significant accounting policies of an enterprise should be included as an integral part of the financial statements.*

A second implication follows—namely, efficient securities markets go hand in hand with full disclosure. If a firm's management possesses relevant information about the firm and if this can be disclosed at little or no cost, management should then disclose this information on a timely basis unless it is certain that the information is already known to investors from other sources. More generally, management should develop and report information about the firm as long as the benefits to investors exceed the costs. The reasons are twofold. First, market efficiency implies that investors will use all available, relevant information as they strive to improve their predictions of future returns, so that additional information will not be "wasted." Second, the more information a firm publishes about itself, the more information is publicly available about that firm. Consequently, investors' confidence in the securities market is enhanced.

Third, market efficiency implies that firms should not be overly concerned about the naive investor—that is, financial statement information need not be presented in a manner so simple that everyone can understand it. The reasoning here is actually quite subtle: if *enough* investors understand the disclosed information, this is sufficient to ensure that the market price of a firm's shares is the same as it would be if all investors understood it. This is because the investors who do understand the financial information will engage in buy/sell decisions on the basis of the disclosed information, which will move the market price towards its efficient level. Also, naive investors can hire other persons (such as financial analysts or investment fund managers) to interpret the information for them, or can mimic the buy/sell decisions of more knowledgeable investors. As a result, any information advantage that the knowledgeable investors may have is quickly dissipated. In other words, the naive investors can *trust* the efficient market to price securities so that they always reflect all that is publicly known about the firms that have issued them, even though these investors may not have complete knowledge and understanding themselves. This is referred to as investors being **price-protected** by the efficient market.

Since Beaver's paper, accountants have recognized that there is a variety of reasons for trading securities. For example, some investors may make a rational decision to rely on market price as a good indicator of future payoffs, rather than incur the costs of becoming informed. Others may trade for a variety of non-portfolio reasons—perhaps an unexpected need for cash has arisen. Consequently, "naive" may not be the best word to describe uninformed investors. This is considered further in Section 4.4.

A final implication is that accountants are in competition with other providers of information, such as financial analysts, media, disclosures by company officials, and so on. That is, belief revision is a continuous process, as pointed out in Section 3.3.3. Thus, if accountants do not provide useful, cost-effective information, we would expect that the usefulness of the accounting function would decline over time as other information sources take over—accountants have no *inherent* right to survive in the competitive marketplace for information.

Empirical evidence about securities market response to financial accounting information is reviewed in Chapter 5.

Beaver's paper was published in 1973. Consequently, it predates SFAC 1 (issued in 1978) and SFAC 2 (1980) by several years. However, it provides a good example of the early enthusiasm of accounting theorists for efficient securities markets. It also highlights the type of disclosure-oriented thinking that led to the formal statement of the usefulness criterion by the FASB in SFAC 1.

4.3.2 SUMMARY

Beaver argues that securities market efficiency has several implications for financial reporting. First, managers and accountants should not be concerned about which accounting policies firms use unless different accounting policies have direct cash flow effects. Many accounting policy alternatives, about which accountants have argued long and hard, do not have such cash flow effects. Second, firms should disclose as much information about themselves as is feasible—the fact of disclosure and not the form it takes is what is important. The efficient market will prefer the least costly form of disclosure, other things equal. One can argue, however, that financial statements are a cost-effective disclosure medium. Third, firms need not be concerned about the naive investor when choosing disclosure policies and formats. Such persons are price-protected, because efficient security prices properly reflect all that is publicly known about those securities. Furthermore, there are a variety of mediums, such as financial analysts and investment funds, whereby investors can take advantage of sophisticated information without needing to fully understand it themselves. Finally, the efficient market is interested in relevant information from any source, not just accounting reports.

4.4   *The Informativeness of Price*

4.4.1   *A LOGICAL INCONSISTENCY*

The careful reader may have noticed an inconsistency in our discussion of efficient securities markets to this point. Recall that efficiency implies that the market price of a security at all times properly reflects all that is publicly known about that security. What is it that drives market price to have this "properly reflects" characteristic? It is the actions of informed investors who are always striving to obtain and process information so as to make good buy/sell decisions.

However, by the definition of market efficiency, all available information is already reflected in market price. That is, the price is **fully informative**.[2] Since information acquisition is costly, and investors could not expect to beat the market when the market price already reflects all publicly known information, investors would simply stop gathering information and rely on market price as the best indicator of future security returns. For example, a simple decision rule would be to buy and hold an investment portfolio, changing its composition only if the risk/return tradeoff of the portfolio gets out of line.

The logical inconsistency, then, is that if prices fully reflect available information, there is no motivation for investors to acquire information; hence, prices will not fully reflect available information. In terms of football forecasting, the forecasters would stop putting effort into their forecasts because they can't beat the consensus forecast, but then the consensus forecast would lose its superior forecasting ability. Technically speaking, the problem here is that stable equilibrium prices do not exist, as shown by Grossman (1976).

This has potentially serious implications for accounting theory, since a lack of equilibrium makes it problematic whether financial statement information is useful to investors. Also, it is contrary to what we observe. SFAC 1 (Section 3.8) certainly implies that investors find financial reporting useful, for example.

However, there is an easy way out of the inconsistency. This is to recognize that there are other sources of demand and supply for securities than the buy/sell decisions of rational informed investors. For example, people may buy or sell securities for a variety of unpredictable reasons—they may decide to retire early, they may need money to pay gambling debts, they may have received a "hot tip," etc. Such persons are called **liquidity traders** or **noise traders**. Their buy/sell decisions will affect a security's market price, but the decisions come at random—they are not based on a rational evaluation of relevant information.

To illustrate how market price is affected by the presence of noise trading, suppose that a rational investor observes a security's price to be higher than he/she had expected based on all the information currently posessed by that investor. Now, our investor knows that other rational investors also have their own information about the security and that this information may well be more favourable. These other investors may be buying and driving up the security's price. As a result, our investor is inclined to raise his/her expectation of the security's value. While the investor does not know what information other investors have, it is rational to believe that the information is favourable and this may be what is driving up the security's price.

However, our investor also knows that the higher-than-expected security price may simply be due to noise trading. Perhaps someone has temporarily invested a large cash windfall in a randomly chosen portfolio of securities, including the security in question. If so, our investor would *not* want to increase his/her expectation of the security's value. Since each scenario is possible, the investor will increase his/her expectation of the security's value, but to an amount *less than* the security's current market price. That is, the rational investor responds by putting some weight on each possibility. In effect, the current share price conveys *some* information about share value but not *all* information as in the fully informative case.

For our purposes, an important point to note is that investors now have an incentive to increase the precision of their beliefs by gathering more information. If they can find out which explanation is the correct one, this can quickly be turned into a profitable investment opportunity. The efforts of investors to do this will then drive share price towards its efficient value. Presumably, at least some of this additional information will come from analysis of financial statements.

When investors behave as just described, they are said to have **rational expectations**. Security prices are said to be **partially informative** in the presence of noise trading and rational expectations. Note that market prices are still efficient in the presence of noise trading, but in an *expected value* sense, since noise has expectation zero. That is, the investor expects that a security's market price fully reflects all publicly available information, but further investigation may reveal that this is not the case.

The extent to which investors gather additional information depends on a number of factors, such as how informative price is, the quality of financial statement information, and the costs of analysis and interpretation. These factors lead to empirical predictions about how security market prices respond to financial statement information. For example, we might expect that price will be more informative for large firms, since they are more "in the news" than small firms, hence their market price will incorporate considerable information. This reduces the ability of financial statements to add to what is already known about such firms. Thus, we would predict that security prices respond less to financial statement information for large firms than for small firms.

Furthermore, note that firm management has an incentive to cater to the desire of investors to ferret out information. For example, management may have inside information that leads it to believe the firm is undervalued. To correct this, management may engage in **voluntary disclosure**, that is, disclosure of information beyond the minimum requirement of GAAP and other reporting standards. Such disclosure can have credibility, even if unaudited, since legal liability imposes discipline on managers' reporting decisions. Unfortunately, there are limitations on voluntary disclosure, not only because the legal system may be unable to completely enforce credibility but because management will not want to reveal information that would give away competitive advantage.

However, voluntary disclosure is much more complex and subtle than simply disclosing information. Management can signal inside information by its choice of accounting policies and, indeed, by the nature and extent of voluntary disclosure itself. This means that there are potential rewards to investors, and analysts, for careful and complete analyses of firms' annual reports. Such analyses may identify mispricing and can quickly be turned into profitable investment decisions.

Also, an increase in the quality of financial statement information, other things equal, should lead investors to increase their utilization of financial statement information relative to price. For example, the requirement by the Ontario Securities Commission (OSC) that firms include **management discussion and analysis (MD&A)** in their annual reports and Section 4250 of the *CICA*

Handbook relating to **future-oriented financial information (FOFI)** may increase market price reactions to annual reports. Annual reports should have higher information content with MD&A and/or FOFI relative to the preexisting information content of market price. MD&A and FOFI are discussed in Section 4.8. Empirical evidence on the decision usefulness of financial statement information will be considered in Chapter 5.

We conclude that the term "properly reflect" in the efficient securities market definition has to be interpreted with care. It does not mean that security prices are fully informative with respect to available information at all points in time. Indeed, if it did, this would have adverse implications for the usefulness of financial statements. Rather, the term should be interpreted as reflecting a tension between the level of informativeness allowed by noise and liquidity traders, and the ability of investors and analysts to identify mispriced securities through analysis of accounting policy choice, the nature and extent of voluntary disclosure, and, indeed, of all other available information. With this interpretation in mind, it is important to point out that the implications of security market efficiency as outlined by Beaver in Section 4.3 continue to apply. In particular, the importance of full disclosure remains.

4.4.2   SUMMARY

While the ability of a market price to *average out* individual differences in information processing, as we saw in the football forecasting example, is on the right track, the process of price formation in securities markets is much more complex than this. Through consideration of ways that rational investors can become more informed by careful analysis of managers' disclosure decisions, and by allowing for other sources of demand and supply for securities than from rational, informed investors, accountants are beginning to understand the role of information in price. The presence of non-rational traders does not necessarily mean that the efficient securities market concept that share prices "properly reflect" information is invalid, but rather that this concept must be interpreted with care.

Improved understanding of the process of price formation leads to empirical predictions of how security prices respond to accounting information and, ultimately, to more useful financial statements.

4.5   A Capital Asset Pricing Model

We are now in a position to formalize the relationship between the efficient market price of a security, its risk, and the expected rate of return on a security. We shall do so by means of the well-known Sharpe-Lintner capital asset pricing model (CAPM) (Sharpe, 1964; Lintner, 1965).

First, we need some preliminaries. Define R_{jt}, the net rate of return on the shares of firm j for time period t, as:

$$R_{jt} = \frac{P_{jt} + D_{jt} - P_{j,t-1}}{P_{j,t-1}} = \frac{P_{jt} + D_{jt}}{P_{j,t-1}} - 1$$

where:

P_{jt} is the market price of firm j's shares at the end of period t

D_{jt} is dividends paid by firm j during period t

$P_{j,t-1}$ is the market price of firm j's shares at the beginning of period t

This is the return concept used in Examples 3.2 and 3.3. It is a *net* rate of return given that the opening market price is subtracted in the numerator. We can also define a *gross rate of return* as $1 + R_{jt}$, where:

$$1 + R_{jt} = \frac{P_{jt} + D_{jt}}{P_{j,t-1}}$$

Since the only difference between the two rate of return concepts is the 1, we can use them interchangeably. In fact, to conform to common practice, we will usually refer to both net and gross rates of return as simply **returns**.

We can think of returns as either *ex post* or *ex ante*. *Ex post*, we are at the end of period t and looking back to calculate the return actually realized during the period. Alternatively, we can stand at the beginning of period t and think of an *ex ante* or expected return as:

$$E(R_{jt}) = \frac{E(P_{jt} + D_{jt})}{P_{j,t-1}} - 1 \tag{4.1}$$

That is, expected return for period t is based on the expected price at the end of the period plus any dividends expected during the period, divided by the beginning-of-period price.

Now, consider an economy with a large number of investors like Toni Difelice (Examples 3.2 and 3.3). Recall that Toni is risk-averse and has a mean-variance utility function. As shown in Tables 3.5 and 3.6, Toni can calculate the expected rates of return, the variances of return, and the covariances of return for each security in the market. Assume that there is a risk-free asset in the economy, with return R_f. Assume also that security markets are efficient and transaction costs are zero. Then, the Sharpe-Lintner CAPM shows that:

$$E(R_{jt}) = R_f(1 - \beta_j) + \beta_j E(R_{Mt}) \tag{4.2}$$

where β_j is the beta of share j and R_{Mt} is the return on the market portfolio for period t.

Note that the model is in terms of the market's *expected* returns. Equation 4.2 states that at the beginning of period t the expected return for the period equals a constant $R_f(1 - \beta_j)$ plus another constant β_j times the expected return on the market portfolio.

Strictly speaking, markets do not have expectations—individuals do. One way to think of the market's expectations is that the price of a share behaves *as if* the market holds a certain expectation about its future performance. More fundamentally, the market price of a share includes a sort of average of the expectations of all informed investors, much like the consensus forecast in the Beaver football example (Section 4.2.2) includes an average expectation of the forecasters.

It is not difficult to see the intuition of the model. Since rational investors will fully diversify when transactions costs are zero, the only risk measure in the formula is β_j. Firm-specific risk does not affect share price because it disappears in fully diversified portfolios. Also, note that the higher is β_j the higher is expected return, other things equal. This is consistent with risk aversion, since risk-averse investors will require a higher expected return to compensate for higher risk.

Note also the role of the current market price $P_{j,t-1}$ in the model. The return demanded by the market on share j for period t, that is, $E(R_{jt})$, is a function only of R_f, R_{Mt}, and β_j. In Equation 4.1, given expected end-of-period price P_{jt} and dividends D_{jt}, we see that $P_{j,t-1}$ in the denominator will adjust so that the right hand side of Equation 4.1 equals $E(R_{jt})$. That is, a share's current price will adjust so that its expected return equals the return demanded by the market for that share.

We can now see how new information affects firm j's share price. Suppose that at time t-1 some new firm-specific information comes along that raises investors' expectations of P_{jt} (and possibly also of D_{jt}), without affecting R_f, β_j or $E(R_{Mt})$. This will throw Equation 4.1 out of balance, since $E(R_{jt})$ from (4.2) does not change. Thus, $P_{j,t-1}$, the current price, must rise to restore equality. This, of course, is consistent with market efficiency, which states that the market price of a security will react immediately to new information.

For our purposes, there are three main uses for the CAPM formula. First, it brings out clearly how share prices depend on investors' expectations of future share price and dividends. If these expectations change (the numerator of Equation 4.1), current price $P_{j,t-1}$ (the denominator) will immediately change to reflect these new expectations. For a given change in expectations, and given R_f and $E(R_{Mt})$, the amount of the change in current price depends only on the share's beta. To put this another way, the larger the change in expectations, the larger the change in price, other things equal.

Second, by reverting to an *ex post* view of returns, the CAPM provides us with a way of separating the realized return on a share into expected and unexpected components. To see this, consider the following version of the model, where we are now at the end of period t and looking back:

$$R_{jt} = \alpha_j + \beta_j R_{Mt} + \epsilon_{jt}$$

This version of CAPM is called the **market model**. It states that the realized return R_{jt} for the period is the sum of the beginning-of-period *expected* return $(\alpha_j + \beta_j R_{Mt})$ and the *unexpected* or **abnormal**[3] return ϵ_{jt}. The expected return comes from the CAPM, with $\alpha_j = R_f(1 - \beta_j)$. The ϵ_{jt} captures the impact on R_{jt} of all those events during period t that were not expected at the beginning of the period. By definition in an efficient market, $E(\epsilon_{jt}) = 0$, since new information comes along randomly. But, in any period t the *realized* value of ϵ_{jt} will not be zero. Thus, the market model enables an *ex post* separation of the realized return R_{jt} into expected $(\alpha_j + \beta_j R_{Mt})$ and unexpected or abnormal (ϵ_{jt}) components.

Third, the market model provides a convenient way to estimate a stock's beta, which, as we saw in Section 3.7, is an important risk measure for investors. Notice that the market model is presented in the form of a regression equation. By obtaining past data on R_{jt} and R_{Mt}, the coefficients of the regression model can be estimated by least-squares regression. If we assume that the market is able to form accurate expectations of R_{Mt} (so that R_{Mt} is a good proxy for $E(R_{Mt})$, which is unobservable), and if we assume that β_j is stationary over time, then the coefficient of R_{Mt} from least-squares regression is a good estimate[4] of β_j. Furthermore, the reasonableness of the estimation can be checked by comparing the estimated coefficient α_j with $(1 - \beta_j)R_f$—the two should be the same.

As we will see in Chapter 5, much empirical research in accounting has required an accurate estimate of beta, and we will return to its estimation in Section 7.6.1. For now, it is important to realize that the CAPM provides an important and useful way to model the market's expectation of a share's returns, and that the model depends crucially on securities market efficiency. Also, it shows clearly how new information affects current share price.

4.6   Information Asymmetry

4.6.1   THE CONCEPT OF INFORMATION ASYMMETRY

In this section, we take a closer look at the notion of "publicly available" information in the efficient securities market definition. This leads directly to what is undoubtedly the most important concept of financial accounting theory—*information asymmetry*. Frequently, one type of participant in the market (sellers, for example) will know something about the asset being traded that another type of participant (buyers) does not know. When this situation exists, the market is said to be characterized by information asymmetry. As mentioned in Section 1.5, there are two major types of information asymmetry—adverse selection and moral hazard. We now consider these in greater detail.

One effect of information asymmetry is to hamper the proper operation of markets. In Examples 2.1 and 2.2, there was no information asymmetry, by the definition of ideal conditions. Then we saw that market values and present values were equal. This is not necessarily true when information asymmetry is present.

These effects were studied by Akerlof (1970). An example of a market characterized by information asymmetry is the used car market. The owner of a car will know more about its true condition, and hence its future stream of benefits, than would a potential buyer. The owner may try to take advantage of this by bringing a "lemon" to market, hoping to get more than it is worth from an unsuspecting buyer. However, the buyers will be aware of this temptation and, since they don't have the information to distinguish between lemons and good cars, will lower the price they are willing to pay for any used car. As a result, many cars—the good ones—will have a market value that is less than the real value of their future stream of benefits. The arbitrage effect, whereby cars of similar service potential must sell for similar prices, operates less effectively when it is difficult to know exactly what the service potential of a used car is. Thus, owners of good cars are less likely to bring them to market. In other words, the market for used cars does not work as well as it might.

In extreme cases, a market may collapse completely as a result of information asymmetry. To illustrate, consider the market for insurance policies. You may wish to buy insurance against the possibility of failing to attain your university or college degree or professional accounting designation. You would be better off with such a policy, at least if the cost was fair. Serious illness or accident, for example, may prevent your completion of the course of studies, and you could eliminate this risk if you had a policy that reimbursed you for your loss of the present value of the increased future income that would follow the attainment of your degree. However, if you owned such a policy, you would probably **shirk** your studies, even if you were perfectly healthy. Why put in all the time and effort to complete your course of studies when, by merely failing, you could receive equivalent compensation from your insurance policy?

As a result, no insurance company would sell you a policy that would reimburse you for your full income loss if you failed to attain your degree. Essentially, the problem is one of information asymmetry. You have a major information advantage over the company, because the company can only observe whether you fail, not whether your illness caused you to fail. This is called a **moral hazard** problem, for you are tempted to cheat the company by shirking your studies. Note that requiring a medical certificate would not be of much use here, because of the difficulty in establishing that it was the illness that led to the failure.

Another difficulty the insurance company would face is that people who were sick would flock to enroll in university programs (called an **adverse selection** problem, because people whose health is adverse to the insurance company's best interests self-select themselves to buy insurance). Then, when their illness led to their failure, they could collect on their policies and still enjoy the monetary fruits of a degree.

Faced with information disadvantages of this magnitude, the company responds by not writing insurance policies of the type described. Hence, no market develops. Obviously, if there is no market for an asset, such as a university degree, it is impossible to value this asset using market value.

It is interesting to note the variety of devices that markets use to reduce the effects of information asymmetry. Thus, used car markets are characterized by guarantees, safety certificates, test drives, dealers who attempt to establish a good reputation, and so on. Insurance markets are characterized by medical examinations for life insurance, co-insurance and deductible clauses for fire insurance, premium reductions for good driving records, and so on. However, because they are costly, these devices do not completely eliminate the problem. Nevertheless, they may be sufficiently effective to at least allow the market to operate, albeit not as properly as it would in the absence of information asymmetry.

The presence of risks, such as the impact of illness on earning power, that individuals would like to protect themselves against but cannot because a market does not develop, is a consequence of incomplete markets. Recall from Section 2.6 that incompleteness results when estimation problems, such as in oil company reserves, prevent market prices from developing. Here, we see that information asymmetry is another source of incompleteness.

Incompleteness of markets also results when markets exist but do not work properly. For example, despite the devices mentioned above that enable the used car market to operate, a used car buyer still bears a risk of buying a vehicle of different quality from what he or she wants and is paying for. That is, if price does not perfectly reflect the quality of a commodity, individuals are unable to buy the exact quality they want, so they bear more risk than they would like. As a result, they would like to see market incompleteness reduced. But because of adverse selection and the cost of devices to overcome it, it may not be cost-effective to eliminate it completely. Nevertheless, we will now argue that financial accounting has a role to play in improving the operation of markets, thereby at least reducing the problem of incompleteness.

One of the reasons why information asymmetry is of such importance to accounting theory is that *securities markets* are subject to information asymmetry problems. This is because of the presence of inside information and insider trading. Even if security market prices fully reflect all publicly available information, including that which can be inferred from firms' accounting policy and disclosure decisions, it is still likely that insiders know more than outsiders about the true quality of the firm. If so, they may take advantage of their information to earn excess profits. This is another example of the adverse selection problem, since insiders will be attracted by this opportunity, which is *adverse* to the interests of investors. Of course, investors will be aware of this possibility and will lower the amounts that they would otherwise be willing to pay for shares, to reflect their expected losses at the hands of insiders. Just like the used car market, the efficient securities market does not work as well as it might.

*We can think of **financial reporting** as a device to reduce the adverse selection problem, thereby improving the operation of securities markets and reducing incompleteness.*

To reduce adverse selection, accountants have adopted policies of **full disclosure**, to expand the set of information that is publicly available. Also, timeliness of reporting will reduce the ability of insiders to profit from their information advantage.

Of course, since financial reporting is costly, it is unlikely that the problem of inside information can be eliminated. Nevertheless, full and timely disclosure will increase the usefulness of financial reporting to investors by expanding the set of publicly available information. This should help with Beaver's concern that accounting is in competition with other information sources, including price itself.

4.6.2   SUMMARY

Under ideal conditions, the firm's market value fully reflects *all* information. When conditions are not ideal, market value fully reflects all *publicly available* information, if security markets are efficient.

The difference between these two information sets includes **inside information**. The ability of insiders to profit from their information advantage is an example of the adverse selection problem. Full and timely disclosure will reduce this problem, thereby making financial reporting more useful to investors and improving the working of securities markets. Since reporting is costly, however, the inside information problem will still be present.

4.7   *The Social Significance of Properly Working Securities Markets*

In a capitalist economy, securities markets are the primary vehicle whereby capital is raised and allocated to competing investment needs. Consequently, it is socially desirable that these markets work properly in the sense that security prices should provide correct values to guide the flow of investment funds. We call a market that does this a **properly working** market. For example, a firm that has high-expected-value capital projects will be encouraged to invest in them if it receives a high price for its securities. Conversely, investment should be discouraged in firms that do not have high-expected-value capital projects. This will happen if security prices properly reflect underlying value. Of course, this is exactly what society wants, since investment capital is in scarce supply. Social welfare will be enhanced if scarce capital goes to the most productive alternatives.

In the previous section, we formally faced up to the existence of information asymmetry and, in particular, the problem of inside information, whereby managers and other insiders have an information advantage over outside investors. It is not hard to see that this adverse selection problem operates against proper securities market operation, since insiders may withhold, delay, or bias the release of relevant information for their own advantage.

It is also important to note that investors will be aware of this possibility. Then, a "lemons" phenomenon, as described in Section 4.6.1 for the used car market, would also come into play here. Investors would recognize that the market is not a "level playing field" and would either withdraw from the market or lower the amount they are willing to pay for *any* security. Then, firms with high-quality investment projects will not receive a high price for their securities, and the market is not working as well as it should. If too many investors withdraw, the market becomes **thin** or, equivalently, it loses **depth**. A problem with thin markets is that investors may not be able to buy or sell all they want of a security at the market price.

Of course, developed capitalist economies have a variety of mechanisms for promoting the proper operation of securities markets. One such approach is to impose **penalties** on the market. Thus, we witness government securities commissions such as the OSC in Ontario and the SEC in the United States. These agencies create and enforce regulations to, for example, control insider trading and promote prompt disclosure of significant events, with penalties for violation.

However, the natural operation of a market can provide **incentives** for the release of inside information even in the absence of penalties for abuse. For example, a variety of mechanisms are available whereby firms with high-quality investment projects can credibly communicate this to the market, thereby enhancing the price they obtain for their securities. **Signalling** is one such mechanism—for example, insiders may retain a substantial equity position in new projects, thereby signalling to the market their beliefs in their high-quality project. The higher the project quality, the greater the incentive to signal. Signals will be considered in greater detail in Chapter 12.

For present purposes, a related incentive mechanism is full disclosure. Firms with high- (or low-) quality projects have an incentive to engage in full disclosure in their financial reports.[5] If such disclosures are credible, investors will remove them from the "lemons" category and will, as a result, be willing to pay higher prices for their securities than they otherwise would.

Obviously, penalty-based and incentive-based mechanisms are not mutually exclusive—we witness both in our economy. The penalty approach is like a "stick" and requires regulation to enforce it. The need for regulation will be reduced, however, to the extent that "carrots" are available to enable firms that wish to do so to credibly reveal their information, thereby enabling them to receive a fair price for their securities.

We may conclude that the social benefits of properly working securities markets will be attained if the following two conditions are met:

- All relevant information is in the public domain, at least up to the ability of penalties and incentives to cost-effectively motivate the release of inside information.
- Securities market prices are efficient relative to this information.

4.8   *Examples of Full Disclosure*

4.8.1   INTRODUCTION

In this section, we will consider two examples of accounting standards of which firms may avail themselves to increase the quality of their financial disclosure. The first is MD&A pursuant to OSC Policy Statement 5.10, issued in 1989. The second is FOFI pursuant to Section 4250 of the *CICA Handbook*, also issued in 1989.

Besides being of interest in their own right, these two standards provide important illustrations of how the amount of relevant information in the public domain can be increased. The MD&A standard is in between the carrot and stick approaches to information release. It is required of firms to which Statement 5.10 applies. However, it is written in fairly general terms so that firms have latitude in the extent to which they release MD&A information. Also, it need only include information available without undue effort or expense and that is not already clear from the financial statements. The second standard (FOFI) is voluntary; hence, it is a carrot approach. Section 4250 applies only if firms decide to release a forecast. The signalling implications of forecasting will be discussed in Chapter 12. Here, our interest is in its full-disclosure aspects.

4.8.2   MANAGEMENT DISCUSSION AND ANALYSIS

Objectives of MD&A

Statement 5.10 requires certain firms in the OSC's jurisdiction to prepare an "Annual Information Form (AIF) and Management's Discussion and Analysis of Financial Condition and Results of Operations (MD&A)." Our coverage will concentrate on MD&A.

The MD&A requirements apply only to relatively large firms, that is, firms with shareholders' equity greater than $10 million and with revenues greater than $10 million.

According to the Introduction to Statement 5.10, the primary objective is to:

enhance investor understanding of the issuer's business by providing supplemental analysis and background material to allow a fuller understanding of the nature of an issuer, its operations and known prospects for the future.

Thus, we see that the objective of MD&A is derived from the decision usefulness approach introduced in Section 3.2. In particular, the emphasis is on assisting the user to assess the future prospects of the firm. Note that this is not accomplished in Statement 5.10 through the financial statements, nor even by direct forecasts of future profits. Rather, the argument is:

There are practical constraints on the amount of information that can be effectively conveyed in financial statements, which are subject to generally accepted accounting and auditing standards. Important transactions, events and conditions are not always fully reflected in the financial statements and some are not easily expressed in dollar amounts. Additional disclosure and analysis beyond the financial statements is necessary to provide an adequate basis for assessment of an issuer's recent history and outlook for the future. This Policy Statement requires such expanded disclosure.

The "additional disclosure and analysis" referred to is oriented to management discussion of its current financial statements and future prospects.

Disclosure Requirements

Generally, the MD&A disclosure requirement is to discuss those aspects of the financial statements and other statistical data that enhance the reader's understanding of financial condition, changes in financial condition, and results of operations. More specifically, discussion is required under the following aspects:

- Discussion of current operations and financial condition is required.

- Specific requirements are set out to disclose information on risks and uncertainties. This is consistent with our discussion of the FASB Conceptual Framework in Section 3.8, in particular with SFAC 1's second objective of financial reporting, which includes assessment of the uncertainty of prospective cash flows and dividends.

- Information about the nature and magnitude of "financial instruments" is required. In addition to bonds and shares, this term includes mortgage-backed securities and hedging instruments. Thus, the Policy Statement requires disclosure of financial instruments that typically do not yet appear on financial statements proper in Canada, such as futures contracts, options, and swaps. This represents a start at bringing "off-balance-sheet financing" into the open.

- Many of the requirements are designed to help users interpret the financial statements. For example, "known trends" that will have a favourable or unfavourable effect on liquidity, capital resources, and continuing operations are to be described. Again, this assists the user to assess the future liquidity and profitability of the firm.

- The Policy Statement contains a number of provisions to assist firms in complying. Thus, firms whose securities are also traded in the United States (and hence must comply with the MD&A requirements of the SEC) can submit their SEC reports to the OSC in satisfaction of the OSC's MD&A requirements. That is, they do not have to prepare the same information twice. Small firms do not have to comply. Firms whose MD&A disclosures could put them at a competitive disadvantage can apply for exemption from reporting of "sensitive information." Also, firms need only include in MD&A information that is available "without undue effort or expense and which does not clearly appear in the issuer's financial statements." Finally, specific auditor involvement in the MD&A disclosures is not required. Presumably, these conditions have been included in response to management concerns about the costs and sensitive nature of compliance. Thus, Statement 5.10 includes a combination of carrot and stick mechanisms to promote information release, as discussed in Section 4.7.

Discussion of MD&A Disclosure

Strictly speaking, MD&A is not part of the financial statements (this explains why MD&A is an OSC standard rather than a *CICA Handbook* standard). Nevertheless, it is not hard to see that it is consistent with the spirit of the Conceptual Framework, where the emphasis is on supplying information to enable investors to assess the future prospects of the enterprise. This forward-looking approach is evident in MD&A, for example in the requirements to describe known trends and uncertainties.

More generally, MD&A is consistent with the decision usefulness approach. The information that it provides should be helpful in better enabling users to assess the probabilities of future profitability, cash flows, or dividends from their investments. Thus, the thrust of MD&A is to assist users in making their own assessments, rather than providing these assessments directly.

In addition, MD&A can improve the proper working of securities markets to the extent that it expands the set of relevant information available to investors. In effect, it has the potential to reduce inside information.

An Example of MD&A Disclosure

Exhibit 4.1 reproduces the risk and uncertainties portion of the MD&A in the 2001 annual report of Mark's Work Wearhouse. The firm's shares are traded on the Toronto Stock Exchange; consequently, it is subject to OSC requirements. The firm also provides extensive discussion of current operations and financial conditions, but this is not reproduced here.

EXHIBIT 4.1 Risk and Uncertainities Portion of MD&A from 2001 Annual Report of Mark's Work Wearhouse

Management's Discussion and Analysis

RISK AND UNCERTAINTIES

Table 17 shows the external and internal risk factors that affect the Company's business, and ultimately its profitability.

Management's responsibility is to mitigate **external risk factors** to the extent possible, and to achieve an appropriate balance among the **internal risk factors,** in order to optimize profits.

The **consumer environment** in Canada as reflected by the growth in total retail sales and in specific segments within the total retail sector has been as outlined in Table 18 over the last five years.

As can be seen from Table 18, total men's wear sales have grown at a slower rate than the growth in total retail sales and sales in men's clothing stores have declined over the last five years. As well, total sales in women's clothing stores have grown at a slower rate than the growth in total retail sales and sales in shoe stores have declined.

Thus, recent economic slow-down concerns notwithstanding, Table 18 does not provide comfort that consumers will continue to purchase apparel at the rates they have historically. In fact, in recent years consumers have shown a marked preference for bigger-ticket items such as furniture, appliances, autos and electronics. The Company is confident that it has mitigated this risk in its Mark's Division by having developed a stable yet evolving product offering, "On Concept" stores, sound marketing programs and is currently growing its ladies' wear and Business-to-Business sales rapidly, and is developing its e-Commerce sales in order to continue growth in its Mark's Division by increasing its market share in the men's wear, ladies' wear and footwear markets in Canada. In addition, the Company introduced its "Corporate Store Strategy" in its Work World Division three years ago and with eight pilot stores is testing the DOCKERS® Stores concept. The addition of the Work World Division is also contributing to the Company's growing market share in the segments of the retail trade in which it operates in Canada and should a DOCKERS® Stores roll out ever become a reality, that would provide a further vehicle to increase the Company's market share in Canada.

RISK FACTOR Table 17

External

Consumer environment	Interest rates
Competion	Unsolicited offer to purchase the Company's outstanding Common Shares
Seasonality	
Weather	Small cap company in current Canadian capital markets
Merchandise sourcing	
Foreign exchange rates	Share trading information

Internal

Customer service

Sales blend

Marketing strategies

Store openings and closings

Expense rates in payroll, advertising, occupancy and systems

Inventory levels

Capital expenditure investments in stores and systems

Number and strength of franchise stores

"Corporate Store Strategy" in the Work World Division Liabilities-to-equity levels

The introduction of new divisions under new store banners, i.e., DOCKERS® Stores Division

Foreign exchange exposure

Interest rate exposure

RETAIL SALES GROWTH Table 18

	Percentage Increase/(Decrease) over Prior Period				
	Total Retail*	Men's Clothing Stores*	Total Men's wear**	Women's Clothing Stores*	Shoe Stores*
Year 2000 over Year 1999	6.3	0.1	3.8	2.7***	(0.4)
Year 1999 over Year 1998	5.8	(2.3)	2.9	1.9	(2.6)
Year 1998 over Year 1997	4/3	(0.2)	5.4	2.8	1.4
Year 1997 over Year 1996	7.3	3.0	3.3	3.6	(1.6)
Year 1996 over Year 1995	2.4	(6.1)	3.9	(1.8)	0.4
Year 2000 over Year 1995	31.3	(3.4)	15.4	12.6	(7.2)

*   Statistics Canada

**   Trendex North America (includes men's wear sales in department stores, men's clothing stores and discount stores)

*** Total sales growth in total ladies' wear which includes ladies' wear sales in department stores, women's clothing stores and discount stores was 1.2% in 2000 over 1999 according to Trendex North America

Competition in the men's wear apparel sector remains fierce as department stores, discount department stores, other discount stores, unisex stores, sporting goods stores and men's specialty stores battle for market share within this market sector. Many of these stores are large U.S.-based retailers. Some mergers and subsequent store consolidations are also occurring within the sector. Management feels that it has mitigated this risk by keeping the Company well-positioned in this market sector by continually developing and introducing new products to enhance product selection for its customers, by offering products across all price points and by offering its customers different geographic shopping locations through its three divisions (e.g., power centres, strip malls, regional malls, etc.). Clearly, the

Company does not believe that it is isolated from the effects of this competition and it intends to continue to be rigorous in maintaining good relationships with its customers, protecting its businesses, generating new customers and continuing to test the introduction of new divisions with new store banners.

The Company's business remains very seasonal with the fourth quarter of the last three fiscal years continuing to produce between 37% and 39% of total system annual sales and most of the annual profits, resulting from the general increase in consumer spending in that period. The sales reporting and merchandise planning modules of the Company's information system assist the Company in mitigating the risk and uncertainties associated with seasonal programs, but cannot remove them completely, as inventory orders, especially for a significant portion of offshore commodities, must be placed well ahead of the season.

Five years ago, approximately 33% of the Company's Mark's Division (the Company's largest division) annual business was in seasonal commodities specifically related to winter weather. Today the Company's Mark's Division does 20% of its annual business in seasonal commodities specifically related to winter weather and does 20% of its annual business in seasonal commodities specifically related to summer weather. While **weather dependency** cannot be totally disassociated from the Company's business, the Company's Mark's Division has clearly spread its winter risk between winter and summer over the last five years. As the Work World Division matures, it will also follow this pattern. The DOCKERS® Stores Division is not a material part of the Company's sales at this time and because of the nature of its assortments it is less weather dependent.

In the area of **merchandise sourcing**, the Company has several sources of supply for most of its key commodities in order to be able to provide a continuous supply of quality products to its customers. While short-term interruptions could occur, the Company continues to work with both its domestic and foreign sources, to ensure that they have the ability and commitment to supply the Company so that customers' needs are met.

As part of its offshore sourcing practice, the Company advises its importers not to provide it with any goods produced in factories that use child labour or unacceptably paid or treated labour. For direct imports, the Company visits and inspects each factory it deals with to determine if the factory employs child or unacceptably paid or treated labour. The Company uses a comprehensive checklist during each inspection to ensure compliance with its ethical sourcing policies. Nevertheless, the Company cannot guarantee that such activities will not occur in the factories of the offshore suppliers with which it deals.

The Company is also a member of the Retail Council of Canada and the Retail Council's Executive Trade Committee and bas adopted the voluntary code of ethical sourcing developed by the Retail Council. In addition, the Company's Corporate Code of Conduct prohibits any employee from accepting gifts, favours or trips other than a nominal amount from anyone with whom they deal on Company business.

The Company's **foreign currency** risk is generally limited to currency fluctuations between the Canadian and U.S. dollars, as most of the Company's offshore suppliers conduct business in U.S. dollars. The Company has no U.S. dollar revenues to use for the purchase of offshore commodities in U.S. dollars The Company's practice is to enter into forward contracts for over 50% of its anticipated U.S. offshore purchases to help manage this risk. At January 27, 2001, the Company had foreign exchange collar arrangements in place for committed and anticipated foreign purchases during the Company's next fiscal year totaling $6,680,000 U.S. Under the terms of the collars, the Company bears the exchange risk on foreign purchases when the Canadian dollar trades against the U.S. dollar within the ranges and for the time periods listed in Note 13 to the Consolidated Financial Statements. At January 27, 2001, there were $102,204 of unrealized gains on the foreign exchange collars based on the January 27, 2001 exchange rate of $1.5063. See Notes 1M and 13 to the Consolidated Financial Statements.

In addition, at January 27, 2001, the Company had foreign exchange fixed contract arrangements in place for committed and anticipated foreign merchandise purchases during the Company's next fiscal year totaling $14,064,500 U.S. Under the terms of the fixed contract arrangements, the Company has fixed its exchange risk on foreign purchases at an average Canadian dollar to the U.S. dollar rate of $1.4738 ($20,728,260 Cdn.). At January 27, 2001, the unrealized gains on these contracts were $456,866 based on a January 27, 2001 exchange rate of $1.5063. See Note 1M and 13 to the Consolidated Financial Statements.

In fiscal 2001, the Company purchased approximately 58% of its merchandise from Canadian manufacturers in Canadian dollars (Mark's Division 57%, Work World Division 65% and DOCKERS® Stores Division 60%).

The Company's **interest rate** risk is a result of its short-term floating rate debt requirements during part of every fiscal year. Interest rate swap contracts are used to hedge the interest rate risk on over 50% of the anticipated short-term floating rate debt requirements for the coming year. At January 27, 2001, the Company had fixed its borrowing rate on $20.0 million of its anticipated short-term borrowing requirements at a 7.295% all-in rate and on $14.5 million of its anticipated short-term borrowing requirements at an all-in rate of 6.965% The mark-to-market value of the interest rate swap contracts is a $7,069 unrecorded gain at January 27, 2001 based on the Company's floating rate interest cost of 7.25% at January 27, 2001. See Notes IM and 13 to the Consolidated Financial Statements.

Since the Company is a public company without a management control-share block, **unsolicited offers to purchase the Company's outstanding Common Shares** could appear from time to time, as happened during fiscal 1998. This possibility may have a higher probability currently, given that institutional investors seem to be **totally disinterested in investing in small cap stocks,** and given the earnings multiple at which the Company's shares are currently trading. See trading multiples at the end of this section. While management has processes in place to have the Company's Board of Directors and non-operations management deal with such matters should they arise; there is s risk that such activities could distract operations management to the point of affecting performance and create expenses which, in combination, could cause the Company to fall short of its forecast range. See Forecast.

The **internal risk factors** are often tied together, and thus action taken to stimulate one factor often results in a negative effect on other factors:

- New store openings may increase sales, but, in the first year or two of operations of a new store, the increase in payroll costs, advertising costs, occupancy costs and interest costs may cause that store to contribute an operating loss, until it becomes a mature store from a sales per square foot perspective.

- Additional advertising campaigns may increase sales, but not sufficiently in the short term to cover the cost of the additional advertising.

- Staff reductions can lower payroll costs, but may cause a loss of sales due to lower sales per customer and customer dissatisfaction with the level of sales service and stock outages in the stores.

Management believes that it is achieving an appropriate balance among the internal risk factors in order to optimize profits.

The Mark's Division franchise operations consisted of 25 franchise stores at January 27, 2001, 88% of which meet Company-set capitalization standards. During fiscal 2001, the Mark's Division purchased four of its franchise stores and converted them to corporate stores. This franchise store purchase activity was higher than normal in fiscal 2001 as three franchisees decided to retire during that fiscal year and offered to sell their stores to the Mark's Division. The Mark's Division franchise operation is very stable and is expected to shrink a little over time with the occasional franchisee selling his or her store to the Corporation.

With a "Corporate Store Strategy" for new store openings (four in fiscal 2001, five in fiscal 2000 and nine in fiscal 1999) and the purchase of franchise stores as they become available (six purchased franchise stores in fiscal 2001, one in fiscal 2000 and 31 in fiscal 1999) and the closure of non-performing franchise stores, the **Work World franchise operation** has reduced to 90 franchise stores at January 27, 2001 from 150 at January 25, 1997. At January 27, 2001, 51% of the remaining Work World franchises meet Company-set capitalization standards that were developed after the December 1, 1996 acquisition date of Work World, as there were no capitalization standards under the previous administration. Every year, the Work World Division introduces at least half a dozen or so new merchandise programs and continually seeks to improve upon existing assortments in order to positively impact a significant part of the merchandise offering and, it is hoped, store sales in both the Work World Division's franchise and corporate stores.

In addition, over the last several years, the Company has put the necessary credit controls in place to control the level of merchandise shipments and other cost risk services provided to the Work World franchisees. Nevertheless, given the capitalization level of many of these stores, there is a risk that more of the stores could close, causing a loss of royalty and other revenues and bad debt write-offs for the Company.

In its purchased franchise stores and in its new corporate stores, the Work World Division expects to generate the appropriate sales per square foot, gross margin rate, and expense rate to produce a front-line contribution higher than the royalty rates earned from franchisees on franchise sales, although this has not yet occurred and remains a risk factor at this time.

During the second half of 1999 (fiscal 2000), the Company launched its **DOCKERS® Stores Division** with the opening of five test stores. Three more test stores were added during 2000 (fiscal 2001). The business formula for the DOCKERS® Stores Division requires that over time, sales per square foot track to mall averages, a 40% gross margin rate be achieved and that sales be made up of an equal blend of men's and women's products and an equal blend of tops and bottoms. As Table 10 (EBITDA) showed, the near-term adverse impact to earnings to launch this new division have been high. As well, there is still a risk that this or any other new division will not blossom. The Company believes that it has mitigated the risk for the DOCKERS® test by basing the store banner on an established, internationally recognized brand, by offering customers additional

DOCKERS® assortments not carried in other stores, by selecting quality store locations and by providing excellent customer service. No additional stores are planned to be added to this test in 2001 (fiscal 2002) as the division will concentrate on improving merchandise assortments as it must get its sales per square foot to track higher in order to succeed.

During the year ended January 27, 2001,the Company's shares **traded at multiples** ranging from 4.5 to 8.3 times earnings per share. This compares to a range of uncalculated negative price-earnings ratios to 99+ times price-earnings ratios for the TSE Merchandising Index and price-earnings ratios ranging from 12.1 to 19.8 times for the TSE Specialty Stores Index during the Company's fiscal 2001 year. Also during fiscal 2001, the Company's share price ranged from 55.7% to 102.5% of the Company's January 27, 2001 book value per share.

Graph 18 compares the yearly percentage changes over the last five years in the cumulative shareholder return on the Common Shares of the Company (assuming a $100 investment was made on January 28, 1996) with the cumulative total return of the TSE 300 Stock Index, the TSE Merchandising Index and the TSE Specialty Stores Index. No dividends have been paid by the Company; therefore it was not necessary to build a dividend reinvestment feature into the graph. The graph spikes upward in fiscal 1998 because, as noted earlier, the Company was subject to an unsolicited offer to purchase the Company's outstanding Common Shares in the fall of 1997.

5-YEAR SHARE PERFORMANCE (Graph 18)
(based on a base of 100)

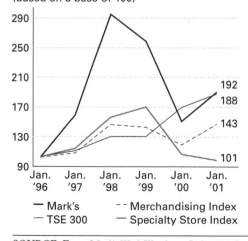

SOURCE: From *Mark's Work Wearhouse Ltd. 2001 Annual Report.* Reprinted with permission.

Note the extensive discussion of the various internal and external risk factors that occupy management's attention in planning future operations, ranging from discussion of trends and risks in the customer and purchasing environments, to risk of takeover offers, to risk of test openings of new concept stores. Also discussed is the company's exposure to foreign currency and interest rate risk, including details of off-balance sheet financial instruments used to manage these risks. Note in general how the information provided goes well beyond what can be learned from the financial statements themselves. Overall, the forward-looking nature of the discussion suggests that Mark's Work Wearhouse has a clear idea of where it wants to go.

Summary

MD&A represents a major step taken by a government regulatory body to set standards that go beyond the requirements of GAAP. The reason for this, presumably, is that the accounting recommendations of the *CICA Handbook* relate primarily to financial statements, whereas the concern of the OSC is with regulating the discussion by management contained elsewhere in the annual report.

The specific requirements of MD&A are of interest in their own right, because they lay out major reporting standards and responsibilities for management. These apply to all firms that are required to register with the OSC. Similar requirements apply to firms registered with the SEC in the United States.

MD&A is also of interest because it further illustrates how the decision usefulness approach to financial reporting has influenced, and been accepted by, a major standard setting body. It has the potential to expand the set of information available to the market.

4.8.3 FUTURE-ORIENTED FINANCIAL INFORMATION (FOFI)

Financial Forecasting Standards

We now consider another standard that has the potential for a further expansion of the information available to investors. In 1989, Section 4250 of *CICA Handbook*, dealing with future-oriented financial information, was issued. According to this section, the objective of presenting FOFI is to provide external users with information that assists them in evaluating the firm's financial prospects.

Section 4250 does not *require* that FOFI be presented. Rather, it provides standards for measurement, presentation, and disclosure for those firms that do decide to disclose FOFI to external users. FOFI is thus an incentive mechanism available to those who wish to develop a reputation for full, timely disclosure.

Despite, or perhaps because of, its voluntary nature, Section 4250 represents a major extension of the full-disclosure principle. It applies both to *forecasts* (prepared using assumptions that reflect the entity's planned courses of action for the period covered) and to *projections* (prepared using assumptions that reflect the entity's planned courses of action for the period covered, together with one or more assumptions that are not necessarily the most probable in management's judgement). Thus, projections are prepared to answer "what if" questions, whereas forecasts are estimates of the most probable outcomes of planned activities. Here, we will consider only forecasts.

Section 4250 recognizes that a forecast is only as good as its underlying assumptions. For example, these should be reasonable and supportable and reflect the *most probable* economic conditions and planned courses of action. Statistically speaking, the most probable value of a random variable is its **mode**, which may differ from the arithmetic mean. Nevertheless, we may take this most probable requirement as being reasonably consistent with an expected value approach to decision-making under uncertainty.

It is interesting that Section 4250 avoids many of the estimation problems of RRA. Thus it requires that the period covered by future-oriented financial information should not extend beyond the point in time for which such information can be reasonably estimated. The section goes on to suggest that this period would normally be one year. Thus, the problems arising from frequent and material revisions to the estimates, which we saw in Chapter 2 as a major problem with the practical application of RRA, should be minimized. Also, because of the short time horizon of the forecast, discounting, and resulting difficult choice of a discount rate, would not normally be needed.

Another interesting point is how Section 4250 takes steps to maximize the usefulness of the FOFI to the user. In addition to requiring disclosure of significant assumptions, it requires that FOFI should be prepared in accordance with the accounting policies expected to be used in presenting historical financial statements for the future period, and that it should be presented in the format of historical financial statements and include at least an income statement. Clearly, the intent here is to present the FOFI in common and well-understood format so as to enhance the user's ability to compare it with past and subsequent actual results.

Thus, we see that Section 4250 provides a major opportunity for improved disclosure. It goes well beyond the simple statement of SFAC1 that users' expectations about future enterprise performance are at least partly based on "evaluations of past enterprise performance." While the responsibility for estimation of future profitability still remains with the user, particularly for projections beyond one year, FOFI disclosures provide an important and potentially useful linkage between past and future. Furthermore, they do this in a manner that does not compromise the integrity of the generally accepted historical cost financial statements.

An Example of a Financial Forecast

Exhibit 4.2 gives extracts from the 2002 financial forecast of Mark's Work Wearhouse, from its 2001 annual report.

EXHIBIT 4.2 Forecast Range and Post Mortem Risk and Uncertainities Portion from 2001 Annual Report of Mark's Work Wearhouse

FORECAST RANGE

Earnings per Common Share, for the 52 weeks ending January 26, 2002 are forecast to be in the range of 31 to 36 cents. This forecast range represents, in management's judgment, the most likely set of conditions and the Company's most likely course of action. The reader is cautioned that some assumptions used while preparing our forecast range, although considered reasonable at the time of preparation, may prove to be incorrect. The actual results achieved during the forecast period will inevitably vary from the forecast range and variations may be material.

KEY ASSUMPTIONS
(Dollars in thousands, except sales per retail sq. ft.)

	Actual 52 Weeks ended January 27, 2001	Forecast Range (unaudited) 52 Weeks ended January 26, 2002	
		Conservative	Optimistic
Growth in GDP	4.7%	2.0%	3.0%
Growth in total retail sales excluding auto, food and drug	5.8%	2.6%	4.5%
Total sales increase—Mark's Division corporate stores	13.3%	13.3%	16.6%
Total sales increase (decrease)— Mark's Division franchise stores	3.8%	(0.3%)	3.2%
Total sales increase—Work World Division corporate stores	23.0%	13.5%	21.4%
Total sales increase (decrease)— Work World Division franchise stores	(2.4%)	(0.4%)	1.9%
Total sales—DOCKERS® Stores Division corporate stores	$7,770	$9,685	$10,569
Number of DOCKER® Stores Division store openings***	3	—	—
Same-store sales increase—Mark's Division corporate stores	10.3%	4.6%	8.0%
Same store sales increase—Mark's Division franchise stores	12.5%	5.0%	8.7%
Same store sales increase—Work World Division corporate stores	4.7%	4.7%	11.1%
Same store sales increase—Work World Division franchise stores	7.8%	5.0%	7.5%

	Actual 52 Weeks ended January 27, 2001	Forecast Range (unaudited) 52 Weeks ended January 26, 2002	
		Conservative	Optimistic
Number of new Mark's Division corporate store openings	2	12	12
Sales from new Mark's Division corporate store openings during year	$1,330	$16,487	$16,487
Number of new Work World Division corporate store openings	4	4	4
Sales from new Work World Division corporate store openings during year	$1,487	$913	$1,774
Number of Mark's Division corporate store expansions, relocations, refurbishments and sales therefrom	8 $24,980	8 $22,732	8 $22,732
Number of Work World Division corporate store expansions, relocations, refurbishments and sales therefrom	2 $2,089	3 $2,410	3 $2,410
Number of Marks Division corporate store closings and sales therefrom	1 $60	1 $593	1 $593
Number of Work World Division corporate store closings and sales therefrom	1 $227	— —	— —
Sales per average retail sq. ft. Mark's Division corporate stores**	$259	$273	$281
Sales per average retail sq. ft. Work World Division corporate stores**	$221	$228	$244
Sales per average retail sq. ft. DOCKERS© Stores Division corporate stores**	$333	$354	$387
Number of Mark's Division franchise stores at year end	25	25	25
Number of Work World Division franchise stores at year end	90	89	89
Mark's Division gross margin rate	41.6%	41.4%	41.3%
Work World Division gross margin rate	37.9%	39.3%	39.7
Consolidated gross margin rate	41.1%	41.1%	41.1%
Consolidated capital expenditures including capital purchases made by capital lease	$11,150	$10,283	$10,283

	Actual 52 Weeks ended January 27, 2001	Forecast Range (unaudited) 52 Weeks ended January 26, 2002	
		Conservative	Optimistic
Operating line—interest rates	7.2%	7.2%	7.2%
Long-term debt financing including capital lease financing and vendor debt on purchase of franchise stores	$14,425	$9,901	$9,901
Consolidated front-line expenses as a percentage of corporate store sales	30.6%	30.7%	30.1%
Consolidated back-line expenses including goodwill amortization as a percentage of total system sales	5.8%	6.3%	6.4%
Weighted average shares outstanding	27,597	26,012	26,012

*   Source: Statistics Canada

**   Calculated on stores open and at the same size for an entire season. The Company divides the year into two seasons. Spring - February through July. Fall - August through January

***   The Company's first five DOCKERS® Stores were opened in fiscal 2000 and three more Dockers® Stores were opened in fiscal 2001.

The Company completed this forecast range on March 22, 2001. The quarterly financial reports issued by the Company to its shareholders during the forecast year will contain either a statement that there are no significant changes to be made to the forecast range or an updated earnings per Common Share forecast or forecast range accompanied by explanations of significant changes. The reader is further cautioned that the fourth quarter of the year continues to produce between 37% and 39% of the Company's total system annual sales and most of its annual profits.

CONSOLIDATED STATEMENT OF EARNINGS
(in thousands, except per Common Share)

	Actual 52 Weeks ended January 27, 2001	Forecast Range (unaudited) 52 Weeks ended January 26, 2002	
		Conservative	Optimistic
Corporate and franchise sales	$487,979	$536,856	$554,874
Franchise sales	124,109	123,668	127,349
Corporate sales	363,870	413,188	427,525
Cost of sales	214,361	243,257	251,916
Gross margin	149,509	169,931	175,609
Front-line expenses	111,248	126,881	128,795

	Actual 52 Weeks ended January 27, 2001	Forecast Range (unaudited) 52 Weeks ended January 26, 2002	
		Conservative	Optimistic
Front-line contribution	38,261	43,050	46,814
Franchise royalties and other	6,558	6,579	6,774
Net front line contribution	44,819	49,629	53,588
Back-line expenses including goodwill amortization	28,293	33,863	35,351
Earnings before income taxes	16,526	15,766	18,237
Income taxes	8,346	7,583	8,772
Net earnings	$8,180	$8,188	$9,465
Earnings per Common Share—basic	30¢	31¢	36¢
Weighted average number of Common Shares outstanding	27,597	26,012	26,012

CONSOLIDATED BALANCE SHEETS
(in thousands)

	Actual 52 Weeks ended January 27, 2001	Forecast Range (unaudited) 52 Weeks ended January 26, 2002	
		Conservative	Optimistic
Assets			
Cash and cash equivalents	$6,993	$1,482	$7,093
Merchandise inventories	84,483	94,248	92,543
Other current assets	18,911	17,244	17,680
	110,387	112,974	117,316
Other assets	1,056	909	909
Capital assets	28,148	26,590	26,590
Future income taxes	2,997	2,597	2,597
Goodwill	14,472	13,867	13,867
	$157,060	$156,937	$161,279
Liabilities			
Accounts payable, accrued liabilities and income taxes payable	$52,317	$48,510	$51,570
Current portion of long-term debt	10,905	11,996	11,996
	63,222	60,506	63,566

Long-term debt	27,016	24,852	24,852
Deferred gains	2,101	2,101	2,101
	92,339	87,459	90,519
Shareholders' equity	31,228	29,790	29,790
Capital stock	33,493	39,688	40,970
Retained earnings	64,721	69,478	70,760
	$157,060	$156,937	$161,279

CONSOLIDATED STATEMENT OF CASH FLOWS
(in thousands)

	Actual 52 Weeks ended January 27, 2001	Forecast Range (unaudited) 52 Weeks ended January 26, 2002	
		Conservative	Optimistic
Cash and cash equivalents generated (deployed)			
Operations	$18,881	$21,029	$22,312
Working capital	2,259	(11,907)	(7,579)
Investing*	(5,807)	(835)	(835)
Financing*	(10,114)	(13,798)	(13,798)
Net cash and cash equivalents generated (deployed)	$5,219	$(5,511)	$100

Post Mortem on the Prior Year's Forecast Range

CONSOLIDATED STATEMENT OF EARNINGS
(in thousands, except per Common Share)

	Actual 52 Weeks ended January 27, 2001	Forecast Range (unaudited) 52 Weeks ended January 27, 2001	
		Conservative	Optimistic
Corporate and franchise store sales	$487,979	$478.937	$492,838
Deduct: Franchise store sales—Mark's	65,754	67,016	70,37
Franchise store sales— Work World	58.355	60,260	61,349
Corporate store sales	363,870	351,661	361,116
Gross margin	149,509	144,418	148,804
Add: Franchise royalties and other	6,558	6,873	7,136

	Actual 52 Weeks ended January 27, 2001	Forecast Range (unaudited) 52 Weeks ended January 27, 2001	
		Conservative	Optimistic
Deduct Expenses including goodwill amortization	139,541	138,166	139,391
Earnings before income taxes	16,526	13,125	16,549
Income taxes	8,346	6,312	7,818
Net earnings	$8,180	$6,813	$8,731
Earnings per Common Share	30¢	25¢	31¢
Weighted average number of Common Shares outstanding	27,597	27,807	27,807

CONSOLIDATED STATEMENTS OF EARNINGS

In its January 29, 2000 annual report, the Company forecast earnings per Common Share in the range of 25 cents to 31 cents for its fiscal year ended January 27, 2001.

In its three quarterly reports issued during fiscal 2001, the Company reported that it was a little ahead or at the upper end of its forecast range and in all cases, advised shareholders that it was staying with its forecast range.

In the final analysis, during the fiscal year ended January 27, 2001, the Company delivered $488.0 million in total system sales—99% of its optimistic forecast. Due to the unplanned purchase of four Mark's Division franchise stores and the purchase of six Work World Division franchise stores, compared to a plan for the purchase of one store during fiscal year 2001, corporate store sales came in $28 million above the optimistic forecast and franchise store sales came in $3.2 million below the conservative forecast. The higher than optimistic forecast corporate store sales also caused the Company to deliver $0.7 million more in gross margin dollars than the optimistic forecast level and 12 basis points below the optimistic forecast level. Franchise royalties and other came in as a percentage of total franchise sales 14 basis points below the rate projected at the optimistic forecast level. The dollar shortfall of $0.6 million in franchise royalties and other from the optimistic forecast level was due to the unplanned conversion of franchise stores to corporate stores as noted above and also due to the fact that franchise store sales, excluding store conversions to corporate came in closer to the conservative forecast level than optimistic forecast level. The Company's total expenses came in $0.2 million higher than the optimistic forecast dollars but at 25 basis points lower (better) as a percentage of corporate store sales.

The net result of all of the above was that the Company delivered $16.5 million in pre-tax income within $23,000 of its optimistic forecast. Income taxes came in at a higher rate than planned, as the Company had not anticipated the immediate adverse impact the substantially enacted decline in future income tax rates would have on its future income tax provision. Lower than planned weighted shares outstanding also helped the earnings per share calculation by 22 basis points.

CONSOLIDATED BALANCE SHEETS

The Company's current assets at January 27, 2001 at $110.4 million essentially came in as expected, ending the 2001 fiscal year within the forecast range. Year-end capital assets came in $4.8 million above the forecast, as the Company spent $1.4 million more than forecast on store capital expenditures, $0.7 million more on system capital expenditures (over half of this overage was on Web system capital expenditures), added $0.6 million of capital assets from unplanned purchases of franchise stores and depreciation was $2.1 million below forecast, due to the timing of capital expenditures and capital lease financing during fiscal 2001.

Goodwill came in $3.7 million higher than planned as a result of the $3.9 million of acquisition goodwill less amortization thereon on the unplanned purchases of franchise stores as summarized in Notes 3 and 8 to the Consolidated Financial Statements

Total liabilities came in $9.9 million higher than the conservative forecast, primarily as a result of the $5.8 million of long-term debt related to the unplanned purchase of the franchise stores and the funding of $2.7 million more in capital lease financing than forecast.

Year-end shareholders' equity came in $3.4 million below the optimistic forecast as $2.9 million more was spent on shares purchased for cancellation under the Company's Normal Course Issuer Bid than had been planned and net earnings came in $0.5 million below forecast, due to a higher than planned tax provision as noted above.

CONSOLIDATED BALANCE SHEETS
(in thousands)

	Actual 52 Weeks ended January 27, 2001	Forecast Range (unaudited) 52 Weeks ended January 27, 2001	
		Conservative	Optimistic
Assets			
Current assets	$110,387	$109,908	$111,176
Other assets	1,056	1,420	1,420
Capital assets	28,148	23,308	23,308
Future income taxes	2,997	3,301	3,301
Goodwill	14,472	10,729	10,729
	$157,060	$148,666	$149,934
Liabilities			
Current liabilities	$63,222	$61,327	$60,677
Long-term debt	27,016	18,935	18,935
Deferred gains	2,101	2,161	2161
	92,339	82,423	81,773
Shareholders' equity			
Capital stock	31,228	32,677	32,677
Retained earnings	33,493	33,566	35,484
	64,721	66,243	68,161
	$157,060	$148,666	$149,934

SOURCE: From *Mark's Work Wearhouse Ltd. 2001 Annual Report.* Reprinted with permission.

The following points should be noted about the Mark's Work Wearhouse forecast. First, the period covered is one year, and no discounting is applied. Also, the forecast information is presented in the same format as the summarized actual 2001 historical cost-based results. Mark's Work Wearhouse has opted for a range forecast, also allowed by Section 4250. Second, notice that key assumptions are given, again in comparison with realized values for the current year. Third, a candid post mortem on the 2001 earnings forecast is provided. Mark's Work Wearhouse's forecast represents an interesting example of what can be done to convey relevant information to financial statement users beyond the minimum requirements of GAAP and MD&A.

Summary

Mark's Work Wearhouse goes well beyond minimal disclosure requirements. It is interesting to contemplate why the firm does this. One reason may be a relatively less litigious environment than other jurisdictions, such as the United States. The company may feel that it is unlikely to be sued by disappointed investors if its financial forecast and other forward-looking information are not satisfied.

However, a more fundamental reason may be that, by communicating inside forward-looking information, Mark's Work Wearhouse wants to increase investor, and even customer, confidence, thereby affecting its cost of capital. Note that it is the *fact* of the extensive disclosure, in addition to its information content, that adds confidence. Another reason may be that Mark's Work Wearhouse, being a relatively small public corporation, may feel a greater need to reveal information about itself than very large corporations, about which more is known from media and other sources.

4.9   Summary and Conclusions

Efficient securities market theory has major implications for financial accounting. One of these is that supplementary information in financial statement notes or elsewhere is just as useful as information in the financial statements proper. Another is that efficiency is defined relative to a stock of publicly known information. Financial reporting has a role to play in improving the amount, timing, and accuracy of this stock.

Examples of full disclosure standards include MD&A and financial forecasts. Both of these standards have the potential to convey information beyond that contained in the conventional historical cost-based financial statements. This potential is not only in the information contained in the disclosure per se. The very act of disclosing or not disclosing a forecast, or the extent to which the firm goes beyond minimal MD&A requirements, also tells the market something about the firm.

Full disclosure has two main benefits, which can be attained simultaneously. One is to enable investors to make better decisions. The other is to improve the ability of securities markets to direct investment to its most productive uses. The reason why these benefits are attained simultaneously, of course, is that better information enables more-informed buy/sell decisions, and it is demand and supply resulting from individual buy and sell decisions that determines market price.

Another implication of efficient securities market theory appears in Beaver's 1973 analysis. This is that the specific accounting policies adopted by firms do not matter as long as they have no differential cash flow effects across those policies, full disclosure is made of the particular policies used, and investors have sufficient information to convert from one policy to another. The reason, according to efficient markets theory, is that investors as a whole will *look through* reported net income to its underlying implications for future cash flows. In so doing, they will take into account the specific accounting policies used in calculating net income. Thus, firms' choices of amortization policy, of successful-efforts or full-cost accounting for oil and gas exploration, of accounting for future tax liabilities, and so on, will not affect the efficient market prices of their securities, providing the specific accounting policies they are using are fully disclosed. Thus, we see that the full-disclosure principle extends to disclosure of accounting policies.

Accountants are improving their understanding of the role of information in determining price. In essence, market price aggregates the collective information processing and decision-making abilities of investors. Thus, market price itself has considerable information content, which individuals may use as input into their decisions. A "buy and hold" investment strategy is an example of a decision that relies on the information content of market price.

This aggregation of information into market price contains a logical contradiction, however. If price is fully informative, no one would bother to collect additional, costly, information. In effect, market price contains within it the seeds of its own destruction. However, we can identify two factors to prevent this from happening:

- Noise and liquidity traders introduce a random component to market price, which prevents market price from being fully informative about future value.

- Information asymmetry, in particular the presence of inside information, means that not all relevant information is in the public domain. Then, investors have the potential to earn extra profits if they can ferret out some of this inside information. Improved disclosure, as in MD&A and forecasting, may provide investors with some help in this regard.

As Beaver (1973) put it, accountants are in competition with other information sources. We now know that market price is one of these other sources. Think of market price as aggregating all relevant "other" information up to the time of release of the financial statements. The question then is: Is it cost-effective for rational investors to inform themselves by utilizing the financial statements?

Again, the accountants' answer is the concept of full disclosure. By increasing the information content of financial reporting, including supplementary information in notes, MD&A and FOFI, not only do accountants help preserve their competitive advantage, they also improve social welfare by reducing the adverse impact of inside information.

If investors do in fact find accounting information useful, this should show up as a response of security prices to this information. In the next chapter, we will examine empirical evidence in this regard.

Questions and Problems

1.   Two firms, of the same size and risk, release their annual reports on the same day. It turns out that they each report the same amount of net income. Following the release, the share price of one firm rose strongly while the other rose hardly at all.

     Explain how it is possible for the market to react positively to one firm's annual report and hardly at all to the other when the firms are similar in size, risk, and reported profitability.

2.   Shares of firm A and firm B are traded on an efficient market. The two firms are of the same size and risk. They both report the same net income. However, you see in the footnotes that firm A uses the LIFO inventory method and declining-balance amortization for capital assets, while firm B uses the FIFO inventory method and straight-line amortization.   (CGA-Canada)

     Which firm's shares should sell at the higher price-to-earnings ratio, all other things being equal? Explain. Assume a period of rising prices.

3.   Using the concept of information asymmetry, answer the following questions:

     a. You observe that used cars sold by new car dealers sell for a higher price, for models of same make, year, and condition, than used cars sold by used car dealers. Why?

     b. Why would a fire insurance policy contain a $150 deductible provision?

     c. Why would a life insurance company require a medical examination before approving applications for new policies?

     d. A firm plans to raise additional capital by means of a new issue of common shares. Before doing so, it hires a well-known investment house to help design and market the issue, and also switches auditors from a small, local firm to a "Big Five" firm. Why?   (CGA-Canada)

4.   To what extent might the financial press provide a relevant source of information for investors? Would this information source conflict with or complement financial statement information? Explain.   (CGA-Canada)

5. On January 21, 1993 *The Wall Street Journal* reported that General Electric Co.'s fourth-quarter 1992 earnings rose 6.2% to $1.34 billion or $1.57 a share, setting a new record and bringing the earnings for 1992 to $4.73 billion or $5.51 a share. After adjusting for extraordinary items, 1992 earnings from continuing operations were up about 10% from the previous year.

   The *Journal* also reported that forecasts made by analysts averaged $1.61 per share for the fourth quarter of 1992, and from $5.50 to $5.60 per share for the whole year. One analyst was quoted as saying that 1992 "wasn't a bad year for GE" despite the downturn in the stock market on the day of the earnings announcement.

   Yet, on the same day the fourth-quarter earnings were announced, General Electric Co.'s stock price fell $1.50 to $82.625 on the New York Stock Exchange.

   Required

   a. Give three reasons to explain why this could happen.

   b. Use the Sharpe-Lintner CAPM (Equations 4.1 and 4.2) to explain how the new information caused the current price slip. Calculations are not required.

6. Atlas Ltd. is a listed public company. It is in a volatile industry. The market price of its shares is highly sensitive to its earnings. The company's annual meeting is to be held soon, and the president is concerned, expecting to be attacked strongly by a dissident group of shareholders.

   One issue the dissidents are expected to focus on is the company's amortization policy. They will claim that the annual declining-balance amortization charges are excessive—that the company's "conservative" amortization policy seriously understates annual earnings per share, causing the shares' market price to be artificially low. Threats have even been made of suing management and the board of directors to "recover the resulting loss in market value, relative to shareholders in companies with less conservative amortization policies, suffered by Atlas shareholders."

   The president has asked you to help prepare a defence against the expected attack on the company's amortization policy.

   Required

   Write a memo summarizing how you would recommend the president respond to this attack. (CGA-Canada)

7. The article "GM to Take Charge of $20.8-Billion" here reproduced from *The Globe and Mail* (February 2, 1993) describes the potential impact of SFAS 106, "Accounting for Postretirement Benefits Other Than Pensions," on General Motors and Ford. For example, it appears that General Motors will be required to record a liability of $20.8 billion, reducing its shareholders' equity from $27.8 billion to $7 billion, about a 75% reduction.

GM TO TAKE CHARGE
OF $20.8-BILLION

ATLANTA—General Motors Corp. will take a $20.8-billion (U.S.) charge against 1992 earnings to account for a new way of estimating retiree health care costs, the auto maker's directors decided yesterday.

The charge, which will not affect the struggling auto maker's cash flow, will leave GM with the largest annual loss of any U.S. corporation, eclipsing the company's 1991 loss of $4.45-billion, which was a record at that time.

Including accounting changes, other charges and losses on its North American operations, GM's 1992 loss could approach $23-billion.

The $20.8-billion is a non-cash charge. It reduces GM's net worth to about $7-billion, still sufficient to pay stock dividends under the laws of Delaware, where GM is incorporated.

Separately, GM said it would take a $744-million fourth-quarter restructuring charge for its National Car Rental Systems business. In a recent U.S. Securities and Exchange Commission filing, GM estimated that charge at about $300-million.

The accounting change, required by the Financial Accounting Standards Board of all publicly traded U.S. companies, has had a major effect on each of the Big Three U.S. auto makers.

Ford Motor Co. said it would take a $7.5-billion charge against 1992 earnings to account for the change. Chrysler Corp. said it has not decided whether to take its $4.7-billion charge as a lump sum in the first quarter or spread it over 20 years, as the standard allows.

GM had estimated its charge for adopting the new accounting standard at $16-billion to $24-billion. The $20.8-billion actual charge includes its workers, GM Hughes Electronics Corp. and its financial subsidiary, General Motors Acceptance Corp.

The company's EDS Corp. subsidiary does not pay health benefits, so it was exempt.

SOURCE: *The Globe and Mail*, February 2, 1993. Reprinted by permission of The Associated Press.

Required

Describe and explain how you would expect the efficient securities market to react to this information.

8.   In 1994, the AICPA established a Special Committee on Financial Reporting. This committee, made up of several leaders in public accounting, industry, and academia, was charged with reviewing the current financial reporting model and making recommendations on what information management should make available to investors and creditors.

In 1994, the committee made several recommendations in a report entitled "Report of the Special Committee on Financial Reporting" that it argued should help investors and other users to improve their assessment of a firm's prospects, thereby improving the usefulness of annual reports. Here is one of its recommendations:

> *Many companies are faced with litigations from investors who feel that they did not live up to their forecasted forward-looking information. "Because of this, managements see disclosure of forward-looking information, even though helpful to users, as providing ammunition for future groundless lawsuits." This means that a lot of managers are reluctant to disclose forward-looking information. In the light of this situation, the Committee recommended that there be "safe harbors" in order to eliminate "unwarranted litigation" when disclosing forward-looking information. The Committee further suggested that standard setters include rules that are "specific enough to enable companies to demonstrate compliance with requirements."*

SOURCE: Excerpt reprinted with permission from report of the AICPA Special Committee on Financial Reporting. © 1994 by American Institute of Certified Public Accountants, Inc.

Required

a. Would relieving firms from legal liability for failing to meet forecasts tend to reduce the credibility and accuracy of forecasted information? Explain. In your answer, consider requirements that would help to control any such tendencies, including the publishing of a post mortem as is done by Mark's Work Wearhouse (Section 4.8.3).

b. What benefits for the proper operation of capital markets would result from increased reporting of credible, accurate forecasts?

9. A major reason for the rarity of forecasts (i.e., FOFI) in annual reports is the possibility of lawsuits if the forecast is not met, particularly in the United States. On November 17, 1995, *The Wall Street Journal* reported that the SEC was supporting a bill before the U.S. Senate to provide protection from legal liability resulting from forecasts, providing that "meaningful cautionary statements" accompanied the forecast.

Required

a. To the extent that firms are discouraged from providing financial forecasts by the prospect of litigation, how could this lead to a negative impact on the proper operation of securities markets? Can you give an argument that a litigious environment might actually help the proper operation of securities markets?

   b. Explain how the passage of a bill such as that mentioned above might benefit investors.

   c. Explain how passage might benefit firms.

10. An article entitled "The Pros Get Trounced in Stock Contest" appeared in *The Wall Street Journal* on March 4, 1993. It describes the outcome of a contest, sponsored by the *Journal*, between four investment analysts and a group using a dart-throwing investment strategy.

   The "Investment Dartboard Stock-Picking" series of contests began in 1988. Each contest runs for a six-month period. The article states that the contest is between four professional investors who choose a portfolio according to their expertise, and reporters who throw darts randomly at the stock listings to choose a "Dartboard Portfolio."

   According to the article, "for the six-month period ended Feb. 28," the team of four experts did their worst picking since the games began in 1988. "The pros trailed the darts by an astonishing margin of 42.3 percentage points." There was a 2.5% rise in the Dow Jones Industrial Average, while the average loss for the pros was 26.7% and the dart-throwers had a gain of 15.6%. However, the cumulative score over all contests now has the analysts leading 18 to 15.

Required

   a. Use efficient securities market theory to explain how "dart-throwing" may be a desirable investment strategy.

   b. To what extent does the cumulative score of 18 to 15 provide evidence in favour of securities market efficiency? Explain.

   c. It appears that the contests do not control for possible risk differences between the analysts' and the dart-throwing portfolios. How would you determine whether risk differences were affecting the results? Suppose that on average the analysts chose riskier strategies than the dart-throwers. Would this affect your answer in part **b**? Explain.

11. For companies with no history of positive earnings, such as startup companies, growth of revenues provides an alternative performance measure and indicator of possible future earning power. This is particularly the case if the new company incurs high R&D costs, advertising, and other startup expenditures which delay the advent of reported earnings. Without reported earnings, such companies may inflate reported revenues to impress investors. In an article in *The Globe and Mail*, December 30, 2000, Janet McFarland discusses some of these practices. They include:

    • Recognizing full revenue even though products or systems can be returned, or when there are future obligations such as servicing the products and systems sold.

- Recording revenue on long-term contracts in advance of billings to the customer (billings may be delayed as a form of vendor financing to the customer, a practice frequently used to attract business from cash-short firms)
- Recording revenue from gross sales when the company is an agent rather than a principal

Examples of such practices include Imax Corp., which reported the (discounted) full amounts of minimum royalties due under 10-year or more leases of its theatre systems (in accordance with GAAP for long-term leases), leaving itself open to the possibility that customers may default on payments due in future. JetForm Corp. recognized revenue from consulting contracts on the percentage-of-completion method, although amounts billed to customers were less. Bid.Com, a firm that conducted on-line auctions as agent for the seller, included the purchase price, rather than its commission on the purchase, as revenue.

One of the problems surrounding reporting of revenue is that while a firm's revenue recognition policy must be disclosed, the disclosure standards in Canada are vague. Thus companies typically state that revenue is recognized as goods are shipped or services rendered, or that revenues on long-term contracts are recognized on a percentage-of-completion basis. These statements are sufficiently general that practices such as the above may be unknown to the market.

Required

a. To what extent can revenue growth substitute for net income as a predictor of future earning power? Explain. Use efficient securities market concepts in your answer, and consider the requirement under GAAP for immediate writeoff of R&D and startup costs.

b. Use the concept of relevance to defend the revenue recognition policies outlined above.

c. Use the concept of reliability to criticize the revenue recognition policies outlined above.

d. To the extent that investors are aware of the possible use of revenue recognition policies that overstate revenues (even though, for a specific firm, they may not know the extent to which that firm is using such policies), what is the effect on the proper operation of the capital market? Explain.

Notes

1. More generally, the random fluctuation could be about a trend line. For example, the price of a security may have an upward trend over time.

2. In Section 3.3.2, we applied the term "informative" to the information system. An informative information system leads the decision-maker to revise his/her prior probabilities. In that context, a *fully* informative information system perfectly reveals the state of nature (see Question 1 of Chapter 3). In the context of this chapter, "fully informative" applies to share price rather than to an information system, but the reasoning is similar—if markets are fully efficient, current share price is fully informative about all publicly available information. Note that if share price is fully informative, the information system formed by financial statements is non-informative—it reveals nothing new about the firm since share price already reveals all. Hence the logical inconsistency—if share prices are fully informative, noone would use financial statements. But, if noone used financial statements, share prices would no longer be fully informative.

3. This abnormal return should not be confused with abnormal earnings of P.V. Ltd. in Example 2.2. While the idea is the same, abnormal security return here refers to a *market* return, whereas abnormal earnings refer to *accounting* net income.

4. Estimating beta by least-squares regression is not inconsistent with the calculation of beta described in Section 3.7.1. The regression approach merely provides a convenient framework to carry out the estimation. To see this, note the definition of the coefficient of an independent variable in a regression model—it is the amount of change in the dependent variable (R_{jt}) for a unit change in the independent variable (R_{Mt}). This is exactly the definition of beta. As explained in Section 3.7.1, beta measures the strength of the variation in a security's return as the market return varies.

5. This argument assumes that the disclosure is truthful. Truthful disclosure can be encouraged by, for example, an audit.

5

The Information Perspective on Decision Usefulness

5.1 Overview

There is a saying that "the proof of the pudding is in the eating." If the efficient markets theory and the decision theories underlying it are reasonable descriptions of reality on average, we should observe the market values of securities responding in predictable ways to new information.

This leads to an examination of empirical research in accounting. Despite the difficulties of designing experiments to test the implications of decision usefulness, accounting research has established that security market prices do respond to accounting information. The first solid evidence of this, security market reaction to earnings announcements, was provided by Ball and Brown in 1968. Since then, a large number of empirical studies have documented additional aspects of securities market response.

On the basis of these studies, it does seem that accounting information is useful to investors in helping them estimate the expected values and risks of security returns. One has only to contemplate the use of Bayes' theorem in Example 3.1 to see that if accounting information did not have information content there would be no revision of beliefs upon receipt, hence no triggering of buy/sell decisions. Without buy/sell decisions, there would be no trading volume or price changes. In essence, information is useful if it leads investors to change their beliefs and actions. Furthermore, the degree of usefulness can be measured by the extent of volume or price change following release of the information.

This equating of usefulness to information content is called the **information perspective** on decision usefulness of financial reporting, an approach that has dominated financial accounting theory and research since 1968, and has only recently begun to yield to a measurement perspective, to be discussed in Chapters

6 and 7. As we have seen in Sections 3.8 and 4.8, the information perspective has also been adopted by major accounting standard setting bodies. This perspective takes the view that investors want to make *their own* predictions of future security returns (instead of having accountants do it for them, as under ideal conditions) and will "gobble up" all useful information in this regard. As mentioned, empirical research has shown that at least some accounting information is perceived as useful. Furthermore, the information approach implies that empirical research can help accountants to further increase usefulness by letting market response guide them as to what information is and is not valued by investors.

> The **information perspective** on decision usefulness is an approach to financial reporting that recognizes individual responsibility for predicting future firm performance and that concentrates on providing useful information for this purpose. The approach assumes securities market efficiency, recognizing that the market will react to useful information from any source, including financial statements.

One must be careful, however, when equating usefulness with the extent of security price change. While accountants may be better off if they base their decisions of what financial statement information to present on the basis of market response to that information, it does *not* follow that *society* will necessarily be better off. Information is a very complex commodity and its private and social values are not the same. One reason is *cost*. Financial statement users do not generally pay directly for this information. As a result, they may find information useful even though it costs society more (in the form of higher product prices to help firms pay for generating and reporting the information) than the increased usefulness is worth. Furthermore, information affects people differently, requiring complex cost-benefit tradeoffs to balance the competing interests of different constituencies.

These social considerations do not invalidate the information perspective. Accountants can still strive to improve their competitive position in the information marketplace by providing useful information. And, it is still true that securities markets will work better to the extent that security prices provide good indicators of investment opportunities. However, what accountants cannot do is claim that the "best" accounting policy is the one that produces the greatest market response.

5.2   *Outline of the Research Problem*

5.2.1   *REASONS FOR MARKET RESPONSE*

We begin by reviewing the reasons why we would predict that the market price of a firm's shares will respond to its financial statement information. For most of this chapter we will confine financial statement information to reported net income. The information content of net income is a topic that has received extensive empirical investigation. Information content of other financial statement components will be discussed in Section 5.7 and in Chapter 7.

Consider the following predictions about investor behaviour, in response to financial statement information:

1. Investors have prior beliefs about the expected return and risk of a firm's shares. These prior beliefs will be based on all available information, including market price, up to just prior to the release of the firm's current net income. Even if they are based on publicly available information, these prior beliefs need not all be the same, because investors will differ in the amount of information they obtain and in their abilities to interpret it. These prior beliefs may also include expectations about the firm's current and future earning power, since future security returns will depend at least in part on profitability.

2. Upon release of current year's net income, certain investors will decide to become more informed, by analyzing the income number. For example, if net income is high, or higher than expected, this may be good news. If so, investors, by means of Bayes' theorem, would revise upward their beliefs about future earning power and returns. Other investors, who perhaps had overly high expectations for what current net income should be, might interpret the same net income number as bad news.

3. Investors who have revised their beliefs about future profitability and returns upward will be inclined to buy the firm's shares at their current market price, and vice versa for those who have revised their beliefs downward. Investors' evaluations of the riskiness of these shares may also be revised.

4. We would expect to observe the volume of shares traded to increase when the firm reports its net income. Furthermore, this volume should be greater the greater are the differences in investors' prior beliefs and in their interpretations of the current financial information. If the investors who interpret reported net income as good news (and hence have increased their expectations of future profitability and returns) outweigh those who interpret it as bad news, we would expect to observe an increase in the market price of the firm's shares, and vice versa.

Beaver (1968), in a classic study, examined trading volume reaction. He found a dramatic increase in volume during the week of release of earnings announcements. Further details of Beaver's findings are included in Question 8 at the end of this chapter. In the balance of this chapter we will concentrate on market price reaction. Market price reaction may provide a stronger test of decision usefulness than volume reaction. For example, the model of Kim and Verrecchia (1997) suggests that volume is noisier than price change as a measure of decision usefulness of financial statement information.

You will recognize that the preceding predictions follow the decision theory and efficient markets theory of Chapters 3 and 4 quite closely. If these theories are to have relevance to accountants, their predictions should be borne out empirically. An empirical researcher could test these predictions by obtaining a sample of firms that issue annual reports and investigating whether the volume and price reactions to good or bad news in earnings occur as the theories lead us to believe. This is not as easy as it might seem, however, for a number of reasons, as we will discuss next.

5.2.2   FINDING THE MARKET RESPONSE

1. Efficient markets theory implies that the market will react quickly to new information. As a result, it is important to know *when* current year's reported net income first became publicly known. If the researcher looked for volume and price effects even a few days too late, no effects may be observed even though they had existed.

    Researchers have solved this problem by using the date the firm's net income was reported in the financial media such as *The Wall Street Journal*. If the efficient market is going to react, it should do so in a **narrow window** of a few days surrounding this date.

2. The good or bad news in reported net income is usually evaluated relative to what investors *expected*. If a firm reported net income of, say, $2 million, and this was what investors had expected (from quarterly reports, speeches by company officials, analysts' predictions, forward-looking information in MD&A and forecasts and, indeed, in share price itself), there would hardly be much information content in reported net income. Investors would have already revised their beliefs on the basis of the earlier information. Things would be different, however, if investors had expected $2 million and reported net income was $3 million. This good news would trigger rapid belief revision about the future prospects of the firm. This means that researchers must obtain a proxy for what investors expected net income to be.

3. There are always many events taking place that affect a firm's share volume and price. This means that a market response to reported net income can be hard to find. For example, suppose a firm released its current year's net income, containing good news, on the same day the federal government first announced a substantial decrease in the deficit. Such a public announcement would probably affect prices of all or most securities on the market, which in turn might swamp the price impact of the firm's earnings release. Thus, it is desirable to separate the impact of market-wide factors on share returns.

5.2.3   *SEPARATING MARKET-WIDE AND FIRM-SPECIFIC FACTORS*

As described in Section 4.5, the market model is widely used to *ex post* separate market-wide and firm-specific factors that affect security returns. Figure 5.1 gives a graphical illustration of the market model for firm j for period t, where we take the length of the period as one day. Longer time periods, such as a week, month, or year, and even shorter periods, are also used by researchers.

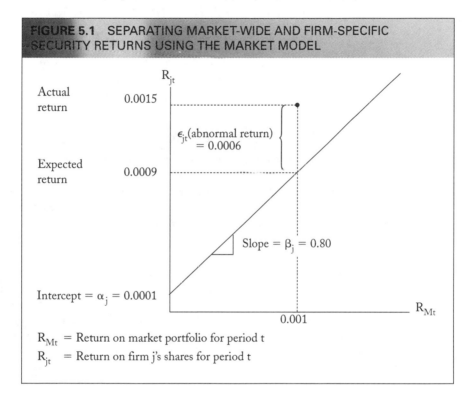

FIGURE 5.1   SEPARATING MARKET-WIDE AND FIRM-SPECIFIC SECURITY RETURNS USING THE MARKET MODEL

R_{Mt} = Return on market portfolio for period t
R_{jt} = Return on firm j's shares for period t

The figure shows the relationship between the return on firm j's shares and the return on the market portfolio (proxied, for example, by the Dow Jones Index).

Consider the equation of the market model, repeated here from Section 4.5:

$$R_{jt} = \alpha_j + \beta_j R_{Mt} + \epsilon_{jt}$$

As described in Section 4.5, the researcher will obtain past data on R_{jt} and R_{Mt} and use regression analysis to estimate the coefficients of the model. Suppose that this yields $\alpha_j = 0.0001$ and $\beta_j = 0.80$, as shown in the figure.[1]

Now, armed with this estimate of the market model for firm j, the researcher can consult *The Wall Street Journal* to find the day of the firm's current earnings announcement. Call this day "day 0." Suppose that for day 0 the return on the Dow Jones Index was 0.001.[2] Then, the estimated market model for firm j is used to predict the return on firm j's shares for this day. As shown in Figure 5.1, this expected return[3] is 0.0009. Now assume that the *actual* return on firm j's shares for day 0 is 0.0015. Then, the difference between actual and expected returns is 0.0006 (that is, $\epsilon_{jt} = 0.0006$ for this day). This 0.0006 is an estimate of the abnormal return on firm j's shares for that day.[4] This abnormal return is also interpreted as the rate of return on firm j's shares for day 0 *after removing* the influence of market-wide factors. Note that this interpretation is consistent with Example 3.3, where we separated the factors that affect share returns into market-wide and firm-specific categories. The present procedure provides an operational way to make this separation.

5.2.4   COMPARING RETURNS AND INCOME

The empirical researcher can now compare the abnormal share return on day 0 as calculated above with the unexpected component of the firm's current reported net income. If this unexpected net income is "good news" (that is, a positive unexpected net income) then, given securities market efficiency, a positive abnormal share return constitutes evidence that investors on average are reacting favourably to the unexpected good news in earnings. A similar line of reasoning applies if the current earnings announcement is bad news.

To increase the power of the investigation, the researcher may wish to similarly compare a few days on either side of day 0. It is possible, for example, that the efficient market might learn of the good or bad earnings news a day or two early. Conversely, positive or negative abnormal returns may continue for a day or two after day 0 while the market digests the information, although market efficiency implies that any excess returns should die out quickly. Consequently, the summing of abnormal returns for a three-to-five-day narrow window around day 0 seems more reasonable than examining day 0 only. It also helps protect against the possibility that the date of publication of current earnings in the financial media may not be a completely accurate estimate of the date of their public availability.

If positive and negative abnormal returns surrounding good or bad earnings news are found to hold across a sample of firms, the researcher may conclude that predictions based on the decision theory and efficient securities market theory are supported. This would in turn support the decision usefulness approach to financial accounting and reporting, because, if investors did not find the reported net income information useful, a market response would hardly be observed.

Of course, this methodology is not foolproof—a number of assumptions and estimations have to be made along the way. One complication is that other firm-specific information frequently comes along around the time of a firm's earnings announcement. For example, if firm j announced a stock split or a change in its dividend on the same day that it released its current earnings, it would be hard to know if a market response was due to one or the other. However, researchers can cope with this by simply removing such firms from the sample.

Another complication is the estimation of a firm's beta, needed to separate market-wide and firm-specific returns as in Figure 5.1. As mentioned, this estimation is usually based on a regression analysis of past data using the market model. Then, the estimated beta is the slope of the regression line. However, as we will discuss in Section 6.2.3, a firm's beta may change over time, for example as it changes its operations and/or its capital structure. If the estimated beta is different from the true beta, this affects the calculation of abnormal return, possibly biasing the results of the investigation.

There is a variety of ways to cope with this complication. For example, it may be possible to get a "second opinion" on beta by estimating it from financial statement information rather than from market data. (This is considered in Section 7.6.1.) Alternatively, beta may be estimated from a period after the earnings announcement and compared with the estimate from a period before the announcement.

Also there are ways to separate market-wide and firm-specific returns that ignore beta. For example, we can estimate firm-specific returns by the difference between firm j's stock return during period 0 and the average return on its shares over some prior period. Or, we can take the difference between firm j's return during period 0 and the return on the market portfolio for the same period. Alternatively, as in Easton and Harris (1991), we can simply work with total share returns and not factor out market-wide returns at all.

The rationale for these simpler procedures is that there is no guarantee that the market model adequately captures the real process generating share returns— the impact of securities market inefficiencies on share returns is discussed in Chapter 6. To the extent it does not, use of the market model may introduce more error in estimating beta and abnormal returns than it reduces by removing market-wide returns and controlling for risk. A further complication is that there is a variety of market portfolio return indices available, of which the Dow Jones Index is only one. Which one should be used?

These issues were examined by Brown and Warner (1980) in a simulation study. Despite modelling and measurement problems such as those mentioned above, Brown and Warner concluded that, for monthly return windows, the market model-based procedure outlined in Section 5.2.3 performed reasonably well relative to alternatives such as those mentioned above. Consequently, this is the procedure we will concentrate on.

Using this procedure, it does appear that the market reacts to earnings information much as the theories predict. We will now review the first solid evidence of this reaction, the famous 1968 Ball and Brown study.

5.3   *The Ball and Brown Study*

5.3.1   *METHODOLOGY AND FINDINGS*

In 1968, Ball and Brown (BB) began a tradition of empirical capital markets research in accounting that continues to this day. They were the first to provide convincing scientific evidence that firms' share returns respond to the information content of financial statements. This type of research is called an **event study**, since it studies the securities market reaction to a specific event, in this case a firm's release of its current net income. A review of the BB paper is worthwhile because its basic methodology, and adaptations and extensions of it, continues to be used. Their paper continues to provide guidance, as well as encouragement, to those who wish to better understand the decision usefulness of financial reporting.

BB examined a sample of 261 New York Stock Exchange (NYSE) firms over nine years from 1957 to 1965. They concentrated on the information content of earnings, to the exclusion of other potentially informative financial statement components such as liquidity and capital structure. One reason for this, as mentioned earlier, was that earnings for NYSE firms were typically announced in the media prior to actual release of the annual report so that it was relatively easy to determine when the information first became publicly available.

BB's first task was to measure the information content of earnings, that is, whether reported earnings were greater than what the market had expected (GN), or less than expected (BN). Of course, this requires a proxy for the market's expectation. One proxy they used was last year's actual earnings, from which it follows that unexpected earnings is simply the change in earnings.[5] Thus, firms with earnings higher than last year's were classified as GN, and vice versa.

The next task was to evaluate the market return on the shares of the sample firms near the time of each earnings announcement. This was done according to the abnormal returns procedure illustrated in Figure 5.1. The only difference was that BB used monthly returns (daily returns were not available on data bases in 1968).

Analogously to Figure 5.1, suppose that firm j reported its 1957 earnings in February 1958, and that these earnings were GN. Suppose also that the return on the NYSE market portfolio in February 1958 was 0.001, yielding an expected firm j return of 0.0009. BB would then calculate the actual return on firm j shares for February 1958. Suppose this was 0.0015, yielding an abnormal return for February of 0.0006. Since firm j's 1957 earnings were reported in February 1958 and since its shares earned 0.0006 over and above the market in this month, one might suspect that the reason for the positive abnormal return was that investors were reacting favourably to the GN information in earnings.

The question then was: Was this pattern repeated across the sample? The answer was yes. If we take all the GN earnings announcements in the sample (there were 1,231), the *average* abnormal security market return in the month of earnings release was strongly positive. Conversely, the average abnormal return for the 1,109 bad news earnings announcements in the sample was strongly negative. This provides substantial evidence that the market did respond to the good or bad news in earnings during a narrow window consisting of the month of earnings announcement release.

An interesting and important aspect of the BB study was that they repeated their abnormal security market returns calculation for a **wide window** consisting of each of the 11 months prior to and the 6 months following the month of earnings release (month 0). BB calculated average abnormal returns for each month of this 18-monthwide window. The results are shown in Figure 5.2, taken from BB.

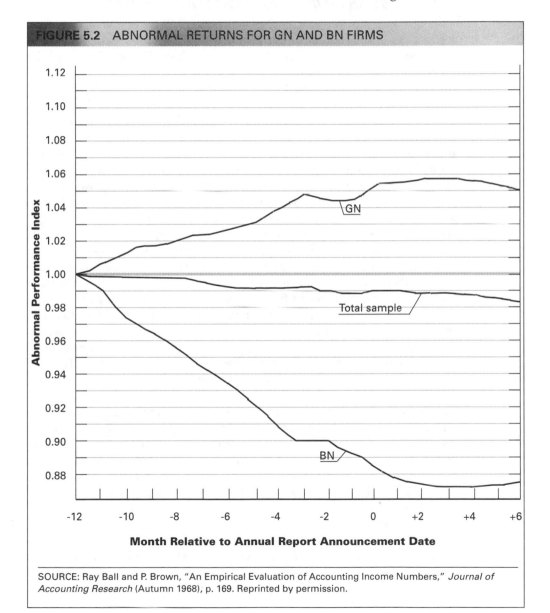

FIGURE 5.2   ABNORMAL RETURNS FOR GN AND BN FIRMS

SOURCE: Ray Ball and P. Brown, "An Empirical Evaluation of Accounting Income Numbers," *Journal of Accounting Research* (Autumn 1968), p. 169. Reprinted by permission.

The upper part of Figure 5.2 shows cumulative average abnormal returns for the GN earnings announcement firms in the sample; the bottom part shows the same for the BN announcement firms. As can be seen, the GN firms strongly outperformed the market, and the BN firms strongly underperformed, over the 11 month period leading up to the month of earnings release.

5.3.2   CAUSATION VERSUS ASSOCIATION

Note that the returns are *cumulative* in the diagram. While there was a substantial increase (for GN) and decrease (for BN) in average abnormal returns in the narrow window consisting of month 0, as described above, Figure 5.2 suggests that the market began to *anticipate* the GN or BN as much as a year early, with the result that returns accumulated steadily over the period. As can be seen, if an investor could have bought the shares of all GN firms one year before the good news was released and held them until the end of the month of release, there would have been an extra return of about 6% over and above the market-wide return. Similarly, an abnormal loss of over 9% would have been incurred on a portfolio of BN firms bought one year before the bad news was released.[6]

This leads to an important distinction between narrow and wide window studies. If a security market reaction to accounting information is observed during a narrow window of a few days (or, in the case of BB, a month) surrounding an earnings announcement, it can be argued that the accounting information is the *cause* of the market reaction. The reason is that during a narrow window there are relatively few other firm-specific events than net income to affect share returns. Also, if other events do occur, such as stock splits or dividend announcements, the affected firms can be removed from the sample, as mentioned. Thus, a narrow-window association between security returns and accounting information suggests that accounting disclosures are the *source* of new information to investors.

Evaluation of security returns over a wide window, however, opens them up to a host of other value-relevant events. For example, a firm may have discovered new oil and gas reserves, be engaged in promising R&D projects, and have rising sales and market share. As the market learns this information from more timely sources, such as media articles, firm announcements, conditions in the economy and industry, quarterly reports, etc, share price would begin to rise. This reflects the partly informative nature of security prices since, in an efficient market, security prices reflect all available information, not just accounting information. Thus, firms that in a real sense are doing well would have much of the effect on their share prices anticipated by the efficient market before the GN appears in the financial statements. That is, *prices lead earnings* over a wide window.

Clearly, this effect was taking place in the BB study. As a result, it cannot be claimed that reported net income *causes* the abnormal returns during the 11 months leading up to month 0. The most that can be argued is that net income and returns are *associated*. That is, for wide windows, it is the real, underlying, economic performance of the firm that generates the association, since both share price and (with a lag) net income reflect real performance.

To pursue this prices lead earnings effect, suppose that we continue to widen the window, perhaps up to several years. We will find that the association between share returns and earnings increases as the window widens. While historical cost-based net income tends to lag behind the market in reflecting value-relevant events, as the window is widened the relative effect of the lag decreases. Over a long period of time the sum of net incomes reported over that period captures more of the effects of economic factors such as those described above, even though there may be a lag in their initial recognition. This effect was studied by Easton, Harris, and Ohlson (1992), who found that the association between security returns and historical cost-based earnings improved as the window was widened, up to 10 years. A similar effect was observed by Warfield and Wild (1992), who found that the association between security returns and earnings for annual reporting periods averaged over 10 times the association for quarterly periods.

In the long run, the total income earned by the firm, regardless of the basis of accounting, will approach total income under ideal conditions (on this point, see question 17). But a narrow window association, as BB found for month 0, provides stronger support for decision usefulness, since it suggests that it is the accounting information that actually causes investor belief revision and hence security returns.

5.3.3 OUTCOMES OF THE BB STUDY

One of the most important outcomes of BB was that it opened up a large number of additional usefulness issues. A logical next step is to ask whether the *magnitude* of unexpected earnings is related to the *magnitude* of the security market response—recall that BB's analysis was based only on the *sign* of unexpected earnings. That is, the information content of earnings in BB's study was classified only into GN or BN, a fairly coarse measure.

The question of magnitude of response was investigated, for example, by Beaver, Clarke, and Wright (BCW) in 1979. They examined a sample of 276 NYSE firms with December 31 year-ends, over the 10-year period from 1965 to 1974. For each sample firm, for each year of the sample period, they estimated the unexpected earnings changes. They then used the market model procedure described in Sections 4.5 and 5.2.3 to estimate the abnormal security returns associated with these unexpected earnings changes.

Upon comparison of unexpected earnings changes with abnormal security returns, BCW found that the greater the change in unexpected earnings, the greater the security market response. This result is consistent with the CAPM (Section 4.5) and with the decision usefulness approach, since the larger are unexpected earnings changes the more investors on average will revise upwards their estimates of future firm earning power and resulting returns from their investments, other things equal.

Also, since 1968, accounting researchers have studied securities market response to net income on other stock exchanges, in other countries, and for quarterly earnings reports, with similar results. The approach has been applied to study market response to the information contained in new accounting standards, auditor changes, etc. Here, however, we will concentrate on what is probably the most important extension of BB, earnings response coefficients. This line of research asks a different question than BCW, namely, for a *given* amount of unexpected earnings, is the security market response greater for some firms than for others?

5.4   *Earnings Response Coefficients*

Recall that the abnormal securities market returns identified by BB were *averages*, that is, they showed that on average their GN firms enjoyed positive abnormal returns, and negative for their BN firms. Of course, an average can conceal wide variation about the average. Thus, it is likely that some firms' abnormal returns were well above average and others' were well below.

This raises the question of *why* the market might respond more strongly to the good or bad news in earnings for some firms than for others. If answers to this question can be found, accountants can improve their understanding of how accounting information is useful to investors. This, in turn, could lead to the preparation of more useful financial statements.

Consequently, one of the most important directions that empirical financial accounting research took since the BB study is the identification and explanation of differential market response to earnings information. This is called **earnings response coefficient (ERC)** research.[7]

> An **earnings response coefficient** *measures the extent of a security's abnormal market return in response to the unexpected component of reported earnings of the firm issuing that security.*

5.4.1   REASONS FOR DIFFERENTIAL MARKET RESPONSE

A number of reasons can be suggested for differential market response to historical cost-based earnings. We will review these in turn.

Beta

The riskier is the sequence of a firm's future expected returns, the lower will be its value to a risk-averse investor, other things equal. For a diversified investor, the relevant risk measure of a security is its beta, explained in Section 3.7. Since investors look to current earnings as an indicator of earning power and future returns, the riskier these future returns are the lower investors' reactions to a given amount of unexpected earnings will be.

To illustrate, think of a typical risk averse, rational investor whose utility increases in the expected value and decreases in the risk of the return on his or her portfolio. Suppose that the investor, upon becoming aware that a portfolio security has just released GN earnings information, revises upwards the expected rate of return on this security, and decides to buy more of it. However, if this security has high beta, this will increase portfolio risk.[8] Consequently, the investor would not buy as much more as if the security was low beta. In effect, the high beta acts as a brake on the investor's demand for the GN security. Since all risk-averse, rational informed investors will think this way, the demand for the GN firm's shares will be lower the higher is its beta, other things equal. Of course, lower demand implies a lower increase in market price and return in response to the GN, hence, a lower ERC.

Empirical evidence of a lower ERC for higher-beta securities has been found by Collins and Kothari (1989) and by Easton and Zmijewski (1989).

Capital Structure

For highly levered firms, an increase, say, in earnings (before interest) adds strength and safety to bonds and other outstanding debt, so that much of the good news in earnings goes to the debtholders rather than the shareholders. Thus, the ERC for a highly levered firm should be lower than that of a firm with little or no debt, other things equal. Empirical evidence of a lower ERC for more highly levered firms has been reported by Dhaliwal, Lee, and Fargher (1991). Billings (1999) also finds lower ERCs for firms with higher debt/equity ratios. As we will point out below in our discussion of the impact of growth opportunities on the ERC, firms with high earnings growth should enjoy reduced market concern about default risk, since earnings growth also adds security to outstanding debt. If this is the case, a high ERC for firms with little or no debt may be driven by high earnings growth rather than low leverage. Nevertheless, when earnings growth is controlled for, Billings finds that ERCs continue to be negatively associated with leverage.

Persistence

We would expect that the ERC will be higher the more the good or bad news in current earnings is expected to **persist** into the future. Thus, if current GN is due to the successful introduction of a new product or vigorous cost-cutting by management, the market response should be higher than if the GN was due to, say, an unanticipated gain on disposal of plant and equipment. In the latter case, the firm's market value increases dollar-for-dollar with the amount of the gain, since there is no reason to expect the unusual gain to recur. This implies a relatively low ERC. In the new product and cost-cutting cases, the ERC should be higher, since the revenue increases or cost savings will persist, to benefit future income statements as well. Evidence that ERCs are higher the higher the persistence of unexpected current earnings changes is presented by Kormendi and Lipe (1987).

Persistence is a challenging and useful concept. One reason, advanced by Ramakrishnan and Thomas (1991) (R&T) is that different components of net income may have different persistence. For example, suppose that in the same year a firm successfully introduces a new product it also reports a gain on disposal of plant and equipment. Then, the persistence of earnings is an average of the differing persistence of the components of earnings. R&T distinguish three types of earnings events:

- Permanent, expected to persist indefinitely
- Transitory, affecting earnings in the current year but not future years
- Price-irrelevant, persistence of zero

The ERCs for these are $(1 + R_f)/R_f$ (where R_f is the risk-free rate of interest under ideal conditions), 1, and 0 respectively.[9]

In effect, there are three ERCs, all of which may be present in the same income statement. R&T suggest that instead of trying to estimate an average ERC, investors should attempt to identify the three types separately and assign different ERCs to each. In so doing, they can identify the firm's permanent, or persistent, earning power. This implies that accountants should provide lots of classification and detail on the income statement.

To understand the ERC for permanent earnings, note that it can be written as $1 + 1/R_f$. Thus, under ideal conditions, the market response to $1 of permanent earnings consists of the current year's "installment" of 1 plus the present value of the perpetuity of future installments of $1/R_f$. (This ignores riskiness of the future installments, which is appropriate if investors are risk-neutral or the permanent earnings are firm-specific.) Writing the ERC this way also shows that when earnings persist beyond the current year, the magnitude of the ERC varies inversely with the interest rate.

Another aspect of ERCs is that their persistence can depend on the firm's accounting policies. For example, suppose that a firm uses fair value accounting, say for a capital asset, and that the value of the asset increases by $100. Assume that the increase results from an increase in the price of the product produced by the asset. Then, assuming that changes in fair value are included in income, net income for the period will include[10] GN of $100. Since unexpected changes in fair value occur randomly, by definition, the market will not expect the $100 to persist. Thus, the ERC is 1.

Suppose instead that the firm uses historical cost accounting for the asset and that the annual increase in contribution margin is $9.09. Then there will be only $9.09 of GN in earnings this year. The reason, of course, is that under historical cost accounting the $100 increase in fair value is brought into income only as it is realized. The efficient market will recognize that the current $9.09 GN is only the "first installment." [11] If it regards the value increase as permanent, the ERC will be 11 (1.10/.10).

Zero-persistence income statement components can result from choice of accounting policy. Suppose, for example, that a firm capitalizes a large amount of organization costs. This could result in GN on the current income statement, which is freed of the costs because of their capitalization. However, assuming the organization costs have no salvage value, the market would not react to the "GN," that is, its persistence is zero. As another example, suppose that a firm writes off research costs currently in accordance with section 3450 of the *CICA Handbook*. This could produce BN in current earnings. However, to the extent the market perceives the research costs as having future value, it would not react to this BN so that, again, persistence is zero, or even negative. The possibility of zero persistence suggests once more the need for detailed income statement disclosure, including a statement of accounting policies.

Earnings Quality

Intuitively, we would expect a higher ERC for higher-quality earnings. Recall from Section 3.3.2 that we define the quality of earnings by the magnitude of the main diagonal probabilities of the associated information system. The higher these probabilities, the higher we would expect the ERC to be, since investors are better able to infer future firm performance from current performance.

As a practical matter, measurement of earnings quality is less clear, since information system probabilities are not directly observable. One approach, discussed in Section 3.3.2, is to infer earnings quality by the magnitude of analysts' earnings forecast revisions following earnings announcements.

A more direct approach was used by Bandyopadhyay (1994), who examined ERCs of successful efforts (SE) versus full cost (FC) oil and gas firms (see Section 2.5.1). Bandyopadhyay predicted that SE firms would have higher ERCs, since the effect of capitalization and subsequent write-off of dry holes under FC introduces price-irrelevant components, to use Ramakrishnan and Thomas' terminology, into reported earnings. That is, SE earnings are of higher quality. Bandyopadhyay also predicted that the higher ERCs for SE firms would be less pronounced during periods of low exploration activity.

For a sample of 39 firms over the period 1982–1985, Bandyopadhyay found a significantly greater ERC for SE firms during two-day windows surrounding the release of their quarterly earnings announcements, compared to FC firms. During the period 1986–1990, when oil and gas exploration activity was relatively low, the ERCs did not differ significantly. These results support Bandyopadhyay's arguments of higher ERCs for higher quality earnings.

Another approach was used by Lev and Thiagarajan (1993) (L&T). They identified 12 "fundamentals" used by financial analysts in evaluating earnings quality. For example, one fundamental was the change in inventories, relative to sales. If inventories increase, this may suggest a decline in earnings quality—the firm may be entering a period of low sales, or simply be managing its inventories less effectively. Other fundamentals were change in capital expenditures, order backlog, etc.

For each firm in their sample, L&T calculated a measure of earnings quality by assigning a score of 1 or 0 to each of that firm's 12 fundamentals, then adding the scores. For example, for inventories, a 1 is assigned if that firm's inventories, relative to sales, are down for the year, suggesting higher earnings quality, and a 0 score is assigned if inventories are up. L&T then partitioned their sample firms each year into five groups of decreasing earnings quality according to their measure. Next, using regression analysis, they estimated average ERCs for each group. They found that the higher-quality-earnings groups had higher ERCs, consistent with the theoretical expectation.

It can also be argued that earnings persistence and earnings quality are positively related. Suppose that a firm reports increased earnings this year and, in addition, inventories relative to sales are down, suggesting an increase in earnings quality. Presumably, the market would expect the GN in earnings to persist. L&T examined the relationship between earnings quality and persistence for their sample firms and found that firms with both high persistence and high earnings quality had higher ERCs, on average, than firms with high persistence and low earnings quality, and similarly for low-persistence firms. These results support a positive relationship between persistence and quality of earnings.

Growth Opportunities

For reasons related to the above persistence and earnings quality arguments, the GN or BN in current earnings may suggest future growth prospects for the firm, and hence a higher ERC. One might think that historical cost-based net income really cannot say anything about the future growth of the firm. However, this is not necessarily the case. Suppose that current net income reveals unexpectedly high profitability for some of the firm's recent investment projects. This may indicate to the market that the firm will enjoy strong growth in the future. One reason, of course, is that to the extent the high profitability persists, the future profits will increase the firm's assets. In addition, success with current projects may suggest to the market that this firm is also capable of identifying and implementing additional successful projects in future, so that it becomes labelled as a growth firm. Such firms can easily attract capital and this is an additional source of growth. Thus, to the extent that current good news in earnings suggests growth opportunities, the ERC will be high.

To illustrate, extend the persistence example above by assuming that the $9.09 of current permanent earnings increase is expected to grow by 5% per year. The present value at 10% of a perpetuity that increases by 5% per year is $1/(0.10 - 0.05) = 20$, greater than $1/0.10 = 10$ under no-growth. Thus, the ERC is 21 rather than 11 as before.

Evidence that the ERC is higher for firms that the market regards as possessing growth opportunities is shown by Collins and Kothari (1989). They use the ratio of market value of equity to book value of equity as a measure of growth opportunities, the rationale being that the efficient market will be aware of the growth opportunities before they are recognized in net income and will bid up share price accordingly. Collins and Kothari find a positive relationship between this measure and the ERCs of their sample firms.

The Similarity of Investor Expectations

Different investors will have different expectations of a firm's next-period earnings, depending on their prior information and the extent of their abilities to evaluate financial statement information. However, these differences will be reduced to the extent that they draw on a common information source, such as analysts' consensus forecasts, when forming their expectations. Consider a firm's announcement of its current earnings. Depending on their expectations, some investors will regard this information as GN, others as BN, hence some will be inclined to buy and some to sell. However, to the extent that investors' earnings expectations were "close together," they will put the same interpretation on the news. For example, if most investors base their earnings expectation on the analysts' consensus forecast, and current earnings are less than forecast, they will all regard this as BN and will be inclined to sell rather than buy. Thus, the more similar the earnings expectations the greater the effect of a dollar of abnormal earnings on share price. In effect, the more precise are analysts' forecasts the more similar are investors' earnings expectations and the greater the ERC, other things equal. For an analysis of conditions under which the ERC is increasing in the precision of analysts' earnings forecasts and how this precision is affected by factors such as earnings quality and number of analysts forecasting the firm, see Abarbanell, Lanen, and Verrecchia (1995).

The Informativeness of Price

We have suggested on several previous occasions that market price itself is partially informative about the future value of the firm. In particular, price is informative about (i.e., leads) future earnings. Recall that the reason is that market price aggregates all publicly known information about the firm, much of which the accounting system recognizes with a lag. Consequently, the more informative is price, the less will be the information content of current accounting earnings, other things equal, hence the lower the ERC.

A proxy for the informativeness of price is *firm size*, since larger firms are more in the news. However, Easton and Zmijewski (1989) found that firm size was not a significant explanatory variable for the ERC. The reason is probably that firm size proxies for other firm characteristics, such as risk and growth, as much as it proxies for the informativeness of share price. Once these factors are controlled for, any significant effect of size on the ERC seems to go away. Collins and Kothari (1989) dealt with size by moving the wide window over which security returns were measured earlier in time for large firms. This substantially improved the relationship between changes in earnings and security returns, the argument being that the market anticipates changes in earning power sooner for large firms. Once this was done, size appeared to have no explanatory power for the ERC.

5.4.2   IMPLICATIONS OF ERC RESEARCH

Be sure that you see the reason *why* accountants should be interested in the market's response to financial accounting information. Essentially, the reason is that improved understanding of market response suggests ways that they can further improve the decision usefulness of financial statements. For example, lower informativeness of price for smaller firms implies that expanded disclosure for these firms would be useful for investors, contrary to a common argument that larger firms should have greater reporting responsibilities.

Also, the finding that ERCs are lower for highly levered firms supports arguments to expand disclosure of the nature and magnitude of financial instruments, including those that are "off-balance-sheet." If the relative size of a firm's liabilities affects the market's response to net income, then it is desirable that all liabilities be disclosed.

The importance of growth opportunities to investors suggests, for example, the desirability of disclosure of segment information, since profitability information by segments would better enable investors to isolate the profitable, and unprofitable, operations of the firm.

Finally, the importance of persistence and quality of earnings to the ERC means that disclosure of the *components* of net income is useful for investors. This implication is discussed further in Section 5.5.

5.4.3   MEASURING INVESTORS' EARNINGS
EXPECTATIONS

As mentioned previously, researchers must obtain a proxy for expected earnings, since the efficient market will only react to that portion of an earnings announcement that it did not expect. If a reasonable proxy is not obtained, the researcher may fail to identify a market reaction when one exists, or may incorrectly conclude that a market reaction exists when it does not. Thus, obtaining a reasonable estimate of earnings expectations is a crucial component of information perspective research.

Under the ideal conditions of Example 2.2, expected earnings is simply accretion of discount on opening firm value. When conditions are not ideal, however, earnings expectations are more complex. One approach is to project the time series formed by the firm's past reported net incomes, that is, to base future expectations on past performance. A reasonable projection, however, depends on earnings persistence. To see this, consider the extremes of 100% persistent earnings and zero persistent earnings. If earnings are completely persistent, expected earnings for the current year are just last year's actual earnings. Then, unexpected earnings are estimated as the *change* from last year. This approach was used by Ball and Brown, as described in Section 5.3. If earnings are of zero persistence, then there is no information in last year's earnings about future earnings, and all of current earnings are unexpected. That is, unexpected earnings are equal to the *level* of current year's earnings. This approach was used by Bill Cautious in Example 3.1. Which extreme is closer to the truth? This can be evaluated by the degree of correlation between security returns and the estimate of unexpected earnings, a question examined by Easton and Harris (1991). Using regression analysis of a large sample of U.S. firms over the period 1969–1986, they documented a correlation between one-year security returns and the change in net income, consistent with the approach of Ball and Brown. However, there was an even stronger correlation between returns and the level of net income. Furthermore, when both earnings changes and levels were used, the two variables combined did a significantly better job of predicting returns than either variable separately. These results suggest that the truth is somewhere in the middle, that is, both changes in and levels of net income are components of the market's earnings expectations, where the relative weights on the two components depend on earnings persistence.

The foregoing discussion is based solely on a time series approach, however. Another source of earnings expectations is analysts' forecasts. These are now widely available for most large firms. If analysts' forecasts are more accurate than time series forecasts, they provide a better estimate of earnings expectations, since rational investors will presumably use the most accurate forecasts. Evidence by Brown, Griffin, Hagerman, and Zmijewski (1987), who studied the quarterly forecasting performance of one forecasting organization (Value Line), suggests that analysts outperform time series models in terms of accuracy. O'Brien (1988) also found that analysts' quarterly earnings forecasts were more accurate than time series forecasts. These results are what we would expect, since analysts can bring to bear information beyond that contained in past earnings when making their earnings projections.

When more than one analyst follows the same firm, it seems reasonable to take the consensus, or average, forecast as the proxy for the market's earnings expectation, following the reasoning underlying the football forecasting example of Section 4.2.2. O'Brien pointed out, however, that the age of a forecast has an important effect on its accuracy. She found that the single most recent earnings forecast provided a more accurate earnings prediction in her sample than the average forecast of all analysts following the firm, where the average ignored how old the individual forecasts were. This suggests that the timeliness of a forecast dominates the cancelling-out-of-errors effect of the average forecast.

Despite evidence that analysts' forecasts tend to be more accurate than forecasts based on time series, other evidence, discussed by Kothari (2001), suggests that analysts' forecasts are optimistically biased, although the bias may have decreased in recent years. Nevertheless, recent studies of the information content of earnings tend to base earnings expectations on analysts' forecasts.

5.4.4   SUMMARY

The information content of reported net income can be measured by the extent of security price change or, equivalently, by the size of the abnormal market return, around the time the market learns the current net income. This is because rational, informed investors will revise their expectations about future earnings and returns on the basis of current earnings information. Revised beliefs trigger buy/sell decisions, as investors move to restore the risk/return tradeoffs in their portfolios to desired levels. If there was no information content in net income there would be no belief revision, no resulting buy/sell decisions, and hence no associated price changes.

For a given amount of unexpected net income, the extent of security price change or abnormal returns depends on factors such as firm size, capital structure, risk, growth prospects, persistence, the similarity of investor expectations, and earnings quality.

Following the pioneering study of Ball and Brown, empirical research has demonstrated a differential market response depending on most of these factors. These empirical results are really quite remarkable. First, they have overcome substantial statistical and experimental design problems. Second, they show that the market is, on average, very sophisticated in its ability to evaluate accounting information. This supports the theory of securities market efficiency and the decision theories that underlie it. Finally, they support the decision usefulness approach to financial reporting.

Indeed, the extent to which historical-cost-based net income can provide "clues" about future firm performance may seem surprising. The key, of course, is the information system probabilities, as shown in Table 3.2. In effect, the higher the main diagonal probabilities, the greater we would expect the ERC to be. This supports the FASB's contention in its Conceptual Framework that investors' expectations are based "at least partly on evaluations of past enterprise performance" (Section 3.8). As accountants gain a better understanding of investor response to financial statement information, their ability to provide useful information to investors will further increase.

5.5   *Unusual, Non-recurring and Extraordinary Items*

In Section 5.4.1, we mentioned Ramakrishnan and Thomas' suggestion (1991) that investors separately estimate permanent, transitory, and price-irrelevant components of earnings. An interesting example of the importance of earnings persistence can be found in the reporting of events that are unusual and/or infrequent. Since these items may not recur regularly, their persistence will be low. This means that they must be fully disclosed; otherwise, the market may get an exaggerated impression of their persistence.

The reporting of **extraordinary items** is specified by Section 3480 of the *CICA Handbook*. In 1989, Section 3480 was revised to introduce greater consistency in the reporting of extraordinary items on the income statement. According to paragraph 3480.02:

Extraordinary items are items that result from transactions or events that have all of the following characteristics:

(a) they are not expected to occur frequently over several years;

(b) they do not typify the normal business activities of the entity;

and

(c) they do not depend primarily on decisions or determinations by management or owners.

The last characteristic in the definition was added in the 1989 revision. Prior to that time, only the first two characteristics applied. The result was to eliminate a large number of former extraordinary items such as, for example, gains or losses on disposals of capital assets. After 1989 such unusual and non-recurring gains or losses would be included *before* income from continuing operations, because management controls the timing of such transactions.

This revision seems to resolve the issue of **classificatory smoothing**, whereby management could smooth (or otherwise manage) earnings from continuing operations by choosing to classify unusual items above or below the operating earnings line. Evidence that managers in the United States behaved as if they smoothed earnings from continuing operations by means of classificatory smoothing was reported by Barnea, Ronen, and Sadan (1976). By requiring those unusual items whose amounts and/or timing could be controlled by management to be consistently reported as part of operating income, the ability to engage in classificatory smoothing was effectively eliminated. It therefore appeared that the new Section 3480 represented an improvement in financial reporting.

However, the nature of the improvement can be questioned, based on the ERC research outlined in Section 5.4. Specifically, unusual items have low persistence. For example, a gain on sale of capital assets would have persistence of 1 or less. Other unusual items could have persistence as low as zero, to the extent that they are not value-relevant at all.

The impact of the 1989 revisions to Section 3480 caused a number of low-persistence unusual and non-recurring items to move from extraordinary items up to the operating section of the income statement. The income statement format following from Section 3480 is summarized as follows (we ignore income taxes for simplicity):

Net income before unusual and non-recurring items, also called core earnings	x x
Unusual and non-recurring items	<u>x x</u>
Income from continuing operations, also called operating income	x x
Extraordinary items	<u>x x</u>
Net income	<u>x x</u>

Core earnings represents the persistent component of income, and is the basis of investors' estimates of future earning power. Unusual and non-recurring items are items that do not qualify as extraordinary items under Section 3480. As mentioned, they are of low persistence, by definition.

We can now see two related problems arising from the 1989 revisions to Section 3480. First, if unusual and non-recurring items are not fully disclosed, investors may overestimate the persistence of operating income. Second, the amounts and timing of the recording of unusual and non-recurring items are subject to strategic manipulation by management. Thus, if management chooses to recognize an unusual loss currently, income from continuing operations is reduced. Furthermore, if the loss had been building up for some time, earnings of previous periods are, in retrospect, overstated. More serious, management may overstate the amount of the loss—the amounts of many losses, such as a writedown of goodwill from acquisitions, are highly subjective and difficult for investors to verify. Then, by excessively relieving *future* periods of charges for amortization, core earnings in future years are overstated. There is no requirement under current GAAP to separate out the effects of prior writedowns from core earnings.[12] Thus, the accounting for unusual and non-recurring items has the potential to confuse the matching of costs and revenues that is at the heart of historical cost-based accounting.

These issues were investigated by Elliott and Hanna (1996), who found a significant decline in the core earnings ERC in quarters following the reporting of a large unusual item (usually, these were losses rather than gains). Furthermore, the ERC declined further if the firm reported numerous large special items over time. This evidence is consistent with the market interpreting the frequency of recording of unusual and non-recurring items as a proxy for their potential misuse. We will return to the impact of extraordinary, unusual, and non-recurring items on core earnings in our discussion of earnings management in Chapter 11.

Thus, the question appears to be open whether Section 3480 actually succeeded in improving financial reporting. From our standpoint, however, Section 3480 represents an interesting example of how theory can be brought to bear to reexamine an issue that was thought resolved.

5.6   *A Caveat About the "Best" Accounting Policy*

To this point, we have argued that accountants can be guided by securities market reaction in determining usefulness of financial accounting information. From this, it is tempting to conclude that the "best" accounting policy is the one that produces the greatest market price response. For example, if net income reported by oil and gas firms under successful-efforts accounting produces a greater market reaction than net income reported under full-cost accounting, successful-efforts should be used, because investors find it more useful.

However, we must be extremely careful about this conclusion. Accountants may be better off to the extent that they provide useful information to investors, but it does not follow that *society* will necessarily be better off.

The reason is that information has characteristics of a **public good**. A public good is a good such that consumption by one person does not destroy it for use by another. Consumption of a **private good**—such as an apple—eliminates its usefulness for other consumers. However, an investor can use the information in an annual report without eliminating its usefulness to other investors. Consequently, suppliers of public goods may have trouble charging for these products, so that we often witness them being supplied by governmental or quasi-governmental agencies—roads and national defence, for example. If a firm tried to charge investors for its annual report, it would probably not attract many customers, because a single annual report, once produced, could be downloaded to many users. Instead, we observe governments through securities legislation and corporations acts, *requiring* firms to issue annual reports.

Of course, firms' annual reports are not "free." Investors will eventually pay for them through higher product prices. Nevertheless, investors perceive them as free, since the extent to which they use the annual report information will not affect the product prices they pay. Also, investors may incur costs to inform themselves, either directly, or indirectly by paying for analyst or other information services. Nevertheless, the basic "raw material" is perceived as free and investors will do what any other rational consumer will do when prices are low—consume more of it. As a result, *investors may perceive accounting information as useful even though from society's standpoint the costs of this information (through higher product prices) outweigh the benefits to investors and capital markets.*

Also, as mentioned in Chapter 1, information affects different people differently. Thus, information may be useful to investors but managers may object to supplying it. As a result, the social value of such information depends on both the benefits to investors and the costs to managers. Such fundamental cost-benefit tradeoffs are extremely difficult to make.

Think of information as a commodity, demanded by investors and supplied by firms through accountants. Because of the public-good aspect of information, we cannot rely on the forces of demand and supply to produce the socially "right" or first-best amount of production, as we can for private goods produced under competition. The essential reason is that the price system does not, and probably cannot, operate to charge investors the full costs of the information they use. Consequently, from a social perspective we cannot rely on the extent of security market response to tell us which accounting policies should be used (or, equivalently, "how much" information to produce). Formal arguments to support this conclusion were given by Gonedes and Dopuch (1974).

We will return to the question of regulation of information production in Chapters 12 and 13. For now, the point to realize is that it is still true that accountants can be guided by market response to maintain and improve their competitive position as suppliers to the marketplace for information. It is also true that securities markets will work better to the extent security prices provide good indications of underlying real investment opportunities. However, these social considerations do suggest that, as a general rule, accounting standard setting bodies should be wary of using securities market response to guide their decisions.

Interestingly, an exception to this rule seems to have occurred with respect to standard setters' decisions to eliminate current cost accounting for capital assets. SFAS 33, which required U.S. firms to report supplemental current cost information for certain assets, was discontinued in 1986. Discontinuance was based in part on the influential study by Beaver and Landsman (1983), who failed to find any incremental securities market reaction to current cost information over and above the information content of historical-cost-based net income.[13] In Canada, Hanna, Kennedy, and Richardson (1990) recommended the discontinuance of Section 4510 of the *CICA Handbook*, which laid down procedures for supplemental current cost disclosures for capital assets. They were unable to find evidence of usefulness of this information and the section was withdrawn in 1992. It is difficult to disagree with decisions to cease production of information that no one finds useful. Nevertheless, from a social perspective, no one knows whether this decision was correct, due to the difficulties of measuring social costs and benefits.

5.7   *The Information Content of RRA*

In this section we depart from our concentration on the information content of historical cost-based net income in order to consider the informativeness of other financial statement information. Specifically, we will consider whether RRA information has additional information content over historical cost net income and book value. Recall from Section 2.4 that SFAS 69 requires oil and gas firms to report supplementary present value information about proved reserves.

A priori, we would expect that if supplemental fair value-oriented information is going to be useful for investors, it would be in the oil and gas industry. One could argue, for example, that historical cost and fair value are especially likely to diverge in this industry—a lucky firm might, at low cost, find a bonanza. More importantly, we pointed out the implications of inside information in Section 4.6. Since so much of the value of an exploring/producing oil company depends on its reserves, shares of such a firm seem especially susceptible to the problems of information asymmetry. Consequently, the market should be particularly interested in reserves information. However, RRA reserves information will only be useful to investors if it enables better predictions of firm performance. Indeed, we will see that empirical tests of RRA decision usefulness are not clear-cut.

The theoretical and empirical ability of RRA to explain the market's evaluation of oil and gas reserves was extensively investigated by Magliolo (1986), in tests conducted on a sample of firms over 1979–1983, inclusive. In one set of tests, Magliolo compared the undiscounted value of net reserves reported in RRA to an estimate of the market's valuation of those reserves. This RRA information did not perform according to theory in its ability to explain market value. Indeed, RRA was outperformed by reserve information provided by an investment service. This service makes a number of adjustments to the current operating data of oil and gas firms to arrive at an economic estimate of revenues and costs. The implication is that RRA, in addition to concerns about reliability, may not be as relevant as competing sources of reserves information.

Magliolo also examined the ability of the elements of an RRA-based income statement (see Table 2.5 for such a statement) to explain *changes* in the market's valuation of reserves. He found that additional reserves proved during the year had significant explanatory power, although some of it appeared to be anticipated by the market, which suggests that other, more timely information sources are available to investors. Other components of the RRA income statement had little explanatory ability. Magliolo concluded that, overall, RRA does not measure the market values of oil and gas reserves as theory would predict.

Other researchers have also investigated the information content of RRA. Doran, Collins, and Dhaliwal (1988) (DCD) studied a sample of 173 producing oil and gas firms over the six-year period 1979–1984. They studied the sub-periods 1979–1981 and 1982–1984 separately.[14]

For each sample observation, DCD calculated monthly abnormal returns as in Figure 5.1 for a 12-month period ending on the firm's year-end (December 31), and summed them for each observation to give a 12-month abnormal return. The question then was, to what extent did RRA information have incremental ability, in addition to the change in historical cost net income, to explain the abnormal return? You will recognize that this approach is similar to that discussed in Sections 5.2 and 5.3, except that now two variables are being used to explain abnormal security returns, rather than one. To the extent that the two-variable model does a better job of explaining abnormal returns than a model using only historical-cost-based net income, it can be argued that the supplemental RRA information is useful for investors, in the sense that it has information content about future share returns over and above the information content of historical cost net income.

Using regression analysis, DCD showed that during 1979–1981 *both* historical cost and RRA information had significant explanatory power, supporting the incremental usefulness of RRA. However, during 1982–1984, *neither* variable had significant explanatory power. Thus, their results were mixed. DCD attributed this to the fact that oil and gas market prices were much more volatile during the earlier period. Consequently, investors would be particularly interested in information about reserves and expected market prices during 1979–1981.

Nevertheless, the fact that they also found historical cost-based net income not to have significant explanatory power for abnormal returns during 1982–1984 is puzzling, since this conflicts with the wealth of evidence about the usefulness of income discussed in Sections 5.3 and 5.4. DCD attribute this result to the fact that the market was expecting an oil glut during 1982–1984 and that the effects of this expectation on oil company share prices swamped the impact of reported net income.[15]

Despite these explanations, DCD's results have to be interpreted as providing, at best, fairly weak evidence in favour of RRA. This lack of strong results also shows up in other studies. For example, Harris and Ohlson (1987) (HO) examined the ability of RRA information to explain the market value of the oil and gas assets[16] of producing firms, rather than abnormal returns as in DCD. Using a sample of 273 observations over the five-year period from 1979 to 1983, they found that the book value of oil and gas assets[17] had significant explanatory power for the market value of these assets. RRA information also had some explanatory power, but less than historical cost.

HO also examined the usefulness of reserve quantity information. SFAS 69 also requires that quantities of proved oil and gas reserves, and changes in the quantities during the year, be disclosed. HO found that quantity information had no incremental explanatory power beyond RRA. In other words, when both quantity information and RRA information are available it seems that investors go for RRA.

It should be pointed out that the DCD study was "wide window," that is, security returns were measured over a 12-month period. Thus, even if a significant association between security returns and RRA was found, this does not mean that the RRA information *causes* abnormal security returns. The most that can be said is that security market price and RRA both reflect the underlying value of future returns from oil and gas properties. This does not necessarily mean that RRA information is not useful, since, knowing that RRA reflects underlying value, investors may use this information in their investment decisions. It does mean, however, that RRA competes with information from other sources. For example, Ghicas and Pastena (1989) also examined the incremental information content of RRA. However, they introduced financial analyst forecasts of oil company values as a *third* explanatory variable. They found that when recent analyst information was available any ability that RRA had to explain oil company value disappeared. Thus, a further constraint on the decision usefulness of RRA is that its potential relevance may be superseded by other, more timely sources of information, consistent with Magliolo's finding.

Even if we ignore the question of timeliness, however, the difficulty that empirical research has had to demonstrate decision usefulness of RRA is surprising. Given the apparent sophistication of security market reaction to reported net income, one would expect a similar reaction to relevant balance sheet and supplementary information.

Several reasons can be suggested for the weak results for RRA. One is reliability, as mentioned. Perhaps RRA is too imprecise to be useful, again consistent with the results of Magliolo. We saw in Section 2.4.2 that management is lukewarm about the usefulness of RRA, claiming low reliability. Second, the research faces more severe methodological difficulties than it does in finding a market reaction to net income. One problem is in finding the point in time that the market first becomes aware of the RRA information. For net income, media publication of the earnings announcement provides a reasonable event date. However, given the inside nature of oil and gas reserves information and its importance to firm value, analysts and others may work particularly hard to ferret it out in advance of the annual report. If a reasonable event date for the release of reserve information cannot be found, return studies must use wide windows, which are open to a large number of influences on price in addition to accounting information.

A third reason may be that historical cost-based information about oil and gas reserves may be more value-relevant than implied by our discussion above. HO suggest that oil companies will not throw money away on exploration and development but, rather, will only spend it if the expected benefits at least equal the costs. This means that the higher is the book value of an oil company's oil and gas properties, the more the company thinks they are worth (allowing for risk), and vice versa. If this argument that book value makes economic sense is combined with the greater reliability of historical cost information than RRA, it is not surprising that the market may find historical cost book value more useful.

In a followup study, HO (1990) investigated the information content of historical cost reserves information more closely. They continued to find that historical cost dominated RRA. Furthermore, their results suggest that the market, if anything, underuses the information content of historical cost reserves information. This finding is of interest because it raises the alternative possibility that securities markets may not be as efficient as the information perspective assumes.

However, one must be cautious in accusing the market of a lack of sophistication. Instead of searching for a direct link between other financial statement information and abnormal security returns, as the above studies have done, there is an indirect approach that links other information to the quality of earnings. To illustrate, suppose that an oil company reports high earnings this year, but supplemental oil and gas information shows that its reserves have declined substantially over the year. An interpretation of this information is that the firm has used up its reserves to increase sales in the short run. If so, the quality of current earnings is reduced, since they contain a non-persistent component that will dissipate if new reserves are not found. Then, the market's reaction to the supplemental reserve information may be more easily found in a low ERC than in a direct reaction to the reserve information itself.

While their study was not specifically oriented to oil and gas firms, this approach was used by Lev and Thiagarajan (1991) (L&T). Parts of their research were reviewed in Section 5.4.1. Recall that they identified 12 fundamental variables that affect earnings quality. Several of these were based on balance sheet information, such as the change in inventories. When L&T added these fundamentals as additional explanatory variables in an ERC regression analysis, there was a substantial increase in ability to explain abnormal security returns beyond the explanatory power of unexpected earnings alone. This suggests that the market, aided perhaps by analysts, is quite sophisticated in its evaluation of earnings, using balance sheet information to augment the information content of the earnings announcement itself.

5.8   *Summary and Conclusions*

The empirical literature in financial accounting is vast, and we have looked only at certain parts of it. Nevertheless, we have seen that, for the most part, the securities market response to reported net income is impressive in terms of its sophistication. Results of empirical research in this area support the efficient markets theory and related decision theories.

What is puzzling, however, is that the market does not seem to respond to non-earnings information as strongly as it does to earnings information. RRA was examined as an example of non-earnings information where, a priori, a strong market response would be expected. The extent to which the lack of strong market response to non-earnings information such as RRA is due to methodological difficulties, to its low reliability, to availability of alternative information sources, or to failure of efficient markets theory itself is not fully understood at the present time, although it may be that investors route their reaction to such information, at least partly, through their perceptions of earnings quality.

As stated earlier, the approach to financial accounting theory that equates the extent of security price change with information content and hence with decision usefulness, is known as the information perspective. The essence of this approach is that investors are viewed as attempting to predict future returns from their investments. They seek all relevant information in this regard, not just accounting information. To maximize their competitive position as suppliers of information, accountants may then seek to use the extent of security market response to various types of accounting information as a guide to its usefulness to investors. This motivates their interest in empirical research on decision usefulness. Furthermore, the more information accountants can move from inside to outside the firm, the better capital markets can guide the flow of scarce investment funds.

Despite these considerations, accountants must be careful of concluding that the accounting policies and disclosures that produce the greatest market response are the best for society. This is not necessarily true, due to the public-good nature of accounting information. Investors will not necessarily demand the "right" amount of information, since they do not bear its full costs. These concerns limit the ability of decision usefulness research to guide accounting standard setters.

Nevertheless, until recently, the information perspective has dominated financial accounting theory and research since the Ball and Brown paper of 1968. It has led to a tremendous amount of empirical investigation that has enriched our understanding of the decision usefulness of accounting information for investors.

Questions and Problems

1. Explain the information perspective on financial reporting. Does it rely on the historical cost basis of accounting? (CGA-Canada)

2. Refer to the separation of market-wide and firm-specific security returns as shown in Figure 5.1. What factors could reduce the accuracy of the estimate of abnormal returns? (CGA-Canada)

3. Explain why the market might begin to anticipate the GN or BN in earnings as much as a year in advance, as Ball and Brown found in Figure 5.2.
(CGA-Canada)

4. Give examples of components of net income with:

   a. High persistence

   b. Persistence of 1

   c. Persistence of 0 (CGA-Canada)

5. Explain why it is desirable to find the exact time that the market first became aware of an item of accounting information if any security price reaction to this information is to be detected. Can such a time always be found? Explain why or why not. What can researchers do when the exact time cannot be isolated?
(CGA-Canada)

6. A researcher finds evidence of a security price reaction to an item of accounting information during a narrow window of three days surrounding the date of release of this information and claims that it was the accounting information that caused the security price reaction. Another researcher finds evidence of security price reaction to a different item of accounting information during a wide window beginning 12 months prior to the release of the financial statements containing that item. This researcher does not claim that the accounting information caused the security price reaction but only that the information and the market price reaction were associated.

   Explain why one can claim causation for a narrow window but not for a wide window. Which price reaction constitutes the stronger evidence for usefulness of accounting information? Explain.

7. XYZ Ltd. is a large retail bookstore chain listed on a major stock exchange, and its reported net income for the year ended December 31, 2000 is $5 million. The earnings were announced to the public on December 31, 2000.

   Financial analysts had predicted the company's net income for 2000 to be $7 million. The financial analysts' prediction of $7 million net income was in effect up until the release of the 2000 earnings on December 31, 2000.

Assumptions

- No other news about XYZ Ltd. was released to the public on December 31, 2000.
- No macroeconomic information was released to the public on December 31, 2000.
- Financial analysts' forecasts about XYZ Ltd.'s net income represented the market's expectations about XYZ Ltd.'s income.

Required

a. Would you expect a change in price of XYZ Ltd.'s common stock on December 31, 2000? If so, why? Explain.

b. Consider the two situations below:

   i. The deviation of forecasted earnings from actual earnings of $2 million ($7 million - $5 million) is completely accounted for by the closing down of a number of its retail outlets.

   ii. The deviation of the forecasted earnings from actual earnings of $2 million is completely accounted for by a fire in XYZ Ltd.'s largest retail outlet, which had caused the outlet to be closed temporarily for six months.

   In which of these two scenarios would you expect the price change of XYZ Ltd.'s common stock to be greater? Explain.

8. In a classic study, Beaver (1968) examined the trading volume of firms' securities around the time of their earnings announcements. Specifically, he examined 506 annual earnings announcements of 143 NYSE firms over the years 1961–1965 inclusive (261 weeks).

For each earnings announcement, Beaver calculated the average daily trading volume (of the shares of the firm making that announcement) for each week of a 17-week window surrounding week 0 (the week in which the earnings announcement was made). For each firm in the sample, he also calculated the average daily trading volume outside its 17-week window. This was taken as the normal trading volume for that firm's shares.

For each week in the 17-week window, Beaver averaged the trading volumes over the 506 earnings announcements in the sample. The results are shown in Figure 5.3 below. The dotted line in the figure shows the average normal trading volume outside the 17-week window.

As can be seen from the figure, there was a dramatic increase in trading volume, relative to normal, in week 0. Also, volume is below normal during most of the weeks leading up to week 0.

FIGURE 5.3   VOLUME ANALYSIS

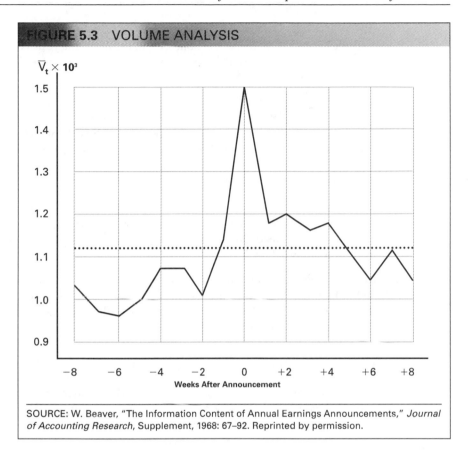

SOURCE: W. Beaver, "The Information Content of Annual Earnings Announcements," *Journal of Accounting Research*, Supplement, 1968: 67–92. Reprinted by permission.

Required

a. Why do you think trading volume increased in week 0?

b. Why do you think trading volume was below normal in the weeks leading up to week 0?

c. Do Beaver's volume results support the decision usefulness of earnings information? Explain.

d. Which is the better indicator of decision usefulness, the abnormal return measure (Figure 5.1) or the volume measure? Explain.   (CGA-Canada)

9. Discuss the impact of firm size on the ERC.

10. X Ltd. is a growth firm that uses conservative, high-quality accounting policies. Y Ltd. is growing more slowly and is a rarity in that it uses fair value accounting for its capital assets and related amortization.

Otherwise, X Ltd. and Y Ltd. are quite similar. They are the same size, and have similar capital structures and similar betas.

Required

a. Both X and Y Ltd. report the same GN in earnings this year. Which firm would you expect to have the greater security market response (ERC) to this good earnings news? Explain.

b. Suppose that X Ltd. had a much higher debt-to-equity ratio and beta than Y Ltd. Would your answer to part **a** change? Explain.

11. On the basis of the empirical evidence presented in this chapter, do you feel the FASB is correct in its claim in SFAC 1 (see Section 3.8) that investors' expectations about future enterprise performance "are commonly based at least partly on evaluations of past enterprise performance?"   (CGA-Canada)

12. By defining extraordinary items to be infrequent, not typical of normal business activities, and not depending on management decision, Section 3480 of the *CICA Handbook* greatly increases the need for adequate disclosure of the components of reported net income. Explain why.

13. In 1998, Stelco Inc. announced plans to alter its capital structure by redeeming $99 million par value of its preferred shares at par. The dividend rate on these shares was about 7.75% of par value. Consequently, after the redemption, the portion of net income going to Stelco's common shareholders will be substantially increased.

Explain the impact of this redemption on the ERC of Stelco's reported net income.

14. Explain why financial statement information has characteristics of a public good? Include a definition of a public good in your answer. What does this imply about using the *extent* of security market reaction to accounting information to guide accountants? Standard setters?

15. You estimate empirically the ERC of firm J as 0.38. Firm K is identical to firm J in terms of size, earning power, persistence of earnings, and risk. Unlike firm J, however, firm K supplements its income statement with a financial forecast. You estimate firm K's ERC as 0.57. Which firm's net income report appears to be more useful to investors? Explain. Does this mean that all firms should be required to prepare financial forecasts? Explain.

16. In 1991, the AICPA established a Special Committee on Financial Reporting. This committee, made up of several leaders in public accounting, industry, and academia, was charged with reviewing the current financial reporting model and making recommendations on what information management should make available to investors and creditors.

In 1994, the Committee made several recommendations in a report entitled "Report of AICPA Special Committee on Financial Reporting" that it argued should help investors and other users to improve their assessment of a firm's prospects, thereby increasing the decision usefulness of annual reports. Here is one of its recommendations:

> *The Committee recommended that companies differentiate between core activities and non-core activities in their income statement, balance sheet, and cash flow statement. "A company's core activities—usual and recurring events—provide the best historical data from which users discern trends and relationships and make their predictions about the future." Non-core activities are defined as "unusual and nonrecurring activities or events (non-core effects) as well as interest charges. Without adjustment, non-core effects can distort or mask an important trend or relationship in the company's ongoing business."*

SOURCE: Excerpt reprinted with permission from report of the AICPA Special Committee on Financial Reporting. © 1994 by American Institute of Certified Public Accountants, Inc.

Required

a. Use the concept of earnings persistence to explain why the Committee recommends separate reporting of the results of "core" activities on the income statement.

b. To what extent does Section 3480 of *CICA Handbook* in Canada (see Section 5.5) ensure that "non-core effects," as the AICPA Committee defines them, are adequately disclosed?

17. It is important to realize that different bases of accounting, such as present value accounting and historical cost-based accounting, do not affect total earnings over the life of the firm, but only the timing of the recognition of those earnings. In effect, over the life of the firm, the firm "earns what it earns," and different bases of accounting will all produce earnings that add up to this total.

If this is so, then we would expect that the greater the number of time periods over which we aggregate a firm's historical cost earnings, the closer the resulting total will be to economic earnings, that is, the earnings total that would be produced over the same periods under ideal conditions.

This was studied by Easton, Harris, and Ohlson (1992) (EHO) and by Warfield and Wild (1992) (WW). EHO proxied economic income by the return on the firm's shares on the securities market. When this return was aggregated over varying periods of time (up to 10 years) and compared with historical cost-based earnings returns for similar periods, the comparison improved as the time period lengthened. WW studied a similar phenomenon for shorter periods. They found, for example, that the association between economic and accounting income for quarterly time periods was on average about 1/10 of their association for an annual period, consistent with historical-cost-based net income lagging behind economic income in its recognition of relevant economic events.

Required

a. In Example 2.1, calculate net income for years 1 and 2 assuming that P.V. Ltd. used straight-line amortization for its capital asset, while retaining all other assumptions. Verify that total net income over the two-year life of P.V. Ltd. equals the total net income that P.V. Ltd. would report using present value amortization.

b. Do the same in Example 2.2, assuming that the state realization is bad and good in years 1 and 2 respectively.

c. Use the fact that accruals reverse to explain why total net income over the two years in **a** and **b** above are the same under economic and straight-line amortization. Are these results consistent with the empirical results of EHO and WW outlined above?

18. On May 8, 2001, the *Financial Post* reported "The Street turns against Canadian Tire." Canadian Tire Corporation's share price had risen by $0.75 to $24.90 on May 2, 2001, following a news release in which Mr. Wayne Sales, president and CEO, said "We are pleased with our ability to deliver double digit growth...." Canadian Tire's reported earnings of $0.37 exceeded analysts' expectations.

The market soon learned, however, that reported earnings included an $8 million one-time gain on sale of certain Canadian Tire assets. Without this gain, earnings were $0.29 per share, 6% below earnings for the same quarter of 2000. Canadian Tire's share price quickly fell back to $22.95.

The *Post* reported that "Passing off" a one-time gain as part of operating earnings "didn't fool or impress analysts" and is something they "hoped not to see again."

Required

a. Use efficient securities market theory to explain the rise in Canadian Tire's share price on May 2, 2001, and the rapid subsequent fall in share price.

b. Was Canadian Tire correct in including the $8 millions one-time gain in operating income? Explain.

c. Evaluate the persistence of Canadian Tire's reported net income of $0.37 per share (no calculations required). Does the fact of Mr. Sale's ignoring of this item in his press release affect your evaluation? Explain why or why not.

19. On October 19, 2000, *The Globe and Mail* reported on Imperial Oil Ltd.'s earnings for the third quarter ended on September 30, 2000, released on October 18. Net income was a record $374 millions, up from $191 millions for the same quarter of the previous year. Return on equity was 25.7%, up from 10.1% a year earlier. Earnings for the quarter included a $60 million gain on Imperial's sale of its Cynthia pipeline and other assets. Cash flow for the quarter was $433 million, up from $270 million in the previous year's third quarter. The reported profit of $374 million was in line with analysts' expectations.

On October 18, the TSE oil and gas index rose by 0.6%, as the market anticipated higher prices for oil and gas. Yet, Imperial's share price fell on the day by $1.25, to close at $37.35. *The Globe and Mail* also reported analysts' comments about a widening discount for heavy crude oil, relative to light crude. Imperial is Canada's biggest producer of heavy crude. Also, Imperial's production from its oil sands projects declined in the quarter, due to maintenance and temporary production problems.

Required

a. Calculate the abnormal return, relative to the TSE oil and gas index, on Imperial Oil's shares for October 18, 2000.

b. Is the abnormal decline in Imperial's share price on October 18 consistent with efficient securities market theory? Explain why or why not. Consider earnings persistence in your answer.

c. In what section of the income statement should the $60 millions gain on the sale of the Cynthia pipeline be reported? Explain.

Notes

1. As mentioned in Section 4.5, this estimate of α_j should equal $(1 - \beta_j)R_f$, where R_f is the risk-free rate of interest. Here, $\alpha_j = 0.0001$ implies $R_f = 0.0005$ per day.

2. The market return for day 0 is calculated as follows:

$$R_{M0} = \frac{\text{Level of DJ Index,} \atop \text{end of day 0} + \text{Dividends on DJ} \atop \text{Index on day 0}}{\text{Level of DJ} \atop \text{Index, beginning of day 0}} - 1$$

Sometimes, because of data problems, the dividends are omitted.

3. Calculated as:

$$E(R_{jt}) = \alpha_j + \beta_j R_{M0}$$
$$= 0.0001 + 0.80 \times 0.001$$
$$= 0.0009$$

4. Again, this abnormal return should not be confused with abnormal earnings of P.V. Ltd. in Example 2.2. While the idea is the same, abnormal return here refers to a *market* return, whereas abnormal earnings refer to *accounting* net income.

5. Other ways to estimate investor expectations are discussed in Section 5.4.3.

6. Note that the loss on bad news firms can be converted into a gain by selling short the shares of the bad news firms.

7. For reasons explained in Section 5.3.2, the interpretation of a narrow-window ERC is different from a wide-window ERC. Here we will refer, somewhat loosely, to both types as simply ERCs.

8. Recall from Section 3.7 that in reasonably diversified portfolios, most of the portfolio risk stems from the betas of the securities in the portfolio. Thus, if the investor were to buy more shares of a security whose beta is greater than the average beta of the securities presently in the portfolio, this will raise the average, hence increasing portfolio risk.

9. These are "market value" ERCs, where the market's response to GN or BN is expressed in terms of the abnormal change in market value, rather than the abnormal return as in our ERC definition. To convert a market value ERC to a rate of return ERC, divide it by opening firm value.

10. This is analogous to the inclusion of unexpected oil price changes in income under RRA. See the alternative format in Table 2.5.

11. This assumes that the market knows that the increase in market value is $100. Possibly, this would be known from sources other than the financial statements. If not, considerable onus is put on the firm for full disclosure. Perhaps MD&A provides a vehicle for management to reveal this information.

12. Note that under RRA, adjustments to prior period estimates are reported separately. Perhaps this approach could be adopted for the effects of current write-offs on future core earnings. If so, this would constitute a major extension of full disclosure. We will return to this possibility in Section 11.7.

13. A number of reasons other than lack of usefulness can be suggested for these results. First, the market may value the information but is able to estimate it from other sources. Second, the information may be relevant but unreliable, since a large number of assumptions and estimates go into its preparation. Third, the market may have reacted to the information but the research methodology was not sufficiently powerful to find it. For example, the Beaver and Landsman (1983) study was criticized by Bernard (1987) on methodological grounds. Indeed, some evidence of security market reaction has been found in studies subsequent to Beaver and Landsman. Thus, Bernard and Ruland (1987) found some information content for current cost information, at least in certain industries.

14. SFAS 69 came into effect in 1982. However, the SEC required disclosure of information similar to RRA information from 1979 to 1981.

15. Note that the procedure to separate economy-wide returns and abnormal returns illustrated in Figure 5.1 does *not* remove industry-wide returns. These will be buried in abnormal returns under the Figure 5.1 procedure, because all firms in DCD's sample were in the oil and gas industry. This illustrates one of the difficulties of working with data from a single industry in empirical studies.

16. HO estimated the market value of oil and gas assets by subtracting the book value of net non-oil and gas assets from the market value of the firm's capital stock and marketable debt.

17. HO's significant result held for both book value on a successful-efforts basis and on a full-cost basis.

6

The Measurement Perspective on Decision Usefulness

6.1 Overview

The **measurement perspective** on decision usefulness implies greater usage of fair values in the financial statements proper. Following from our discussion in Section 2.5.1, greater use of fair values suggests a balance sheet approach to financial reporting, as opposed to the income statement approach which underlies the research described in Chapter 5. This, in turn, implies a larger role for the financial statements proper to assist investors in predicting the firm's **fundamental value**, that is, the value the firm's shares would have if all relevant information was in the public domain. *We define the measurement perspective as follows:*

> *The **measurement perspective** on decision usefulness is an approach to financial reporting under which accountants undertake a responsibility to incorporate fair values into the financial statements proper, providing that this can be done with reasonable reliability, thereby recognizing an increased obligation to assist investors to predict fundamental firm value.*

Of course, if a measurement perspective is to be useful, it must not be at the cost of a substantial reduction in reliability. While it is unlikely that a measurement perspective will *replace* the historical cost basis of accounting, it does seem to be the case that the relative balance of cost-based versus fair value-based information in the financial statements is moving in the fair value direction. This may seem strange, given the problems that techniques such as RRA accounting have experienced. However, a number of reasons can be suggested for the change in emphasis.

One such reason involves securities market efficiency. Despite the impressive results outlined in Chapter 5 in favour of the decision usefulness of reported net income, recent years have seen increasing theory and evidence suggesting that securities markets may not be as efficient as originally believed. This suggestion has major implications for accounting. To the extent that securities markets are not fully efficient, the reliance on efficient markets to justify historical cost-based financial statements supplemented by much supplementary disclosure, which underlies the information perspective's approach to decision usefulness, is threatened. For example, if investors collectively are not as adept at processing information as efficiency theory assumes, perhaps usefulness would be enhanced by greater use of fair values in the financial statements proper. Furthermore, while beta is the only relevant risk measure according to the CAPM, perhaps accountants should take more responsibility for reporting on firm risk if markets are not fully efficient.

Other reasons derive from a low proportion of share price variability explained by historical cost-based net income, from the Ohlson clean surplus theory that provides support for increased measurement, and from the legal liability to which accountants are exposed when firms become financialy distressed.

In this chapter we will outline and discuss these various reasons.

6.2   *Are Securities Markets Efficient?*

6.2.1   *INTRODUCTION*

In recent years, increasing questions have been raised about the extent of securities market efficiency. These questions are of considerable importance to accountants since, if they are valid, the practice of relying on supplementary information in notes and elsewhere to augment the basic historical cost-based financial statements may not be completely effective in conveying useful information to investors. Furthermore, to the extent that securities markets are not fully efficient, improved financial reporting may be helpful in reducing inefficiencies, thereby improving the proper operation of securities markets. That is, better reporting of firm value will enable investors to better estimate fundamental value, thereby more easily identifying mispriced securities. In this section, we will outline and discuss the major questions that have been raised about market efficiency.

The basic premise of these questions is that average investor behaviour may not correspond with the rational decision theory and investment models outlined in Chapter 3. Investors may be biased in their reaction to information, relative to how they should react according to Bayes' theorem. For example, psychological evidence suggests that individuals tend to be **overconfident**—they overestimate the precision of information they collect themselves (see, for example, the discussion in Odean (1998)). If an individual's information collecting activities reveal GN, for example, he or she will revise their subjective probability of high future earnings by more than they should according to Bayes' theorem. If, on average, investors behave this way, share price will overreact.

Another attribute of many individuals is **self-attribution bias,** whereby individuals feel that good decision outcomes are due to their abilities, whereas bad outcomes are due to unfortunate realizations of states of nature, hence not their fault. Suppose that following an overconfident investor's decision to purchase a firm's shares, its share price rises (for whatever reason). Then, the investor's faith in his or her investment ability rises. If share price falls, faith in ability does not fall. If the average investor behaves this way, share price **momentum** will develop. That is, reinforced confidence following a rise in share price leads to the purchase of more shares, and share price rises further. Confidence is again reinforced, and the process feeds upon itself, that is, it gains momentum. Daniel, Hirshleifer and Subrahmanyam (1998) present a model whereby momentum develops when investors are overconfident and self-attribution biased. Daniel and Titman (1999), in an empirical study, report that over the period 1968–1997 a strategy of buying portfolios of high-momentum shares and short-selling low-momentum ones earned high and persistent abnormal returns (i.e., higher than the return from holding the market portfolio), consistent with the overconfidence and momentum arguments.[1]

Self-attribution bias and momentum are, of course, inconsistent with securities market efficiency and underlying decision theory. According to the CAPM, higher returns can only be earned if higher beta risk is borne. Yet Daniel and Titman report that the average beta risk of their momentum portfolios was less than that of the market portfolio. Furthermore, share price momentum implies positive serial correlation of returns, contrary to the random walk behaviour of returns under market efficiency.

The study of behavioural-based securities market efficiencies is called **behavioural finance.** For a comprehensive review of the theory and evidence of behavioural finance, see Hirshleifer (2001). We now review several other questions about efficiency that have been raised in this theory.

6.2.2   PROSPECT THEORY

The **prospect theory** of Kahneman and Tversky (1979) provides a behavioural-based alternative to the rational decision theory described in Section 3.3. According to prospect theory, an investor considering a risky investment (a "prospect") will separately evaluate prospective gains and losses. This contrasts with decision theory where investors evaluate decisions in terms of their effects on their total wealth (see Chapter 3, Note 4). Separate evaluation of gains and losses about a reference point is an implication of the psychological concept of **narrow framing,** whereby individuals analyze problems in too isolated a manner, as a way of economizing on the mental effort of decision making. This mental effort may derive from information overload (i.e., more information than the individual can handle) and/or from a feeling that it is not worth the effort to acquire more information. As a result, an individual's utility in prospect theory is defined over deviations from zero for the prospect in question, rather than over total wealth.

The investor's utility for gains is assumed to exhibit the familiar risk averse, concave shape as illustrated in Figure 3.2. However, at the point where the investment starts to lose in value, the investor's rate of utility loss is greater than the rate of utility increase for a gain in value.[2] Indeed, the utility for losses is assumed to be convex rather than concave, so that the investor exhibits "risk taking" behaviour with respect to losses. This assumption derives from **loss aversion**, a behavioural concept whereby individuals are averse to even very small losses. This leads to a **disposition effect**, whereby the investor holds on to losers and sell winners. This effect was studied by Shefrin and Statman (1985). They identified a sample of investors whose rational decision was to sell loser securities before the end of the taxation year. They found, however, that the investors tended to avoid selling, consistent with the disposition effect.

Figure 6.1 shows a typical investor utility function under prospect theory.

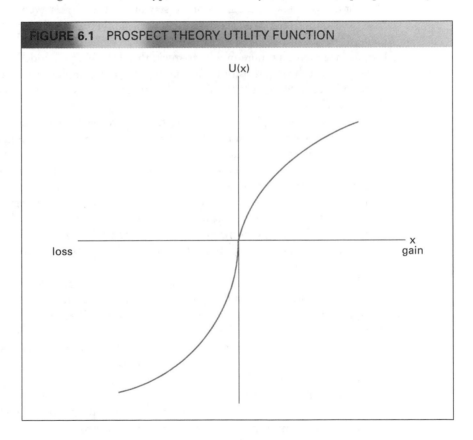

FIGURE 6.1　PROSPECT THEORY UTILITY FUNCTION

Prospect theory also assumes that when calculating the expected value of a prospect, individuals "weight" their probabilities. This weighting is a ramification of overconfidence. Thus, evidence (e.g., GN) that a state (e.g., high earning power) is likely to happen will be underweighted, particularly if the evidence is abstract, statistical, and highly relevant. In effect, by underweighting evidence that a state is likely to happen, the main diagonal probabilities of the information system are perceived by the overconfident investor as lower than they actually are. As a result, the individual's posterior probability of the state is also too low. However, individuals tend to overweight salient, anecdotal, and extreme evidence (e.g., a media article claiming that a stock is about to take off), even though realization of such states is a rare event.

These tendencies lead to "too-low" posterior probabilities on states that are likely to happen, and "too high" on states that are unlikely to happen. The posterior probabilities need not sum to one.

The combination of separate evaluation of gains and losses and the weighting of probabilities can lead to a wide variety of "irrational" behaviours. For example, fear of losses may cause investors to stay out of the market even if prospects have positive expected value according to a decision theory calculation. Also, they may underreact to bad news by holding on to "losers" so as to avoid realizing a loss, or may even buy more of a loser stock, thereby taking on added risk. Thus, under prospect theory, investor behaviour depends in a complex way on the levels of payoff probabilities, risk aversion with respect to gains and risk taking with respect to losses.

There are few empirical accounting tests of prospect theory, relative to the empirical tests based on rational investor behaviour described in Chapter 5. One such test, however, was conducted by Burgstahler and Dichev (1997). In a large sample of U.S. firms from 1974–1976, these researchers documented that relatively few firms in their sample reported small losses. A relatively large number of firms reported small positive earnings. Burgstahler and Dichev interpreted this result as evidence that firms that would otherwise report a small loss manipulate cash flows and accruals to manage their reported earnings upwards, so as to instead show small positive earnings (techniques of earnings management are discussed in Chapter 11).

As Burgstahler and Dichev point out, this result is consistent with prospect theory. To see why, recall first that prospect theory assumes that investors evaluate gains and losses relative to a reference point of zero—if earnings are positive, share value, hence investor wealth and utility, increases, and vice versa if earnings are negative. Now observe from Figure 6.1 that the rate at which investor utility increases is greatest for small gains, and the rate at which it decreases is even greater for small losses. This implies a *very* strong rate of negative investor reaction to a small reported loss, and a strong rate of positive reaction to small reported positive earnings. Managers of firms that would otherwise report a small loss thus have an incentive to avoid this negative investor reaction, and enjoy a positive reaction, by managing reported earnings upwards. (Of course, managers of firms with *large* losses have similar incentives, but as the loss increases it becomes more difficult to manage earnings sufficiently to avoid the loss. Also, the incentive to manage earnings upwards declines for larger losses since the rate of negative investor reaction is not as great, and runs into a disposition effect.)

However, Burgstahler and Dichev suggest that their evidence is also consistent with rational behaviour. Lenders will demand better terms from firms that report losses, for example. Also, suppliers may cut the firm off, or demand immediate payment for goods shipped. To avoid these consequences, managers have an incentive to avoid reporting losses if possible. As a result, the extent to which Burgstahler and Dichev's findings support prospect theory is unclear.

6.2.3 IS BETA DEAD?

As mentioned in Section 4.5, an implication of the CAPM is that a stock's beta is the sole firm-specific determinant of the expected return on that stock. If the CAPM reasonably captures rational investor behaviour, share returns should be increasing in β_j and should be unaffected by other measures of firm-specific risk, which are diversified away. However, in a large sample of firms traded on major U.S. stock exchanges over the period 1963–1990, Fama and French (1992) found that beta had little ability to explain stock returns. Instead, they found significant explanatory power for the book-to-market ratio (ratio of book value of common equity to market value) and for firm size. Their results suggest that rather than looking to beta as a risk measure, the market acts as if firm risk increases with book-to-market and decreases with firm size. These results led some to suggest that beta is "dead."

Different results are reported by Kothari, Shanken, and Sloan (1995), however. They found that over a longer period of time (1941–1990) beta *was* a significant predictor of return. Book-to-market also predicted return, but its effect was relatively weak. They attributed the difference between their results and those of Fama and French to differences in methodology and time period studied.

The status of the CAPM thus seems unclear. A possible way to "rescue" beta is to recognize that it may change over time. Our discussion in Section 4.5 assumed that beta was **stationary**. However, events such as changes in interest rates and firms' capital structures, improvements in firms' abilities to manage risk, and development of global markets may affect the relationship between the return on individual firms' shares and the marketwide return, thereby affecting the value of firms' betas. If so, evidence of volatility that appears to conflict with the CAPM could perhaps be explained by shifts in beta.

If betas are non-stationary, rational investors will want to know when and by how much they have changed. This is a difficult question to answer in a timely manner, and different investors will have different opinions. This introduces differences in their investment decisions, even though they all have access to the same information and proceed rationally with respect to their opinion as to what beta is. In effect, an additional source of uncertainty, beyond the uncertainty resulting from random states of nature, is introduced into the market. This uncertainty arises from the mistakes investors make in evaluating new values of non-stationary share price parameters. As a result, additional volatility is introduced into share price behaviour but beta remains as the only variable that explains this behaviour. That is, the CAPM implication that beta is the sole firm specific risk variable is reinstated, with the proviso that beta is non-stationary. Models that assume rational investor behaviour in the face of non-stationarity[3] are presented by Kurz (1997). Evidence that non-stationarity of beta explains much of the apparent anomalous behaviour of share prices is provided by Ball and Kothari (1989).

Behavioural finance, however, provides a different perspective on the validity of the CAPM. Daniel, Hirshleifer, and Subrahmanyam (2001) present a model that assumes two types of investors—rational and overconfident. Because of rational investors, a stock's beta is positively related to its returns, as in the CAPM. However, overconfident investors overreact as they gather information. In the case of GN, this drives share price too high, thereby driving down the firm's book-to-market ratio. Over time, share price reverts towards its efficient level as the overconfidence is revealed. As a result, both beta and book-to-market ratio are positively related to future share returns, consistent with the results of Kothari, Shanken, and Sloan, and inconsistent with the CAPM's prediction that beta is the only firm-specific return predictor.

From an accounting standpoint, to the extent that beta is not the only relevant firm-specific risk measure, this can only increase the role of financial statements in reporting useful risk information (the book-to-market ratio is an accounting-based variable, for example). Nevertheless, in the face of the mixed evidence reported above, we conclude that beta is not dead. However, it may change over time and may have to "move over" to share its status as a risk measure with accounting-based variables.

6.2.4 EXCESS STOCK MARKET VOLATILITY

Further questions about securities market efficiency derive from evidence of excess stock price volatility at the market level. Recall from the CAPM (equation 4.2) that, holding beta and the risk-free interest rate constant, a change in the expected return on the market portfolio, $E(R_{Mt})$, is the only reason for a change in the expected return of firm j's shares. Now the fundamental determinant of $E(R_{Mt})$ is the aggregate expected dividends across all firms in the market—the higher are aggregate expected dividends the more investors will invest in the market, increasing demand for shares and driving the stock market index up (and vice versa). Consequently, if the market is efficient, changes in $E(R_{Mt})$ should not exceed changes in aggregate expected dividends.

This reasoning was investigated by Shiller (1981), who found that the variability of the stock market index was several times greater than the variability of aggregate dividends. Shiller interpreted this result as evidence of market inefficiency.

Subsequently, Ackert and Smith (1993) pointed out that while expected future dividends are the fundamental determinant of firm value, they should be defined broadly to include all cash distributions to shareholders, such as share repurchases and distributions following takeovers, as well as ordinary dividends. In a study covering the years 1950–1991, Ackert and Smith showed that when these additional items were included, excess volatility disappeared.

However, despite Ackert and Smith's results, there are reasons why excess volatility may exist. One reason, consistent with efficiency, derives from non-stationarity, as outlined in the previous section. Other reasons derive from behavioural factors. The momentum model of Daniel, Hirshleifer, and Subrahmanyam (1998) implies excess market volatility as share prices overshoot and then fall back. A different argument is made by DeLong, Shleifer, Summers, and Waldmann (1990). They assume a capital market with both rational and positive feedback investors. Positive feedback investors are those who buy in when share price begins to rise, and vice versa. One might expect that rational investors would then sell short, anticipating the share price decline that will follow the price run-up caused by positive feedback buying. However, the authors argue that rational investors will instead "jump on the bandwagon," to take advantage of the price run-up while it lasts. As a result, there is excess volatility in the market.

In sum, it seems that the question of excess market volatility raised by Shiller is unresolved. The results of Ackert and Smith suggest it does not exist if dividends are defined broadly. Even if excess volatility does exist, it can possibly be explained by rational models based on non-stationarity. Alternatively, volatility may be driven by behavioural factors, inconsistent with market efficiency.

6.2.5 STOCK MARKET BUBBLES

Stock market bubbles, wherein share prices rise far above rational values, represent an extreme case of market volatility. Shiller (2001) investigates bubble behaviour with specific reference to the surge in share prices of technology companies in the United States in the years leading up to 2001. Bubbles, according to Shiller, derive from a combination of biased self-attribution and resulting momentum, positive feedback trading, and to "herd" behaviour reinforced by optimistic media predictions of market "experts." These reasons underlie Federal Reserve Board Chairman Greenspan's famous "irrational exuberance" comment on the stock market in a 1996 speech.

Shiller argues that bubble behaviour can continue for some time, and that it is difficult to predict when it will end. Eventually, however, it will burst because of growing beliefs of, say, impending recession or increasing inflation.

6.2.6 EFFICIENT SECURITIES MARKET ANOMALIES

We conclude this section with evidence of market inefficiency that specifically involves financial accounting information. Recall that the evidence described in Chapter 5 generally supports efficiency, and the rational investor behaviour underlying it. There is, however, other evidence suggesting that the market may not respond to information exactly as the efficiency theory predicts. For example, share prices sometimes take some time to fully react to financial statement information, so that abnormal security returns persist for some time following the release of the information. Also, it appears that the market may not always extract all the information content from financial statements. Cases such as these that appear inconsistent with securities market efficiency are called **efficient securities market anomalies**. We now consider three such anomalies.

Post-announcement Drift

Once a firm's current earnings become known, the information content should be quickly digested by investors and incorporated into the efficient market price. However, it has long been known that this is not exactly what happens. For firms that report good news in quarterly earnings, their abnormal security returns tend to drift upwards for at least 60 days following their earnings announcement. Similarly, firms that report bad news in earnings tend to have their abnormal security returns drift downwards for a similar period. This phenomenon is called **post-announcement drift**. Traces of this behaviour can be seen in the Ball and Brown study reviewed in Section 5.3—see Figure 5.2 and notice that abnormal share returns drift upwards and downwards for some time following the month of release of GN and BN, respectively.

Reasons for post-announcement drift have been extensively studied. For example, Foster, Olsen, and Shevlin (1984) examined several possible explanations for its existence. Their results suggested that apparent post-announcement drift may be an artifact of the earnings expectation model used by the researcher. As outlined in Chapter 5, most studies of securities market response to earnings announcements measure their information content by some proxy for unexpected earnings, on the grounds that the market will only respond to that portion of a current earnings announcement that it did not expect. When these authors proxied unexpected earnings by the change in earnings from the same quarter last year, they found strong evidence of post-announcement drift. However, with other proxies for unexpected earnings, there appeared to be no such drift. Since we do not know which earnings expectation model is the correct one, or, for that matter, even whether unexpected earnings is the best construct for measuring investor reaction (see Section 5.4.3), the Foster, Olsen, and Shevlin results tended to leave the existence of post-announcement drift up in the air, so to speak.

Be sure you see the significance of post-announcement drift. If it exists, investors could earn arbitrage profits, at least before transactions costs and before taking risk into account, by buying shares of good news firms on the day they announced their earnings and selling short shares of bad news firms. But, if investors scrambled to do this, the prices of good news firms' shares would rise right away, and those of bad news firms' shares would fall, thereby eliminating the post-announcement drift.

Bernard and Thomas (1989) (BT) further examined this issue. In a large sample of firms over the period 1974–1986, they documented the presence of post-announcement drift in quarterly earnings. Indeed, an investor following the strategy of buying the shares of GN firms and selling short BN on the day of earnings announcement, and holding for 60 days, would have earned an average return of 18%, over and above the marketwide return, before transactions costs, in their sample.

An explanation is that *investors appear to underestimate the implications of current earnings for future earnings.* As BT point out, it is a known fact that quarterly seasonal earnings changes are positively correlated. That is, if a firm reports, say, GN this quarter, in the sense that this quarter's earnings are greater than the same quarter last year, there is a greater than 50% chance that its next-quarter earnings will also be greater than last year's. Rational investors should anticipate this and, as they bid up the price of the firm's shares in response to the *current* GN, they should bid them up some more due to the increased probability of GN in *future* periods. However, BT's evidence suggests that this does not happen. The implication is that post-announcement drift results from the market taking considerable time to figure this out, or at least that it underestimates the magnitude of the correlation (Ball and Bartov, 1996). In terms of the information system given in Table 3.2, BT's results suggest that Bill Cautious evaluates the main diagonal probabilities as less than they really are.

Researchers continue to try to solve the post-announcement drift puzzle. For example, Bartov, Radhakrishnan, and Krinsky (2000) point out that the market contains sophisticated and unsophisticated investors. They find that post-announcement drift is less if a greater proportion of a firm's shares is held by institutional investors. To the extent that institutions are a good proxy for sophisticated investors, their results suggest that post-announcement drift is driven by unsophisticated investors who, presumably, do not comprehend the full information in current quarterly earnings. Also, Brown and Han (2000) find that post-announcement drift holds, in their sample, only for firms with poor information environments (small firms, firms with little analyst following, and firms with few institutional investors).

While studies such as these increase our understanding of post-announcement drift, they do not fully explain why it continues to exist. Thus, post-announcement drift continues to represent a serious and important challenge to securities market efficiency.

Market Efficiency with Respect to Financial Ratios

The results of several studies suggest that the market does not respond fully to certain balance sheet information. Rather, it may wait until the balance sheet information shows up in earnings or cash flows before reacting. If so, this raises further questions about securities market efficiency, and it should be possible to devise an investment strategy that uses balance sheet information to "beat the market." Evidence that the market does wait, and details of a strategy that did appear to beat the market, appear in a paper by Ou and Penman (1989) (OP).

OP began their study by deriving a list of 68 financial ratios. They obtained a large sample of firms and, for each firm, calculated each ratio for each of the years 1965 to 1972 inclusive. Then, for each ratio, they investigated how well that ratio predicted whether net income would rise or fall in the next year. Some ratios predicted better than others did. For example, the return on total assets proved to be highly associated with the change in next year's net income—the higher the ratio in one year the greater the probability that net income would increase the next. However, the ratio of sales to accounts receivable, also called accounts receivable turnover, did not predict the change in next year's net income very well.

OP then took the 16 ratios that predicted *best* in the above investigation and used them as independent variables to estimate a *multivariate* regression model to predict changes in next year's net incomes. This model then represents their sample's best predictor of next year's earning changes, since it takes the 68 ratios they began with, distills them to the 16 best on an individual-ratio basis, and uses these 16 in a multivariate prediction model.

Armed with this model, OP then applied it to predicting the earnings changes of their sample firms during 1973 to 1983. That is, the prediction model was estimated over the period from 1968 to 1972 and then used to make predictions from 1973 to 1983. For each firm and for each of the years 1973 to 1983, the prediction from the multivariate model is in the form of a *probability* that net income will rise in the following year.

OP then used these predictions as the basis for the following investment strategy. For each firm and for each year, *buy* that firm's shares at the market price *three months* after the firm's year-end *if* the multivariate regression model predicts that the probability of that firm's net income rising next year is 0.6 or more (the three months is to allow sufficient time for the firm's financial statements to be released and for the market to digest their contents). Conversely, if the model's prediction is that the probability of net income rising is 0.4 or less, *sell short* that firm's shares three months after its year-end.

Notice that this investment strategy is implementable—it is based on information that is actually available to investors at the time. Also, in theory, the strategy need not require any capital investment by the investor because the proceeds from the short sales can be used to pay for the shares that are bought. (In practice, some capital would be required due to restrictions on short sales and, of course, brokerage fees and other transactions costs.)

In the OP model, once bought, shares were held for 24 months and then sold at the market price at that time. Shares sold short were purchased at the market price 24 months later to satisfy the short-sale obligation.

The reasoning behind this investment strategy is straightforward. We know from Chapter 5 that the share prices respond to earnings announcements. If we can predict in advance, using ratio information, which firms will report GN and which BN, then we can exploit these predictions by the above investment strategy.

The question then was, did this investment strategy beat the market? To answer this question, OP calculated the profit or loss on each transaction, which was then converted into a rate of return. These returns were then aggregated to give the total return over all transactions. Next, it was necessary to adjust for the market-wide rate of return on stocks, so as to express returns net of the performance of the market as a whole. For example, if OP's investment strategy produced a return of 8%, but the whole market rose by 10%, one could hardly say that the strategy beat the market. However, when market-wide returns were removed, OP found that their strategy earned a return of 14.53% over two years, *in excess of market-wide return*, before transactions costs. As the chances of this happening by chance are almost zero, their investment strategy appeared to have been successful in beating the market.

OP's results were surprising, because under efficient markets theory those results should not have occurred. The investment strategy was based solely on information that was available to all investors—financial ratios from firms' financial statements. Efficient market theory suggests that this ratio information will quickly and efficiently be incorporated into market prices. The share prices of the firms that OP bought or sold short should have already adjusted to reflect the probable increases or decreases in next year's net incomes by the time they bought them, in which case their investment strategy would not have earned excess returns. The fact that OP did earn excess returns suggests that the market did not fully digest all the information contained in financial ratios. Rather, the market price only adjusted as the next two years' earnings increases or decreases were actually announced. But by then, OP had already bought or sold short. Consequently, the OP results served as another anomaly for efficient securities market theory.

Market Response to Accruals

Sloan (1996), for a large sample of 40,769 annual earnings announcements over the years 1962–1991, separated reported net income into operating cash flow and accrual components. This can be done by noting that:

Net income = operating cash flows ± net accruals

where net accruals, which can be positive or negative, include amortization expense, and net changes in non-cash working capital such as receivables, allowance for doubtful accounts, inventories, accounts payable, etc.

Sloan points out that, other things equal, the efficient market should react more strongly to a dollar of good news in net income if that dollar comes from operating cash flow than from accruals. The reason is familiar from elementary accounting—accruals reverse. Thus, looking ahead, a dollar of operating cash flow this period is more likely to be repeated next period than a dollar of accruals, since the effects of accruals on earnings reverse in future periods. In other words, cash flow is more persistent. Sloan estimated separately the persistence of the operating cash flows and accruals components of net income for the firms in his sample, and found that operating cash flows had higher persistence than accruals. That is, consistent with the above "accruals reverse" argument, next year's reported net income was more highly associated with the operating cash flow component of the current year's income than with the accrual component.

If this is the case, we would expect the efficient market to respond more strongly to the GN or BN in earnings the greater is the cash flow component relative to the accrual component in that GN or BN, and vice versa. Sloan found that this was not the case. While the market did respond to the GN or BN in earnings, it did not seem to "fine-tune" its response to take into account the cash flow and accruals composition of those earnings. Indeed, by designing an investment strategy to exploit the market mispricing of shares with a high or low accruals component in earnings, Sloan demonstrated a one-year return of 10.4% over and above the market return.

Sloan's results raise further questions about securities market efficiency.

Discussion of Efficient Securities Market Anomalies

Numerous investigators have tried to explain anomalies without abandoning efficient securities market theory. One possibility is risk. If the investment strategies that appear to earn anomalous returns identify firms that have high betas, then what appear to be arbitrage profits are really a reward for holding risky stocks.[4] The authors of the above three anomaly studies were aware of this possibility, of course, and conducted tests of the riskiness of their investment strategies. In all cases, they concluded that risk effects were not driving their results.

However, others have investigated the risk explanation. Greig (1992) reexamined the OP results and concluded that their excess returns were more likely due to the effects of firm size on expected returns than on the failure of the market to fully evaluate accounting information. The evidence of Fama and French (1992) suggests that firm size explains share returns in addition to beta (see Section 6.2.3. See also Banz (1981)). On the basis of more elaborate controls for firm size than in OP, Greig's results suggest that OP's excess returns go away when size is fully taken into account.

Stober (1992) confirmed excess returns to the OP investment strategy. He showed, however, that the excess returns continued for up to six years following the release of the financial statements. If the OP excess returns were due to a deviation of share prices from their efficient market value, one would hardly expect that it would take six years before the market caught on. In other words, while the market may wait until the information in financial ratios shows up in earnings, this would hardly take six years. This suggests that the OP results reflect some permanent difference in expected returns such as firm size or risk rather than a deviation from fundamental value.

Different results are reported by Abarbanell and Bushee (1998), however. In a large sample of firms over the years 1974–1988, they also documented an excess return; to a strategy of buying and short-selling shares based on non-earnings financial statement information such as changes in sales, accounts receivable, inventories, and capital expenditures. Unlike Stober, however, the excess returns did not continue beyond a year, lending support to OP's results.

Another possible explanation for the anomalies is transactions costs. The investment strategies required to earn arbitrage profits may be quite costly in terms of investor time and effort, requiring not only brokerage costs but continuous monitoring of earnings announcements, annual reports, and market prices, including development of the required expertise.[5] Bernard and Thomas (1989) present some evidence that transactions costs limit the ability of investors to exploit post-announcement drift. Thus, their 18% annual return, as well as the 14.53% over two years reported by Ou and Penman, and Sloan's 10.4% may appear to be anomalous only because the costs of the investment strategies required to earn them are at least this high.

If we accept this argument, securities market efficiency can be reconciled with the anomalies, at least up to the level of transactions costs. To put it another way, we would hardly expect the market to be efficient with respect to more information than it is cost-effective for investors to acquire.

The problem with a transactions cost-based defence of efficiency, however, is that *any* apparent anomaly can be dismissed on cost grounds. If cost is used to explain everything, then it explains nothing. That is, unless we know what the costs of an investment strategy *should* be, we do not know whether the profits earned by that strategy are anomalous. We conclude that the efficient securities market anomalies continue to raise challenging questions about the extent of securities market efficiency.

6.2.7   IMPLICATIONS OF SECURITIES MARKET INEFFICIENCY FOR FINANCIAL REPORTING

To the extent that securities markets are not fully efficient, this can only increase the importance of financial reporting. To see why, let us expand the concept of noise traders introduced in Section 4.4.1, as suggested by Lee (2001). Specifically, now define noise traders to also include investors subject to the behavioural biases outlined above. An immediate consequence is that noise no longer has expectation zero. That is, even in terms of expectation, share prices may be biased up or down relative to their fundamental values. Over time, however, rational investors, including analysts, will discover such mispricing and take advantage of it, driving prices towards fundamental values.

Improved financial reporting, by giving investors more help in predicting fundamental firm value, will " speed up" this arbitrage process. Indeed, by reducing the costs of rational analysis, better reporting may reduce the extent of investors' behavioural biases. In effect, securities market inefficiency supports a measurement perspective.

6.2.8   CONCLUSIONS ABOUT SECURITIES MARKET EFFICIENCY

Collectively, the theory and evidence discussed in the previous sections raise serious questions about the extent of securities market efficiency. Fama (1998), however, evaluates much of this evidence and concludes that it does not yet explain the "big picture." That is, while there is evidence of market behaviour inconsistent with efficiency, there is not a unified alternative theory that predicts and integrates the anomalous evidence. For example, Fama points out that apparent overreaction of share prices to information is about as common as underreaction. Thus, post-announcement drift and the Ou and Penman financial ratio anomaly involve underreaction to accounting information whereas the Sloan accruals anomaly involves overreaction to the accrual component of net income. What is needed to meet Fama's concern is a theory that predicts when the market will overreact and when it will underreact.

This lack of a unified theory may be changing. The models of Daniel, Hirshleifer, and Subrahmanyam (see Sections 6.2.1 and 6.2.3) incorporate behavioural variables into rigorous economic models of the capital market. They generate predictions of momentum, volatility, and drift that are consistent with many of the empirical observations.

Fama also criticizes the methodology of many of the empirical inefficiency studies, arguing that many of the anomalies tend to disappear with changes in how security returns are measured. Kothari (2001) gives an extensive discussion of these issues, cautioning that much apparent inefficiency may instead be the result of methodological problems. Consideration and evaluation of these problems is beyond our scope here.

Studies that claim to show market inefficiencies are often disputed on the grounds that the "smart money," that is, rational investors, will step in and immediately arbitrage away any share mispricing. Defenders of behavioural finance argue that this is not necessarily the case. One argument is that rational, risk averse investors will be unsure of the extent of irrational investor behaviour, and will not be sure how long momentum and bubbles will last. As a result, they hesitate to take positions that fully eliminate mispricing. Another argument (DeLong, Shleifer, Summers, and Waldmann (1990)—see Section 6.2.4) is that rational investors may jump on the bandwagon to take advantage of momentum-driven price rises while they last. In effect, behavioural finance argues that "irrational" behaviour may persist.

There is evidence that biased investor behaviour and resultant mispricing is strongest for firms for which financial evaluation is difficult, such as firms with a large amount of unrecorded intangible assets, growth firms and, generally, firms where information asymmetry between insiders and outsiders is high. For example, Daniel and Titman (1999)—see Section 6.2.1—found greater momentum in stocks with low book-to-market ratios than in stocks with high ratios. Firms with low book-to-market ratios are likely to be growth firms, firms with unrecorded intangibles, etc. This suggests that greater use of a measurement perspective for intangible assets, such as goodwill (to be discussed in Section 7.5), has a role to play in reducing investor biases and controlling market inefficiencies. Kothari (2001) cautions, however, that studies that claim to find evidence of inefficiencies for firms in poor information environments are particularly subject to method-ological problems, since, by definition, data on such firms are less reliable.

Finally, notwithstanding the title of this section, whether securities markets are or are not efficient is really not the right question. Instead, the question is one of the *extent* of efficiency. The evidence described in Chapter 5, for example, sug-gests considerable efficiency. To the extent that markets are reasonably efficient, the rational decision theory which underlies efficiency continues to provide guid-ance to accountants about investors' decision needs. A more important question for accountants is the extent to which a measurement perspective will increase deci-sion usefulness, thereby reducing any securities market inefficiencies that exist.

We conclude that the efficient securities market model is still the most useful model to guide financial reporting, but that the theory and evidence of ineffi-ciency has accumulated to the point where it supports a measurement perspective, even though this may involve a sacrifice of some reliability for increased relevance.

6.3 OTHER REASONS SUPPORTING A MEASUREMENT PERSPECTIVE

A number of considerations come together to suggest that the decision usefulness of financial reporting may be enhanced by increased attention to measurement. As just discussed, securities markets may not be as efficient as previously believed. Thus, investors may need more help in assessing probabilities of future earnings and cash flows than they obtain from historical cost statements. Also, we shall see that reported net income explains only a small part of the variation of security prices around the date of earnings announcements, and the portion explained may be decreasing. This raises questions about the relevance of historical cost-based reporting.

From a theoretical direction, the clean surplus theory of Ohlson shows that the market value of the firm can be expressed in terms of income statement and balance sheet variables. While the clean surplus theory applies to any basis of accounting, its demonstration that firm value depends on fundamental account-ing variables is consistent with a measurement perspective.

Finally, increased attention to measurement is supported by more practical considerations. In recent years, auditors have been subjected to major lawsuits, particularly following failures of financial institutions. In retrospect, it appears that asset values of failed institutions were seriously overstated. Accounting stan-dards that require marking-to-market, ceiling tests, and other fair value-based techniques may help to reduce auditor liability in this regard.

We now review these other considerations in more detail.

6.4   THE VALUE RELEVANCE OF FINANCIAL STATEMENT INFORMATION

In Chapter 5 we saw that empirical accounting research has established that security prices do respond to the information content of net income. The ERC research, in particular, suggests that the market is quite sophisticated in its ability to extract value implications from financial statements prepared on the historical cost basis.

However, Lev (1989) pointed out that the market's response to the good or bad news in earnings is really quite small, even *after* the impact of economy-wide events has been allowed for as explained in Figure 5.1. In fact, only 2 to 5% of the abnormal variability of narrow-window security returns around the date of release of earnings information can be attributed to earnings itself.[6] The proportion of variability explained goes up somewhat for wider windows—see our discussion in Section 5.3.2. Nevertheless, most of the variability of security returns seems due to factors other than the change of earnings. This finding has led to studies of the **value relevance** of financial statement information, that is, the extent to which financial statement information affect share returns and prices.

An understanding of Lev's point requires an appreciation of the difference between **statistical significance** and **practical significance**. Statistics that measure value relevance such as R^2 (see Note 6) and the ERC can be significantly different from zero in a statistical sense, but yet can be quite small. Thus, we can be quite sure that there *is* a security market response to earnings (as opposed to *no* response) but at the same time we can be disappointed that the response is not larger than it is. To put it another way, suppose that, on average, security prices change by $1 during a narrow window of three or four days around the date of earnings announcements. Then, Lev's point is that only about two to five cents of this change is due to the earnings announcement itself, even after allowing for market-wide price changes during this period.

Indeed, value relevance seems to be deteriorating. Brown, Lo, and Lys (1999), for a large sample of U.S. stocks, conclude that R^2 has decreased over the period 1958–1996. They also examined the trend of the ERC over the same period—recall from Section 5.4.2 that the ERC is a measure of the usefulness of earnings. Brown, Lo, and Lys found that the ERC also had declined over 1958–1966. Lev and Zarowin (1999), in a study covering 1978–1996, found similar results of declining R^2 and ERC. A falling ERC is more ominous than a falling R^2, since a falling R^2 is perhaps due to an increased impact over time of other information sources on share price, rather than a decline in the value relevance of accounting information. The ERC, however, is a direct measure of accounting value relevance, regardless of the magnitude of other information sources.

Of course, we would never expect net income to explain *all* of a security's abnormal return, except under ideal conditions. The information perspective recognizes that there is always a large number of other relevant information sources and that net income lags in its recognition of much economically significant information, such as the value of intangibles. Recognition lag lowers R^2 by waiting "too long" before recognizing value-relevant events. Collins, Kothari, Shanken, and Sloan (1994) present evidence of the lack of timeliness of historical cost-based earnings.

Even if accountants were the *only* source of information to the market, our discussion of the informativeness of price in Section 4.4, and the resulting need to recognize the presence of noise and liquidity traders, tells us that accounting information cannot explain all of abnormal return variability. Also, non-stationarity of parameters such as beta (Section 6.2.3) and excess volatility introduced by non-rational investors (Section 6.2.4) further increase the amount of share price volatility to be explained.

Nevertheless, a "market share" for net income of only 2 to 5% and falling seems low, even after the above counterarguments are taken into account. Lev attributed this low share to poor earnings quality, which leads to a suggestion that earnings quality could be improved by introducing a measurement perspective into the financial statements. At the very least, evidence of low value relevance of earnings suggests that there is still plenty of room for accountants to improve the usefulness of financial statement information.

6.5   Ohlson's Clean Surplus Theory

6.5.1   THREE FORMULAE FOR FIRM VALUE

The Ohlson **clean surplus** theory provides a framework consistent with the measurement perspective, by showing how the market value of the firm can be expressed in terms of fundamental balance sheet and income statement components. The theory assumes ideal conditions in capital markets, including dividend irrelevancy.[7] Nevertheless, it has had some success in explaining and predicting actual firm value. Our outline of the theory is based on a simplified version of Feltham and Ohlson (1995) (F&O). The clean surplus theory model is also called the **residual income** model.

Much of the theory has already been included in earlier discussions, particularly Example 2.2 of P.V. Ltd. operating under ideal conditions of uncertainty. You may wish to review Example 2.2 at this time. In this section we will pull together these earlier discussions, and extend the P.V. Ltd. example to allow for earnings persistence. The F&O model can be applied to value the firm at any point in time for which financial statements are available. For purposes of illustration, we will apply it at time 1 in Example 2.2, that is, at the end of the first year of operation.

F&O begin by pointing out that the fundamental determinant of a firm's value is its dividend stream. Assume, for P.V. Ltd. in Example 2.2, that the bad-economy state was realized in year 1 and recall that P.V. pays no dividends, until a liquidating dividend at time 2. Then, the expected present value of dividends at time 1 is just the expected present value of the firm's cash on hand at time 2:

$$PA_1 = \frac{0.5}{1.10}(\$110 + \$100) + \frac{0.5}{1.10}(\$110 + \$200)$$

$$= \$95.45 + \$140.91$$

$$= \$236.36$$

Recall that cash flows per period are $100 if the bad state happens and $200 for the good state. The first term inside the brackets represents the cash on hand at time 1 invested at a return of $R_f = 0.10$ in period 2.

Given dividend irrelevancy, P.V.'s market value can also be expressed in terms of its future cash flows. Continuing our assumption that the bad state happened in period 1:

$$PA_1 = \$100 + 0.5 \times \frac{\$100}{1.10} + 0.5 \times \frac{\$200}{1.10}$$

$$= \$100 + \$136.36$$

$$= \$236.36$$

where the first term is cash on hand at time 1, that is, the present value of $100 cash is just $100.

The market value of the firm can also be expressed in terms of financial statement variables. F&O show that:

$$PA_t = bv_t + g_t \tag{6.1}$$

at any time t, where bv_t is the net book value of the firm's assets per the balance sheet and g_t is the expected present value of future abnormal earnings, also called **goodwill**. For this relationship to hold it is necessary that all items of gain or loss go through the income statement, which is the source of the term "clean surplus" in the theory.

To evaluate goodwill for P.V. Ltd. as at time t = 1, we look ahead over the remainder of the firm's life (1 year in our example).[8] Recall that **abnormal earnings** are the difference between actual and expected earnings. Using F&O's notation, define ox_2 as earnings for year 2 and ox_2^a as abnormal earnings for that year.[9] From Example 2.2, we have:

If the bad state happens for year 2, net income for year 2 is

$$(100 \times 0.10) + 100 - 136.36 = -\$26.36,$$

where the first bracketed expression is interest earned on opening cash. If the good state happens, net income is

$$10 + 200 - 136.36 = \$73.64$$

Since each state is equally likely, expected net income for year 2 is

$$E\{ox_2\} = 0.5 \times -26.36 + 0.5 \times 73.64 = \$23.64$$

Expected abnormal earnings for year 2, the difference between expected earnings as just calculated and accretion of discount on opening book value, is thus

$$E\{ox_2{}^a\} = 23.64 - .10 \times 236.36 = \$0$$

Goodwill, the expected present value of future abnormal earnings, is then

$$g_1 = 0/1.10 = 0$$

Thus, for P.V. Ltd. in Example 2.2 with no persistence of abnormal earnings, goodwill is zero. This is because, under ideal conditions, arbitrage ensures that the firm expects to earn only the given the interest rate on the opening value of its net assets. As a result, we can read firm value directly from the balance sheet:

$$\begin{aligned} PA_1 &= \$236.36 + \$0 \\ &= \$236.36 \end{aligned}$$

Zero goodwill represents a special case of the F&O model called **unbiased accounting,** that is, all assets and liabilities are valued at fair value. When accounting is unbiased, and abnormal earnings do not persist, all of firm value appears on the balance sheet. In effect, the income statement has no information content, as we noted in Example 2.2.

Unbiased accounting represents the extreme of the measurement perspective. Of course, as a practical matter, firms do not account for all assets and liabilities this way. For example, if P.V. Ltd. uses historical cost accounting for its capital asset, bv_1 may be biased downwards relative to fair value. F&O call this **biased accounting.** When accounting is biased, the firm has *unrecorded* goodwill g_t. However, the clean surplus formula (6.1) for PA_t holds for any basis of accounting, not just unbiased accounting under ideal conditions. To illustrate, suppose that P.V. Ltd. uses straight line amortization for its capital asset, writing off

$130.17 in year 1 and $130.16 in year 2. Note that year 1 present value-based amortization in Example 2.2 is $123.97. Thus, with straight line amortization, earnings for year 1 and capital assets as at the end of year 1 are biased downwards relative to their ideal conditions counterparts. We now repeat the calculation of goodwill and firm value as at the end of year 1, continuing the assumption of bad state realization for year 1.

With straight line amortization, expected net income for year 2 is:

$$E\{ox_2\} = (100 \times .10) + 0.5(100 - 130.16) + 0.5(200 - 130.16) = \$29.84$$

Expected abnormal earnings for year 2 is:

$$E\{ox_2^a\} = 29.84 - .10 \times 230.16 = \$6.82,$$

where $230.16 is the firm's book value at time 1, being $100 cash plus the capital asset book value on a straight line basis of $130.16.

Goodwill is then

$$g_1 = 6.82/1.10 = \$6.20,$$

giving firm market value of

$$\begin{aligned} PA_1 &= 230.16 + 6.20 \\ &= \$236.36, \end{aligned}$$

the same as the unbiased accounting case.

While firm value is the same, the goodwill of $6.20 is unrecorded on the firm's books. This again illustrates the point made in Section 2.5.1 that under historical cost accounting net income lags real economic performance. Here, historical cost-based net income for year 1 is $100 − $130.17 = −$30.17, less than net income of −$23.97 in Example 2.2. Nevertheless, if unrecorded goodwill is correctly valued, the resulting firm value is also correct.

This ability of the F&O model to generate the same firm value regardless of the accounting policies used by the firm has an upside and a downside. On the upside, an investor who may wish to use the model to predict firm value does not have to be concerned about the firm's choice of accounting policies. If the firm manager biases reported net income upwards to improve apparent performance, or biases net income downwards by means of a major asset writedown, the firm value as calculated by the model is the same.[10] The reason is that changes in unrecorded goodwill induced by accounting policy choice are offset by equal but opposite changes in book values. The downside, however, is that the model can provide no guidance as to what accounting policies *should* be used.

We now see the sense in which the Ohlson clean surplus theory supports the measurement perspective. Fair value accounting for P.V.'s assets reduces the extent of biased accounting. In doing so, it moves more of the value of the firm onto the balance sheet, thereby reducing the amount of unrecorded goodwill that the investor has to estimate. While the sum of book value and unrecorded goodwill is the same in theory, whether or not the firm uses fair value accounting; in practice the firm can presumably prepare a more accurate estimate of fair value than can the investor. If so, and if the estimate is reasonably reliable, decision usefulness of the financial statements is increased, since a greater proportion of firm value can simply be read from the balance sheet. This is particularly so for investors who may not be fully rational, and who may need more help in determining firm value than they receive under the information perspective.

6.5.2 EARNINGS PERSISTENCE

F&O then introduce the important concept of *earnings persistence* into the theory. Specifically, they assume that operating earnings are generated according to the following formula:

$$\text{ox}_t^{\,a} = \omega \text{ox}_{t-1}^{\,a} + \upsilon_{t-1} + \widetilde{\epsilon}_t \tag{6.2}$$

F&O call this formula an **earnings dynamic**. The $\widetilde{\epsilon}_t$ are the effects of state realization in period t on abnormal earnings, where the "~" indicates that these effects are random, as at the beginning of the period. As in Example 2.2, the expected value of state realization is zero and realizations are independent from one period to the next.

The ω is a persistence parameter, where $0 \leq \omega < 1$. For $\omega = 0$, we have the case of Example 2.2, that is, abnormal earnings do not persist. However, $\omega > 0$ is not unreasonable. Often, the effects of state realization in one year will persist into future years. For example, the bad-state realization in year 1 of Example 2.2 may be because of a rise in interest rates, the economic effects of which will likely persist beyond the current year. Then, ω captures the proportion of the $50 abnormal earnings in year 1 that would continue into the following year.

However, note that $\omega < 1$ in the F&O model. That is, abnormal earnings of any particular year will die out over time. For example, the effects of a rise in interest rates will eventually dissipate. More generally, forces of competition will eventually eliminate positive, or negative, abnormal earnings, at a rate that ultimately depends on the firm's business strategy.

Note also that persistence is related to its empirical counterpart in the ERC research. Recall from Section 5.4.1 that ERCs are higher the greater the persistence in earnings. As we will see in Example 6.1 below, this is exactly what clean surplus theory predicts—the higher ω is, the greater the impact of the income statement on firm value.

The term v_{t-1} represents the effect of other information becoming known in year $t - 1$ (i.e., other than the information in year t-1's abnormal earnings) that affects the abnormal earnings of year t. When accounting is unbiased, $v_{t-1} = 0$. To see this, consider the case of R&D. If R&D was accounted for on a fair value basis (i.e., unbiased accounting) then year t-1's abnormal earnings includes the change in value brought about by R&D activities during that year. Of this change in value, the proportion ω will continue into next year's earnings. That is, if R&D is valued at fair value, there is no relevant other information about future earnings from R&D—current earnings includes it all.

When accounting is biased, v_{t-1} assumes a much more important role. Thus, if R&D costs are written off as incurred, as is the case under current GAAP, year $t - 1$'s abnormal earnings contain no information about future abnormal earnings from R&D activities. As a result, to predict year t's abnormal earnings it is necessary to add in as other information an outside estimate of the abnormal earnings in year t that will result from the R&D activities of year $t - 1$. That is, v_{t-1} represents next period's earnings from year $t - 1$'s R&D.

In sum, the earnings dynamic models current year's abnormal earnings as a proportion ω of the previous year's abnormal earnings, plus the effects of other information (if accounting is biased), plus the effects of random state realization.

Finally, note that the theory assumes that the set of possible values of $\tilde{\epsilon}_t$ and their probabilities are known to investors, consistent with ideal conditions. It is also assumed that investors know ω. If these assumptions are relaxed, rational investors will want information about $\tilde{\epsilon}_t$ and ω and can use Bayes' theorem to update their subjective state probabilities. Thus, nothing in the theory conflicts with the role of decision theory that was explained in Chapter 3.

EXAMPLE 6.1   PRESENT VALUE MODEL UNDER UNCERTAINTY AND PERSISTENCE

We now extend Example 2.2 to allow for persistence. Continue all the assumptions of that example and add the further assumption $\omega = 0.40$. Since we assume ideal conditions, $v_{t-1} = 0$. Recall that abnormal earnings for year 1 are −$50 or $50, depending on whether the bad state or good state happens. Now, 40% of year 1 abnormal earnings will persist to affect operating earnings in year 2.

We begin with the amortization schedule for P.V.'s capital asset, based on the expected decline in the asset's present value as at time 0. This amortization schedule is the same as in Example 2.2, that is:

```
Amortization, year 1 = $260.33 − $136.36 = $123.97
Amortization, year 2 = $136.36 − 0       = $136.36
                                            $260.33
```

Now, assume that the bad state happens in year 1. (A similar analysis applies if the good state happens.) Then, we calculate P.V.'s market value at time 1. We begin with the formula based on expected future dividends.

$$PA_1 = \frac{0.5}{1.10}(\$110 - 0.40 \times \$50 + \$100) + \frac{0.5}{1.10}(\$110 - 0.40 \times \$50 + \$200)$$

$$= \frac{0.5}{1.10} \times \$190 + \frac{0.5}{1.10} \times \$290$$

$$= \$86.36 + \$131.82$$

$$= \$218.18$$

Note the effect of persistence—40% of year 1 abnormal earnings will persist to reduce year 2 cash flows. Otherwise, the calculation is identical with Example 2.2. We see that the effect of persistence of the bad state is to reduce the time 1 firm value by $236.36 - 218.18 = \$18.18$, the present value of the \$20 of reduced future cash flows.

Now, moving from the dividends formula to the clean surplus formula for firm value (6.1), F&O use the earnings dynamic equation (6.2) to show that that the firm's goodwill g_t can be expressed in terms of the current year's abnormal earnings, giving a market value of:

$$PA_t = bv_t + \alpha \times ox_t^a \tag{6.3}$$

where $\alpha = \omega/(1 + R_f)$ is a capitalization factor.[11] Note, as mentioned above, that the higher is the persistence parameter ω the higher is the impact of current earnings information on share price PA_t. In our example, for $t = 1$:

Cash on hand	= \$100.00
Book value of asset, based on amortization schedule, $\$260.33 - \$123.97$	= $\underline{\$136.36}$
bv_t	= $\underline{\$236.36}$

This gives:

$$PA_t = bv_t + \alpha \times ox_t^a$$

$$= \$236.36 + \frac{0.40}{1.10} \times -\$50$$

$$= \$236.36 - \$18.18$$

$$= \$218.18$$

which agrees with the market value based on expected future dividends.

The implications of the F&O model with persistence are twofold. First, even under ideal conditions, *all the action is no longer on the balance sheet*. The income statement is important too, because it reveals the current year's abnormal earnings, 40% of which will persist into future periods. Thus, we can regard abnormal earnings as 40% persistent in this example.

Second, the formula (6.2) implies that investors will want information to help them assess persistent earnings, since these are important to the future performance of the firm. Our discussion of extraordinary items in Section 5.5 showed how accountants can help in this regard by appropriate classification of items with low persistence. Also, the formula is consistent with the empirical impact of persistence on the ERC as outlined in Section 5.4.1, where we saw that greater persistence is associated with stronger investor reaction to current earnings.[12]

6.5.3   *ESTIMATING FIRM VALUE*

The F&O model can be used to estimate the value of a firm's shares. This can then be compared to the actual market value, to indicate possible over- or under-valuation by the market, and to aid in investment decisions. The following example applies the model to Bombardier Inc. The methodology used in this example is based on the procedures outlined in Lee (1996).

EXAMPLE 6.2   ESTIMATING THE VALUE OF COMMON SHARES OF BOMBARDIER INC.

From Bombardier's 2001 annual report (not reproduced here), we take 2001 net income (NI_{2001}) as $988.6, before unusual items and after preferred share dividends (all dollar figures are in millions), its book value as $3,512.4 at January 31, 2001 and $3,311.8 at January 31, 2000. (both after deducting preferred shares). This gives Bombardier's 2001 return on opening equity (ROE_{2001}) as .300. Somewhat arbitrarily, we assume that this return will continue for the next seven years, after which return will equal Bombardier's cost of capital. This assumption implies a persistence parameter of $\omega = 1$ for seven years. We will return to this assumption shortly.

Common dividends totalled $186.3 for 2001, giving a dividend payout ratio of 186.3/988.6 = .188. We assume that this ratio will also continue for seven years.

To estimate Bombardier's cost of capital, we use the CAPM (Section 4.5):

$$E(R_{jt}) = R_f(1 - \beta_j) + \beta_j E(R_{Mt}),$$

where firm j is Bombardier and t is January 31, 2001. We take the risk-free rate of interest as $R_f = .04$, and $E(R_{Mt})$, somewhat arbitrarily, as .10.

Bombardier's equity β was obtained from Globeinvestor.com as about .80. Then, our estimate of the firm's cost of equity capital is:

$$E(R_{jt}) = .04(1 - .8) + .80 \times .10$$

$$= .09$$

We assume that this 9% cost of capital will stay constant.

Next, we evaluate Bombardier's unrecorded goodwill. As stated earlier, goodwill is the present value of expected future abnormal earnings, which we evaluate over a seven-year horizon from January 2001. First, we use the clean surplus relation to project end-of-year book values:

$$bv_{2002} = bv_{2001} + NI_{2002} - d_{2003}$$

where d is dividends. Using the relationship $d_t = kNI_t$, where k is the dividend payout ratio, this becomes:

$$bv_{2002} = bv_{2001} + (1 - k)NI_{2002}$$

$$= bv_{2001} [1 + (1 - k)ROE]$$

$$= 3512.4 (1 + .812 \times .3)$$

$$= \$4,369$$

Similar calculations give:

$$bv_{2003} = \$5,435$$

$$bv_{2004} = \$6,761$$

$$bv_{2005} = \$8,411$$

$$bv_{2006} = \$10,463$$

$$bv_{2007} = \$13,016$$

Now abnormal earnings are defined as the difference between expected and actual earnings. We take expected earnings as cost of capital times opening book value. Actual earnings for a given year are projected as ROE times opening book value. Thus expected abnormal earnings for 2002 are:

$$ox^a_{2002} = [ROE - E(R_j)]bv_{2001}$$

$$= (.30 - .09)3,512.4$$

$$= \$737.6$$

Similar calculations give:

$$ox^a_{2003} = \$917.5$$

$$ox^a_{2004} = \$1,141.4$$

$$ox^a_{2005} = \$1,419.8$$

$$ox^a_{2006} = \$1,766.3$$

$$ox^a_{2007} = \$2,197.2$$

$$ox^a_{2008} = \$2,733.4$$

The present value of these abnormal earnings, that is, goodwill, at January 31, 2001, discounted at Bombardier's cost of capital, is

$$g_{2001} = \frac{737.6}{1.09} + \frac{917.5}{1.09^2} + \frac{1,141.4}{1.09^3} + \frac{1,419.8}{1.09^4} + \frac{1,766.3}{1.09^5} + \frac{2,197.2}{1.09^6} + \frac{2,733.4}{1.09^7}$$

$$= \$7,289.5$$

Finally, we add in January 31, 2001 book value (i.e., bv_{2001}):

$$PA_{2001} = 3,512.4 + 7,289.5$$

$$= \$10,801.9$$

Bombardier had 1,366.051 million common shares outstanding[13] as at January 31, 2001, giving an estimated value per share of $7.91.

Bombardier's actual share price around the middle of March, 2001, which we take as the date that the market became aware of the contents of the financial statements[14] was approximately $20, over twice the amount of our estimate! While one could adjust estimates of the risk-free interest rate, dividend payout ratio and cost of capital, reasonable changes to these estimates would not affect the calculation significantly.

Our estimate of abnormal earnings is more problematic. In effect, we have ignored abnormal earnings beyond seven years. If we were to extend the number of years, this would increase the estimated share value in our example. For example, an assumption that ROE of 30% will continue for 10 and 12 years raises estimated share value to $14.68 and $19.45, respectively. However, it is not clear that this should be done. Note that earnings at the rate of cost of capital (i.e., ROE = $E(R_j)$) have zero effect on PA_{2001}. Thus, in effect, we have assumed that Bombardier earns .30 ROE for seven years and .09 thereafter. As mentioned above, competitive pressures operate to eliminate abnormal earnings over time. Nevertheless, it appears that the market's expectation of Bombardier's future earning power is substantially higher than we can justify. In this regard, it should be noted that on October 31, 2001, Bombardier shares traded as low as $9.19, closing at $10.30. This is still somewhat higher than our estimate of $7.91, however.

Despite discrepancies such as this between estimated and actual share value, the F&O model can be useful for investment decision making. To see how, suppose that you carry out a similar analysis for another firm—call it Firm X—and obtain an estimated share value of $5. Which firm would you sooner invest in if they were both trading at $20? Bombardier may be the better choice, since it has a higher ratio of model value to share value. That is, more of its share value is "backed up" by book value and expected abnormal earnings. Indeed, Frankel and Lee (1998), who applied the methodology of Example 6.2 to a large sample of U.S. firms during 1977–1992, found that the ratio of estimated market value to actual market value was a good predictor of share returns for two to three years into the future. Thus, for the years following 2001, Frankel and Lee's results suggest that Bombardier's share return should outperform that of Firm X.

Nevertheless, the discrepancy between estimated and actual share price in Example 6.2 seems rather large. One possibility is that Bombardier's shares are affected by the momentum and bubble behaviour described in Sections 6.2.1 and 6.2.5. Indeed, Dechow, Hutton, and Sloan (1999) (DHS), in a large sample of U.S. firms over the period 1976–1995, present tentative evidence that investors may not fully anticipate the extent to which abnormal earnings decline over time. This evidence supports our refusal above to extend the period of abnormal earnings beyond seven years.

Another possibility, however, is that our estimate did not fully use all available information. DHS also report that estimates of firm value based on the F&O model that ignored other information were too low, consistent with our results for Bombardier. This brings us back to the v_{t-1} term in the earnings dynamic (6.2). Recall that this term represents additional information in year $t-1$, beyond that contained in ox_{t-1}^a, that affects earnings in year t, and that it is non-zero when accounting is biased. Biased accounting is certainly the case. For example, Bombardier deducted R&D expenses of $123.4 millions in 2001. As you know, under GAAP, most R&D costs are written off in the year they are incurred, even though they may have significant impact on future earnings. To the extent that R&D will increase *future* earnings, we may wish to increase our projected ROE above 30% by adding back to reported earnings all or part of 2001 R&D expense.[15] This would increase our estimate of share value. However, as a practical matter, estimating the future value of R&D is difficult, and we are reluctant to do this here.

Another source of additional information is analysts' forecasts of earnings. Analysts will consider additional information in preparing their forecasts, not just the information from current earnings as we did for Bombardier. If we had taken analysts' earnings forecasts into account in our estimates of future periods' earnings, this may have improved our estimate of share price. Bombardier's earnings per common share for 2001 were $0.70, and, from Globeinvestor.com in mid-July, 2001, the average analyst forecast of Bombardier's earnings per share for 2002 and 2003 are $0.90 and $1.14, respectively. Thus analysts are forecasting an increase in earnings per share of 28.57% for 2002 and 26.67% for 2003, greater than the (ROE $\times$ (1 − k) =) 24.36% increase implicit in Example 6.2. This suggests that we may wish to increase our estimate of Bombardier's future profitability beyond 30% ROE. Supporting this suggestion, DHS report that undervaluations of share price were reduced (but not eliminated) in their sample when analysts' forecasts were included in their predictions. Nevertheless, in view of the possibility of analyst optimistic bias pointed out in Section 5.4.3, we are hesitant to increase our estimate further.

We conclude that while our procedure to estimate Bombardier's share price is on the right track, it may not have fully exploited all the financial statement and analyst information that is available. This leads to an examination of empirical studies of the ability of the clean surplus approach to predict earnings and share price.

6.5.4   EMPIRICAL STUDIES OF THE CLEAN SURPLUS MODEL

Clean surplus theory has generated much empirical research. One aspect of this research compares the relative predictive ability of the dividend, cash flow and residual income models. Recall from Section 6.5.1 that under ideal conditions all three models produce identical valuations. However, when conditions are not ideal, the model that produces the best predictions is an empirical matter. For example, it is often argued that the clean surplus model has an advantage because it uses balance sheet information and, as a result, has to project only abnormal or residual income. Cash flow and dividend models must predict total future flows. Thus, the clean surplus model has "less" to predict and is thereby less subject to error. It is also argued that the clean surplus model is more convenient to apply than the cash flow model. It uses readily-available financial statement information and does not have to back cash flows out of accrual accounting-based reports.

A major practical problem in applying all three models is the choice of forecast horizon, and what value, if any, to assign to flows beyond the horizon (called the terminal value problem). Our Bombardier estimate used a forecast horizon of seven years, with a terminal value of zero on the grounds that competitive pressures are expected to eliminate abnormal returns beyond that time. Of course, this zero terminal value assumption is rather arbitrary. Perhaps a better (but still arbitrary) assumption is that Bombardier's abnormal earnings would not fall to zero, but rather start to decline after seven years. Then, terminal value is greater than zero, which would increase our value estimate.

An alternative assumption is to base terminal value on analysts' long-range forecasts. In this regard, Courteau, Kao, and Richardson (2001), for a sample of U.S. firms over the period 1992–1996, studied the relative predictive ability of the three models, using analyst's predictions of earnings in place of predictions from the earnings dynamic equation (6.2), and a five-year forecast horizon. They found that predictions using arbitrary terminal value assumptions, as we did for Bombardier, substantially underestimated share market prices. When terminal values were based on analyst's long-range forecasts, predictions were much more accurate. Furthermore, the three models were then roughly equal in their forecasting ability, consistent with our theoretical expectation.

A second type of empirical clean surplus research studies the prediction of future earnings, since future earnings are a main input into the goodwill estimate. In particular, this research examines how other information can improve earnings and share price predictions. This represents a significant change in emphasis from research under the information perspective, which studies the association between financial statement information and share returns. As an example of this change in emphasis, consider the study of Abarbanell and Bushee (1997). In an extension of the approach used by Ou and Penman (1989) (Section 6.2.6) and Lev and Thiagarajan (1993) (Section 5.4.1), they showed how certain "fundamental signals" from the current financial statements, such as changes in sales, accounts receivable, inventories, gross margin, and capital expenditure could improve the prediction of next year's earnings changes. They went on to show that analysts appeared to underuse the fundamental signals when predicting earnings, suggesting that their earnings forecasts would benefit from greater attention to the full information potential of financial statements. Myers (1999) adds order backlog as other information in the earnings dynamic, but finds this does not remove a tendency for under-prediction of firm value by the clean surplus model. Begley and Feltham (2002) add analysts' forecasts and current capital expenditures as other information. They find that these variables significantly improve prediction of unrecorded goodwill for their sample firms. Overall, these results suggest considerable promise for the usefulness of financial statement information, beyond the information in current earnings, in improving earnings and share price predictions.

A third type of research relates to the earnings dynamic itself. Instead of using the earnings dynamic to predict abnormal earnings, why not simply use analysts' earnings forecasts? These are readily available for up to five years ahead. Furthermore, despite the results of Abarbanell and Bushee (1997), outlined above, that analysts appear to underuse fundamental signals, they presumably use a large amount of other information, in addition to current earnings, when preparing their forecasts. As a result, the investor can be less concerned about what other information should be added in the earnings dynamic. Dechow, Hutton, and Sloan (1999), in their evaluation of different earnings prediction models, found that a simple projection of abnormal earnings based on analysts' one-year ahead earnings forecasts predicted share price as well as a full application of the earnings dynamic equation (6.2). Also, the study of Courteau, Kao, and Richardson (2001) referred to above uses analyst forecasts throughout. It seems clear that the question of the best earnings prediction model, and the extent to which accounting information is useful in this process, is unsettled.

Finally, another use of the theory is to estimate a firm's cost of capital. In Example 6.2, note that any four of the five variables—share price, book value, expected future earnings, risk-free interest rate, and cost of capital—can be used, in principle, to solve for the other one. This approach was used by Botosan (1997). In a study to be discussed in Section 12.3, Botosan used the clean surplus model to estimate the costs of capital of the firms in her sample, and then went on to demonstrate conditions under which high quality financial statement disclosure lowered cost of capital. Thus, the clean surplus model provides an alternative to the CAPM for cost of capital estimation.

6.5.5   SUMMARY

Clean surplus theory has had a major impact on financial accounting theory and research. By demonstrating that firm value can equally well be expressed in terms of financial accounting variables as in terms of dividends or cash flows, it has led to increased research attention to earnings prediction. Much of this research explores how current financial statement information can be used to improve this prediction. Better earnings prediction enables better estimates of unrecorded goodwill, leading to better predictions of firm value and hence better investment decisions.

The theory also leads to a measurement perspective, since the more fair values are reported on the balance sheet the less the proportion of firm value included in unrecorded goodwill, hence the less the potential for investor mistakes in estimating this complex component of firm value. This can improve investor decision making and proper securities market operation, particularly if securities markets are not as fully efficient as once believed.

6.6   *Auditors' Legal Liability*

Perhaps the main source of pressure in favour of the measurement perspective, however, comes as a reaction to spectacular failures of large firms, particularly financial institutions. Many such failures have taken place in the United States. For example, an article in *The Wall Street Journal* (March 11, 1994, p. A2) reported that Resolution Trust Corp. had lawsuits against the audit firm of Deloitte and Touche totalling $1.4 billion, and the Federal Deposit Insurance Corp. had lawsuits of another $450 million. The charges arose from alleged clean audit opinions issued to savings and loan associations that, in retrospect, were insolvent. The article describes a proposed settlement of these lawsuits in excess of $300 million. While considerably less than the amounts at suit, this would still be the second-largest liability settlement surrounding the savings and loan debacle. (The largest was a $400-million settlement by Ernst and Young for similar charges.)

Under historical cost accounting, it can happen that firms that are here today, in the sense that their balance sheets and income statements show them to be going concerns, are gone tomorrow. While accountants and auditors may claim that information about impending failure was implicit in the notes or other sources, or was not their responsibility, there is a certain logic to questions raised by those who ask why the financial statements proper did not more clearly foretell the disaster. Auditors often have considerable difficulty in defending themselves from the lawsuits that usually accompany business failure.

Furthermore, these legal liability pressures are likely to continue to increase. For example, Jensen (1993) points out that as technology advances, more and more firms are finding themselves with substantial excess capacity. The resulting need to downsize leads to mergers and acquisitions, reorganizations, layoffs, or bankruptcy. All of these events put severe pressure on the adequacy of historical-cost-based net income and asset valuation.

In addition, firms are facing increasing pressures to behave in socially and environmentally responsible ways. Many firms face substantial future liabilities in this regard, for example in site restoration costs, which severely strain the concept of matching costs and revenues.

One way that accountants and auditors can protect themselves against these pressures is to adopt a measurement perspective, that is, introduce more fair values into the accounts. Then, they can point out that the financial statements *anticipated* the value changes leading to bankruptcy, merger, downsizing, environmental liabilities, etc. Of course, this requires greater use of estimates and judgement but, because of legal liability, accountants may be more willing to adopt at least those fair valuations that can be attained without substantial loss of reliability.

6.7   Conclusions

Recall that the information perspective on financial reporting is content to accept the historical cost basis of accounting, and rely on full disclosure to enhance usefulness to investors. The form of disclosure does not matter, since it is assumed that there are enough rational, informed investors to quickly and correctly incorporate any reasonable form into the efficient market price. Empirical research has confirmed that the market finds net income information at least to be useful. In effect, empirical research under the information perspective tends to accept the efficient market price and to evaluate the usefulness of accounting information in terms of its association with this market price.

However, there are a number of questions about the information perspective. First, securities markets may not be as fully efficient as had previously been believed, suggesting that investors might need some help in figuring out the full implications of accounting information for future returns. Second, a "market share" of 2 to 5% for net income seems low and, despite theoretical support, it has been difficult to find much direct market reaction at all to non-earnings accounting information. In addition, legal liability may force accountants to increase the use of fair values in the financial statements. These questions are reinforced by the development of the Ohlson clean surplus theory, which emphasizes the fundamental role of financial accounting information in determining firm value. This theory implies a more basic role for financial statements in reporting on firm value than the information perspective, which views accounting information as one of many information sources competing for the attention of the efficient market. Thus, the clean surplus theory leads naturally to the measurement perspective.

Of course, for reasons of reliability, the measurement perspective would never extend to a complete set of financial statements on a fair value basis. Historical cost is unlikely to be displaced as the primary accounting basis for capital assets, for example. Rather, the question is one of degree—to what degree will fair values supplant costs in useful financial reporting? Consequently, in the next chapter we review GAAP from a valuation perspective. There always has been a substantial present value and market value component to the financial statements. But, as we shall see, recent years have witnessed a number of new fair value standards.

Questions and Problems

1. Why does a measurement perspective on decision usefulness suggest more value-relevant information in the financial statements proper, when efficient securities market theory implies that financial statement notes or other disclosure would be just as useful?

2. What will be the impact on relevance, reliability and decision usefulness of financial statement information as accountants adopt the measurement perspective?

3. Explain what "post-announcement drift" is. Why is this an anomaly for securities market efficiency?

4. An investor considers two mutual funds. Based on past experience, the first fund has expected return of .08 and standard deviation of .05. The second fund has expected return of .07 and standard deviation of .06. There is no reason to assume that future performance of these funds will differ from past performance. However, the second fund has a guarantee attached that return in any year will not be negative.

    The investor buys the second fund. Use prospect theory to explain why.

5. Lev, in his article "On the Usefulness of Earnings" (1989), points out the low ability of reported net income to explain variations in security prices around the date of release of earnings information. Lev attributes this low explanatory power to low earnings quality.

    Required

    a. Define earnings quality. Relate your answer to the concept of an information system in single-person decision theory.

b. What other reasons might there be for the low explanatory power of earnings?

c. How might an increased measurement perspective in financial statements increase earnings quality, and hence the impact of earnings on security prices?

6. In Section 6.4, The concept of *value relevance* of net income is introduced. It appears that the value relevance of reported earnings, as measured by R^2 or ERC, is low, and falling over time. Use single person decision theory to explain why value relevance of reported earnings can be measured by R^2 or ERC.

7. On January 26, 1995, *The Wall Street Journal* reported that Compaq Computer Corp. posted record 1994 fourth-quarter results. Despite $20.5 million in losses from the December, 1993, Mexican currency devaluation, and losses on currency hedging, earnings grew to $0.90 per share from $0.58 in the same quarter of 1993, on a revenue growth of 48%. Furthermore, Compaq captured the No. 1 market share spot, with shipments up 50% from 1993 and with slightly higher profit margin.

Nevertheless, on the same day, Compaq's share price fell by $5.00, a decline of about 12%. The *Journal* reported that analysts had been expecting earnings of about $0.95 per share. Also, there were concerns about Compaq's scheduled introduction of new products in March 1995, following a warning by Compaq's CEO Eckhard Feiffer that first-quarter, 1995 earnings were likely to be "flat."

Required

a. Use single-person decision theory and efficient securities market theory to explain why the market price fell.

b. Assume that the $20.5 million in losses from peso devaluation and currency hedging are a *provision*, not a realized cash loss, at the end of the fourth quarter (i.e., an *accrual*). Use the anomalous securities market results of Sloan (1996) to explain why the market price fell.

c. The *Journal* quoted an analyst as stating "the market overreacted." Use prospect theory to explain why the market might overreact to less-than-expected earnings news.

d. Which of the above three explanations for the fall in Compaq's share price do you find most reasonable? Explain.

8. For what reasons might transactions costs, including investors' time to figure out and operate strategies that appear to beat the market, not be a completely adequate explanation for the apparent efficient securities market anomalies?

9. Reproduced on page 208 is the Economic Value Added (EVA) disclosure from the MD&A section of the 1996 annual report of Domtar, Inc. Some of the uses of EVA are outlined in Domtar's discussion in the disclosure. Of interest here is the close relationship between the EVA measurement formula and the clean surplus-based valuation procedure outlined in Example 6.2. Note that the EVA

for a given year is equivalent to abnormal earnings (ox_t^a) for that year in our example. Recall that goodwill is calculated as the present value of expected future abnormal earnings.

ECONOMIC VALUE ADDED (EVA)

At the end of 1995, the Corporation adopted a new management system known as Economic Value Added, or EVA®, to ensure that the decision-making process at Domtar is aligned with the objective of increasing shareholder value.

In 1996, this concept was implemented throughout the Corporation and is being used for measuring performance, evaluating investment decisions, improving communication and for incentive compensation. EVA® training courses were developed and are being provided to a large number of employees in on-going efforts to develop a value creation culture at Domtar.

The EVA® measurement formula is as follows:

$$EVA^® = NOPAT^1 - \text{Capital Charge}^2$$

[1] Net operating profit after tax

[2] Capital employed × Cost of capital for the Corporation

This simple formula highlights the notion that in order to create value for Domtar shareholders, every business unit must generate returns at least equal to its cost of capital, including both debt and shareholders' equity.

Following a record year in 1995 when $316 million of EVA® was created, EVA® for Domtar in 1996 was $120 million negative, due to the decline in selling prices.

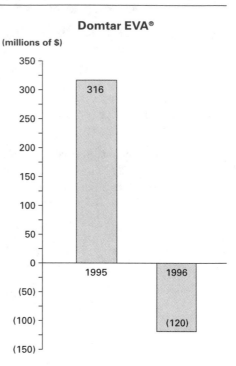

Domtar EVA®

(millions of $)

EVA®	=	NOPAT	−	Capital Charge
1995	316 =	539	−	223
1996	(120) =	88	−	208

Domtar remains committed to creating long-term shareholder value and will intensify its efforts in 1997, especially in areas under its control, such as productivity, costs, customer service and capital management. Domtar will also benefit from an overall lower cost of capital going forward as a result of its debt management program completed in 1996.

Required

a. Evaluate the usefulness of this approach to communicating information to investors. Consider both relevance and reliability issues.

b. If you were the top manager of a company using EVA, would its use encourage or discourage you from initiating major, capital intensive expansion projects? Explain why or why not.

c. You are an investor in a fast-growing, high-tech company that reports EVA. The assets of the company are primarily intangible (patents, skilled workforce), hence not included in the EVA capital charge. How would the largely intangible nature of the assets of such a company affect your interpretation of its EVA? Explain.

d. Note that reporting of EVA is voluntary. Domtar reports this information for 1996 even though its EVA is negative. Does Domtar's willingness to report this information add credibility to its claim that it "will intensify its efforts in 1997?" Explain.

10. Recent years have seen considerable litigation against auditors in the United States, despite changes to litigation laws in 1995 that made it more difficult for investors to sue auditors.

A major source of this litigation arises from the pressure firms feel to meet analysts' earnings expectations. To avoid reporting lower-than-expected earnings, firms sometimes use earnings management, such as premature revenue recognition and other devices, to raise reported net income. To avoid a qualified audit report, the firm may pressure its auditor to "stretch" GAAP. This puts the auditor in a difficult position. If the auditor goes along, he or she will inevitably be drawn into lawsuits when the earnings management becomes known (as it eventually must, since accruals reverse).

For example, Waste Management Inc. overstated its earnings during a five-year period in the 1990s, using a variety of earnings management devices such as lengthening the useful life of capital assets, increasing their estimated salvage value, and understating liabilities for rehabilitating contaminated waste disposal sites. In December, 1998, Waste Management's auditor, Arthur Andersen, offered $220 millions to settle class action lawsuits following revelation of these practices.

One can sympathize with company managers for wanting to meet earnings expectations. The market will severely penalize their stock price if they do not. For example, in 1997, Eastman Kodak announced that revenue would not meet expectations due to the high value of the U.S. dollar, and analysts reduced their estimate of first quarter, 1997, earnings from $0.90 per share to $0.80. Kodak's share price fell by $9.25 to $79 in heavy trading. Subsequently, Kodak reported earnings per share for the quarter of $0.81, and share price rose $2.25 to $75.37.

This market reaction has been repeated many times since. An article in *The Wall Street Journal* in April, 2000 quoted a principal of Bogle Investment Management as saying that the market is "overdiscounting" changes in earnings expectations and that it is "reacting too much."

Required

a. Why might an auditor be tempted to "cave in" to client pressure to manage reported earnings so as to meet analysts' expectations?

b. To what extent would increased use of a measurement perspective in financial reporting reduce auditor exposure to client pressure and lawsuits?

c. Use concepts from behavioural finance to explain why the market may "overreact" to changes in earnings expectations.

d. Is the $9.25 reduction in Kodak's share price reported above inconsistent with efficient securities market theory? Explain why or why not.

Notes

1. It should be noted that Daniel and Titman's investment strategy used hindsight to pick stocks with high and low momentum. The strategy would not be implementable in real time.

2. In mathematical terms, the utility function is continuous but not differentiable at zero.

3. Non-stationarity provides an alternative to noise trading, discussed in Section 4.4.1, for the non-collapse of share prices on an efficient market. When share price parameters, such as beta, are non-stationary, investors will have differing opinions as to whether current share prices reflect their current beta values, and will trade on the basis of these opinions.

4. For example, firms' betas may shift when they announce good or bad earnings news. If the beta shifts were positive for GN firms and negative for BN, this could explain post-announcement drift as simply an artifact of the higher (for GN firms) and lower (for BN) returns that investors would demand to compensate for the changes in risk, since, as discussed in Sections 3.4, 3.5, and 3.6,

investors trade off risk and return. While BT present evidence that, following earnings announcements, betas do shift in the manner described above, the magnitude of the shifts is much smaller than what would be required to explain the magnitude of the post-announcement drift.

5. Suppose that transactions costs were 5% of the amount invested. Then, if it was possible to gross 5% by a strategy of buying GN firms and selling short BN firms, transactions costs would consume the 5% profit, so investors would not bother. Thus, what might appear to be a profitable investment strategy may merely reflect the level of transactions costs required to earn those profits.

6. The proportion of variability is measured by the R^2 statistic from the regression of abnormal security returns on unexpected earnings.

7. The clean surplus model can be extended to allow for some information asymmetry, although under restrictive conditions. See Feltham and Ohlson (1996), reviewed in Section 11.6.

8. In the F&O model, the firm's life is assumed infinite.

9. The "o" stands for "operating." If the firm has financial assets, such as cash or securities, these are assumed to earn the risk-free rate of interest. Consequently, financial assets do not contribute to goodwill, which is the ability to earn *abnormal* earnings.

10. The investor may wonder *why* the manager chose these particular accounting policies, however. That is, the manager's choice of accounting policies may itself reveal inside information to the market. Then, it is not completely correct to say that the investor need not be concerned about accounting policy choice. This is considered in Chapter 11.

11. Our expression for α differs slightly from that of F&O. They assume that the firm has an infinite life, whereas our assumption is that P.V. Ltd. has a two-year life.

12. The persistence parameter ω can be related to the three types of earnings events distinguished by Ramakrishnan and Thomas (1991) (R&T) (Section 5.4.1), namely permanent, transitory, and price-irrelevant, with ERCs of $(1 + R_f)/R_f$, 1, and 0, respectively. First, consider a \$1 permanent abnormal earnings event occurring in year t for a firm with an infinite life. This will increase bv_t, in F&O notation, by \$1. In addition, ω of this will persist to year t + 1, ω^2 to year t + 2, etc. Thus, the total effect, discounted at the rate R_f, of the \$1 of year t abnormal earnings on PA_t, that is, the ERC, is

$$\text{ERC} = 1 + \frac{\omega}{1 + R_f} + \frac{\omega^2}{(1 + R_f)^2} + \frac{\omega^3}{(1 + R_f)^3} + \cdots$$

$$= \frac{1 + R_f}{1 + R_f - \omega}$$

In R&T terms, permanent abnormal earnings have an ERC of $(1 + R_f)/R_f$. To express this ERC in terms of ω, we have

$$\frac{1 + R_f}{1 + R_f - \omega} = \frac{1 + R_f}{R_f},$$

which holds for $\omega = 1$.

Thus permanent abnormal earnings have $\omega = 1$. Note that this is outside the range of ω in the earnings dynamic (6.2). That is, for an infinite firm horizon the F&O model is not defined for permanent earnings.

R&T transitory abnormal earnings have an ERC of 1. Thus

$$\frac{1 + R_f}{1 + R_f - \omega} = 1,$$

which holds for $\omega = 0$. Thus, transitory earnings have an ω of zero.

For price-irrelevant abnormal earnings, with ERC of 0, we have

$$\frac{1 + R_f}{1 + R_f - \omega} = 0,$$

which is satisfied only in the limit as $\omega \to \pm \infty$. Since this is again outside the allowed range for ω, the F&O model is not defined for price-irrelevant abnormal earnings.

13. Bombardier Inc. has 2 classes of common shares outstanding—A & B. They differ with respect to voting rights and dividend preference. However, their market values and betas are almost identical. For purposes of this example, we combine the 2 classes.

14. This is the date the financial statements for the year ended January 31, 2001 were signed.

15. This is equivalent to adding in other information in the earnings dynamic equation 6.2.

7 *Measurement Perspective Applications*

7.1 Introduction

Despite the pressures for a measurement perspective as discussed in Chapter 6, the movement of accounting practice in this direction encounters two formidable obstacles. The first is reliability. The decision usefulness of fair value-based financial statements will be compromised if too much reliability is sacrificed for greater relevance. Second, management's skepticism about RRA that we saw in Section 2.4.2 carries over to fair value accounting in general, particularly since the measurement perspective implies that fair values are incorporated into the financial statements proper. Management's concerns are particularly enhanced if unrealized gains and losses from changes in fair values are included in net income.

Nevertheless, recent years have seen major new measurement-oriented standards, with more on the horizon. In this chapter, we review and evaluate some of these standards.

7.2 Longstanding Measurement Examples

Even though financial statements are conventionally referred to as based on historical cost, they contain a substantial fair value component. To preface a discussion of recent measurement-oriented standards, we will review some common longstanding instances of market and present value-based valuations.

7.2.1 ACCOUNTS RECEIVABLE AND PAYABLE

For most firms, current accounts receivable and accounts payable are valued at the expected amount of cash to be received or paid. Since the length of time to payment is short, the discount factor is negligible, and this basis of valuation approximates present value.

7.2.2 *CASH FLOWS FIXED BY CONTRACT*

There are numerous instances where cash flows are fixed by contract. Then, valuation is frequently based on present value, since the contract often provides reliable estimates of amounts and timing of future cash flows and interest rate. Thus, if a firm issues long-term debt and uses the compound interest method to amortize any premium or discount, it can be shown that the resulting net book value of the debt equals the present value of the future interest and principal payments, discounted at the effective rate of interest of the debt established at the time of issue.

As another example, Section 3065 of *CICA Handbook* requires capital lease contracts and related leased assets to be valued at the present value of minimum lease payments, using the lower of the interest rate implicit in the lease and the lessee's current borrowing rate.

It should be noted, however, that if market interest rates change during the life of the contract, present values of outstanding debt or leases are not adjusted. As far as interest rates are concerned, the accounting for leases and debt is still on a historical cost basis. Consequently, the accounting for long-term debt and leases is only a partial application of the measurement perspective.

7.2.3 *THE LOWER-OF-COST-OR-MARKET RULE*

The lower-of-cost-or-market rule is another long-established example of a measurement perspective. Under this rule, when the market value of a temporary investment falls below its carrying value, Section 3010 of *CICA Handbook* requires a writedown to market value. A similar rule is traditionally applied to inventories. Also, if the value of a long-term investment falls below its carrying value, and the decline in value is not temporary, it should be written down under Section 3050 of the *Handbook*.

Note that while asset values are written down under lower-of-cost-or-market, they are not written up. Indeed, once an asset is written down, the written-down value becomes the new "cost," which may not be written up again.

The lower-of-cost-or-market rule is usually justified in terms of conservatism. It is more difficult to justify in terms of decision usefulness, however, since one would think that if market value information is useful, it would be useful when value is greater than cost as well as when it is less than cost. Presumably, accountants, and auditors, must feel that their exposure to legal liability is greater for an asset overstatement than for an equivalent amount of understatement. Nevertheless, the rule remains as an interesting and important partial application of the measurement perspective.

7.2.4   CEILING TEST FOR CAPITAL ASSETS

Section 3060 of *CICA Handbook* imposes a **ceiling test for capital assets**. While the primary basis of accounting for capital assets continues to be historical cost, Section 3060 requires a write-down when the net carrying value of the capital assets exceeds the net recoverable amount.

The calculation of the net recoverable amount requires the estimation of future net cash flows from use of the capital assets. The net cash flows are essentially the assets's operating cash inflows less related cash outflows, including any future removal and site restoration costs, plus residual or salvage value.

The estimation of the net recoverable amount is to be based on the "most probable set of economic conditions." Thus, it constitutes an application of the present value model under uncertainty, as in Example 2.2. However, there is a major difference. Under Section 3060, the estimated future cash flows are not discounted in computing net recoverable amount on the grounds that the purpose of the calculation is to determine cost recovery, not valuation.

This orientation to cost recovery rather than valuation seems hard to justify. For example, timing of future cash flows will differ across assets. Yet, without discounting, two assets with the same total cash flows will be valued identically, even though the cash flows of one asset are expected to be realized later than the other. Furthermore, the rate of return reported on subsequent use of the asset will be downward biased. A cynical explanation for the lack of discounting is that because a low discount rate means high present value, other things equal, the standard setters wish to minimize the number of times a write-down will need to be recorded. At the very least, this could seriously delay the recording of losses. An alternate explanation, however, is a reluctance of the standard setter to allow firms to specify a discount rate, since this may decrease the reliability of the ceiling calculation. Consequently, a uniform discount rate of zero is required (note that not requiring discounting is the same thing as requiring a discount rate of zero).

The ceiling test under U.S. GAAP moves a bit closer to a measurement perspective. SFAS 121 of the FASB proceeds in a two-step manner. First, an impairment test is applied. If the undiscounted expected future cash flows from a capital asset, or group of assets, is less than carrying value in the accounts, the assets are deemed impaired. Second, if deemed impaired, they are written down to fair value, with an impairment loss recognized on the income statement. Generally, fair value means market value, but, if market value is unavailable, fair value can be estimated by means of discounted present value, using a risk-adjusted interest rate.

Another difference from Example 2.2, of course, is the asymmetric nature of ceiling tests. That is, capital assets may be written down, but not written up, to net recoverable value. In this regard, the ceiling test is similar to the lower-of-cost-or-market rule.

We should also point out that the ceiling test applies to oil and gas reserves. Unlike RRA, however, future net revenues are not discounted in the calculation of the ceiling under the Canadian standard. Any excess of book values over the ceiling should be written off, but (also unlike RRA) no write-up is applied if the ceiling is greater than book value.

Nevertheless, despite the partial nature of its application, and despite its denial of discounting in Canada, the ceiling test represents an important extension of the measurement perspective to a major class of assets.

7.2.5   PUSH-DOWN ACCOUNTING

When one firm acquires all, or virtually all, of another firm in an arm's-length transaction, Section 1625 of *CICA Handbook* allows (but does not require) the assets and liabilities of the acquired firm to be comprehensively revalued, with the resulting values recorded on the books of the acquired firm. This is called **push-down accounting**. The result is that the assets and liabilities are recorded on the books of the acquired firm at their fair values as established in the acquisition transaction. In addition, Section 1625 requires comprehensive revaluation following a financial reorganization, provided that the reorganization is significant enough to result in a substantial realignment of interests. Thus, Section 1625 constitutes another major example of the introduction of a measurement perspective into financial reporting.

7.2.6   CONCLUSIONS

The above is only a partial listing of longstanding fair-value-based measurements in generally accepted accounting principles. For a more complete discussion, see Weil (1990). For our purposes, the main point to realize is that a considerable amount of measurement perspective is already inherent in financial statements, even though those statements are regarded as primarily historical cost-based.

The foregoing examples, however, understate the extent of measurement perspective in current GAAP. We now turn to a consideration of more recent fair-value-oriented accounting standards.

7.3   *More Recent Fair Value-Oriented Standards*

7.3.1   PENSIONS AND OTHER POST-EMPLOYMENT BENEFITS

Defined benefit pension plans[1] are accounted for on a present value basis under Section 3461 of *CICA Handbook*—pension liabilities are based on expected present value of pension benefits earned by the employee to date, taking into account projected compensation to expected retirement. Pension fund assets are valued at fair value. Pension expense for a period includes service cost—the expected present value of benefits earned by employees under the plan for the period, including for projected increases in earnings, plus accretion of discount on opening pension liability, reduced by earnings on pension plan assets.

Effective in 2001, Section 3461 also applies to other post-employment benefits (OPEBs), such as health care and insurance provided to current and retired employees. Section 3461 regards OPEBs as a form of deferred compensation that, like pensions, should be recorded as employee services are rendered. The accumulated OPEB liability is based on the expected present value of benefits to be paid on behalf of current and retired employees. Also, the expense for the period includes service cost and accretion of discount, net of any return on plan assets.

Prior to the effective date of Section 3461, most firms accounted for OPEBs on a pay-as-you-go basis, recognizing an expense only as cash payments were made. Thus, adoption of fair value accounting usually results in the recording of a substantial liability to "catch up" for accumulated OPEB obligations to current and retired employees. Section 3461 allows the offsetting charge to go directly to retained earnings (retroactive application); or to be amortized over future years (prospective application), thus avoiding a substantial earnings "hit" in the year of adoption.

Section 3461 is quite similar to SFAS 106 in the United States, which has been in effect for some time. For firms that used the retrospective option, the amount of the writeoff was often surprisingly large. For example, *The Globe and Mail* (February 2, 1993) reported a $20.8-billion one-time charge by General Motors Corp. to record its OPEB obligation upon adoption of SFAS 106 (see Chapter 4, Question 7). This reduced its shareholders' equity by about 75%!

For our purposes, the important aspect of pension and OPEB accounting is their use of discounted present value to calculate expense and accumulated liabilities. As such, they represent a major example of the measurement perspective in financial accounting.

As we would expect, accounting for pensions and OPEBs on a present value basis entails a substantial loss of reliability, due to the many assumptions and estimates that have to be made, including the choice of a discount rate. Recall that low reliability is a possible explanation for the apparent lack of decision usefulness of RRA, as discussed in Section 5.7. The usefulness of OPEB information was investigated by Amir (1993), who studied the impact on firms' share prices of the estimated amounts of their OPEB liabilities. For a 1992 sample of 231 U.S. firms, Amir documented a negative relationship, suggesting that investors used OPEB information in their decision-making. Presumably, in contrast to RRA, the contractual nature of most pension and OPEB plans endows their future cash flows with sufficient certainty that increased relevance is not negated by lower reliability.

7.3.2 IMPAIRED LOANS

Section 3025 of the *CICA Handbook*, released in 1994, relates to impaired loans. This standard requires that loans be written down by the lender to their **estimated realizable amount** when they become impaired or restructured. This amount is based on the expected future cash flows to be derived from the loans, discounted at the rate of interest implicit in the loan transaction. Any loss resulting from such a write-down is to be recorded in current income. Furthermore, under certain conditions the net carrying value of impaired loans is to be adjusted for subsequent changes in the estimated realizable amount, with the resulting charge or credit reflected in the income statement.

It is this latter provision, which allows subsequent writeup if loan quality improves, that is of particular interest, suggesting a movement away from the lower-of-cost-or-market rule. Thus, the impaired loans standard indicates a clear extension of the measurement perspective by standard setters. This is confirmed in paragraph 3025.55, which states that disclosure of the net charge or credit to income resulting from loan impairment allows users of financial statements to assess the effect on net income of changes in expectations of the amounts and timing of future cash flows from loans.

7.4   *Financial Instruments*

7.4.1   *INTRODUCTION*

In Canada, accounting for **financial instruments** is laid down by Section 3860 of the *CICA Handbook*, issued in 1995. Section 3860 deals primarily with the definition and disclosure of financial instruments. It does not specify how they should be valued on firms' books. Consequently, this standard is more in keeping with the information perspective than with application of the measurement perspective, the topic of this chapter. Nevertheless, we will include it in our discussion here for continuity. Standard setters in the United States have gone further in the direction of the measurement perspective with respect to financial instruments than is currently the case in Canada. Consequently, we will supplement our discussion by reference to U.S. standards where appropriate.

In part, the delay in moving towards a measurement perspective for financial instruments in Canada is because the AcSB is participating in the development of a major new international standard that will require fair value accounting for all financial instruments. We will review a draft version of this standard below.

Financial instruments are defined in Section 3860 as follows:

A financial instrument is any contract that gives rise to both a financial asset of one party and a financial liability or equity instrument of another party.

Financial assets and liabilities are defined quite broadly. Thus, Section 3860 defines a financial asset as:

(i)   cash;

(ii) a contractual right to receive cash or another financial asset from another party;

(iii) a contractual right to exchange financial instruments with another party under conditions that are potentially favourable;

(iv) an equity instrument of another entity.

Similarly, a financial liability is any liability that is a contractual obligation:

(i) to deliver cash or another financial asset to another party;

(ii) to exchange financial instruments with another party under conditions that are potentially unfavourable.

Thus, financial assets and liabilities include items such as accounts and notes receivable and payable, debt and equity securities held by the firm, and bonds outstanding. These are referred to as primary instruments. Also included are **derivative instruments**, to be discussed in Section 7.4.3.

As mentioned, Section 3860 is information-perspective-oriented. For example, it requires disclosure of fair values of financial instruments as supplementary information. Thus, it does not lay down rules for financial instrument valuation in the accounts, although the valuation of certain types of primary financial instruments, such as receivables, impaired loans, and capital leases are prescribed in other sections. However, a measurement perspective for financial instruments has developed much further in the United States. It is instructive to look at these developments to see some of the problems that must be overcome in moving to fair value financial instrument accounting.

7.4.2   VALUATION OF DEBT AND EQUITY SECURITIES

SFAS 115 of the FASB applies to investments in debt securities and to investments in equity securities with readily determinable fair values. It requires that these assets be classified at acquisition into one of three categories:

- **Held-to-Maturity** Debt securities for which the entity has a "positive intent and ability" to hold to maturity
- **Trading Securities** Held for a short time for the purpose of selling them
- **Available-for-Sale** All other securities to which SFAS 115 applies

While held-to-maturity securities are valued at amortized cost, both trading and available-for-sale securities are valued at fair value. For trading securities, unrealized gains and losses from such valuations are included in income. For available-for-sale securities, unrealized gains and losses are included in other comprehensive income.

A statement of **other comprehensive income** is required in the United States by SFAS 130, effective for fiscal years beginning after December 15, 1997. Other comprehensive income includes adjustments to fair value of available-for-sale securities, foreign currency translation adjustments, and several other types of unrealized gains and losses, and is reported after net income. As these gains and losses are realized, they are transferred to net income. SFAS 130 is discussed in Section 13.6.2.

To understand SFAS 115's seemingly inconsistent juxtaposition of accounting policies, two major problems need to be pointed out. The first problem is **gains trading**, also called "cherry picking." This is a practice that financial institutions, in particular, have been suspected of using as a way to manage their reported earnings. Gains trading can be employed when investment portfolios are valued at cost or amortized cost, and when at least some securities have risen in value. Then, the institution can realize a gain by selling securities that have risen in value, while continuing to hold securities that may have fallen in value. No loss is recognized on these latter securities, because they continue to be carried on a cost basis on grounds that they will be held to maturity.

Note that gains trading is not possible if securities are valued at fair value, with unrealized gains and losses included in income—if changes in fair value are recorded as they occur, then there is no gain or loss on disposal. Thus, the firm has no discretion to cherry pick. However, it is interesting to note that SFAS 115 has the potential to make the problem of gains trading worse rather than better. When securities are transferred from held-to-maturity to trading, SFAS 115 requires that the transfer be accounted for at fair value, with any gain or loss included in income. Thus, to gains trade, the firm need only reclassify held-to-maturity securities as trading—no sale of securities is needed.

However, SFAS 115 protects against this possibility by placing stringent conditions on transfers into and out of held-to-maturity. For example, if a firm intends to hold a debt security for an indefinite period, this does not qualify as held-to-maturity. Also, transfers out of held-to-maturity require events that are "isolated, nonrecurring, and unusual for the reporting enterprise that could not have been reasonably anticipated...."

The second problem is one of volatility of reported net income. SFAS 115 applies only to financial assets. However, financial institutions may coordinate the duration and other characteristics of their financial assets and liabilities in order to create a **natural hedge** of changes in values. It then seems reasonable that if financial assets are carried at fair values so should financial liabilities. Otherwise, the volatility of net income that results from recognizing unrealized gains and losses from only financial assets is greater than the real volatility the firm has chosen through its natural hedging activities. It is for this reason, presumably, that SFAS 115 stipulates that certain securities (held-to-maturity) need not be carried at fair value and that gains and losses on others (available-for-sale) are excluded from net income. If unrealized gains and losses on these financial assets do not enter into net income, they cannot contribute to excess volatility.

One might ask why SFAS 115 does not simply require that financial liabilities also be carried at fair value, rather than going through the contortions just described. The difficulty is that financial institutions are a major industry affected by SFAS 115 and that, to date, a generally accepted method of fair-valuing the demand deposit liabilities of financial institutions does not exist. It may seem reasonable to value demand deposits at their face value, since this is the amount that depositors can demand. This is the way demand deposits are currently valued. However, this basis of valuation ignores the value of **core deposit intangibles**. These can arise from customers' acceptance of a lower-than-market rate of interest on their deposits, due to goodwill, habit, location, etc. As a simple example, suppose that a bank pays 1% interest on a customer's $100 deposit but lends the customer's money at 5%. Then, as long as the customer keeps the $100 on deposit, the bank's $100 deposit liability is offset by a core deposit intangible asset that will generate $4 per year. The face amount of deposit liabilities should be reduced by this intangible asset for a fair valuation. Yet this introduces problems of estimating the timing of withdrawals and discounting, which are currently unresolved. In the face of these difficulties, SFAS 115 opts not to require fair value accounting for any financial liabilities, and to control resulting excess volatility of net income by retention of historical cost accounting for held-to-maturity securities, and exclusion of unrealized gains and losses on available-for-sale securities from net income. While retention of historical cost for held-to-maturity securities does not eliminate the possibility of gains trading, the FASB must feel that the stringent controls over transfers between categories will keep the problem within bounds.

Despite these compromises, SFAS 115 represents a clear extension of the measurement perspective beyond the realm of supplemental disclosure and into the financial statements proper. Major classes of financial assets are to be fair-valued with unrealized gains and losses included either in net income or other comprehensive income.

7.4.3 DERIVATIVE INSTRUMENTS

Derivative instruments are contracts, the value of which depends on some **underlying** price, interest rate, foreign exchange rate, or other variable. A common example is an option, such as a call option, that gives the holder a right to buy, say, 100 shares of a firm's common stock for $20 each during, or at the end of, some specified period. The notional amount of the contract is 100 (shares). The underlying is the market price of the shares. The higher the market price, the higher the value of the option, other things equal. Other examples of derivatives include futures, forward and swap contracts, interest rate caps and floors, and fixed-rate loan commitments. Generally, these instruments convey a benefit to the holder if there is a favourable movement in the underlying. If the underlying moves unfavourably, there may or may not be a loss to the holder.

A characteristic of derivative instruments is that they require or permit settlement in cash—delivery of the asset associated with the underlying need not take place. Thus, the option contract above need not involve the holder actually buying the shares, but only receiving the value of the option in cash at time of settlement. As another example, suppose a firm needs to borrow a large sum of money in six months time. It is concerned that interest rates may rise over this period. It buys a bond futures contract giving it the right to sell government bonds at a specified price on a settlement date six months hence. If interest rates go up, the underlying market value of the bonds goes down, and the value of the futures contract rises to offset the higher borrowing cost. If this contract had to be settled physically, the firm would have to enter the bond market on the settlement date, buy the requisite amount of government bonds, and sell them to the party on the other side of the contract at the contract price to realize the value of the contract. With cash settlement, the firm can simply receive a cash payment equal to the value of the contract, thereby saving both sides the costs of physical buying and selling. The ability to settle derivative instruments in cash has contributed to the great increase in their use over the past number of years.

Derivative instruments may or may not require an initial net investment. For example, a firm may enter into an interest rate swap contract that requires no cash outlay. If an initial investment is required, it is for less than the notional amount times the underlying. In the option example above, if the current share price is, say, $18, the cost to the holder of the option contract will certainly be less than $1,800, the amount that would be required to buy the shares outright. This is reasonable, because while the holder of the option will participate in any price increase of the shares during the option term, other rights of ownership, such as dividends, are excluded. In effect, the option holder is buying only the rights to future appreciation in value over some time period, not the shares themselves. In our bond futures contract example, the firm could also have protected itself by borrowing now, to lock in the current interest rate. But, this would require an additional interest cost for six months on the full amount needed.

These three examples illustrate the leverage aspect of derivatives—a lot of protection can be acquired at relatively low cost. Leverage is another reason for the great increase in the use of derivatives in recent years. Of course, leverage is a two-edged sword. If derivatives are used to speculate on the underlying price rather than to manage risk, the amount that can be lost, for a low initial investment, can be very large indeed.[2] This low initial investment characteristic of derivatives is a reason why accountants have found them difficult to deal with under historical cost accounting. Since there is little or no cost to account for, all or part of the contract is off-balance sheet.

For this reason, standard setting bodies have required supplementary disclosure of information about financial instruments, including derivatives. As mentioned, Section 3860 of *CICA Handbook* requires fair value information to be disclosed for financial instrument assets and liabilities, both recognized and unrecognized, as well as details of their terms and conditions. Information about **credit risk** of financial assets is also required, where credit risk is the risk that the other party to the contract will not fulfill its obligations. Related requirements are now contained in SFAS 107 of the FASB.

The accounting for derivative instruments has been moved substantially towards a measurement perspective, however, by SFAS 133 of the FASB, effective for fiscal periods beginning after June 15, 2000. This standard requires that all derivatives be measured at fair value for balance sheet purposes. If a derivative is traded, fair value would be measured by its market value. If it is not traded, models of derivative value can be used.

How can we model the fair value of an option? To illustrate, consider our example of an option to purchase 100 shares at $20, where the current market price is $18 per share. Assume that the option can be exercised at the end of two months. Assume also that the shares change their price only at the end of each month, and that these price changes follow a random walk (see Section 4.2.1). Specifically, assume that share price will increase each month by $2 with probability 0.5 or decrease by $2 with probability 0.5. This price behaviour is depicted in Figure 7.1.

Looking ahead from time 0 (now), at the end of the first month the 100 shares will have a market value of $2,000 with probability 0.5, and a value of $1,600 with probability 0.5. At the end of the second month (the expiry date of the option) their market value will be $2,200 with probability 0.25 (i.e., 0.5 × 0.5), $1,800 with probability 0.5 (0.25 + 0.25) or $1,400 with probability 0.25.

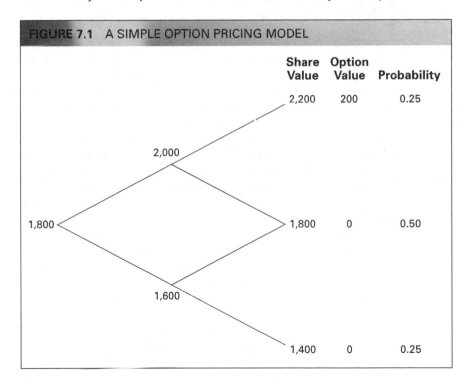

FIGURE 7.1   A SIMPLE OPTION PRICING MODEL

	Share Value	Option Value	Probability
	2,200	200	0.25
2,000			
1,800	1,800	0	0.50
1,600			
	1,400	0	0.25

Now the option will only be exercised if the value of the shares is $2,200. Since the exercise price is $20 per share, or $2,000 in total, the value of the option is then $200. For the other two possible share values, the option will not be exercised, so that its value is then $0.

The question then is, what is the fair value of the option at time 0, its date of issuance? If we assume that the risk-free interest rate in the economy is zero, this fair value is simply $200 × 0.25 = $50, the expected value of the option at maturity.[3]

Of course, our assumption that the share price changes only at the end of each month is unrealistic. In reality, many share prices change almost continuously. This can be modelled in our example by increasing the number of times that price changes in Figure 7.1 (but holding the time to expiration constant at two months). As the number of times the price changes goes to infinity (i.e., share price varies continuously) the fair value of the option is given by the famous Black/Scholes (1973) option pricing formula,[4] which values the option as a function of the following five variables:

- Current market price of the share—$18
- Variability of return of the share
- Exercise price of option—$20
- Time to expiration
- Risk-free interest rate

The first two of these inputs to the formula are characteristics of the underlying share price. Thus, given values for the last three variables, we see how the value of the option derives from the current market price and return variability of the share. The higher the current price, the more valuable is the option. The greater the variability of the price, the more valuable is the option since there is a greater likelihood that the price will rise by the expiry date (there is also a greater likelihood that the price will fall but, in that case, the option need not be exercised). Since Black/Scholes, models to value other, more complex derivative instruments have been developed. Thus, under appropriate conditions,[5] models provide a way to implement the fair-value calculations required by Section 3860, SFAS 107 and SFAS 133.

Changes in fair value of derivative instruments are recognized in net income under SFAS 133, except for certain hedging contracts, which are discussed in Section 7.4.4.

It is noteworthy that SFAS 133 applies only to derivatives, not to all financial instruments. Debt and equity securities continue to be accounted for, in the United States, under SFAS 115, discussed in Section 7.4.2. Implementation of fair-value accounting for all financial instruments will require dealing with problems of core deposit intangibles and income volatility that were discussed in that section. We return to these problems in Section 7.4.5.

7.4.4 HEDGE ACCOUNTING

Firms issue or acquire financial instruments for a variety of reasons. For example, they may manage their capital structure by means of convertible debt. They may manage their cash flows by issuing zero-coupon debt. Interest rate swaps and bond futures contracts may enable lower financing costs. Perhaps the major reason why firms deal in financial instruments, however, is to *manage risk*.[6] It is this role of financial instruments that we concentrate on here.

The term "manage" risk is used advisedly. The goal of risk management is to produce a desired level of firm-specific risk, not necessarily to reduce it to zero. Zero risk may be too costly, or not even possible. Indeed, it may not even be desirable, since investors can reduce firm-specific risk for themselves through portfolio diversification.

As mentioned in Section 7.4.2, firms are, to some extent, protected against risks by natural hedging. For example, if a firm owns securities and at the same time has interest-bearing debt outstanding, the market value of the assets will tend to move in the opposite direction to the market value of the debt. This will particularly be the case if the firm tailors the amounts, duration and other characteristics of the debt to match the risk characteristics of the securities.

While we will consider only hedging by means of derivative instruments, it should be noted that natural hedges are ultimately a management decision and any evaluation of a firm's susceptibility to risk should also consider natural hedging. Here, we simplify by viewing hedging by means of derivative instruments as a way of reducing *specific* risks, such as the risk of interest rate changes on floating-rate debt or foreign exchange risk on anticipated future sales. Natural hedging is viewed as reducing *total*, or non-specific, firm risk. In effect, hedging with derivative instruments takes over where natural hedging leaves off.

As suggested above, a variety of complex financial instruments has been developed to enable firms to better manage risks. Many of these risks are **price risks**, arising from changes in interest rates, commodity prices and foreign exchange rates. Other risks arise from credit risk. The accounting for these complex instruments involves difficult issues of recognition and valuation, which standard setting bodies are currently addressing.

The essence of a hedge is that if a firm owns, say, a risky asset, it can hedge this risk by acquiring a **hedging instrument**—some other asset or liability whose value moves in the direction opposite to that of the **hedged item**. Accounting for hedges of transactions that take place entirely within the current period is relatively straightforward. The gain or loss on the hedged item and the loss or gain on the hedging instrument can both be recorded in current net income, which then includes a realized loss or gain only to the extent the hedge is not completely effective. Hedges may not be completely effective because there may not exist a hedging instrument that will completely offset the hedged item's gain or loss. For example, a bank may have trouble finding a perfect hedge for the risk of changing interest rates on its deposit liabilities. The risk resulting from the absence of a perfectly effective hedge is called **basis risk**.

For hedging transactions that extend into future periods, hedge accounting has traditionally laid down conditions under which unrealized gains or losses on these transactions can be deferred. Thus, under Section 1650.54 of *CICA Handbook*, an exchange gain or loss on a foreign currency-denominated monetary asset should be deferred if the hedging instrument is a non-monetary item, until the settlement date of the hedging instrument. Also, many firms hedge anticipated future transactions, such as the foreign exchange risk of next year's expected sales in a foreign country. Section 3860.92 of the *Handbook* envisages the deferral of gains or losses on financial instruments designated as hedges of anticipated future transactions, until those transactions take place.

The rationale of these deferrals is not hard to see—the matching concept of historical cost accounting is violated if gains or losses on hedged items and related hedging instruments are recognized in different periods. Also, the volatility of net income is increased. Hedge accounting then operates to get the gains and losses into the same period. Note, however, that deferral of gains and losses is a creature of historical cost accounting and the information perspective. Deferred gains and losses should not appear on the balance sheet under a measurement perspective, because they do not generate future cash flows. In this regard, the AcSB is moving to eliminate deferrals in Canada. To gain some appreciation of how hedges are accounted for under the measurement perspective, we again look at practice in the United States.

SFAS 133 has also resulted in major changes in hedge accounting. For derivative instruments designated as hedges of recognized assets and liabilities, called **fair value hedges,** the gain or loss on the hedging instrument is included in current earnings under SFAS 133. The related loss or gain on the hedged item is also included in current earnings. This means, in effect, that if the hedged item is still on the books at period-end, it is marked-to-market. For example, if a firm hedges a risk of changes in the fair value of its inventory by means of a forward contract where the underlying is, say, the price of some major component of that inventory, it would adjust the carrying value of its inventory by the change in the fair value of the hedged component, despite the traditional cost or lower-of-cost-or-market basis of inventory valuation. The forward contract is also marked-to-market, with the result that net income is affected only to the extent that the hedge is not completely effective.

SFAS 133 also eliminates deferrals of gains and losses on hedged items and hedging instruments, on the grounds that deferred gains and losses are not assets and liabilities. As mentioned above, this characterizes the balance sheet approach that underlies the measurement perspective. Since deferred gains and losses do not involve future economic benefits or payments, they are not included on the balance sheet. Under the income statement approach that underlies the information perspective and historical cost accounting, deferred gains and losses can be included on the balance sheet, since they are "by-products" of matching of costs and revenues.

Instead of deferral, SFAS 133 allows unrealized gains and losses on derivative instruments designated as hedges of forecasted transactions, called **cash flow hedges**, to be included in other comprehensive income until the transactions affect net income. Then, any accumulated gain or loss is transferred into net income for that period.

An instrument must meet certain criteria if it is to be eligible for hedge accounting under SFAS 133. Non-derivative instruments are generally prohibited from being eligible. This rules out hedge accounting for natural hedges. Also, options issued as stock-based compensation are excluded. For instruments that are eligible, management must **designate** the instrument as a hedge at the inception of the hedge, identify the hedged item and document the nature of the risk being hedged. The rationale is that reported net income would lose reliability if management had the discretion to designate a hedging instrument at any time it wanted. For example, faced with a major loss on derivatives not held as a hedge, management could decide to retroactively designate them as cash flow hedges of forecasted transactions. Then, the loss could be put into other comprehensive income, thereby at least delaying its impact on net income.

Note that if a derivative cannot be designated, it does not enjoy the benefits of hedge accounting, such as offsetting of losses on the derivative by fair-valuing the hedged item (fair value hedge) or delaying loss recognition to other comprehensive income (cash flow hedge). Denial of these benefits increases the volatility of reported earnings. High earnings volatility can have adverse effects on firms with high debt loads by increasing the probability of financial distress, and on growth firms who may want to hedge their risks but may have relatively few hedgeable items. Such firms would need to rely on natural hedges. In effect, SFAS 133 enables hedge accounting for specific risks, but does not facilitate the reduction of total firm risk which, as mentioned, would benefit highly levered and high-growth firms. For further discussion of these issues, see Guay (1999).

Another criterion for designation as a hedge is that the derivative instrument must be "highly effective" in offsetting changes in the fair value of the hedged item. SFAS 133 does not lay down rules for determining high effectiveness except that management's documentation of hedge effectiveness should be consistent with the entity's established risk management strategy. However, highly effective essentially means that there is high negative correlation between the fair values of the hedging instrument and the hedged item.

One way of estimating this correlation is the *cumulative dollar offset* method. For example, suppose that a firm hedges the risk of a variable interest rate liability by purchasing a treasury bill futures contract, whereby it undertakes to buy a given amount of treasury bills at some future date at a fixed price. Due to rising interest rates, the fair value of its liability has decreased by $1,500 to date, and the fair value of its treasury bill futures contract has fallen by $1,300. Then the ratio of gain to loss is $+ 1,500/-1,300 = -1.15$. Since this is reasonably close to a perfect ratio of -1, this supports continuing the designation of the futures contract as a hedge.

Whether an instrument is regarded as a hedge or not can have extreme consequences. A case in point is Franklin Savings Association of Ottawa, Kansas.[7] Franklin, during the 1980s, engaged in an aggressive strategy of using funds from deposits to buy risky derivative financial instruments. It hedged the interest rate risk of these derivatives by the use of sophisticated and complex hedging instruments. At the end of its 1989 fiscal year, Franklin had accumulated losses on these hedging instruments of $365 million, which it deferred under the hedge accounting standards in effect at the time.

The U.S. regulatory body with responsibility for Franklin, the Office of Thrift Supervision, became increasingly concerned about Franklin's investment and hedging strategies and questioned the deferral of the $365 million in losses. The issue boiled down to one of correlation between losses and gains resulting from interest rate changes under the firm's hedging strategy. By some measures of hedge effectiveness, Franklin "passed." By other methods, including a version of the cumulative dollar offset method described above, it "failed."

In the face of this conflicting evidence, the Office of Thrift Supervision decided that the deferred losses be written off. Since Franklin's statutory capital was only $380 million, this put it into technical insolvency, takeover by the regulatory authorities, and possible liquidation.

It is interesting to speculate whether this sequence of events would have happened had SFAS 133 been in place at the time. Presumably, SFAS 133's requirement to document the assessment of hedge effectiveness at inception would have made it clearer to management and the Office of Thrift Supervision whether or not the hedging strategy was "highly effective," and so would have prevented matters going as far as they did. One thing is clear, however. With the advent of SFAS 133, hedge accounting joins the movement towards a measurement perspective.

7.4.5   THE JOINT WORKING GROUP DRAFT STANDARD

In 2000, the Financial Instruments Joint Working Group of Standard Setters (JWG), an international group of accounting standard setters[8] issued a draft standard, *Financial Instruments and Similar Items*. This draft standard proposes fair value accounting for almost all financial instruments, with gains and losses from adjusting to market included in net income. The JWG points out that fair values are the most relevant values for financial statement users, and argues that fair values of derivatives can be determined with reasonable reliability. The draft standard contains important extensions of the measurement perspective as applied to financial instruments. We now evaluate some of these extensions.

As pointed out in Section 7.2.2, current GAAP does not allow adjustment of the carrying value of financial liabilities resulting from changes in market interest rates. Furthermore, there is no adjustment if the fair values of the firm's financial liabilities change due to changes in the firm's credit rating. The draft standard would require such adjustments. For example, suppose that a firm has just suffered a downgrade by a credit rating agency, with the result that the market value of its outstanding debt falls. Then, under the draft standard, the firm would reduce the carrying value of its debt to the lower value, with the resulting credit included in income. Recording of a gain following a credit downgrade may take some getting used to. However, as the JWG argues, a real gain has occurred since the firm's debt is worth less than before.

There is, however, a danger of circularity in the JWG's reasoning here. A major role for financial reporting is to increase the quantity and quality of information available to investors. In our credit rating example, the agency's revision is already known to the market, and reflected in the new market price of the debt. Fair valuing the firm's debt at the new market price adds nothing to what the market already knows. Hence the fair value information is not decision useful. Only if the firm were to adjust the fair value of its debt to some other value than market value, reflecting its inside information about its true financial condition and prospects, would decision useful information be generated. However, the draft standard elsewhere (para. 121) states that the firm is not expected to adjust the observed market price of a financial liability for information that would affect its credit standing if it became known. The circularity, then, is that fair value information intended to increase usefulness of financial reporting does not do so if fair value reflects only the market's existing information.

A second extension of the measurement perspective in the draft standard relates to the demand deposit liabilities of financial institutions. Recall from Section 7.4.2 that SFAS 115 does not require that demand deposits be fair valued, because of the lack of an accepted method of valuing core deposit intangibles. This is a major reason why SFAS 115 applies only to financial assets. If all financial instruments are to be fair valued, the draft standard must circumvent this difficulty. It does so by arguing that core deposit intangibles are separate from the deposit liabilities to which they relate, and that consideration of the accounting for intangibles is beyond its scope. This enables the draft standard to require that demand deposits be fair valued, but that the value of core deposit intangibles not be deducted in determining this value.

The draft standard also deals with hedge accounting. Like SFAS 133, the JWG rejects deferring of unrealized gains and losses on hedges of anticipated future transactions on the balance sheet. Unlike SFAS 133, however, it requires that these unrealized gains and losses be included in net income. This would seem to increase the volatility of reported net income. To see the JWG's reasoning, however, consider the following illustration:

A firm intends to buy a large amount of an essential raw material in six months time, which puts the transaction into the next accounting period. It decides to hedge against the possibility of an increase in the price of the raw material over the next six months, and purchases an option to buy the required amount of material at the current market price. By the end of the current period, the raw material price has increased, and the option has correspondingly increased in value, by $1,000. Under the draft standard, the balance sheet valuation of the option is increased by $1,000 to its current fair value, and the resulting credit is included in the current year's net income. No recognition is given to the anticipated future purchase since there is no commitment to buy and the transaction has not yet taken place. The firm objects, arguing that the $1,000 credit should be shown on the balance sheet rather than in net income, on the grounds that it has a "liability" to apply the gain to reduce the cost of the purchase next period. Furthermore, the firm argues, its designation of the derivative as a hedge of an anticipated future transaction serves as sufficient commitment to validate the future purchase. Including the gain in current year's income induces greater volatility of net income than the firm has chosen through its hedging activities.

The JWG defends its position, however, by pointing out that whether the future purchase actually takes place depends on management's continuing intent to enter into the transaction. That is, an expected future transaction cannot be used to justify an obligation to use the gain to offset a future loss. As a result, the gain must be included in current net income. There is no excess volatility of income, JWG argues, because the gain reflects what has actually happened, and only what has actually happened, to date. In effect, the volatility of reported net income reflects the inherent volatility of a hedge of an anticipated transaction.

The extent to which the draft standard will find its way into the accounting standards of the jurisdictions involved is difficult to say. It may take some time to overcome the skepticism that managers tend to show towards fair value accounting (see, for example, problem 7). Nevertheless, given its influential source, the proposal will be difficult to ignore and, no doubt, will be effective in moving the accounting for financial instruments even further in a measurement direction.

7.5   *Accounting for Intangibles*

7.5.1   *INTRODUCTION*

Accounting for intangibles is the ultimate test for the measurement perspective. While intangible assets, such as patents, trademarks, franchises, good workforce, location, restructurings, and information technology, are important assets for many firms and, for some firms, comprise most of firm value, their fair values are difficult to establish reliably, particularly if they are self-developed. This is because the costs of intangibles may be spread over many years and, as these costs are incurred, it may not be known whether they will ever produce future benefits. An example is the costs of research and development, the results of which are often an important component of many firms' intangible assets. Since it is so difficult to predict future payoffs from these costs, it is simply not known whether they will be recovered, let alone what their fair value is. As a result, Section 3450 of *CICA Handbook* requires that research costs not appear on the balance sheet at all—they are charged to expense as incurred. Costs of developing a product or process resulting from research may be capitalized only if their future benefits are reasonably certain. In the United States, SFAS 2 requires that all R&D costs be written off in the year they are incurred.

It is important to realize that intangibles are "there" even if they are not on the balance sheet—recall our demonstration of this in Section 6.5.1. Instead, due to recognition lag, they appear through the income statement—recall that our estimate of goodwill for Bombardier is based on a projection of future earnings. That is, since the historical cost accounting system waits until an intangible's value is realized as sales and earnings, the income statement contains the current "installment" of the value of intangibles. Only if an intangible enables abnormal earnings, over and above the cost of the capital used to generate those earnings, does that intangible have value. In effect, under current GAAP, accounting for intangibles such as those resulting from the firm's R&D activities is firmly within the information perspective of historical cost accounting.

Recall from Section 6.5.1 that goodwill is defined as the present value of future abnormal earnings. We now see the connection between intangible assets and goodwill. A firm has goodwill if its intangible assets generate abnormal earnings. To simplify the discussion, we will usually refer to goodwill for the remainder of this section. However, we should remember that goodwill arises from one or more underlying intangible assets.

The question then is, should goodwill remain off the balance sheet, with the implication that the income statement reports on it as realized, or should its fair value be measured and reported on the balance sheet? Reporting the fair value of goodwill has potential for increased decision usefulness, since this may reveal management's inside information about future expected earning power, and it is management that has the best information about what this earning power is. But, reporting the fair value of goodwill creates serious problems of reliability.

At this point, it is helpful to distinguish between self-developed goodwill and purchased goodwill. We first consider purchased goodwill.

7.5.2   ACCOUNTING FOR PURCHASED GOODWILL

When one firm acquires another in a business combination, the **purchase method** of accounting for the transaction requires that the tangible and identifiable intangible assets, and the liabilities of the acquired company be valued at their fair values for purposes of the consolidated financial statements.[9] Goodwill is then the difference between the net amount of these fair values and the total purchase price paid by the acquiring company. We illustrate the accounting for purchased goodwill with an example.

EXAMPLE 7.1   ACCOUNTING FOR PURCHASED GOODWILL

JDN Ltd. is a rapidly expanding "hi-tech" firm. As at January 1, 2000, it has 100 shares outstanding, trading at $10. Its balance sheet is as follows:

JDN LTD.
BALANCE SHEET
As at January 1, 2000

Capital Assets	$500	Liabilities	$100
		Shareholders' Equity	400
	$500		$500

S Ltd. is also growing rapidly, and is in a business similar to that of JDN. Its balance sheet as at January 1, 2000 is as follows:

S LTD.
BALANCE SHEET
As at January 1, 2000

Capital Assets	$300	Liabilities	$140
		Shareholders' Equity	160
	$300		$300

On January 1, 2000, JDN purchases all the 160 outstanding shares of S Ltd. in exchange for 40 shares of JDN's stock valued at $10 each, for a total purchase price of $400. The balance sheet of JDN immediately after the acquisition is:

JDN LTD.
BALANCE SHEET (POST-ACQUISITION)
As at January 1, 2000

Capital Assets, excluding		Liabilities	$100
investment in S	$500		
Investment in S	400	Shareholders' Equity	800
	$900		$900

As mentioned, the identifiable assets and liabilities of the purchased company must be valued at their fair values for purposes of preparing a consolidated balance sheet, with any excess of the purchase price over net fair value reflected as goodwill. Assume that as at the date of acquisition the fair value of S Ltd.'s capital assets is estimated as $340, and of its liabilities as $140. The consolidated balance sheet of JDN and its wholly-owned subsidiary S Ltd. as at date of acquisition is thus:

JDN LTD. AND SUBSIDIARY
CONSOLIDATED BALANCE SHEET
As at January 1, 2000

Capital Assets, excluding goodwill	$840	Liabilities	$240
Goodwill	200	Shareholders' Equity	800
	$1,040		1,040

Goodwill is determined as the amount paid for S Ltd. ($400) less the fair value of net assets acquired ($200).

Now assume that for 2000 the consolidated sales of JDN and its subsidiary are $1,000; less consolidated expenses, exclusive of amortization, of $850. Assume also that capital assets, exclusive of goodwill, are amortized at the rate of 10% per annum.

The question now is, should goodwill be amortized? Until recently, the answer was "yes." Under historical cost-based accounting, goodwill should be amortized over its useful life, so as to match its costs with the additional revenues generated by the intangible assets created by the merger.

However, standard setters, including the AcSB in Canada, have now eliminated the amortization of goodwill. This was accomplished in the United States by SFAS 142, adopted in July 2001. In Canada, Section 3062 of CICA Handbook contains similar requirements. These standards constitute a substantial movement towards the measurement perspective. Specifically, goodwill is retained on the consolidated balance sheet at its value established at time of purchase, unless there is evidence of impairment, in which case a ceiling test is to be applied to write goodwill down to its new fair value.

It is instructive, however, to examine the accounting for purchased goodwill prior to SFAS 142, so as to understand the pressures leading to the elimination of goodwill amortization. Consequently, assume in our example that goodwill is to be amortized over a five-year period. Then, the consolidated income statement for 2000 is:

JDN LTD. AND SUBSIDIARY
CONSOLIDATED INCOME STATEMENT
For the Year 2000

Sales	$1,000
Cost of sales and other expenses	850
Amortization of capital assets (10% of $840)	84
Amortization of goodwill (20% of $200)	40
	974
Net income	$ 26

Note that net income is only 2.6% of sales and 2.5% of opening total assets. The management of a firm in a situation such as this typically feels that such a result does not reflect its performance during and following an acquisition. That is, management feels that consolidated net income following the acquisition should show the beneficial effects of its business judgement, without being penalized by mandatory amortization of goodwill.

Consequently, management tried to circumvent the amortization requirement. We shall illustrate two ways to do this. One way was to account for the acquisition as a **pooling of interests**, or simply a pooling. A pooling is essentially a merger of equals, rather than a purchase of one firm by another.

Like goodwill amortization, pooling of interests accounting is now also removed from GAAP. SFAS 141, adopted in July, 2001, requires that all business combinations be accounted for as purchases. Section 1581 of *CICA Handbook* contains a similar requirement. Nevertheless, the method is still of interest since it illustrates the strength of management's determination to avoid goodwill amortization.

If the merger had been accounted for as a pooling, the post-acquisition balance sheet would appear as follows:

JDN + S LTD. (POOLING OF INTERESTS BASIS) As at January 1, 2000			
Capital Assets	$800	Liabilities	$240
		Shareholders' Equity	560
	$800		$800

As can be seen, the balance sheet components of the two firms are simply added together to form the pooled balance sheet. No fair valuing of capital assets is required, and no goodwill appears. The former shareholders of JDN now own 400/560 of the new enterprise, with the former shareholders of S Ltd. owning the remaining 160/560 of the shares. The year 2000 income statement now becomes:

JDN + S LTD. INCOME STATEMENT (POOLING OF INTERESTS BASIS) For the Year 2000	
Sales	$1,000
Cost of sales and other expenses	850
Amortization of capital assets (10% of $800)	80
	930
Net income	$ 70

As can be seen, net income is substantially higher, since there is no increased amortization from the fair-valued assets and no goodwill amortization. Consequently, given a choice, management would prefer the pooling method to the purchase method.

However, even prior to the recent discontinuance of pooling accounting under GAAP, accounting for this transaction as a pooling would not have been allowed under Canadian GAAP. Section 1540.14 of *CICA Handbook*, as it existed in 2000, stated that the proportionate interest in the new firm should normally be 50% for each group of former shareholders, whereas in our example the former shareholders of JDN Ltd. hold a 400/560 interest. This merger would probably have been allowed as a pooling of interests under U.S. GAAP in effect for 2000, however, under which the rules allowing pooling were less strict. Consequently, Canadian managers were even more opposed to goodwill amortization than their American counterparts, since they were less likely to be able to avoid it through the pooling route.

This leads to a second way to circumvent the effects of goodwill amortization. This is to account for the acquisition as a purchase, but to emphasize **cash income**, (sometimes called "pro-forma" income) rather than net income, where cash income is defined as net income before goodwill amortization and any related restructuring charges.[10] Under this tactic, the income statement itself is not affected—consolidated net income remains at $26 as in our example. However, cash income is emphasized in earnings announcements, messages to shareholders, MD&A, etc. In this way, management seeks to convince investors that goodwill amortization does not "matter," in the sense that it is not relevant to the evaluation of the performance of the consolidated entity. In our example, cash income for 2000 is $26 + 40 = $66.

Note that to the extent management succeeds in convincing investors that cash income is a better performance measure than net income, there is less discipline for managers to avoid overpaying in business acquisitions. In our example, if JDN had paid $600 rather than $400 for S Ltd., consolidated net income would turn into a loss of $14, but cash income would be unaffected.

As a further illustration of cash income, consider the 2000 Annual Report of the Toronto-Dominion Bank (TD Bank). In its MD&A, TD Bank reported operating cash basis net income of $2,018, $1,472, and $1,183 ($millions) for 2000, 1999, and 1998, respectively, explaining that these amounts exclude items that are not "part of our normal operations." The bank's reported net incomes for these three years as per its consolidated income statement were $1,025, $2,981, and $1,138, respectively. For 2000, the difference is due to the after-tax effects of $1,203 amortization of goodwill arising from TD Bank's acquisition of Canada Trust in that year, plus $475 of restructuring costs from the same transaction. Clearly, the two earnings sequences give different impressions of TD Bank's operations.

It will be interesting to see whether the mandatory use of purchase accounting, but without a requirement to amortize the resulting goodwill, will reduce management's emphasis on cash accounting. It may not, since should goodwill become impaired, massive writeoffs can result from application of the ceiling test. For example, JDS Uniphase Corporation reported a preliminary net loss for its fiscal year ended June 30, 2001 of $50.558 billion, reportedly the largest loss ever incurred by a North American corporation. This loss included a writedown of purchased goodwill of $44.774 billion,[11] in addition to amortization of remaining purchased goodwill of $5.475 billions. Nevertheless, in a news announcement accompanying the release of its 2001 preliminary loss, JDS reported a pro forma profit of $67.4 millions (see Problem 13).

7.5.3   SELF-DEVELOPED GOODWILL

Unlike purchased goodwill, no readily identifiable transactions exist to determine the cost of self-developed goodwill. Consequently, costs that may create goodwill, such as R&D, are usually written off as incurred. As mentioned, any goodwill that develops from these costs shows up in subsequent income statements. This recognition lag is a major reason why share price responds to earnings announcements, as documented in Chapter 5. The market watches net income carefully for clues as to future earning power.

Nevertheless, the proportion of abnormal share return explained by net income is low, and seems to be declining over time, as discussed in Section 6.4. Reasons for this low "market share" were examined by Lev & Zarowin (LZ) (1999). Recall that their study was introduced in Section 6.4, where we noted their findings of declining earnings value relevance over time. Here, we consider LZ's investigation into reasons for this falling market share. They argue that this is due primarily to a failure to account properly for self-developed intangibles.

To see LZ's argument, consider a firm's current income statement. As mentioned, under current GAAP, current net income includes the realization, if any, of the value of *past* expenditures on self-developed intangibles. This impact forces current reported net income *up*. However, this is not the end of the story. The firm will also be incurring *current* costs to develop goodwill, such as R&D. These cost force current net income *down*. If the firm has had past successes in its R&D efforts, the ERC with respect to these current R&D costs may well be zero or negative. That is, the market will not penalize the firm for the reduction in current reported earnings caused by current R&D, and may even reward it, if it feels that based on past experience, current R&D costs will enhance future earnings. Obviously, if the firm's share price responds positively to costs that force current net income down, this will show up as a low association between abnormal share return and net income. Furthermore, LZ suggest, most firms' expenditures on self-developed intangibles increase over time, driven by deregulation, innovation, and competition. If so, the low association intensifies. In effect, current accounting for R&D results in a *mismatch* of the costs of intangibles with the revenues generated by those intangibles. These effects, LZ argue, are a prime contributor to low and declining R^2s and ERCs.

To investigate this argument, LZ examine a sample of U.S. firms with high research intensity, that is, firms whose R&D costs have grown at an increasing rate. While R&D is only one intangible, they focus on it on grounds that R&D is a major contributor to self-developed goodwill. LZ find a significantly lower association between share returns and reported earnings for this sample than for a second sample of firms with low R&D intensity, consistent with their argument.

The question then is, what might be done to improve the accounting for intangibles? LZ make two suggestions. The first is for a type of successful efforts accounting for R&D. They propose that the costs of R&D be capitalized if they pass a "feasibility test," such as a working model or a successful clinical trial. Capitalization at this point, they argue, provides a reasonable tradeoff between relevance and reliability, and reveals inside information about the success of R&D efforts to the market. The capitalized costs would then be amortized over their estimated useful life.

The second suggestion is to restate current and previous financial statements as evidence that past expenditures on intangibles are paying off becomes available. For example, suppose that three years ago a firm charged to expense a $100,000 provision for restructuring. It is now apparent that the restructuring was successful. That is, the restructuring cost has led to an intangible asset, although this was not known at the time it was recorded. LZ's suggestion is to retroactively capitalize the restructuring costs and amortize them over their expected useful life. The current year's financial statement, plus revised financial statements for the two previous years, would be issued to give effect to this capitalization and amortization. This will improve matching and, LZ argue, will better enable the market to interpret the intangible asset created by the restructuring.

7.5.4   THE CLEAN SURPLUS MODEL REVISITED

Another approach to valuing goodwill is to use the clean surplus model discussed in Section 6.5. Recall that our valuation of the share value of Bombardier Inc. in Section 6.5.3 resulted in a goodwill estimate of $7,289.5 (million). Perhaps this amount could be formally incorporated into the financial statements as the fair value of Bombardier's goodwill. While we discussed at the time some of the reliability issues surrounding this estimate, if the estimate was to be prepared by management it would convey relevant information about Bombardier's expected future earning power.[12]

Alternatively, the clean surplus goodwill calculation could possibly serve as a ceiling test for purchased goodwill. If, in the case of Bombardier, the book value of its purchased goodwill exceeds $7,289.5, this suggests that purchased goodwill should be written down so as not to exceed this value.[13] Such a procedure, however, clouds the distinction between purchased and self-developed goodwill. For example, the purchased goodwill might be worthless, in which case it should be written down to zero, and the $7,289.5 would then be entirely self-developed. For further discussion of the possible use of the clean surplus model to account for goodwill, see AAA Financial Accounting Standards Committee (2001).

7.5.5   SUMMARY

Application of the measurement perspective to accounting for goodwill creates severe reliability problems. These problems may be somewhat mitigated for purchased goodwill, since at least a cost figure is available. Yet, even for purchased goodwill, amortization was essentially arbitrary due to the difficulty of establishing useful life. Furthermore, management disliked being charged for goodwill amortization and took steps to avoid it. Standard setters are moving towards a measurement perspective to purchased goodwill by introducing new standards to write it down only if there is evidence of impairment. The clean surplus model may provide a framework to structure the estimation of the fair value of goodwill.

When goodwill is self-developed, further reliability problems arise, and standard setters usually react by requiring immediate expensing of the costs of intangibles that underlie self-developed goodwill. However, this creates problems of matching of costs and revenues, and is the root cause of low value-relevance of reported earnings. Suggestions to improve the accounting for self-developed goodwill include capitalization and amortization of successful research projects, and restatement of past financial statements to correct premature writeoffs of intangible costs in the light of more recent information.

7.6   *Reporting on Risk*

7.6.1   BETA RISK

In SFAC 1 and Section 3860 of *CICA Handbook*, professional accounting bodies recognize that investors need risk information. The theory underlying the CAPM suggests (Section 4.5) that a stock's beta is the sole firm-specific risk measure for a rational investor's diversified portfolio. The usual way to estimate beta is by means of a regression analysis based on the market model.

These considerations seem to suggest that there is little role for financial reporting of firm risk. However, this is not the case. One reason is that beta and various accounting-based risk measures are correlated. This is of significance given the likelihood, discussed in Section 6.2.3, that a stock's beta is not stationary. Financial statement-based risk measures may indicate the direction and magnitude of a change in beta sooner than the market model, which would require several periods of new data for re-estimation.

Beaver, Kettler, and Scholes (1970) (BKS) were the first to examine formally the relationship between beta and financial-statement-based risk measures. For a sample of 307 New York Stock Exchange firms over two time periods,

1947–1956 and 1957–1965, they used a market model regression analysis to estimate betas for their sample firms for each time period. Then they calculated various financial statement-based risk measures for the same periods. The correlations between three of these risk measures and betas were as follows:

TABLE 7.1   CORRELATION COEFFICIENTS BETWEEN ACCOUNTING RISK MEASURES AND BETA, FOR FIVE-SECURITY PORTFOLIOS

	PERIOD 1 1947–56	PERIOD 2 1957–65
Dividend payout	−0.79	−0.50
Leverage	0.41	0.48
Earnings variability	0.90	0.82

SOURCE: BKS, Table 5. Reprinted by permission.

Dividend payout is the ratio of common share cash dividends to net income. Leverage is the ratio of senior debt securities to total assets. Earnings variability is the standard deviation of the firm's price/earnings ratio over the period.

Notice that the signs of the correlations are what we would expect (for example, the higher the dividend payout, the lower the risk) and that most of the correlations are quite high. Furthermore, there is reasonable consistency between Period 1 and 2. Indeed, BKS report that their most highly correlated accounting variable was a better predictor of a stock's beta than its current beta, supporting our suggestion above that accounting-based risk measures may provide timely indications of shifts in beta.

These correlation results may seem surprising since, a priori, it is not obvious why a market-based risk measure has anything to do with accounting variables. However, Hamada (1972) showed that, under ideal conditions, there is a direct relationship between debt-to-equity and beta. Lev (1974) showed a direct relationship, also under ideal conditions, between operating leverage and beta (operating leverage is the ratio of fixed to variable operating costs). BKS' results suggest that these relationships carry over at least in part to non-ideal conditions. The rationale for these results is not hard to see. The higher a firm's financial and operating leverage, the more it will benefit if business conditions improve, and suffer if they deteriorate, since high leverage means a high proportion of fixed costs in the firm's cost structure, hence high sensitivity of earnings to changes in the level of activity. The efficient market will be aware of this and, the higher the leverage, the more it will bid up share price when business conditions improve, and vice versa. The stock market index will also rise and fall with business conditions. Since beta measures how strongly the firm's share price varies as the market varies, the greater the leverage the higher is beta.

BKS' findings have financial reporting implications. Hamada's study implies that off-balance-sheet liabilities should be brought onto the balance sheet at fair value to maximize correlation of debt-to-equity with beta. Section 3065 of CICA Handbook, which requires present-value accounting for capital leases, is a longstanding partial example. SFAS 133, described in Section 7.4.4, requires derivative instruments, many of which were previously off-balance-sheet, to be recorded at fair value.

Lev's study implies that firms should separate fixed and variable operating costs, if investors are to infer beta from the financial statements. Surprisingly, financial reporting seems of little help here. Indeed, Ryan (1997) points out that absorption cost accounting, which includes fixed operating costs in inventory, actually increases the difficulty of evaluating operating leverage.

In the face of these complications, commercial services have sprung up to sell beta estimates to investors. At least some of these base their estimates in part on accounting risk measures. To the extent that these services earn a profit, this speaks well for the ability of financial statements to provide useful risk measures.

7.6.2   STOCK MARKET REACTION TO OTHER RISKS

Over the past few years, standard setters have been requiring increased risk-related information in annual reports. We have already seen in Section 4.8.2 that MD&A requires a discussion of risks and uncertainties, particularly with respect to downside risk. Also, many of the disclosures required by Section 3860 and SFASs 107 and 133 (see Section 7.4.3) are risk-related. These include supplementary information about exposures to market and credit risks and about the firm's risk management policies, for example.

At first glance, one might question the relevance for investors of firm-specific risk information. However, as discussed in Section 6.2, there is theory and evidence that the CAPM does not completely capture the risk factors used by the market in setting share prices, and that investors may not always behave as the rational decision theory leading to the CAPM predicts. Consequently, the decision usefulness of risk information such as that required by Section 3860 and SFASs 107 and 133 is an empirical question.

Much of the empirical research in this area relates to financial institutions. For such firms, financial assets and liabilities comprise most of book value, and it is to financial assets and liabilities that many of the risk-related disclosure standards relate. Barth, Beaver and Landsman (1996) (BBL) examined the effects of supplemental SFAS 107 fair-value disclosures on the market value of equity for a sample of 136 U.S. banks for 1992 and 1993. They found a market response to the fair values of banks' loans portfolios, which suggests that the relevance of fair-value reporting of these assets outweighs reliability difficulties in measuring loan value. This result extends the finding by Barth (1994) that fair values of banks' investment securities (another major class of bank assets) also is related to the market value of banks' shares.

Interestingly, BBL found that the market response to fair value of loans was smaller for banks in lower-than-average financial condition (measured by their regulatory capital ratios). This implies that the market evaluates such banks as riskier—a bank in poor financial condition is less likely to be around to realize the unrealized gains and losses on its loan portfolio. BBL also found that banks' share values were negatively affected by non-performing loans and amounts of interest-sensitive liabilities, and positively affected by amounts of interest-sensitive assets. This means that these sources of risk were not fully hedged, which is consistent with our discussion of the costs of hedging in Section 7.4.4. Schrand (1997) studied the effect on interest rate risk of derivatives-based hedging activities, for a sample of 208 savings and loans associations during 1984–1988. She measured the interest rate sensitivity of her sample firms by their one-year "maturity gap," the amount of their interest-sensitive assets maturing in one year less their interest-sensitive liabilities maturing in one year. The greater the gap, the greater the sensitivity of their share returns to unexpected changes in interest rates.

Note that maturity gap corresponds to the concept of natural hedging introduced in Section 7.4.2—the narrower the gap the more the institution is coordinating the maturities of its on-balance-sheet, interest-sensitive assets and liabilities so as to reduce its interest rate risk. For most of her sample firms, Schrand found that the gap was negative. That is, consistent with BBL, Schrand's firms were not completely eliminating their risk by means of natural hedging (if they were, gap would be zero). For each sample firm, Schrand then evaluated the effect of the firm's (off-balance-sheet) derivatives hedging activities on its one-year maturity gap. She found that the more a firm reduced its gap in this way, the less sensitive its share price was to unexpected interest rate changes, particularly for the larger institutions in her sample (which were more active users of derivatives).

Collectively, the results of BBL and Schrand suggest that the stock market is sensitive to interest rate risk, over and above its sensitivity to beta. Furthermore, both the firm's on-balance-sheet natural hedging as well as its off-balance-sheet derivatives hedging (Schrand's study predates SFAS 133) affect the magnitude of the market response.

We would expect that if other sources of risk than beta were to be useful for investors, it would be for interest rate risk of financial institutions. However, firms in other industries also face price risks, which raises the question of whether the market is also sensitive to these. Wong (1998) examined the foreign exchange risk of a sample of 145 manufacturing firms during 1994–1996. He found that, for some firms in his sample, share price was sensitive to foreign currency exposure. However, unlike Schrand, neither the fair value nor the notional amount (i.e., face value) of firms' foreign exchange derivatives positions explained the magnitude of the sensitivity. One possible explanation is that investors sufficiently diversify their holdings that they are not sensitive to firms' foreign exchange risks. However, Wong attributed the lack of results to shortcomings of hedging disclosures in annual reports (much of Schrand's data was taken from regulatory filings, which would not be available for industrial firms). He recommended more disaggregated disclosures in annual reports of notional amounts, fair values, long and short positions and maturities by class of instrument.

7.6.3   *A MEASUREMENT PERSPECTIVE ON RISK REPORTING*

The disclosures discussed in the previous section are primarily oriented to the information perspective—they involve the communication of information to enable investors to make their own risk evaluations. However, like valuations of assets and liabilities, reporting on risk is also moving towards a measurement perspective.

In this regard, consider the risk disclosure requirements laid down by the SEC (1997), as described by Linsmeier and Pearson (1997). These include "quantitative" price risk disclosures, which can take the following forms: (1) a **tabular presentation** of fair values and contract terms sufficient to enable investors to determine a firm's future cash flows from financial instruments by maturity date; (2) a **sensitivity analysis** showing the impact on earnings, cash flows or fair values of financial instruments, resulting from changes in relevant commodity prices, interest rates and foreign exchange rates; or, (3) **value at risk**, being the loss in earnings, cash flows or fair values resulting from future price changes sufficiently large that they have a specified low probability of occurring.

While the tabular presentation is oriented to an information perspective, the latter two alternatives are of interest because they are measurement-oriented. The firm, rather than investors, prepares the quantitative risk assessments. We would expect that it is the firm that has the most accurate estimates of its own risks. Hence, these latter two risk measures have the greater potential for decision usefulness.

Table 7.2 shows a sensitivities disclosure from the 1997 annual report of Beau Canada Exploration Ltd. The table shows the impact on cash flows and earnings of relevant commodity price, interest rate and foreign exchange rate risks.

Note that oil price sensitivity is given before and after hedging activities are taken into account. Presumably, the after-hedging sensitivities are of greater relevance, which raises the question of why other risks are reported before hedging. The notes to the company's financial statements (not reproduced here) report that there are no foreign exchange hedges outstanding as at the year-end, although hedges were in effect for interest rate risk. Perhaps the company plans to alter the extent of its hedging activities over the coming year, or it may feel that pre-hedging sensitivities provide a "worst case" estimate of the impact of price risks on operations.

Sensitivity estimates are subject to relevant range problems. Thus, if the price of oil were to change by, say, $3/bbl, it is unlikely that the impact on earnings would be three times the impact of the $1/bbl change given in the table. Another problem is with co-movements in prices. It is unlikely that changes in the bank prime rate are independent of changes in the $U.S./Can exchange rate, for example. Yet, each change estimate in Table 7.2 holds the other prices constant.

TABLE 7.2 BEAU CANADA EXPLORATION LTD. 1997 ANNUAL REPORT. PRICE RISK SENSITIVITIES				
SENSITIVITY—1998 ESTIMATES	**CASH FLOW**		**EARNINGS**	
	net *(millions)*	per share	net *(millions)*	per share
Change of $1.00/bbl US in WTI oil price excluding hedges	$3.9	4¢	$2.3	3¢
Change of $1.00/bbl US in WTI oil price including hedges	$1.9	2¢	$1.1	1¢
Change of $0.10/mcf in price of natural gas	$3.1	4¢	$1.9	2¢
Change of 1% in bank prime excluding swaps	$1.4	2¢	$0.8	1¢
Change of $0.01 in US/Canadian exchange rate[1]	$1.4	2¢	$0.8	1¢

[1] a stronger US$ improves cash flow, earnings.

SOURCE: Beau Canada annual report, 1997. Reprinted by permission.

Finally, nothing is said about the probabilities of price changes. These would have to be assessed by the investor.

The value at risk approach addresses some of these problems. Consider, for example, a firm's portfolio of financial instruments at year-end. To calculate value at risk, the firm first needs to assess a joint probability distribution of the various price risks that affect the fair value of the portfolio over some holding period, say 90 days. This, in turn, is converted into a distribution of the changes in the fair value of the portfolio. The value at risk is then the loss in fair value that has only a 5% (or some other low probability) chance of occurring over the 90-day holding period. In effect, a loss greater than the value at risk is a rare event. The approach can also be extended to cash flow and earnings value at risk.

Microsoft Corporation is a well-known user of value at risk. It faces foreign currency, interest rate, and securities price risks, which it hedges by means of options. Microsoft does not fully hedge these risks—this is likely to be too costly. However, it uses value at risk to estimate its unhedged exposure, and reports the results in its annual report. Presumably, Microsoft adjusts the extent of its hedging activities so as to attain the level of price risk it is willing to bear.

To illustrate, Microsoft's 2000 Annual Report discloses that there is a 97 1/2% probability that the loss on its interest-sensitive investments would not exceed $211 millions over a 20-day holding period (thus, only a 2 1/2% probability of a loss greater than this amount). Microsoft also holds large amounts of equity investments, many for strategic reasons—its June 30, 2000 balance sheet shows $17,726 (millions) of such investments. Value at risk, based on 2 1/2% probability and a 20-day holding period, is reported as $1,020 millions.

While primarily geared to downside risk, there appears to be no reason why value at risk could not be applied to upside risk as well. A challenging aspect of value at risk, however, is the need to assess the joint price distribution, including correlations between the price risks. Keeping track of past price changes is one way to do this. Nevertheless, if there are, say, 10 price risks faced by a portfolio, then 10 expected values, 10 variances and 45 correlations need to be estimated. Microsoft does not explain in its annual report how it assesses its price risk distribution.

7.6.4   CONCLUSIONS

We conclude that information about firm risk, in addition to beta, is valued by the stock market, at least for financial institutions. This is documented by the sensitivity of share returns of these institutions to risk exposures and to the impact of hedging on these exposures. Financial reporting has responded by increased reporting of fair values for financial instruments, supplemented by discussion of risks and how they are managed, and by disclosure of financial instrument contract information. This enables investors to better evaluate the amounts, timing and uncertainty of returns on their investments. It can be suggested that increased disaggregation of financial instrument information would further assist investors in this regard.

Financial reporting is also moving towards providing investors with quantitative risk information, such as sensitivity analyses and value at risk. Despite methodological challenges, these represent important steps in moving risk disclosures towards a measurement perspective.

7.7   Summary and Conclusions

There are numerous instances of the use of fair values in financial reporting, and the list is growing. Many longstanding uses involve only partial application of a measurement perspective, as in lower-of-cost-or-market, long-term debt, ceiling tests, and push-down accounting. Thus, under lower-of-cost-or-market and ceiling tests, written-down assets are not written up again if value increases. Also, under current GAAP, the present value of long-term debt is not adjusted for changes in interest rates, and once subsidiary asset values are pushed down they are not revalued subsequently. Nevertheless, partial applications of fair value have the potential to be decision useful to the extent they reveal a material change in the firm's financial position and prospects.

However, recent standards extend the measurement perspective so as to periodically measure both value increases and decreases. Thus, under Section 3025 of the *CICA Handbook*, impaired loans may be written up if impairment is reduced. Under SFAS 115, in the United States, trading and available-for-sale securities are marked-to-market each period. Furthermore, pensions and OPEBs are reported at present value each period in Canada and the United States. While the information is supplemental, Section 3860, as well as SFAS 107 in the United States, require periodic disclosure of fair value and risk information for a variety of financial instruments. Even the accounting for business combinations and purchased goodwill is becoming measurement-oriented, as witnessed by recent standards, which eliminate the pooling-of-interest method and apply a ceiling test to goodwill. Also, SEC regulations require disclosure of quantitative risk measures.

Certainly, it appears that decision usefulness is moving more and more into the arena of measurement. Reasons for this were suggested in Chapter 6. They include the low value relevance of historical cost-based net income, reactions to theory and evidence that securities markets may not be as fully efficient as originally believed, increasing acceptance of a theory that expresses firm value in terms of accounting variables, and auditor legal liability resulting from abuses of the historical cost system. The combined effect of these factors seems to have convinced accounting standard setters that striving for greater relevance is worthwhile, even at the cost of some sacrifice of reliability.

Whether the recent measurement-oriented standards described in this chapter will increase the market share of financial accounting information in explaining share returns, and will reduce auditor liability, remains to be seen. Furthermore, only time will tell whether the recent downturn in economic activity triggered by the collapse of share prices of many technology firms will slow down or accelerate the measurement perspective. On the one hand, this collapse may remind accountants of the lesson from the Great Depression of the 1930s, that values are fleeting, thereby reinforcing the historical cost basis. On the other hand, the measurement perspective may be reinforced, as accountants strive to ensure that new, lower values for assets such as purchased goodwill are promptly and fully reported.

Questions and Problems

1. Under generally accepted accounting principles, certain current assets such as cash, accounts receivable, and marketable securities (when fair value is below cost) are carried at present value and/or market value. Does this violate the historical cost basis of accounting? Explain.

    Note: A good answer will consider the point in the operating cycle at which revenue is realized.

2. Explain why the reporting of deferred assets and liabilities on the balance sheet is inconsistent with the measurement perspective.

3. Explain why a firm may not necessarily reduce its price risks to zero by means of hedging transactions.   (CGA-Canada)

4. On August 31, 1999, an article in *The Globe and Mail*, "2000: New year, new accounting, new costs," anticipated the introduction of Section 3461 of *CICA Handbook*, requiring accrual accounting for OPEBs. The article noted that firms have the option of recording the accumulated OPEB liability as a direct charge to retained earnings, or to amortize the liability over the next several years. The article quotes Mr. Ken Vallillee, a partner of a large accounting firm, as saying "Most companies will opt for the onetime charge if they can." The article also points out that Section 3461 replaces the previous method of accounting for OPEBs, charging cash payments for OPEBs to expense as they are made.

Required

a. Explain the extent to which the new standard will increase the decision usefulness of financial statements for investors. Consider both issues of relevance and reliability in your answer.

b. Do you agree With Mr. Vallillee that most firms will opt for the onetime charge? Explain why or why not.

c. What effects will the reporting of the OPEB liability have on the market value of affected firms' shares? Will the effect depend on how the firm chooses to record the liability? In your answer, consider situations where share price might fall, remain unchanged, or rise. Assume in your answer that securities markets are efficient.

5. The ceiling test for capital assets imposed by Section 3060 of *CICA Handbook* can have important implications for investors, and auditors. A case in point is Bramalea Inc., a Canadian real estate developer, which went bankrupt in 1995 during a period of falling real estate values, with $3.5 billion of debt.

   Bramalea's auditor, KPMG Peat Marwick Thorne, was subsequently sued by senior debenture holders. The lawsuit claimed that the auditor had been negligent by allowing an $800 to 900-million overstatement of the company's property values. KPMG denied liability.

Required

a. To what extent is the ceiling test of Section 3060 consistent with the measurement perspective on decision usefulness?

b. In applying the ceiling test, the net recoverable amount is to be based on the "most probable set of economic conditions." If unfavourable state realization subsequent to the balance sheet date results in balance sheet values, in retrospect, having been overstated, is this grounds for legal liability? Discuss. In your discussion, include consideration of whether it would have been useful to have disclosed a measure of the riskiness of Bramalea's real estate values.

   c. Would discounting of future expected cash flows from real estate at the firm's cost of capital reduce the likelihood of investor lawsuits such as the one against KPMG? Explain.

   d. Does the threat of lawsuits, if balance sheet values turn out to be in error, affect the credibility of financial reporting? Explain why or why not.

6. Share prices of many "hi-tech" firms are quite volatile relative to the stock market index. In an article in *The Wall Street Journal*, (reprinted in *The Globe and Mail*, May 16, 2001), Greg Ip discusses a reason why. He points out that hi-tech firms have high fixed costs, consisting mainly of R&D driven by rapid technological progress. They also have low variable costs, since the direct production costs of their products tend to be very low. In effect, high-tech firms have high operating leverage.

For example, Yahoo Inc. incurred a drop in revenue of 42% in the first quarter of 2001, but its costs barely dropped. It reported an operating loss of $33 millions for the quarter, compared to a profit of $87 millions in the last quarter of 2000.

Required

   a. Use high operating leverage to explain high stock price variability.

   b. Use the argument that beta is non-stationary (Section 6.2.3) to explain high stock price volatility.

   c. Use the behavioural finance concepts of momentum and bubbles to explain high stock price volatility.

   d. Are these three sources of volatility mutually exclusive? Explain.

7. Reproduced here is "Banks Anticipate the Crunch of New Accounting Rule," from *The Wall Street Journal* (January 5, 1995). The article describes concerns by bankers in the United States following the passage of SFAS 115.

BANKS ANTICIPATE THE CRUNCH OF NEW ACCOUNTING RULE

New York—Bank capital is at a high level. Many banks are flush with cash. And bank stocks seem to have bottomed out after declining most of last fall.

So why are many bank executives unhappy? For one thing, unexpected jumps in interest rates have driven down the market value of their bond and derivative portfolios. But bankers are even more upset that new accounting rules will prevent them from selling the "dogs" in these portfolios in 1995.

The Financial Accounting Standards Board, the chief rule-making body for accountants, issued an accounting rule early in 1993 that forces banks to value debt securities at current market prices. The rule is effective for 1994 financial statements, due early this year.

The FASB's new rule allows banks to carry old debt securities at the original cost—even if the current market value is lower—so long as that debt is intended to be held to maturity. But if the banks decide to sell any of that debt, then the entire portfolio must be valued at current prices. For that reason, most banks are likely to hold onto their debt rather than sell it, say accountants and bank analysts.

SHARP REDUCTIONS

With interest rates rising—and bond principal therefore falling—banks that sold some bonds would face sharp reductions in the amount of equity reported to shareholders. Although reported earnings would not be affected—only the balance sheet—bankers fear that some investors would sour on bank stocks, making it harder for many banks to raise new capital in the stock market.

Last month, federal bank regulators dropped a proposal that would have required the separate financial statements used for regulatory purposes to also reflect declining market values. Under the proposal, these declines would have forced banks to reduce the capital on their regulatory books, lowering their capacity to make loans.

While bankers applaud the federal regulators' decision to kill the proposal, many are still upset by the FASB rule. Consider the situation at PNC Bank Corp., Pittsburgh, which has almost $18 billion in bonds in a portfolio that it promises to hold to maturity. A bank spokesman says that if interest rates rise by two percentage points in 1995, the bank's net interest

income may drop by at least 15% from the 1994 level.

Bankers "want to be able to pick the bonds they want to sell at a profit, despite promising they would hold them to maturity, and not recognize unrealized losses on other bonds they hold," says Timothy Lucas, the Financial Accounting Standards Board's research director.

If they were free to sell the bonds, banks could use deftly timed sales to produce profits and offset declines in interest income. But the FASB rule hinders the sale of held-to-maturity bonds, bankers say. The rule considerably "limits our flexibility to respond to" interest-rate declines, the PNC spokesman says.

Thomas Rice, senior vice president for investor relations of Shawmut National Corp., Hartford, Conn., says that a rise in interest rates by a percentage point this year could "cost us $22 million in pretax net interest income." Shawmut has an $8.2 billion portfolio of held-to-maturity bonds; the sale of only a few of those bonds could force the bank to deduct unrealized losses in the entire portfolio from bank equity.

Mr. Rice says that "securities markets are very fluid these days and we would like to do what is rational for our bank without having to worry about how accounting numbers change." The FASB rule "ties our hands for a long period of time, and life would be much better if it weren't there," he adds.

Others agree. The FASB rule on bonds held to maturity "limits banks' ability to address interest-rate imbalances," says Dennis Shea, a bank analyst with Morgan Stanley & Co. Moshe Orenbuch, a bank analyst with Sanford C. Bernstein & Co., says that the rule-making body "puts accounting principles ahead of the needs of users of financial statements."

But Timothy Lucas, the FASB's research director, retorts that the rule is designed to improve disclosure for investors. Bankers "want their cake and want to eat it, too," he asserts. "They want to be able to pick the bonds they want to sell at a profit, despite promising they would hold them to maturity, and not recognize unrealized losses on other bonds they hold."

Accounting rule-makers also say the new rule resulted from many banks' "cherry-picking" bonds to sell from their holdings to create instant profits without valuing the rest of their bonds. Dennis Beresford, the FASB's chairman, also says that banks are getting the brunt of rule-makers' attention because "they are doing much more complex and risky transactions such as hedging and derivatives nowadays."

Indeed, PNC, for one, recently said that its unrealized losses from derivatives amounted to $500 million. Derivatives are contracts with values linked to underlying assets and those involving hedges against interest-rate moves can be used by banks to speculate on such moves.

Banks are also unhappy with certain other FASB rules. William J. Roberts, senior vice president and controller of First Chicago Corp., who is chairman of the American Bankers Association's accounting committee, cites an account-ing rule on impaired loans. The rule, effective for 1995 financial statements, could reduce First Chicago's profits by 1% to 5% during the next economic downturn, he estimates.

The rule requires banks to revalue not only the loan's principal as under current accounting rules but also the interest expected to be earned on the loan. "It makes no sense because we've already boosted our loan-loss reserves to cover such events," Mr. Roberts says.

PRESSURE TO BREAK DOWN RESULTS

Meanwhile, pressure—from both FASB and the Securities and Exchange Commission—is mounting on banks to break down their financial results into separate segments for consumer banking, venture capital, mutual-fund processing and other lines of business. Some banks still report in single segments, but since early 1993, others have become more willing to break down their financial results.

A survey by accountants Ernst & Young shows that 20 of the 50 biggest banks provide such breakdowns in their financial reviews while only 13 of the second 50 biggest banks do this. Some bankers say they resist such breakdowns because they reveal competitive data to other banks.

SOURCE: "Banks Anticipate the Crunch of New Accounting Rule," *The Wall Street Journal*, January 5, 1995. Reprinted by permission of *The Wall Street Journal*, © 1995 Dow Jones & Company Inc. All rights reserved worldwide.

Required

a. Describe the method, and the effects on the financial statements, of gains trading, or "cherry-picking" as the article refers to it.

b. Under SFAS 115, if a firm sells any held-to-maturity bonds prior to maturity, its whole remaining held-to-maturity portfolio may be reclassified as available-for-sale. What is the effect of this reclassification on the balance sheet valuation of the portfolio? Why does SFAS 115 do this?

c. If a bank is required to reclassify its held-to-maturity portfolio to available-for-sale, this does not affect reported earnings, as the article indicates. What is affected? Why does SFAS 115 exclude from net income the unrealized gains and losses from marking available-for-sale securities to market? Explain fully.

d. If there is no effect on net income of marking available-for-sale securities to market, why are bankers concerned about the "crunch" of the new accounting rule? Consider both income statement and balance sheet-oriented reasons in your answer.

e. Use efficient securities market theory to evaluate the claim referred to in the article that, with interest rates rising and bond values falling, the resulting "sharp reductions in the amount of equity" would cause investors to "sour" on bank stocks. In your answer, consider the finding of Barth (1994) that the market values of banks' shares are affected by information about the fair values of their investment securities.

f. The article refers to another FASB standard, on impaired loans. This standard is similar to Section 3025 of CICA Handbook, outlined in Section 7.3.2. Apparently, bankers are concerned that this standard could reduce profits "by 1% to 5% during the next economic downturn." Given the finding of Barth, Beaver, and Landsman (1996) of a securities market response to information about the fair values of banks' loans portfolios, explain the bankers' concerns. Do you agree with these concerns from the standpoint of an investor in banks' shares? Explain why or why not.

8. While ceiling tests for all capital assets were not yet in place in the United States in 1992, the SEC did enforce a ceiling test on the oil and gas reserves of producers. Essentially, a write-down was required if the book value of reserves exceeded their present value. In this regard, the SEC ceiling test was similar to that of Section 3060 of *CICA Handbook*.

An article entitled "Natural-Gas Producers Bristle at 'Snapshot' Accounting" appeared in *The Wall Street Journal* on April 17, 1992. It described the annoyance of affected firms, some of whom were forced to make substantial write-downs as a result of the ceiling test.

The SEC's ceiling test requires corporations to value their energy reserves at a price that "is whatever the company is able to sell its gas or oil for on the last day of the accounting period." According to the article, the SEC states that this test is necessary in order "'to insure that investors receive disclosures based on accounting that reflects recoverable value of assets.'" However, Bob Alexander, president of Alexander Energy Co., feels that this is not a good rule because "'the ceiling calculation takes a snapshot of a price on one day.'" Mr. Alexander, along with others, feels that this rule should be replaced by "a 12-month weighted average price to eliminate seasonal fluctuations."

Not all companies are required to use the ceiling test on their oil and gas reserves; the test is only for those companies that use full-cost accounting, which excludes successful-effort users.

According to the article, if the book value of oil and gas reserves is higher than the ceiling calculation, the company must write down the reserves to the ceiling. The article, for example, states that Enserch Exploration had to take a $50 million write-down of its reserves in 1991. These large write-downs often lead to a decrease in stock price even though it is a non-cash adjustment. Analyst Catherine Montgomery "believes the market sometimes reads too much into the write-downs," adding "I think that serious investors, institutions and analysts understand these write-downs....But the average investor out there has a knee-jerk response and stock prices may be affected."

Required

a. Explain why firms using the full-cost method of accounting for reserves are more likely than successful-effort firms to be affected by the ceiling test. The article stated that full-cost firms "have to apply the ceiling test to their oil and gas reserves every quarter; successful efforts users never do." Do you agree that successful-effort firms never have to apply a ceiling test? Explain.

b. Use efficient securities market theory to critically evaluate a claim made in the article that ceiling test write-downs can adversely affect stock price. Do you agree with this claim? Explain.

c. The article pointed out that once ceiling test write-downs are made, assets cannot be written up again if prices recover. Presumably, this accounts for the concern expressed by oil company managers about "snapshot" accounting. Why does the ceiling test impose write-downs but not allow subsequent write-ups? As an informed investor in the oil and gas industry, would you support regular adjustment of book values of oil and gas reserves to market value? Explain.

9. An article entitled "Presidential Life Is Accused by SEC of Overstatement" appeared in *The Wall Street Journal* on September 23, 1992. It describes a "cease and desist" order issued by the SEC following a claimed overstatement by Presidential Life Corporation of the fair value of certain of its security investments.

According to the article, the SEC believed that Presidential Life did not use generally accepted accounting principles to account for its junk bonds, and did not disclose the risks of the portfolio. Many of these bonds "had declined sharply in market price in 1989 and...most of the issuers of its junk bonds were either in bankruptcy or near default."

According to the SEC, this led to a $20.7-million overstatement of Presidential's 1989 pre-tax profit. "The SEC also alleged that Presidential misled investors when the company told investors in 1989 that 'the company believes its investments in high yield/high risk obligations will have no material adverse effects.'"

Required

a. To what extent would SFAS 115, had it been in effect at the time, have prevented the claimed misstatements? Explain.

b. The corporation plans to contest the SEC's charge. Suppose that you were in charge of preparing counterarguments to the SEC. What would these arguments be?

10. Under SFAS 115, most loan assets held by U.S. banks are held in the "held-to-maturity" category, where they are valued at amortized cost. Of course, if the fair value of a loan should fall below this amount, the impaired loans standard requires a writedown. With the recent economic downturn, investors watch loan writedowns with particular care. Major writedowns will likely result in a decline in the bank's share price, as investors interpret the writedown as a sign of loan quality problems to come. For example, in Canada, *The Globe and Mail*, March 7, 2001, reports "Scotiabank profit overshadowed by impaired loans." The bank reported a substantial increase in first quarter, 2001 net income. However, it also reported a 44% increase in impaired loans. Its share price on the Toronto Stock Exchange fell by $3.46, closing at $42.44.

Faced with reactions such as these, banks may wish to disguise the extent of major loan writedowns. An article in *The Economist*, March 22, 2001, "Shell game," describes how some U.S. banks have responded.

The trick, according to *The Economist*, is to transfer problem loans to the "available-for-sale" category. Under SFAS 115, available-for-sale securities are valued at their fair value. Thus, the transferred loans must be written down. However, the writedown will be buried in larger totals and the market would not know how much of the total adjustment to fair value belongs to the loans transferred from held-to-maturity impaired loans. Furthermore, unrealized gains and losses from fair valuing available-for-sale securities are included in other comprehensive income under SFAS 115, so that writedowns do not affect net income. Another consequence is that the book value of held-to-maturity loans on the balance sheet is reduced, so that any existing loan loss allowance will appear more adequate.

Whether banks actually sell the transferred problem loans is an open question. *The Economist* points out that the dollar amount of secondary trading has risen dramatically in recent years. However, the length of time that banks can hold loans in the available-for-sale category without selling them is a "grey area." Presumably, the banks' auditors will be aware of these practices and will take steps to discourage them. However, *The Economist* quotes an official of the Office of the Comptroller of the Currency (a U.S. banking regulator) as saying auditors "too often side with their clients" in grey areas.

Required

a. What is the likely effect on banks' share prices and on the proper operation of capital markets of the above practice? Explain.

b. Why does SFAS 115 allow held-to-maturity loans to be valued at cost, or amortized cost, instead of at fair value like trading and available-for-sale securities? Explain. To what extent would amending SFAS 115 to require fair value accounting for all financial instruments eliminate the practice? Explain.

c. If you were the auditor of a bank engaging in the above practice, would you qualify your audit report if the bank refused your request to stop? Discuss why or why not.

11. On March 11, 2000, *The Globe and Mail* reported "Ballard losses double." The reference is to Ballard Power Systems Inc., a Canadian developer of fuel cell technology. On March 10, 2000, Ballard reported an operating loss of $26 millions for the fourth quarter of 1999, bringing its loss for the year to $75.2 millions on revenues of $33.2 millions. Its loss for 1998 was $36.2 millions on revenues of $25.1 millions. The reason for the increased loss in 1999, according to Ballard, was a huge increase in R&D spending for its fuel cell technology.

On March 10, 2000, Ballard's share price closed at $189 on the Toronto Stock Exchange, up $14 on the day for an increase of 8%.

Required

a. Does the increase in Ballard's share price on March 10, 2000 on the same day that it reported an increased loss imply a high or low R^2 and ERC for the relationship between the return on Ballard's shares and abnormal earnings? Explain, using the arguments of Lev and Zarowin (1999). Assume that the increase in the TSE 300 index on March 10, 2000 was less than 8%.

b. How do Lev and Zarowin propose to improve the accounting for R&D? Explain how this proposal could affect R^2 and the ERC.

c. Does Ballard's share price behaviour on March 10, 2000 suggest securities market efficiency or inefficiency? Explain.

12. Consider the concept of cash income discussed in Section 7.5.2. Do you agree with management that amortization of purchased goodwill is not part of normal operations? Explain why or why not. In your answer, consider efficient securities market theory and how the efficient market would react to cash income. Why do you think management emphasizes cash income?

13. As mentioned in Section 7.5.2, JDS Uniphase Corporation reported a preliminary loss of $50.558 billions for the year ended June 30, 2001. In a July 26, 2001 news release accompanying its financial statements, JDS also presented a "pro-forma" income statement that showed a profit for the year of $67.4 millions. The difference is summarized as follows ($ millions):

Net loss, as reported	$50,558.0
Add:	
Write off of purchased goodwill	$44,774.3
Writeoff of tangible and intangible assets from acquisitions	5,939.2
Losses on equity investments	1,453.3
Gain on sale of subsidiary	(1,768.1)
Non-cash stock option compensation	385.6
Income tax	(158.9)
	50,625.4
Pro-forma net income	$ 67.4

Required

a. The purchased goodwill arises primarily from business acquisitions paid for in shares of JDS Uniphase. In *The Globe and Mail*, 27 July 27, 2001, Fabrice Taylor states that in JDS' case, "most of the goodwill on the books comes from overvalued stock." In a separate article, Showwei Chu quotes a senior technology analyst as "They paid what the companies were worth at the time." While currently trading in the $8 range, JDS' shares were trading between $100 and $200 when most of the acquisitions were made.

   i) Assume securities markets are fully efficient. Does the $44, 774.3 writeoff of purchased goodwill represent a real loss to JDS Uniphase, even though no cash is involved? If so, state precisely the nature of the loss and who ultimately bears it.

   ii) Would your answer change if securities markets are subject to momentum and bubble behaviour? Explain.

b. What additional information is added to the publicly available information about JDS Uniphase as a result of the supplementary pro-forma income disclosure?

c. Why does JDS Uniphase management present the pro-forma income disclosure?

d. To the extent that investors accept pro-forma income as a measure of management performance, how might this affect management's propensity to overpay for future acquisitions? Explain.

14. In the MD&A section of its 2000 Annual Report, Royal Bank of Canada reports "economic profit." This consists of cash operating earnings less a capital charge of 13.5%, being the bank's cost of common equity capital. The amounts for the last two years are as follows:

	2000	1999
Net income after preferred share dividends ($ millions)	$2,140	$1,600
Add amortization of goodwill, other intangibles, and one-time items	87	168
Cash operating earnings	2,227	1,768
Capital charge	(1,460)	(1,386)
Economic income	$ 767	$ 382

Required

a. Relate the concept of economic income here to the clean surplus valuation procedure in Example 6.2. Does Royal Bank have unrecorded goodwill? (No calculations needed.)

b. Royal Bank also breaks down results for its major business segments. For example, the personal and commercial financial services segment contributed $469 millions of the $767 total economic income for 2000. If you were the manager of a Royal Bank segment, would your propensity to incur large capital expenditures be affected by your knowledge that economic income was a factor in evaluating your performance? Explain why or why not.

c. What new information, if any, is conveyed to the market by Royal Bank's disclosure of cash income and economic income? Why does Royal Bank make these disclosures?

15. The sensitivity analysis from the MD&A section of the 1997 annual report of Suncor Energy Inc. is reproduced below. The analysis discloses the potential effects of changes in crude oil and product prices, and of changes in the Can/US dollar exchange rate, on 1997 cash flows and earnings.

Required

a. Evaluate the relevance and reliability of this method of disclosing risk information.

b. The analysis does not indicate whether the sensitivities are evaluated before or after hedging activities are taken into account. Presumably, they are before hedging. What would be some of the problems of analyzing sensitivities net of hedging activities?

c. Suncor's price risks arise from changes in the market prices of crude oil, natural gas and refined products, with associated foreign exchange risk because market prices are largely based on the U.S. dollar. Suncor reports elsewhere in its MD&A (not reproduced) that its Board of Directors has approved hedging of up to 30% of product volume against price risks. Why would Suncor's Board impose this limitation on management's ability to manage risk? Give reasons based on internal control, cost, and investor diversification considerations.

TABLE 6.3   SUNCOR ENERGY INC., SENSITIVITY ANALYSIS

The sensitivity analysis (below) shows the main factors affecting Suncor's annual pre-tax cash flow from operations and after-tax earnings, based on actual levels of operation in 1997. It illustrates the potential financial impact of these factors on Suncor's 1997 financial results. A change in any one factor could compound or off-set other factors. Because this table does not incorporate potential cross-relationships, it cannot necessarily predict accurate results.

($ millions)	1997 Average	Change	APPROXIMATE CHANGE IN	
			Pre-tax cash flow from operations	After-tax earnings
Oil Sands				
Price of crude oil ($/barrel)	**26.36**	U.S.$1.00	14	9
Sales (barrels per day)	**78 100**	1 000	9	6
Exploration and Production				
Price of crude oil ($/barrel)	**22.22**	U.S.$1.00	3	2
Price of natural gas ($/thousand cubic feet)	**1.93**	0.10	7	4
Production of natural gas (millions of cubic feet per day)	**240**	10	6	3
Sunoco				
Retail gasoline margin (cents/litre)	**6.8**	0.1	2	1
Refining/wholesale margin (cents/litre)	**4.6**	0.1	5	3
Consolidated				
Exchange rate: Cdn $: U.S. $	**0.72**	0.01	7	4

This sensitivity analysis excludes the impact of crown environmental credit of $31 million received in 1997, but not available in future years.

SOURCE: Suncor Energy Inc, annual report 1997. Reprinted by permission.

Notes

1. A defined benefit pension plan specifies the benefits to be received by an employee, such as 75% of salary at time of retirement. This type of plan is distinguished from a defined contribution plan, where the contribution to be made by the employer is specified. In a defined contribution plan, the pension benefits received by the employee depend on the amounts contributed and the earnings of the plan assets.

2. Examples of speculation using derivatives that resulted in bankruptcy or near bankruptcy include Orange County, California; Barings Bank, and Long term Capital Management. For accounts of these disasters, see Boyle & Boyle (2001), Chapter 8.

3. If the risk-free interest rate is greater than zero, the option fair value is more complex. Also, options are usually fair-valued by an equivalent approach, called a **replicating portfolio**. This is a portfolio consisting of an investment in the underlying share plus a short position in a risk-free asset, where the amounts of each security are determined each period so that the replicating portfolio yields the same return as the option for each possible end-of-period value of the option. Since the underlying share and the risk-free asset have readily available market values, and since the return on the option is the same as that of the replicating portfolio, arbitrage forces the fair value of the option to equal the value of the replicating portfolio. For details, see Boyle & Boyle (2001), Chapter 4.

4. Boyle & Boyle (2001), Chapter 5, page 89, call this formula the Black/Scholes/ Merton formula, due to important contributions by Robert Merton (1973).

5. It should be pointed out that these valuation models assume that the markets on which the underlying securities are traded work well. If, because of adverse selection or other problems, they do not work well, then just as the market price of the underlying security may not reflect true value, the model value of the derivative security may not reflect its true value. Thus, the availability of valuation models in no way reduces the need for financial reporting to be an effective vehicle for fully disclosing information to the market, as discussed in Section 4.7.

6. It should be apparent that risk goes both ways. That is, assets (and liabilities) may decrease or increase in value. Thus, if an asset is fully hedged against price risk, the firm will not suffer from a decline in asset value but will not enjoy an increase in value either. This is a statistical notion of risk. Nevertheless, we will sometimes use the term risk in the sense of downside risk only. Credit risk, for

example, is the risk of loss from the failure of the other party to a contract to fulfil its obligations.

7. I am indebted to Mark Finn, Northwestern University, for material on Franklin Savings Association. For further information on Franklin, see Milligan (1991).

8. The JWG comprises members of accounting standard setters or professional organizations in Australia, Canada, France, Germany, Japan, New Zealand, five Nordic countries, the United Kingdom, the United States, and the International Accounting Standards Board.

9. These fair values may or may not be pushed down to the books of the acquired company. See Section 7.2.5.

10. Of course, this is not really "cash" income since it includes other accruals, such as sales on credit. It is not known where the term originated.

11. The company's preliminary net loss for the year was increased by further goodwill write-downs of $5.3 billion reported in its audited financial statements for the year.

12. Management may not be willing to reveal this estimate, on grounds that it may reveal important information to competitors.

13. This requires that purchased goodwill be excluded from opening book value for purposes of the clean surplus goodwill calculations.

8

Economic Consequences and Positive Accounting Theory

8.1 Overview

You may have noticed that there has been little discussion of management's interests in financial reporting to this point other than several references to management scepticism about fair value accounting. As mentioned earlier, a thesis of this book is that motivation of responsible manager performance is an equally important role of financial accounting as the provision of useful information to investors. If so, it is necessary that accountants understand and appreciate management's interests in financial reporting.

This will involve us in a new line of thought that, at first glance, differs sharply from the investor decision-based and efficient market-oriented theories discussed earlier. Our first task is to understand the concept of **economic consequences.** In the process, we will also learn about some of the accounting problems in three major areas of accounting policy choice—stock-based compensation, government assistance, and costs of oil and gas exploration.

> **Economic consequences** *is a concept that asserts that, despite the implications of efficient securities market theory, accounting policy choice can affect firm value.*

Essentially, the notion of economic consequences is that firms' accounting policies, and changes in policies, *matter*. Primarily, they matter to management. But, if they matter to management, accounting policies matter to the investors who own the firms, because managers may well change the actual operation of their firms due to changes in accounting policies. An example would be changes in accounting policies relating to oil and gas company reserves. Changes in such accounting policies, according to economic consequences arguments, may alter managers' exploration and development activities, which in turn may affect firm value. If these changes are potentially negative and if many investors are affected, investors may bring pressure to bear on their elected representatives. Indeed, managers will lobby these same representatives if they feel that a proposed accounting standard negatively affects their interests. Consequently, politicians will also be interested in firms' accounting policies and in the standard setting bodies that determine them.

It is important to point out that the term "accounting policy" refers to *any* accounting policy, not just one that affects a firm's cash flows. Suppose that a firm changes from declining-balance to straight-line amortization. This will not in itself affect the firm's cash flows. Nor will there be any effect on income taxes paid, since tax authorities have their own capital cost allowance regulations. However, the new amortization policy will certainly affect reported net income. Thus, according to economic consequences doctrine, the accounting policy change will matter, despite the lack of cash flow effects. Under efficient markets theory the change will not matter (although the market may ask *why* the firm changed the policy) because future cash flows, and hence the market value of the firm, are not directly affected.

An understanding of the concept of economic consequences of accounting policy choice is important for two reasons. First, the concept is interesting in its own right. Many of the most interesting events in accounting practice derive from economic consequences. Second, a suggestion that accounting policies do not matter is at odds with accountants' experience. Much of financial accounting is devoted to discussion and argument about which accounting policies should be used in various circumstances, and many debates and conflicts over financial statement presentation involve accounting policy choice. Economic consequences are consistent with real-world experience.

The presence of economic consequences raises the question of why they exist. To begin to answer this question, we introduce **positive accounting theory.** This theory is based on the contracts that firms enter into, in particular executive compensation contracts and debt contracts. These contracts are frequently based on financial accounting variables, such as net income and the ratio of debt to equity. Since accounting policies affect the values of these variables, and since management is responsible for the firm's contracts, it is natural that management be concerned about accounting policy choice. Indeed, management may choose accounting policies so as to maximize the firm's interests, or its own interests, relative to these contracts. Positive accounting theory attempts to predict what accounting policies managers will choose in order to do this.

8.2   *The Rise of Economic Consequences*

One of the most persuasive accounts of the existence of economic consequences appears in an early article by Stephen Zeff (1978) entitled "The Rise of 'Economic Consequences.'" The basic questions that it raises are still relevant today.

Zeff defines economic consequences as "the impact of accounting reports on the decision-making behavior of business, government and creditors." The essence of the definition is that accounting reports can *affect* the real decisions made by managers and others, rather than simply *reflecting* the results of these decisions.

Zeff documents several instances in the United States where business, industry associations, and governments attempted to influence, or did influence, accounting standards set by the Accounting Principles Board (predecessor to the FASB) and its predecessor, the Committee on Accounting Procedure (CAP).

This "third-party intervention," as Zeff calls it, greatly complicated the setting of accounting standards. If accounting policies did not matter, choice of such policies would be strictly between the standard setting bodies and the accountants and auditors whose task was to implement the standards. If only these parties were involved, the traditional accounting model, based on well-known concepts such as matching of costs and revenues, realization, and conservatism, could be applied and no one other than the parties involved would care what specific policies were used. In other words, accounting policy choice would be *neutral* in its effects.

As an example of an economic consequences argument, Zeff discusses the attempts by several U.S. corporations to implement replacement cost accounting during 1947 to 1948, a period of high inflation. Here, the third-party constituency that intervened was management, who argued in favour of replacement cost amortization to bolster arguments for lower taxes and lower wage increases, and to counter a public perception of excess profitability. The efficient market argument would be that such intervention was unnecessary because the market would see through the high reported net incomes produced by historical cost amortization during inflation. If so, it should not be necessary to "remind" users by formal adoption of replacement cost amortization. It is interesting to note that the CAP held its ground in 1948 and reaffirmed historical cost accounting.

Zeff goes on to outline the response of standard setting bodies to these various interventions. One response was to broaden the representation on the standard setting bodies themselves; for example, the Financial Executives Institute, representing management, is represented on the Financial Accounting Foundation (the body that oversees the FASB). Also, the use of exposure drafts of proposed new standards became common as a device to allow a variety of constituencies to comment on proposed accounting policy changes.

As Zeff puts it, standard setting bodies face a dilemma. To retain credibility with accountants, they need to set accounting policies in accordance with the financial accounting model and its traditional concepts of matching and realization (recall that Zeff is describing practices prior to the increased emphasis on the measurement perspective). Yet, as we have seen in Section 2.5, such historical cost-based concepts seldom lead to a unique accounting policy choice. That is, since net income does not exist as a well-defined economic construct under nonideal conditions, there is no theory that clearly prescribes what accounting policies should be used, other than a vague requirement that some tradeoff between relevance and reliability is necessary. This opens the door for various other constituencies to get into the act and argue for their preferred accounting policies. In short, standard setting bodies must operate not only in the accounting theory domain, but also in the political domain. Zeff refers to this as a "delicate balancing" act. That is, without a theory to guide accounting policy choice, we must find some way of reaching a consensus on accounting policies. In a democratic setting, this implies involvement in the political domain. While a need for delicate balancing complicates the task of standard setters, it makes the study of the standard setting process, and of accounting theory in general, much more challenging and interesting.

Summary

Despite the implications of efficient market theory, it appears that accounting policy choices have economic consequences for the various constituencies of financial statement users, even if these policies do not directly affect firm cash flows. Furthermore, different constituencies may prefer different accounting policies. Specifically, management's preferred policies may be at odds with those that best inform investors.

Economic consequences complicate the setting of accounting standards, which require a delicate balancing of accounting and political considerations. Standard setting bodies have responded by bringing different constituencies in to their boards and by issuing exposure drafts to give all interested parties an opportunity to comment on proposed standards.

8.3   *Employee Stock Options*

We now examine three areas where economic consequences have been particularly apparent. The first of these is accounting for stock options issued to management and, in some cases, to other employees, giving them the right to buy company stock over some time period. We will refer to these options as **ESOs.**

Accounting for ESOs in the United States has traditionally been based on the 1972 Opinion 25 of the Accounting Principles Board (APB 25). This standard required firms issuing fixed[1] ESOs to record an expense equal to the difference between the market value of the shares on the date the option was granted to the employee (the **grant date**) and the exercise, or strike, price of the option. This difference is called the **intrinsic value** of the option. Most firms granting ESOs set the exercise price equal to the grant date market value, so that the intrinsic value is zero. As a result, no expense for ESO compensation need be recorded. For example, if the underlying share has a market value of $10 on the grant date, setting the exercise price at $10 triggers no expense recognition, whereas setting the exercise price at $8 triggers an expense of $2 per ESO granted.

In the years following issuance of APB 25, this basis of accounting became widely recognized as inadequate. Even if there is no intrinsic value, an option has a **fair value** on the grant date, since the price of the underlying share may rise over the term to expiry (the **expiry date**) of the option. Thus failure to record an expense understates compensation cost and overstates net income. Furthermore, a lack of earnings comparability across firms results, since different firms have different proportions of options in their total compensation packages. These problems worsened as a result of a dramatic increase in the use of ESO compensation since 1972, particularly for small, start-up, hi-tech firms. These firms particularly like the non-cash-requiring aspect of ESOs and their motivational impact on the workforce, as well as the higher reported profits that result compared to other forms of compensation.

Also during this period, executive compensation came under political scrutiny, due to the high amounts of compensation that top executives received. Firms were perhaps motivated to award seemingly excessive amounts of ESO compensation since such compensation was "free." Charging the fair value of ESOs to expense would, some felt, help investors to see the real cost of this component of compensation. Indeed, in February, 1992 a bill was introduced into the U.S. Congress requiring ESOs to be valued and expensed.

One of the reasons why the APB had not required fair value accounting for ESOs was the difficulty of establishing this value. This situation changed somewhat with the advent of the Black/Scholes option pricing formula (see Section 7.4.3). However, several aspects of ESOs are not captured by Black/Scholes. For example, the model assumes that options can be freely traded, whereas ESOs cannot be exercised until the **vesting date**, which is typically one or more years after they are granted. Also, if the employee leaves the firm prior to vesting the options are forfeited or, if exercised, there may be restrictions on the employee's ability to sell the acquired shares. In addition, the Black/Scholes formula assumes that the option cannot be exercised prior to expiry (a European option), whereas ESOs are American (can be exercised prior to expiry). Nevertheless, it was felt by many that Black/Scholes provided a reasonable basis for reliable estimation of ESO fair value.

Consequently, in June, 1993, the FASB issued an exposure draft of a proposed new standard. The exposure draft proposed that firms record compensation expense equal to the fair value at the grant date of ESOs issued during the period. Fair value could be determined by Black/Scholes or other option pricing formula, with adjustment for the possibility of employee retirement prior to vesting and for the possibility of early exercise. Early exercise, for example, was dealt with by using the *expected* time to exercise based on past experience, rather than the time to expiry, in the Black/Scholes formula.

The exposure draft attracted extreme opposition from business, which soon extended into the Congress. Concerns were expressed about the economic consequences of the lower reported profits that would result. These claimed consequences included lower share prices, higher cost of capital, a shortage of managerial talent, and inadequate motivation. This would particularly disadvantage small start-up companies that, as mentioned, were heavy options users. To preserve their bottom lines, firms would be forced to reduce ESO usage, with negative effects on cash flows, employee motivation, and innovation. This, it was claimed, would threaten the competitive position of American industry. Business was also concerned that the draft proposal was politically motivated. If so, opponents of the proposal would feel justified in attacking it with every means at their disposal.

Another series of questions related to the ability of Black/Scholes to reliably measure ESO fair value. To see these concerns, we first need to consider just what the costs of ESOs are, since, unlike most costs, they do not require any cash outlay. Essentially, the cost is borne by the firm's shareholders through dilution of their proportionate interests in the firm. Thus, if an ESO is exercised at a price of, say, $10 when the market value of the share is $30, the ex post cost to the firm and its shareholders is $20. By admitting the new shareholder at $10, the firm foregoes the opportunity to issue the share at the market price of $30. That is, the $20 opportunity cost measures the dilution of the existing shareholders' interests. The fair value of the ESO at the grant date is then the expected present value of this opportunity cost.[2]

However, this expected value is very difficult to measure. As mentioned, the employee may exercise the option at any time after vesting up to expiry. The ex post cost to the firm will then depend on the difference between the market value of the share and the exercise price at that time. In order to know the fair value of the ESO it is necessary to know the employee's optimal exercise strategy.

This strategy is modelled by Huddart (1994). As Huddart points out, determining the employee's strategy requires knowledge of the process generating the firm's future stock price, the employee's wealth and utility function (in particular the degree of risk aversion), whether the employee holds or sells the acquired shares (many firms require senior officers to hold large amounts of company stock) and, if sold, what investment alternatives are available. Matters are further complicated if the firm pays dividends on its shares and if the motivational impact of the ESO affects share price.

By making some simplifying assumptions (including no dividends, no motivational impact), Huddart showed that the Black/Scholes formula can substantially overstate the fair value of an ESO at the grant date. To see why, we first note three option characteristics:

1. The expected return from holding an option exceeds the expected return on the underlying share. This is because the option cannot be worth less than zero, but the share price can fall below the option's exercise price. As a result, a risk-neutral employee would not normally exercise an ESO before maturity.

2. The "upside potential" of an American option (its propensity to increase in value) increases with the time to maturity. The longer the time, the greater the likelihood that during this interval the underlying share price

will take off, making the option more valuable. Early exercise sacrifices some of this upside potential.

3. If an option is "deep-in-the-money," that is, if the value of the underlying share greatly exceeds the exercise price, the set of possible payoffs from holding the option and their probabilities closely resembles the set of pay-offs and probabilities from holding the underlying share. This is because for a deep-in-the-money option the probability of share price falling below exercise price is low. Then, every realization of share price induces a similar realization in the option value. As a result, if the employee is required to hold the shares acquired, he or she might as well hold the option to maturity. The payoffs are the same and, due, to the time value of money, paying the exercise price at expiry dominates paying it sooner.

The question then is, are there circumstances where the employee *will* exercise the option early? Huddart identifies two. First, if the ESO is only slightly in-the-money (substantial risk of zero payoff), the time to maturity is short (little sacrifice of upside potential), and the employee is required to hold the shares acquired, risk aversion can trigger early exercise. Since there is substantial risk of zero return, the risk-averse employee (who trades off risk and return) may feel that the reduction in risk from exercising the option now rather than continuing to hold it outweighs the lower expected return from holding the share.

The second circumstance occurs when the ESO is deep-in-the-money, the time to expiry is short, and the employee can either hold the acquired share or sell it and invest the proceeds in a riskless asset. If the employee is sufficiently risk averse, the riskless asset is preferred to the share. Because the option is deep-in-the-money, the payoffs and their probabilities are similar for the share and ESO. Thus the employee is indifferent to holding the ESO or the share. Since holding the riskless asset is preferred to holding the share, it is also preferred to holding the option. Then, the employee will exercise the option, sell the share, and buy the riskless asset.

In a follow-up empirical study to test the early exercise predictions, Huddart and Lang (1996) examined the ESO exercise patterns of the employees of eight large U.S. corporations over a ten-year period. They found that early exercise was common, consistent with Huddart's risk aversion assumption. They also found that the variables that explained empirically the early exercises, such as time to expiration and extent to which the ESO was in-the- money, were "broadly consistent" with the predictions of the model.

The significance of early exercise is that the fair value of ESOs at grant date (hence the expense to be recorded under the FASB exposure draft) is less than the fair value determined by Black/Scholes. This is particularly apparent for the first early exercise scenario outlined above. If the ESO is barely in-the-money, the ex post cost of the option to the employer (share price less exercise price) is low. Since the Black/Scholes formula assumes the option is held to maturity, it does not allow for cost reductions such as this. While the cost savings from the second circumstance are less, the cost to the employer is still less than Black/Scholes, as Huddart shows.[3]

As one can imagine, theory and evidence suggesting that the exposure draft, if implemented, may not produce reliable estimates of ESO cost would be seized upon by critics, particularly if the estimates tended to be too high. As a result, in December, 1994, the FASB announced that it was dropping the exposure draft, on the grounds that it did not have sufficient support. Instead, the FASB turned to supplementary disclosure. In SFAS 123, issued in 1995, it urged firms to use the fair value approach suggested in the exposure draft, but allowed the APB 25 intrinsic value approach provided the firm gave supplementary disclosure of fair value-based ESO expense.

As an example of supplementary disclosure under SFAS 123, consider the following summary from the 2000 annual report of Microsoft Corporation:

	As Reported	SFAS 123
Revenue ($millions)	$22,956	$22,956
Operating expenses	12,019	13,912
Operating income	10,937	9,044
Other income	3,338	3,338
Income taxes	(4,854)	(4,210)
Net income	$ 9,421	$ 8,172
Earnings per share	$ 1.70	$ 1.48

SFAS 123 amounts are based on the Black/Scholes formula with an expected time to exercise of 6.2 years. The decline in net income and earnings per share is about 13%. The decline in operating income of $1,893, or over 17%, is even more striking. This material effect on income is consistent with the results of Botosan and Plumlee (2001), who found, in a 1998 sample of 100 fastest-growing U.S. firms, that earnings were reduced on average by about 14% on application of SFAS 123.

Above, we outlined Huddart's result that early ESO exercise can be triggered by risk aversion. This, however, is not the only possible explanation for early exercise. More recently, Aboody and Krasznik (2000) (AK) studied the information release practices of CEOs around ESO grant dates. They confined their study to CEOs because it is the CEO that controls the firm's release of information. Their results are based on a sample of 4,426 ESO awards to CEOs of 1,264 different U.S. firms during 1992–1996. Of these awards, 2,039 were by firms with *scheduled* grant dates. That is, awards were made on the same dates each year.[4] Thus, CEOs of these firms knew when the ESO awards were coming.[5]

AK found that, on average, CEOs of firms with scheduled ESOs used a variety of tactics to manipulate share price downwards just prior to the grant date, and to manipulate price up shortly after. One tactic was to make an early announcement of an impending BN quarterly earnings report, but to make no such announcement for an impending GN report. Other tactics included influencing analysts' earnings forecasts and selective timing of release of their own forecasts.

Since the exercise price of an ESO is usually set equal to share price on the grant date to avoid expense recognition under APB 25, a low share price on this date increases the extent to which the ESO will be in the money during the exercise period. This increases the expected value of the award to the CEO. It also increases the likelihood of early exercise since, according to Huddart's analysis, deep-in-the-money ESOs are more likely to be exercised early. Thus, to the extent early exercise leads the Black/Scholes formula to overstate the fair value of ESOs, the problem is worsened. Furthermore, if implementation of the FASB exposure draft would cause compensation committees to reduce usage of ESOs, the ability of CEOs to engage in this opportunistic behaviour would be reduced, further increasing the intensity of their objections.

Since the exposure draft was abandoned, we do not know whether its economic consequences would have been as severe as its critics claimed. The firm's cash flows would not be directly affected by the recording of an expense for stock options. Nevertheless, despite the prediction of efficient securities market theory that accounting policy changes without cash flow effects will not affect share price, business *did* perceive economic consequences. Otherwise, it would not have opposed the exposure draft to the extent it did.

8.4   *Accounting for Government Assistance*

Governments frequently provide benefits to firms in order to influence those firms' decisions in a manner desired by government policy. For example, governments may provide incentives for firms to locate in designated areas, ranging from grants, conditional on the firm meeting certain commitments, to municipal tax relief. Other programs may be designed to encourage firms to become more capital-intensive, to assist the capital goods sector of the economy and/or to enhance international competitiveness. Assistance to stimulate research and development is another common government policy.

Government assistance plans that do not involve capital items are relatively straightforward in terms of accounting. Thus, if a firm receives a payment representing a reduction of municipal taxes in a particular year, this should go to reduce the municipal tax cost of that year. These suggestions are consistent with the *CICA Handbook*, which states, "Government assistance towards current expenses or revenues should be included in the determination of net income for the period" (paragraph 3800.20).

Accounting for government assistance with respect to capital items can be considerably more complex. For example, assume that a firm receives a substantial grant for locating its new plant in a designated area. Under historical cost accounting, we can immediately see several possible alternatives to account for the grant:

1. The amount of the grant could be brought into income in the year in which it is received (more precisely, in the year in which the firm becomes

entitled to receive it). Because the firm has done what is required to earn the grant, it should be recognized as income of that period.

2. The grant could be credited to the cost of the new plant. Because the grant was given to encourage the firm to locate its plant in the designated area, the cost of the plant should be reduced accordingly.

3. The grant could be regarded as deferred revenue and brought into revenue over the life of the plant. Clearly, this alternative would tend to have the same effect on net income as the second alternative, although the balance sheet would be different—it would show a deferred credit for the unrecognized portion of the grant, whereas the second alternative would show a lower valuation for capital assets and related amortization.

It is important to note that the choice of alternative can have a material effect on reported net income. While, as mentioned, alternatives two and three would tend to produce a similar net income, alternative one would result in a substantially higher net income in the first year of the grant, with lower incomes in subsequent years.

Historical cost accounting theory seems incapable of resolving the question of which method is best. The matching of cost and revenue principle produces ambiguous results. It could be used to justify alternative one by arguing that the effort required to earn the grant was carried out when the plant was built in the designated area. Consequently the grant should be matched with this effort by bringing it into revenue as soon as the firm qualifies for it. This argument would be particularly valid if the costs of constructing and operating the plant were not materially higher in the designated area. However, the same matching principle can be used to justify alternatives two and three, by arguing that since the grant was received specifically for the new plant, it belongs to the whole useful life of the plant. Consequently, it should be used to reduce amortization expense (alternative two) or recognized as revenue over this period (alternative three). Only then would the revenues generated from the new plant be properly matched with the costs of earning them.

The lack of resolution of arguments such as these has made it necessary for a standard setting body to step in. Indeed, since 1975 the *CICA Handbook* (paragraph 3800.26) has required that:

Government assistance towards the acquisition of fixed assets should be either:

(a) deducted from the related fixed assets with any depreciation calculated on the net amount, or

(b) deferred and amortized to income on the same basis as the related depreciable fixed assets are depreciated. The amount of the deferral and the basis of amortization should be disclosed.

Thus, in terms of our example, the *CICA Handbook* allows alternatives two and three and does not allow alternative one.

8.4.1 THE PIP GRANT ACCOUNTING CONTROVERSY

A particularly interesting example of economic consequences took place in Canada with respect to the accounting for government grants to encourage exploration for oil and gas. This occurred during the early 1980s when the Liberal government introduced the National Energy Policy (NEP), whose goal was the energy self-sufficiency of Canada. One aspect of the NEP was a new 8% tax on revenue from producing oil and gas wells. The Petroleum and Gas Revenue Tax (PGRT) was to be paid by all oil companies in Canada.

A second aspect of the NEP was the Petroleum Incentive Program (PIP), a system of government grants based on exploration expenditures. To qualify for the maximum grant (80% of exploration expenditures) a firm had to be largely Canadian-owned and explore in remote areas, such as the Beaufort Sea or off Canada's east coast.

Clearly, the NEP and, in particular, the PIP grants program were fraught with political implications. It could be interpreted as discriminating against Alberta, because oil and gas exploration in that province was not in a remote area, and as discriminating against foreign-owned oil companies. For an interesting account of the PIP grant controversy, see Crandall (1983).

Some of the accounting implications of the NEP program were noncontroversial. The new PGRT was straightforward. It would reduce the reported net incomes and cash flows of all oil companies operating in Canada by 8% of oil and gas revenues.

The PIP grants were more complex. Since oil and gas wells are long-term assets, they would fall under paragraph 3800.26 of the *CICA Handbook*; that is, the PIP grants had to be reflected in revenue over the useful life of the related exploration expenditures. In Canada, the full-cost method of accounting for oil and gas exploration expenditures was widespread around the time of the NEP. Consequently, the useful life of exploration expenditures would be quite long, regardless of whether those expenditures resulted in successful wells. In other words, the PIP grants would be reflected in net income only over an extended period, despite the fact that the cash flow from grants would be received right away.

Clearly, combining the accounting impacts of the PGRT and PIP would result in a drop in reported net income, even for firms that qualified for the maximum PIP. The 8% PGRT would reduce net income currently, but the offsetting PIP grants were to be taken into income only over a period of years. Executives of affected oil companies became extremely concerned about this implication.

This raises the question of why the executives were so concerned. As Crandall points out, "the cash flow prospects were favourable or neutral." Thus, on balance, there seemed to be no reduction in prospects of future cash flows for firms that qualified for maximum PIP. Hence, according to efficient markets theory, the securities market valuation for such firms should either rise or be unaffected. Yet, according to Crandall:

Most of them knew they would have to go to the financial markets to raise the funds needed for the exploration contemplated by the NEP. They believed that the underwriters would want to price their securities at a less favourable rate if they reported a lower net income because of the CICA stand. The validity of this view is controversial, but there is no question that it was widely believed.

Certainly, something was bothering the oil company executives, to the point where they brought pressure to bear on the federal government to remedy the situation. It seems that efficient securities market theory is not able to explain these reactions.

The federal government shared the oil companies' concerns, fearing that lower oil company reported profits would hamper attainment of the goals of the NEP. It brought pressure to bear on the CICA to amend or waive the requirements of Section 3800, even to the point of threatening legislation if the CICA failed to act. Apparently, the federal government did not subscribe to efficient securities market theory either.

In the face of these pressures, the CICA held its ground. Ultimately, the government decided not to legislate. The CICA had the support of other powerful constituencies, such as the Ontario Securities Commission. Also, it may have felt that direct intervention would compromise the integrity of the standard setting process in Canada.

In this particular instance the CICA won. Regardless of the outcome, however, the PIP grant controversy has enlightened us about economic consequences. It certainly demonstrates that accounting standards cannot be set in a vacuum and that their economic consequences can extend well into the political system.

8.4.2 SUMMARY

Two aspects of the accounting for government assistance are worthy of note. First, we have another example of our by-now-familiar argument that the matching of costs and revenues concept usually allows different ways to account for the same thing. Uniform policies to account for government assistance are in place only because they are mandated by the *CICA Handbook*. The second aspect is that the PIP grants controversy, a specific instance of disagreement over the accounting for government grants, represents an important and close-to-home example of economic consequences in action.

8.5 Stock Market Reaction to Successful-Efforts Accounting in the Oil and Gas Industry

Our third illustration of economic consequences also pertains to oil and gas, although its focus is somewhat different. The previous two examples have been concerned with management and government reaction to accounting policies. Here we will look at investor reaction. Recall again that under the efficient markets theory developed in Chapter 4, there should be no effect on the market price of firms' shares arising from a change in accounting policy if that policy change does not influence cash flows. Consequently, if a share price reaction is observed following a change in accounting policy that has no cash flow effects, such an observation would raise further questions about efficient securities market theory and/or reinforce economic consequences arguments. It should by no means be taken for granted that such a share price reaction would be observed, however. Empirical research is needed to investigate this issue.

Our coverage here is based on an article by Lev, "The Impact of Accounting Regulation on the Stock Market: The Case of Oil and Gas Companies" (1979). Lev's study concerns SFAS 19, issued in 1977. That statement required that all U.S. oil and gas firms account for their exploration costs using the successful-efforts (SE) method. Recall that we discussed SE in relation to the alternative full-cost (FC) method in Section 2.5.1; you may wish to review the discussion at this time. While use of successful efforts is no longer required under GAAP, Lev's article is still relevant today, because it remains one of the few studies to document a market response to an accounting policy change that had no cash flow effects.

Since the choice of accounting policy for oil and gas exploration costs represents another instance of policy choice with no direct cash flow effects, efficient securities market theory predicts that there should be no managerial or governmental objections to the use of SE. Yet, economic consequence arguments were very much in evidence with respect to SFAS 19. In particular, there were concerns about possible adverse impacts on competition in the oil and gas industry and on oil and gas exploration. The source of these concerns was that most small oil and gas firms used FC. Since SE tended to produce lower reported net income than FC, especially for actively exploring firms,[6] it was feared that the lower reported net incomes would make it more difficult for small firms to raise capital, thus reducing competition and extent of exploration.

Consequently, Lev set out to determine whether the security prices of oil and gas firms were affected by the imposition of SE. If the concerns about SE, expressed by the government and the smaller oil and gas firms, were well founded, the answer should be yes, strengthening the economic consequences argument.

While the publication of an earnings announcement in the financial press works well as an estimate of the date on which the market becomes aware of current earnings, it can be much more difficult to establish the comparable date for a non-earnings events study. Lev took the event date as July 18, 1977, the date that the FASB issued the exposure draft for SFAS 19. It was always possible that some other event occurring around this date could trigger oil stock price changes, rather than the event of interest. However, Lev carefully examined news reports surrounding July 18 that might have related to oil and gas and concluded that this was not the case.

Lev secured a sample of 49 FC firms (firms that had been using FC and hence would be required to switch to SE under SFAS 19) and a control sample of 34 SE firms. The daily stock returns for these firms were examined for a seven-day period surrounding July 18, using the same abnormal returns procedure that was described in Section 5.2 and used by Ball and Brown and in ERC studies.

He found a significant average negative, abnormal return for the shares of the 49 sample FC firms affected by SE on the day following the release of the exposure draft. For the 34 sample firms that were already using SE, and were relatively unaffected by the exposure draft, there was little average negative return.

Lev reran his analysis using the "raw" returns, that is, the total daily share returns without separation into economy-wide and firm-specific components. He found roughly similar results, consistent with no major economy-wide events taking place on or about July 18, 1977.

Other researchers have also investigated security price reaction to changes in accounting standards. With respect to oil and gas, Dyckman and Smith (1979) and Kross (1982) found no significant reaction, while Lys (1984) did. It is instructive to contemplate possible reasons for market reaction. As discussed by Lev, one possibility is securities market inefficiency—perhaps this is another anomaly. In view of the questions raised in Section 6.2 about the extent of securities market efficiency, this is a possibility. However, other reasons can be suggested. One is that managers of FC firms may run into difficulties raising capital and/or may reduce their exploration activities once they were forced to use SE. Another reason is that the reduction in reported net income and shareholders' equity following a switch to SE might affect management bonuses and debt covenant ratios. The market could have been reacting to possible dysfunctional manager response to problems such as these. In the final analysis, however, we simply do not know why the market reacted as it did in Lev's study.

Nevertheless, while we may not know the reason, Lev's result does suggest that the market *did* react to an accounting event with no cash flow implications. Consequently, it is evidence that mandated accounting policy changes *can* have security price effects, thereby strengthening the economic consequences argument.

8.6   *The Relationship Between Efficient Securities Market Theory and Economic Consequences*

At this point, we may have another anomaly. Efficient securities market theory predicts no price reaction to accounting policy changes that do not impact underlying profitability and cash flows. If there is no securities price reaction (implying no change in firms' costs of capital), it is unclear why management and governments should be particularly concerned about the accounting policies that firms use. In other words, efficient markets theory implies the importance of full disclosure, including disclosure of accounting policies. However, once full disclosure of accounting policies is made, the market will interpret the value of the firm's securities in the light of the policies used and will not be fooled by variations in reported net income that arise solely from differences in accounting policies.

Yet, in three important areas of accounting policy choice, we have seen that three major constituencies of financial statement users—management, government, and investors—have indeed reacted to paper changes in accounting policy. The strength of management reaction seems particularly surprising, even involving appeals to government authority to intervene on its behalf. These various reactions are summarized in the concept of economic consequences. That is, accounting policy choice can matter even in the absence of cash flow effects.

Thus, accounting policies have the potential to affect real management decisions, including decisions to intervene either for or against proposed accounting standards. This "tail wagging the dog" aspect of economic consequences is all the more interesting in view of the empirical results described in Chapter 5. These results are remarkable in the sophistication they document of the market's response to financial accounting information. The question then is, does the existence of economic consequences reinforce the theory and evidence that securities markets are not fully efficient, as discussed in Section 6.2, or can efficient securities markets and economic consequences be reconciled?

Our next task is to do what any discipline does when confronted with observations, specifically, economic consequences, that are inconsistent with existing theory. We search for a more general theory that may include the existing theory but that also has the potential to explain the inconsistent observations. This brings us to positive accounting theory.

8.7 The Positive Theory of Accounting

8.7.1 OUTLINE OF POSITIVE ACCOUNTING THEORY

For our purposes, the term "positive" refers to a theory that attempts to make good predictions of real-world events. Thus:

> *Positive accounting theory (PAT)* is concerned with predicting such actions as the choices of accounting policies by firm managers and how managers will respond to proposed new accounting standards.

For example, can we predict which oil and gas firm managers will choose the successful-efforts accounting policy for their exploration costs and which will choose full-cost? Can we predict which managers will react favourably to new fair value accounting standards for financial instruments, and which will be opposed?

PAT takes the view that firms[7] organize themselves in the most efficient manner, so as to maximize their prospects for survival[8]— some firms are more decentralized than others, some firms conduct activities inside while other firms contract out the same activities, some firms finance more with debt than others, etc. The most efficient form of organization for a particular firm depends on factors such as its legal and institutional environment, its technology, and the degree of competition in its industry. Taken together, these factors determine the set of investment opportunities available to the firm, and hence its prospects.

A firm can be viewed as a **nexus of contracts**, that is, its organization can be largely described by the set of contracts it enters into. For example, contracts with employees (including managers), with suppliers, and with capital providers are central to the firm's operations. The firm will want to minimize the various **contracting costs** associated with these contracts, such as costs of negotiation, monitoring of contract performance, costs of possible renegotiation or contract violation should unanticipated events arise during the term of the contract, and expected costs of bankruptcy and other types of financial distress.

Many of these contracts involve accounting variables. Thus, employee promotion and remuneration may be based on accounting-based performance measures such as net income, or the meeting of preset individual targets, such as cost control. Contracts with suppliers may depend on liquidity and financing variables. Lenders may demand protection in the form of maintenance of certain financial ratios such as debt-to-equity or times interest earned, or minimum levels of working capital or equity.

PAT argues that firms' accounting policies will be chosen as part of the broader problem of attaining efficient corporate governance. Efficient governance requires trading off cost of capital and contracting costs. Cost of capital can be reduced by accounting policies that fully inform the market, thereby reducing investor concerns about adverse selection. However, policies that fully inform the market may reduce the correlation between firm performance and manager effort, thereby increasing costs of controlling moral hazard. Total costs will typically be minimized by some tradeoff between the two.

As an illustration of efficient corporate governance, consider the study by Mian and Smith (1990), who examine the accounting policy choice of whether to consolidate a subsidiary company. They argue that the greater the interdependence between parent and subsidiary the more efficient it is (that is, the lower the contracting costs) to prepare consolidated financial statements. The reason is that the greater the interdependence the more desirable it is to evaluate the *joint* results of parent and subsidiary operations. Consolidated financial statements provide a basis for joint evaluation. It is more efficient to monitor manager performance by use of consolidated financial statement-based performance measures than by performance measures based on separate parent and subsidiary financial statements when interdependence is high. Thus Mian and Smith predict that the greater the integration between parent and subsidiary the more likely the parent will prepare consolidated statements. This argument can be extended to predict that if consolidated financial statements are prepared for internal monitoring of manager performance it is less costly to also prepare consolidated statements for external reporting. Mian and Smith present empirical evidence consistent with these predictions.

It should be noted that PAT does not go so far as to suggest that firms (and standard setters) should completely specify the accounting policies they will use. This would be too costly. It is desirable to give managers some flexibility to choose from a set of available accounting policies so that they can adapt to new or unforseen circumstances. For example, a new accounting standard may increase firms' debt-to-equity ratios (Section 3461 of *CICA Handbook* dealing with postretirement benefits is such a standard—see Section 7.3.1) to the point where violation of debt covenants is of concern. It would probably be less costly for management to, say, switch from the LIFO to the FIFO inventory method, or to liquidate LIFO inventory layers, or to issue preferred stock in place of debt, as a way to increase equity even after allowing for income tax effects, rather than to renegotiate the debt contract or suffer the expected costs of technical violation.

Usually, the set of available accounting policies can be taken as those allowed under GAAP, although there is no reason, other than cost, why the set cannot be further restricted by contract. However, giving management flexibility to choose from a set of accounting policies opens up the possibility of **opportunistic behaviour** *ex post*. That is, given the available set, managers may choose accounting policies from the set for their own purposes.

This recognition of the possibility of opportunistic behaviour points out an important assumption. PAT assumes that **managers are rational** (like investors) and will choose accounting policies in their own best interests if able to do so. That is, managers maximize their own expected utility. Thus, PAT does *not* assume that the manager will simply act so as to maximize firm profits. Rather, the manager will only maximize profits if he/she perceives this to be in his/her own best interests. For example, managers of actively exploring oil companies whose remuneration contracts are based on reported net income may choose full-cost accounting over successful-efforts so as to smooth out income and increase the expected utility of their bonus streams, even though higher reported income under full-cost may increase firm taxes and encourage entry of additional firms into the industry. Of course, such opportunistic behaviour will be anticipated when the manager's remuneration contract is being negotiated and the firm will price-protect itself by lowering the manager's formal remuneration by the expected amount of opportunism. That is, given competition in the labour market for managers, managers will be willing to work for a lower compensation from the company if they can augment their utility by means of opportunistic behaviour. As a result, given the remuneration contract, managers have an incentive to behave opportunistically to the extent they have the ability to choose from a set of accounting policies.

The optimal set of accounting policies for the firm then represents a compromise. On the one hand, tightly prescribing accounting policies beforehand will minimize opportunistic accounting policy choice by managers, but incur costs of lack of accounting flexibility to meet changing circumstances. On the other hand, allowing the manager to choose from a broad array of accounting policies will reduce costs of accounting inflexibility but expose the firm to the costs of opportunistic manager behaviour.

PAT emphasizes the need for empirical investigation to determine how the tradeoff between cost of capital and contracting costs, the flexibility for managers to choose from a set of accounting policies, and, indeed, the corporate governance structure itself, varies from firm to firm depending on its environment. Ultimately the objective of the theory is to understand and predict managerial accounting policy choice across different firms.

Thus, PAT does not attempt to tell individuals or constituencies what they *should* do. Theories that do this are called **normative**. This book draws on both positive and normative theories. The single-person decision theory and the theory of investment described in Chapter 3 can be interpreted as normative theories—if individuals wish to make a decision in the face of uncertainty so as to maximize expected utility, they should proceed as the theories recommend.

Whether normative theories have good predictive abilities depends on the extent to which individuals actually make decisions as those theories prescribe. Certainly, some normative theories have predictive ability—we do observe individuals diversifying their portfolio investments, for example. However, we can still have a good normative theory even though it may not make good predictions. One reason is that it may take time for people to figure out the theory. Individuals may not follow a normative theory because they do not understand it, because they prefer some other theory, or simply because of inertia. For example, investors may not follow a diversified investment strategy because they believe in technical analysis[9] and may concentrate their investments in firms that technical analysts recommend. But, if a normative theory is a good one, we should see it being increasingly adopted over time as people learn about it. However, unlike a positive theory, predictive ability is not the main criterion by which a normative theory should be judged. Rather, it is judged by its logical consistency with underlying assumptions of how rational individuals should behave.

Some people become engaged in the question of which theoretical approach is the correct one. See, for example, Boland and Gordon (1992) and Demski (1988). For our purposes, however, it is sufficient to recognize that both normative and positive approaches to theory development and testing are valuable. To the extent that decision-makers proceed normatively, positive and normative theories will make similar predictions. By insisting on empirical testing of these predictions, positive theory helps to keep the normative predictions on track. In effect, the two approaches complement each other.

8.7.2   THE THREE HYPOTHESES OF POSITIVE ACCOUNTING THEORY

The predictions made by PAT are largely organized around three hypotheses, formulated by Watts and Zimmerman (1986). We will give these hypotheses in their "opportunistic" form, since according to Watts and Zimmerman (1990), this is how they have most frequently been interpreted. By opportunistic form we mean that managers choose accounting policies in their own best interests, which may not necessarily also be in the firm's best interests.

1. **The bonus plan hypothesis** All other things being equal, managers of firms with bonus plans are more likely to choose accounting procedures that shift reported earnings from future periods to the current period.

   This hypothesis seems reasonable. Firm managers, like everyone else, would like high remuneration. If their remuneration depends, at least in part, on a bonus related to reported net income, then they may be able to increase their current bonus by reporting as high a net income as possible. One way to do this is to choose accounting policies that increase current reported earnings. Of course, because of the nature of the accrual process, this will tend to lower future reported earnings and bonuses, other things equal. However, the present value of the manager's utility from his or her future bonus stream will be increased by shifting it towards the present.

   Note also that if the manager is risk-averse, he/she will prefer accounting policies that smooth reported earnings, since a less variable bonus stream has higher expected utility than a volatile one, other things equal.

2. **The debt covenant hypothesis** All other things being equal, the closer a firm is to violation of accounting-based debt covenants, the more likely the firm manager is to select accounting procedures that shift reported earnings from future periods to the current period.

   The reasoning is that increasing reported net income will reduce the probability of technical default. Most debt agreements contain covenants that the borrower must meet during the term of the agreement. For example, a borrowing firm may covenant to maintain specified levels of debt-to-equity, interest coverage, working capital, and/or shareholders' equity. If such covenants are violated, the debt agreement may impose penalties, such as constraints on dividends or additional borrowing.

   Clearly, the prospect of covenant violation constrains management's actions in running the firm. To prevent, or at least postpone, such violation, management may adopt accounting policies to raise current earnings. According to the debt covenant hypothesis, as the firm approaches default, or if it actually is in default, it is more likely to do this.

   Again, the manager may object to accounting policies that increase earnings volatility, since this increases the probability of future covenant violation.

3. **The political cost hypothesis** All other things being equal, the greater the political costs faced by a firm, the more likely the manager is to choose accounting procedures that defer reported earnings from current to future periods.

The political cost hypothesis introduces a political dimension into accounting policy choice. For example, political costs can be imposed by high profitability, which may attract media and consumer attention. Such attention can quickly translate into political "heat" on the firm and politicians may respond with new taxes or other regulations. This has happened to oil companies, for example, during periods of restricted crude oil supply and rising gasoline prices. Resulting public anger has led, in the United States, to special taxes on oil companies to take back the excess profits. As a result, oil company managers may feel that, for example, switching to LIFO would reduce the likelihood of this happening again.

Often, sheer size can lead to political costs. Very large firms may be held to higher performance standards, for example with respect to environmental responsibility, simply because they are felt to be large and powerful. If the large firms are also highly profitable, such political costs will be magnified.

Also, firms may face political costs at particular points in time. Foreign competition may lead to reduced profitability unless affected firms can influence the political process to grant import protection. One way to do this would be to adopt income-decreasing accounting policies in an attempt to convince the government that profits are suffering.

These three hypotheses form an important component of PAT. Note that they all lead to empirically testable predictions. For example, managers of firms with bonus plans are predicted to choose less conservative and less volatile accounting policies, such as full cost accounting, than managers of firms without such plans. Also, we would expect that managers of firms with bonus plans would oppose proposed accounting standards that may lower reported net income, such as the bringing of PIP grants into income only over the life of related assets. Such standards would make it more difficult to maximize current reported earnings by choice of accounting policy. Also, managers may object to volatility-increasing accounting standards, such as those based on fair value accounting, if unrealized gains and losses are included in income.

Similarly, the debt covenant hypothesis predicts that managers of firms with high debt-to-equity ratios will choose less conservative accounting policies than managers of firms with low ratios, and will be more likely to oppose new standards that limit their ability to do this and/or that increase earnings volatility. The political cost hypothesis predicts that managers of very large firms will choose more conservative accounting policies than managers of smaller firms, and will be less likely to oppose new standards that may lower reported net income.

These hypotheses can also be interpreted from an efficient contracting perspective. For example, with respect to the bonus hypothesis, firms may want to exclude accounting policies that produce volatile earnings from their accounting policy set. Otherwise, the resulting earnings volatility will reduce the expected utility of future bonuses for risk-averse managers, forcing the firm to pay more to compensate. With respect to the debt covenant hypothesis, an increase in the probability of debt covenant violation increases the firm's expected costs of financial distress. With respect to the political cost hypothesis, the firm will benefit from avoidance of political costs.

8.7.3 EMPIRICAL PAT RESEARCH

Positive accounting theory has generated a large amount of empirical research. For example, the Lev (1979) paper discussed in Section 8.5 is a PAT study. Lev makes no recommendations on how firms and investors *should* react to the SFAS 19 exposure draft. Rather, the emphasis is on how investors *did* react to the prospect of full-cost oil and gas firms being required to switch to successful efforts. Thus Lev's study helps us to understand *why* different firms may choose different accounting policies, why some managers may object to changes in these policies, and why investors may react to the potential impact of an accounting policy change on net income. Indeed, Lev includes both the bonus plan and debt covenant hypotheses as possible reasons for the market's unfavourable reaction to the prospect of full-cost firms being forced to switch to successful-efforts. To the extent that the firms' contracting becomes less efficient, and to the extent that managers would behave opportunistically to preserve their bonuses and avoid debt covenant violation, the securities market would be expected to react negatively.

Much PAT research has been devoted to testing the implications of the three hypotheses described above. For example, the bonus plan hypothesis was investigated by Healy (1985), who found evidence that managers of firms with bonus plans based on reported net income systematically adopted accrual policies so as to maximize their expected bonuses. Healy's paper and some of the research that followed from it are discussed in Section 11.2.

Sweeney (1994) reports on tests of the debt covenant hypothesis. She studied a sample of 130 U.S. manufacturing firms that were first-time debt covenant violators during the period 1980–1989, plus a control sample of 130 firms of similar size and industry that did not violate debt covenants.

Sweeney obtained information about the existence and nature of debt covenant violations from firms' annual reports, including MD&A. She found that the most frequently violated covenants were with respect to maintenance of working capital and shareholders' equity. Debt-to-equity and interest coverage ratios were violated relatively infrequently. Many of the sample firms disclosed the nature of the costs they incurred because of covenant violation. These included increased security, restrictions on further borrowing, and higher interest rates.

Sweeney found that in an eight-year period beginning five years prior to the year of default, the defaulting firms made, on average, significantly more voluntary income-increasing accounting policy changes than the control sample firms, and that the average cumulative impact on reported net income of these changes was significantly greater for the defaulting firms. Examples of income-increasing accounting changes include changes in pension plan assumptions, pension terminations, adoption of FIFO inventory, and liquidation of LIFO inventory layers.

In addition to voluntary changes in accounting policies such as those just mentioned, firms may be able to manipulate reported net income by the timing of adoption of new accounting standards. For example, Section 3461 of *CICA Handbook* requires fair value accounting for pensions and OPEBS. Issued in March, 1999, it is effective for fiscal years beginning on or after January 1, 2000, with earlier adoption encouraged. This means that a firm with a December 31 year-end could wait until its December 31, 2000 annual report before adopting Section 3461, or could adopt as early as its December 31, 1999 annual report. A firm whose reported net income would decrease under Section 3461 relative to its income under the previous pay-as-you-go accounting for OPEBS would adopt as late as possible if it was close to or in violation of debt covenants, according to the debt covenant hypothesis. Sweeney found that her sample of defaulting firms did tend to adopt mandatory income-decreasing standards late, and adopt income-increasing standards early. The control sample firms did not exhibit this behaviour. Sweeney's voluntary and mandatory accounting policy results are consistent with opportunistic accounting policy choice by managers, at the expense of creditors, as predicted by the debt covenant hypothesis.

Sweeney also reports that of her 130 sample defaulting firms, only 53 firms actually made accounting policy changes during the eight-year period surrounding violation. That is, the results given above are despite the fact that 77 firms made no income-increasing changes at all. This raises a question as to the generality of the opportunistic form of the debt covenant hypothesis.

To investigate why some defaulting firms adopted accounting policies to increase reported net income and why some did not, Sweeney identified those defaulting firms that had both "accounting flexibility" and low default costs. If firms had little flexibility to make income-increasing accounting changes (for example, they may already be using FIFO inventory accounting and straight-line amortization) and if they bore no costs of covenant violation (firms that did not report costs of violation in their annual reports were taken as not bearing such costs), they would hardly be expected to make income-increasing accounting changes. She found that firms in her defaulting sample that had both little flexibility and low default costs made significantly fewer income-increasing changes than firms that did not have these characteristics, suggesting that managers appear to trade off the costs of accounting policy change against the benefits.

This result is of interest, because it implies that the opportunistic version of the debt covenant hypothesis does not tell the whole story, and that the efficient contracting version of PAT is also operative—managers would be less concerned about costs to the firm of accounting policy change if they were behaving opportunistically. We will return to efficient contracting below.

With respect to the political cost hypothesis, much empirical investigation has been based on firm size. However, this measure of political cost is complicated by the correlation of size with other firm characteristics, such as profitability and risk. Also, the bonus plan and debt covenant hypotheses work in the opposite direction to size in their accounting policy predictions, so that it is necessary to control for their effects.

These considerations suggest that empirical investigation of the political cost hypothesis should look at situations where political costs are particularly salient. One such situation occurs when firms are under pressure from foreign imports.

Jones (1991) studied the actions of firms to lower reported net income during import relief investigations. The granting of relief to firms that are affected by foreign competition is, in part, a political decision. Trade legislation allows for the granting of assistance such as tariff protection to firms in industries that are unfairly affected by foreign competition. In the United States, the International Trade Commission (ITC) is responsible for investigating whether there is injury. This investigation will consider economic factors such as sales and profits of affected firms. However, there is also a considerable political dimension to the granting of relief, since consumers will end up paying higher prices, and there may be retaliation by foreign countries. A determination of injury by the ITC goes initially to the president, who has 60 days to decide whether to grant relief. If relief is not granted, Congress may step in and override the president.

Thus, it is by no means clear that a deterioration of profitability is sufficient for relief to be granted. As a result, affected firms have an incentive to choose accounting policies to lower their reported net income even more, so as to bolster their case. Of course, this incentive will be known to the ITC, politicians, and the public. However, as Jones points out, these constituencies may not have the motivation to adjust for any opportunistic downward manipulation of earnings. For example, the effect of higher prices which would follow the granting of relief to an industry may not be sufficiently great for it to be cost-effective for consumers to lobby against it. Even the ITC may not be fully motivated to adjust for manipulation of earnings if it was a priori sympathetic to the petitioning firms. These disincentives to unwind any earnings manipulation are strengthened if it is difficult to detect.

An effective way to reduce reported earnings in a hard-to-detect manner is to manipulate accounting policies relating to accruals. For example, a firm may increase amortization charges, it may record excessive liabilities for product guarantees, contingencies, and rebates, and it may record generous provisions for doubtful accounts and obsolescence of inventories. These are called **discretionary accruals**.

Jones examined whether firms used discretionary accruals to lower reported earnings. She collected a sample of 23 firms from five industries involved in six import relief investigations by the ITC over the period 1980–1985 inclusive.

It is easy to determine a firm's **total accruals** for the year. One approach, pointed out in Section 6.2.6, is to take the difference between operating cash flows and net income. Accruals are interpreted quite broadly here, being the net effect of all recorded operating events during the year other than cash flows. Changes in accounts receivable and payable are accruals, as are changes in inventories. Amortization expense is a negative accrual, being that portion of the cost of capital assets that is written off in the year. Jones used an equivalent approach, by taking the change in non-cash working capital for the year from the comparative balance sheets, plus amortization expense, as her measure of total accruals.

However, separating total accruals into discretionary and non-discretionary components presents a major challenge. This is because non-discretionary accruals are correlated with the level of business activity. For example, if a firm is suffering from foreign competition it may have lower receivables, it may have to delay payment of current liabilities, and it may have to write off large amounts of slow-moving inventory. These are negative accruals, but they can hardly be regarded as discretionary. How can the researcher, who does not have access to the firm's records and so must work from the financial statements, separate them out of total accruals so as to get at the discretionary component?

Jones' approach to this problem was to estimate the following regression equation for each firm j in her sample, over a period prior to the year of the ITC investigation:[10]

$$TA_{jt} = \alpha_j + \beta_{1j}\Delta REV_{jt} + \beta_{2j}PPE_{jt} + \varepsilon_{jt}$$

where:

TA_{jt} = total accruals for firm j in year t

ΔREV_{jt} = revenues for firm j in year t less revenues for year $t - 1$

PPE_{jt} = gross property, plant, and equipment in year t for firm j

ε_{jt} = a residual term that captures all impacts on TA_{jt} other than those from ΔREV_{jt} and PPE_{jt}

α_j, β_{1j}, and β_{2j} are constants to be estimated.

The purpose of ΔREV_{jt} is to control for non-discretionary accruals of current assets and liabilities, on the grounds that these depend on changes in business activity as measured by revenues. Also, PPE_{jt} controls for the non-discretionary component of amortization expense, on the grounds that this depends on the firm's investment in capital assets.

With this regression model estimated for each sample firm, Jones used it to predict non-discretionary accruals during the ITC investigation years. That is:

$$U_{jp} = TA_{jp} - (\alpha_j + \beta_{1j}\Delta REV_{jp} + \beta_{2j}PPE_{jp})$$

where p is the year of investigation, TA_{jp} is firm j's total accruals for this year, and the quantity in brackets is the predicted non-discretionary accruals for the year from the regression model. The term U_{jp} is thus an estimate of discretionary accruals for year p for firm j.[11] The political cost hypothesis predicts that the U_{jp} will be negative, that is, that firms use discretionary accruals to force down reported net income.

Jones found evidence of the predicted behaviour. For almost all firms in the sample, discretionary accruals as measured above were significantly negative in the ITC investigation years. Significant negative accruals were not found in the years immediately preceding and following the investigations. These results, while perhaps not as strong as might be expected, suggest that affected firms were systematically choosing accrual policies so as to improve their case for import protection, consistent with the political cost hypothesis.

The above are just a few of numerous studies to test the predictions of PAT. More extensive discussions are contained in Watts and Zimmerman (1986, 1990). It does appear that these three hypotheses have empirical validity in explaining differential manager reaction to accounting policy choices. Estimation of discretionary accruals is an important component of much PAT research. We will return to it in our review of earnings management in Chapter 11.

While these three PAT hypotheses may explain manager reaction, the evidence is less strong that they can explain *investor* reaction to accounting policy change. In fact, the Lev study reviewed in Section 8.5 is one of the few to find a clear security market reaction to a paper policy change. However, even Lev does not clarify whether his results were due to positive theory variables or to securities market inefficiency. More generally, Bernard (1989) states that evidence that the market responds to the economic consequences of other standards than oil and gas has been hard to come by. Whether market value effects are present, but existing empirical methodology cannot uncover them, or whether the three hypotheses are not good predictors of security market reaction to economic consequences appears to be an open question.

8.7.4 DISTINGUISHING THE OPPORTUNISTIC AND EFFICIENT CONTRACTING VERSIONS OF PAT

As mentioned, the three hypotheses of PAT have been stated above in opportunistic form, that is, they assume that managers choose accounting policies to maximize their own expected utility relative to their given remuneration and debt contracts and political costs. As mentioned, these hypotheses can also be stated in "efficiency" form, on the assumption that compensation contracts and internal control systems, including monitoring by the board of directors, limit opportunism, and motivate managers to choose accounting policies that minimize the firm's cost of capital and contracting costs.

Frequently, these two forms of PAT make similar predictions. For example, from the bonus plan hypothesis a manager may choose straight-line amortization over, say, declining-balance so as to opportunistically increase remuneration. However, this same policy could be chosen under the bonus hypothesis for efficiency reasons. Suppose that straight-line amortization best measures the opportunity cost to the firm of using its fixed assets. Then, straight-line amortization results in a reported income that better measures manager performance. As a result, this policy would more efficiently motivate the manager (which is the purpose of the bonus in the first place) relative to other possible amortization policies. Also, as Sweeney (1994) points out, if a firm in danger of default on its debt covenants runs down its LIFO inventory, this could be regarded as an opportunistic increase in profits at the expense of creditors. Alternatively, if the threatened default arises from a fall in business activity, reducing inventories could be an efficient business strategy to increase cash flows, particularly if the firm is in a tax loss position.

Consequently, it can be difficult to tell whether firms' observed accounting policy choices are driven by opportunism or efficiency. Yet, without being able to distinguish these possibilities, it can hardly be said that we understand the process of accounting policy choice.

PAT research addresses this problem. We have already referred to the study of Mian and Smith in Section 8.7.1, who report evidence that firms make efficient decisions with respect to preparation of consolidated financial statements. Also, Christie and Zimmerman (1994) investigated the extent of income-increasing accounting choices in a sample of firms that had become takeover targets. Their reasoning was that if opportunistic accounting policy choice was taking place, it would be most rampant in firms that subsequently were taken over, as existing management struggled to maintain their jobs and reputations by maximizing reported net income and financial position. Christie and Zimmerman found that, even in such a sample, the effects of income-increasing accounting choices were relatively small. From this, they reasoned that the extent of opportunism in the population of firms at large was even less.

Earlier, we mentioned that Sweeney (1994) found that managers were mindful of the costs versus benefits of accounting policy change, and appeared to change accounting policies in the face of debt covenant problems only when it was cost-effective to do so. If only the opportunistic version of the debt covenant hypothesis held, managers would be less concerned about costs in their attempts to manoeuvre out of their covenant problems.

Sweeney presents additional evidence in favour of the efficiency version of PAT, by identifying four firms in her sample that could have delayed default by switching from LIFO but chose not to do so. All of these firms would have incurred substantial tax costs if they had switched. She identified another three firms that apparently decided not to incur the costs of changing accounting policies because the income effects of doing so would not have been large enough to delay default.

Overall, Sweeney's results support both versions of PAT but suggest that a detailed, firm-specific analysis is needed to separate the two.

The research of Dechow (1994) also relates to the two versions of PAT. She argued that if accruals are largely the result of opportunistic manipulation of reported earnings, the efficient market will reject them in favour of cash flows, in which case cash flows should be more highly associated with share returns than net income. Alternatively, if accruals reflect efficient contracting, net income should be more highly associated with share returns than cash flows. Her empirical tests found net income to be more highly associated with returns than cash flows.

Dechow also argued that when accruals are relatively large (as, for example, in rapidly growing firms), net income should be even more highly associated with share returns, relative to cash flows, than when the firm is in steady state (in which case cash flows and net income will be equal). Her empirical tests found this to be the case, adding further support to efficient contracting.

Guay (1999) studied the derivatives activities of firms in the year that they first began to use them. Guay pointed out that, from an opportunistic perspective, managers have incentives to increase firm risk. For example, shareholders of a firm with outstanding debt will benefit from an increase in firm risk since, if the firm becomes financially distressed, their liability is limited and the debtholders will bear much of the loss. However, if the firm prospers, the shareholders reap all the benefits. Thus the manager who wants to please the shareholders will increase firm risk, other things equal. Furthermore, to the extent the manager owns firm shares personally, this risk-increasing incentive operates on the manager directly. Also, if the manager owns stock options acquired as part of executive compensation, a similar risk-increasing incentive operates, since the lowest value for the option is zero but, if share price rises, the options can be very lucrative.

From an efficient contracting perspective, however, excessive risk is costly to the firm. One reason is that excessive risk both raises the firm's cost of capital and increases the probability that the firm will have to go to the capital market. A second reason is that risk increases the probability of financial distress and resulting costs. Third, for highly levered firms, prospective profits on new investment projects will go primarily to increase the security of the debtholders rather than the shareholders. This reduces the incentive for the manager to pursue profitable projects (the underinvestment problem). Finally, executive compensation plans impose risk on the manager by basing compensation at least in part on net income or some other measure of performance. If the firm's performance is excessively risky, the expected utility of the risk averse manager's bonus stream is reduced, meaning that the firm will have to pay the manager more.

The efficient contracting version of PAT suggests that the firm limit its risk. Derivatives are a powerful and effective way to do this. The way that a firm uses derivatives can be used to test which version of PAT is operative. If firms that initiate the use of derivatives do so primarily to hedge, the efficient contracting version is supported. If they use derivatives primarily to speculate, this suggests the opportunistic version.

In a test sample of 254 U.S. firms which first began to use derivatives during the period 1991 to 1994, inclusive, Guay found that these new users experienced a significant reduction in several measures of firm risk[12] relative to a control sample of firms that did not initiate new derivatives activity, consistent with a hedging motivation. He also documented a consistency between type of risk exposure and type of hedging instrument used. For example, a majority of test firms with high interest rate risk used hedging instruments that reduced interest rate risk, such as interest rate swaps. Furthermore, the variability of daily share returns (a measure of total firm risk) of the test sample firms fell in a manner consistent with efficient contracting following initiation of derivatives use. For example, firms with high leverage experienced high risk reductions, and vice versa. This suggests that those firms with the greatest incentive to hedge their risk did in fact make greater use of derivatives.

Collectively, these various results support the efficient contracting version of PAT.

8.7.5   CONCLUSIONS

PAT attempts to understand and predict firms' accounting policy choices. At its most general level it asserts that accounting policy choice is part of the firm's overall need to minimize its cost of capital and contracting costs. The accounting policies that do this are largely determined by the firm's organizational structure, which in turn is determined by its environment. Thus, accounting policy choice is part of the overall process of corporate governance.

PAT has led to a rich body of empirical literature. Three aspects of the firm's organizational structure and environment have been particularly singled out for study—its management compensation contracts, its capital structure, and its exposure to political costs.

PAT does not imply that a firm's accounting policy choice should be uniquely specified. Rather, it is usually more efficient to have a set of accounting policies, from which management may choose. This set can be taken as the set of policies allowed by GAAP or it can be further restricted by contract. Allowing management some flexibility in accounting policy choice enables a flexible response to changes in the firm's environment and to unforeseen contract outcomes. However, it also opens the door to opportunistic management behaviour in accounting policy choice.

From the perspective of PAT, it is not hard to see why accounting policies can have economic consequences. From an efficiency perspective, the set of available policies affects the firm's flexibility. From an opportunistic perspective, the ability of management to select accounting policies for its own advantage is affected. Either way, changes in the set of available policies will matter to management. Accounting standards may restrict the allowable accounting policies, as in the accounting for government assistance under Section 3800 of *CICA Handbook*. Other standards may lower reported net income, as in the accounting for OPEBs under Section 3461, or in proposed standards to record an expense for executive and employee stock options. Still other standards may increase earnings volatility, as in draft proposals to fair value all financial instruments. Thus, we would expect management to react, and the more a new standard interferes with existing contracts and/or reduces accounting policy choice, the stronger this reaction should be. Note that nothing in this argument necessarily conflicts with securities market efficiency.

While, as mentioned, managers' concerns about accounting policies and standards may be driven by opportunism or by efficient contracting, there is significant evidence in favour of the efficient contracting version of PAT. This suggests that firms are able to align managers' interests with those of shareholders. We now turn to consideration of how this alignment may be accomplished.

Questions and Problems

1. Explain the difference between a normative and a positive theory. Give an example of each.

2. Can a positive theory make good predictions even though it may not capture exactly the underlying decision processes by which individuals make decisions? Explain.

3. How is a firm's susceptibility to political costs often measured in positive accounting theory? Do you think this is a good measure? Explain.

4. In his article "The Impact of Accounting Regulation on the Stock Market: The Case of Oil and Gas Companies" (Section 8.5), Lev examined the daily returns on a portfolio of oil and gas company's common shares affected by SFAS 19. At the time, this standard would have required firms to use the successful-efforts method of accounting for the costs of oil and gas exploration.

   Lev found that there was an average decline of 4.5% in the share prices of firms that would be affected by the new standard during a three-day period following the release of the exposure draft (July 18, 1977), which announced the FASB's intention to impose successful-efforts accounting. This illustrates the economic consequences of an accounting policy change that would have no direct impact on affected firms' cash flows.

   Required
   a. Why did Lev examine share returns around the date of the exposure draft (July 18, 1977) rather than the date SFAS 19 was issued (December 5, 1977)?
   b. Why did Lev examine daily stock returns instead of returns over a longer period, such as a week?
   c. Lev chronicled other events that may have affected oil company share prices around July 18, 1977, such as political developments, developments in the oil and gas market, etc. Why did he do this? (CGA-Canada)

5. In his article "The Impact of Accounting Regulation on the Stock Market: The Case of Oil and Gas Companies," Lev refers to the negative reaction to the oil and gas exposure draft by small oil and gas producers that were currently using the full-cost method. These small producers argued that successful-efforts accounting would reduce their ability to raise capital, with consequent effects on oil and gas exploration and on the level of competition in the industry.

Required

Evaluate these arguments from the standpoint of efficient securities market theory.

6. Lev, in his study "The Impact of Accounting Regulation on the Stock Market: The Case of Oil and Gas Companies" (Section 8.5), found a significant negative abnormal securities market return for a sample of firms that were to be required by SFAS 19 to switch from full-cost to successful-efforts accounting for the costs of oil and gas exploration.

Required

a. Use the bonus plan hypothesis of positive accounting theory to explain this negative securities market reaction.

b. Use the debt covenant hypothesis to explain this negative securities market reaction.

c. Explain, for a specific affected firm, how you would distinguish which of these two hypotheses was most likely to be driving that firm's negative share price reaction.

7. Use the efficienct contracting form of positive accounting theory to explain why managers would prefer to have GAAP allow a *set* of generally accepted accounting policies from which to choose, rather than have GAAP set so restrictively as to completely prescribe accounting policy choice.

Use the opportunistic form of positive accounting theory to explain the same thing.

8. A new accounting standard requires a firm to accrue major new liabilities for employee pensions and benefits. As a result, its debt-to-equity ratio rises to the point where technical violation of covenants in its borrowing agreements is threatened. Management knows that renegotiation of these covenants would be difficult and costly.

Suggest some accounting policy choices that could reduce the likelihood of technical violation. Ideally, any changes in policies should not violate GAAP, not affect the firm's real operations, and not reduce cash flows. Justify your suggestions.

9. The Joint Working Group Draft Standard, that proposes fair value accounting for all financial instruments, was reviewed in Section 7.4.5. An article in *The Economist*, "Shining a light on company accounts," August 18, 2001, also discussed this proposal, suggesting that standard setters are in for "a bruiser of a

battle." The article states that "Banks and companies hate the idea," and threaten severe economic consequences. For example, the article reports the reaction of banks in France that fair value accounting for all financial instruments would "threaten the stability of entire banking systems." British banks claim that their role of providing long-term credit to firms with changeable credit ratings "might be compromised." Corporate treasurers are quoted as saying that the JWG's requirement to include gains and losses on cash flow hedges in income, rather than their present practice of deferring such gains and losses might have the effect of "discouraging risk management."

Required

a. Explain why the banks and corporate treasurers dislike the JWG proposal and explain, from their point of view, why its implementation may result in the claimed economic consequences. Use the bonus plan and debt covenant hypotheses of PAT in your answer.

b. Instead of the JWG proposal, would the cash flow hedge accounting procedures allowed under SFAS 133 eliminate the concerns of the corporate treasurers? Explain.

10. SFAS 123 of the FASB requires firms to disclose as supplementary information the cost of stock options awarded to executives and other employees during the year, where the cost is based on the fair value of the options awarded. Fair value may be determined by the market value of the options or, if no market value is available, based on the Black/Scholes option pricing formula (see Section 7.4.3). A similar standard is in place in Canada, effective in 2002.

Compaq Computer Corp., in its 2000 annual report, reports net income of $569 millions. In Note 8 to the financial statements, in accordance with SFAS 123, it reports an after-tax cost of employee stock options on a fair value basis of $378 millions. This reduces its net income to $191 millions and its earnings per share from $0.33 to $0.11.

Required

a. Explain why the two net income numbers are so different.

b. Which net income number best measures Compaq's performance for 2000? Explain.

c. SFAS 123 encourages firms to use the fair value method of valuing stock option compensation in their accounts and financial statements proper. Very few firms do. Use positive accounting theory to explain why Compaq prefers to report this information in the notes to its financial statements.

d. If the FASB were to amend SFAS 123 to require firms to use the fair value method in their accounts, would there be economic consequences? Explain.

11. An article entitled "Accounting Rule-Making Board's Proposal Draws Fire," by Lee Berton, appeared in *The Wall Street Journal* on January 5, 1994. It described the concerns of small businesses about a FASB proposal to charge the value of employee stock options to expense. Under current GAAP, there is usually no expense recorded for such options.

    According to the article, small businesses felt that this new proposal would hurt them the most, because they use stock option plans instead of high salaries to lure top executives. This enables smaller businesses to compete with larger businesses "for executive talent."

    The article referred to a Coopers & Lybrand survey that found the FASB proposal would reduce reported profits of start-up or high-tech firms by 27%, compared with 3.4% for mature, larger firms.

    Craig M. Swanson, vice president of finance for Protocol Systems Inc., a medical equipment maker, was quoted in the article as saying that 200 of their 250 employees receive stock options. However, if the FASB proposal were implemented, he would only give stock options to the top executives. Mr. Swanson stated that "without options, talented people won't want to take the risk of growing with us."

    In addition, the article gave an example of a restaurant chain, Outback Steakhouse Inc., where Robert Merritt, senior vice president and chief financial officer, stated that they use stock options in order to keep their employees "interested in the overall performance of the company." He insisted that dropping stock options "could make it harder to convince employees that their hard work enhances their own wealth."

    In defence of the proposal, the article quoted FASB chairman Dennis Beresford as saying "We are aware of the concerns of small businesses....But we feel that issuing stock options without any cost gives the issuing company an unfair advantage and is an accounting loophole that needs to be addressed."

    Required

    a. What economic consequences might there be if the FASB proposal goes through?

    b. Do you agree with Mr. Beresford's reply, despite possible economic consequences? Explain why or why not.

12. Before 1993 in the United States, and before 2001 in Canada, other postretirement benefits (OPEBs) were accounted for on a cash basis, allowing companies to account for these benefits as they were paid to employees. However, after December 15, 1992, FASB implemented SFAS 106, a standard that requires companies to account for postretirement benefits on an accrual basis. Section 3461 of *CICA Handbook* contains similar provisions. (See Section 7.3.1.)

According to SFAS 106 (paragraph 124), "accrual accounting will more appropriately reflect the financial effects of an employer's existing promise to provide those benefits and the events that affect that promise in financial statements, as those events occur." Furthermore, SFAS 106 (paragraph 20) states that "the expected postretirement benefit obligation for an employee is the actuarial present value as of a particular date of the postretirement benefits expected to be paid by the employer's plan to or for the employee."

This new rule has had economic consequences, whereby firms moved to reduce their postretirement benefits. For example, as reported in *The Wall Street Journal* (November 4, 1992), McDonnell Douglas Corp. cut benefits to retired employees upon realizing that it faced a $1.2-billion charge against earnings from SFAS 106.

Required

a. What is the after-tax impact on a firm's cash flows following adoption of SFAS 106 or Section 3461 of *CICA Handbook*, assuming benefits are not cut?

b. Why would some firms move to reduce retiree benefits following adoption of SFAS 106 or Section 3461?

c. Give an argument how a firm's share price might rise following the reporting of a major charge for adoption of SFAS 106 or Section 3461.

13. An article in the *Calgary Herald* (October 22, 1994), described a proposed new *CICA Handbook* standard that would require a switch to accrual accounting from pay-as-you-go for the costs of other post-employment benefits (OPEBs), such as health care and life insurance (now Section 3461—see Section 7.3.1). Many firms grant such benefits to retired employees. The proposed accrual accounting is similar to the accounting already in place for OPEBs in the United States.

According to the article, the total annual costs on the books of affected Canadian firms would increase from $2.1 billion annually to $6.7 billion, on top of extraordinary charges of about $52 billion to record the accumulated liability upon adoption of the standard.

Required

a. Will the cash paid to or on behalf of retired employees for OPEBs be affected by the new standard?

b. The article states that most employers significantly underestimate the costs of providing OPEBs. Give an argument, based on efficient securities market theory, that the share prices of affected firms will fall following adoption of the new standard.

c. The article also states that the number of companies offering life insurance to retired employees has dropped significantly over the past few years. Give an argument, also based on efficient securities market theory, that the share prices of affected firms might rise.

14. Reproduced on page 293 is an article, "Pooling of interests strategy key to two planned mergers," from *The Globe and Mail* (January 26, 1998). The article describes aspects of the proposed merger between Royal Bank of Canada and Bank of Montreal. The proposal had been arranged so as to qualify as a pooling of interests under Section 1580 of *CICA Handbook* (now discontinued). Under this section, when a business combination qualified as a pooling of interests, the assets and liabilities appearing on the balance sheets of the combining entities were simply transferred at their respective book values to the books of the new entity. This is in contrast with the purchase method of accounting for a business combination. Then, one of the combining entities is viewed as acquiring the other, in which case Section 1580 (now in Section 1581) required that the assets and liabilities appearing on the books of the acquired entity be brought onto the books of the acquirer at fair value. Any excess of the purchase price over the fair value of these net assets is allocated to goodwill. Section 1580 required that this goodwill be amortized against earnings over a period of not more than 40 years.

Since most purchases involve a substantial premium over the fair values of the net assets appearing on the books of the acquired entity, amortization of the resulting goodwill forces down the reported earnings of the acquiring company in the years following the acquisition. This does not happen under a pooling, since no goodwill is recorded in the first place.

To avoid this earnings "penalty," business combinations were usually structured as poolings of interests if at all possible. However, Section 1580 imposed strict requirements. In effect, the shareholders of one of the combining entities must hold "not significantly more" than 50% (in the article, this is interpreted as less than 55%) of the voting shares of the new entity. That is, the combining entities should be of similar size and value.

Note: For an illustration of purchase v. pooling accounting, see Section 7.5.2.

Required

a. Does the method of accounting for a business combination—purchase or pooling—affect the cash flows of the new entity following the combination?

b. The article reports that the market price of Bank of Montreal shares rose by 15% on the day that the merger proposal was announced, whereas the market price of Royal Bank shares rose by only 5%. Why did the Bank of Montreal's shares rise so much more?

c. Why would the Royal Bank's management be willing to offer a premium to Bank of Montreal shareholders in order to meet the pooling of interests criteria of *CICA Handbook*?

POOLING OF INTERESTS STRATEGY KEY TO TWO PLANNED MERGERS

Accounting treatment will avert earnings hit from various costs

Without accountants, the two largest mergers in Canadian history would not be taking place. Both **Royal Bank of Canada's** proposed $40-billion union with **Bank of Montreal** and **Trans-Canada Pipelines Ltd.**'s $14-billion marriage with **Nova Corp.** depend on an accounting treatment known as a "pooling of interest." The approach has already worked to the benefit of B of M shareholders.

A pooling of interests allows both the two banks and the two pipeline companies to combine their business into one new company without taking the earnings hit that comes from costs such as good will.

In a takeover, good will is the money paid for a company above what its net assets are worth, a concept that takes in what's paid for intangibles such as dominant market share or a strong brand name. Because good will must be written off against earnings, any company trying to justify a takeover must be able to overcome good will by wringing additional profit out of the combined business.

However, no good will is taken into account when a true merger takes place, one that meets the standards that accountants set for a pooling of interests.

The key criterion is that one company can own no more than 55 per cent of the merged entity, with the other partner owning no less that 45 per cent. While relatively common in the United States, pooling-of-interest mergers are seldom seen in Canada because accounting rules here are stricter.

The bank merger, unveiled Friday, was clearly crafted to fit the pooling-of-interest guidelines.

While terms of TransCanada Pipelines' deal with Nova were not public yesterday, executives at the two Calgary-based companies had previously indicated they were negotiating a marriage of equals.

If it goes forward, Royal Bank's union with B of M would see shareholders in both banks exchange their shares for a stake in a new company at a ratio already fixed. Shareholders in Royal Bank, the country's largest bank, would get one new bank share for each Royal share held. For shareholders of B of M, the nation's No. 3 bank, the ratio is 0.97 of a new bank share for each existing B of M share.

If the transaction takes place, Royal Bank shareholders will end up owning 54.9 per cent of the new institution, while B of M shareholders will have a 45.1-per-cent stake.

To get B of M's ownership in the new bank above the 45-per-cent threshold for a pooling of interest, the exchange ratio had to be set at a level that put a premium on B of M's share price, compared with what it was trading at prior to the deal's announcement.

When the merger was unveiled Friday, investors pushed up B of M shares to reflect that premium. B of M stock rose $10.45 on Friday to close at $67.70 on the Toronto Stock Exchange, a staggering 15-per-cent one-day increase in its market capitalization. In comparison, Royal Bank was up $3.90 to $75.75, a 5-per-cent gain.

"Coming at this as a merger of equals, makes B of M a much more attractive partner than the other banks, such as Bank of Nova Scotia, where you'd be forced to do a takeover," one Royal Bank adviser said.

SOURCE: Reprinted with permission from *The Globe and Mail.*

---

15. The article reproduced here from the *New York Times* (September 16, 1990), "Fearing Backlash, Big Oil Companies Will Trim Profits," describes strategies of oil industry executives to hold down their reported profits in the wake of increasing crude oil prices following the Iraqi invasion of Kuwait.

    While the impact on profits of holding down the selling price of gasoline is obvious, the article describes another strategy, namely "to increase the amount of money they set aside, or hold in reserve, for future environmental expenses, for…maintenance programs and for potential legal claims."

FEARING BACKLASH, BIG OIL COMPANIES WILL TRIM PROFITS

Fearful of public and Congressional outcry over the large profits that many oil companies are likely to report for the fiscal quarter that ends in two weeks, industry executives are trying to find ways to hold down those profits.

Their strategy takes two tacks. One is to hold down the increases in the retail price of gasoline. That may be news to motorists who have seen gas prices rise an average of 23 cents a gallon since the Iraqi invasion of Kuwait last month, but oil industry executives say a 36-cent-a-gallon increase would have been needed to offset the sharp increase in crude oil prices, which have nearly doubled this summer.

The oil companies' second strategy for reducing profits is to increase the amount of money they set aside, or hold in reserve, for future environmental expenses, for refinery and chemical-plant maintenance programs and for potential legal claims. Such a step is commonplace in the industry and conforms with accounting standards.

In trying to hold down profits, the oil industry is heeding the advice of the White House and senior Republicans in Congress.

CALLS FOR RESTRAINT

In a speech on Aug. 8, President Bush urged the oil companies to show restraint in raising gasoline prices. The next day, Senator Bob Dole of Kansas, the minority leader, sent a telegram to the chief executives of 11 major oil companies, warning that if gasoline price increases were not checked, the outcry would be overwhelming.

"I can assure you that it will be very difficult to stop legislation controlling the prices of petroleum products or taxing profits resulting from these increases should no action be taken by the oil industry," he said in the telegram.

The industry is anxious to avoid a replay of the 1970s, when angry consumers and legislators pilloried Big Oil as oil prices and company profits soared. A windfall profit tax took several billion dollars away from oil companies before crude oil prices plunged below $10 after 1985. Bryan Jacoboski, an analyst at Paine Webber, said oil executives suppose now that "the best way to avoid any windfall profit tax is not to report any windfall profits."

One warning of potential backlash came Thursday, when Senator Kent Conrad, a North Dakota Democrat, told Energy Secretary James D. Watkins, "There will be universal outrage" if reports of soaring oil profits appear.

Mr. Watkins replied that antitrust officials in the Justice Department were the Administration's first line of defense against profiteering. He also said oil companies that engaged in the practice would be "hammered" by the Administration.

Senator Conrad said in an interview Friday: "If there is a significant surge in profits, we all know there will be a public reaction. I'm not engaged in oil-industry bashing. I am trying to understand what the President means when he says we will not allow profiteering. Where is the plan?"

Nonetheless, profit increases of more than 40 percent from those reported in the comparable fiscal quarter last year seem certain for at least four major oil companies, and many others are expected to show profits of close to 20 percent, Wall Street securities analysts say. In general, oil companies that will profit the most are those that produce a great deal of crude oil and thus will benefit from the near-doubling of crude oil prices.

"It's a great time to be a producer of oil, but it's a bad time to be a retail seller of gasoline," Mr. Jacoboski said.

Holding down prices at the gas pump could also help the larger oil companies in the future because smaller competitors might be squeezed out of gasoline retailing.

Required

a. What pricing and accounting policy behaviour is predicted by the bonus plan and debt covenant hypotheses of positive accounting theory, in response to increasing crude oil prices? Explain.

b. The article implies that "Big Oil" companies are the ones concerned about a possible backlash. Use the political cost hypothesis of positive accounting theory to explain why only "Big Oil" companies would be so concerned.

c. What inventory accounting policy would "Big Oil" companies find most effective in holding down profits? Explain.

d. In view of efficient securities market theory, do you think the strategy of holding down reported profits by means of accounting policy choice will be effective in avoiding a backlash? Explain why or why not.

16. In late 1992, the FASB was preparing to release its proposal to charge the cost of stock options issued to executives and employees to expense. An article, "American Accounting: Optional," appeared in *The Economist*, October 17, 1992. It described some of the problems of determining the cost of executive and employee stock options and of convincing firms to deduct this cost on their income statements.

According to the article, critics of the proposal attacked the Black/Scholes approach to valuing options issued to executives and employees, claiming that the actual cost to the firm is zero. Many firms were also concerned about the impact of the proposal on their bottom lines. Furthermore, there were concerns that the proposal was politically motivated

Mr. Denis Beresford, the FASB chairman, replied that options issued to executives and employees did indeed have a cost. The article quoted Mr. Beresford as saying that accountants must "tell it the way it is."

Required

a. Use positive accounting theory to explain why many firms were concerned about the impact of the proposal on their bottom line.

b. Use the three hypotheses of positive accounting theory to predict which firms would be most opposed to the FASB proposal for expensing stock options.

c. Critics of the proposed standard claimed that the cost of ESOs is zero. Explain to these critics why their claim is incorrect.

d. Given that net income does not exist as a well-defined economic construct under non-ideal conditions, explain whether you agree with FASB chairman Beresford's statement that accountants must "tell it the way it is."

Notes

1. APB 25 distinguishes between variable and fixed ESO plans. A variable plan is one under which the number of shares the employee may acquire and/or the price to be paid are not determinable until some time after the grant date. Under a fixed plan, the number of shares and the exercise price are known at the grant date.

2. This assumes that the number of shares to be issued by means of options is not large enough to affect the market price of the firm's shares.

3. Huddart also shows that the proposed correction for early exercise (expected time to exercise) can still result in overstating fair value.

4. AK's argument assumes that investors do not know the scheduled date. If they did, they could discount the CEO's information release to adjust for manager biases. AK argue that there is considerable uncertainty that a firm will maintain its scheduled ESO grant dates, and whether or not it does is not known until after the fact. Also, it would take several years before the market could identify that the firm was, in fact, adhering to a fixed schedule. AK present evidence in support of their argument.

5. AK study firms with scheduled ESO award dates to rule out the possibility that instead of manipulating information release managers may manipulate the award date itself. This latter possibility was investigated by Yermack (1997), who reports evidence suggesting that managers pressure compensation committees to grant unscheduled ESOs shortly before good earnings news. This gives the CEO low exercise price and subsequent benefit as share price rises in response to the GN.

6. Lev refers to a FASB staff study of the impact of SFAS 19, which found 64% of firms using FC would have their reported earnings decreased by 5% or more under SFAS 19. Also, 74% of FC firms would have their shareholders' equity reduced by 5% or more.

7. In the following discussion it will be helpful to distinguish between the firm and its manager. We can think of the firm as represented by the board of directors.

8. This is the "economic Darwinism" argument of Alchian (1950).

9. Technical analysis is an approach to investing that studies past market performance for systematic patterns and attempts to predict future market performance by projecting these patterns. It is inconsistent with securities market efficiency, which predicts that share return fluctuations will be random.

10. To standardize for firm size, Jones divides both sides of this equation by total assets.

11. This procedure, called the "Jones model," will be recognized as conceptually related to the use of the CAPM to separate security returns into expected and abnormal components, as illustrated in Figure 5.1.

12. Risk measures used by Guay include interest rate exposure, exchange rate exposure, "total" risk (based on the standard deviation of the firm's daily stock returns), firm-specific risk (based on the standard deviation of the firm's daily stock returns after using the market model to remove economy-wide effects), and beta. By and large, Guay's result that new derivatives users do so to reduce risk holds for all of these risk concepts.

9

An Analysis of Conflict

9.1   *Overview*

In this chapter, we consider the managerial motivation that underlies economic consequences and positive accounting theory in more detail. To properly understand management's interests in financial reporting, it is necessary to consider some models from **game theory**. Game theory attempts to model and predict the outcome of **conflict** between rational individuals. Certainly, economic consequences are characterized by conflict. We will also consider **agency theory**. This is a version of game theory that models the process of **contracting** between two or more persons. Since each party to a contract attempts to get the best deal for him/herself, agency theory also involves conflict.

As pointed out in Chapter 8, business firms enter into many contracts. Two particularly important contracts are **employment contracts** between the firm and its managers and **lending contracts** between the firm and its lenders. Both of these types of contracts often depend on the firm's reported net income. Employment contracts frequently base managerial bonuses on net income, and lending contracts usually incorporate protection for the lenders in the form of covenants that, for example, bind the firm not to exceed a certain debt-to-equity ratio, or not to pay dividends if working capital falls below a specified level.

Game theory can help us understand how managers, investors, and other affected parties can rationally deal with the economic consequences of financial reporting. Consequently, game theory and agency theory are relevant to accounting. Accounting policies can have economic consequences when important contracts are affected by those policies. Game theory helps us to see why contracts frequently depend on financial statements.

It can be argued that the historical cost basis of accounting has desirable properties that make it useful for contracting purposes. These properties are not necessarily the same as those that provide the most useful information to investors, leading to the fundamental problem of financial accounting theory outlined in Section 1.6.

Finally, the contract-based role for financial statements that emerges from game theory helps us to see how the theory of efficient securities markets is not necessarily inconsistent with economic consequences. Securities markets can be efficient and accounting policies can have economic consequences once the conflict implications for financial reporting are understood.

9.2   *Understanding Game Theory*

In this chapter, we will study the **economic theory of games**, or **game theory** for short. This is a large topic—we can only scratch the surface here. Nevertheless, we will see that game theory underlies many of the current issues in financial accounting theory.

Essentially, game theory models the interaction of two or more *players*. Frequently, this interaction occurs in the presence of uncertainty and information asymmetry. Each player is assumed to maximize his or her expected utility, just as the investors did in our decision theory and investment decision examples in Chapter 3. The difference is that game theory, in addition to taking into account any uncertainty arising from random realization of states of nature, requires that the players formally take the actions of the other players into account. Actions of other players can be extremely difficult to predict, because the action chosen by one player will depend on what action that player thinks the other players will take, and vice versa. Consequently, game theory tends to be more complex than decision theory and the theory of investment. However, the formal recognition of conflict between rational parties greatly expands the range of situations addressed by the theory.

Another way to view game theory is that the actual number of players lies "in between" the number in single-person decision theory and in markets. On the one hand, in decision theory, there is a *single* player, playing a game against nature—nature's play may be thought of as the realization of one of the states of nature. At the other extreme, we can think of a market as a game with a *large* number of players. If the market is perfect in the economic sense, the number of players is so large that the actions of any one player cannot influence what happens on the market—this is the notion of a *price-taker* in economics, as in our investment decisions in Examples 3.1 and 3.2, where the decision makers took the market prices of securities as given.

However, in game theory the number of players, while greater than one, is sufficiently small that the actions of one player *do* influence the other players—hence the conflict aspect of a game where the players take the actions of the other players into account. The decision problems facing firms in cartels or in oligopolistic industries (where each of a few producers affect, but do not control, the market) can be modelled as games, for example.

There are many different types of games. One basis for classifying games is as **cooperative** or **non-cooperative**. In a cooperative game, the parties can enter into a **binding agreement**. A cartel is an example of a cooperative game. Cartels work best where it is possible to enforce binding agreements on members not to bolt the cartel in favour of high short-term profits. If such agreements are not possible, the cartel would be more like a non-cooperative game. An oligopolistic industry is an example of a non-cooperative game, at least in jurisdictions where agreements in restraint of trade are illegal. We will illustrate both types of games in our development.

9.3   *A Non-cooperative Game Model of Manager-Investor Conflict*

In Section 3.2, we introduced the concept of **constituencies** of financial statement users. Conflict between constituencies can be modelled as a game, since the decision needs of different constituencies may not coincide. As we explored in Chapter 3, investors will desire relevant and reliable financial statement information to assist in assessing the expected values and risks of their investments. Managers, however, may not wish to reveal all the information that investors desire. They may prefer to omit certain liabilities from the balance sheet, on the grounds that this will make it easier to raise capital by facilitating contracts with lenders. Also, they may prefer not to reveal which accounting policies are being used so as to have room to "manage" reported profits by change of accounting policy if necessary. In addition, management may fear that releasing too much information will benefit their competition. These are just some of the actions that managers may take to present the firm in the best light by biasing, or otherwise manipulating, the financial statements for either efficient contracting or opportunistic purposes. The investor, of course, will be aware of this possibility and will take it into account when making an investment decision. Firm management, in turn, will be aware of possible investor reaction when preparing the financial statements. Game theory provides a formal framework for studying this conflict situation and for predicting the decisions the parties will make.

We will model this situation as a **non-cooperative game**, since it is difficult to envisage a binding agreement between manager and investor about what specific information is to be supplied. For one thing, such an agreement could be very costly, since similar agreements would have to be negotiated with all users. But different users may have varied decision problems and hence different information needs, so that many different sets of financial statements would be needed. Even if such binding agreements were made, they would be difficult and costly to enforce, because each user would need to conduct, or hire, an audit investigation of the firm to monitor management compliance with the agreement. In other contexts, binding agreements may be illegal, as when an oligopolistic industry enters into an agreement in restraint of trade.

To illustrate this game between the manager and the investor, consider Example 9.1.

EXAMPLE 9.1 MANAGER-INVESTOR RELATIONS AS A NON-COOPERATIVE GAME

We assume the manager has two strategies, one of which must be chosen. (See Table 9.1). We will call the first of these "distort" (D), which we can think of as underinvesting in the internal control system and choosing accounting policies to maximize or otherwise bias reported net income. The second strategy is to choose "honest" (H), which we can think of as maintaining a strong internal control system and preparing relevant and reliable financial statements. The investor also has two strategies—to buy shares in the manager's firm or to refuse to buy, denoted by B and R respectively.

TABLE 9.1 UTILITY PAYOFFS IN A NON-COOPERATIVE GAME

		Manager	
		HONEST (H)	**DISTORT (D)**
	BUY (B)	60, 40	20, 80
Investor			
	REFUSE TO BUY (R)	35, 20	35, 30

The numbers in Table 9.1 represent the utility payoffs to the investor and manager respectively for each possible strategy combination. Thus, if the manager chooses H and the investor B, the investor receives a utility of 60 and the manager receives 40, and so on for the other three pairs of numbers in the table. You should analyze the relationship between the payoffs to make sure they appear reasonable. For example, if the investor chooses B, a higher utility is attained by the investor when the manager is honest (60) than when the manager distorts the information (20). Similarly, if the investor refuses to buy, the manager would prefer to choose D (if the manager distorts the information, less money and effort is put into the internal control system and into relevant and reliable reporting).

It is important to emphasize the assumption that each party has *complete information* about the other. Thus, the investor knows the strategies available to the manager and the manager's payoffs and vice versa. Game theory can be extended to relax these assumptions, but this is beyond our scope. This completeness of information does not extend to choice of strategy, however. Each player in this example chooses his or her strategy without knowing the strategy choice of the other in this game.

What **strategy pair** will be chosen? The term means simply a statement of the strategy chosen by each player. Thus, BH is a strategy pair whereby the investor buys (B) and the manager is honest (H). Review Table 9.1 and make your own prediction before reading on.

We can rule out the RH and BD strategy pairs easily. If the manager were to choose H, the investor will reason that it would be better to choose B, because it yields a utility of 60 as opposed to one of 35 from R. Thus, RH would be unlikely to happen. Similarly, if the manager were to choose D, the investor would reason that it would be better to choose R, so BD would be unlikely.

Now consider the BH pair. If the investor were to choose B, the manager would then prefer D. Thus, it seems BH must be ruled out also. The only strategy pair not subject to this problem is RD. If the manager were to choose D, the investor would prefer R. Similarly, if the investor were to choose R, the manager would prefer D. RD is the only strategy pair such that *given* the strategy choice of the other player, each player is content with his or her strategy. Such a strategy pair is called a **Nash equilibrium**. Thus, RD is the predicted outcome of the game.

However, RD is not a completely satisfactory outcome of the game in Example 9.1. Notice that *both parties would be better off* if BH were chosen rather than RD. But if the investor were to choose B rather than R, he or she knows that the rational manager would then prefer D and the investor would end up with 20 rather than the 35 from choosing R. Consequently, the investor would not choose B. The Nash equilibrium outcome RD in this game is unfortunate, because it means, at least for payoff values assumed, that the market for the firm's shares would not work very well—no one would buy them.

It is interesting to speculate what might happen next. Perhaps the parties would get together and enter into a binding agreement to choose BH, after all. However, the investor would have to be convinced the agreement was in fact binding on the manager and could be enforced. Another possibility would be to change the payoffs of the game, by introducing severe penalties for distortion. This may lower the manager's payoffs for BD and RD to, say, zero. Then it can be verified that BH would be a Nash equilibrium. This would require the intervention of some central authority, however.

Yet another approach would be to think of the game in a *long-run* perspective. If this game were repeated many times, and the manager always chose H, a reputation for honesty would be established and investors would start choosing B. This would give the manager a long-run average of 40, rather than the 30 that would be obtained on a one-shot basis. Extensions of game theory to incorporate these possibilities are beyond the scope of this example. Nevertheless, game theory provides a powerful and flexible methodology for studying problems of conflict.

Note the essential difference between single-person decision theory and game theory approaches. In our earlier decision theory Example 3.1, Bill Cautious assessed *probabilities* of what would happen—he ended up with a 0.77

probability of the high payoff, and so on. The assumption in decision theory is that the high or low payoffs are generated by some random mechanism called **nature**. Thus, a decision theory problem is sometimes called a game against nature, because some impartial force (nature) is assumed to generate the high or low payoffs with the probabilities as given. While we gave considerable attention to how investors may assess these probabilities and revise them as new information is obtained, we made an implicit assumption throughout Example 3.1 that the particular decision chosen by the investor would not affect what these probabilities were. That is, nature does not "think."

This assumption is fine for many decision problems. Indeed, as we outlined in Chapters 3 and 4, much progress has been made in understanding the decision needs of users through study of the decision theory approach. However, the approach breaks down when the payoffs are generated by a *thinking opponent* (the manager) rather than by nature. In Example 9.1, the manager will reason that if the investor buys, his or her best act is to distort, and the investor knows this. Thus, it is not correct for the investor to assign probabilities to the manager's action choice when the manager's action is not chosen probabilistically. Similarly, it would not be correct for the manager to assign probabilities to the investor's action.[1] Such behaviour, by either or both decision-makers, would be unlikely to lead to good decisions in the conflict situation.

How can we use a game such as the one modelled in Example 9.1 in financial accounting theory? The essential point to realize here is that such models enable us to *better understand the process of accounting policy choice*. Recall that in Chapter 3 we developed a considerable body of theory to enable us to understand the information needs of investors. In that chapter we showed that major professional accounting standard setting bodies appear to have adopted the decision usefulness approach that follows from the theory. What we did *not* consider in those chapters, however, was whether firm management would be *willing* to adopt the full disclosure policies that accounting standard setters have proposed. Indeed, the important message in Chapter 8 was that managers appear unwilling to sit idly by, and adopt whatever accounting policies are suggested by the standard setters (representing the interests of investors). The assumption of positive accounting theory that managers are rational, leading to the possibility of opportunistic behaviour, makes it clear that management has *its own* interests at stake in accounting policy choice and cannot be assumed to necessarily adopt full-disclosure or other accounting policies solely on the grounds that they will be useful to shareholders and other investors. This is shown in our Example 9.1 by the utility of the manager being lower under H than under D. In essence, the interests of the investor and manager constituencies may *conflict*.

By modelling this conflict situation as a game, we can understand the problems surrounding policy choice more clearly. In particular, we see that, depending on the payoffs of the game, it may indeed be in a manager's interests to distort the financial statements, at least in the short run. Any accounting body concerned about implementing a new pronouncement must be concerned with the resulting payoffs to *both* investors and management. Only by ensuring that the payoffs to management are such that management will accept the new policy can a smooth implementation be assured.

Of course, any accountant with practical experience in choosing a firm's accounting policies will know about management's interest in and concern about these policies, without having to be convinced by a game theory example. Our point is that such interest and concern is exactly what is predicted by the game theory. Better understanding of this conflict situation by accounting standard setters will result in more realistic accounting policy choices, which should avoid the economic consequences disputes that were documented in Chapter 8.

There are other conflict situations in financial accounting that can be studied in a game context. For example, Darrough and Stoughton (1990) (D&S) analyze a game between a monopolistic firm (the incumbent) and a potential entrant to the industry (the entrant). The incumbent needs to raise equity capital for a new project. It has inside information about itself that can be either favourable or unfavourable about its future prospects. If the information is favourable, its disclosure will lower the incumbent's cost of capital for its new equity issue. However, the favourable news will also encourage the entrant to enter the industry. If the information is unfavourable, its disclosure[2] will deter the entrant but raise cost of capital. What should the incumbent do—disclose or not disclose?

The answer depends on how profitable the incumbent is. If existing monopoly profits are high and the need for equity capital is moderate, the dominant consideration for the incumbent is to deter entry. Then, D&S show that if the entrant has high prior probability that the incumbent's inside information is favourable and/or the costs of entry to the industry are low, the incumbent firm will fully disclose its inside information, good or bad. If its inside information is unfavourable, its loss of profits if the entrant enters outweighs the higher cost of capital, so the incumbent will disclose. If its inside information is favourable, the incumbent will disclose even if this attracts entry since profits will still be satisfactory, particularly in view of the lower cost of capital following the favourable disclosure.

Other outcomes are possible, however. D&S show that if the entrant has low prior probability that the incumbent's inside information is favourable, the incumbent will not disclose favourable or unfavourable information. Even the incumbent with favourable news will be better off not disclosing if the higher profits from discouraging entry outweigh the increased cost of capital that results.

These conclusions are of interest, because they suggest that the question of full disclosure extends into industry structure. In the D&S model, the greater the competition in an industry (measured by the threat of entry), the better the disclosure. This reinforces our conclusion from positive accounting theory that full disclosure to investors is not the only consideration affecting managers' accounting policy choices.

Indeed, it also reinforces the claim of Merino and Nymark (Section 1.2) that, prior to the creation of the SEC in 1933, the primary role of full disclosure was to enable potential entrants to identify high-profit industries. Presumably, the higher an incumbent firm's monopoly profits the more incentive it had to engage in manipulative financial reporting.

We see then that implications of the D&S analysis have a deeper significance. By delineating conditions under which firms may or may not disclose voluntarily, conditions under which standard setting may or may not be needed are identified.

Since D&S, other papers have refined and extended the above considerations. See, for example, Darrough (1993), Newman and Sansing (1993), and Feltham and Xie (1994).

9.3.1 SUMMARY

Non-cooperative game theory enables us to model the conflict situation that often exists between different constituencies of financial statement users. Even a very simple game-theoretic model shows that an accounting standard setting body that fails to consider the interests of all constituencies affected by accounting policy choice is in danger of making policy recommendations that are difficult to implement. Furthermore, conflict analysis can be used to examine conditions under which standards may or may not be needed, since under some conditions firms may be motivated to release even unfavourable information voluntarily.

9.4   *Some Models of Cooperative Game Theory*

9.4.1 INTRODUCTION

While the non-cooperative game in Example 9.1 illustrates some of the implications of conflict between user constituencies, many other areas of accounting exhibit **cooperative** behaviour. Recall that the essence of cooperation here is that the players in a game situation can enter into agreements that they perceive as binding. Such agreements are often called **contracts**. There are many such contractual agreements that have accounting implications.

In this section we will be concerned with two important types of contracts that have implications for financial accounting theory. These are **employment contracts** between the firm and its top manager and **lending contracts** between the firm manager and the bondholder. In these contracts, we can think of one of the parties as the principal, and the other the agent. For example, in an employment contract, the firm owner is the principal and the top manager is the agent hired to run the firm on the owner's behalf. This type of game theory is called **agency theory**.

> ***Agency theory*** *is a branch of game theory that studies the design of contracts to motivate a rational agent to act on behalf of a principal when the agent's interests would otherwise conflict with those of the principal.*

Actually, agency theory contracts have characteristics of both cooperative and non-cooperative games. They are non-cooperative in that both parties choose their actions non-cooperatively. The two parties do not specifically agree to take certain actions; rather, the actions are motivated by the contract itself. Nevertheless, each party must be able to commit to the contract, that is, to bind him/herself to "play by the rules." For example, it is assumed that the manager in an employment contract will not grab the total firm profits and head for a foreign jurisdiction. Such commitment may be enforced by the legal system, by use of bonding or escrow arrangements or, perhaps, by the reputations of the contracting parties. Consequently, for our discussion, we will include them under cooperative games.

9.4.2   *AGENCY THEORY: AN EMPLOYMENT CONTRACT BETWEEN FIRM OWNER AND MANAGER*

Much of agency theory can be introduced by means of a simple owner-manager contract illustration.

It should be noted in the following example that the use of two persons is a modelling device to keep the example as simple as possible. The owner and the manager are proxies for a large number of similar investors and managers with conflicting interests. In effect, the firm exhibits a separation of ownership and control, captured by modelling the firm as two rational individuals with conflicting interests.

EXAMPLE 9.2 A FIRM OWNER-MANAGER AGENCY PROBLEM

Consider a simple firm consisting of a single owner (the principal) and a single manager (the agent). The firm operates for one period. It faces uncertainty, which, as usual, we express in the form of random states of nature. Assume that there are two such states, denoted by θ_1 and θ_2. State θ_1 represents "good times" and θ_2 "bad times." If good times occur, the firm's end-of-period payoff will be $x_1 = \$100$. Given bad times, the end-of-period payoff will be $x_2 = \$50$.

We will think of the payoff here as the firm's net income. [3] (Note, however, that in a one-period model, net income, cash flows, and dividends are identical.)

Each state realization leads to a specific payoff. If θ_1 occurs, net income $= x_1 = \$100$, and if θ_2 occurs, $x_2 = \$50$. Thus, we can work just as well with the probabilities of the payoffs as with the probabilities of the states of nature themselves. That is, the probability that θ_1 happens is the same as the probability that the payoff is x_1, and so on. If the probability of θ_1 is 0.6, we can say that the probability of x_1 is 0.6, rather than the more awkward "the probability of θ_1 is 0.6 and, if θ_1 occurs, $x_1 = \$100$." Consequently, we will suppress direct reference to states of nature for the remainder of the example.

Now, assume that the owner does not operate the firm. This responsibility lies with the manager. Assume also that, after being hired, the manager has two action choices—**work hard**, denoted by a_1, or **shirk**, denoted by a_2. The action choice of the manager will affect the probability distribution of the payoffs. Let these probability distributions be as follows:

- If the manager works hard:

  $P(x_1/a_1)$ = 0.6
  $P(x_2/a_1)$ = 0.4
  ____
  1.0

- If the manager shirks:

  $P(x_1/a_2)$ = 0.4
  $P(x_2/a_2)$ = 0.6
  ____
  1.0

Recall that x_1 represents the high payoff. If the manager works hard the probability of x_1 is greater (0.6) than it would be under shirking (0.4). In statistical terms, the payoff distribution conditional on a_1 stochastically dominates (in the first degree) the distribution conditional on a_2. This is a critical point to realize—the action of the agent affects the distribution of the payoffs. In particular, the greater the effort put into the operation of the firm by the manager, the higher the probability of the high payoff and the lower the probability of the low payoff.

Of course, this is just what we would expect. Harder work by the manager increases the probability that the firm will do well. It is still possible for low payoff to occur—it is unlikely that the manager's efforts could completely ensure the high payoff, because of factors beyond his or her control—but the probability of the low payoff decreases as effort increases. In other words, at least some of the factors affecting the payoff are under managerial control.

It should also be pointed out that effort should be interpreted quite broadly. Effort goes beyond a literal interpretation as the number of hours worked, and includes such factors as the care the manager takes in running the firm, the diligence with which subordinates are motivated and supervised, the absence of perquisite-taking, and so on. In effect, effort is a modelling device that encompasses the whole range of activities undertaken by a manager.

We summarize the example up to this point in Table 9.2. The dollar amounts in the table represent reported net incomes under each of the four payoff/act combinations. The probabilities are conditional on the chosen act, that is, if a_1 is chosen by the manager the probability of x_1 is 0.6, whereas it is 0.4 if a_2 is chosen, and so on.[4]

TABLE 9.2 PAYOFFS FOR AGENCY EXAMPLE				
	Manager's Effort			
	a_1 (work hard)		**a_2 (shirk)**	
	Payoff	Probability	Payoff	Probability
x_1 (high payoff)	$100	0.6	$100	0.4
x_2 (low payoff)	50	0.4	50	0.6

We assume that the payoff is *observable* to both parties. Note that this puts the onus on the firm's accounting system and financial statements to report information fully and accurately, so that both players in the game are willing to accept reported net income as a measure of the payoff. We will return to this point in Section 9.5.1.

Now, consider this problem from the standpoint of the owner of the firm. The owner wishes to hire the manager to operate the firm, that is, the owner will have no direct control over the act taken. The owner would like the manager to work hard, that is, to choose a_1, because the probability of the high payoff is higher conditional on a_1 than on a_2.

To illustrate this more formally, assume that the owner is risk-neutral, and that the owner's utility from a given payoff is equal to the dollar amount of that payoff. Assume also that the manager receives a fixed salary of $25. Then, the owner's expected utility conditional on each act is:

$$
\begin{aligned}
EU_O(a_1) &= 0.6(100 - 25) + 0.4(50 - 25) \\
&= 0.6 \times 75 + 0.4 \times 25 \\
&= 45 + 10 \\
&= 55
\end{aligned}
$$

$$
\begin{aligned}
EU_O(a_2) &= 0.4(100 - 25) + 0.6(50 - 25) \\
&= 0.4 \times 75 + 0.6 \times 25 \\
&= 30 + 15 \\
&= 45
\end{aligned}
$$

where $EU_O(a_1)$ denotes the owner's expected utility given that the manager chooses a_1, and similarly for a_2. Just as in decision theory, we assume the players' wish to maximize their expected utilities. Consequently, the owner wants the manager to choose a_1, because its expected utility to the owner is greater. It should be clear that this result will hold for any probabilities such that the probability of x_1 given a_1 is greater than it is given a_2. Also, our assumption that the owner is risk-neutral could be relaxed and replaced by an assumption of risk aversion.

Now consider matters from the manager's standpoint. Let the manager be risk-averse. Specifically, assume that his or her utility from remuneration equals the square root of the remuneration.

Will the manager *want* to work for the owner? Most managers have alternative opportunities for the use of their time. We will assume that the manager's **reservation utility** is 3 (that is, the manager's expected utility from operating the firm must be at least 3 units or he or she would go elsewhere). Of course, the manager would prefer to receive a utility greater than 3, if possible. However, other managers would also like to work for this firm. If the manager asks for more than 3, the owner may well hire someone else. Consequently, given reasonable competition in the labour market for managers, we expect the manager to be willing to work for a utility of 3.

Now, given that the manager is hired, will a_1 in fact be chosen, as desired by the owner? First, it is important to remind ourselves again that in game theory, and in agency theory in particular, one player will not choose an act desired by another player just because that player says so. Rather, each player chooses that act that maximizes his or her own expected utility. This observation is consistent with positive accounting theory, as discussed in Chapter 8.

Consequently, if the manager chooses a_1, it must be because the manager's expected utility is at least as great for a_1 as for a_2. Note that this assumption differs from much economic analysis, where it is assumed that firms act in a manner to maximize their profits. This expected utility maximizing behaviour by all parties is one of the important and distinguishing characteristics of positive accounting theory and the economic theory of games.

Next, assume that the manager is **effort-averse**. This means that the manager dislikes effort and that the greater the level of effort the greater the dislike. In effect, the disutility of effort is subtracted from the utility of remuneration.

Consequently, we will assume:

Disutility of effort level $a_1 = 2$

Disutility of effort level $a_2 = 1.7$

We can now calculate the manager's expected utility, net of the disutility of effort, for each act. Recall that the manager is assumed to receive a salary of $25.

$$EU_m(a_1) = \sqrt{25} - 2 \quad = 3$$

$$EU_m(a_2) = \sqrt{25} - 1.7 \quad = 3.3$$

where $EU_m(a_1)$ denotes the expected utility of the manager, given that the manager chooses a_1, and similarly for a_2.

We see, then, that the manager will prefer to choose a_2, contrary to the wishes of the owner. This result is not very surprising. Most people, even managers, would prefer to take it easy, all other things being equal. Here, other things *are* equal, because the manager receives a salary of $25 regardless. This tendency of an agent to shirk is an example of moral hazard.

Designing a Contract to Control Moral Hazard

The question now is, what should the owner do in a situation such as that described in Example 9.2? One possibility is for the owner to refuse to hire the manager, but any other rational salaried manager would also choose a_2. Consequently, the owner could either go out of business or run the firm him/herself. These latter two possibilities are unlikely, however. The running of an organization is a complex and specialized task for which the owner may not have the required skills, and, after all, we do witness a separation of ownership and management in all but the smallest organizations. In fact, our owner has a number of other options, which we will now consider.

Hire the Manager and Put Up with a_2   The owner could proceed anyway, letting the manager get away with a_2 and putting up with a utility of 45 rather than 55. This also seems unlikely, however, since we will see that the owner can do better than this.

Direct Monitoring   If the owner could costlessly observe the manager's chosen act, this would solve the problem. Then, the contract could be amended to pay the manager a salary of $25 if a_1 was taken and, say, $12 otherwise. It is easy to verify that the manager would then choose a_1, because choosing a_2 would result in only $12 remuneration and expected utility of 1.76.

This type of contract is called **first-best**. It gives the owner the maximum attainable utility (55) and gives the agent the reservation utility (3). Under the assumptions of Example 9.2, no other contract can improve on this.

The first-best contract also has desirable **risk-sharing** properties. Note that under this contract the manager bears no risk, because a fixed salary is received regardless of the payoff. Since the manager is risk-averse, this is desirable. The owner bears all the risk of the random payoff. Since the owner is risk-neutral, he or she does not mind bearing risk. Indeed, we could argue that a function of business ownership is to bear risk. If the owner was risk-averse, rather than risk-neutral, the first-best contract would involve the owner and manager sharing the risk. However, demonstration of this is beyond our scope.

Unfortunately, the first-best contract is frequently unattainable. This would seem to be the case in an owner-manager contract, because it is unlikely that the owner could monitor the agent's effort in a managerial setting. The nature of managerial effort is so complex that it would be effectively impossible for a remote owner to establish whether the manager was in fact "working hard." We thus have a case of information asymmetry—the manager knows the effort level, but the owner does not. As mentioned previously, this particular form of information asymmetry is called moral hazard.

Indirect Monitoring   Given that managerial effort is not directly observable, it may be possible under some conditions to impute the effort. To illustrate, let us change our example slightly. See Table 9.3. The only difference between this table and Table 9.2 is that the payoff for (x_2, a_2) is now \$40 rather than \$50. In agency theory terms, this is a case of **moving support**, that is, the set of possible payoffs is different (it moves) depending on which act is taken. Table 9.2 is a case of **fixed support**—the set of possible payoffs is fixed at (100, 50), regardless of the action choice.

TABLE 9.3 PAYOFFS FOR AGENCY EXAMPLE				
	Manager's Effort			
	a_1 (work hard)		a_2 (shirk)	
	Payoff	Probability	Payoff	Probability
x_1 (high payoff)	\$100	0.6	\$100	0.4
x_2 (low payoff)	50	0.4	40	0.6

It is apparent from Table 9.3 that if the owner observes a payoff of \$40 it will be known that the manager chose a_2 even though effort is not directly observable. Then the owner could amend the contract to offer the manager a salary of \$25 unless the payoff was \$40, in which case the salary would be \$12. It is easy to check that the manager would then choose a_1:

$$EU_m(a_1) = \sqrt{25} - 2 \qquad\qquad = 3$$
$$EU_m(a_2) = 0.4\sqrt{25} + 0.6\sqrt{12} - 1.7 = 2.38$$

The penalty of \$13 if the \$40 payoff happens is sufficient cause for the agent to choose a_1.

Indirect monitoring will *not* work for the fixed-support case of Table 9.2, however. The reason is that if a payoff of \$50 is observed, this is consistent with either a_1 or a_2, and similarly for the \$100 payoff. Thus, the owner cannot impute the act from payoff observability.

It seems, then, that we cannot rely on indirect monitoring to ensure that the first-best contract will be attained. First, many contracting situations may be characterized by fixed support. For example, reported net income can be any positive or negative number. If a firm reports, say, a loss of \$1 million the owner cannot be certain whether this loss resulted from low manager effort or an unfortunate realization of the state of nature.

Second, even if moving support holds, legal and institutional factors may prevent the owner from penalizing the manager sufficiently to force a_1. For example, minimum wage laws may prevent the owner from being able to impose a remuneration of \$12.

Owner Rents Firm to the Manager   At this point, the owner may well be tempted to say to the manager, "O.K., I give up—you take the firm and run it and pay me a rental of $47.38." Then, the owner no longer cares what action the manager takes, since a rental of $47.38 is received regardless. This is referred to as internalizing the manager's decision problem.

Such arrangements do exist, or they have existed in the past, in the form of tenant farming. Tenant farming is usually regarded as inefficient, however, and it is easy to see why. The manager's expected utility would be:

$$
\begin{aligned}
EU_m(a_1) &= 0.6\sqrt{100 - 47.38} + 0.4\sqrt{50 - 47.38} - 2 \\
&= 0.6 \times 7.25 + 0.4 \times 1.62 - 2 \\
&= 4.35 + 0.65 - 2 \\
&= 3.00
\end{aligned}
$$

$$
\begin{aligned}
EU_m(a_2) &= 0.4\sqrt{100 - 47.38} + 0.6\sqrt{50 - 47.38} - 1.7 \\
&= 0.4 \times 7.25 + 0.6 \times 1.62 - 1.7 \\
&= 2.90 + .97 - 1.7 \\
&= 2.17
\end{aligned}
$$

Thus, the manager will choose a_1 and receive reservation utility of 3.

Note, however, that the owner receives a utility of 47.38 in this contract, compared to 55 in the first-best contract. Consequently, the owner is worse off. The reason is that this contracting arrangement has inefficient risk-sharing characteristics. The owner is risk-neutral, and hence is willing to bear risk, but there is no risk for the owner because a fixed rental is received. The risk-averse manager, who dislikes risk, is forced to bear it all. The owner must lower the rental from $55 to $47.38 to enable the manager to receive reservation utility of 3, costing the owner $7.62 in lost utility. The $7.62 is called an **agency cost** (Jensen and Meckling, 1976), and is another component of contracting costs, which the owner will want to minimize.

Give the Manager a Share of the Payoff   Finally, we come to what is often the most efficient alternative if the first-best contract is not attainable. This is to give the manager a share of the payoff. Suppose that the owner offers the manager 32% of the payoff. Then, the manager's expected utility from each act is as follows:

$$
\begin{aligned}
EU_m(a_1) &= 0.6\sqrt{0.32 \times 100} + 0.4\sqrt{0.32 \times 50} - 2 \\
&= 0.6 \times 5.66 + 0.4 \times 4.00 - 2 \\
&= 3.40 + 1.60 - 2 \\
&= 3.00
\end{aligned}
$$

$$EU_m(a_2) = 0.4\sqrt{0.32 \times 100} + 0.6\sqrt{0.32 \times 50} - 1.7$$
$$= 0.4 \times 5.66 + 0.6 \times 4.00 - 1.7$$
$$= 2.26 + 2.40 - 1.7$$
$$= 2.96$$

Thus, the manager will choose a_1 instead of a_2, as desired by the principal.

Note that it is the *contract* that provides the motivation here, as we mentioned earlier.[5] Given the terms of the contract, the manager *wants* to take a_1. This aspect of the contract is called **incentive-compatibility**, since the agent's incentive to take a_1 is compatible with the owner's best interests. (The first-best contract, if it is attainable, is also incentive-compatible, because the prospect of low remuneration following a_2 motivates the manager to take a_1.) We then say that the owner's and manager's interests are **aligned**, since they both want the firm to do well.

It is instructive to look more closely at the owner's expected utility in this payoff-sharing contract:

$$EU_O(a_1) = 0.6(100 - 32) + 0.4(50 - 16)$$
$$= 0.6 \times 68 + 0.4 \times 34$$
$$= 40.8 + 13.6$$
$$= 54.4$$

This is less than the owner's utility of 55 in the first-best contract. The agency cost of this contract is thus 0.6, less than the 7.62 agency cost of the rental contract. The profit sharing contract is more efficient than the rental contract. The reason is not difficult to see. In the rental contract the risk-averse manager bears all the risk. Here, manager and owner share the risk. While both contracts motivate a_1, a lower **risk premium** (0.6 compared to 7.62) is needed to enable the manager's reservation utility to be attained. This lower risk premium translates into increased expected utility for the owner (54.4 compared to 47.38).

However, while the profit sharing contract may be more efficient, it is not first-best. The most efficient contract short of first-best is called **second-best.** The agency cost of the second-best contract is the irreducible minimum resulting from the unobservability of the agent's effort and resulting moral hazard problem. It is the cost to the principal of motivating the agent's effort by means of a profit sharing contract. To put this another way, the manager needs to bear *some* risk to convince the owner that the work-hard effort alternative will be chosen.

Agency costs are one of the costs of contracting that are part of positive accounting theory. As discussed in Section 8.7.1, the firm will want to arrange its contracts as efficiently as possible, and we pointed out there that the efficient contracts will depend on the firm's form of organization and its environment. We can now see more clearly the nature of this dependence. For example, consider a firm in a high-tech industry. Survival in such an environment requires a great deal of research and development, most of which must be written off currently under Section 3450 of the *CICA Handbook*. Consequently, reported net income of such firms is not a good measure of manager effort, to the extent that current research costs have benefits for the future. Thus, positive accounting theory predicts that high-tech firms will tend to base manager remuneration on some other payoff measure than net income, such as share price,[6] and that the remuneration contract would include stock options that may reduce the risk to the manager of share price volatility. Such a contract would have a strong incentive effect while minimizing agency costs resulting from the risk imposed on the manager.

As another example, consider a closely held firm. The organization structure of such a firm would exhibit high manager share ownership and manager representation on the board of directors. Then, the manager's incentive to exert effort is at least partly internalized, and the most efficient remuneration contract would need to impose only relatively low risk on the manager (since risk is already imposed by share ownership). Note also that membership on the board of directors gives the manager some control over risk through the ability to influence firm operating and financing policies. Then, positive accounting theory predicts that there will be a lower profit sharing component in the manager's remuneration contract, relative to those of firms that are widely held. Research by Lambert and Larcker (1987) that found evidence of efficiencies such as these is outlined in Section 10.6.

Summary

We can make the following observations:

1. Observability of an agent's effort seems unlikely in an owner-manager context, because of the separation of ownership and control that characterizes firms in a developed industrial society. This is an example of information asymmetry leading to moral hazard, in that, after the contract is signed, the rational manager will, if possible, take advantage of the lack of effort observability to shirk. Agency theory, a branch of game theory, studies the problem of designing a contract to control moral hazard. The optimal contract does so with the lowest possible agency cost.

2. The nature of the optimal contract depends crucially on what can be jointly observed. Contracts can only be written in terms of performance measures that are jointly observable by both principal and agent:

   • If the agent's effort can be jointly observed, directly or indirectly, a fixed salary (subject to a penalty if the contracted-for effort level is not taken) will be optimal when the principal is risk-neutral. Such a contract is called first-best. Here, *effort* is the performance measure.

   • If the agent's effort cannot be jointly observed, but payoff can, the optimal contract will give the agent a share of the payoff. This will motivate the agent to work hard, but is second-best, because it imposes additional risk on the agent. Here, the *payoff* is the performance measure. Since the payoff is frequently expressed in terms of net income, this creates an opportunity for the accounting system to report a net income number that reflects as closely as possible the results of the manager's effort in running the firm (see Note 3). The higher the correlation of net income with effort, the closer the second-best contract to first-best, and hence the lower the agency costs borne by the owner. We denote such an income measure as "hard."

- If neither effort nor payoff can be observed, the optimal contract is a rental contract, whereby the principal rents the firm to the manager for a fixed rental fee, thus internalizing the agent's effort decision. Here, there is *no* performance measure. Such contracts tend to be unsatisfactory, because they impose all of the risk on the agent.

3. There are alternative measures of firm performance to net income, such as share price. The most efficient payoff measure, or combination of measures, depends on the firm's organizational structure and environment.

9.4.3 AGENCY THEORY: A BONDHOLDER-MANAGER LENDING CONTRACT

We now consider another moral hazard problem, namely a contract between a lender and a firm, such as a bondholder and the firm manager. We will regard the bondholder as the principal and the manager as the agent.

EXAMPLE 9.3 A LENDER-MANAGER AGENCY PROBLEM

A risk-neutral lender faces a choice of lending $100 to a firm or investing the $100 in government bonds yielding 10%. The firm offers 12% interest, contracting to repay the loan one year later, that is, to repay $112. However, unlike for government bonds, there is credit risk, that is, a possibility that the firm will go bankrupt, in which case the lender would lose both the principal and the interest.

The firm manager can choose one of two acts. The first act, denoted by a_1, is to pay no dividends while the loan is outstanding. The second act, a_2, is to pay high dividends. If the manager chooses a_1, assume that the lender assesses the probability of bankruptcy as 0.01, so that there is a 0.99 probability of receiving repayment, including $12 interest. However, if a_2 is chosen, the lender assesses the probability of bankruptcy as 0.1, because the high dividends will reduce the firm's solvency. Thus, under a_2, the probability of repayment will be only 0.9.

Assume that the manager is paid by means of an incentive contract consisting of a salary plus a bonus based on the firm's net income. Then, since dividends are not charged against income, the manager's remuneration is unaffected by the act chosen, that is, the manager is indifferent between the two acts. Thus, there is no compelling reason to assume that the manager will or will not take a_1, the lender's preferred act. After thinking about this, the lender assesses equal probabilities for each act of the manager, that is, the probability of a_1 is 0.5 and similarly for a_2. Table 9.4 summarizes this scenario.

TABLE 9.4 PAYOFFS FOR LENDER-MANAGER CONTRACT

	Manager's Act			
	a_1 (no dividends)		a_2 (high dividends)	
	Payoff	Probability	Payoff	Probability
x_1 (interest paid)	$ 12	0.99	$ 12	0.9
x_2 (bankrupt)	−100	0.01	−100	0.1

The payoff amounts in the table exclude the $100 loaned. Thus, the lender either earns an interest income of $12 or loses the $100 investment. We could add $100 to each payoff, to express returns gross of the $100 loaned, without affecting the results.

The probabilities in the table are conditional on the manager's chosen act. Thus, if a_1 is taken, the probability of the lender receiving the interest is 0.99; hence, the probability of the lender receiving nothing is $1.00 - 0.99 = 0.01$, and so on. Recall that we have also assumed that the chances are 50/50 that a_1 will be chosen.

Will the lender be willing to lend $100 to the firm? The alternative is to buy government bonds, with a return of 10%, or $10 in total. The expected profit from investing in the firm is:

$$ETR = 0.5(12 \times 0.99 - 100 \times 0.01) + 0.5(12 \times 0.9 - 100 \times 0.1)$$
$$= 0.5 \times 10.88 + 0.5 \times 0.80$$
$$= 5.44 + 0.40$$
$$= 5.84$$

where ETR denotes expected total return.

The first term in brackets represents the lender's expected return conditional on a_1. There is a 0.5 probability that a_1 will be chosen. Similarly, the second term in brackets is the expected return conditional on a_2, also multiplied by the 0.5 probability that a_2 will be chosen.

Thus, the ETR is only $5.84 or 5.84% on the amount loaned. The reason, or course, is the probability of bankruptcy, particularly if a_2 is taken, which forces the expected return down to well below the nominal rate of 12%. Our lender, who can earn 10% elsewhere, will not make the loan.

What nominal rate would the firm have to offer in order to attract the lender? This can be calculated as follows:

10.00 = 0.5(0.99R − 100 × 0.01) + 0.5(0.9R − 100 × 0.1)

where R is the required nominal rate. The left side is the lender's required total return. Upon solving for R, we obtain:

$$R = \frac{15.50}{0.945} = 16.40$$

Thus, the firm would have to offer a nominal rate of return of over 16% in order to attract the lender.

The 16% interest rate in Example 9.3 would probably seem too high to the manager, particularly since he or she shares in net income. Consequently, the manager may try to find some more efficient contractual arrangement that would lower the interest rate. One possibility would be to *commit* to take a_1. This could be done by writing a covenant into the lending agreement. An example of a covenant would be to pay no dividends if the interest coverage ratio (ratio of net income before interest and taxes to annual interest payments) is below a specified level. Another example would be to not undertake any additional borrowing (which would dilute the security of existing lenders) if the debt-to-equity ratio is above a specified level. Since covenants are legally binding, the lender will change the assessed probabilities of the acts. Assume the probability that the manager will take a_1 is now assessed by the lender as 1, and 0 for a_2. Thus, if the firm offers a nominal rate of 12%, the lender's ETR is:

1(12 × 0.99 − 100 × 0.01) + 0(12 × 0.9 − 100 × 0.1) = 10.88

Since this exceeds the required $10, the lender would now make the loan.

Summary

The main point to realize in Example 9.3 is the existence of a moral hazard problem between lenders and firm managers—managers may act contrary to the best interests of the lenders. Rational lenders will anticipate this behaviour, however, and thereby raise the interest rates they demand for their loans. As a result, the manager has an incentive to commit not to act in a manner that is against the lenders' interests. This can be done by inserting covenants into the lending agreement whereby the manager agrees to limit dividends or additional borrowing while the loan is outstanding. Consequently, the firm is able to borrow at lower rates.

9.5   *Implications of Agency Theory for Accounting*

9.5.1   *HOLMSTRÖM'S AGENCY MODEL*

In a widely referenced paper, Holmström (1979) gives a rigorous development of the agency model. We now review aspects of his model from an accounting perspective.

Holmström assumes that the agent's effort is unobservable by the principal but that the payoff is jointly observable, consistent with Example 9.2. This reminds us that if a payoff is to serve as a basis for contracting, it must be observable to both parties. The question then is: Is net income sufficiently observable that principal and agent are willing to use it as a measure of payoff? If not, other payoff measures, such as share price, may take over.

The answer to this question is not obvious. Granted, both parties can observe a number called net income. But, since the manager controls the firm's accounting system and accounting policies, is net income sufficiently credible that the owner is willing to pay a bonus to the manager based on that reported number? By credible, we mean that the owner knows that the manager has an incentive to disclose truthfully. If the owner does not accept the report of net income as credible, he or she would be unwilling to enter into a contract based on net income.

Thus, we see that contracting implies a role for GAAP and for an audit. GAAP are needed as a cost-effective way to put limits on the manager's incentive to influence reported net income by selecting from alternative accounting policies. Both parties should know the rules as to how net income is calculated. GAAP serve to provide this needed structure.

Auditing is needed to add credibility to the reported net income number. This credibility has several sources. First, the owner can be reasonably certain of the integrity of the audited internal control systems underlying the firm's accounting system so that the likelihood of fraud or error in net income is low. Second, the auditor will ensure that GAAP are adhered to, so that net income is determined in accordance with a set of publicly known rules. Third, the professional status of the auditor reassures the owner that the auditor is independent and unlikely to be unduly influenced by the manager. Certainly, agency theory implies that a strong and active auditing profession, which enforces competent and ethical behaviour by its members, is key to the financial reporting process.

The usefulness of net income for contracting also depends on the basis of accounting. It can be argued that historical cost-based income has desirable properties in this regard. For example, it may be less susceptible to manager manipulation and bias than fair value-based net income, at least when markets do not work well. Also, fair value-based net income may be volatile, since market values fluctuate over time, and this volatility may not be correlated with manager effort. Thus, historical cost-based income may be harder than income based on current values.

Given payoff observability, Holmström shows formally that a contract based on the payoff is less efficient than first-best, as illustrated by our Example 9.2. As in our example, the source of the efficiency loss is the necessity for the risk-averse agent to bear additional risk in order to overcome the tendency to shirk.

This raises the question of whether the second-best contract could be made more efficient by basing it on a second variable in addition to payoff. For example, as we have implied earlier, share price also conveys information about manager performance. Rather than using one measure or the other, would basing the contract on *both* net income and share price reduce the agency costs of the second-best contract?

Holmström shows that the answer to this question is yes, provided that the second variable is also jointly observable, and conveys some information about manager effort beyond that contained in the payoff measure itself.[7] This will typically be the case for share price. As discussed above, net income is not a perfectly hard measure of effort—despite GAAP and auditing, some manager ability to manipulate and bias net income within GAAP remains. Indeed, our discussion of auditor liability in Section 6.6 suggests that auditors may go along with such manipulation and bias. A further argument in favour of share price is that the efficient securities market price is based on more information than just accounting information, so that we would expect it to convey additional information about manager effort.

Of course, share price tends to be quite volatile, being affected by economy-wide events. Nevertheless, Holmström's analysis shows that no matter how noisy the second variable is, it can be used to increase the efficiency of the second-best contract if it contains at least some additional effort information.[8]

Thus, an interesting implication of the Holmström model is that, just as net income competes with other information sources for investors under efficient securities market theory, it competes with other information sources for motivating managers under agency theory. As we will see in Chapter 10, this prediction is borne out in practice.

To meet this competition as a measure of manager performance, net income should be hard. As mentioned earlier, hardness will be affected by the relative proportions of historical cost-based and fair value-based measurements in net income. This leads directly to the fundamental problem of financial accounting theory stated in Section 1.6. To the extent that historical-cost-based net income is highly correlated with manager effort, it will be useful for contracting. But fair value-based net income can be useful for investor decision-making, due to its greater relevance. Then, the best measure of net income for informing investors need not be the same as the best measure for contracting, as recognized by Gjesdal (1981).

9.5.2 RIGIDITY OF CONTRACTS

Agency theory assumes that the courts will costlessly enforce contract provisions. While the parties to a contract could agree among themselves to amend contract provisions, this can be surprisingly difficult. Contracts tend to be *rigid* once signed. The reasons for this rigidity need some discussion. Otherwise, we might ask, if economic consequences have their roots in the contracts that managers enter into, why not just *renegotiate* the contracts following a change in GAAP, or other unforeseen state realization.

Note first that it is generally impossible to anticipate all contingencies when entering into a contract. For example, unless the contract is of very short duration, it would be difficult to predict changes in GAAP that could affect the contract. Contracts that do not anticipate all possible state realizations are termed **incomplete**. The contracts in Examples 9.2 and 9.3 are **complete**. Thus, in Example 9.2, the only possible state realizations are θ_1 and θ_2, leading to payoffs x_1 and x_2, respectively. While the set of possible state realizations could be expanded in the examples, in an actual contract the parties could not anticipate all possibilities. New accounting standards issued while the contract is in effect, and which change the way net income or covenant ratios are calculated, are examples of state realizations that are hard to predict.

Given incomplete contracts, renegotiation might be possible to some extent, but it does not seem that the possibility of renegotiation following a change in GAAP is sufficient to alleviate management's concerns about accounting policies (perhaps introducing provisions for renegotiation into a contract *before* it is signed would be useful, but this is beyond our scope). For example, suppose that a new GAAP accounting policy lowers reported net income and increases its variability. The manager goes to the bondholder and explains that, through no one's fault, the accounting rules have changed and requests that the coverage ratio covenant be reduced from 2.5:1 to 2:1. This, the manager argues, would restore the bondholder's protection to what it was before the rule change. Why should the bondholder agree to such a request? In doing so, he or she is giving something away—namely the increased protection against excessive dividends that resulted from the new accounting policy. To be willing to do this, the bondholder may well require something in return, such as a higher interest rate. The problem for the manager is further complicated if, as is usually the case, there are many bondholders. Agreement would then be required from all of them, or, at least, a majority.

The manager's compensation contract with the firm owner would be similarly difficult to amend. If the manager requests, say, a higher bonus rate, to correct for an accounting policy change that lowers reported net income, the compensation committee of the board of directors may want something in return, or even reopen the entire contract for renegotiation.

In effect, a consequence of entering into contracts is just that—they are contracts, and hence tend towards rigidity. Thus, unforseen state realizations impose costs on the firm and/or the manager. The manager who is unfavourably affected by a change of the accounting rules in midstream may be forced to take out his or her displeasure on the accountants who introduced the rule change rather than on the other parties to the contract. It is contract incompleteness that drives the economic consequences discussed in Chapter 8.

9.6   Reconciliation of Efficient Securities Market Theory with Economic Consequences

We have seen how firms are able to align manager and shareholder interests, consistent with the efficient contracting version of positive accounting theory. Agency theory demonstrates that the best attainable compensation contract usually bases manager compensation on one or more measures of firm performance. Managers then have an incentive to maximize this performance, a goal also desired by shareholders.

This alignment enables us to see why accounting policies have economic consequences, despite the implications of efficient securities market theory. Under efficient securities market theory, only accounting policy choices that affect expected cash flows create economic consequences. The contracting-based argument we have given for economic consequences does not depend on accounting policy choices having direct cash flow effects. This argument is the same whether direct cash flow effects are present or not.

Rather, it is the rigidities produced by the signing of binding, incomplete contracts that create managers' concerns, and that lead to their intervention in the standard setting process. These rigidities have nothing to do with whether accounting policy changes affect cash flows.

Therefore, economic consequences and efficient securities markets are not inconsistent. They can be reconciled by positive accounting theory, with normative support from agency theory that suggests *why* firms enter into employment and debt contracts that depend on accounting information. Nothing in the above arguments leading to managerial concern about accounting policies conflicts with securities market efficiency.

Similarly, nothing in the theory of efficient securities markets conflicts with managerial concern about accounting policies. Joint consideration of both theories, though, helps us to see that managers may well intervene in accounting policies, even though those policies would improve the decision usefulness of financial statements to investors. In the final analysis, the interaction between managers and investors is a game, as modelled in Sections 9.3 and 9.4.

While game theory is consistent with *managers'* concerns about accounting policies, the theory also helps us to understand Lev's finding (Section 8.5), that *investors* were also concerned about such policies. One interpretation of Lev's finding is that the securities market is inefficient. Security prices fell in response to the prospect of an accounting policy change that would tend to lower reported net income of affected firms but would not affect their cash flows.

An alternative interpretation, however, is that Lev's finding is evidence of market efficiency, rather than inefficiency. To see this, consider once again the impact of successful-efforts on reported net income, namely, that it will tend to lower income and make it more volatile. Both of these effects will increase the probability of violation of covenants in borrowing agreements. Since violation of debt covenants can have serious implications, the efficient market bids down the share prices accordingly. Also, these effects reduce the expected utility of risk-averse managers' bonus streams. This may lead managers to change the way they operate the firm. For example, in response to the increased volatility of reported net income, managers of firms affected by the switch to successful-efforts may adopt safer exploration policies. Since these policies may offer significantly lower expected returns than the policies they replace, investors may bid down share prices in response. Thus, when contracting effects are recognized, securities market reaction to a paper change in accounting policy may support the theory of market efficiency rather than inefficiency.

While basing managers' compensation on firm performance aligns their interests with those of shareholders it should be noted that this alignment is not complete. As a result, some manager opportunism may remain. This is because net income and/or share price do not *perfectly* reveal manager effort—recall in Example 9.2 that firm payoff is also affected by the realization of the state of nature. A favourable state realization may allow the manager to shirk and still collect high compensation. Alternatively, or in addition, managers may be able to disguise shirking, at least in the short run, by choosing accounting policies that maximize reported earnings, particularly if they can hide the earnings management behind poor disclosure. Dysfunctional effects such as these will be reduced (but not eliminated) by efficient compensation contract design.

9.7   *Summary and Conclusions*

The various conflict-based theories described in this chapter have important implications for financial accounting theory. These can be summarized as follows:

1. Conflict theories enable a reconciliation of efficient securities markets and economic consequences. Early applications of efficient market theory to financial accounting (as, for example, in Beaver's early article, discussed in Section 4.3) suggested that accountants concentrate on full disclosure of information useful for investors' decision needs. The form of disclosure and the particular accounting policies used did not matter, as the market would see through these to their ultimate cash flow implications.

   Certainly, accountants have adopted the decision usefulness approach and its full-disclosure implications. Frequently, however, as noted in Chapter 8, management intervened in the standard setting process. This was not predicted by efficient securities market theory, since under that theory the market value of a firm's securities should be independent of its accounting policies, unless cash flows were affected. Why would management care about accounting policies if these do not affect its cost of capital? An answer is that changes in accounting policies can affect provisions in contracts that firm managers have entered into, thereby affecting their welfare and the welfare of the firm.

The reason why accounting policies can affect manager and firm welfare should be carefully considered. The basic problem is one of information asymmetry. In an owner-manager context, the manager knows his or her own effort in running the firm on the owner's behalf, but typically the owner cannot observe this effort. Knowing this, the manager faces a temptation to shirk. Thus, there is a moral hazard problem between owner and manager. To control moral hazard, the owner can offer the manager a share of reported net income. This sharing in the results of personal effort motivates the manager to work harder. However, it also means that the manager has a personal interest in how net income is measured. The firm will want to induce the desired effort as efficiently as possible.

When managers enter into borrowing contracts with lenders, similar implications for manager and firm welfare occur. Borrowing contracts typically contain covenants that restrict the payment of dividends depending on the values of certain financial statement-based ratios, such as interest coverage. Since covenant violations can be costly to the firm, both the manager and the firm will have a personal interest in accounting policy changes that affect the probability of covenant violation, particularly if they share in firm profits.

Economic consequences can be seen as a rational result of the rigidities introduced by entering into binding, incomplete contracts. The conflict situation between managers, who may object to accounting policies that have adverse economic consequences for them and their firms, and investors, who desire full disclosure, can be modelled as a non-cooperative game.

2. Another implication of agency theory is that historical cost-based net income has desirable properties for contracting purposes, including the fact that its rules are well known, so that contracting parties have a good "feel" for how it responds to differing economic circumstances. Also, historical cost-based net income is reasonably reliable, relative to fair-value-based alternatives, and it appears to be reasonably correlated with manager effort[9]. These hardness properties of historical cost-based net income lead, however, to the fundamental problem of financial accounting theory, namely the reconciliation of the information needs of investors with those of contracting.

3. Finally, agency theory implies that generally accepted accounting principles and auditing are important to giving net income the credibility it needs to serve as a basis for contracting.

For these reasons, game theory is an important component of financial accounting theory. In addition to enabling a better understanding of the conflicting interests of various constituencies affected by financial reporting, it has encouraged research into executive compensation and earnings management. Chapters 10 and 11 will review some of this research.

Questions and Problems

1. The instability of economic cartels such as OPEC (Organization of Petroleum Exporting Countries) can be explained, at least in part, by game theory considerations. Typically such cartels attempt to agree to restrict oil production and keep prices to customers high. Frequently, however, some countries violate these agreements.

   Use the following depiction of a two-country non-cooperative game to explain why violation occurs. That is, explain in words which strategy pair is likely to be played in this game and why. Identify the Nash equilibrium of this game.

		Country 1	
		Keep	**Violate**
Country 2	**Keep**	100, 100	40, 200
	Violate	200, 40	50, 50

   In each box, the first number represents country 2's payoff and the second country 1's payoff.　　　　　　　　　　　　　　　　　　　　(CGA-Canada)

2. U-Haul, a "do-it-yourself" moving company, is doing a booming business these days. The reason is that some companies relocating employees are changing the way they reimburse moving expenses. Before the change, moves were very expensive, because the companies paid for everything. Now, the companies pay a fixed amount to the employee, who can keep the savings, if there are any. Explain this change using agency theory concepts. Also, U-Haul offers to reimburse customers for the cost of oil used during the move, while customers have to pay for their own gasoline. Why?

3. A manufacturer of farm equipment is headed for financial distress. Bonuses of management are based on net income relative to budget. There has been a recent change in management, occurring in early 2001. To the surprise of the new manager, the outgoing manager had sharply increased 2000 production, resulting in excessive levels of inventory on hand at the end of 2000. The manufacturer uses absorption costing for its inventories.

   Required

   a. Explain why the old management increased production and inventories.

     b. How might the remuneration plan of management be changed to reduce the likelihood that this would happen in the future?   (CGA-Canada)

4.   Suppose a company has a number of divisions that are profit centres, all sharing a production facility (for example, a machine shop). The user divisions are always submitting rush orders to the operator of the common production facility. The division involved (division A) claims the order is urgent and that delay will result in significant profit losses to the company, a claim that is very difficult for the operator of the common facility to verify or refute. This sometimes results in a job being given priority, which causes the delay of another division's job, where the cost of delay to the company (forgone profits due to, say, impatient customers going elsewhere) is well in excess of the cost of delay to division A. Assume that each division manager receives a bonus based solely on the profits of his or her division, in addition to fixed salary.

Required

     a. Explain why the behaviour of division A's manager is predictable, in terms of agency theory.

     b. Can you think of a solution to this agency problem? Explain why your solution works.

5.   The PIP grant accounting controversy discussed in Section 8.4.1 can be analyzed as a non-cooperative game. Let the two players be the government and the CICA. Each player faces two strategies: the "cooperate" strategy happens when one player goes along with the preferred accounting policy of the other; the "strong" strategy involves one player sticking to its own policy regardless of the wishes of the other.

Hypothetical, but reasonable, payoffs for each player are summarized in the following table.

		CICA	
		Cooperate	**Strong**
	Cooperate	50, 50	8, 60
Government	**Strong**	20, 10	12, 15

In each box, the first number represents the government's payoff and the second number the CICA's payoff. To illustrate, consider the lower left box. Here, the government plays strong, that is, it demands that the CICA waive the requirements of Section 3800 and the CICA agrees. The government receives a payoff of 20 in this case, because it is seen as the dominant player. However, because this strategy erodes its relationship with the CICA and with other constituencies who feel that standard setting should be done in the private sector, its payoff is less than the 50 it would receive if both players had cooperated. The CICA receives a very low payoff of 10, because it is perceived as capitulating to the government's demands. Similar reasoning applies to the other three boxes of the table.

Required

a. On the basis of the discussion in Section 8.4.1, which strategy pair did the players choose?

b. Is this strategy pair a Nash equilibrium? Explain.

c. Both parties would have been better off if they had cooperated. Based on the payoffs shown in the table, explain, why this strategy pair was unlikely to have been chosen.

6. The shareholders of X Ltd. will vote at the forthcoming annual meeting on a proposal to establish a bonus plan, based on firm performance, for X Ltd. management. Proponents of the plan argue that management will work harder under a bonus plan and that expected cash flows will thereby increase. However, a dissident shareholder group argues that there is little point in granting a bonus plan, because management will bias or otherwise manage earnings to increase their bonus, rather than working harder.

Upon investigation, you estimate that if the bonus plan is granted, expected cash flows will be $150 if management does not manage earnings, and $140 if it does, *before* management remuneration in each case (cash flows are lower in the latter case because management uses earnings management to disguise shirking). Management remuneration, including the bonus, would be $50 if it does not manage earnings and $60 if it does. Assume that cash flows not paid as management remuneration will go to the shareholders.

If the bonus plan is not granted, expected cash flows will be $140 before management remuneration if management does not manage earnings and $100 if it does. Management remuneration would be $30 in either case, with the balance of cash flows going to the shareholders.

Required

a. Prepare a payoff table for the above game between shareholders and management.

b. Which strategy pair will be chosen? That is, identify a Nash equilibrium for the game. Assume both players are risk-neutral.

c. What is the main advantage of a game theory approach to modelling the management's decision whether to manage earnings, rather than modelling it as a single-person decision theory problem of the manager?

7. Mr. Kao, the owner of Kao Industries, wants to hire a manager to operate the firm while he takes an extended trip abroad. He wants the manager to work hard (60 hours per week) rather than shirk (40 hours per week). The payoff table for Kao Industries under each alternative is as follows:

KAO INDUSTRIES PAYOFF TABLE FOR YEAR		
Net Income for Year (before manager remuneration)	Probability (a_1 = 60 hours)	Probability (a_2 = 40 hours)
$400	0.7	0.2
200	0.2	0.3
0	0.1	0.5

Kao is negotiating with a potential manager about the remuneration contract. The manager's disutility for effort for the year is:

$$\text{Disutility of effort} = \frac{h^2}{800}$$

where h is the number of hours worked per week.

Required

a. Show calculations to verify that for a fixed annual salary paid to the manager, Mr. Kao will prefer that the manager work hard. Mr. Kao is risk-neutral.

b. For any fixed annual salary, will the manager prefer to work hard or to shirk? Explain.

c. Suppose that Mr. Kao offers the manager a fixed annual salary of $10, plus 10% of net income. The manager's utility for money is equal to the square root of the money received. Assuming that the manager takes the job, which act would he or she take? Show your calculations.   (CGA-Canada)

8. The shareholders of UVW Ltd. are unhappy about the top manager's performance. While the manager's effort in running the firm cannot be observed, it is felt that he puts in effort equivalent to about 40 hours a week. The manager's annual salary at present is $160,000.

A new incentive contract is being considered by the shareholders, whereby the manager would receive a salary of $100,000 per annum plus a bonus of 25% of reported net income before salary and bonus.

You are asked to analyze the expected impact of the new bonus plan on the manager. You estimate that if the manager puts in about 60 hours per week (a_1), net income before manager remuneration will be $1,040,000 per annum with probability of 0.7, and $90,000 per year with probability of 0.3. Under the present salary-based remuneration, whereby the manager's effort is 40 hours per week (a_2), analysis of past profitability shows that annual net income has been $1,040,000 only 0.1 of the time and $90,000 the other 0.9.

You also ascertain that the manager's utility for money is equal to the square root of the money received, and that disutility for effort is four times the number of hours worked per week.

Required

a. Show calculations to verify that under the present salary-based remuneration plan the manager will prefer to work 40 hours per week over 60 hours.

b. Which act, a_1 or a_2, will the manager prefer under the new incentive contract? Show calculations.

c. A new accounting standard is proposed that, while it will not change future expected net income, will greatly increase the volatility of net income. Explain why the manager would object to the proposed new standard.

9. Mr. K is contemplating a one-year 8% loan of $500 to firm J. Mr. K demands at least a 6% expected return per annum on loans like this.

K is concerned that the firm may not be able to pay the interest and/or principal at the end of the year. A further concern is that if he makes the loan, firm J may engage in additional borrowing. If so, K's security would be diluted and the firm would become more risky. Since firm J is growing rapidly, K is sure that the firm would engage in additional borrowing if he makes the loan.

K examines firm J's most recent annual report and calculates an interest coverage ratio (ratio of net income before interest and taxes to interest expense) of 4, including the contemplated $500 loan.

Upon considering all of these matters, K assesses the following probabilities:

Payoff	Probability
θ_1: Interest and principal repaid	0.80
θ_2: Reorganization, principal repaid but not interest	0.18
θ_3: Bankruptcy, nothing repaid	0.02
	1.00

Required

a. Should Mr. K make the loan? Show calculations.

b. Firm J offers to add a covenant to its lending agreement with Mr. K, undertaking not to engage in any additional borrowing if its interest coverage ratio falls below 4 before the next year-end. Mr. K estimates that there is a 60% probability that the interest coverage ratio will fall below 4. If it does, the covenant will prevent dilution of his equity by additional borrowing, and he feels the lower coverage ratio would still be adequate. He assesses that his payoff probabilities would then be:

Payoff	Probability
θ_1	0.95
θ_2	0.04
θ_3	0.01

If the coverage ratio does not fall below 4, the resulting additional borrowing and dilution of security would cause him to assess payoff probabilities as:

Payoff	Probability
θ_1	0.85
θ_2	0.14
θ_3	0.01

Should Mr. K now make the loan? Show calculations.

10. One of the problems of entering into contracts, including executive compensation contracts, is incompleteness. That is, it is generally impossible to foresee all relevant events that might happen and build provisions for them into the contract. An example of contract rigidity in the face of an unforeseen event appeared in *The Wall Street Journal* (April 15, 1993) in an article entitled "Firms Get Around Big One-Time Earnings Hits to Save Executive Bonuses."

The article discusses SFAS 106, which requires that firms accrue employees' OPEBs benefits, rather than waiting until they are paid (see Section 7.3.1). The article states that because of SFAS 106 "many compensation committees want to use operating earnings—not net after the accounting change—to calculate top managers' bonuses."

For example, Chrysler Corp., which had a charge for retiree health costs of $4.7 billion in 1993, plans to ask its shareholders if it could exclude the charge to calculate bonuses. However, there is opposition by the United Shareholders Association, who believe that charges such as postretirement benefits "should be deemed a regular business cost, not an unusual expense to be ignored by board compensation committees." However, consulting firm Wyatt Co. "says it's simpler to exclude the new annual charges than to alter bonus formulas."

Required

a. If you were a Chrysler shareholder, would you agree to this request? Explain why or why not.

b. If you were a senior Chrysler executive affected by SFAS 106 and your request was turned down, how would you react? Explain why.

11. Non-cooperative game theory is a way of modelling the conflict situation that exists between a firm manager and investors. Consider the following depiction of a game between a manager/entrepreneur and a potential investor in the firm.

		Manager/Entrepreneur	
		Work hard	**Shirk**
Investor	**Invest**	7, 6	2, 7
	Do not invest	5, 3	6, 5

The manager may choose to work hard or shirk. The number pairs show the payoffs to the investor (first number) and the manager (second number) for each manager/investor strategy pair. For example, if the investor invests and the manager works hard, they receive payoffs of 7 and 6 respectively.

Required

a. Identify the cooperative solution and explain why it is not a Nash equilibrium.

b. Identify a Nash equilibrium and explain why it is the predicted outcome of a single play of the game.

c. Suppose that the assumption of a non-cooperative game is relaxed, so that the parties can enter into a binding agreement, that is, a contract. Suggest two ways that the manager may convince the investor that he or she will work hard in such a contract, so that the investor will invest.

d. Suppose that the first payoffs above, that is, the payoffs to the investor, are interpreted as net income, net of manager compensation. What properties should net income have if the investor is to be willing to accept it as a valid payoff measure?

12. Growth Ltd. is a high-tech firm whose owner does not have the required management expertise to run the firm. The owner wants to hire a manager with the required expertise. The continued success of Growth depends crucially on how hard the new manager works.

If the manager works hard (a_1), firm profit is $500 with probability .7 and $200 with probability .3. If the manager shirks (a_2), firm profit is $500 with probability .2 and $200 with probability .8. In both cases, profits are before manager compensation.

The owner is interviewing a prospective manager, and finds out that she is risk-averse, with utility for compensation equal to the square root of the dollar compensation received. Like most people, however, she is also effort-averse. If she works hard, she suffers a disutility of effort of 2 units of utility. If she shirks, her effort disutility is zero.

Required

a. Growth Ltd. offers the manager a salary of $41 per period plus 20% of firm profit before manager compensation. Will the manager take a_1 or a_2? Show your calculations.

b. Instead, Growth offers the manager zero salary plus 30% of profits before manager compensation. Will she take a_1 or a_2? Show your calculations.

c. Does the manager's effort decision change between parts **a** and **b** above? Explain why or why not.

d. Many executive compensation contracts base the manager's compensation on *both* net income and share price performance. Explain an advantage of using two performance measures rather than only one in compensation contracts.

13. Toni Difelice is contemplating lending $10,000 to Tech Enterprises Ltd. Tech offers her 8% interest with the principal to be repaid at the end of the year.

Toni carefully examines the financial statements of Tech Enterprises and is concerned about its interest coverage ratio, which is currently at 1.8:1. She feels that there is a 5% chance that Tech will go bankrupt, in which case she would only recover $2,000 of her principal and no interest. She suggests a debt covenant in the lending contract, whereby Tech promises not to issue any more debt beyond what Toni invests if its interest coverage ratio falls below 1.6:1. With such covenant protection, Toni assesses only a 1% probability of bankruptcy and subsequent recovery of only $2,000.

The manager of Tech Enterprises agrees to this request, providing that Toni reduce her interest rate to 5%.

Toni is risk-averse, with a mean-variance utility function:

$$U(a) = 2x_a - \sigma_a^2$$

where a is her investment act, x_a is the expected return on a, and σ_a^2 is the variance of the return of a.

Required

a. Which act should Toni take?

    a_1 : 8% interest, no debt covenant

    a_2 : 5% interest, debt covenant

b. Explain why the manager of Tech Enterprises would be concerned about new accounting standards that may come into effect after the lending contract with Toni is concluded. Consider both standards that will tend to lower reported net income and standards that will increase its volatility.

14. Henri owns and operates a small successful sporting goods store. He has not had a holiday for three years. He decides to take an extensive one-year trip around the world, and is negotiating with Marie to operate the store while he is away. The store's earnings, before manager compensation, are highly dependent on how hard the manager works, as per the following table:

	a_1: Work Hard		a_2: Shirk	
	Payoff	Prob.	Payoff	Prob.
x_1: High Earnings	$260	0.7	$260	0.2
x_2: Low Earnings	$80	0.3	$80	0.8

Marie, like most people, is risk-averse and effort-averse. Her utility for money is equal to the square root of the amount of money received. If she works hard, her effort disutility is 2. If she shirks, her effort disutility is 1.

Marie informs Henri that she is willing to accept the manager position but that she must receive at least an expected utility of 3.4, or she would be better off to work somewhere else. After some calculation, Henri offers Marie a salary of $20 plus 5% of the store earnings (after deducting salary).

Required

a. Will Marie accept Henri's contract offer? Show calculations.

Hint: First calculate which act Marie would take.

b. Henri insists that if he hires Marie the store's annual earnings must be audited by a professional accountant. Explain why.

c. Assume that Henri hires Marie under the contract proposed, that is, $20 salary plus 5% of profits after salary. Shortly after he leaves, a new accounting standard requires that estimated customer liability be accrued. This lowers the high earnings to $220 and the low earnings to $40 in the table above. The payoff probabilities are unaffected. Which act will Marie now take? Show calculations.

15. A problem with many games is that they can have multiple Nash equilibria. This makes it difficult to predict the outcome of the game.

As an illustration of a non-cooperative game with multiple equilibria, consider the following payoff table, which is a slight adjustment of the game in question 1:

		Country 1	
		Keep	Violate
Country 2	Keep	100, 100	50, 200
	Violate	200, 50	50, 50

Required

a. Identify three Nash equilibria of this game.

b. Suppose that this game will be repeated a known, finite number of times. Suppose that the current equilibrium is in the lower left portion of the table. Describe an action by country 1 that would cause a shift to a new equilibrium.

c. Suppose that the game will be repeated an infinite number of times. What equilibrium would you then predict? Explain.

Notes

1. The discussion here assumes only pure strategies, that is, strategies where one act is chosen with probability 1. It is possible to have mixed-strategy solutions, where players randomize between acts over which they are indifferent. Then, this statement would need modification.

2. Darrough and Stoughton assume that if disclosure is made, it is honest. This assumption can be motivated by an audit and/or by severe penalties for fraudulent disclosure.

3. Our use of net income as a payoff measure assumes that it captures all aspects of the manager's performance for the period. In a one-period model, this seems reasonable. However, as we shall discuss in Chapter 10, in a multi-period setting, net income may not capture all aspects of performance. Consider, for example, manager effort in the current period with respect to R&D. Since the revenue generated by current R&D will not be recognized until some later period, net income lags the full effects of current manager performance. Then, other payoff measures are possible, such as physical output and/or share price. More generally, we could view net income, physical output, and/or share price as different information systems that convey, with noise, information *about* the payoff. A more complete formulation of the agency problem includes the choice by the principle of the best information system.

4. There is an implicit assumption throughout Example 9.2 that principal and agent have the same state probabilities. This assumption is made in most agency theory models. However, some models allow the agent to possess or obtain superior

information. Then, in addition to moral hazard, the principal faces an adverse selection problem, since the agent may use this information for his/her own advantage. For example, the agent may obtain private information about the state realization prior to selecting an action (called **pre-decision** information). Then, by reporting a lower-than-actual state realization, the agent may use this information to shirk, as demonstrated by Christensen (1981), who also shows how the principal, at a cost, can truthfully extract this information from the agent.

5. Note that the employment contract here is linear in the payoff, that is, 32% of net income. When there are more than two states of nature, it is possible that a non-linear contract would be more efficient. This is beyond our scope here.

6. There is an implicit assumption of efficient securities markets here.

7. More precisely, for the second variable to reduce agency costs it must be false that the payoff measure is a sufficient statistic for the pair of variables (payoff, second variable) with respect to effort.

8. Holmström points out that if the contract with the manager is confined to a limited class, such as the linear contract assumed in Example 9.2, this result may not hold.

9. It may be the case that certain aspects of fair value accounting could increase the correlation of net income with manager effort, if they reduce the recognition lag between effort and payoff. For example, capitalization and amortization of certain R&D costs, as discussed in Section 7.5.3, may better reflect current manager effort than writing these costs off as incurred. Even here, however, problems of reliability may reduce, rather than increase, correlation with effort. See also Note 3 above.

Executive Compensation

10.1 Overview

In this chapter we consider **executive compensation plans**. We will see that real incentive plans follow from the agency theory developed in Chapter 9, but are more complex and detailed. They involve a delicate mix of incentive, risk, and decision horizon considerations.

> *An **executive compensation plan** is an agency contract between the firm and its manager that attempts to align the interests of owners and manager by basing the manager's compensation on one or more measures of the manager's effort in operating the firm.*

Many compensation plans are based on two measures of manager effort—net income and share price. That is, the amounts of bonus, shares, options, and other components of executive pay that are awarded in a particular year depend on both net income and share price performance. As we shall see, basing compensation on both net income and share price helps control the amount of risk these plans impose on managers, and the length of their decision horizons.

With respect to net income, its role in compensation plans is equally as important as its role in informing investors, since motivation of responsible executive performance and enhancing the proper operation of managerial labour markets is as desirable a social goal as enabling good investment decisions and proper securities market operation. Consequently, an understanding of the properties that net income needs in order to fulfill a performance-motivating role is important for accountants. Unless net income has desirable hardness qualities, it will be "squeezed out" of efficient compensation plans since, as mentioned, it competes with share price performance in this role. If so, a major source of competitive advantage for accountants will be lost.

10.2   *Are Incentive Contracts Necessary?*

Fama (1980) makes the case that incentive contracts of the type studied in Section 9.4.2 are not necessary because the managerial labour market controls moral hazard. If a manager can establish a reputation for creating high payoffs for owners, that manager's market value (i.e., the compensation he or she can command) will increase. Conversely, a manager who shirks, thus reporting lower payoffs on average, will suffer a decline in market value. As a manager who is tempted to shirk looks ahead to future periods, the present value of reduced future compensation, Fama argues, will be equal to or greater than the immediate benefits of shirking. Thus, the manager will not shirk. This argument, of course, assumes an efficient managerial labour market.

Fama also argues that for lower-level managers, any shirking will be detected and reported by managers below them, who want to get ahead. That is, a process of "internal monitoring" operates to discipline managers who may be less subject to the discipline of the managerial labour market itself.

The agency model of Section 9.4.2 is single-period. Thus, it cannot deal directly with the multi-period horizon that is needed for reputation formation and internal monitoring. Recall that in the single-period model, the manager's market value enters only through the reservation utility constraint—the utility of the compensation of the next-best available position. In a one-period model, this utility is taken as a constant. Fama's argument is that if the manager contemplates the downwards effect of current shirking on the reservation utility of future employment contracts, shirking will be deterred.

The agency model can be extended to deal with these considerations. With respect to internal monitoring, we outline the study of Arya, Fellingham, and Glover (1997) (AFG). They design a two-period model with one owner and two risk-averse managers. The managers' efforts produce a joint, observable payoff in each period. The owner cannot observe either manager's effort but each manager knows the effort of the other. One way for the owner to motivate the managers to work hard is to offer each of them an incentive contract similar to the one in Section 9.4.2, in each period. However, AFG show that the owner can offer a more efficient contract by exploiting the ability of each manager to observe the other's effort. Since the payoff is a joint effort, shirking by either manager will reduce the payoff for *both*. Then, in the AGF contract, each manager threatens the other that he or she will shirk in the second period if the other shirks in the first. If the contract is designed properly, the threat is credible and each manager works hard in both periods. The resulting two-period contract is more efficient because it imposes less risk than a sequence of two single-period contracts. As a result, managers can attain their reservation utility with lower expected compensation.

The important point for our purposes is that the contract continues to base manager compensation on the payoff. In effect, while exploitation of the ability of managers to monitor each other can *reduce* agency costs of moral hazard, it does not eliminate them. Thus, AFG's model suggests that an incentive contract for lower-level managers is still necessary.

With respect to the ability of manager reputation to control moral hazard, Fama's argument does not consider that the manager may be able to disguise the effects of shirking, at least in the short run, by managing the release of information. That is, in addition to the moral hazard problem, the managerial labour market is subject to similar adverse selection problems as the securities market— the manager may withhold, delay, bias, or otherwise manage the release of information. Then, just as share price may not reflect underlying firm value, neither will the labour market reflect underlying manager value. That is, market forces of reputation may not be completely effective in controlling moral hazard when the manager has private information and can control its release.

In this regard, evidence on the extent of the market's ability to control the manager's incentive to shirk is presented by Wolfson (1985). He examined contracts of oil and gas limited partnerships in the United States. These are tax-advantaged contracts between a general partner (agent) and limited partners (principal) to drill for oil and gas. The general partner provides the expertise and pays some of the costs. The bulk of the capital is provided by the limited partners.

Such contracts are particularly subject to moral hazard and adverse selection problems, due to the highly technical nature of oil and gas exploration. For example, the general partner privately learns the results of the drilling. This leads to the "noncompletion incentive problem." Once drilled, a well should be completed if its expected revenues—call them R—exceed the costs of completion. However, for tax reasons, completion costs are paid by the general partner. If the general partner receives, say, 40% of the revenues, then, from his or her perspective, it is worthwhile to complete only if .40R is greater than the completion costs. Given that only the general partner knows R, a well may not be completed (i.e., the manager covers up shirking by withholding information about R) unless R is very high.

Wolfson studied two types of well-drilling: exploratory wells and development wells. The noncompletion problem is not as great for exploratory wells since, if an exploratory well does come in, the chances are that R will be high indeed.

Investors will be aware of this noncompletion problem, of course, and will bid down the price they are willing to pay to buy in, possibly to the point where the general partner cannot attract limited partners at all. The question then is, can a general partner ease investor concerns by establishing a reputation, thereby increasing his or her market value and the amounts that investors are willing to pay?

To measure reputation, Wolfson collected information on the past performance of a sample of general partners over 1977–1980. The higher a general partner's past success in generating a return for limited partners, the higher that partner's reputation was taken to be. Wolfson found that the higher the reputation of a general partner, the more he or she received from limited partners to buy in, suggesting that investors were responding to the manager's reputation.

However, Wolfson also found that investors paid significantly less to buy into developmental wells than into exploratory wells. As mentioned, the undercompletion problem is greater for development wells.

Combination of these two findings suggests that while market forces can *reduce* the managers' moral hazard problem, *they do not eliminate it*. If reputation-building completely eliminated the undercompletion problem, we would not see investors paying less when the problem is greater.

While Wolfson's results apply only to a small sample of oil and gas contracts, they are of more general interest because of their implication that the managerial labour market is not completely effective in controlling moral hazard, contrary to Fama's argument. An agent's past success in generating payoffs for investors does not perfectly predict that the agent will not succumb to moral hazard in the current period.

We may conclude that while internal and market forces do help to control managers' tendencies to shirk, they do not eliminate them. Thus, effort incentives based on the payoff are still necessary. We now turn to an examination of an actual managerial compensation contract of a large corporation. As we will see, incentives loom large.

10.3   *A Managerial Compensation Plan*

In this section, we present an example of a managerial compensation plan. The following exhibit describes the plan of BCE Inc., a large Canadian corporation with shares traded on the Toronto, New York, and Swiss stock exchanges. The exhibit is reproduced from the Management Proxy Circular, dated February 28, 2001, mailed to shareholders.

EXHIBIT 10.1   Directors' and officers' remuneration: Report on executive compensation

COMPENSATION PHILOSOPHY

The objectives of BCE's executive compensation policy are to assist in attracting and retaining executives, and to motivate them to achieve and surpass individual and group performance objectives consistent with creating shareholder value and advancing BCE's corporate success.

The compensation philosophy of BCE is to offer total compensation based on a comparator group of major Canadian and U.S. corporations. A substantial portion of the cash compensation is contingent upon corporate performance. In addition, there are long-term incentive programs designed to motivate the attainment of longer-term objectives, to align executive and shareholder interests and to ensure opportunities for capital accumulation as share prices increase.

Underlying BCE's compensation programs is an emphasis on share ownership, and officers of BCE are required to attain specified share ownership levels over a five-gear period. Such levels are expressed as a percentage of annual base salary and range from 200 per cent for the lowest officer position to 500 per cent for the Chief Executive Officer.

The Management Resources and Compensation Committee (the "MRCC") undertakes periodic reviews of BCE's executive compensation policy to ensure its continued effectiveness in meeting the foregoing objectives.

COMPOSITION OF THE COMPENSATION COMMITTEE

The MRCC is responsible for the administration of BCE's executive compensation policy. The MRCC reports and makes recommendations on executive compensation matters to the Board of Directors.

The members of the MRCC are Messrs. Richard J. Currie, Brian M. Levitt, John H. McArthur and Paul M. Tellier. Mr. Ralph M. Barford was a member and the Chairman of the MRCC until April 26, 2000, on which date Mr. Currie became Chairman of the committee. Mrs. Micheline Charest was a member until March 6, 2000. The MRCC met eight times during 2000. As a corporate practice, in 2000, the Chairman and Chief Executive Officer of BCE also attended MRCC meetings except when matters pertaining to him were discussed. He does not vote at MRCC meetings.

TOTAL COMPENSATION

Total compensation, which comprises salary, annual short-term incentive awards, long-term incentives, benefits and perquisites, is compared to a group of widely-held Canadian and U.S. corporations. This comparator group of companies is reviewed from time to time by the MRCC to ensure comparability in the current context. Total compensation levels are set to reflect both the marketplace (to ensure competitiveness) and the responsibility of each position (to ensure internal equity). The total compensation policy is positioned between the 50th and the 75th percentile based on individual contribution and on meeting certain financial threshold targets, e.g. if positioned at the 75th percentile, 25 per cent of the companies paid more and 75 per cent of the companies pay less.

Salary

The target salary is the mid-point of a salary range for an executive officer which is set at median levels in the comparator group to reflect similar positions in these companies using a direct comparison of responsibilities. Base salaries for executive officers are then determined by the MRCC within the above policy.

The salary of Mr. Jean C. Monty of $1,218,000 per annum as Chief Executive Officer for 2000 was set at the mid-point of the foregoing salary range, consistent with the above philosophy.

Annual Short-Term Incentive Awards

As part of the executive compensation policy, the MRCC established annual short-term incentive target awards ranging in 2000 from 35 per cent of the salary for the lowest eligible officer position to 90 per cent for the Chief Executive Officer.

Annual awards are based upon two factors:

(1) corporate performance — this is assessed on the basis of various strategic business objectives and quantifiable financial targets both set at the beginning of the year as the Corporate Mandate by the Board of Directors (see *Strategic Planning (Corporate Mandate)* under **Mandate Of The Board** on page 19). Strategic business objectives might include, for example, a specific corporate objective with respect to a particular subsidiary, the development of new businesses, the improvement of management development, or the strengthening of certain relationships. Quantifiable financial targets might include, for example, baseline earnings per share or contribution to earnings from core businesses. Although the corporate performance objectives have different relative weights, primary consideration is generally given to the quantifiable financial targets for BCE and its principal business units; and

(2) individual contribution — this is evaluated on the basis of criteria which affect corporate performance, such as creativity and initiative in addressing business issues, succession planning and management development.

On the basis of the above factors, the MRCC determines the size of the annual short-term incentive awards. More specifically, the amount of the awards is computed based on the product of the corporate performance factor and of the individual contribution factor. Actual awards may vary between zero and three times the target awards depending on achievement of the above two factors.

They are paid at the beginning of a year with respect to performance in the previous year. Executive officers who participate in The BCE Inc. Share Unit Plan for Senior Executives and Other Key Employees (1997) (the "Executive Share Unit Plan") and who receive share units cannot be paid short-term incentive awards for the same achievements (see **Share Units** on page 10).

Given his receipt of share units, no short-term incentive award was granted for the year 2000 to Mr. Monty in his capacity as Chief Executive Officer.

LONG-TERM COMPENSATION
Stock Options

Options to purchase BCE common shares may be granted under stock option plans of the Corporation to officers and other key employees of the Corporation and of certain of its subsidiaries (such stock option plans being herein collectively referred to as the "BCE Stock Option Program"). Stock option awards vary according to salary level and do not take outstanding options into account. Grant levels depend on the position of the incumbent and the total compensation relative to the market. They are based on the value required to attain the applicable percentile (i.e. between the 50th and 75th percentile in total market compensation, as previously discussed on page 9 under **Total Compensation**) and translated to options based on the market value of the Corporation's common shares on the day prior to the effective date of the grant of the options ("Subscription Price").

In addition, special grants of stock options may be approved to recognize singular achievements or, exceptionally, to retain and motivate executives in order to further align executive and shareholder interests and to motivate key employees ("Special Grants").

The term of an option is normally ten years from the date of the grant except in the case of retirement, cessation of employment, death or an optionee's employer ceasing to be the Corporation or a subsidiary of the Corporation, in which case the term is reduced in accordance with the provisions of the BCE Stock Option Program or in accordance with decisions made from time to time by the MRCC under such program.

Except as indicated below, the right to exercise an option in its entirety accrues by 25 per cent annual increments over a period of four years from the date of grant unless otherwise determined by the MRCC at the time of grant. For example, in the case of the Special Grants of options, the right to exercise such options may accrue over a longer period of time or, in the case of options subject to forfeiture if certain financial objectives of the optionee's employer are not met in the year of grant, the right to exercise such options accrues only in the event such financial objectives are achieved. Furthermore, the BCE Stock Option Program was modified in 1999 to provide special vesting provisions in the event of a Change of Control (as defined below) of the Corporation. If there occurs a Change of Control of the Corporation and an optionee's employment is terminated by the Corporation other than for cause or by the optionee for good reason (as set out in more detail in the BCE Stock Option Program, an "Unjustified Termination") within 18 months following such Change of Control, the options then held by such optionee with respect to which the right to exercise has not yet accrued become exercisable in full for a period of 90 days there-

after, or such longer period as the MRCC may determine. "Change of Control" is defined, in essence, as (i) an offeror acquiring 50% or more of the outstanding securities of a class of voting or equity securities of the Corporation; (ii) certain changes to the composition of the majority of the Board of Directors of the Corporation, or (iii) the approval by the shareholders of the Corporation of plans or agreements providing for the disposition of all or substantially all the assets of the Corporation, the liquidation or dissolution of the Corporation or, in certain cases, the merger, consolidation or amalgamation of the Corporation. Options held by an optionee principally employed in a BCE business unit, such as Bell Canada or such other direct or indirect subsidiary of the Corporation identified by the MRCC (a "Designated Business Unit"), with respect to which the right to exercise has not yet accrued will, in the event that the Corporation ceases to hold at least a 50% interest but continues to hold at least a 20% interest in such Designated Business Unit and the employment of the optionee is terminated in a manner which constitutes an Unjustified Termination within 18 months following the decrease in the Corporation's interest in the Designated Business Unit, become exercisable in the same manner as described above with respect to a Change of Control. Options held by an optionee principally employed in a Designated Business Unit with respect to which the right to exercise has not yet accrued will, in the event that the Corporation ceases to hold at least a 20% interest in such Designated Business Unit, become exercisable in full, effective upon the earlier of the date one year following the occurrence of such event or the date of an Unjustified Termination of the optionee, for a period of 90 days thereafter or such longer period as the MRCC may determine.

The exercise price payable for each common share covered by an option is generally the Subscription Price except where the MRCC makes a determination that the exercise price should be higher than the Subscription Price or where the MRCC establishes, subject to any required approval of the stock exchanges on which the common shares of the Corporation are listed and posted for trading, that the exercise price should be less than the Subscription Price in the event that an option to acquire shares of a subsidiary of the Corporation or a company which is proposed to become a subsidiary of the Corporation is intended to be converted into an option to acquire common shares of the Corporation so that the economic position of the optionee is not affected by such conversion.

Simultaneously with the granting of an option, rights to a Special Compensation Payment ("SCP") may be granted by the optionee's employer. A SCP is a cash payment representing the excess of the market value of the shares on the date of exercise over their Subscription Price. When SCPs are attached to options, the SCPs are triggered when the options are exercised. No SCPs have been granted since November 1999.

Upon assuming the responsibility of Chief Executive Officer in 1998, Mr. Monty received a special grant of 400,000 options. This special grant represents the normal allocation of options for the years 1998 to 2000.

Share Units

To increase the alignment of executive and shareholder interests, BCE established the Executive Share Unit Plan pursuant to which share units ("Units"), each one being equivalent in value to one BCE common share, may be awarded to certain officers and other key employees of the Corporation and of certain BCE subsidiaries (the "Participants"). Unit awards may be annual awards or may be special awards to recognize singular achievements or to achieve certain corporate objectives.

On each BCE common share dividend payment date, additional Units are credited to the account of the Participants in an amount equivalent to dividends on outstanding BCE common shares. Following cessation of employment of a Participant, Units are paid, after remittance of applicable withholding taxes, in BCE common shares purchased on the open market.

There are no vesting conditions under the terms of the Executive Share Unit Plan. Furthermore, the number and terms of outstanding Units are not taken into account when determining whether and how many new Units will be awarded.

The MRCC determines the size of the Unit awards as a percentage of salary upon the same factors and weighting as those described under **Annual Short-Term Incentive Awards**. Target awards are also the same as those for short-term incentive awards. The number of Units awarded is determined on the basis of the market value of the Corporation's common shares on the day prior to the effective date of the award of the Units. Persons who are paid annual short-term incentive awards cannot receive Units for the same achievements. The MRCC may, with respect to any particular year, require an eligible officer or key employee to participate in the Executive Share Unit Plan.

Mr. Monty received 14,067 Units based on a special share unit award of

$470,000 to ensure his total 2000 compensation reached the 75th percentile of the market, as provided for in BCE's compensation policies. Share units in lieu of stock options were awarded to Mr. Monty in order to reach the 75th percentile of the market because, as previously indicated, Mr. Monty already received in 1998 his normal allocation of options for the years 1998 to 2000.

In addition, the MRCC determined that Mr. Monty exceeded the objectives of the Corporate Mandate and therefore recommended, and the Board of Directors approved, that Mr. Monty receive 39,861 Units based on an award of $1,644,300 in respect of 2000. The determination of the award reflects the fact that, in 2000,

BCE's baseline earnings per share exceeded the Corporate Mandate's target. In addition, 2000 marked significant progress in all core areas, particularly for Bell Canada. Furthermore, key strategic initiatives were realized in 2000, including the Arrangement pursuant to which BCE distributed an approximate 35% ownership interest in Nortel Networks Corporation ("Nortel Networks") to its shareholders and the CRTCs approval of the acquisition of CTV. With respect to the individual contribution factor, the determination of the award reflects Mr. Monty's exceptional leadership which played a key role in the realization of the above-mentioned corporate achievements.

SOURCE: Reprinted with permission from *BCE Inc., Management Proxy Circular*, February 28, 2001.

Several aspects of this compensation plan should be noted. First, note that officers are required to hold a significant amount of BCE shares, ranging from 2 to 5 times base salary. Second, there are three main compensation components: salary; annual short-term incentive awards, consisting of cash bonuses or, for senior officers, share units; and stock options. Observe that the short-term incentive awards depend on "quantitative financial targets," such as earnings per share (a net income-based measure of performance), and individual creativity and initiative. The more senior the manager, the more the award depends on quantitative factors. Stock options are awarded under the long-term component of the plan. Since the value of the stock options depends on BCE's share price, share price constitutes a market-based measure of performance.

Third, many compensation plans require that a certain level of earnings, or other performance measure, be reached before incentive compensation becomes payable. The threshold level of performance is called the **bogey**. Also, many plans contain an upper limit to compensation, called the **cap**.

In BCE's case, no formal bogey or cap is stated. However, these seem to be implicit. We are told that total compensation is positioned between the 50th and 75th percentiles of a group of comparable companies, thereby placing an upper limit on compensation. Also, the amounts of short-term incentive awards are geared to targets set at the beginning of the year. If these bogeys are not met, the awards are, presumably, zero. Also, the short-term awards are capped at three times the amount based on the target.

It should be noted that the compensation committee of BCE's Board of Directors (MRCC) has the ultimate say in the amounts of salary, bonus, and option awards, within the above guidelines. The compensation committee is a corporate governance device, to deal with the fact that the BCE plan, like all real compensation contracts, is *incomplete* (see the discussion of complete and incomplete contracts in Section 9.5.2). While contracts tend to be rigid, the compensation committee may have some discretion to deal with the effects on compensation of an unanticipated outcome if it feels that management has done a good job in the face of this outcome.

Fourth, the incentive effects of BCE's compensation plan should be apparent. For highest-ranking officers, annual incentive awards are based primarily on attainment of financial targets, such as earnings per share, and are credited to the officer in the form of "share units," not shares themselves. It appears that these share units cannot be redeemed until retirement, cessation of employment, or death. Since the number of share units awarded is determined by the current year's performance, this creates a short-term incentive to maximize the current year's level of the performance measure. Note, however, that maximizing current reported performance may be at the expense of the firm's longer-run interests, possibly leading to dysfunctional tactics such as deferral of maintenance, underinvestment in R&D, premature disposal of facilities in order to realize a gain, and taking advantage of other segments of the organization. However, the effective share ownership that the share units create also gives the high-ranking officers involved a longer-term interest in the success of the firm. Presumably, this reduces the temptation to engage in dysfunctional practices such as those mentioned. It is interesting to note that executives below the highest-ranking levels receive their annual incentive awards in cash. It seems that the intent is to motivate these executives to maximize the short run efficiency of day-to-day operations, within longer-term guidelines set by the senior officers.

To reinforce these longer-term considerations, all executives and other key employees participate in the stock option-based long-term incentive plan. Here, recipients will benefit to the extent that BCE's common share price when an option is exercised exceeds the price when the option is granted. Note that the exercise price of the option is generally equal to the market value of a BCE share on the day prior to the effective date of the grant (the subscription price). In terms of our discussion of ESOs in Section 8.3, the option's intrinsic value is zero. As a result, no expense is recognized by BCE for options granted.

The options have a 10-year term, and the right to exercise early is not fully available until four years after the grant date. Early exercise is further constrained by the requirement that officers hold substantial share positions. For example, the CEO is required to hold at least five times base salary in common shares.

Fifth, the *mix* of short- and long-term incentive components in a compensation plan is important. As mentioned above, a high proportion of long-term incentive components produces a longer manager decision horizon, and vice versa. The MRCC can influence the mix. We are told that "the MRCC determines the size of the annual short-term incentive awards." Given that options are awarded to bring an executive's total compensation up to the 50th to 75th percentile of that of comparable corporations, the greater the size of the short-term award the smaller the options award and vice versa, other things equal. We will outline in Section 10.4 why some flexibility in the short-term/long-term incentives mix is desirable.

Finally, consider the risk aspects of BCE's plan. Certainly, compensation is risky for BCE managers since economy and industry-wide events that may not be controllable or informative about the manager's effort will affect both earnings per share and share price. However, aspects of the BCE plan operate to control compensation risk. Base salary, of course, is relatively risk-free. Also, the lower limit on both short-term incentive awards and stock option value is zero. This reduces downside risk since, if the bogey is not attained or if share value falls below the exercise price, the manager does not have to pay the firm. In addition, as mentioned, total compensation is adjusted to the 50th to 75th percentile of that of the comparison group. By setting total compensation in this way, an averaging effect is introduced, which would tend to make a BCE executive's total compensation less subject to variations in the performance of BCE itself.

In sum, the BCE compensation structure appears to be quite sophisticated in terms of its incentives, decision horizon, and risk properties. For our purposes, the most important point to note is that there are two main incentive components: short-term bonus and share units, and longer-term stock options whose value depends on share price performance. Thus, both accounting and market-based performance measures are embedded in the plan. These give management a vital interest in how net income is determined, both because earnings per share is a direct input into compensation and because, as we saw in Chapter 5, net income affects share price.

We now turn to a more general consideration of the compensation issues raised above.

10.4   The Theory of Executive Compensation

In Chapter 9 we suggested that basing manager compensation on the payoff was often the only feasible way to motivate manager effort in the presence of moral hazard. From an accounting perspective, it seemed natural to regard net income as the payoff, so that the compensation contract was based on net income. Then, the properties of net income as a proxy for manager effort become important. Essentially, the higher the correlation between net income and effort the more efficient the contract, in the sense of lower agency costs. We suggested at the time that historical cost-based net income may have this desirable quality. Reasons were that historical cost net income tends to be harder, hence more reliable, than fair value accounting, at least when markets do not work well. It is also less volatile, in the sense that it is less subject than share price to economy-wide events that are out of manager control and uninformative about effort.

While this efficient contracting role for net income is on the right track, the BCE compensation plan suggests that real plans are more complex and detailed, involving a mix of incentive, risk, and decision horizon considerations. Consistent with Holmström's 1979 analysis (Section 9.5.1), it seems that net income must compete with other performance measures in compensation plans, just as it competes with other information sources for investors under efficient securities market theory. Consequently, an understanding of the role of net income in manager compensation plans is important to accountants. To the extent that accountants can improve the quality of net income for efficient contracting, this will enhance their competitive advantage as well as promote responsible manager performance.

Given that compensation plans contain more than one performance measure, what determines the relative proportions of each measure (i.e., the mix) in determining the amount of compensation? Banker and Datar (1989), demonstrated conditions under which the mix of performance measures depends on the product of the **precision** and **sensitivity** of those measures, where precision is the reciprocal of the variance of the performance measure and sensitivity is the rate at which the expected value of the measure responds to manager effort. Thus, the lower the noise in net income and the greater its sensitivity to manager effort, the greater the proportion of net income to share price in the optimal contract.

There are a number of ways accountants can increase the sensitivity and precision of net income. Sensitivity will be increased by limiting the manager's ability to opportunistically manipulate reported net income. This can be accomplished, for example, by ensuring full disclosure of unusual and non-recurring items (earnings management is discussed in Chapter 11). Full disclosure of unusual and non-recurring items increases earnings sensitivity by enabling the compensation committee to better evaluate earnings persistence. Persistent earnings are a more informative measure of manager effort than transitory or price-irrelevant earnings. Earnings precision will be increased if adjustments of assets and liabilities to fair value are fully disclosed, or included in other comprehensive income, so that they can be excluded from net income for bonus purposes to the extent they are not informative about manager effort.

Another factor, however, seriously reduces the sensitivity of net income with respect to effort. Namely, the full impact on net income of current manager effort is not observable in the year the effort is exerted, despite our assumption that it was in the single-period models of Chapter 9. For example, profit on inventory acquired during the current period is not typically recognized if it is unsold at period-end, even though purchasing is part of current manager effort. Even for inventory sold, losses on credit sales for the period have to be estimated, despite marketing and credit policy being part of current effort.

This sensitivity problem is even greater if we recognize that manager effort is a *set* of activities, rather than a single activity. Some of these activities have longer-run implications than others. For example, payoffs from effort devoted to advertising, capital expenditure, acquisitions, divestitures, R&D, etc. may not be known for years, yet managers must be compensated periodically. In effect, current net income captures the payoffs from some current manager activities later than others and may completely omit the payoffs from some of them.

Given these problems of using current net income as a payoff measure, we can see why share price might be more sensitive than net income to effort. With efficient securities markets, share prices will "properly reflect" all that is known about prospective payoffs from current manager actions. For example, share price will incorporate the future prospects of current R&D efforts, even though most R&D costs are written off currently under Section 3450 of *CICA Handbook*. Furthermore, as we saw in Sections 5.3 and 5.4, share price includes the value relevant information content of net income itself.

Consequently, one might ask, why not base manager compensation only on share price? The reason is that while it may be more sensitive, share price is less precise than net income. This is because it is affected by a host of economy-wide events such as interest rate changes, exchange rate movements, and trade agreements, which impose risks beyond those inherent in the firm's production processes themselves. While hedging may reduce some of these risks, it is unlikely that their complete elimination is cost effective, as discussed in Section 7.4.4. Also, as discussed in Section 4.4.1, the presence of noise traders means that share prices do not perfectly aggregate even public information. Further problems with precision arise to the extent that securities markets are not fully efficient. Consequently, the use of share price as a payoff measure may impose excess compensation risk on managers and lead to misallocation of effort across activities.

To the extent that net income is relatively insensitive to economy-wide factors, noise trading and market inefficiency, inclusion of *both* share price and net income in the compensation contract improves compensation contract efficiency. Indeed, this has been demonstrated by Bushman and Indjejikian (1992), Kim and Suh (1993), and Feltham and Xie (1994), whose analyses show that, in the presence of noise trading, the optimal contract includes both share price and net income as performance measures, even though share price fully incorporates the value relevant information in net income. The reason derives from the fundamental problem of financial accounting theory, which implies that net income tells us something about manager performance beyond what share price tells us, even though share price reflects the good or bad news in net income (i.e., share price is not a sufficient statistic for share price and net income with respect to manager effort; see Chapter 9, Note 7). Then, inclusion of both variables, as in the BCE plan, increases contracting efficiency.

Recognition of manager effort as a set of activities, with both current and longer-term payoffs, generates a potential for further contracting efficiencies.

Specifically, the firm may wish to encourage some activities more than others. This would not be possible with share price as the only performance measure, since share price aggregates the expected payoffs from *all* activities. However, with both share price and net income as performance measures, the firm can adjust the relative proportions of each to exploit the fact that current net income includes the payoffs from only some manager activities in the current period. For example, suppose a firm wants to encourage the manager to undertake more R&D. Then, it can reduce the proportion of the manager's compensation on the basis of net income and increase the proportion on the basis of share price. Compensation will now rise more strongly due to securities market response to an increase in R&D, and there will be less compensation penalty from writing R&D costs off currently. Consequently, it will be in the manager's interest to increase R&D. More generally, firms with substantial investment opportunities will want to increase the proportion of share price-based compensation,[1] since it can take some time for the results of investment projects to show up in net income.

As another example, suppose that the firm has to cut costs in the short run. Net income will reflect the favourable cash flow effects of cost cutting quickly and accurately, perhaps even more so than share price, particularly if the cost-cutting measures are complex or constitute inside information, or the market is concerned about the longer-run effects of short-run cost cutting. Also, as mentioned, share price may not perfectly aggregate the cost-cutting information in the presence of noise trading or market inefficiencies. Then, the firm may wish to increase the weight of net income relative to share price in the manager's compensation.

In effect, when share price and net income differentially reflect the short- and long-run payoffs of current manager actions, the length of the manager's decision horizon can be controlled by the mix of share price-based and net income-based compensation—more share-based compensation produces a longer decision horizon and vice versa. This was demonstrated theoretically by Bushman and Indjejikian (1993). As we pointed out in Section 10.3, it seems that the BCE compensation plan allows the Compensation Committee some flexibility with respect to the mix of short- and long-term compensation.

10.5   *The Role of Risk in Executive Compensation*

Forcing managers to bear compensation risk is consistent with agency theory, which tells us that if unobservable effort is to be motivated the manager must be "under the gun" by bearing risk. Note, however, that managers, like other rational, risk-averse individuals, trade off risk and return. Consequently, the more risk managers bear the higher must be their *expected* compensation if reservation utility is to be attained. Thus, to motivate the manager at the lowest cost, designers of incentive compensation plans try to get the most motivation for a given amount of risk imposed or, equivalently, the least risk for a given level of motivation.

Nevertheless, the manager must bear some compensation risk if effort is to be motivated. Consequently, it is desirable that the manager not be able to work out from under whatever risk the compensation plan imposes. The manager can shed compensation risk by, for example, selling shares and options acquired and investing the proceeds in a risk-free asset and/or a diversified portfolio. However, compensation plans typically reduce this possibility by constraining the manager's ability to dispose of shares and options acquired. Thus the BCE plan requires officers to hold from 2 to 5 times annual base salary in BCE shares. Also, stock options are not fully exercisable until four years after the grant date.

It is important to note that risk can affect how the manager operates the firm. On the one hand, the compensation committee may be overly generous in not penalizing the manager for state realizations that are not his or her "fault," thereby destroying contract rigidity. For example, outstanding ESOs are sometimes "repriced" to a lower exercise price (see Problems 9 and 11). Or, the manager may be allowed to engage in excessive hedging. Then, the incentive to exert effort will suffer since not enough risk is imposed on the manager. In this regard, Suncor Energy Inc., in its 2000 annual report MD&A, describes its oil and gas cash flow hedging program. Suncor's Board meets regularly with management to assess the extent of hedging. The Board has restricted cash flow hedging to a maximum of 50% of 2000 and 2001 oil production and to 30% for 2002, 3, and 4.

On the other hand, too much risk can also be dysfunctional. Some limitation of the manager's downside risk is desirable because even managers do not have unlimited wealth, and fear of personal bankruptcy is probably not the best way to motivate a manager to work hard. The reason is that the manager may then adopt only "safe" operating and investment strategies whereas diversified shareholders' interests may be better served by riskier ones. As mentioned, the compensation plan bogey, and stock options, limit downside risk.

But, if the manager's downside risk is limited, it seems reasonable for his or her upside risk to be limited too; otherwise the manager would have everything to gain and little to lose.[2] Compensation plans that impose a bogey but not a cap encourage opportunistic risk taking since there will be large rewards to the manager if the risks pay off but little penalty if they do not. Stock options have similar characteristics. Some consequences for the firm of excessive risk taking were outlined in Section 8.7.4. Note that the BCE plan imposes a cap on short-term incentive awards of three times the award based on the target. Similar constraints are not apparent for stock options, however. The period from exercise to expiry of BCE's option awards is up to six years, suggesting considerable upside potential.

Another risk-reducing device is **relative performance evaluation (RPE)**. RPE has the potential to reduce the manager's risk while maintaining incentives. The theory of RPE was developed by Holmström (1982). By setting bonuses or other incentive awards *relative* to the average performance of other firms in the industry, the systematic or common risk that the industry faces will be filtered out of the incentive plan, especially if the number of firms in the industry is large. Since economy- or industry-wide risks are likely to be uncontrollable and uninformative about manager effort, basing the performance measure or measures on the difference between the firm's performance and the average performance of the industry will tighten up the correlation between effort and performance measure that is needed for an efficient contract. To see why, recall that net income is a noisy measure of firm performance (despite our argument above that it is less noisy than share price). As a result, the realization of random states of nature clouds the relationship between manager effort and firm performance (recall that, by definition, no one can control state realization), thereby imposing risk on the manager. But just as a consensus football forecast has qualities superior to those of individual forecasters (Section 4.2.2), so the average performance of firms in an industry has superior qualities as a measure of the impact of state realization on the firm. In effect, basing the manager's compensation on firm performance relative to the industry average filters out the common industry and economy risk, leaving a performance measure that is more highly correlated with manager effort than net income itself, and hence less risky.

The BCE compensation plan contains aspects of RPE. As mentioned, total compensation is positioned at the 50th to 75th percentile of a group of comparable companies. This introduces an averaging effect, since the total compensation of a BCE manager depends not only on BCE's performance but also on the performance of a group of comparable companies.

Despite the theoretical appeal of RPE, strong statistical evidence that managers are compensated this way has been hard to come by. Antle and Smith (1986) found weak evidence for RPE, and according to Pavlik, Scott, and Tiessen (1993), a survey of RPE articles shows that the ability of RPE to predict manager compensation is modest. A possible reason for the weak empirical support is given by Sloan (1993), who argues, as we have above, that net income is relatively insensitive to economy-wide risks. Inclusion of net income as a performance measure in addition to share price shields manager compensation from these economy-wide effects. As a result, RPE is not needed, since basing compensation on both share price and net income accomplishes a similar result.

10.6   *Empirical Compensation Research*

These various theoretical considerations raise the question of whether real compensation plans are designed as the theory suggests. This was studied by Lambert and Larcker (1987) (LL). Using a sample of 370 U.S. firms over 1970–1984 inclusive, LL investigated the relative ability of return on shares and return on equity to explain managers' cash compensation (salary plus bonus). If, for example, compensation plans and compensation committees primarily use share return as a manager performance measure, then share return should be significantly related to cash compensation. Alternatively, if they primarily use net income as a performance measure, return on equity (a ratio based on net income) should be significantly related to cash compensation.

Note that LL examined only cash compensation. Empirically, accounting variables do not seem to explain the options component of manager compensation. Indeed, this can be seen in the BCE plan. While short-term incentive awards are based on individual contributions and net income, stock option awards are not. Rather, they are made to bring total compensation up to the 50th to 75th percentiles of the group of comparison companies. Consequently, most studies of the role of net income in compensation concentrate on cash awards.

LL found that return on equity was more highly related to cash compensation than was return on shares. Indeed, several other studies have found the same thing. This supports the risk-reduction and decision horizon-controlling roles for net income in compensation plans that were suggested in Section 10.4, and implies that net income, at least as GAAP existed during the period 1970–1984, has characteristics that make it an important input into the bonus component of compensation.

LL also found that the relationship of these two payoff measures to cash compensation varied in systematic ways. For example, they showed that the relationship between return on equity and cash compensation strengthened when net income was less noisy relative to return on shares. They measured the relative noisiness of net income by the ratio of the variability of return on equity over 1970–1984 to the variability of return on shares over the same period. The lower the noise in net income, the better it reflects manager effort. This finding is consistent with Banker and Datar's analysis.

LL discovered that compensation for growth firms' executives tended to have a lower relationship with return on equity than average. This is also consistent with Banker and Datar, since, for growth firms, net income is relatively less sensitive to manager effort than it is for the average firm. Historical cost-based net income tends particularly to lag behind the real economic performance of a growth firm, because this basis of accounting does not recognize value increases until they are realized. The efficient market, however, will look through to real economic performance and value the shares accordingly. Thus, return on equity should be less highly related to compensation than share return for such firms, consistent with what LL found.

Perhaps the most interesting finding of LL, however, was that for firms where the correlation between share return and return on equity was low, there tended to be a higher weight on return on equity in the compensation plan, and vice versa. In other words, when net income is relatively uninformative to investors (low correlation between share return and return on equity) that same net income is relatively informative about manager effort (higher weight on return on equity in the compensation plan). This provides empirical evidence on the impact of the fundamental problem of financial accounting theory—the investor-informing and the manager-performance-motivating dimensions of usefulness must be traded off.

Also in an empirical study, Bushman, Indjejikian, and Smith (1996) found that CEOs of growth firms, and of firms with long product development and life cycles, derived a greater proportion of their compensation from individual performance measures relative to net income- and stock price-based measures. Recall that BCE's compensation plan bases short-term incentive awards on *individual* creativity and initiative in addition to earnings, primarily for less senior executives. When net income, and perhaps even stock price, are relatively insensitive to manager effort, it seems that this approach extends to CEOs as well.

In Section 10.4, we suggested that accountants could improve the sensitivity of net income to manager effort by enabling identification of persistent earnings by the compensation committee. Evidence that suggests compensation committees do indeed value persistent earnings more highly for compensation purposes than transitory or price-irrelevant earnings is provided by Baber, Kang, and Kumar (1999) (BKK). In a sample of 712 firms over the years 1992 and 1993, their results include a finding that the effect of earnings changes on compensation increases with the persistence of those earnings changes.

To understand BKK's result, consider the following example. A firm's earnings persistence is 0.85. That is, 85% of the change in earnings during the year will persist into future years. Assume that current earnings are $100, and that last year's earnings were $80, so that the change in earnings is $20. Current earnings include $15 of transitory items (non-recurring and unusual items, extraordinary items), and no price-irrelevant items. To simplify, suppose that last year's earnings were all unexpected and contained no transitory or price-irrelevant items. Then, 85% of last year's earnings, or $68, are expected this year. This $68 corresponds to the "quantifiable financial targets" in the BCE plan. Current year's unexpected earnings of $32 ($100 − $68) corresponds to achievement in excess of target. It is this excess over target that determines BCE's short- term incentive award for the year.

Now, current year's $32 unexpected earnings includes $15 of transitory earnings (unexpected by definition) and $17 ($20 × .85) of earnings that will persist into future years. We would expect the compensation committee to put more weight on the high persistence component ($17) of excess over target than the low persistence component ($15), since earnings that persist are better evidence of manager effort than earnings that do not. The BKK result is consistent with this expectation.

In sum, the above empirical results suggest that, like investors, compensation committees are on average quite sophisticated in their use of accounting information. Just as full disclosure of value relevant information will increase investors' use of this information, full disclosure of "effort relevant" information will increase its usage by compensation committees, thereby maintaining and increasing the role of net income in motivating responsible manager performance.

10.7   The Politics of Executive Compensation

The question of manager compensation has been a longstanding one in the United States and Canada. Many have argued that top managers are overpaid, especially in comparison to those in other countries, such as Japan.

In 1990, Jensen and Murphy (JM) published a controversial article about top manager compensation. They argued that CEOs were not overpaid, but that their compensation was far too unrelated to performance, where performance was measured as the change in the firm's market value (that is, the change in shareholder wealth). They examined the salary plus bonus of the CEOs of the 250 largest U.S. corporations over the 15 years from 1974 to 1988. For each year, they added the current year's and next year's salary and bonus and found that on average the CEOs received an extra 6.7 cents compensation over the two years for every $1,000 increase in shareholder wealth. When they added in other compensation components, including stock options and direct share holdings, the CEOs still received only $2.59 per $1,000 increase in shareholder wealth.

Other aspects of JM's investigation were consistent with these findings. For example, the variability (as measured by the standard deviation) over time of CEOs' and regular workers' compensations were almost the same. JM concluded that CEOs did not bear enough risk to motivate good performance, and consequently recommended larger stock holdings by managers. With respect to the BCE plan, note again from Exhibit 10.1 that there are guidelines that require substantial stock holdings by officers.

Nevertheless, some counterarguments can be made to JM.[3] First, we would *expect* the relationship between pay and performance to be low for large firms, simply because of a size effect. Suppose that a large corporation increased in value by $5 billions last year (for example, BCE Inc's 2000 net income was $4.861 billions). An increase of even 1% of this amount in the CEO's remuneration would be large enough to attract media attention.

Second, for large corporations at least, it is difficult to put much downside risk on an executive, as we argued in Section 10.5. An executive whose pay is highly related to performance would have so much to lose from even a small decline in firm value that this would probably lead to excessive avoidance of risky projects. If, in addition, upside risk is limited, this means a low pay-performance relationship.

In this regard, it is interesting to note that, in 1997, BCE Inc. reported a net loss of $1.536 billion, compared to net earnings of $1.152 billion for 1996. Nevertheless, 60,881 share units were awarded to six senior officers for 1997 under the short-term compensation plan, compared to 55,299 share units in 1996. Salaries were also up for 1997, as were stock options awarded under the long-term incentive plan. BCE's 1997 net loss resulted from an extraordinary item of $2.950 billion for "stranded costs." That is, increasing competition as a result of telecommunications deregulation in Canada resulted in BCE's inability to recover the full costs of certain assets from revenues. The extraordinary charge represented a write-down of these assets to estimated future cash flows, consistent with the ceiling test of Section 3060 of *CICA Handbook*, discussed in Section 7.2.4. BCE's 1997 earnings before this extraordinary item were $1.414 billion.

One could argue that deregulation of the telecommunications industry has little to do with manager effort, consistent with BCE's treatment of the write-down as an extraordinary item under Section 3480 of *CICA Handbook* (see Section 5.5). In effect, the item is transitory, hence of low persistence. As we argued in the previous section, low persistence supports a low weighting in determining compensation. Nevertheless, its exclusion for bonus purposes also supports an argument that a low pay-performance relationship is to be expected.

This exclusion by BCE is consistent with the results of Gaver and Gaver (1998). For a sample of 376 large U.S. firms over the years 1970–1996, these authors found that while extraordinary gains tended to be reflected in CEO cash compensation, extraordinary losses were not. This result suggests that compensation committees feel that reducing manager compensation for extraordinary losses imposes excessive risk on the manager, since the extraordinary loss may be the result of a market downturn rather than manager shirking.

Finally, it should be pointed out that the value of a given amount of compensation to a manager is lower than it might appear at first glance. Much of compensation is granted in the form of shares and options. But since the right to freely sell these is usually restricted, as we saw in the case of BCE, they are worth less to the manager than their current fair value. The more risk-averse the manager, the greater this reduction in value.

To illustrate, assume that firms use the Black-Scholes option pricing formula to estimate the fair value of stock options to the executive. As discussed in Section 8.3, this formula assumes that options can be freely traded. Lambert, Larcker, and Verrecchia (1991) calculated the cash-equivalent value to a manager of 10,000 options with a Black-Scholes value of $351,260. If the manager is moderately risk-averse and if 50% of the manager's wealth is tied to the firm's stock price, the value of the options to the manager who cannot freely trade them is only $152,300, according to their calculations.[4] If the manager is highly risk-averse this value falls to $65,900. While fair value may represent the opportunity cost to the firm, it exceeds the options' value to the managers.

Nevertheless, studies such as JM's have strengthened the longstanding concern about executive salaries. The following cartoon reflects this concern.

Of course, if labour markets are to work well, they must know how much compensation the manager is receiving. It is interesting to note that in 1993 the Ontario Securities Commission adopted regulations to require firms to give more disclosure of their executive compensation. These regulations are similar to those of the SEC (1992) in the United States. For example, a detailed explanation of

SOURCE: Jim Berry. Reprinted by permission of Newspaper Enterprise Association.

the compensation of firms' five highest-paid executives is required, as is a report from the compensation committee justifying the pay levels. Presumably, the securities commissions feel that if shareholders and others have enough information to intelligently evaluate manager compensation levels and components, they will take appropriate action if these appear out of line. Whether these measures will suffice to stem the concern or whether stronger action will be taken (for example, to limit the amount of manager compensation deductible for tax purposes, as has been done in the United States) remains to be seen.

10.8   *Summary*

Managerial labour markets undoubtedly reduce the severity of moral hazard. However, past manager performance is not an iron-clad indicator of future performance. Also, labour markets are subject to adverse selection problems, since managers may withhold relevant information to disguise shirking. Consequently, incentive contracts are still necessary.

Executive compensation contracts involve a delicate balancing of incentives, risk, and decision horizon. To properly align the interests of managers and shareholders, an efficient contract needs to achieve a high level of motivation while avoiding the imposition of too much risk on the manager. Too much risk can have dysfunctional consequences such as shortening a manager's decision horizon, adoption of earnings-increasing tactics that are against the firm's longer-run interests, and avoidance of risky projects. Managers are particularly sensitive to risk, because they cannot diversify it away as can shareholders.

To attain proper alignment, incentive plans usually feature a combination of salary, bonus, and various types of stock plans including options. These components of compensation are usually based on two performance measures—net income and share price. We can think of these as two noisy measures of the unobservable payoff from current-period manager effort. Theory predicts that the relative proportion of each in the compensation plan depends on both their relative precision and sensitivity, and the length of manager decision horizon that the firm wants to motivate. Empirically, it appears that executive compensation is related to performance but that the strength of the relationship is low. However, for large firms at least, this low relationship is to be expected. Also, the relative proportion of net income-based and share price-based compensation components seems to vary as the theory predicts.

Executive compensation is surrounded by political controversy. Regulators have responded by expanding the information available to shareholders and others, on the assumption that they will take action to eliminate inefficient plans, or the managers and firms that have them. Whether this is sufficient to reduce compensation concerns remains to be seen.

We may conclude that financial reporting has an important role in motivating executive performance. This role extends to improving the working of managerial labour markets by reducing the extent to which manager reputation may be based on incomplete or biased information, and to serving as a payoff measure in compensation contracts. This role is equally important as its role in promoting good investment decisions and improving the operation of securities markets.

Questions and Problems

1. Below is a portion of a 2001 proxy form sent to shareholders of Miracle Corporation. It reveals that Miracle has a bonus plan for its three senior executives that allocates them 10% of before-tax profits. Also, under the Employee Stock Option Plan, share options up to 12% of capitalization may be granted to directors or employees.

MIRACLE CORP.

Executive and Management Compensation

The Corporation's five executive officers were remunerated, in total, $440,000 by way of fees, salaries and bonuses for the fiscal year ended May 31, 2001.

Included in the aforesaid sum was $280,000 paid to the three senior executive officers as full-time employees of the Corporation, pursuant to individual four-year Management Agreements made between the Corporation and those senior executive officers, effective June 1, 1997. Under the terms of the Agreements, the three senior executives are entitled to receive an aggregate bonus of 10% of before-tax profits earned by the company and their base salaries are to be increased 10% per year. For the 2001 fiscal year, the three senior executive officers waived their bonus entitlements to the extent that each received dividends on shares of the Corporation held by them which dividend was declared and paid for the fiscal year ended May 31, 2001.

It is to be noted that the Directors have adopted a form of Employee Stock Option Plan under which share options of up to 12% of the capitalization of the Corporation may be granted to Directors or employees. There are presently reserved, to that end, 930,000 common shares of the Corporation; but the Corporation has not granted any option to any Director or employees as of the date of this Information Circular.

Required

a. Explain the reason for the 10% bonus plan for senior executives. Are there any possible dysfunctional consequences of the bonus plan resulting from the apparent lack of a cap? Why is the bonus based on before-tax profits, rather than after-tax?

b. Explain why there is also an Employee Stock Option Plan.

c. To what extent would the bonus plan cause management to be concerned about accounting policies and changes in GAAP?

2. Agency theory suggests that one way to motivate managers to act in the best interests of the owners/shareholders is to link managerial compensation to

firms' payoffs, such as net income or share returns. However, such a linkage imposes risk on the manager.

Required

a. Why is it important to control or reduce some of the risk thus imposed on managers? Explain.

b. Discuss *two* methods by which risk imposed on the managers could be reduced.

c. Many managerial compensation packages impose restrictions on *when* managers can sell stocks granted to them as a part of their compensation. For example, some compensation packages indicate that stocks may be forfeited unless the manager continues to work for the firm for a certain number of years after the granting of the stock. Discuss the justification behind such restrictions.

d. Inclusion of shares and options in managerial compensation packages has been attributed to the desire of the owners/shareholders to provide managers an incentive to undertake policies that benefit the firm's long-term rather than short-term interests. If this is true, why not compensate the manager only on the basis of share return (for example, only by stock options)? In other words, under these circumstances, what is the justification for having a cash or a bonus element in the compensation package?

3. Firms A and B are roughly the same size, but operate in different industries. Firm A bases a high proportion of its executive compensation on net income and a relatively low proportion on share price performance. For firm B, these proportions are reversed. Yet, both firms appear to be well managed, consistently profitable, and growing. Use the concepts of sensitivity and precision of a performance measure to explain why both firms' compensation plans are efficient, despite the differing proportions.

4. An article entitled "Study of CEOs' Compensation Finds Surprises" appeared in the *The Wall Street Journal* on November 18, 1991. The article described the findings of a study done on executive pay by Graef S. Crystal, a professor at the University of California at Berkeley, who looked at "the 1990 compensation of 1,000 chief executives." Professor Crystal "concludes that while 30% of the difference in executives' pay can be traced to company size, 'no more than 4% can be accounted for by differences in company performance.'" Thus, the article documents a very low pay-performance relationship for the companies studied. This prompted Ralph Whitworth, president of the United Shareholders Association that sponsored the study, to say: "There's just no correlation between pay and performance."

According to the article, "Mr. Crystal takes the exercise another step, tallying up the 1,000 executives' pay and redistributing it to those whom the study showed to be more deserving." For example, the article points out that David Glass, an executive at Wal-Mart Stores Inc., received $980,000 in pay. However, according to the study, Mr. Glass should have received $11 million due to the retailer's size and growth.

On the other hand, Time Warner Inc.'s co-chiefs, Steven Ross and N.J. Nicholas, together amassed almost $100 million in compensation, which was "heavily bolstered by money made in the merger of their respective companies." However, according to the study, Mr. Ross and Mr. Nicholas should have received a combined $2.5 million.

Required

a. What are the problems of measuring company performance in a study such as this? In your answer, include problems with both stock-based and net-income-based performance measures.

b. Give reasons why we would expect a low pay-performance relationship for large corporations.

5. An article entitled "Former Critic of Big Stock Plans for CEOs Now Supports Them" that appeared in the *The Wall Street Journal* on December 16, 1992 describes a study of executive compensation that found firms with a higher "pay-performance sensitivity" produced higher returns for shareholders, where pay-performance sensitivity is the rate at which a CEO's pay changes with changes in firm performance.

According to the article, the United Shareholders Association, a Washington shareholder-rights group that once criticized the use of stock and/or stock options as a form of compensation for top executives, had changed its tune. Its spokespersons now believed that "stock-based pay" was the best way to motivate top executives "to boost the value of a company's stock and, therefore, the payoff for shareholders."

The Association's new view came from a study conducted by Kevin J. Murphy, at the time an associate professor with Harvard Business School, who "suggests that companies that reward executives for stock-price increases with stock-based pay consistently perform better than those that don't."

The Murphy study, based on the 1,000 largest U.S. companies, "calculates how much the top U.S. chief executive officers earned in 1991 for each $1,000 their shareholders as a group gained in stock-price appreciation and dividends."

According to the article, the study found that Philip H. Knight of Nike Inc. was at the top of the "pay-performance sensitivity" because he earned $680.77 per $1,000 change in shareholder value. On the other hand, John E. Lobbia of Detroit Edison Co. was at the bottom of the "pay-performance sensitivity" for earning only two cents for each $1,000. Also, "the median sensitivity level was $5.44 per $1,000."

The study concluded that those "companies with higher sensitivity levels—whose chief executives had greater stock incentives—produced higher returns for shareholders over the past one, five and 10 years."

However, the article pointed out that there is no conclusive proof of the theory that larger "incentives" produce better "performance." Indeed, there has been some criticism of the study from companies that have low "pay-performance sensitivity" rankings. They argue that the study did not effectively take into account other "incentive plans that aren't stock based or…tied to measures other than stock-price improvement." For example, Detroit Edison Co., the company with the lowest ranking, made a comment that it had had high shareholder returns in past years even though it lacked financial rewards for its CEO.

Required

a. Explain why basing executive compensation on a stock price-based performance measure implicitly assumes securities market efficiency.

b. According to the article, the study cautions that the finding of a positive sensitivity-return association does not prove that higher sensitivity *causes* higher returns to shareholders. Use the theory of executive compensation to explain how there might in fact be a causal link.

c. Presumably, the author of the study controlled for firm size and risk before reaching his conclusion. Explain how firm size could affect pay-performance sensitivity, other things being equal. Do the same for firm risk.

d. The United Shareholders Association changed its position to support share price as a performance measure, instead of "long used" measures such as earnings per share, which provide "only a weak incentive for an executive to boost shareholder value." Do you agree? In your answer, consider the problem of controlling the executive's time horizon.

6. In 1993, the OSC implemented new executive compensation disclosure rules (OSC, Form 40, Securities Act, Regulation 638/93). These require that shareholder proxy statements contain tables spelling out compensation for the five highest-paid executives, plus a report from the board's compensation committee explaining the firm's compensation practices.

Required

a. To what extent do you think that such disclosure requirements will assist the proper operation of an efficient managerial labour market? Explain.

b. If the managerial labour market is fully efficient (that is, analogous to an efficient securities market), would manager incentive plans based on risky performance measures such as share price and reported net income be needed? Explain why or why not.

7. An article entitled "Taking Stock—Big Firms Rely More on Options But Fail to End Pay Criticism" that appeared in *The Wall Street Journal* on March 11, 1992 describes the emphasis in many firms on issuing stock options to executives. According to the article, stock options "tend to be generous" when measured at their face value, defined as the number of shares awarded under option times the market price of the stock on the date the option is granted.

The article points out that Anthony Luiso, chairman of International Multifoods Corp., "talked its board into tripling his option grants in exchange for forgoing $1 million in pay over five years."

The article states that stock options have become very appealing, because they allow companies to decrease their large cash compensation packages for executives in exchange for stock options. Companies tell their executives that they "won't benefit unless ordinary stockholders do."

There has been some criticism about granting stock options as compensation. For instance, David Norr, an investment advisor who testified before a Senate subcommittee, states "that it is [not] necessary to provide options to retain and attract people." Furthermore, he believes that being a CEO at a major corporation should be incentive enough. Even Mr. Luiso, mentioned earlier, cannot say that stock options give him incentive to improve his performance: "I can't sit here and say if I didn't have this [stock option] program, then my decision-making process would be less good than it is now."

Furthermore, "some experts suggest tying option grants to achieving some corporate goals. The options would become available to executives only when the company, for example, improved its return on equity." Some companies such as AT&T have adopted a plan whereby stock options are granted at a higher price than the market price on the date the option is granted. Thus, the executive would only be rewarded when the stock price rises above this higher price.

Required

a. Would granting stock options to executives with a higher exercise price than the stock price on the grant date trigger the recording of compensation expense under APB 25? (See Section 8.3) Explain why or why not.

b. The article defines face value of an option award as the number of options granted times the market value of the stock on the grant date. Is face value a reasonable measure of the fair value of the option award? Explain why or why not.

c. The article states that stock options are "the fastest growing segment of executive pay." Why do firms issue options, in addition to or in place of other components of executive compensation?

d. Explain why the value of options to an executive may be less than the face value of the award.

e. Do you agree that options do not cost the company anything? Explain.

f. According to the article, "most option plans reward executives for success but don't penalize them for failure." Discuss the incentive effects of this aspect of options. In your answer, consider how the risk imposed on the manager by such plans may affect the manager's actions.

8.   Reproduced below are the 1997 consolidated statement of operations and Note 2 to the financial statements of BCE Inc. The statement of operations shows an extraordinary charge of $2.950 billion for stranded costs, described in Note 2. After this extraordinary charge, operations showed a net loss for the year of $1.536 billion.

CONSOLIDATED FINANCIAL STATEMENTS—BCE INC.
CONSOLIDATED STATEMENT OF OPERATIONS

For the years ended December 31	($ millions, except per share amounts)		
	1997	1996	1995
Revenues	33,191	28,167	24,624
Operating expenses	25,795	22,011	19,434
Research and development expense	2,911	2,471	2,134
Operating profit	4,485	3,685	3,056
Other income	365	393	238
Operating earnings	4,850	4,078	3,294
Interest expense – long-term debt	1,111	1,160	1,154
– other debt	121	141	172
Total interest expense	1,232	1,301	1,326
Earnings before taxes, non-controlling interest and extraordinary item	3,618	2,777	1,968
Income taxes	(1,522)	(1,118)	(819)
Non-controlling interest	(682)	(507)	(367)
Net earnings before extraordinary item	1,414	1,152	782
Extraordinary item	(2,950)	—	—
Net earnings (loss)	(1,536)	1,152	782
Dividends on preferred shares	(74)	(76)	(87)
Net earnings (loss) applicable to common shares	(1,610)	1,076	695
Earnings (loss) per common share[1]			
Net earnings before extraordinary item	2.11	1.70	1.12
Extraordinary item	(4.64)	—	—
Net earnings (loss)	(2.53)	1.70	1.12
Dividends per common share[1]	1.36	1.36	1.36
Average number of common shares outstanding (millions)[1]	636.0	632.7	622.9

1   Reflects the subdivision of common shares on a two-for-one basis on May 14, 1997.

EXTRAORDINARY ITEM

As at December 31, 1997, BCE determined that most of its telecommunications subsidiary and associated companies no longer met the criteria necessary for the continued application of regulatory accounting provisions. As a result, BCE recorded an extraordinary non-cash charge of $2,950 million, net of an income tax benefit of $1,892 million and a non-controlling interest of $38 million. Also included in the extraordinary item is an after-tax charge of $97 million representing BCE's share of the related extraordinary item of its associated companies.

The operations of most of BCE's telecommunications subsidiary and associated companies no longer met the criteria for application of regulatory accounting provisions due to significant changes in regulation including the implementation of price cap regulation which replaced rate-of-return regulation effective January 1, 1998 and the concurrent introduction of competition in the local exchange market. Accordingly, BCE adjusted the net carrying values of assets and liabilities as at December 31, 1997 to reflect values appropriate under GAAP for enterprises no longer subject to rate-of-return regulation.

The determination by BCE that most of its telecommunications subsidiary and associated companies no longer met the criteria for the continuing application of regulatory accounting provisions is the result of a review, which began in 1997, to assess the impact of the introduction of price cap regulation coupled with the introduction of competition in the local exchange market. Before the advent of these two factors, accounting practices were based on a regulatory regime which provided reasonable assurance of the recovery of costs through rates set by the regulator and charged to customers. These regulatory accounting provisions resulted in the recognition of certain assets and liabilities along with capital asset lives which were substantially different from enterprises not subject to rate-of-return regulation.

The extraordinary charge consists of a pre-tax charge of $3,602 million related to capital assets and a pre-tax charge of $1,181 million to adjust the carrying values of other assets and liabilities to arrive at carrying values appropriate for enterprises not subject to rate-of-return regulation. The amount of the charge related to capital assets was determined based upon an estimate of the underlying cash flows using management's best estimate assumptions concerning the most likely course of action and other factors relating to competition, technological changes and the evolution of products and services. The net carrying values of capital assets were adjusted primarily through an increase in accumulated depreciation. The primary component of the $1,181 million charge relates to the write-off of deferred business transformation and workforce reduction costs.

SOURCE: BCE Inc., *1997 Annual Report*. Reprinted by permission.

Required

a. Does the charge for stranded costs meet the definition of an extraordinary item under Section 3480 of *CICA Handbook* (see Section 5.5)? Discuss.

b. Regardless of whether or not the $2.950 billion is an extraordinary item, as a member of BCE's executive compensation committee would you support exclusion of the charge from earnings for the purpose of managers' short-term incentive awards? Discuss.

c. What is the persistence of the $2.950 billion component of 1997 earnings? Your answer should be in the range [0-1]. Explain your answer.

d. What will be the effect of the $2.950 billion charge on future years' earnings, compared to what earnings would have been if the charge had not been recorded? Given that the 1997 charge was excluded from earnings for executive compensation purposes, would you, as a member of BCE's executive compensation committee, support the inclusion in future years' earnings for compensation purposes of the after-effects of the 1997 charge? Why or why not?

9. Following major declines in their share prices, firms frequently "reprice" outstanding stock options issued to executives and employees as part of their incentive compensation. Reproduced here is an article from the *Financial Post* (April 3, 1997), describing such a repricing by Rogers Communications Inc. According to the article, Rogers' stock options with exercise prices ranging from $12.64 to $19.38 were lowered to an exercise price of $8.31.

ROGERS REPRICES COMPENSATION OPTIONS

Rogers Communications Inc. repriced all the options its executives and other employees have received as part of their compensation packages in 1994 and 1995 because the company's share price has fallen so far, Rogers' annual shareholder circular says.

The options' new exercise price is $8.31, significantly lower than the earlier prices, said Rogers spokeswoman Jan Innes.

Previously, exercise prices ranged from $12.64 to $19.38. Also, the exercise period was extended to 2006.

"If you've got options and they're well above what the stock is trading at, they're certainly not very interesting," explained Jan Innes.

Rogers' circular says the company awards options to "focus executives' attention on the long-term interests of the corporation and its shareholders."

Analysts were surprised by the move.

"I can imagine that shareholders will be a bit perturbed," said one. "After all, their shares didn't get repriced. But I suppose it will help keep people motivated."

Rogers shares have fallen drastically since 1993, when they hit a $21.88 high. The shares (RCIb/TSE) closed yesterday at $8, down 55¢.

Ted Rogers' options, along with other non-management directors' options, will not be repriced.

Rogers' class A shareholders, the only ones entitled to vote, will vote on the arrangement at the company's annual meeting May 2. Ted Rogers controls over 90% of the A shares, so the vote should pass.

Meanwhile, working two jobs is paying off for Ted Rogers, president and chief executive of Rogers Communications and acting president of Rogers Cable-systems Ltd.

Rogers got a 21% salary increase to $600,000 for 1996, plus a 160% rise in his bonus, to $260,110, for a total of $860,110. In addition, he was given 300,000 new options.

But he was not the highest paid executive at the cable and telecommunications company he founded.

That distinction went to Stan Kabala, chief operating officer of telecommunications and chief executive of Rogers Cantel Mobile Communications Inc.

Kabala, who joined Rogers Jan. 1, 1996, got a salary of $600,000, plus a bonus of $925,000, for a total of $1,525,000. He was also awarded 119,000 stock options.

Kabala's big bonus was related to a deal completed in November 1996 with U.S. phone giant AT&T Corp., as well as for Cantel's performance.

The last time Rogers paid bonuses of such magnitude was in 1994 after it completed its takeover of Maclean Hunter Ltd.

SOURCE: *The National Post*, April 3, 1997. Reprinted by permission.

Required

a. Give reasons why firms frequently issue stock options to executives and senior employees as part of their incentive compensation.

b. If options are always repriced when share prices fall, what effects may there be on the incentives to work hard of officers and employees involved?

c. If you were a shareholder of Rogers Communications, how would you react to the repricing?

d. It has been argued that options held by the CEO should not be repriced, even if repricing is extended to less senior executives and employees. Note that the article reports that options held by Ted Rogers, president and CEO of Rogers Communications, are not being repriced. Why?

10. Ittner, Larcker, and Rajan (1997) studied the relative weights placed on financial and non-financial performance measures in CEO bonus contracts for a sample of 317 U.S. firms across 48 industries for 1993–1994. Recall that BCE Inc. (Section 10.3) has both types of performance measures in its short-term incentive awards, with the relative weight placed on individual non-financial performance measures increasing as the rank of the officer gets lower. Non-financial performance measures in the BCE plan include creativity and initiative, succession planning and management development. For the highest-ranking officers, performance measures are primarily financial, such as earnings per share.

Ittner, Larcker, and Rajan find empirical support for the following hypotheses about the relative weights on financial and non-financial performance measures in compensation plans:

   i. Noise. The higher the correlation between manager effort and net income (measured by the correlation between stock market and accounting-based returns), the greater the relative weight on financial performance measures.

   ii. Firm strategy. "Prospector firms" (growth and innovation oriented, identify and adapt quickly to new product/service opportunities) will have greater relative weight on non-financial performance measures than "defender" firms (stable set of products/services, emphasis on increasing efficiency to reduce operating costs).

iii. Product quality. The greater the firm commitment to quality, the greater the relative weight on non-financial performance measures.

iv. Regulation. Regulated firms will have greater relative weight on non-financial performance measures than non-regulated firms.

Required

a. Give intuitive arguments to explain these four hypotheses.

b. Which of these four hypotheses might explain the increasing weight placed by BCE Inc. on non-financial performance measures for lower-ranking officers?

11. Many firms "reprice" employee stock options (ESOs) following major declines in their share price, by lowering the exercise price. This is because ESOs issued before the decline are deep out of the money, hence unlikely to be of any value. Such moves usually outrage shareholders, who have seen the value of their shares also fall but who receive no comparable benefits.

Saly (1994) studied repricing of ESOs. Her analysis applies to repricing after a market downturn, not to a firm-specific fall in share price that may be due to manager shirking.

As Saly points out, compensation contracts are incomplete. That is, it is unlikely that provision for adjustments to compensation following a market downturn are anticipated and written into the compensation plan. The question then is, should the contract be "renegotiated" following a market downturn, by repricing ESOs. If so, this would violate the general rule that, once signed, contracts tend to be rigid.

In Saly's model, the answer is yes. Renegotiation of the ESOs' strike price increases the correlation between manager effort and the performance measure (share price), since a market downturn is not a result of low manager effort. Without the possibility of renegotiation, the risk-averse manager would have to be compensated for the risk inherent in the possibility of a market downturn, to attain reservation utility. If a downturn occurs and there is no repricing, the manager's expected utility will fall, since the expected proceeds from ESOs are effectively zero. This will cause him/her to either shirk or leave the company.

In June, 2001, Nortel Networks Corp. announced that it was canceling its existing ESOs and replacing them with new ESOs with a lower strike price. Nortel's share price, which had been in excess of $100 when many of the ESO's were issued, suffered following the market collapse of share prices of high-tech firms, and was trading in the $20 range at the time of the announcement. Nortel's move was widely reported in the financial media and drew significant negative comment. For example, *The Globe and Mail* (5 June 2001) quoted Carol Bowie of the Investor Responsibility Research Center as saying "...you can't make the 50-yard kick. So we'll cut it down to 35." It also quoted J. Richard Finlay, head of the Center for Corporate and Public Governance as saying "We'd all like to be told our high school physics test where we got 35 out of 100 is now 35 out of 50, but shareholders don't have that luxury."

Nortel defended its move by claiming it was necessary to retain key employees, pointing out that top manager ESOs were not being repriced (this would require shareholder approval) but only those of lower level employees. In the same issue of the *Globe*, Brian Milner pointed out that the cost to Nortel of repricing the ESOs is zero, and that no further dilution of shareholders' equity will result since the old ESOs are being cancelled. Nevertheless, Milner comments that in the public eye the repricing is still "a reward for crummy performance."

Required

a. In the light of Saly's model, do you agree with Nortel's ESO repricing? Explain why or why not.

b. In Nortel's repricing proposal, the new options will not be issued until 6 months plus 1 day after the old ones are cancelled. What is the possible effect on employee effort during this 6-month period? Explain.

c. Nortel plans to cancel existing ESOs and replace them with new ones, rather than simply repricing the existing options to a lower exercise price. Use the provisions of APB 25 (See Section 8.3) to explain why repricing leads to the recording of an expense but issuing new ones does not.

Notes

1. For a methodology to estimate a firm's investment opportunities, and evidence that the proportion of share price-based compensation in firms' compensation contracts increases with investment opportunities, see Baber, Janakiraman, and Kang (1996).

2. In technical terms, compensation plans that limit downside risk but not upside risk are convex.

3. These arguments are based on R.A. Lambert and D.F. Larcker, "Firm Performance and the Compensation of Chief Executive Officers," working paper, January 1993.

4. Recall that the expected utility of a risk-averse individual declines with risk, holding expected value constant. The interpretation of the $152,300 is that the manager would be indifferent between a riskless payment of $152,300 and options with an expected value of $351,260. The options are risky because their market value will fluctuate with the value of the underlying shares and, because of restrictions laid down in the compensation contract, the manager cannot shed this risk by selling them. A similar interpretation applies to the $65,900.

Earnings Management

11.1 Overview

Earnings management can be viewed from both a contracting and a financial reporting perspective. From a contracting perspective, earnings management can be used as a low-cost way of protecting the firm from the consequences of unforeseen state realizations in the presence of rigid and incomplete contracts.

From a financial reporting perspective, managers may be able to affect the market value of their firm's shares by earnings management. For example, they may want to create the impression of smooth and growing earnings over time. Given securities market efficiency, this requires them to draw on their inside information. Thus, earnings management can be a vehicle for the communication of management's inside information to investors. Both of these perspectives lead to the interesting, and perhaps surprising, conclusion that a little bit of earnings management can be "good."

However, some managers may abuse earnings management. From a contracting perspective, they may use earnings management opportunistically to benefit themselves at the expense of other contracting parties. With respect to financial reporting, they may record excessive writeoffs, or emphasize earnings constructs other than net income, such as "pro forma" earnings. Some of these tactics suggest that managers do not fully accept securities market efficiency. At the very least, excessive earnings management reduces the reliability of financial reporting.

For whatever reason, it should be apparent that managers have a strong interest in the bottom line. Given that managers can choose accounting policies from a set of policies (for example, GAAP), it is natural to expect that they will choose policies so as to maximize their own utility and/or the market value of the firm. This is called **earnings management**. An understanding of earnings management is important to accountants, because it enables an improved understanding of the usefulness of net income, both for reporting to investors and for contracting.

> **Earnings management** *is the choice by a manager of accounting policies so as to achieve some specific objective.*

It should be mentioned that choice of accounting policies is interpreted quite broadly. While the dividing line is not clear-cut, it is convenient to divide accounting policy choice into two categories. One is the choice of accounting policies per se, such as straight-line versus declining-balance amortization, or policies for revenue recognition. The other category is discretionary accruals, such as provisions for credit losses, warranty costs, inventory values, and timing and amounts of non-recurring and extraordinary items such as writeoffs and provisions for reorganization.

Regardless of its rationale, it is important to realize that there is an "iron law" surrounding earnings management, which will be familiar from introductory accounting. This is that *accruals reverse.* Thus, a manager who manages current earnings upwards will find that the reversal of these accruals in subsequent periods will force future earnings downwards just as surely as current earnings were raised. Then, even more earnings management is needed if reporting of losses is to be further postponed. In effect, if a firm is performing poorly, earnings management cannot indefinitely postpone the day of reckoning. Thus, the possibility that a bit of earnings management can be good should not be used to rationalize misleading or fraudulent reporting. There is a fine line between earnings management and earnings mismanagement. Ultimately, the location of this line must be determined by standard setters, security commissions, and the courts.

11.2 Evidence of Earnings Management for Bonus Purposes

A paper by Healy (1985), entitled "The Effect of Bonus Schemes on Accounting Decisions," is a seminal investigation of a contractual motivation for earnings management. Healy observes that managers have inside information on the firm's net income before earnings management. Since outside parties, including the Board itself, may be unable to learn what this number is, he predicted that managers would opportunistically manage net income so as to maximize their bonuses under their firms' compensation plans. Here, we will review Healy's methods and findings.

Healy's paper is based on positive accounting theory (Section 8.7). It attempts to explain and predict managers' choices of accounting policies. More specifically, it is an extension of the bonus plan hypothesis, which states that managers of firms with bonus plans will maximize current earnings. By looking more closely at the structure of bonus plans, Healy comes up with specific predictions of how and under what circumstances managers will engage in this type of earnings management.

Healy's study was confined to firms whose compensation plans are based on current reported net income only. These will be called **bonus schemes** for the rest of this section. As we saw for BCE Inc. in Section 10.3, cash bonuses are typically based on net income. We also saw that, for risk reduction reasons, bonus schemes have bogies. To control possible excessive risk-taking, they may also have caps. In Healy's sample, not all schemes have caps, although they all have bogeys. Figure 11.1 illustrates a typical bonus scheme.

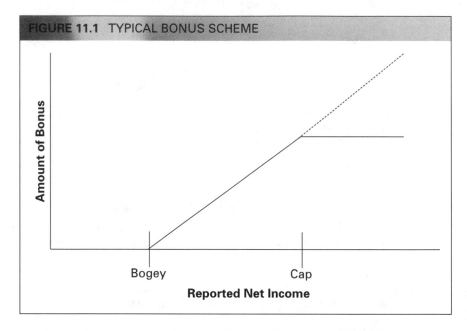

FIGURE 11.1   TYPICAL BONUS SCHEME

In the figure the bonus increases linearly (for example, 10% of net income) between the bogey and the cap. Below the bogey, bonus is zero. If there is no cap, the bonus would increase along the dotted line. Otherwise, the bonus becomes a constant for net income greater than the cap. The bonus scheme depicted in Figure 11.1 is simpler than that of BCE's short-term incentive plan, where the bogey and cap are implicit. Nevertheless, the basic idea carries over.

Now, consider the incentives to manage reported net income faced by a manager subject to such a scheme. If net income is low (that is, below the bogey), the manager has an incentive to lower it even further,[1] which is called **taking a bath**. If no bonus is to be received anyway, the manager might as well adopt accounting policies to further reduce reported net income. In so doing, the probability of receiving a bonus the following year is increased, since current writeoffs will reduce future amortization charges. Similarly, if net income is high (above the cap), there is motivation again to adopt accounting policies to reduce reported net income, because a bonus would be permanently lost on reported net income greater than the cap.

Only if net income is between the bogey and cap is the manager motivated to adopt accounting policies to increase reported net income. Thus, Healy refines the bonus plan hypothesis—it really only applies when net income is between the bogey and the cap.

How does a manager manage net income? Healy considers two approaches. The first is by controlling various accruals, where accruals are defined broadly to include that portion of revenue and expense items on the income statement that is not represented by cash flows. The second is by changing accounting policies per se. Let us consider first the accruals procedure.

To illustrate how accruals may be used to manage earnings, we begin by repeating the formula first given in Section 6.2.6:

$$\text{Net income} = \text{operating cash flows} \pm \text{net accruals}$$

This can be broken down into:

$$\text{Net income} = \text{operating cash flows} \pm \text{net non-discretionary accruals} \pm \text{net discretionary accruals.}$$

The concept of discretionary accruals was introduced in Section 8.7.3. These are accruals over which the manager can exercise some control. As pointed out there, the estimation of discretionary accruals by researchers poses a major challenge. As described, the Jones (1991) model is the currently accepted estimation methodology. However, other approaches are possible. One of these is an item-by-item procedure, which considers each accrual and classifies it as primarily discretionary or primarily non-discretionary.

To illustrate, consider the hypothetical example in Table 11.1. In the table, a positive sign for an accrual means that, for given cash flow, it increases net income, and vice versa. For simplicity, we have assumed that there are no extraor-

TABLE 11.1 DISCRETIONARY AND NON-DISCRETIONARY ACCRUALS		
Operating cash flow, as per cash flow statement		$1,000
Less: Amortization expense	− 50	
Add: Increase in (net) accounts receivable during the year	+ 40	
Add: Increase in inventory during the year	+100	
Add: Decrease in accounts payable and accrued liabilities during the year	+ 30	120
Net income, as per income statement		$1,120

dinary income statement items and no income tax expense. Assume that explanations for the four accrual items are as follows:

- **Amortization expense** Annual amortization expense is laid down by the firm's amortization policy and its estimates of assets' useful lives. Given this policy, amortization expense is a non-discretionary accrual.

- **Increase in net accounts receivable** Assume that this derives from a decrease in the allowance for doubtful accounts, resulting from a less conservative estimate than in previous years. This accrual is discretionary, because management has some flexibility to control the amount. Other reasons for the increase could include a more generous credit policy, keeping the books open beyond the year-end, or simply an increase in volume of business. The first two of these accruals are discretionary, the third is non-discretionary.

  Thus, we see that there can be several reasons for an increase in receivables. A researcher with access only to the comparative financial statements would be unlikely to know what particular reason or reasons accounted for the increase or whether the increase was discretionary or non-discretionary or both. Nevertheless, it is clear that the manager who wishes to increase reported net income through accounts receivable accruals has several means available.

- **Increase in inventory** Assume that this derives from the firm manufacturing for stock during a period of excess manufacturing capacity. The result is to include fixed overhead costs in inventory rather than charging them off to expense as unfavourable volume variances.

- **Decrease in accounts payable and accrual liabilities** Assume that this derives from the firm being more optimistic about warranty claims on its products than it has been in previous years. Alternatively, or in addition, the decrease could be due to regarding certain borderline items as contingencies rather than accruals. Again, we see that there can be ample room for discretionary accruals in accounts payable.

The main point to note is that the manager has considerable discretion to manage reported net income within the rules of GAAP. Notice also that, for many of these discretionary accruals, it would be difficult for the firm's auditors to discover the earnings management or, if they did discover it, to object, since all of the techniques mentioned, with the exception of holding the books open past the year-end, are within GAAP. It is also clear that a similar set of discretionary accruals to decrease reported net income are available to the manager, simply by reversing those described above.

Healy did not have access to the books and records of his sample firms. Consequently, he was unable to determine the specific discretionary accruals made by those firms' managers. As a result, he used another approach, namely to take total accruals as a proxy for discretionary accruals (his study preceded the Jones model). Thus, in our example, he would estimate discretionary accruals as +$120, instead of the +$170 that would be used if he had full information. The +$170 of discretionary accruals will raise total accruals by $170, regardless of what other non-discretionary accruals may be present; that is, higher total accruals contain higher discretionary accruals, and vice versa. However, using total accruals as a proxy for discretionary accruals may get the researcher into trouble if non-discretionary accruals are large relative to discretionary. Then, finding evidence of earnings management is like finding a needle in a haystack.

Healy obtained a sample of 94 of the largest U.S. industrial companies. He followed each company over the period 1930–1980 and obtained a total of 1,527 usable observations, that is, 1,527 firm years where the bogey and (if applicable) cap for a firm's bonus scheme could be calculated. Of these, 447 observations included both a bogey and a cap.

Each observation was then classified into one of three categories, or "portfolios" as Healy calls them. Portfolio UPP consisted of observations where earnings were above the cap, portfolio LOW of observations where earnings were below the bogey, and portfolio MID where they were between the bogey and cap. The theory underlying Table 11.1 predicts that total accruals should be greater for the MID portfolio than for UPP and LOW—recall that income-increasing accruals have a positive sign in Table 11.1.

For the 447 observations that had both a bogey and a cap, the results are summarized in Table 11.2. We see that 46% of the 281 observations in the MID portfolio had total accruals that were positive, that is, income-increasing. This is consistent with our firm in Table 11.1, where total accruals were +$120. The average accrual of these 281 observations was +0.0021 of total assets (accruals were deflated by total assets so that they could be compared across firms of differ-

TABLE 11.2 OBSERVATIONS WITH BOTH A BOGEY AND A CAP

	Proportion of Accruals with Given Sign		Number of Observations	Average Accruals
	Positive	**Negative**		
LOW	0.09	0.91	22	–0.0671
MID	0.46	0.54	281	+0.0021
UPP	0.10	0.90	<u>144</u>	–0.0536
			<u>447</u>	

SOURCE: P. M. Healy, "The Effect of Bonus Schemes on Accounting Decisions," *Journal of Accounting and Economics* (April 1985), p. 96, Table 2. Reprinted by permission.

ent sizes). For the observations in the LOW and UPP portfolios, the proportions with positive total accruals was were much lower—only 9% and 10% respectively. In fact, the average accruals for these observations were negative (income-decreasing). These results are consistent with Healy's arguments (see Figure 11.1), that firm managers whose net incomes are below the bogey and above the cap will tend to adopt income-decreasing accruals and only managers with net income between the two will tend to adopt income-increasing accruals. Thus, Healy's predictions of earnings management by managers subject to bonus schemes were supported by the empirical results.

TABLE 11.3 OBSERVATIONS WITH BOGEY ONLY				
	Proportion of Accruals with Given Sign		Number of Observations	Average Accruals
	Positive	**Negative**		
LOW	0.38	0.62	74	−0.0367
MID	0.36	0.64	1,006	−0.0155
			1,080	

SOURCE: P. M. Healy, "The Effect of Bonus Schemes on Accounting Decisions," *Journal of Accounting and Economics* (April 1985), p. 96, Table 2. Reprinted by permission.

Results for observations where the bonus scheme had only a bogey are summarized in Table 11.3. Here, there is no UPP portfolio. The proportions of positive and negative accruals are about the same for each portfolio. However, the average accrual is significantly greater for MID, being −0.0155 of total assets compared to −0.0367 for LOW. Thus, we can conclude that while the MID observations did not engage in a higher proportion of positive accruals, the accruals they did make were significantly larger (that is, less negative) on average. These results, while perhaps not as dramatic as those of Table 11.2, also are significantly consistent with Healy's arguments for earnings management by managers subject to bonus schemes.

The second approach to searching for evidence consistent with earnings management is to examine voluntary changes in accounting policies. From the firms in his sample, Healy collected 242 accounting policy changes over the 12 years 1968 to 1980 for which the effect on net income could be determined.

As Healy notes, accounting policy changes are not as desirable an opportunistic earnings management vehicle as accruals. Reasons are that such changes are highly visible compared to accruals—they have to be disclosed in the annual report—and that the standard of consistency prevents a particular policy from being changed very often. Thus, accounting policy changes tend to be a blunt and inflexible weapon. Healy did not find that his sample firms used accounting policy changes the same way they used accruals. That is, policy changes were not used to increase annual reported net income in the MID range and to decrease it for LOW and HIGH incomes. Presumably, a reason is that accruals are a more effective way to accomplish this objective.

Nevertheless, it can be argued that if managers are going to change accounting policies, a good time to do it is just after introduction or amendment of a bonus plan. A manager may be motivated at that time to adopt an income-increasing accounting policy change (for example, a switch from accelerated to straight-line amortization). This policy change would increase the expected bonus in future years, particularly if there was no cap on the bonus scheme.

To test this reasoning, Healy classified his sample companies into two portfolios for each year from 1968 to 1980. One portfolio consisted of firms that adopted or modified their bonus plan in the year; the other consisted of firms that did not. If the above argument is correct, the first portfolio should have more accounting policy changes than the second.

Healy found that in 9 of the 12 years over which comparisons were made, the portfolio of firms with bonus plan changes did in fact have more accounting policy changes. This provides significant evidence that managers also use such changes as an earnings management vehicle.

However, in view of the finding that managers did not use accounting policy changes to influence individual years' net income, it seems that their use of accounting policy changes is a longer-run earnings management device. Such changes can be used to give a general upward or downward influence on net income over a period of time extending from adoption or modification of a bonus plan. Presumably, individual years in this time period can then have their reported net incomes fine-tuned by means of accruals.

It should be emphasized that earnings management studies face severe methodological problems. As mentioned earlier, a major difficulty is that discretionary accruals cannot be directly observed. Consequently, some proxy must be used. Using total accruals, as Healy did, introduces measurement error into the discretionary accruals variable, which makes it more difficult to detect earnings management should it exist. Another problem arises if the amount of non-discretionary accruals is correlated with net income. For example, as Kaplan (1985) has pointed out, a firm with reported net income above the cap of its bonus plan may have low non-discretionary accruals if its high income is due to an unexpected increase in demand that runs down inventory. Then, the low total accruals that are used to infer earnings management are really due to the level of the firm's real economic activity and not to low discretionary accruals. Healy was aware of these problems and conducted additional tests to control for them, which he interpreted as confirming his findings. As mentioned above, the methodology used by Jones (1991) provides a more refined way to estimate non-discretionary accruals.

For further discussion of methodological issues in this area see McNichols and Wilson (1988), Schipper (1989), Dechow, Sloan, and Sweeney (1995), and Bernard and Skinner (1996).

McNichols and Wilson (1988) also studied the behaviour of accruals in a bonus context. They confined their investigation to the provision for bad debts, on the grounds that a precise estimate of what the bad debts allowance should be (that is, the non-discretionary portion of the bad debts accrual), can be made. Then, discretionary accruals can be taken as the difference between this estimate and the actual bad debts provision. A precise estimate of non-discretionary accruals will reduce the problem of measurement error in the discretionary accruals variable. This approach also reduces the problem of correlation between net income and non-discretionary accruals, since the impact on the bad debts provision of the firm's level of economic activity is captured by their estimate of what the bad debts allowance should be. They found that, over the period 1969–1985, discretionary bad debt accruals were significantly income-reducing both for firm years that were very unprofitable and those that were very profitable (and thus likely to be below and above the bogeys and caps, respectively, of the bonus agreements). For firm years that were between these profitability extremes, discretionary accruals were much lower, and usually income-increasing. These results are consistent with those of Healy.

More recently, Holthausen, Larcker, and Sloan (1995) (HLS) studied managers' accruals behaviour for bonus purposes. They were able to obtain data on whether managers' annual earnings-based bonuses were in fact zero, greater than zero but less than the maximum bonus, or at the maximum. These are substantially better data than Healy, who had to estimate whether earnings before discretionary accruals were below bogey, between bogey and cap, or above cap on the basis of available descriptions of bonus contracts, and *assume* that if earnings were below the bogey the manager would not receive a bonus, etc.

Using a version of the Jones (1991) model to estimate non-discretionary accruals for a sample of 443 firm-year observations over 1982–1990, HLS found that managers who were at their bonus maxima managed accruals so as to lower reported earnings. This is consistent with Healy's results—see row 3 of Table 11.2. However, HLS did not find that managers who received zero bonus also used accruals to manage earnings downward, which differed from Healy's findings (row 1, Table 11.2). HLS concluded that methodological problems arising from Healy's procedures for estimating discretionary accruals explained why he appeared to find negative accruals for his low portfolio.

In summary, we may conclude that, despite methodological challenges, there is significant evidence that, on average, managers use accruals to manage earnings so as to maximize their bonuses, particularly when earnings are high. This evidence is consistent with the bonus plan hypothesis of positive accounting theory.

11.3   Other Motivations for Earnings Management

Managers may engage in earnings management for a variety of reasons, besides a bonus scheme. Now, we will look at these briefly.

11.3.1 OTHER CONTRACTUAL MOTIVATIONS

There are two complementary ways to think about earnings management from a contracting perspective. First, we can think of it as opportunistic behaviour by managers to maximize their utility in the face of compensation and debt contracts and political costs.

However, we can also think about earnings management from an efficient contracting perspective. When setting compensation contracts, firms will anticipate managers' incentives to manage earnings and will allow for this in the amount of compensation they offer. Lenders will do the same thing in deciding on the interest rates they demand. Contracts are then more efficient since they anticipate the earnings management and adjust payments accordingly. Also, since contracts are rigid and incomplete, earnings management gives managers some flexibility to protect the firm in the face of unanticipated state realizations, to the advantage of all the contracting parties.

Healy's investigation suggests that earnings management to affect bonuses does exist. The incentive for earnings management arises from the characteristics of bonus schemes, which are contracts between the firm and its managers that set forth the basis of managerial compensation.

Another important situation where contracts depend on accounting variables arises from the moral hazard problem between manager and lender analyzed in Section 9.4.3. To control this problem, long-term lending contracts typically contain covenants to protect against actions by managers that are against the lenders' best interests, such as excessive dividends, additional borrowing, or letting working capital or shareholders' equity fall below specified levels, all of which dilute the security of existing lenders.

Earnings management for covenant purposes is predicted by the debt covenant hypothesis of positive accounting theory. Given that covenant violation can impose heavy costs, firm managers will be expected to avoid them. Indeed, they will even try to avoid being close to violation, because this will constrain their freedom of action in operating the firm. Thus, earnings management can arise as a device to reduce the probability of covenant violation in debt contracts.

Earnings management in a debt covenant context was investigated by Sweeney (1994), reviewed in Section 8.7.3. For a sample of firms that had defaulted on debt contracts, Sweeney found significantly greater use of income-increasing accounting changes relative to a control sample, and also found that defaulting firms tended to undertake early adoption of new accounting standards when these increased reported net income, and vice versa.

DeFond and Jiambalvo (1994) also examined earnings management by firms disclosing a debt covenant violation during 1985–1988. They found evidence of the use of discretionary accruals to increase reported income in the year prior to and, to a lesser extent in the year of, the covenant violation.

Somewhat different results are reported by DeAngelo, DeAngelo, and Skinner (1994), however. They studied a sample of 76 large, troubled firms. These were firms that had three or more consecutive loss years during 1980–1985 and that had reduced dividends during the loss period. For 29 of these firms, the cut in dividends was forced by binding debt covenant constraints.

After controlling for the influence of declining sales and cash flows on accruals, DeAngelo et al. failed to find evidence that these 29 firms used accruals to manage earnings upward in years prior to the cut in dividends, relative to the remaining sample firms that did not face debt covenant constraints. Rather, all the sample firms exhibited large negative (that is, earnings-reducing) accruals extending for at least three years beyond the year of the dividend cut. DeAngelo et al. attribute this behaviour as due in part to large, discretionary non-cash write-offs. Apparently, these were to signal to lenders, shareholders, unions, and others that the firm was facing up to its troubles, and to prepare the ground for subsequent contract renegotiations that frequently took place.

It thus seems that when its troubles are profound, the firm's behaviour transcends that which is predicted by the debt covenant hypothesis and, instead, earnings management becomes part of the firm's (and its manager's) overall strategy for survival.

Earnings management incentives also derive from **implicit contracts**, also called relational contracts. These are not formal contracts, such as the compensation and debt contracts just considered. Rather, they arise from continuing relationships between the firm and its stakeholders (shareholders, employees, suppliers, lenders, customers) and represent expected behaviour based on past business dealings. For example, if the firm and its manager develop a reputation for always meeting formal contract commitments they will receive better terms from suppliers, lower interest rates from lenders, etc. In effect, the parties act *as if* such favourable contracts exist. In terms of our game theory Example 9.1, the manager and the firm's stakeholders trust each other sufficiently that they play the cooperative solution rather than the Nash equilibrium.

Earnings management for implicit contracting purposes was investigated by Bowen, DuCharme, and Shores (1995) (BDS). They argued that the manager's implicit contracting reputation can be bolstered by high reported profits, which increase stakeholders' confidence that the manager will continue to meet contractual obligations.[2] For example, they predicted that firms with relatively high cost of goods sold and notes payable (used as proxies for high continuing involvement with suppliers and short-term creditors, respectively) would be more likely to choose FIFO inventory and straight-line amortization accounting policies than LIFO and accelerated amortization policies. FIFO and straight-line amortization are regarded as income-increasing since they tend to produce higher reported earnings over time than their LIFO and accelerated amortization counterparts.

Based on a large sample over 1981–1993, BDS found that firms with a high level of continuing involvement with stakeholders were more likely to choose FIFO and accelerated amortization policies than firms with lower levels of continuing involvement, consistent with their prediction. Furthermore, this tendency was still evident even after they controlled for other earnings management motivations, such as those arising from the compensation and debt contracts discussed above.

11.3.2 POLITICAL MOTIVATIONS

Many firms are quite politically visible. This is the case for very large firms, simply because their activities touch large numbers of people. Also, firms in strategic industries, such as oil and gas, will be visible, as will monopolistic or near-monopolistic firms such as airlines and power companies. Such firms may want to manage earnings so as to reduce their visibility. This would entail, for example, accounting practices and procedures to minimize reported net income, particularly during periods of high prosperity. Otherwise, public pressure may arise for the government to step in with increased regulation or other means to lower profitability. You will recognize that this motivation underlies the political cost hypothesis of positive accounting theory.

Jones (1991), reviewed in Section 8.7.3, found that her sample firms made significantly greater income-decreasing accruals during the year of ITC investigation than in years outside the investigation year. Also, Cahan (1992), using methodology similar to Jones, found that a sample of firms under investigation for monopolistic practices by the U.S. Department of Justice and the Federal Trade Commission during 1970–1983 used more income-decreasing accruals during investigation years relative to other years in the sample period.

11.3.3 TAXATION MOTIVATIONS

Income taxation is perhaps the most obvious motivation for earnings management. However, taxation authorities tend to impose their own accounting rules for calculation of taxable income, thereby reducing firms' room to manoeuvre. Consequently, taxation should not play a major role in earnings management decisions in general.

An exception, however, occurs with respect to the choice of the LIFO versus FIFO inventory method. In the United States, firms that use LIFO for tax purposes must also use it for financial reporting. During periods of rising prices, LIFO will usually result in lower reported profits and lower taxes, relative to FIFO. Yet, even when prices are rising, we observe that not all U.S. firms switch to LIFO. In effect, firms can either manage income down by choosing LIFO, resulting in lower taxes and increased cash flows, or manage income up by choosing FIFO, at the cost of higher taxes and lower cash flows. The question then is why.

Much positive theory research has tried to explain and predict firms' inventory policy choices. It does appear that tax savings are an important factor. For example, Dopuch and Pincus (1988) report evidence that tax savings are high for LIFO firms and that firms who remain on FIFO do not suffer large tax consequences, for reasons such as low amounts of inventory, high variability of inventory levels, high inventory turnover, and low effective tax rates. Lindahl (1989) also reports results consistent with these reasons.

From an efficient securities market perspective, we would expect that cash savings would dominate the effects of a lower reported net income under LIFO. Then, we would expect a favourable effect on firms' share prices upon switching from FIFO to LIFO when prices are rising. Sunder (1973) was the first to document such an effect. However, subsequent research, for example Abdel-khalik and McKeown (1978), suggests the market may react negatively. This issue is still unresolved.

From a contracting perspective, one can suggest why some firms may forgo tax savings in favour of higher reported earnings under FIFO. Managerial bonuses may be favourably affected by higher reported profits, and the probability of technical violation of debt covenants will fall. However, empirical evidence that contracting variables explain LIFO/FIFO choices is not strong. For example, Abdel-khalik (1985) found that managers of LIFO firms did not suffer adverse bonus effects. Also, Hunt (1985) failed to find evidence of bonus plan effects. There is some evidence that firms with high debt-to-equity levels are more likely to use FIFO, reported by Cushing and LeClere (1992), Lindahl (1989), and Hunt (1985). However, Lee and Hsieh (1985) and Dopuch and Pincus (1988) do not find the debt-to-equity ratio to be significant.

Overall, the evidence seems to support tax savings as the most important factor in LIFO/FIFO choice. Firms that switch to LIFO have the most to gain tax-wise, and vice versa. However, to the extent that firms are willing to accept lower reported earnings to gain tax savings, this raises questions about the strength of the bonus plan and debt covenant hypotheses. Perhaps, though, other methods that do not require a cash flow sacrifice, such as accruals management and paper accounting policy changes, are sufficient for managers concerned about contract rigidities.

11.3.4 CHANGES OF CEO

A variety of income management motivations exist around the time of a change of CEO. For example, the bonus plan hypothesis predicts that CEOs approaching retirement would be particularly likely to engage in a strategy of income maximization, to increase their bonuses. Similarly CEOs of poorly performing firms may income-maximize to prevent, or postpone, being fired. Alternatively, consistent with the findings of DeAngelo et al. (1994) as discussed above, such CEOs may take a bath so as to increase the probability of positive future earnings. This motivation also applies to new CEOs, especially if large writeoffs can be blamed on the previous CEO.

These motivations were studied by Murphy and Zimmerman (1993) (MZ). They examined the behaviour of four discretionary variables (that is, variables with earnings management potential), namely research and development (R&D), advertising, capital expenditures, and accruals. Their study included a large sample of CEO changes in U.S. companies during the period from 1971 to 1989.

Note that three of the variables examined by MZ affect the firm's real operations. While reducing R&D, advertising, and capital expenditures may be an effective way to increase current earnings, they are potentially quite costly to the firm, since its competitive position may be adversely affected in future. The accrual and accounting policy variables that we have considered to this point are less costly, since with the exception of LIFO inventory they are strictly paper devices with no direct effect on current or future cash flows. The possibility of using real variables such as R&D alerts us to the fact the managers have more scope to manage earnings than might be thought at first.[3] Also, it emphasizes that while GAAP may serve to constrain earnings management, it is unlikely they could ever eliminate it.

Studies such as MZ also face difficult methodological problems. For example, the probability of CEO change is affected by the firm's operating performance. But operating performance will also affect the magnitude of discretionary variables. Thus, accounts receivable may be lower if sales are down, and financially stressed firms may simply not have the cash to maintain R&D, advertising, and capital expenditures. If lower accruals, and lower expenditures on the other three discretionary variables, are observed, is this due to earnings management or to poor operating performance? Another problem is that it may be difficult to tell, in the transition year, whether any apparent earnings management is due to the new CEO or the old.

After controlling for problems such as these, MZ concluded that most of the unusual behaviour of the four discretionary variables was due to poor operating performance. For example, they found no evidence that CEOs approaching retirement income-maximized. Perhaps surprisingly, they also found little evidence that CEOs of poorly performing firms income-maximized either, although it should be emphasized that all these CEOs subsequently left the firm. Both of these findings are inconsistent with the opportunistic form of the bonus plan hypothesis. However, MZ did find evidence that incoming CEOs of poorly performing firms took baths.

It is interesting to speculate on these findings of a lack of earnings management by outgoing executives. Pourciau (1993), in a study of non-routine executive change, finds a similar result and gives extensive discussion of possible reasons. If methodological problems are ruled out, one possibility is that the outgoing executive engaged in income-increasing earnings management in years prior to departure, and earnings in the departure year are forced down by the iron law of reversal of these earlier discretionary accruals. Yet another possibility is that boards of directors monitor the activities of poorly performing and outgoing managers with particular care, particularly with respect to real variables such as R&D, so that opportunistic earnings management would be nipped in the bud. Furthermore, the extent of board monitoring may vary with the firm's corporate governance structure. For example, an entrenched manager who dominates the board may feel less need to manage earnings. Smith (1993) gives further discussion of issues such as these.

It is also possible that some managers use earnings management successfully to avoid being fired. If so, they would not have appeared in the MZ sample. In this regard, DeFond and Park (1997) report evidence of managers' use of discretionary accruals to "borrow" earnings from future periods when future earnings are expected to be good relative to current earnings. Similarly, managers appear to "save" current earnings when future earnings are expected to be poor relative to current earnings. The reason for such smoothing, according to DeFond and Park, is that managers are likely to be fired when current earnings are poor, regardless of past earnings performance. Consequently, income smoothing to avoid reporting poor earnings enhances job security.

11.3.5 INITIAL PUBLIC OFFERINGS

By definition, firms making initial public offerings (IPOs) do not have an established market price. This raises the question of how to value the shares of such firms. Presumably, financial accounting information included in the prospectus is a useful information source. For example, Hughes (1986) shows analytically that information such as net income can be useful in helping to signal firm value to investors, and Clarkson, Dontoh, Richardson, and Sefcik (1992) find empirical evidence that the market responds positively to earnings forecasts as a signal of firm value. This raises the possibility that managers of firms going public may manage the earnings reported in their prospectuses in the hope of receiving a higher price for their shares.

Friedlan (1994) investigated this issue. For a sample of 155 U.S. IPOs during 1981–1984 he examined whether the firms managed earnings upward in the latest accounting period prior to the IPO by means of discretionary accruals. Since IPO firms are usually growing rapidly, it is particularly difficult to estimate their discretionary accruals, because growth itself drives an increase in accruals, such as accounts receivable, inventories, etc. After extensive tests to control for this problem, Friedlan concluded that IPO firms did indeed make income-increasing discretionary accruals in the latest period prior to the IPO, relative to accruals in a comparable previous period. Furthermore, accruals management seemed to be concentrated in the poorer-performing sample firms as measured by operating cash flows (such firms presumably have greater motivation to increase reported income) and in the smaller sample firms (about which less may be known).

11.3.6 *TO COMMUNICATE INFORMATION TO INVESTORS*

The use of earnings management to communicate information to investors may seem questionable in view of efficient securities market theory. As we have argued in Section 4.3.1, investors will look through firms' accounting policy choices when evaluating and comparing earnings performance. Recall, however, that we define market efficiency relative to publicly available information. If earnings management can reveal inside information, it can actually improve the informativeness of financial reporting.

To pursue this, recall from Example 3.1 that rational investors are primarily interested in future firm performance, and use current reported earnings to revise their probabilities of what this future performance will be. Now it is management that typically has the best (inside) information about future earnings prospects. If reported earnings are managed to a number that represents management's best estimate of persistent earning power, and the market realizes this, share price will quickly reflect this inside information. In effect, responsible use of earnings management can increase the main diagonal probabilities of the information system (Table 3.2). We will return to this argument in Section 11.6.

11.4 *Patterns of Earnings Management*

From the foregoing discussion, it is apparent that managers may engage in a variety of earnings management patterns. Here, we will collect and briefly summarize these patterns.

1. **Taking a bath** This can take place during periods of organizational stress or reorganization, including the hiring of a new CEO. If a firm must report a loss, management may feel compelled to report a large one—it has little to lose at this point. Consequently, it will write off assets, provide for expected future costs, and generally "clear the decks." This will enhance the probability of future reported profits. Healy also mentions that managers whose net income is below the bogey of the bonus plan may also take a bath, for a similar reason—it will enhance the probability of future bonuses. In effect, the recording of large writeoffs puts future earnings "in the bank."

2. **Income minimization** This is similar to taking a bath, but less extreme. Such a pattern may be chosen by a politically visible firm during periods of high profitability. Policies that suggest income minimization include rapid writeoffs of capital assets and intangibles, expensing of advertising and R&D expenditures, successful-efforts accounting for oil and gas exploration costs, and so on. Income taxation, such as for

LIFO inventory, provides another set of motivations for this pattern, as does enhancement of arguments for relief from foreign competition.

3. **Income maximization**   As we saw in Healy's study, managers may engage in a pattern of maximization of reported net income for bonus purposes, providing this does not put them above the cap. Firms that are close to debt covenant violations may also maximize income.

4. **Income smoothing**   This is perhaps the most interesting earnings management pattern. We saw from Healy that managers have an incentive to smooth income sufficiently that it remains between the bogey and cap. Otherwise, earnings may be temporarily or permanently lost for bonus purposes. Furthermore, if managers are risk-averse, they will prefer a less variable bonus stream, and hence may want to smooth net income.

   We considered covenants in long-term lending agreements in Section 9.4.3. The more volatile the stream of reported net income, the higher the probability that covenant violation will occur. This provides another smoothing incentive: to reduce volatility of reported net income so as to smooth covenant ratios.

   Managers may also smooth income to reduce the likelihood of being fired.

   Finally, firms may smooth reported net income for external reporting purposes. This can convey inside information to the market by enabling the firm to communicate its expected persistent earning power.

It should be apparent that these various earnings management patterns can be in conflict. Over time, the pattern chosen by a firm may vary due to changes in contracts, changes in levels of profitability, changes in CEO, capital needs, and changes in political visibility. Even at a given point in time, the firm may face conflicting needs to, say, reduce reported net income for political reasons, but to smooth it for borrowing purposes.

11.5   *Why Does Earnings Management Persist?*

Probably, most people would feel that earnings management is "bad," since, as we have suggested, it implies a reduction in the reliability of financial statement information. This raises the question of why it seems to persist. Why can't boards of directors, lenders, government agencies, and investors "unravel" the earnings management, so that there is no point in engaging in it?

One reason, as pointed out by Schipper (1989), is that it is prohibitively costly for others to find out managers' inside information. For example, amounts of discretionary accruals would be very difficult to discover, even by boards of directors. Also, other more visible earnings management techniques such as accounting policy changes, timing of capital gains and losses, and provisions for restructuring can be difficult for outsiders to interpret. For example, is a firm's sale of one of its divisions driven by necessity or by timing considerations, or is a provision for restructuring excessive? Answers to questions such as these are typically private, inside information. There must be some blockage of manager/board or manager/investor communication, or earnings management will be unravelled.

It should be emphasized that "prohibitively costly" does not mean that the unravelling of earnings management is impossible, but simply that it is not cost-effective. For example, the board of directors may be able to determine the extent of accruals manipulation by hiring an auditor to give a complete report. However, it may not feel that this is worth the cost, particularly if it had anticipated some earnings management when setting the manager's compensation contract in the first place. Also, evaluating the reasonableness of gains and losses on sales of capital assets or of the adequacy of restructuring provisions could be very costly even for analysts, large blockholders, and other sophisticated investors. Large corporations are extremely complex, often spanning several industries and conducting operations worldwide.

Also, Jones (1991) argues that individual consumers may not feel it is worth becoming informed about applications for tariff protection before the ITC, since the impact on them of price increases following a successful application would be small. Even the ITC may not bother to investigate for earnings management if it does not receive complaints from consumers.

Given that earnings management persists, we now consider the question of whether it is, on balance, good or bad.

11.6   The "Good" Side of Earnings Management

Another reason for the persistence of earnings management is that there is a "good" side to it. As mentioned, we can consider the good side of earnings management from both a contracting and a financial reporting perspective. From a contracting perspective the extent to which earnings management can be good is related to the efficient contracting versus opportunistic forms of positive accounting theory, as discussed in Chapter 8. Under efficient contracting, it is desirable to give managers some ability to manage earnings in the face of incomplete and rigid contracts. We must be careful not to necessarily interpret evidence of earnings management for bonus, debt covenant, and political reasons as bad. Such an interpretation would only be valid if managers go too far and behave opportunistically with respect to existing contracts. Thus, we would expect some earnings management to persist for efficient contracting reasons.

Also, as mentioned in Section 11.3.6, earnings management can be a device to convey inside information to the market, enabling share price to better reflect the firm's future prospects. To see how this could come about, consider the blocked communication concept of Demski and Sappington (1987) (DS).

Frequently, agents obtain specialized information as part of their expertise, and this information can be prohibitively costly to communicate to the principal, that is, its communication is **blocked**. For example, it may be difficult for a physician to communicate to the patient exact details of an examination and diagnosis. Then, the physician's act (for example, operating on the patient) must stand in not only for the physician's surgical skills but also for the information acquired during the diagnosis. DS show that the presence of blocked communication can reduce the efficiency of agency contracts, since the agent may shirk on information acquisition and compensate by taking an act that, from the principal's standpoint, is sub-optimal—the physician may simply sew up a badly cut hand on the basis of a cursory examination that fails to check for possible tendon or nerve damage, for example. If so, the principal has an incentive to try to eliminate or reduce the blocked communication.

In a financial reporting context, earnings management can be a device to do this. To illustrate, suppose that the board of directors (the principal) wants to encourage the manager (the agent) to communicate the firm's long-run, persistent earnings potential. This is complex inside information of the manager. If the manager simply announced this information, the announcement would not likely be credible, since the board or the market would find it prohibitively costly to verify. Suppose, however, that the firm has just realized a profit of $200 millions from the sale of a division. Rather than report a net income substantially higher than what is sustainable in the long run, the manager decides to record a provision for restructuring of, say, $180 millions, thereby reducing current earnings to what the manager feels will persist.

Of course, this type of behaviour can be pushed too far. If the $180 millions is grossly in excess of what is needed for restructuring, future earnings will be overstated through lower amortization charges. This is discussed in the next section. Nevertheless, "unblocking" the manager's inside information by offsetting one large accrual against another to produce a desired result has some credibility, since it involves the financial statements, for which the manager has formal responsibility. If the manager reported a provision for restructuring that differed materially from internal plans, this could result in auditor objection and possible legal liability. However, if the $180 millions exceeds actual restructuring needs, a variety of other discretionary accruals is available to make up the difference and give the manager the reported net income he or she wants. Thus, the board may allow a reasonable amount of earnings management as a way to communicate blocked, inside information to the market. Notice that the market cannot unravel this earnings management, since it is based on inside information about sustainable earning power. However, the market can use the earnings management to infer what this inside information is.

This argument that net income can convey inside information to investors while at the same time being useful for contracting purposes has been further explored by DS (1990). We can think, for example, of operating cash flows or some other relatively unmanaged performance measure, such as net income before non-recurring and extraordinary items (i.e., core earnings—see Section 5.5), as reporting on manager effort. Then, DS show that judicious choice and disclosure of accruals, such as the provision for restructuring mentioned above, can in addition convey value-relevant information to investors.

This "dual purpose" role for net income is encouraging and helps to meet the fundamental problem of financial accounting theory, since the board may base manager compensation on the relatively hard, unmanaged core performance measure while the more value-relevant net income number is still available to investors. However, as DS (1990) point out, the information conveyed by the financial statements in their model does not purport to fully convey the value of the firm. All that is claimed is that *some* value-relevant information is conveyed by net income. That is, their model does not get around our general observation that net income is only well defined under ideal conditions. Consequently, it is still the case that the best net income for contracting need not be the same as the most useful net income for informing investors.

Finally, Feltham and Ohlson (1996) show conditions under which managers, by choice of amortization policy (a discretionary accrual), can reveal inside information to investors about the goodwill component of firm value. Recall from the clean surplus valuation equation (Section 6.5) that firm value is composed of book value plus unrecorded goodwill. Better knowledge by investors of the value of goodwill thus enables better estimates of firm value.

Feltham and Ohlson assume ideal conditions of uncertainty, but with a further assumption that management learns inside information about future cash flows. Then, given some (restrictive) assumptions, Feltham and Ohlson show that management can communicate this information by appropriate choice of amortization policy. That is, the resulting earnings number enables investors to infer the firm's goodwill, hence the firm's value. Feltham and Ohlson's analysis complements DS (1990) in demonstrating that earnings management can be good if management uses it responsibly.

The theoretical works just reviewed suggest that there is an economic role for earnings management. However, given the variety of motivations for earnings management, and the difficulty of discovering and interpreting discretionary accruals including extraordinary items, it is a complex task to establish empirically whether the stock market reacts to earnings management as the theory predicts. In particular, does the market react to earnings management as if it is good or bad? The answer to this question is important to accountants since they are prominently involved in the techniques and implementation of earnings management, and will get drawn into the negative publicity and lawsuits that inevitably follow the revelation of bad earnings management practices. Also, to the extent that earnings management is good, standard setting, which typically limits accounting choice, may actually reduce the ability of financial reporting to reveal inside information.

Subramanyam (1996) provides some evidence on this issue. He separated accruals into discretionary and non-discretionary components, using the Jones model (Section 8.7.3), for a sample of 2,808 firms over the years 1973–1993, for a total of 21,135 firm-year observations. Subramanyam found, after controlling for the effects of operating cash flows and non-discretionary accruals on share returns, that the stock market responded positively to discretionary accruals, consistent with managers, on average, using earnings management responsibly to reveal inside information about future earning power.

As Subramanyam points out, however, this finding is subject to different interpretations. For example, the market may be responding naively to the higher/ lower reported earnings that result from high/low discretionary accruals. If so, a securities market anomaly similar to that of Sloan (Section 6.2.6) may be operating.

Subramanyam conducts extensive tests, though, that tend to support that the market responds efficiently to the discretionary accruals. We will return to Subramanyam's study in the next section.

Subramanyam also points out that his findings depend on the ability of the Jones model to separate accruals into discretionary and non-discretionary components in a manner consistent with how the market interprets them. This suggests that alternate approaches to studying the market's reaction to earnings management are desirable. For example, Liu, Ryan, and Whalen (1997) examine the quarterly loan loss accruals (a form of earnings management) of a sample of 104 U.S. banks over 1984–1991. After separating these accruals into expected and unexpected components, they find a significantly positive share price reaction to unexpected increases in loan loss provisions for "at risk" banks (banks with regulatory capital close to legal minimums), but only in the fourth quarter. For banks not at risk, share price reaction to unexpected loan loss provisions was negative. These results suggest that at risk banks, by managing their earnings downwards, credibly convey to the market that they are taking steps to resolve their problems, which should improve their future performance. This good news was strong enough to outweigh the bad news of the fact of the loan writedowns per se. For banks not at risk, there is less need to take steps to resolve problems, with the result that the bad news component dominated the market's reaction. The reason why the at-risk banks' share prices rose only in the fourth quarter appears to be due to auditor involvement in that quarter. Presumably, management, and the market, take loan loss provisions much more seriously when auditors are involved.

In addition to providing further evidence of how earnings management can convey inside information, Liu, Ryan, and Whalen's results suggest considerable sophistication in the securities market's response, supporting Subramanyam's efficient market interpretation of his findings.

Additional evidence consistent with responsible earnings management is provided by Barth, Elliott, and Finn (1999). From a large sample of U.S. corporations over the years 1982–1992, they report evidence that firms with patterns of steadily increasing earnings for five years and longer enjoy higher price/earnings multiples than firms with equivalent levels and variability of earnings growth but absent the steadily increasing pattern. To the extent the steadily increasing earnings patterns are created by earnings management, the market appears to reward earnings management that does not overstate future earning power.

It should be noted that in deriving their result, Barth, Elliott, and Finn control for earnings persistence. The increased market valuation of their subject firms derives from factors beyond the use of earnings management to reveal persistent earning power. The most likely explanation, they suggest, is that the increasing earnings patterns reveal inside information about growth opportunities. For a specific example of a firm that reports steadily increasing earnings, see Problem 9.

11.7   The "Bad" Side of Earnings Management

Despite theory and evidence of responsible use of earnings management, there is also evidence of "bad" earnings management. From a contracting perspective, this can result from opportunistic manager behaviour. The tendency of managers to use earnings management to maximize their bonuses, as documented by Healy, can be interpreted this way, for example.

Further evidence is supplied by Dechow, Sloan, and Sweeney (1996), who examined the earnings management practices of a test sample of 92 firms charged in the United States by the SEC with alleged violation of GAAP, in comparison with a control sample of firms of similar size and industry. Their investigation revealed a number of motivations for earnings management. A common one was closeness to debt covenant constraints. The firms in their test sample had, on average, significantly greater leverage and significantly more debt covenant violations than the control sample.

Dye (1988) modelled earnings management from a capital markets perspective. He envisaged two generations of shareholders—current and future. The current shareholders will sell their shares to the next generation in a future period. Given inside information, and given that it is prohibitively costly for the future shareholders to unravel the firm's earnings management, Dye showed that a manager acting on behalf of the current shareholders has an ability and incentive to manage earnings so as to maximize the selling price received by the current shareholders.

To illustrate this motivation, consider a manager who intends to raise new share capital. A variety of discretionary accruals can be used to increase reported net income in the short run, such as speeding up revenue recognition, lengthening the useful life of capital assets, underprovision for environmental and restoration costs, etc. The iron law of accruals reversal is of less concern due to the short decision horizon. To the extent that earnings management raises the issue price of new share capital, the current shareholders benefit at the expense of new ones.

Dechow, Sloan, and Sweeney (1996), mentioned above, also studied the financing decisions of their sample firms. They found that their charged firms (which, by definition, were heavy users of earnings management) issued, on average, significantly more securities during the period of earnings manipulation than the control sample. This result is consistent with the prediction of Dye's model. For a specific example of this type of behaviour, see Problem 10.

Hanna (1999) discusses another type of earnings management. This is the frequent recording of excessive charges for non-recurring items such as write-downs under ceiling test standards, and provisions for reorganization. Hanna points out that manager bonuses are typically based on core earnings. Furthermore, analysts' forecasts are typically of core earnings. Thus non-recurring charges do not affect manager bonuses and do not take away from the ability to meet earnings forecasts. But, excessive non-recurring charges increase *future core earnings*, by putting them in the bank through reduced future amortization charges and absorption of future costs that would otherwise be charged to expense. Then, the manager benefits both ways. Major costs that may have been accumulating for several years (i.e., the non-recurring charges) do not affect bonuses or ability to meet earnings forecasts, and the future expense reductions increase core earnings, on which the manager *is* evaluated.

Furthermore, the upwards effect on future core earnings is very difficult to detect, since reduced future amortization charges and other expense reductions are buried in larger totals. In effect, poor disclosure of the effects of past non-recurring charges enables managers to engage in this type of earning management. Nevertheless, the market does appear to react to earnings management of this nature. As mentioned in Section 5.5, Elliott and Hanna (1996) found that the ERC for a dollar of quarterly core earnings is lower for firms that have frequently recorded large unusual and non-recurring charges than for firms that have not recorded such charges. This is consistent with the market using the frequency of non-recurring charges as a proxy for the extent to which core earnings may be overstated. Of course, if accountants would disclose the effect on core earnings of past non-recurring writeoffs, a proxy such as this would not be needed.

The earnings management techniques just outlined are not necessarily inconsistent with securities market efficiency. As mentioned, they rely on poor disclosure to keep the extent of earnings management as inside information. Yet, other results question efficiency itself. In the previous section, we discussed Subramanyam's (1996) study, which he interpreted as providing evidence for good earnings management. However, a recent study by Xie (2001) casts doubt on this interpretation. For a large sample of firms over the period 1971–1992, Xie used the Jones model to estimate discretionary and non-discretionary accruals for each firm-year observation. He then estimated the persistence of these two accruals components. As we would expect, he found the persistence of discretionary accruals to be less than that of non-discretionary accruals. As a result, the efficient market should assign a lower ERC to a dollar of discretionary accruals than to a dollar of non-discretionary. However, Xie found that the ERCs for discretionary accruals in his sample was significantly higher than their low persistence would suggest. In other words, the market appears to overvalue discretionary accruals.

Thus, Subramanyam's efficient markets interpretation of his results is questioned. It may be that the favourable market reaction to discretionary accruals in Subramanyam's study is driven simply by market overreaction to them rather than by their information content. That is, managers may be exploiting another efficient securities market anomaly.

In a similar vein, we reported in the previous section on the finding of Barth, Elliott, and Finn (1999) that the market favours firms with steadily increasing earnings patterns. Their interpretation is that the efficient market responds to the persistence and growth information implicit in the increasing earnings. However, Barth, Elliott, and Finn do not rule out an alternative, inefficient market, interpretation, which is that momentum trading (see Section 6.2.1) in response to the increasing earnings pattern drives the favourable market reaction.

Schrand and Walther (2000) report yet another form of earnings management. They analyze a sample of firms that reported a material, non-recurring gain or loss on disposal of property, plant and equipment in the *prior* quarter but no such gain or loss in the *current* quarter. In news releases that typically accompany earnings announcements, managers compare the current quarter's performance with a prior quarter. The question then is, in these news releases, do managers "remind" investors of the non-recurring gain or loss in the prior quarter? Schrand and Walther found that the likelihood of such a reminder was significantly greater if the prior quarter's non-recurring item was a gain rather than a loss. In this way, the lowest possible prior period benchmark was emphasized, thereby showing the change in earnings from the prior quarter in the most favourable light.

Furthermore, while their sample size was small (130), Schrand and Walther found that at the earnings announcement date, investors did not seem to see through this opportunistic strategy. Share prices responded more positively than expected for the "remind" firms but did not respond less positively for the firms that did not remind. It should be noted, though, that the mispricing was corrected when the actual financial statements were released some time later.

The interesting point from Schrand and Walther is that management of *past* reported earnings cannot possibly be driven by contracting considerations. This suggests that contracting variables do not completely explain economic consequences and earnings management. Rather, at least some managers behave as if they believe they can "fool" the market by means of earnings management.

These various results suggest that managers may not fully believe in securities market efficiency. To the extent that the market does not identify and punish the actions that follow, bad earnings management is encouraged.

The implication for accountants, however, is not to reject market efficiency, but rather to give the market a greater chance to operate. That is, the antidote to bad earnings management is to **improve disclosure**. If accountants ensured that low persistence items were fully disclosed, and ensured that the effects on core earnings of previous writeoffs were fully disclosed, the efficient market would more quickly discover bad earnings management and react accordingly. Managers would bear the full consequences of their actions and bad earnings management would decrease.

11.8   *Summary and Conclusions*

Earnings management is made possible by the fact that GAAP do not completely constrain managers' choices of accounting policies and procedures. Such choices are much more complex and challenging than simply selecting those policies and procedures that best inform investors. Rather, managers' accounting policy choices are often motivated by strategic considerations, such as contracts that depend on financial accounting variables, CEO retirement, managers' attempts to avoid being fired, new share issues, takeover bids, appeals for tariff protection, discouraging of potential competition, and unblocking of inside information. In effect, accounting policy choice has characteristics of a game. Economic consequences are created when changes in GAAP adversely affect managers' abilities to play the game. That is, managers will react against rule changes that reduce their flexibility of accounting choice. As a result, accountants need to be aware of the legitimate needs of management, as well as of investors. Actual financial reporting represents a compromise between the needs of these two major constituencies.

Despite the reduction of reliability that accompanies earnings management, a strong case can be made that it is useful if kept within bounds. First, it gives managers flexibility to react to unanticipated state realizations when contracts are rigid and incomplete.

Second, the flexibility allowed by GAAP enables earnings management to serve as a vehicle for the credible communication of inside information to investors. Both of these arguments are consistent with efficient securities markets and the efficiency version of positive accounting theory.

Nevertheless, some managers may abuse the communications potential of GAAP by pushing earnings management too far, with the result that persistent earning power is overstated, at least temporarily. This behaviour can result from a failure to accept securities market efficiency or from an ability to hide bad earnings management behind poor disclosure, or both. To the extent managers do not accept securities market efficiency, believing instead that they can fool the market by their disclosure decisions, positive accounting theory does not fully reconcile market efficiency and economic consequences.

Whether earnings management is good or bad depends on how it is used. Accountants can reduce the extent of bad earnings management by bringing it out into the open. This can be accomplished by improved disclosure of low-persistent items and by reporting on the effect of previous writeoffs on core earnings.

Questions and Problems

1   Explain why a firm's manager might both believe in securities market efficiency and engage in earnings management.

2. For an income management strategy of taking a bath, the probability of the manager receiving a bonus in a future year rises. Explain why.   (CGA-Canada)

3. A manager increases reported earnings by $1,300 this year. This was done by reducing the allowance for credit losses by $500 below the expected amount, and reducing the accrual for warranty costs expense to $800 below the expected amount. Explain why, other things equal, this will lower next year's earnings by $1,300.

4. You are a CEO operating under a bonus plan similar to the one assumed by Healy (Section 11.2). Explain whether you would react favourably or negatively to an exposure draft of a proposed change in GAAP that has the following effects on your financial statements. Treat each effect as independent of the others.

    a. The effect will be to increase liabilities. Examples of such GAAP changes include capitalization of long-term leases (*CICA Handbook*, Section 3065), recording of pension plan obligations, and other postretirement benefits for employees (*CICA Handbook*, Section 3461).

    b. The effect will be to increase the volatility of reported net income. An example would be the proposed accounting for cash flow hedges by the Joint Working Group draft standard (Section 7.4.5).

    c. The effect will be to exert downward pressure on reported net income. An example is the PIP grant accounting controversy (see Section 8.4.1).

    d. The effect will be to eliminate alternative ways of accounting for the same thing. Section 3065 of CICA Handbook imposed uniform standards for accounting for leases is an example.

5. The firms in Healy's study of earnings management (Section 11.2) would have been using the historical cost basis of accounting. Given that firms are moving to greater use of fair value accounting for financial instruments, as described in Section 7.4.2, would this increase or decrease the potential for opportunistic earnings management for bonus purposes? Explain.

6. Shown below are the income statement and comparative balance sheets of ACR Ltd., from its year 2003 annual report. The year 2003 statement of changes in financial position of ACR Ltd. (not shown) shows operating cash flow as $2,386.

    Required

    a. What is the amount of net accruals included in ACR Ltd.'s year 2003 net income?

    b. Use the information in the income statement and balance sheets of ACR Ltd. to calculate the various individual accruals and reconcile to the net total in part **a.**

c. Upon comparing operating cash flow and net income, we see that the accruals have substantially lowered the reported income for the year. Give three reasons why management may want to manage income downwards in this manner.

ACR LTD.
INCOME STATEMENT
Year Ended December 31, 2003

Contract income	$11,684
Cost of contracts	9,073
Gross profit	2,611
General and administrative expenses	1,346
Amortization	276
Interest	16
	1,638
Operating profit	973
Equity income from affiliates	165
Other income	52
	217
Income before income taxes and extraordinary items	1,190
Income taxes:	
Current	584
Future	59
	643
Income before extraordinary items	547
Extraordinary items	—
Net income for year	$ 547

ACR LTD.
BALANCE SHEETS
As at December 31

	2003	2002
Assets		
Current assets:		
Cash	$ 693	$ —
Trade accounts receivable	2,107	3,464
Income taxes recoverable	—	506
Inventories	810	410
Prepaid expenses	61	99
	3,671	4,479
Investments in affiliated companies	405	203
Machinery and equipment	1,532	1,632
	$5,608	$6,314

	2003	2002
Liabilities		
Current liabilities:		
Bank indebtedness	$ —	$1,291
Accounts payable and accrued liabilities	398	497
Income taxes payable	282	34
Liability for future income taxes	83	64
	763	1,886
Future income tax liability	62	22
	825	1,908
Shareholders' Equity		
Share capital	2,268	2,268
Capital contributed on issue of warrants	80	80
Retained earnings	3,895	3,275
Excess of appraised value of fixed		
assets over amortized cost	1,175	1,307
	7,418	6,930
Less: Cost of shares purchased	2,635	2,524
	4,783	4,406
	$5,608	$6,314

7. A way to manage earnings is to manipulate the point in the operating cycle at which revenue is regarded as earned. An article entitled "Bausch & Lomb Posts 4th-Quarter Loss, Says SEC Has Begun Accounting Probe" appeared in *The Wall Street Journal* on January 26, 1995.

   The article reports on questions raised by the SEC about Bausch & Lomb Inc.'s premature recording of revenue from products shipped to distributors in 1993. "Bausch & Lomb oversupplied distributors with contact lenses and sunglasses at the end of 1993 through an aggressive marketing plan, and was forced to buy back a large portion of the inventory [in 1994] when consumer demand didn't meet expectations." The oversupply amounted to around $10 million, which Bausch & Lomb claimed was not "material."

   In addition, the article points out that in the fourth quarter of 1994 Bausch & Lomb had incurred $20 million in "one-time expenses," which included expenses from "previously announced staff cuts of about 2,000." Also, in the fourth quarter Bausch & Lomb took a $75 million charge in its oral-care division in order "to reduce unamortized goodwill that it recorded when Bausch & Lomb bought the business in 1988." Many analysts are saying that Bausch & Lomb are looking to sell the oral-care division, and this reduction of unamortized goodwill will make the division look better.

Required

a. What earnings management policy did Bausch & Lomb appear to be following in 1993?

b. Evaluate revenue recognition policy as an earnings management device, from management's standpoint.

c. The article refers to a $20 million writeoff in 1994 relating to staff cuts, and another $75 million writeoff in Bausch & Lomb's oral-care division. What earnings management strategy does the firm appear to have followed in 1994? Why?

d. Do Bausch & Lomb's 1993 and 1994 earnings management strategies suggest that its management does not accept efficient securities market theory? Explain why or why not.

8. Earnings management extends into the realm of new share offerings (IPOs), since the prospectus for a new offering includes current and recent financial statements. An article entitled "RJR Nabisco's Use of Accounting Technique Dealing with Goodwill Is Getting a Hard Look," which appeared in *The Wall Street Journal* on April 8, 1993, describes some earnings management considerations surrounding a $1.5 billion new share offering of Nabisco, a food subsidiary of RJR Nabisco Holdings.

According to the article, the parent, RJR Nabisco Holdings, has substantial goodwill on its books arising from its acquisition of Nabisco, which is being amortized at a rate of $607 million annually (at the time, both the *CICA Handbook*, and, in the United States, APB 17 required that goodwill from acquisitions be amortized over a period of up to 40 years). However, this goodwill amortization appears only on the books of the parent—not on those of Nabisco.

According to the article, "What RJR is doing is presenting Nabisco's annual earnings without the burden of $206 million of 1992 'goodwill,' leaving this earnings-depressing item with the parent company instead." This resulted in Nabisco increasing its 1992 after-tax profit from $179 million to $345 million or from 48 cents a share to 93 cents a share.

The article further states "Nabisco executives indicated the food company could generate 1993 earnings of as much as $1.30 a share. That earnings level might justify the proposed selling price of $17 to $19 a share for the new Nabisco shares, analysts say."

The article questions whether RJR is managing the reported net income of its Nabisco subsidiary by not "pushing down" (see Section 7.2.5) goodwill to Nabisco.

Required

a. What pattern of earnings management is RJR following? Why?

b. Without considering any strategic issues surrounding the pricing of the new shares, do you think that goodwill should be pushed down to the subsidiary company?

c. Do you think the strategy of not pushing down the goodwill will be successful in raising the issue price of the new shares? Explain why or why not.

9. The article by Randall Smith, Steven Lipin, and Amal Kumar Naj, here reproduced from *The Wall Street Journal* (November 3, 1994), "Managing Profits" describes some of the earnings management devices used by General Electric to report strong, consistent earnings growth over the last decade.

MANAGING PROFITS

How General Electric Damps Fluctuations in Its Annual Earnings

The debacle at Kidder, Peabody & Co. might ruin the year for most companies.

But the roughly $750 million in losses and after-tax charges that General Electric Co. will incur this year before finally unloading Kidder will barely dent GE's smooth, consistent earnings growth. Despite those losses, some analysts believe, GE may be able to match or top last year's profit of $5.15 billion before accounting charges.

In the past decade, GE's earnings have risen every year, although net income fell in 1991 and 1993 because of accounting changes related to post-retirement benefits. The gains, ranging between 1.7% and 17%, have been fairly steady—especially for a company in a lot of cyclical businesses. As a result, GE almost seems able to override the business cycle.

How does GE do it? One undeniable explanation is the fundamental growth of its eight industrial businesses and 24 financial-services units. "We're the best company in the world," declares Dennis Dammerman, GE's chief financial officer.

But another way is "earnings management," the orchestrated timing of gains and losses to smooth out bumps and, especially, avoid a decline. Among big companies, GE is "certainly a relatively aggressive practitioner of earnings management," says Martin Sankey, a CS First Boston Inc. analyst.

To smooth out fluctuations, GE frequently offsets one-time gains from big asset sales with restructuring charges; that keeps earnings from rising so high that they can't be topped the following year. GE also times sales of some equity stakes and even acquisitions to produce profit gains when needed.

Asked several times about earnings management, Mr. Dammerman declines to discuss directly whether GE engages in the practice. Asked whether offsetting one-time gains with one-time charges could be considered earnings management, he says, "I've never looked at it in that manner." He also declines to say whether other companies use such tactics.

Most U.S. companies do try to smooth profit growth. Walt Disney Co., for example, can decide when it wants profits from a videocassette re-release of *Snow White*. Banks and insurance companies do a lot of smoothing by adjusting the level of their reserves, and many companies time write-offs carefully.

A look at GE illustrates how analysts say one giant corporation manages earnings. They add that few companies have maneuvered so successfully for so long on so large a scale. GE's size and diversity give it an unusual array of opportunities, of course. Moreover, Chairman Jack Welch relentlessly monitors GE's profit growth.

A DISMAYED MR. WELCH

Last April, when announcing that a bond-trading scheme at Kidder had generated false 1993 profits and triggered a $210 million first-quarter charge, Mr. Welch said investors prize GE's ability "to deliver strong, consistent earnings growth in a myriad of global economic conditions. Having this reprehensible scheme ... break our more-than-decade-long string of 'no surprises' has all of us damn mad."

His dislike of surprises extends beyond what GE's operating executives tell him to what GE tells Wall Street. Russell Leavitt, a Salomon Brothers analyst, says GE executives "give you some guidance" on what other analysts' estimates are and how reasonable they are. The result, says Ben Zacks of Zacks Investment Research, is that analysts' GE estimates fall in a "very, very tight range."

GE especially prizes consistent growth because it has so many different businesses

that most analysts can't track them all. For example, GE is followed by electrical-equipment analysts, most of whom have a loose grasp of financial services.

NARROWING THE DISCOUNT

GE's two major parts are an industrial conglomerate and a financial-services conglomerate, and both segments outdo their market peers. According to an analysis of data from Morgan Stanley & Co., industrial conglomerates sold at an average 20% discount to the market as of Sept. 30, based on their multiple of price to next year's anticipated earnings, while financial-services companies—banks, finance and insurance—were at a 35% discount. But partly because of its consistent earnings growth, GE sold at a discount of only 11%.

One financial calculation that helped smooth earnings at GE a few years ago was an increase in the assumed rate of future investment returns on pension funds. In 1991, a weak year at many companies, GE raised its return-rate assumption a full percentage point, to 9.5% from the 8.5% in effect for five years.

That change, by reducing GE's pension costs, helped lift what it terms the profits on its pension fund to $696 million in 1991 from $380 million in 1990, a pretax swing of $316 million. For companies like GE with overfunded pension plans, accounting rules require such changes to be reflected in corporate profits.

How much did GE's overall profit rise in 1991? Just $132 million after tax.

However, GE says the increase in its assumed return on pension assets reflected the lofty investment returns in the 1980s and wasn't any higher than rates assumed by other big companies. It says the change wasn't designed to raise reported 1991 profits.

The clearest way GE manages earnings is through restructuring charges. When GE sells a business at a profit or takes an unusual gain, it generally takes an offsetting restructuring charge of roughly equal size. In six of the years since 1983, GE has taken charges totaling $3.95 billion in this way.

Last year, when GE booked a $1.43 billion pretax gain on the sale of its aerospace business, for example, it took a $1.01 billion charge to cover costs of "closing and downsizing and streamlining of certain production, service and administrative facilities world-wide." After tax, the gain and the charge matched up exactly at $678 million.

And that 1993 charge, by anticipating some specific 1994 expenses such as "asset write-offs, lease terminations and severance benefits," is helping GE report better profit this year. Without the 1993 charge, some of those expenses could have reduced this year's net income. Because some of the expenses eventually would have to be paid anyway, First Boston's Mr. Sankey says, this reporting strategy allows GE to "transmute" one-time gains into future operating income.

One rationale for using this tactic: GE executives believe that many investors ignore one-time gains from asset sales in valuing companies. But clearly, taking an offsetting charge against a big gain prevents GE's earnings from getting too high in any one year; by spreading the gain into future years, the company can more easily report the steady growth that investors prefer.

Mr. Dammerman, the finance chief, says that whenever GE anticipates a gain on an asset sale or a tax or accounting change, its executives "sit down with our businesses and say, 'What are some strategic decisions that you would make to make the business better going forward?' " He says GE's use of such charges is one way it pursues both short-term and long-term goals; without such gains, he adds, some of the spending wouldn't have been planned or would have been timed differently.

PRACTICE UNDER SCRUTINY

Richard Leftwich, an expert in financial-statement analysis at the University of

HOW GE OFFSETS GAINS FROM ASSET SALES

Year	Pretax Gain (millions)	Source of the Gain	Pretax Restructuring Charges (millions)
1993	$1,430	Sale of aerospace unit to Martin Marietta	$1,011
1987	858	Change in accounting for taxes and inventory	1,027
1986	50	Sale of foreign affiliate	311
1985	518	Sale of three coal properties and 37% cable stake	447
1984	617	Sales of Utal Int'l, small appliance unit, cable company	636
1983	117	Sale of radio/TV stations and Gearhart Industrial stake	147

SOURCE: General Electric Co.

Chicago business school, says analysts and regulators are questioning U.S. corporations' widespread use of restructuring charges. He wonders how companies distinguish between everyday expenses needed to remain competitive and truly extraordinary events. Such use of restructuring charges "raises real issues for how to think about what the future profits mean," he adds, "because the costs are being written off now, but the profits are being reported in the future."

Later this month, accounting rule- makers, under prodding by the Securities and Exchange Commission, are expected to sharply limit such big one-time write-offs. The new rules would force companies to spread such charges over future years or take them when the relevant expenses are actually paid rather than when planned.

While conceding the SEC "hates" such charges, Mr. Dammerman adds: "It's not like we're creating some big cookie jar" from which GE takes profits at will.

Another way GE manages its earnings is by literally buying them—by acquiring companies or assets that are immediately profitable because they throw off more income than GE's cost of financing. Much of the growth in GE Capital's earnings in the past few years has been generated by a spate of acquisitions.

"Of course we're buying earnings when we do an acquisition," says James Parke, GE Capital's chief financial officer. The financial-services subsidiary acquired assets totaling $16.9 billion in 1993 alone.

Daniel Porter, GE Capital's North American chief of retailer financial services, says he and his colleagues may hunt for acquisitions if his division might miss its annual earnings target. He says they ask: "Gee, does somebody else have some income? Is there some other deals we can make?"

RISK IN HASTY ACTION

The danger, of course, is that a headlong rush into acquisitions to book earnings could lead to unwise decisions. Management's ambitious growth targets create GE Capital's biggest business risk, according to Sanjay Sharma, a Moody's Investors Service analyst.

"As growth in the commercial finance sector has become difficult to achieve because of growing bank and nonbank competition, an aggressive strategy in this sector can only be accomplished by paying higher premiums for portfolio acquisitions—in effect, by taking greater risks," Mr. Sharma says. Already, he notes, the returns on GE Capital's mushrooming trove of assets are slipping, to 1.4% in 1993 from 1.61% in 1989. To keep growing so fast without major gains from operations, GE would have to make more and more acquisitions, possibly compounding the risk.

Isn't it unsound to have earnings-report considerations drive the timing of acquisitions? Mr. Dammerman says that as long as executives keep both long-term and short-term goals in mind, "I see nothing wrong with someone saying, 'Look, I have an earnings objective for the year, and to achieve that earnings objective maybe I need to go make an acquisition.' That's fine if the individual can come up with a good acquisition."

Two former GE Capital executives say GE's financial business contains a wealth of hidden value—which they call reserves—that can be tapped to get income as needed. "Are there hidden values there? Absolutely," Mr. Parke says, though they are "impossible to measure."

One way GE stores profits for future use is, ironically, by following fairly conservative accounting practices. In fact, John W. Stanger, GE Capital's president from 1975 to 1984, says those practices would occasionally annoy managers who believed the company was "trying to bury profits" that they had racked up in a stellar year.

HANDLING USED AIRCRAFT

GE Capital also has considerable discretion over the timing of sales of warrants or equity kickers obtained in the course of lending and in deciding whether to sell or re-lease aircraft coming off lease. GE Capital has "significant ability to come up with earnings on demand," First Boston's Mr. Sankey says, because of its "diversified portfolio" and "very large amount of flexibility in how you report earnings."

Take the hypothetical example of an aircraft nearing the end of a 15-year lease. GE may have already written off most of the plane's cost, leaving its book value low. GE can potentially book a gain if it then sells the plane, Mr. Sankey says, but not if the jet is re-leased to another airline.

Mr. Parke denies that GE Capital fattens its earnings by selling aircraft. It has some discretion, he says, but this is limited because "you have to have a buyer, and you have to have the right market conditions in order to maximize the value."

The timing of sales of equity interests obtained through warrants—the equity operations that GE often gets for lending on especially risky buyouts—also is "very discretionary," Mr. Sankey says. But GE executives say they have only a little discretion because such sales usually depend on when a company goes public. Now holding a potentially valuable 50% stake in Montgomery Ward, however, GE Capital would have considerable say over when the retailer went public.

Such maneuvers are particularly difficult to monitor at GE Capital because the amount of information it discloses is relatively scant compared with the wealth of information about its parent company. GE Capital, for example, doesn't differentiate its income from asset sales.

"You look at their financial reports—they are pretty skinny. A lot of analysts feel frustrated because it's such a complex organization," says Richard Schmidt of Standard & Poor's Corp., the credit-rating agency. He concedes that many commercial finance companies keep their numbers close to the vest, too.

As an unregulated financial-services company, GE Capital also has more flexibility to defer write-offs than do highly regulated U.S. banks. During the 1990-91 recession, regulators required banks to take write-downs, add reserves and sell assets. But GE Capital contends that it writes off bad assets *faster* than banks do and that rating agencies and the markets are tougher than bank regulators.

THE RCA ACQUISITION

One of GE's most intriguing moves to boost its net income was in its accounting for its $6.4 billion acquisition of RCA Corp. in 1986. Anytime an acquisition is made for a price exceeding the book value of the business, the premium over book value must be recorded on the buyer's books.

In the case of RCA, one former GE executive recalls that GE allocated a disproportionate amount of this so-called goodwill to NBC, increasing the TV network's book value while reducing that of other RCA assets. GE's own annual reports appear to substantiate his recollection. In 1987, the year after the acquisition, GE raised NBC's book value to $3.8 billion from $3.4 billion. The higher book value for NBC and the resulting lower value for other RCA assets raised GE's profits on sales of some of RCA's non-NBC assets.

Among the RCA units sold, GE recorded a $110 million gain on the disposition in 1991 of NBC's interest in an RCA-Columbia home-video joint venture. And the aerospace business was sold in 1993 at a pretax profit of $1.43 billion. That leaves NBC as the last major piece of RCA still on GE's books.

Mr. Dammerman says that boosting gains from future non-NBC asset sales didn't enter into how NBC was valued and that GE didn't know at the time which businesses would be sold. He adds that GE couldn't record profits from some RCA assets sold soon after the acquisition.

However, one consequence of assigning a higher book value to NBC eventually became apparent when GE began considering the sale of the network in the early 1990s. The higher book value raised the price GE would have had to obtain to avoid booking a loss. When GE held talks about selling NBC to Paramount Communications Inc. (now owned by Viacom Inc.), Paramount proposed to structure the sale financing in a way that would help GE avoid an immediate write-down, according to two people familiar with the negotiations. Mr. Dammerman says that although GE wanted to avoid a loss, the proposed transaction wasn't structured with that aim.

Despite some experts' doubts about earnings management, some accountants say it can be helpful as long as corporate executives try to convey a fair picture. "Some people would say maybe smoothing makes sense because it gives the best indication of the future and the long-term trend," says Peter Wilson, who specializes in financial-statement analysis at the Sloan School of Management at Massachusetts Institute of Technology.

But Howard Schilit, an accounting professor at American University in Washington, comments: "Earnings management can be very dangerous for the investor because you are creating something artificial. The numbers should reflect how the company is actually doing."

GE executives differ in how much smoothing they acknowledge. In an initial interview, GE Capital Chairman Gary Wendt said, "We do a little, not a lot." His financial chief, Mr. Parke, said, "We have a lot of assets in this business.... Obviously, there are timing issues associated with when those assets are sold."

Required

a. Evaluate the effectiveness of restructuring charges as an earnings management device. Do you agree with Professor Leftwich's reservations about such charges and with the SEC's expected limitations on such provisions? Explain.

b. Explain whether you agree with Peter Wilson, who says "maybe smoothing makes sense" or with Howard Schilit, who says "earnings management can be very dangerous."

    c. One of the most interesting aspects of the article is its implications for securities market efficiency. If large, complex firms such as GE have "so many different businesses that most analysts can't track them all," how can the market price of GE's shares properly reflect all that is known about the firm? To what extent do you think earnings management is a substitute for analysts in informing the market about the firm's value and prospects?

10. The article "Dangerous Games," by Jonathan Laing is here reproduced from *Barron's* (June 8, 1998). The article describes apparent earnings management devices used by Sunbeam Corp., with "Chainsaw Al" Dunlap as CEO, to "largely manufacture" its 1997 reported earnings of $109.4 million.

DANGEROUS GAMES

Did "Chainsaw Al" Dunlap manufacture Sunbeam's earnings last year?

Albert Dunlap likes to tell how confidants warned him in 1996 that taking the top job at the small-appliance maker Sunbeam Corp. would likely be his Vietnam. For a time, the 60-year-old West Point graduate seemingly proved the Cassandras wrong. As the poster boy of 'Nineties-style corporate cost-cutting, he delivered exactly the huge body counts and punishing airstrikes that Wall Street loved. He dumped half of Sunbeam's 12,000 employees by either laying them off or selling the operations where they worked. In all, he shuttered or sold about 80 of Sunbeam's 114 plants, offices and warehouses.

Sunbeam's sales and earnings responded, and so did its stock price, rising from $12.50 a share the day Dunlap took over in July 1996 to a high of 53 in early March of this year.

But last month Sunbeam suffered a reversal of fortune that was as sudden and traumatic for Dunlap as the Viet Cong's Tet offensive was to U.S. forces in 1968. After several mild warnings of a possible revenue disappointment, Sunbeam shocked Wall Street by reporting a loss of $44.6 million for the first quarter on a sales decline of 3.6%. In a trice, the Sunbeam cost-cutting story was dead, along with "Chainsaw Al" Dunlap's image as the supreme maximizer of shareholder value. Now Sunbeam stock has fallen more than 50% from its peak, to a recent 22.

And just as suddenly, what was supposed to be an easy sprint, Dunlap's last hurrah as a corporate turnaround artist, has turned into a grinding marathon. Lying in tatters is his growth scenario for Sunbeam, based on supposedly sexy new offerings such as soft-ice cream makers, fancy grills, home water purifiers and air-filter appliances. Many of the new products have bombed in the marketplace or run into serious quality problems. Moreover, Sunbeam has run into all manner of production, quality and delivery problems. It recently announced the closing of two Mexican manufacturing facilities with some 2,800 workers, citing the facilities' lamentable performance. Dozens of key executives, members of what Dunlap just months ago called his Dream

Team, are bailing out. And now he faces another year or more of the wrenching restructuring that's needed to meld Sunbeam with its recently announced acquisitions, including the camping-equipment maker Coleman Co., the smoke detector producer First Alert and Signature Brands USA, best known for its Mr. Coffee line of appliances. These acquisitions will double the size of a company whose wheels are coming off. This may not be Vietnam, but it sure ain't Kansas, Toto.

Sunbeam declined to discuss the company's problems with *Barron's*. In some ways, Dunlap seems to have morphed into a latter-day Colonel Kurtz of the movie *Apocalypse Now*, increasingly out of touch with the grim realities of Sunbeam's situation and suspicious of friend and foe alike. For example, Wall Street is still buzzing over a confrontation that Dunlap had with PaineWebber analyst Andrew Shore at a Sunbeam meeting with the financial community in New York three weeks ago. Shore had the temerity to ask several questions that Dunlap deemed impertinent, and Dunlap snarled, "You son of a bitch. If you want to come after me, I'll come after you twice as hard."

Shore, the first major analyst to downgrade Sunbeam's stock in April when word began to circulate of a possible first-quarter earnings debacle, is still upset over the incident. "As far as I'm concerned, Al is the most overrated CEO in America," he grouses. "He's nothing but a bully who speaks in sound bites and completely lacks substance."

Despite Sunbeam's latest reversal of fortune, don't expect Al Dunlap to be headed for the poorhouse any time soon. Though the swoon in Sunbeam shares has vaporized the value of the options held by most of the company's executives and managers, Dunlap's large option and stock grants are still worth about $70 million, down from a peak value of over $300 million when the stock was at its high. Moreover, in February Dunlap negotiated a new contract, doubling his annual base salary of $2 million. Under a rich benefits package, Sunbeam even foots the bill for Dunlap and his wife's first-class air fare from Florida, where Sunbeam is headquartered, to Philadelphia so that Dunlap can visit his personal dentist to keep his latest bridge comfy and pearly white. Limo charges and overnights at the Four Seasons hotel are included as well. All this from the self-styled champion of shareholder value.

We can't say we are surprised by Sunbeam's current woes. In a cover story last year entitled "Careful, Al" (June 16), we cast a skeptical eye on Dunlap's growth objectives in the low-margin, cutthroat small-appliance industry. We also pointed out the yawning gap between Sunbeam's performance claims and reality. We took special note of Sunbeam's accounting gimmickry, which appeared to have transmogrified through accounting wizardry the company's monster 1996 restructuring charge ($337 million before taxes) into 1997's eye-popping sales and earnings rebound. But to no avail. Wall Street remained impressed by Sunbeam's earnings, and the stock continued to rise from a price of 37 at the time of the story.

Sunbeam's financials under Dunlap look like an exercise in high-energy physics, in which time and space seem to fuse and bend. They are a veritable cloud chamber. Income and costs move almost imperceptibly back and forth between the income statement and balance sheet like charged ions, whose vapor trail has long since dissipated by the end of any quarter, when results are reported. There are also some signs of other accounting shenanigans and puffery, including sales and related profits booked in periods before the goods were actually shipped or payment received. Booking sales and earnings in advance can comply with accounting regulations under certain strict circumstances.

"We had an amazing year," Dunlap crowed in Sunbeam's recently released 1997 annual report, taking an impromptu victory lap for the profit of $109.4 million, or $1.41 a share, on sales of $1.2 billion. Sunbeam had every incentive to try to shoot the lights out in 1997. Dunlap and crew were convinced they would be able to attract a buyer for the company just as they had done in the second year of their restructuring of Scott Paper in 1995, when Dunlap managed to fob Scott off on Kimberly Clark for $9 billion. They openly shopped Sunbeam around in the second half of last year, but the offer never came. The rising stock price made the company too expensive, and would-be buyers were also deterred by the nightmares Kimberly Clark experienced after buying Scott.

Yet, sad to say, the earnings from Sunbeam's supposed breakthrough year appear to be largely manufactured. That, at least, is our conclusion after close perusal of the company's recently released 10-K, with a little help from some people close to the company.

Start with the fact that in the 1996 restructuring, Sunbeam chose to write down to zero some $90 million of its inventory for product lines being discontinued and other perfectly good items. Even if Sunbeam realized just 50 cents on the dollar by selling these goods in 1997 (in some cases, they reportedly did even better), that would account for about a third of last year's net income of $109.4 million.

One has to go to the 1997 year-end balance sheet to detect more of mother's little helpers. One notes a striking $23.2 million drop, from $40.4 million in 1996 to $17.2 million in 1997, in pre-paid expenses and other current assets. There's no mystery here, according to a former Sunbeam financial type. The huge restructuring charge in 1996 made it a lost year anyway, so Sunbeam prepaid everything it could, ranging from advertising and packaging costs to insurance premiums and various inventory expenses. The result: Costs expensed for 1997 were reduced markedly, if unnaturally. This artifice alone probably yielded an additional $15 million or so in 1997 after-tax income.

Why did Sunbeam's "Other Current Liabilities" mysteriously drop by $18.1 million and "Other Long-Term Liabilities" fall by $19 million in 1997? The answer is simple, according to folks close to the company. Various reserves for product warranties and other items that were set aside during Sunbeam's giant 1996 restructuring were drained down in 1997, creating perhaps an additional $25 million or so in additional net income for the year.

On top of all that, as part of the 1996 restructuring charge, Sunbeam reduced the value of its property, plant, equipment and trademarks by $92 million. Though some of these charges applied to assets Sunbeam was selling off, the bulk of the charge related to ongoing operations. This allowed Sunbeam to lower its depreciation and amortization expense on the 1997 income statement by nearly $9 million. That would create about $6 million of additional after-tax income.

Oddly enough, the figure for net property, plant and equipment on Sunbeam's balance sheet still rose during 1997, to $241 million from $220 million the year before. This is likely an indication that such costs as product development, new packaging and some advertising and marketing initiatives were capitalized or put straight on the balance sheet instead of being expensed in the year they were incurred, as was the previous practice. In this manner, expense could have been shifted from 1997 into future years, when they can be burned off at a slower, more decorous pace afforded by multi-year depreciation schedules. Why else would Sunbeam's advertising and promotion expense drop by some $15 million, from $71.5 million in 1996 to $56.4 million last year? Particularly when Sunbeam trotted out a splashy national television ad campaign in 1997 to boost consumer demand for its new products. This advertising shortfall alone contributed another $10 million to Sunbeam's 1997 profits.

The company also got a nice boost from a 61% drop in its allowance for doubtful accounts and cash discounts, from $23.4 million in 1996 to $8.4 million in 1997. And this decline occurred despite a 19% rise in Sunbeam's sales last year. The milking of this bad debt reserve in 1997 likely puffed net income by an additional $10 million or so.

Then there's the mystery of why Sunbeam's inventories exploded by some 40%, or $93 million, during 1997. Quite possibly, Sunbeam was playing games with its inventories to help the income statement. By running plants flat out and building inventories, a company can shift fixed overhead costs from the income statement to the balance sheet where they remain ensconced as part of the value of the inventory until such time as the inventory is sold. To be conservative, let's assume this inventory buildup might have helped Sunbeam's profits to the tune of, say, $10 million.

Lastly, there are more than superficial indications that Sunbeam jammed as many sales as it could in 1997 to pump both the top and bottom lines. The revenue games began innocently enough early last year. Sales were apparently delayed in late 1996, a lost year anyway, and rammed into 1997. Likewise, The Wall Street Journal reported several instances of "inventory stuffing" during 1997, in which Sunbeam either sent more goods than had been ordered by customers or shipped goods even after an order had been cancelled. But these are comparatively venial sins that companies engage in all the time to make a quarter's results look better. Besides, Sunbeam gave the plausible excuse at the time that glitches in a computer system consolidation in the first quarter had them flying blind for a time.

But as 1997 dragged on and the pressure to perform for Wall Street intensified, Sunbeam began to take greater and greater liberties with sales terms to puff current results. The latest 10-K, for example, discloses that in the fourth quarter of last year Sunbeam recorded some $50 million in sales of cooking grills under an "early buy" program that allowed retailers to delay payment for the items as long as six months. Moreover, some $35 million of these "early buys" were categorized "bill and hold" sales and never even left Sunbeam's warehouses.

Sunbeam engaged in bill-and-hold transactions in other product lines, too, according to a number of people in the appliance industry. In the second quarter, for example, Sunbeam booked a sale and "shipped" some $10 million of blankets to a warehouse it had rented in Mississippi near its Hattiesburg distribution center. They were held there for some weeks for Wal-Mart. The company also pumped millions of dollars of goods into several national small-appliance distributors on such easy payment terms as to call into question whether a sale ever took place. Some with knowledge of Sunbeam's business practices say the appliance maker in some instances transferred title for the goods to distributors but then agreed to not only delay payment but actually pay the distributors what amounted to a storage charge for taking the goods. These sources also said that in some cases distributors also had the right to return the items to Sunbeam without suffering any loss.

How much did various types of questionable sales add to 1997's net income? No outsider can know for sure. But we can make an educated guess based on the fact that Sunbeam's receivables, or unpaid customer accounts, jumped by 38%, or $82 million, in 1997. Taking into account Sunbeam's profit margins, it seems that questionable sales could have boosted 1997 net income by as much as $8 million.

We by no means are privy to all Sunbeam's techniques for harvesting current earnings from past restructuring charges and future sales. Deconstructing Al Dunlap is a daunting task. But to save our gentle readers the effort, our total estimate of artificial profit boosters in 1997 came to around $120 million compared with the $109.4 million profit the company actually reported. Thus, one is left to wonder whether Sunbeam made anything at all from its actual operations, despite

Dunlap's claim to have realized some $225 million in cost savings as a result of his restructuring prowess.

Our dour view of Sunbeam's current financial health is only confirmed by the company's consolidated statement of cash flow in the latest 10-K. These numbers, of course, are harder to finesse because they track the actual cash that flowed in and out of the company during 1997. And the statement doesn't paint a pretty picture. Despite 1997's eye-catching $109.4 million net profit, Sunbeam still suffered negative cash flow from operations of $8.2 million, after taking into account the explosion in Sunbeam's inventory and accounts receivable during the year. And that operating cash flow deficit would have been an even larger $67.2 million if not for the sale of $59 million in receivables in the last week of 1997. After capital expenditures of $58.3 million is thrown into the equation, Sunbeam's free cash flow deficit amounts to more than $125 million.

Sunbeam's first-quarter earnings debacle is yet another sign of a company that's in anything but the pink of health. Despite management assertions into April that Sunbeam's first-quarter sales would finish comfortably ahead of those for the first quarter of 1997, they ended up declining 4%. Even more shocking to Dunlap's fans was the $44.6 million loss in the March quarter compared with a profit in the year earlier period of $6.9 million. Sure, $36.8 million of that first-quarter loss was the result of nonrecurring charges, mostly a handsome new pay package Dunlap managed to negotiate in February. But the operating loss Sunbeam suffered of $7.8 million was a clear sign of its true earnings power once the tank from the 1996 restructuring charge had run dry.

Dunlap trotted out a whole raft of excuses for the company's lamentable first-quarter performance. He cited dumb deals his former No. 3 executive had made with major retailers before Chainsaw fired him in April, the effect of bad weather on grill sales caused by El Nino, and so forth.

Whatever the case, the first-quarter disaster wasn't the result of any lack of effort on Sunbeam's part to pump up the results. The company recorded $29 million of additional "buy now, pay later" grill sales. In fact, the company is now holding so many grills, in various warehouses around its Neosho, Missouri, grill plant that it has had to lease warehouse space in nearby Oklahoma. Who knows how many of these grills will ever make it to the selling floor?

Sunbeam also extended its quarter by three days, from March 28 to March 31. This allowed the company to book an extra $20 million in sales both from ongoing Sunbeam operations and two days of sales from Coleman (its acquisition closed on March 30). But to no avail. Sunbeam still fell $9 million short of last year's sales of $253.5 million.

Reports are rife that Sunbeam tried to strong-arm suppliers into "recutting" their invoices for various goods and services so that Sunbeam would officially owe less money. The proviso was that the suppliers would be allowed to add back the amount forgone, plus interest, in invoices submitted after the first quarter had ended. A Sunbeam financial official denies the "recutting" charge and characterizes the activity by the company's procurement department as the normal give-and-take that goes on between suppliers and companies seeking rebates.

But that's not the understanding held by an official at one China-based supplier. When contacted by *Barron's*, this official readily acknowledged that he had sent Sunbeam a check for $500,000, or 5% of the business he does annually with the company, in late March. "The only reason I sent them a check rather than a new invoice is that we had no invoices outstanding at the time we received the call," he explained. "We figure our contribution dropped right down to the bottom line if Sunbeam actually booked it. I don't know what happened, though."

For the next few quarters, expect the recent acquisition of Coleman, First Alert and Mr. Coffee to restore a measure of calm to Sunbeam's financial performance. The giant restructuring charges that Sunbeam is taking to integrate the new units, at $390 million before taxes, will give the company plenty of fodder with which to play earnings games. The company is even forecasting earnings of $1 a share this year and $2 next year—before extraordinary items, naturally.

But Dunlap's days at Sunbeam may be numbered. The already-ailing company now has to struggle under $2 billion of additional debt and a negative tangible net worth of $800 million. And his enemies, including disenchanted shareholders, angry securities analysts, and bitter former employees, are growing in number and circling ever closer to the company's headquarters in Delray Beach. Of course, Dunlap could always escape by using the building's flat roof to chopper out, should it come to that. One can only hope he'll remember to take the American flag with him.

Required

a. Jonathan Laing notes that Sunbeam's prepaid expenses declined from $40.4 million at 31 December 31, 1996 to $17.2 at 31 December 31, 1997, a reduction of $23.2 million. He points out that 1996 was a "lost year anyway" (because of a 1996 restructuring charge of $337 million), so Sunbeam "prepaid everything it could." Laing then states that this "artifice alone probably yielded" $15 million in 1997 after-tax income.

Do you agree with Laing's analysis of the effect of the decline in prepaid expenses during 1997 on 1997 net income? Explain why or why not.

b. Laing reports that 1997 operating cash flow was -$8.2 million. Since net income was reported as $109.4 million, net income-increasing accruals must have totalled $117.6 million. Use the information in the article to itemize the impacts on net income of the various earnings management devices described. How close does your itemized list come to $117.6 million? In arriving at your itemized total, take your answer to **a** into account.

Do you agree with Laing's statement that 1997 earnings "appear to be largely manufactured"? Explain why or why not.

c. On the last page, the article refers to Sunbeam's acquisition of Coleman, First Alert and Mr. Coffee, indicating that Sunbeam is taking restructuring charges of $390 millions to integrate these firms into its operations. Explain how this will "give the company plenty of fodder with which to play earnings games."

d. Use the "iron law" of accruals reversal to help explain why there was a substantial first quarter 1998 loss.

11. Barton (2001) studied managers' use of derivatives and discretionary accruals to smooth reported earnings. As Barton points out, both of these devices have smoothing potential—since earnings can be expressed as the sum of operating cash flow and total accruals, smoothing can be accomplished through operating cash flows (which can be hedged by derivatives) and/or through accruals (by means of the discretionary portion).

From a sample of large U.S. firms during 1994–1996, incl., Barton found that managers trade off the use of derivatives and discretionary accruals in order to maintain (i.e., smooth) earnings volatility at a desired level. Specifically, firms that were heavy derivatives users tended to be low users of discretionary accruals, and vice versa. Other things equal, this suggests that managers are sensitive to the costs of smoothing earnings. That is, firms appear to use the combination of smoothing devices that are, for it, the least costly.

Required

a. Give reasons why managers may want to smooth earnings.

b. What are some of the costs of smoothing earnings? Why would managers trade off these 2 earnings smoothing devices, rather than using only one or the other?

c. Suppose that the JWG draft standard (see Section 7.4.5) comes into effect. Would this be likely to increase or decrease the use of derivatives for smoothing purposes? Explain.

d. Are Barton's results more consistent with the opportunistic or efficient contracting version of positive accounting theory? Why?

Notes

1. Healy points out that if net income is just below the bogey, the manager might instead adopt policies to increase net income, so that at least some bonus would be received.

2. This assumes that stakeholders do not unwind the earnings management. BDS argue that it is not cost-effective them to do so, since it is difficult to isolate the effects on reported income of continuing use of FIFO or accelerated amortization, particularly since many stakeholders have limited ability to process information and may not have enough at stake to warrant careful evaluation of reported earnings.

3. It should be noted that levels of expenditure on real variables may not be inside information of the manager, particularly if there is full disclosure. The reasons for changes in these variables may be inside information, however.

Standard Setting: Economic Issues

12.1 Overview

We now return to the role of standard setting that was introduced in Chapter 1. Recall that we view the standard setter as a mediator between the conflicting interests of investors and managers. The fundamental problem of financial accounting theory is how to conduct this mediation, that is, how to reconcile the financial reporting and efficient contracting roles of accounting information or, equivalently, how to determine the socially "right" amount of information. We define the "right" amount as that amount that equates the marginal social benefits of information to the marginal social costs.[1]

Of course, we should not take for granted that regulation is necessary for this reconciliation. Much of the required mediation can be accomplished by market forces. Nevertheless, substantial arguments can be made that market forces alone are unable to drive the right amount of information production. Our purpose in this chapter is to review and evaluate these arguments.

The extent of standard setting is a challenging one for accountants. Many aspects of firms' information production are regulated, and many of these regulations are laid down by accounting standard setting bodies themselves, in the form of GAAP. Furthermore, the extent of regulation is increasing all the time, as more and more accounting standards are promulgated.

As you are aware, many industries in recent years have been deregulated. Airlines, trucking, financial services, telecommunications, and electric power generation are examples of industries that have seen substantial deregulation. What would happen if the information industry was deregulated? Would this produce a flood of competition and innovation, or would information production collapse into chaos? At present, the answers to these questions are not known. However, discussion of the pros and cons of standard setting helps us to see the tradeoffs that are involved and to appreciate the crucial role of information in society.

12.2   *Regulation of Economic Activity*

There are numerous instances of regulation of economic activity in our economy. Firms that have a monopoly, such as electricity distribution, local telephone companies, and transportation companies are common examples. Here, regulation typically takes the form of regulation of rates, regulation of the rate of return on invested capital, or both. Public safety is an area subject to frequent regulation as, for example, in elevator inspection laws, standards for automobile tire construction, and fire protection regulations. Communications is another area that, in many countries, is deemed sufficiently sensitive to attract regulation.

Other sets of regulations affect financial institutions and securities markets. The primary reason for such regulation is to protect individuals who are at an information disadvantage. This points up the fact that information asymmetry underlies the question of regulation of information production. If there was no information asymmetry, so that managerial actions and inside information were freely observable by all, there would be no need to protect individuals from the consequences of information disadvantage.

Information asymmetry is thus frequently used to justify regulations to protect the information-disadvantaged. Insider trading rules and regulations to ensure full disclosure in prospectuses are examples. In addition to protecting ordinary investors, such regulations are also intended to improve the operation of capital markets by enhancing public confidence in their fairness.

Accounting practice is also strongly affected by regulations designed to protect against information asymmetry. An important role of accounting and auditing is to report relevant and reliable information, thereby reducing information asymmetry between firm insiders, the investing public, and other users. However, this role requires that accountants and auditors be credible and competent. Thus, there are laws to regulate the accounting professions that control entry and maintain high standards. Many other regulations also affect accountants. Minimum disclosure requirements for annual reports are required by corporations acts. Government statistical agencies and taxation authorities require financial information. Quasi-governmental bodies such as the OSC and the SEC require a variety of information disclosures for firms whose shares are publicly traded. Private bodies such as stock exchanges require periodic disclosures from firms whose securities are traded on the exchange. Finally, other private bodies, such as the AcSB and the FASB, set accounting and auditing standards.

Thus, we see that accounting is a highly regulated area of economic activity. Governments are directly involved in this regulation through laws to control the creation of professional accounting bodies and their rights to public practice, and also through minimum disclosure requirements for annual reports and prospectuses, as laid down in corporations acts. Indirect government involvement comes, for example, through the creation of securities commissions. Furthermore, the professions themselves do much of their own regulating by formulating and monitoring accounting and auditing standards. Henceforth, we will use the term **central authority** to refer to any of these regulatory bodies.

In this chapter our primary concerns are the regulation of minimum disclosure requirements, generally accepted accounting and auditing standards, and the requirement that public companies have audits. We will use the term **standard setting** to denote the establishment of these various rules and regulations. Note that standard setting involves the regulation of firms' external information production decisions. For our purposes, it does not matter whether these standards are set by direct or indirect regulation. In the case of indirect regulation, such as AcSB and FASB standards, authority to set standards is clearly delegated by, or allowed by, the government. The main point to realize is that firms are not completely free to control the amount and timing of the information they produce about themselves. Rather, they must do so under a host of regulations that we will call standards, laid down by some central authority.

> ***Standard setting*** *is the regulation of firms' external information production decisions by some central authority.*

In considering issues of information production, it is helpful to distinguish between two types of information that a manager may possess. The first type is called **proprietary information**. This is information that, if released, would directly affect future cash flows of the firm. [2] Examples are technical information about valuable patents, and plans for strategic initiatives such as takeover bids or mergers. The costs to the manager and firm of releasing proprietary information can be quite high.

The second type is called **nonproprietary information**. This is information that does not directly affect firm cash flows. It includes financial statement information, earnings forecasts, details of new financing, and so on. The audit is also included in nonproprietary information.

12.3   *Private Incentives for Information Production*

12.3.1 *WAYS TO CHARACTERIZE INFORMATION PRODUCTION*

While the term "production" of information may take some getting used to, we use it for two reasons. First, we want to think of information as a commodity that can be produced and sold. Then, it is natural to consider separately the costs and benefits of information production.

Second, we want a unified way of thinking about the various ways information production can be accomplished. Information is a complex commodity. Just what do we mean when we speak of the quantity of information produced? There are several ways to answer this question.

First, we can think of **finer information**. For example, a thermometer that tells you the temperature in degrees is a finer information system than one that only tells you if the temperature is above or below freezing—the first thermometer tells you everything that the second one does, and more. It enables a finer reading of the temperature. In an accounting context, a finer reporting system adds more detail to the existing historical cost-based statements. Examples of finer reporting include expanded note disclosure, additional line items on the financial statements, segment reporting, and so on. In terms of our decision theory discussion of Chapter 3, finer information production means a better ability to discriminate between realizations of the states of nature. For example, in a decision problem where the relevant set of states of nature is the temperature, a thermometer that tells you degrees enables better discrimination between different temperature states than one that only tells you if the temperature is above or below freezing. We can also think of the information perspective on decision usefulness, discussed in Chapter 5, as implying finer information production, since the information perspective encourages elaboration of the financial statements proper by means of MD&A and notes.

Second, we can think of **additional information**. For example, we might add a barometer to our thermometer. In an accounting context, additional information means the introduction of new information systems to report on matters not covered by the historical cost system. Examples would include fair value accounting, which introduces the effects of changing values into financial reporting, and future-oriented financial information, which expands reporting responsibility to include expected future operations. In decision theory terms, additional information means an expansion of the set of relevant states of nature upon which the firm's performance depends. Thus a thermometer-barometer reports on atmospheric pressure as well as temperature. In effect, additional information can produce greater relevance in reporting. We can think of the measurement perspective on decision usefulness discussed in Chapter 6 as a move towards producing additional value-relevant information.

A third way to think about information production is in terms of its **credibility**. The essence of credibility is that the receiver knows that the supplier of information has an incentive to disclose truthfully. In our thermometer example, the purchaser knows that the manufacturer must produce an accurate product in order to stay in business. Thus, the purchaser accepts the thermometer as a credible representation of the temperature. In an accounting context, it is often suggested that a "Big Five" audit is more credible than a "non-Big Five" audit because a large audit firm has more to lose,[3] both in terms of reputation and "deep pockets;" hence, it will maintain high audit standards. Also, the greater the penalties for managers who divulge false information, the more credibility investors attach to managers' disclosures.

In this chapter we will not need to distinguish these different ways to produce information and will refer to them all, rather loosely, as **information production**.

Note that however we think of its production, more information will require higher costs, some of which may be proprietary.

12.3.2 CONTRACTUAL INCENTIVES FOR INFORMATION PRODUCTION

Incentives for private information production arise from the contracts that firms enter into. As we saw in Chapter 9, information is necessary to monitor compliance with contracts. For example, if managerial effort is unobservable, this leads to an incentive contract based on the results of the firm's operations. Then, information about net income is needed to provide a measure of results. Also, an audit adds credibility to the reported net income, so that both the owner and the manager of the firm are willing to accept reported net income as a reliable measure of managerial performance.

Similarly, when a firm issues debt, it typically includes debt covenants in the contract. Information is needed about the various ratios on which the covenants are based, so that the firm's adherence to its covenants can be monitored over the life of the debt issue. Again, an audit adds credibility to the covenant information.

Another contractual reason for private information production arises when a privately owned firm goes public. This was modelled by Jensen and Meckling (1976). The owner-manager of a firm going public, after selling all or part interest, has a motivation to increase shirking. Note that prior to the IPO the shirking problem was internalized—the owner-manager bore all the costs. The costs of shirking are the reduced profits that result. Subsequent to the new issue, the owner-manager does not bear all the costs—the new owners will bear their proportionate share. Thus, shirking costs the owner-manager less after going public, so he or she will engage in more of it. This is an agency cost to the new owners of the firm.

Investors will be aware of this motivation, however, and will bid down the amount they are willing to pay for the new issue by the expected amount of agency costs. In effect, the firm's cost of capital rises. Consequently, the owner-manager has an incentive to contract to limit his or her shirking and thereby raise the issue price. For example, the contract between the owner-manager and the new investors in the firm may include a forecast, which the owner-manager will be motivated to meet (this will be recognized as the production of additional information). Alternatively, the contract may provide for a lot of detail in the financial statements (finer information), to make it more difficult for the owner-manager to hide or bury costs of perquisites. Also, the contract may provide for an audit to increase the credibility of the information production. In all of these cases, the owner-manager commits by contract to produce information that will convince investors that he or she will in fact continue to manage diligently. Investors, realizing this, will be willing to pay more for an interest in the firm than they would otherwise.

The key point here is that the firm has a private incentive to produce information in all of these contracting scenarios—no central authority is needed to force information production. Furthermore, since the types and amounts of information to be produced under the contract are negotiated and agreed to by all contracting parties, the right amount of information is produced, by definition. That is, the information production decision is internalized between the contracting parties. Then, the question of whether too much or too little information is produced does not arise. Failure to provide for information production in the contract will make it more incomplete, hence more difficult or impossible to enforce.

In principle, the contractual motivation for information production can be extended to any group of contracting parties. Consider, for example, the relationship between the firm manager and investors. The investor's decision problem was reviewed in Chapter 3, where we concluded that rational investors want information about the expected return and risk of their investments. The firm manager and each investor could contract for the desired amount of information about the firm's future cash flows, financial position, and so on. The contract could provide that the investor pay for this information or, perhaps, the manager would offer it free to raise the demand for the firm's shares. Note that different investors would, in general, want different amounts of information about the firm. One investor, adept at financial analysis, might demand a very fine projection of future operations, from which to prepare an estimate of future cash flows and returns on investment. Another investor may simply want information about the firm's dividend policy. A very risk-averse investor might demand a very credible audit, at a correspondingly high cost, while another investor would prefer the least costly audit available. Other investors may not demand any information at all, particularly if their investment portfolios are well diversified. Instead, they might rely on market efficiency to price-protect them.

Unfortunately, while direct contracting for information production may be fine in principle, it will not always work in practice. The reason should be apparent from the previous paragraph. In many cases there are simply too many parties for contracts to be feasible. If the firm manager was to attempt to negotiate a contract for information production with every potential investor, the negotiation costs alone would be prohibitive. In addition, to the extent that different investors want different information, the firm's costs of information production would also be prohibitive. If, as an alternative, the manager attempted to negotiate a single contract with all investors, these investors would have to agree on what information they wanted. Again, given the disparate information needs of different investors, this process would be extremely time-consuming and costly if, indeed, it was possible at all. Hence, the contracting approach only seems feasible when there are a few parties involved. The owner-manager incentive contracts studied in Section 9.4.2 involved only two persons. Our long-term lending contract example in Section 9.4.3 involved a manager and a lender.

Even if contracting parties do reach an information production agreement, another problem arises. Unless the agreement can be enforced (as in a cooperative game), parties to the agreement may be tempted to violate it for their own short-run benefit. For example, suppose that a managerial compensation contract provides for a year-end audit. Knowing this, the manager works hard during the year. Then, since the manager's effort has already been exerted, the principal would benefit from cancelling the audit, thereby saving the audit costs. But, cancelling the audit this year will reduce the incentive for the manager to work hard next year.

It seems that while contracts are an important source of private information production, we cannot rely on them completely for the information needs of society. Accordingly, we now turn to a second set of private incentives for firms' information production. We will call these **market-based** incentives.

12.3.3 MARKET-BASED INCENTIVES FOR INFORMATION PRODUCTION

Private incentives for managers to produce information about their firms also derive from market forces. Several markets are involved.

The *managerial labour market* constantly evaluates manager performance. As a result, managers who release false, incomplete, or biased information will suffer damage to their reputations. While reputation considerations do not completely remove the need for incentive contracts, as discussed in Section 10.2, they do reduce the amount of incentives needed. In terms of our agency example in Section 9.4.2 where the manager received a 32% profit share, a profit share of, say, 20% may be sufficient when reputation considerations are taken into account.[4] Consequently, less risk is imposed on the (risk-averse) manager, thereby making him/her less reluctant to release information that affects firm value. Thus, the managerial labour market provides important incentives for information production.

Similar incentives are provided by *capital markets*. Managers are motivated by reputation and contracting considerations to increase firm value. This creates an incentive to release information to the market. The reason is that more information, by reducing concerns about adverse selection, increases investor confidence in the firm, with the result that the market prices of its securities will rise or, equivalently, its cost of capital will fall, other things being equal. This will show up in enhanced firm profitability and value, hence enhanced market value for the manager. The financial forecast of Mark's Work Wearhouse (Section 4.8.3) provides a good example of a high level of information release.

Another market that disciplines managers is the *takeover market*, also called the market for corporate control. If the manager does not increase firm value, the firm may be subject to a takeover bid, which, if successful, frequently results in replacement of the manager. The more disgruntled the shareholders are, the more likely that such a takeover bid will be successful. Consequently, the takeover market also motivates managers to increase firm value, with implications for information production similar to those of the managerial labour and capital markets.

Formal models that relate information release to the firm's market value are presented by, for example, Merton (1987) and Diamond and Verrecchia (1991). In the Merton model, information asymmetry is modelled as only a subset of investors knowing about each firm. If the firm can increase the size of this subset, say by the voluntary release of information, its market value will rise, other things equal. In the Diamond and Verrecchia model, voluntary disclosure reduces information asymmetry between the firm and the market, which facilitates trading in its shares. The resulting increase in **market liquidity**[5] attracts large institutional investors who, if they have to do so in future, can then sell large blocks of shares without lowering the price they receive. The firm's share price increases as a result of this greater demand.[6]

Thus, labour markets and the market for corporate control, along with efficient securities markets, are important noncontractual sources of private information production. In all cases, it is market prices that provide the motivation—security prices and managers' market values on the labour market are affected by the quality of firms' information production decisions.

12.3.4 SECURITIES MARKET RESPONSE TO FULL DISCLOSURE

The theoretical arguments in Section 12.3.3 predict that the securities market will respond positively to increased disclosure. In this section, we review some empirical studies of this prediction. The Merton model was tested by Lang and Lundholm (1996). They used financial analysts' ratings of disclosure quality, based on evaluations of firms' quarterly and annual reports and investor relations, for a large sample of firms over the years 1985–1989. The authors found that, other things equal, the higher the disclosure quality as judged by the analysts, the greater the number of analysts following the firm. This result is not obvious, a priori, because one could argue that better information production by a firm reduces the need for analysts to interpret it for investors. The finding that analyst following increased suggests that analysts can do a better job when they have more information to work with; that is, increased analyst following leads to increased investor interest. Merton's model then predicts increased demand for the firm's shares, or, equivalently, lower cost of capital.

Healy, Hutton, and Palepu (1999) tested implications of the Diamond and Verrecchia model. Using the same analysts' disclosure quality ratings as Lang and Lundholm, they found that firms with improved disclosure ratings were associated with a significantly improved share price performance in the year following the rating increase, compared to other firms in their same industry. They also found a significant increase in institutional ownership. Both of these results are predicted by Diamond and Verrecchia.

Welker (1995) investigated the effect of disclosure quality on the bid-ask spread component of market liquidity (see Note 5). He predicted that shares of firms with better disclosure policies would have lower spreads, the reason being that better disclosure policy implied less investor concern about insider trading and other adverse selection problems. After controlling for other factors that also affect spread, such as trading volume,[7] Welker found a significant negative relationship between disclosure quality (as measured by analysts' disclosure quality ratings) and bid-ask spread. Again, this result is consistent with the Diamond and Verrecchia model.

Botosan (1997) reported the results of a direct test of disclosure quality and cost of capital. For a sample of 122 U.S. manufacturing corporations, Botosan evaluated their disclosure quality by the extent of voluntary disclosure in their 1990 annual reports. She also estimated the cost of capital for each firm using the clean surplus model (see Section 6.5.4). Botosan found higher quality disclosure to be significantly associated with lower cost of capital, but only for firms with low analyst following. Since analysts typically access a wider variety of information sources than just the annual report, it seems that for a firm that has high analyst following, the reports they generate swamp the effects of voluntary annual report disclosure.

Sengupta (1998) investigated the impact of disclosure quality on the cost of debt. He found that, on average, his sample firms enjoyed a .02% reduction in interest cost for every 1% increase in their disclosure quality as rated by financial analysts over 1987–1991. He also found that this result strengthened for riskier firms, where a firm's riskiness was measured by the standard deviation of the return on its shares. The reason for this favourable impact, according to Sengupta, was that lenders assigned lower credit risk to firms with superior disclosure policies.

The market response to *lack of* full disclosure is also worth noting. In their study of firms under investigation by the SEC for violations of GAAP, Dechow, Sloan, and Sweeney (1996) report an average drop of 9% in share price on the day the investigation is announced. When investors lose faith in a firm's financial reporting, the consequences can be severe indeed.

Enron, Corp., a large Texas-based energy conglomerate, provides a dramatic example of these consequences. In the fall of 2001, the SEC launched a formal investigation into Enron's financial accounting, leading to revelations that the company had overstated earnings during 1997–2001 by $591 millions, or about 40%. This was accomplished through dealings with a large number of limited partnerships, some of which were controlled by senior executives and thus not at arms length. Apparently, Enron had recognized profits on sales and other dealings with these partnerships, and had failed to record losses suffered by some of them. Since they were not at arm's length, these partnerships should have had their financial results consolidated with those of Enron, in which case the profits on the intercompany transactions would have been eliminated and the losses recognized. However, this was not done. Furthermore, large debts incurred by these limited partnerships had not been recognized by Enron. When this off-balance-sheet financing was revealed it became apparent that Enron was in violation of its debt covenants, leading to downgrades by credit rating agencies and the immediate maturing of much of its debt.

Investor confidence in Enron quickly collapsed. Its share price, which was in the range of $50 to $80 during the first half of 2001, fell to $0.61 on November 28, creating hugh losses for employees, creditors, and investors, and triggering numerous lawsuits. In addition to the SEC probe, The U.S. Congress initiated its own investigations. On December 2, Enron filed for bankruptcy protection. Its cost of capital had effectively become infinite.

Collectively, these results suggest that firms with high quality disclosure enjoy lower costs of debt and equity capital, and vice versa. They support our theoretical arguments that market forces encourage information production.

12.3.5   OTHER INFORMATION PRODUCTION INCENTIVES

The Disclosure Principle

A simple argument can be made that suggests that a manager will release all information, good or bad. This is known as the **disclosure principle**.[8] If investors know that the manager has the information, but do not know what it is, they will assume that if it was favourable the manager would release it. Thus, if investors do not observe the manager releasing it, they will assume the worst and bid down the market value of the firm's shares accordingly. For example, suppose that investors know that a manager possesses a forecast of next year's earnings, but they do not know what the forecast is. The manager may as well release it, as failure to do so would be interpreted by the market as the lowest possible forecast.

This argument is reinforced by the manager's incentive to keep the firm's share price from falling. A fall in share price will harm the manager through lower remuneration, if remuneration depends on share price, and/or through lower value on the labour market for managers. Since the market will assume the worst if the information is not released, any release of credible information will prevent share price and market value from falling as low as it would otherwise.

Undoubtedly, the disclosure principle operates in many situations. However, as Dye (1985) discusses, it does not always work. Note that it requires that investors know that the manager has the information. If they do not know this, the argument breaks down. For example, the firm may not have prepared earnings forecasts in the past and the market may not be sure whether one has been prepared this year.

A second reason for failure of the disclosure principle derives from costs of disclosure. This was examined by Verrecchia (1983), who sought to reconcile the disclosure principle with the empirical observation that managers do not always fully disclose. For example, they may delay the release of bad news. Verrecchia assumes that, if disclosure is made, it is truthful. However, he also assumes that there is a cost of disclosure. The cost is constant, independent of the nature of the news. For example, there may be a proprietary cost of releasing valuable patent information. Investors know that the manager has the news, and know its cost of disclosure, but do not know what the news is.Then, if the information is withheld, investors do not know whether it is withheld because it is bad news or because it is good news but not sufficiently good to overcome the disclosure cost, and the disclosure principle fails.

If we rank the nature of the news on a continuum from bad to good, Verrecchia shows that for given disclosure cost there is a threshold level of disclosure. The lower the disclosure cost, the lower the threshold, and if disclosure cost is zero, as it would be for non-proprietary information, the disclosure principle is reinstated.

However, consistent with the disclosure principle, Verrecchia assumed that the market knows that the manager has the information. But, the market may be unsure about this. For example, as mentioned above, the firm may or may not have prepared a forecast. Then, failure to disclose cannot be interpreted by investors as the lowest possible forecast. This assumption limits the generality of a conclusion that the disclosure principle is reinstated for non-proprietary information.

These considerations were modeled by Penno (1997). He assumed that the manager's non-proprietary information is noisy, with the quality of the information measured by the noise term's variance. He also assumed that the market has only a probability (as opposed to knowing for sure) that the manager has the information and that this probability is decreasing in information quality (i.e., higher quality information is more difficult to obtain). Penno shows that, similar to Verrecchia, there is a threshold level of forecasted profits below which the manager would not disclose. In Penno's model, the likelihood of disclosure decreases as the manager's information quality increases. Thus, release of high quality forecasts such as those of Mark's Work Wearhouse is predicted to be somewhat rare, since they will only be disclosed when the forecast is relatively favourable. In this regard, it is interesting to note that Mark's Work Wearhouse did not release a forecast for 1992, a year in which it was expecting a loss. We may conclude that, even for non-proprietary information, the disclosure principle is prone to failure.

Information released under the disclosure principle must be credible. That is, the market must know that the manager has an incentive to reveal it truthfully. Obviously, if a manager lies about next year's forecast of net income it can hardly be said that information is being disclosed. Information that is subject to verification after the event, such as a forecast, will be credible to the extent that penalties can be applied for deliberate misstatement. Another way to secure credibility is to have released information attested to by a third party, such as an auditor. However, because much inside information is not verifiable even after the fact, or subject to audit, truthful disclosure cannot always be attained.

The need for truthful disclosure has been relaxed somewhat by Newman and Sansing (1993) (NS). They analyze a two-period model consisting of an incumbent firm, a representative shareholder, and a potential entrant to the industry. The firm, which is assumed to act in the shareholder's best interests, knows its value exactly. If it were not for the potential entrant, the shareholder's best interests would be served by disclosing this value, since the shareholder could then optimally plan consumption and investment over the two periods. However, this may trigger entry, in which case the incumbent firm will suffer a loss of profits and value. How should the firm report?

The answer depends on the costs to the entrant should it decide to enter the industry, and the resulting loss of profits to the incumbent. For example, if entry costs are high and there is substantial loss of profits upon entry, the incumbent firm may disclose imprecise information about its value. That is, instead of an exact disclosure, it will disclose an interval within which its value lies. If it reported its value exactly, its disclosures would not be credible, since everyone knows it has an incentive to deter entry.

Disclosure in the NS model is truthful in the sense that the firm credibly reveals an interval within which its value lies. Nevertheless, the disclosure principle fails in the sense that the firm does not report its value exactly. The NS model is consistent with range forecasts of earnings, as for Mark's Work Wearhouse (Section 4.8.3).

Finally, as shown by Dye (1985), the disclosure principle can break down if there is a conflict between information desired by investors and information needed for contracting purposes. Suppose, contrary to our suggestion in Section 10.4, that the market price of a firm's shares better reflects manager effort than does net income. This could be the case if there are relatively few economy-wide events affecting share price. Then, share price is a more efficient variable upon which to base manager compensation than net income.

Suppose, however, that the manager has a forecast of future profitability that, if reported, would affect share price. Furthermore, assume the market knows the manager has this forecast. Reporting the forecast would reduce the ability of share price to reflect manager effort, since this ability would be swamped by the impact of the forecast on price. Thus, from a contracting perspective it may be desirable to discourage the reporting of forecasts even though a forecast provides useful information to investors. In effect, the best information for contracting may not be the best information for investor decision-making, and the investor information may not be reported for contracting reasons. Then, the disclosure principle breaks down. Dye's model provides a supplement to legal liability as a reason why reporting of forecasts is rare.

In sum, the disclosure principle is a simple and compelling argument for release of inside information. However, it breaks down in numerous instances, and hence cannot be relied upon to ensure that firms always release full information.

Signalling

It frequently happens that firms differ in quality. For example, a firm may have better investment opportunities than other firms. Alternatively, a firm may conduct superior R&D, leading to potentially valuable patents. Such information would be of considerable usefulness to investors. Yet, disclosure of the details of high-quality projects and technology may reveal valuable proprietary information. Furthermore, even if the manager did disclose the details, he or she may not be believed by a skeptical marketplace. How can the manager credibly reveal the firm's **type**, as these underlying quality differences are called, without incurring the excessive costs?

This problem of separating firms of different types has been extensively considered by means of signalling models.

> *A **signal** is an action taken by a high-type manager that would not be rational if that manager was low-type.*

A crucial requirement for a signal is that it be less costly for a high-type manager than for a low-type. This is what gives a signal its credibility, since it is then irrational for a low-type to mimic a high-type, and the market knows this.

Spence (1973) was the first to formally model signalling equilibria. He did so in the context of a job market. Given that it is less costly to a high-type job applicant to obtain a specified level of education than to a low-type, Spence showed that equilibria exist where employers can rely on the applicant's chosen level of education as a credible signal of that person's underlying competence.

A number of signals have been suggested that are relevant to accounting. One such signal is **direct disclosure**. Hughes (1986) showed how such disclosure can be a credible signal. In her model, a manager wants to reveal his or her expectation of firm value, by making a direct disclosure at the beginning of the period. Investors observe the firm's cash flows at the end of the period. They then infer the probability of the realized cash flow contingent on the manager's disclosure. For example, if the manager disclosed a high firm value but cash flow is very low, investors will assess a high probability that the disclosure was untrue, and penalties will be applied. Knowing this, the manager is motivated to report truthfully, so that in equilibrium investors can correctly infer his or her expectation of firm value.

While Hughes' model does not apply to the moral hazard problem (the manager's expectation of firm value is independent of his or her effort), it does demonstrate how direct disclosure can operate to reduce adverse selection. Firms of different types can separate themselves, so that the market value of their securities properly reflects firm value.

A variety of **indirect signals** has been studied to further understand disclosure issues. As Leland and Pyle (1977) show for an entrepreneur going public, the proportion of equity retained is a signal, because it would not be rational for a bad-news manager to retain a high equity position. Also, audit quality can be a signal of the value of a new securities issue. A rational manager would be unlikely to retain a high-quality (and high-cost) auditor when the firm is a low-type. Similar arguments relate to the choice of underwriter for a new issue. Titman and Trueman (1986) and Datar, Feltham, and Hughes (1991) developed models where audit quality is a signal.

A firm's capital structure has signalling properties. There is evidence, for example, that the market value of existing common shares falls when the firm issues new shares. While dilution of existing shareholders' equity is one possibility, another explanation is the market's concern that the new shares may be issued by a low-type firm—a high-type firm would be more likely to issue bonds or finance internally. One reason is that the high value increments would then accrue to existing shareholders. Another reason is that a high-type firm would assess its probability of bankruptcy as low (thus, the probability that the bondholders would take over the firm is low).

Dividend policy can also be a signal. A high payout ratio may signal a firm as having a confident future. However, a high payout ratio could also mean that the firm sees little prospect for profitable internal financing from retained earnings. Thus, dividend policy may not be as effective a signal as others.

Accounting policy choice also has signalling properties. For example, a firm may adopt a number of conservative accounting policies. A high-type firm can do this and still report profits, while a low-type firm would report losses. Thus, conservative accounting policies can signal a manager's confident view of the firm's future. The signalling properties of accounting policy choice are related to the use of earnings management to credibly reveal inside information, as discussed in Section 11.6.

Publication of forecasts, in jurisdictions where forecasting is voluntary, is another signal. Why should a low-type firm voluntarily publish a forecast of its low type?

Note that for signals to be applicable, the manager must have a *choice*. For example, if some central authority imposed a uniform standard of audit quality on all firms, audit quality would not be available as a signal. Indeed, Spence (1973) shows that for a viable signalling equilibrium to exist there must be a sufficient number of signals available to the manager.

This argument, that standards to enforce uniform accounting destroy managers' abilities to signal, is important for standard setting. In Section 2.5.1 we suggested that the major problem with historical cost accounting is that there is no unique way to match costs with revenues. We also suggested that standard setting bodies may then have to step in to impose uniformity. The clear implication was that diversity in reporting practices was "bad." This implication is correct, as far as it goes. Diversity in reporting practices imposes costs on investors who want to compare the performance of different entities, because it is necessary to restate the entities' financial statements to a common basis before valid comparisons can be made.

However, if we reconsider this implication in the light of signalling theory, we see that diversity may not be as bad as first suggested. To the extent that firms' choices of accounting policies signal credible information about those firms, diversity of reporting practices is desirable. This argument is reinforced by our discussion of earnings management in Chapter 11. We argued there that a little bit of earnings management is a good thing, since it gives some flexibility in the face of contract rigidities and can serve as a vehicle for the release of inside information. Obviously, earnings management by means of accounting policy choice is only possible if there is a sufficiently rich set of accounting policies, such as GAAP, from which to choose. Signalling theory serves as a counterargument to the continual refinement of GAAP so as to eliminate accounting policy choice.

Thus, we can see a tradeoff with respect to diversity of reporting practices. The optimal amount of diversity is not zero, despite the costs that diversity imposes, because of signalling considerations. It is important for standard setting bodies to realize the signalling potential of accounting policy choice.

Financial Policy as a Signal

In this section we review a paper by Healy and Palepu (1993) (HP). HP address the question of what managers might do to signal their inside information to the efficient market. We have already discussed how market forces motivate managers to communicate information so as to maximize their firm's market value. But since, as we shall see, these forces are subject to various degrees of market failure, and also since noise trading can distort a firm's share price, managers of some firms may find their firms undervalued by the capital market relative to their inside information. The question then is, how can they signal the real value of the firm?

HP provide a specific illustration of the above problem. Patten Corp.[9] acquires large undeveloped tracts of land, subdivides them into lots, and sells them, with up to 90% of the financing supplied by Patten. Revenue is recognized upon sale, that is, when at least 10% of the purchase price has been received and collection of the balance is reasonably assured. This creates a potential problem of bad debt losses. However, in its 1986 financial statements Patten provided a bad debt allowance of only $10,000 on accounts receivable of $29.4 million. The firm claimed that this low amount was justified by past experience and a low current delinquency rate.

In 1987, concern appeared in the financial media that Patten's bad debt allowance was too low. Specifically, the fear was expressed that past delinquency rates may not be representative of future delinquency. Patten's share price plunged following the publication of these concerns, as investors quickly revised their beliefs about Patten's future prospects.

HP suggest several possible manager responses to convince the market of their inside information that the value of the accounts receivable is substantially as shown in the financial statements. One response is direct disclosure of credit granting and collection procedures, so as to inform the market of their integrity. Direct disclosure should be a credible signal here, since management would be foolish to overly expose itself to penalties such as loss of reputation and legal liability by disclosing incorrect information at such a critical time.

However, details of the firm's credit and collection policies are likely to be proprietary information, which could harm its competitive position—recall our discussion of the Darrough and Stoughton model in Section 9.3 and of Newman and Sansing in this section. Consequently, HP suggest several financial policies that could serve as indirect signals of management's information.

One such policy would be to raise private financing and/or to sell accounts receivable without recourse to a financial institution. Our discussion of contractual incentives for information production in Section 12.3.2 suggests that when there are only a few parties involved in a contract they can agree among themselves what information to provide. Here, it may be less costly for Patten to provide a private lender with information about the real value of its receivables than to provide it to the market, since, as mentioned, providing it to the market would require public release of proprietary information. The market, upon becoming aware of the private financing, would realize that this is an indirect signal and would raise its evaluation of Patten.

Another possibility would be for Patten to engage in a hedging strategy. Then, credit losses on accounts receivable would be offset by gains on the hedging instrument. Such a policy would be prohibitively expensive if large credit losses were anticipated. Consequently, it should be a credible signal. However, Patten would have to be careful not to get into the aggressive derivatives strategies that brought down Franklin Savings (Section 7.4.4).

Yet another signalling strategy would be for management to increase its holdings of Patten shares. This would load additional risk on to management, thereby increasing their incentive to work hard as well as giving them a longer-run perspective in operating the firm.

Note the common theme in all of these signalling strategies. Management would be foolish to undertake any of them unless it really believed its inside information about asset values. This is what gives signals their credibility. The market will realize this, with the result that the fall of Patten's share price should be reversed. HP's article insightfully demonstrates the rich variety of signals available for credible communication of inside information to an efficient market.

Private Information Search

To this point, our investigation of private incentives for release of inside information has centred on the manager. The argument has been that a high level of information release will improve the manager's reputation and lower the firm's cost of capital, to the manager's benefit. Thus, the onus is on the manager to release information.

Implicit in this line of reasoning is that investors are passive. They merely react to whatever information the manager releases in deciding on their demand for the firm's securities. In effect, they are price-protected by the market. It may be, however, that many investors will be active in seeking out information, particularly in the presence of noise traders or securities market inefficiencies. For example, they may conduct their own investigations and analyses of fundamental firm value, or hire financial analysts and other experts to assist them. They may watch closely persons that they suspect have inside information and mimic their actions.

Thus, there is a variety of ways that investors can conduct a **private information search**. Bill Cautious, in Example 3.1, did so by analysis of the annual report, using Bayes' theorem to process the resulting information. To the extent that such activities are successful, inside information is very quickly transferred to the public domain. By limiting the ability of insiders to capitalize on inside information, the severity of the adverse selection problem is reduced.

Unfortunately, private information search can be quite costly, from society's perspective, since more than one investor incurs costs to discover the same information. It would be cheaper, in terms of total resources used to generate information, if the firm produced and publicized the information only once, so that each investor would not have to rediscover it.

Hirschleifer's (1971) analysis is a classic in the area of private information search. Hirschleifer considered an exchange economy, that is, an economy without production, so that there is no scope for information search to affect the manager's effort. Then, Hirschleifer showed that the social value of information search is negative, even though individual investors may perceive it as valuable. The reason is that, without production, the amount of goods and services in the economy is fixed, so that private information search just redistributes wealth, it does not create wealth. Then, since information search has a cost, the net social effect is negative.

If we consider a production economy, private information search may improve the proper operation of markets, with resulting impacts on firms' costs of capital and manager effort. However, to the extent that a redistributive component to private information search remains, this will still constitute a cost to society.

One such cost is unequal distribution of information across investors, as discussed by Beaver (1989). For example, the "big guys" may have more resources to find and analyze information, leaving the small investor at a disadvantage. This leads to suggestions, such as by Lev (1988), for regulation to require firms to release information to everyone, thereby enhancing public confidence in a fair marketplace and contributing to market liquidity. Interestingly, the SEC has recently done just this. Regulation FD, adopted in August, 2001, prohibits companies from selectively disclosing information. In Canada, the Ontario Securities Act prohibits companies from releasing information to selected individuals before releasing it to the general public.

12.3.6 CONCLUSIONS

There are many private vehicles and incentives for managers to produce information. Furthermore, it does appear that firms and managers are rewarded for superior disclosure decisions, and punished when misleading information release is discovered. However, it should be emphasized that market forces will not motivate the release of all inside information, since there are costs to the firm of information release. In addition to proprietary costs, as discussed above, agency costs arise from the fundamental problem of financial accounting theory.[10] As pointed out in Section 9.5.1, full disclosure can reduce the hardness of net income, rendering it less correlated with manager effort. As a result, compensation contracts become less efficient. Consequently, information release is a tradeoff between the benefits of lower cost of capital and higher costs of motivating the manager. Baiman and Verrecchia (1996) present a model that demonstrates this tradeoff.

Assuming that firms choose the lowest cost point of this tradeoff, it might seem that market forces can drive the right amount of information production from society's perspective. However, we now review some counterarguments, called **market failures**, which suggest that regulation may still be needed.

12.4   *Sources of Market Failure*

12.4.1 *EXTERNALITIES AND FREE-RIDING*

Frequently, information released by one firm will convey information about other firms. For example, if a firm reveals a sharp increase in sales and profits, this may affect the market's expectations for other firms in the industry. Also, if a firm releases proprietary information (for example, details about a valuable patent) this could affect the market's expectations of future earnings of competing firms. Interactive effects such as these are called **externalities**.

The effect of externalities is to cause the private and social values of information to diverge. The Darrough and Stoughton (1990) model, reviewed in Section 9.3, of a game between a monopolist incumbent and a potential entrant to the industry also illustrates the effect of externalities. Under some conditions, the monopoly firm does not release information, so as to deter entry. While this may benefit the monopolist, it does reduce the flow of information to the market, thereby imposing a cost on society.

In Section 5.6, we noted that accounting information has characteristics of a public good. We pointed out that this makes it difficult for the firm to charge for producing this information. In effect, when the use of information by one individual does not destroy it for use by another, other investors can "free-ride" on this information. Since all investors will realize this, no one has an incentive to pay. Then, if the firm cannot recover the costs of information production it will produce less than it would otherwise.

> An **externality** is an action taken by a firm or individual that imposes costs or benefits on other firms or individuals for which the entity creating the externality is not charged or does not receive revenue. **Free-riding** is the receipt by a firm or individual of a benefit from an externality.

The crucial aspect of both externalities and free-riding is that the costs and benefits of information production as perceived by the firm differ from the costs and benefits to society. For example, if accounting information produced by one firm informs investors about other firms, this is a benefit to society for which the producing firm receives no benefit. Hence, the firm will underproduce relative to the first-best amount for society. A similar phenomenon operates for the free-rider problem.

Externalities and free-riding are well-known reasons used to justify regulation. The regulator steps in to try to restore the socially right amount of production because market forces alone fall short.

12.4.2 THE ADVERSE SELECTION PROBLEM

Given our conclusion in Section 12.3.6 that market forces do not motivate full information release, some inside information remains. Then, the adverse selection problem arises. Persons with access to this inside information may well exploit their advantage at the expense of outside investors.

In our context, there are two versions of the adverse selection problem. First, we have the problem of insider trading, which was introduced in Section 4.6.1. If opportunities exist for insiders, including managers, to generate excessive profits by trading on the basis of their insider information, persons willing to do this will be attracted to the opportunity. Then, outside investors will not perceive the securities market as a level playing field and may withdraw. This will reduce market liquidity. For the market to operate properly, it is necessary that there be enough traders that the buy or sell decisions of any one of them does not affect the market price of a security. This will not happen unless the market is sufficiently liquid. Thus, the ability of insiders to earn excessive trading profits constitutes a securities market failure.

A second version of adverse selection arises when managers who are privy to bad news about the firm's future do not release that information, thereby avoiding, or at least postponing, the negative firm consequences. This has two adverse effects. First, investors are less able to distinguish between securities of different qualities. Then managers with low-quality, bad-news securities will be encouraged to bring them to market and managers with good-news securities may not bring them to market (if the market cannot distinguish between securities of different qualities then the market price will reflect the average quality—this is called **pooling**). Second, since owners do not know that the bad news firm is doing badly, the ability of the takeover market to purge poor managers is reduced, so that the average quality of managers is lowered.

Both of these effects of failure to release bad news mean that investors have a continuing concern about adverse selection.

12.4.3 THE MORAL HAZARD PROBLEM

We suggested in Section 12.3.3 that reputation formation on the managerial labour market, in conjunction with incentive-based compensation contracts, operates to encourage managers' information production. However, these forces may not be completely effective. The reason is that managers may be able to disguise shirking by opportunistic use of earnings management. Thus, DeFond and Park (1997), as outlined in Section 11.3.4, documented a tendency of managers to cover up periods of low profitability by borrowing earnings from other periods. One reason for low profitability, of course, is manager shirking. Thus, despite managerial labour markets and incentive contracts, investors will also be concerned about (bad) earnings management.

12.4.4 UNANIMITY

A characteristic of economies with markets that do not work properly is a lack of unanimity, which derives from the effects of adverse selection and moral hazard just described. With properly working markets, firm shareholders will be unanimously in favour of the manager maximizing the market value of the firm. When markets do not work properly, this need not be the case. Eckern and Wilson (1974) studied this problem with respect to the physical production of the firm—that is, the types and quantities of products to be produced—and showed that the manager's choice of production plan to maximize the market value of the firm would not in general be approved by all shareholders under certain market conditions.

A similar result applies to firms' production of information. Blazenko and Scott (1986) demonstrated that in an economy where the information market does not work properly, due to adverse selection, the firm manager was motivated to choose that audit quality that would maximize firm market value (recall that an audit is a form of information production). All shareholders, however, would prefer a higher-quality audit. The reason is that from the shareholders' perspective, there are two valuable functions of the audit. One is to add credibility to the firm's financial statements, as we have mentioned. The other is that, if the audit catches the manager in fraud or shirking, the shareholders may recover damages. Since only the first function has value to the manager, the audit is of greater value to the shareholders. Consequently, they will demand more of it than the manager wishes to supply.

To put this argument another way, an effect of investor concerns about adverse selection and moral hazard is that firms' share prices will be slightly lower than their fundamental values. Even if a manager does engage in information release to maximize firm value, this maximization is with respect to a share price that is "too low." Thus, shareholders would prefer the manager to release more information than the manager feels is optimal.

12.4.5 CONCLUSIONS

Markets for information are characterized by externalities and free-riding. These problems, if sufficiently serious, can justify central authority intervention. Furthermore, since market forces do not motivate full information release, securities and managerial labour markets do not fully protect investors from the consequences of insider trading and earnings management. As a result, shareholders will not be unanimous in their support of manager policies, even policies that involve firm value maximization.

12.5   *How Much Information Is Enough?*

Starting from the standard economic prescription that firms should produce information to the point where its marginal social benefit equals its marginal social cost, we see that private market forces are unlikely to produce this result. One reason is externalities and free-riding—market forces are unable to give firms the full social benefits of their information production decisions and are unable to fully internalize the costs of these decisions. Even if they could, the forces of moral hazard and adverse selection lead to a fundamental lack of unanimity between managers' decisions and investors' interests, motivating investors to demand regulation to protect their interests.

Nevertheless, we must not assume that ever-increasing regulation is necessarily socially desirable. This is because regulation carries with it substantial costs. These include direct costs of the bureaucracy needed to establish and administer the regulations, and compliance costs imposed on firms. Of possibly greater magnitude are indirect costs. One such indirect cost arises from the fact that when standards are set to enforce uniform accounting and reporting, managers' opportunity to signal is reduced. Uniform audit standards for all firms and mandatory forecasting requirements are examples of standards that would reduce signalling potential.

A second indirect cost arises because the regulator may not, and indeed probably will not, be able to calculate the socially optimal amount of information to require. This is because information is such a complex commodity, because there are conflicts between decision usefulness and contracting needs for information, and because different investors have different decision needs.[11] Since information regulations affect firms' financing, investment, and production decisions, the indirect costs of any "wrong" amount of information production can be large indeed.

Given these complex cost-benefit considerations, we simply do not know how much regulation is enough. However, it is safe to say that complete deregulation would not be socially desirable. The uncontrolled impacts of externalities, adverse selection and moral hazard would be sufficiently serious that markets would probably cease to function. Nor is complete regulation desirable, since the costs to completely eliminate accounting policy choice would be astronomic. However, this leaves a considerable range over which to debate the extent of regulation. Much more knowledge of the benefits and costs of financial reporting will be needed before the question of extent of regulation can be answered.

However, we can still ask if the efficiency of regulation can be improved. That is, how might standards generate more information at less cost? In the next section, we consider a suggestion in this regard.

12.6   *Decentralized Regulation*

Information about firm segments—where segmentation may be on the basis of product lines, subsidiary companies, geography—has been required disclosure in firms' annual reports for some time. For example, Section 1700 of *CICA Handbook* required such disclosure. Segment information should be useful to investors, since, in evaluating the expected performance and risk of large and complex firms, relevant information may be buried in consolidated totals. With segment disclosure, it is more difficult to disguise poor performance in one segment by means of good performance in another.

In 1997, a replacement, Section 1701, was issued by the AcSB in conjunction with a similar standard by the FASB. Of interest is the basis of segmentation in these revised standards. They require that the firm report segment information on the same basis as it organizes its segments internally for top management decision-making and performance evaluation. For our purposes, two aspects of this requirement are of interest. First, of the various bases of segmentation that are possible, reporting on a basis consistent with the internal organization should be of greatest usefulness to investors, since it is management that knows best how to organize the business. Thus, reporting externally on the same basis will give investors the best insights into the firm's operations. Second, the costs to the firm of complying with the new standard should be low since the firm is already preparing the required information internally.[12]

Another example of this approach is the SEC's (1997) requirement for risk disclosure, discussed in Section 7.6.3. This standard also allows management a choice of how best to report on the riskiness of its operations. Presumably, the best way to report on risk is in a manner consistent with the firm's internal risk management procedures.

We call this approach "decentralized regulation." While there is regulation involved, compliance is decentralized to the internal decisions of management.[13] This improves relevance of reporting and at the same time is less costly. Note that, unlike most standards, management retains the ability to signal through its choice of reporting methods.

12.7   *Summary*

The question of the extent to which standards for information production should be imposed is a complex and important one for a market economy. At present, we witness substantial regulation of firms' information production decisions. These regulations include insider trading laws and laws to regulate full disclosure. They also include laws to establish accounting and auditing professions. These professions, in turn, may form bodies empowered to establish GAAP, such as the AcSB and the FASB. However, it can be argued, by analogy with other industries where regulation has been eased, that deregulation of the information "industry" would result in a flood of innovation and competition, to society's advantage.

Indeed, theory suggests a number of reasons why firms would produce information in the absence of standards. These derive from the information needs of contracts and from market forces. Parties to contracts will want information to motivate effort and to reward accomplishment. Managerial labour markets and takeover markets interact with securities markets to motivate managers to release information so as to maximize market value. Signalling is an important vehicle for credible information release.

Such private forces undoubtedly result in much information production. Theory also suggests, however, that even if we ignore externalities and free-riding, the amount produced by private forces alone may fall short of society's demands. The reason can be seen by means of a two-stage argument. First, contracts for information production break down when a large number of persons are involved. Consequently, we cannot rely on contracts for all of society's information needs.

Second, when contracts break down, market prices (for managerial services and for securities) must take over as motivators of information production. However, market forces do not motivate full information release, since there are costs of releasing information and firms will trade off the costs with the benefits. As a result, some inside information remains, creating a fundamental lack of unanimity between managers' information production decisions and information demanded by investors. Investors may then turn to regulation to remedy the perceived deficiency.

However, it is important to realize that private forces need not completely eliminate market failures to preclude regulation. This is because regulation also has costs. These include direct costs, such as a bureaucracy to set and enforce the standards, and compliance costs imposed on firms. More importantly, however, they include indirect costs imposed on society if the central authority mandates the "wrong" amount of information. Since information is such a complex commodity, this is quite likely to happen. Given the impact of information on firms' production, financing, and investment decisions, the costs to society here can be significant.

The question of standard setting then boils down to a cost-benefit tradeoff. The costs of regulation include not only the enforcement costs, but also the costs of any wrong decisions made by the regulator. The benefits lie in reduced market failures that persist after private market forces have done their best. At present, the extent to which the benefits of regulation exceed the costs is not known, although giving firms some flexibility in how they meet reporting standards may be worthwhile.

Finally, it should be noted that lack of unanimity leads directly to questions about the fairness of the distribution of information. That is, standard setting may need to draw on political theory as well as economics. We will explore this suggestion in Chapter 13.

Questions and Problems

1. Information has both costs and benefits to a firm. What are the costs and benefits of information production to a firm? How much information should the firm produce?   (CGA-Canada)

2. Explain why a voluntary forecast can be an indirect signal but a mandated forecast cannot.   (CGA-Canada)

3. "Contracting internalizes the problem of information production." Explain what this statement means.   (CGA-Canada)

4. Describe the difference between a direct and an indirect signal, using a voluntary forecast as prescribed by the *CICA Handbook*, Section 4250 (see Section 4.8.3) as an example.   (CGA-Canada)

5. To what extent do (i) security market forces and (ii) managerial labour market forces operate to motivate managers to operate their firms in the best interests of the shareholders. In your answer, identify how financial accounting information enables the market forces to operate.

6. The notion of a market for information, unlike markets for agricultural commodities, transportation services, and so on, may be unfamiliar to most people. A main reason for this is that information is a very complex commodity.

   List three ways that we can think about the quantity of information and explain each briefly.

7. An adverse selection problem can arise from information asymmetry between issuer and buyer of securities.

   Required

   a. Explain what the adverse selection problem is in this context.

   b. How can financial accounting information reduce the adverse selection problem?

   c. Can financial accounting information eliminate the problem completely? Explain.

   d. What other ways are used to reduce the problem of inside information?

8. The failure of managers to release bad news is a version of the adverse selection problem. Such failure indicates that the securities market is not working properly.

   Required

   a. Why might a manager withhold bad news?

   b. To what extent does the disclosure principle operate to reduce the incentive of a manager to withhold bad news? Explain.   (CGA-Canada)

9. In February, 1998, Newbridge Networks Corp., a telecommunications equipment maker based in Kanata, Ontario, announced that its revenues and profits for the quarter ending on February 1, 1998 would be substantially below analysts' estimates. Its share price immediately fell by 23% on the Toronto and New York stock exchanges.

   The sale, in December, 1997, of over $5 million of the company's shares by an inside director of Newbridge was widely reported in the financial media during February, 1998. Details of sales by other Newbridge insiders, including its CEO, during previous months were also reported. The implication of these media reports was that these persons had taken advantage of inside information about disappointing sales of a new product line.

   Required
   a. Which source of market failure is implied by these media reports?
   b. What effects on investors, and on liquidity of trading in Newbridge shares, would media reports of such insider sales be expected to create?
   c. Suppose that Newbridge's management felt that its share price was undervalued by the market after the February earnings announcement. Describe some signals that management and directors could engage in to counter the public impression of lower-than-expected profitability.

10. In November, 1997, Philip Services Corp., a large recycler of scrap metal based in Hamilton, Ontario, floated a share issue on the New York Stock Exchange at U.S. $16.50 per share. In the months that followed, revelations of substantial losses led to several large writedowns on Philip's books, totalling about $400 million. Matters were made worse by a lack of clear and complete explanations by the company as to what the sources of the losses were. By September, 1998, Philip's shares were trading at under $2.

   A lawsuit followed on behalf of the purchasers of the November, 1997 share issue. It claimed that Philip had deliberately engaged in earnings management so as to postpone the market's knowledge of the impending losses until after the share issue. Accounting policies allegedly used to do this included capitalization of losses at one of Philip's facilities as employee training costs, inclusion of profits from trading in metals contracts as ordinary revenue, and inflating the carrying values of inventories. Allegations also appeared in the financial media that Philip had revealed inside information to certain analysts.

   Required
   a. Why would managerial labour and capital markets not operate to prevent the earnings management practices that Philip's management was accused of?
   b. Explain why Philip's failure to communicate promptly and fully the reasons for the $400 million of writedowns would contribute to the fall in its share price.

c. Philip's auditor, Deloitte and Touche, were included as defendants in the lawsuit, on the grounds that they had allowed the alleged earnings management. Based on the information in the question, what arguments could you make to defend yourself if you were the auditor?

d. If you were a financial accounting regulator, such as a member of the OSC or the AcSB, what new regulations, if any, would you put into place, assuming the lawsuit has merit, to prevent similar incidents in future?

11. The article below, reproduced from the *Toronto Star*, July 16, 1998, describes some of the recommendations from a study of the information production practices of gold mining companies, following the infamous Bre-X Minerals Ltd. scandal. Bre-X, a Canadian gold mining development company with shares traded on the Toronto Stock Exchange, was exploring an Indonesian gold property claimed to be the world's largest, until the claim was revealed to be a hoax.

MINING FIRMS TOLD TO CAN ALL THEIR HYPE

Gold mining companies must become clearer and less promotional in their communications with the public and investment analysts if they want to attract shareholders and financing, a recent study shows.

The study, conducted by communications firm Wertheim & Co. Inc., found that clear, honest, timely and relevant information has become even more important for investors in the wake of the confidence-damaging scandal surrounding Bre-X Minerals Ltd.

Shares in Calgary-based Bre-X, once the darling of the stock markets, collapsed when its property in Indonesia was found to not have the huge gold deposit the company had been promoting. At one point its Busang property was believed to have the world's largest gold find. Bre-X is now in bankruptcy protection.

Most of the 35 investment analysts and institutional investors surveyed said that junior mining companies in particular need to become less promotional.

Asked what they would advise mining companies to do differently, many respondents cited the need for companies to provide independent, third-party verification of their finds or test results.

Other recommendations included providing better and more regular disclosure, and offering more information on the testing methods the companies used.

Some respondents said the content of many press releases needed improving, with one suggesting "there are going to have to be some guidelines as to when you can start telling the public about things, and what should be included in some of those early comments."

"Many of the company reports are unintelligible to the average investor," said Richard Wertheim, managing partner of Wertheim & Co.

One institutional investor surveyed for the study said investors are now placing "a higher burden of proof on the company seeking the financing to show that they actually have what they say they have, rather than just making statements that there is, you know, excellent potential, etc."

He said "there is going to be greater demand for information, for audited information by independent sources, and if they can't come up with it and are not willing to spend the money to do it, then they won't get the financing—from us, anyway."

Another analyst said he's always been amazed that junior mining companies "can start reporting just the barest of information."

"They don't wait until they have a number of drill holes completed before they release the results," he said.

"I mean, actually they're releasing results right from the time they grab the specimen off the property, or there's a trench and they throw out a result. I think they're releasing results far too early in the program."

Another piece of advice was that companies need to improve the communications effort when stock markets or gold bullion prices are depressed and investors are less enthusiastic.

There was a feeling that companies time the release of their news according to when it may be most favorably received and have the most impact on the stock price.

A few respondents suggested improved disclosure in prospectus documents, and formalizing what defines proven and probable reserves or mineable ore.

Others suggested more punitive measures of accountability for directors and management.

SOURCE: Reprinted with permission—The Toronto Star Syndicate.

Required

a. What well-known problem of information asymmetry does the article illustrate? Explain.

b. Explain why decreased public confidence in gold mining companies will reduce or eliminate their ability to obtain financing. What are the social costs of a reduced ability of gold mining companies to obtain financing?

c. The article identifies several proposals for increased regulation of information production. These include additional information about testing methods and definitions of proven and probable reserves, understandability of reporting, timing of reporting, increased credibility of reporting through audits, and more severe punishment of managers who violate full and fair disclosure. To what extent will these recommendations, if implemented, provide cost-effective protection for investors against similar scandals in future? Explain your answer.

12. XYZ Ltd. is an owner-managed retail hardware store that went public on January 1, 2000. Afterwards, Tom Harris, the fun-loving owner-manager, held 70% of the common stock and remained the chief executive of the company.

Required

a. Why is it likely that Tom Harris will shirk more as a majority shareholder relative to the time he was the owner-manager of the company prior to January 1, 2000?

b. How might potential investors protect themselves from the adverse effects of likely excessive shirking by the CEO/majority shareholder, Tom Harris, after the issuance of shares?

c. Prior to going public, does Tom Harris have an incentive to convince potential shareholders that he will not engage in excessive shirking? Discuss.

d. What steps can Tom Harris take to convince potential shareholders that he will not engage in excessive shirking? (CGA-Canada)

13. Regulation FD of the SEC came into effect in October, 2000. This new standard requires firms that release material information which may affect their share price to release it to all investors simultaneously. The purpose is to stop "selective disclosure," whereby managers release information, such as changes in earnings forecasts, to a select group of analysts and institutional investors, relying on these persons to convey the information to the market.

Required

a. Explain the market failure that has led to this new standard.

b. Describe the effects on market liquidity of selective disclosure.

c. In an article in *The Globe and Mail*, November 8, 2000, Paul Hill notes that an effect of Regulation FD has been to cause firms to reduce the amount of information they release. This suggests that the regulation has increased the costs of information production. Describe and explain two sources of increased cost resulting from this regulation.

d. Do you feel that Regulation FD will improve the operation of securities markets? Explain why or why not.

14. In October, 1999, DaimlerChrysler AG started to give more information to analysts, including production forecasts and earnings outlooks. This increased transparency followed a sharp drop in the firm's share price following its second quarter, 1999 earnings report, which revealed flat earnings compared to the previous year. Apparently, DaimlerChrysler managers felt that much of the share price decline was a result of investors having been "taken by surprise," rather than of the flat earnings as such.

The article also reported on a recent meeting of DaimlerChrysler managers in Washington, DC. The meeting was "upbeat," with discussion of plans for several new vehicles and of continued cost cutting progress.

Required

a. Use the disclosure principle to explain why DaimlerChrysler will reveal this new information.

b. Does the increased disclosure constitute a signal? Explain why or why not. Suggest ways that DaimlerChrysler management could credibly signal its upbeat information to the market.

15. On October 7, 2000, *The Globe and Mail* reported that Air Canada had slashed its 3rd and 4th quarter, 2000 earnings forecasts. The company had revealed this information by phone calls to a select group of analysts. Air Canada's share price dropped by 12% on the day it revealed this information, and by another 3% on the next trading day.

The selective disclosure to certain analysts immediately produced strong negative reactions by angry investors and media, and led to calls for investigation by the OSC and TSE.

This episode was particularly embarrassing to Canadian securities regulators since, a few weeks previously, the SEC had passed Regulation FD in the United States. This was a fair disclosure regulation that prohibits material information from being revealed only to investment analysts. Canadian regulators said at the time that a similar regulation was not needed in Canada because Canadian laws already prohibited such selective disclosure.

Air Canada defended its disclosure policy by claiming that the information underlying the lower earnings forecasts (e.g., higher fuel prices and increased payments to pilots) was already in the public domain. It was attempting to remind analysts that they had not properly incorporated this information into their earnings forecasts.

Subsequently, Air Canada agreed to pay a fine of $1,080,000 in settlement of the charges.

Required

a. Why would Air Canada want to disclose information about lower-than-expected earnings prior to the actual release of its quarterly income statements?

b. Give two reasons why share price fell in the days following the selective disclosure.

c. Explain the impact of selective disclosure practices on the proper operation of the securities market.

d. *The Globe and Mail* also reported that a huge block of Air Canada shares had traded on the day prior to the selective disclosure. What problem of information asymmetry is suggested by this trade? Explain.

e. Canadian securities legislation prohibits use for personal gain of such material information by the analysts to whom it is given. Assuming that the analysts did not use the information for personal gain, do you think that Air Canada should have been charged? Explain why or why not.

16. The article reproduced below, "Sears' monthly figures reveal worrying trends" appeared in *The Globe and Mail*, November 11, 2000. The article reports that Sears Canada Inc. has started to release monthly sales figures. Apparently, the market was disappointed in the first figures released. Sears' share price fell by $1.50 on learning the sales news for October, 2000.

SEARS' MONTHLY FIGURES REVEAL WORRYING TRENDS

Continued slump in big-ticket item sales could signal business slowdown: analysis

---

Sears Canada Inc. has started releasing monthly sales figures in an effort to meet growing demands for "timely" disclosure of information—and the first batch of data pointed to disappointing trends.

Sears sales figures showed a continuing weakening in sales of big-ticket items such as furniture, a trend that could signal a general slowdown in business, retail analysts warned.

The figures also may point to a weaker holiday season than many had anticipated, some observers cautioned.

Last week Canadian Tire Corp. Ltd., another major retailer, reported a disappointing financial performance for its third quarter.

On Thursday night, Sears Canada said its October sales climbed a modest 3.8 per cent to $57.7-million from $55.9-million for the same period last year. More worrying, however, was the 1.7 percent drop in crucial same-store sales at outlets open for at least a year. The figure doesn't take into account added sales flowing from new-store openings.

Sears' catalogue sales fell 4.3 percent, off-mall sales gained 19.7 percent, but same-store sales in those outlets slipped 4.5 percent, the company said. Same-store sales are considered a key measure in retail.

"The sales trend for October was significantly below our expectations," Paul Walters, Sears Canada chairman and chief executive officer, said in a news release. "We continued to experience soft revenues in our big-ticket business for the third consecutive month, impacting growth in both our full-line and off-mall formats."

Investors appeared worried about the latest figures, pushing Sears' share down $1.50 to finish at $23.30 on the Toronto Stock Exchange yesterday. The share price has been falling over the past couple of months in the face of weaker results and delays in opening seven new Eatons stores, which are set to relaunch on Nov. 25.

Sears spokeswoman Christine Hudson said the retailer has decided to release quarterly revenue data as a "proactive position" on disclosing more information to shareholders in light of similar moves among North American companies. "There exists an emerging trend in both Canada and the U.S. towards more complete and timely disclosure," she said.

She noted that major U.S. retailers publish monthly sales figures, although the big chains in Canada up until now only issued quarterly results.

Canadian Tire spokesman Scott Bonikowsky said it is also looking at fuller disclosure "just as every other company in Canada is, because of all the changes that are under way."

In last week's quarterly results, he said, Canadian Tire issued more information than usual, including consolidated balance sheets and retained earnings that give a picture of cash flows.

"We're going to continue to look at a range of options, just to make sure we have excellent disclosure," he said.

Rob Moore a spokesman for Hudson's Bay Co., said it is considering releasing monthly revenues, among other things—but not in the short term. Its next quarterly results will be issued on Dec. 7.

"There's not a lot of benefit to be derived from not meeting the expectations of the investment community, in terms of what you disclose," he said.

Analysts said weaker results from Sears and Canadian Tire—as well as many U.S. retailers—are not very encouraging.

"It looks to me like we're not looking for a very buoyant Christmas," said analyst Keith Howlett at Research Capital Corp, in Toronto. "It's hard to be too optimistic at that moment."

Concerns about disclosure were heightened last month after Air Canada officials told a select group of analysts some critical date in late-night phone calls—and the stock price plummeted the next day.

SOURCE: Used by permission of *The Globe and Mail.*

Required

a. Why would Sears release its October, 2000 sales even though it must have known that the market would interpret them as bad news?

b. Suppose that Sears had not released October sales in a "timely" manner, and that the market only learned of them several months later. Would the decline in share price when the market finally learned of them be more or less than $1.50, other things equal? Explain.

c. According to the article, Hudson's Bay Co. has decided not to disclose monthly sales. As an investor, how would you react to Hudson's Bay's lack of disclosure? Explain.

17. In *The Wall Street Journal*, June 30, 1997, Suzanne McGee describes how institutional investors, such as mutual fund managers, are searching for highly liquid stocks to invest in. If the market for a stock is not liquid, these large investors

will have to pay a higher price to buy in, and receive a lower price if they sell out, simply because the quantities they deal in are large enough to affect share price. These concerns are heightened, according to McGee, because many large investors adopt a strategy of selling out at the first sign of trouble and buying back in at the first sign of recovery.

McGee points out that liquidity has a favourable effect on share price. For example, highly liquid stocks such as Coca-Cola are selling at 46 times earnings, whereas the Standard & Poor's 500-stock index trades at 22 times earnings. In effect, McGee argues, the market pays a premium for liquidity.

Required

a. Given its size and number of shares outstanding, how can a firm increase the liquidity of its shares? Consider both depth and bid-ask spread in your answer.

b. What are some of the costs to a firm of increased disclosure?

Note: See Notes 5, 6, 7, and 8.

18. The following article by John Partridge appeared in *The Globe and Mail*, August 23, 2001. It discusses the decision by Canadian Imperial Bank of Commerce (CIBC) to discontinue separate disclosure of gains on sales of portions of its "bonanza" investment in Global Crossing Ltd.

SILENCE ON GLOBAL GAINS SEEN HELPING CIBC

When Canadian Imperial Bank of Commerce reported its third-quarter results on Monday, it kept its mouth firmly shut about its bonanza investment in Global Crossing Ltd. for the first time since 1999.

Analysts say that CIBC's sudden reticence about the rich gains it has been making on its original $30-million (U.S.) stake in the Bermuda-based telecommunications company could help start a recovery in the bank's lagging stock market valuation—although some of them contend that the change in disclosure is a step backwards.

"We debated whether we should continue to disclose the [gains on] Global Crossing and other large merchant banking investment, and we concluded that we wouldn't going forward," Tom Woods, CIBC's chief financial officer, told analysts during the quarterly conference call.

Despite the new vow of silence, Global Crossing has given CIBC a lot to crow about.

Back in 1999, the value of the bank's initial investment in Global Crossing soared to more than $4.3-billion as the Bermuda company caught the updraft of the telecom and high-tech boom. Its shares skyrocketed to a high of $54.

CIBC made a pretax gain of $583-million (Canadian) by selling some of its Global Crossing stock that year, and another $697-million in 2000. This second sale translated to $397-million after tax, equal to nearly 20 percent of the bank's $2.06-billion profit last year.

And in this year's second quarter, when CIBC put a total of $426-million on the bottom line, Global Crossing gains brought it another tidy $314-million before taxes.

The Bermuda company's shares have plummeted to less than $5 (U.S.) apiece in the telecom and tech meltdown, but CIBC had already hedged much of its remaining stake in the company through forward sales contracts. According to its annual report for 2000, the hedges mature between this year and 2003, and are at prices ranging from a "floor" or low of $20 to $28 a share to a "ceiling' of $46 to $64.

Analysts figure CIBC still has about $1.5-billion (Canadian) in unrealized but locked-in gains on its big score. "It's a huge number," one said.

During Monday's conference call, Mr. Woods didn't explain why the bank has decided to stop breaking out these gains.

But analysts are pretty sure they know the reason. CIBC, they say, figures it has been penalized for disclosing them, and is betting that silence on the topic may be golden for its share price.

That price could unquestionably do with a bit of help. Despite rallying this week, CIBC's stock currently carries the worst "beta" or volatility rating among the five biggest domestic banks, and the lowest price-earnings multiple.

"Everybody would strip out the Global Crossing gains from the numbers," one analyst said, explaining how he and his colleagues have used the information until now.

"They're saying "Well, how is it that when we do well you take it out, but when we do badly you analysts leave it in? We're not getting any credit for it, so we're going to bury it in our earnings, and you guys can do whatever you want to do.'"

CIBC's new approach will instead allow it to use the Global Crossing gains to discreetly smooth and manage—and make more predictable—its overall financial results, without observers being able to divine precisely how this was done. This is a practice already widely followed by other banks in similar situations, and as another analyst put it, CIBC was simply "trying to be too honourable."

Some observers are unhappy that the bank has decided to go quiet on Global Crossing. For instance, in a report issued Tuesday, analyst James Bantis of Credit Suisse First Boston called the move "a step back" after two years in which the bank has "made great strides towards improving the level of financial disclosure and source of earnings."

Mr. Bantis complained that no longer disclosing the Global Crossing gains—which he considers non-recurring— "reduces the quality and transparency of CIBC's earnings over the medium term."

Still, the view is that over time, CIBC's market valuation will benefit because there are few things investors like banks to have more than "earnings visibility," that is, predictable results.

"Historically, CIBC has not been prepared to smooth their earnings, but that changed in this quarter," one of the analysts said. "What it means is that there's going to be much better earnings visibility out of the Commerce, because they've got $1.5-billion in gains left and total flexibility about bringing it in whenever they want…Intuitively, they're going to book them when they most need them."

Another analyst concurred, saying that the new approach will likely be a positive influence on Bay Street's profit forecasts for the bank, and that this, in turn, "will be positive for their valuation."

SOURCE: Used by permission of *The Globe and Mail*

Required

a. Will this reduction of disclosure affect the market's ability to evaluate the persistence of CIBC's earnings? Explain.

b. Section 1520.03(l) of *CICA Handbook* requires separate income statement disclosure of gains and losses that do not have all of the characteristics of extraordinary items but which are not expected to occur frequently over several years or do not typify normal business activities. Do you feel that CIBC's reduction of disclosure violates this requirement? Explain why or why not.

c. How do you think the securities market will react to this reduction of disclosure? Explain.

d. In this case, it seems that private market forces to motivate information production have failed. Should new regulations be put into place to require separate disclosure of gains and losses on sales of this nature? Explain why or why not.

Notes

1. This is a purely economic definition. Note that it is in terms of *total* information production. The benefits and costs of information production are aggregated across all members of society. The reason why economists define the socially right amount of information this way derives from a desire to attain the largest possible information "pie" in the economy (equating marginal total benefits with marginal total costs does this). Also of concern, however is the *distribution* of total information across investors. Economists may not feel that they have a comparative advantage in advising how the pie should be carved up. To illustrate, hold total information production constant at a level that satisfies the def-

inition and consider two scenarios. In the first, 80% of the benefits of information production go to the wealthiest 10% of investors. In the second, the benefits are distributed equally across all investors. Most people would not feel that the two scenarios were equivalent. Thus, issues of distribution quickly get caught up in ethical and political debate—they are no longer strictly economic.

In this chapter, we are primarily concerned about aggregate information production. In Chapter 13, we examine the role of accounting standard setting bodies in promoting distribution of information in a manner that is fair to managers and investors.

2.   The dividing line between proprietary and nonproprietary information is somewhat ambiguous. For example, as we saw in our review of Darrough and Stoughton (Section 9.3), the release of information that may seem nonproprietary (such as a financial forecast) could affect future cash flows if it attracts entry to the industry. Nevertheless, the distinction is a useful one. For further discussion of the interrelationships between proprietary and nonproprietary information see Dye (1986).

3.   See, for example, L. DeAngelo (1981).

4.   It would be necessary to top up the manager's contract with, say, a fixed salary to meet the manager's reservation utility.

5.   By market liquidity we mean the ability of investors to quickly buy and sell large quantities of securities at the market price with reasonable transactions costs. Liquidity is a composite of market **depth**—the number of shares that investors are willing to buy or sell at any given price—and the **bid-ask spread**—the contemporaneous difference between buying price and selling price of a share. Information asymmetry is one of the factors affecting the spread. The more investors are wary of buying a lemon, the greater the asymmetry—the market protects itself from asymmetry by increasing the spread. Information asymmetry also reduces depth, by causing investors to leave the market.

6.   For these effects on cost of capital to operate, the market must perceive the information released to be credible. Devices to attain credibility include lawsuits, audits, and stock exchange or country of listing. Hiring a higher quality auditor implies a commitment to greater information release. Alternatively, or in addition, a manager could commit to a higher level of information production by moving the firm to an exchange, possibly in a different country, with higher information standards.

7.   Lee, Mucklow, and Ready (1993) find that a share's spread increases when its trading volume is unusually high. They suggest that the market interprets the high volume as due to insiders or other traders with superior information trading on the basis of this information. Without knowing what this information is, the market becomes more uncertain about the share's future return prospects, and increases the spread to protect itself.

8. The disclosure principle is attributed to Grossman (1981) and Milgrom (1981).

9. For further discussion see Healy and Palepu (1993). Data on Patten Corp. are from Harvard Business School case #9-188-027.

10. Another cost arises if we recognize more than one type of investor. Large institutional investors will have greater ability and resources to analyze information than ordinary investors. Ordinary investors may feel that this disadvantage will increase as more firm information is released, and they may reduce their demand for the firm's shares at the same time that demand from institutional investors is increasing. (As an example, consider the practice of many firms of giving "guidance" to analysts, or releasing information in conference calls with a select group of analysts and large institutions. The SEC has recently prohibited this practice, on the grounds that it puts ordinary investors at a disadvantage—see problem 13.) If ordinary investors leave the market, this puts a brake on the increase in market liquidity, which will cause the firm to stop short of full information release.

11. Indeed, this complexity is recognized by standard setters. Thus SFAC 1.23 of the FASB (see Section 3.8) states "…the benefits from financial information are usually difficult or impossible to measure objectively, and the costs often are; different persons will honestly disagree about whether the benefits of information justify its costs."

12. This assumes that the external reporting of internal information does not incur substantial proprietary costs. Indeed, this standard could have economic consequences, since it is possible that the firm may change its internal organization to reduce proprietary costs.

13. Section 1701 of the *CICA Handbook* calls this the "management approach."

13

Standard Setting: Political Issues

13.1 Overview

In Chapter 12 we saw that, from the perspective of economic theory, the question of the extent of regulation of accounting and reporting standards is unsettled. While we can suggest a number of contractual and market-based incentives for private information production, we simply do not know whether increased market failures that would follow from deregulation of firms' information production decisions would be more or less costly to society than the various costs of the standard setting process. It does appear, however, that the problem of market failure is quite fundamental. Information asymmetry (and the resulting problems of moral hazard and adverse selection), which creates the demand for information production by firms, also creates a demand for regulation of that information production. This is because of the problem of unanimity—the amount of information that firms would privately produce need not, and in general will not, equal the amount that investors want. As a result, investors may push for regulation to remedy the perceived deficiency.

This suggests that standard setting is fundamentally as much a political process as an economic one. Such a viewpoint is consistent with the concept of constituencies of accounting, with the political cost hypothesis of positive accounting theory in Section 8.7.2, and with the game theoretic and agency theoretic views of constituency conflict in Chapter 9. It seems natural to expect that the various accounting constituencies would appeal to the political process when their conflicting interests cannot be resolved by contractual or market forces.

Our first objective in this chapter is to review two theories of regulation. The first, the **public interest theory**, takes the view that regulation should maximize social welfare. This was the viewpoint of Chapter 12. The second, the **interest**

group theory of regulation, suggests that individuals form coalitions, or constituencies, to protect and promote their interests by lobbying the government. These coalitions are viewed as in conflict with each other, to obtain their share of benefits from regulation.

Our second objective is to examine the *processes* of standard setting. Besides being of interest in their own right, we will learn that these processes are largely consistent with the interest group theory of regulation.

Our third objective is to consider the criteria that standard setters need to consider if their standards are to be acceptable. While decision usefulness and reduction of information asymmetry are necessary for any standard, we shall see that much more is needed. Specifically, the standard must be acceptable to its various constituencies. This requires a careful attention to due process by the standard setter.

13.2   *Two Theories of Regulation*

13.2.1 *THE PUBLIC INTEREST THEORY*

The public interest theory of regulation was implicit in our examination of standard setting in Chapter 12. This theory suggests that regulation is the result of a public demand for correction of market failures. In this theory, the central authority, also called the regulatory body or the regulator, is assumed to have the best interests of society at heart. It does its best to regulate so as to maximize social welfare. Consequently, regulation is thought of as a tradeoff between the costs of regulation and its social benefits in the form of improved operation of markets. Chapter 12 addressed these various costs and benefits.

While this view represents an ideal of how regulation should be carried out, there are problems with its implementation. It can be argued, from the standpoint of how regulation works in practice, that the theory is superficial and perhaps naive. Our discussion here is based on Stigler (1971), Posner (1974), and Peltzman (1976).

One problem with the public interest theory is the very complex task of deciding on the right amount of regulation. This is particularly true for a complex commodity like information where, as Chapter 12 makes clear, it is effectively impossible to please everyone. Then, the door is left open for other theories of how the amount of regulation is determined.

An even more serious problem, however, lies in the motivation of the regulatory body. Given the complex nature of its task, it is difficult for a legislature to monitor the operations of the regulator. In effect, the ability of the legislature to force the regulatory body to act in the public interest is weak, because of the complex nature of regulation and the fact that costly and lengthy hearings would be needed for the legislature to know whether the regulator is doing a good job. This opens up the possibility that the regulatory agency will operate on its own behalf rather than on behalf of the public. The situation here is reminiscent of the manager in our agency theory discussion of Example 9.2, who was motivated to shirk because his or her action was unobservable to the owner. Thus, the public interest theory represents a sort of first-best approach to regulation. In practice, the first-best solution may not be attainable, because of problems of implementation. This leads directly to another theory.

13.2.2 THE INTEREST GROUP THEORY

The interest group theory of regulation takes the view that an industry operates in the presence of a number of interest groups (or constituencies, as we have used the term in earlier chapters). Consider any manufacturing industry as an example. The firms in the industry compose an obvious interest group, as do the firms' customers. Another interest group would be environmentalists, who would be concerned about the industry's social responsibility. These various interest groups will lobby the legislature for various amounts and types of regulation. For example, the industry itself may demand regulation to protect it against foreign price competition or against encroachments on its operations by related industries. Customers may form groups to lobby for quality standards or price controls. Environmentalists may lobby for emission control regulations and greater disclosure of environmental performance. These various constituencies can be thought of as demanders of regulation. Note that the nature and extent of the regulation they demand will differ across constituencies.

The political authority, or legislature, can also be thought of as an interest group, which has the power to supply regulation. The interests of the political authority lie in retaining power. Consequently, it will supply regulation to those constituencies that it believes will be most effective and useful in helping it retain power. The regulatory body is then in the middle. It is the vehicle whereby regulation is supplied. It attempts to maximize its own welfare while at the same time balancing the demands of the various constituencies.

In effect, the interest group theory of regulation regards regulation as a commodity for which there is a demand and a supply. The commodity will be allocated to those constituencies that are most politically effective in convincing the legislature to grant them regulatory favours.

While it may seem rather cynical, the interest group theory may well be a better predictor of how regulation really works than the public interest theory. Before considering the extent to which the theory fits the regulation of the information industry, we will examine the standard setting process.

13.3   *Standard Setting in Canada and the United States*

13.3.1 *THE CANADIAN INSTITUTE OF CHARTERED ACCOUNTANTS (CICA)*

Accounting Standards Committee

The *CICA Handbook* contains standards for financial accounting and for auditing, as laid down by the Accounting Standards Board (AcSB) and the Auditing Standards Board (AuSB) respectively of the Canadian Institute of Chartered Accountants. The *CICA Handbook* is the major source of accounting and auditing standards in Canada. Its authority is enhanced because it has a special legal status. For example, the Canada Business Corporations Act, Regulation 44, states:

> *The financial statements referred to in paragraph 155(1)(a) of the Act shall, except as otherwise provided by this Part, be prepared in accordance with the standards, as they exist from time to time, of the Canadian Institute of Chartered Accountants set out in the* CICA Handbook.

The AcSB is authorized by the Board of Governors of the Canadian Institute of Chartered Accountants to publish reports on its own responsibility. The CICA Board of Governors has also authorized the AuSB to publish reports on its own responsibility. There is also a third CICA standard setting body, the Public Sector Accounting and Auditing Committee (PSAAC).

Process of Standard Setting   The following points should be noted about the process of setting standards for the CICA Handbook:

- The AcSB publishes accounting standards "on its own authority." Presumably, this is to give it a measure of independence from the CICA itself and reduce the possibility of interference in its deliberations.

- New standards require the approval of at least two-thirds of the members of the Board. This is an example of **super-majority voting**, which decreases the possibility of approval of a standard that is only marginally acceptable to the Board. This will also tend to produce a process of compromise in the creation of a new standard. Dissenting members will be in a stronger position than they would be if only a simple majority was required and thus would be less likely to feel that their views and concerns had been ignored.

- Two-thirds or more of the Board's members must be members of the CICA. This may water down the two-thirds voting requirement—to the extent that CICA members who "think alike" may gang up on non-CICA members. However, Board members will be selected to represent both official languages and also major geographical regions. In addition, they should comprise a broad range of occupational backgrounds and experience. It is noteworthy that provision is made for the appointment of five members from organizations representing financial analysts, business executives, academics, and other professional accounting organizations. Thus, while the CICA retains majority representation on the Board, some attempt has been made to broaden representation, both from different areas of the CICA and from other accounting constituencies.

- While not mentioned explicitly in the terms of reference, it should be noted that exposure drafts enable interested parties to react to a proposed standard before it is finalized. It is possible that significant change will be made in a new standard before it is finalized, depending on constituent reaction.

- Membership on the AcSB is voluntary, that is, with the exception of the Chairperson, these are not full-time, salaried positions. In effect, the organizations that employ the Board members bear the costs. Whether this is a desirable state of affairs is difficult to say. An alternative scenario might be one in which Board members were full-time, paid employees (like FASB members in the United States). Of course, this would require that considerably more money be raised to support the Board's activities. To the extent that this was raised from a variety of different constituencies, this would broaden the base of financial support for the standard setting process. However, we saw in Chapter 12 that the direct costs of setting and administering standards were only a part, and probably a small part, of the overall costs of standard setting. Nevertheless, such an alternative scenario might reduce any possible concerns arising from the fact that, at present, the organizations that employ the Board members, mainly professional accounting firms, may "call the tune." Yet another possibility would be to discontinue the AcSB, and adopt GAAP as laid down by the FASB (Section 13.3.3) and/or the International Accounting Standards Board (Section 13.4). The CICA, however, has rejected these alternatives, at least for the time being.

- The *CICA Handbook* says little about how a particular topic is placed on the agenda of the AcSB. Presumably, Board members and full-time Institute staff are close enough to public practice to know what topics require attention. Also, the AcSB is advised by the Standards Advisory Board. This is a body with widely based membership set up to provide an outside perspective on priorities for possible new standards.

- It should be apparent that the issuance of a new standard will require considerable time. First, background research is needed. Then, a project proposal must be prepared and approved, followed by a statement of principles. The exposure draft stage will also take considerable time. It seems that the procedures for due process in establishing a new standard carry a time penalty. This reduces the ability of the Board to respond to new issues as they arise. In effect, the Board may be able to react to problems only after they have arisen.

However, the Board can also issue **Guidelines**. These are interpretations of existing *CICA Handbook* recommendations or opinions on other matters for which a *CICA Handbook* provision does not exist. While Guidelines do not have the authority of *CICA Handbook* recommendations, they do have the potential to enable a relatively quick reaction when a need arises.

- Also, the **Emerging Issues Committee (EIC)** was established in 1988 by the AcSB to provide a forum for timely review of emerging accounting issues that are likely to receive divergent or unsatisfactory treatment in practice in the absence of some guidance. The EIC has 14 voting members, including 10 from public practice and four from industry, two of which are nominated by the Financial Executives Institute. Its pronouncements require a consensus, defined as the existence of no more than two dissenting members of those present at the meeting. The EIC represents a major step towards improving the timeliness of the standard setting process.

Our main observation from this discussion is that the various steps to create a new standard suggest that the process is quite "political." In other words, many of the various constituencies of accounting are invited to take part, either as part of the process leading to insertion of an item into the Board agenda, as members of the Board itself, or as respondents to exposure drafts. If the process was strictly economic, as was implicit in our discussion in Chapter 12, such broad-based representation would not be necessary.

13.3.2 THE ONTARIO SECURITIES COMMISSION (OSC)

Here, we examine the securities commission of Ontario. The Ontario Securities Commission (OSC) administers securities legislation in Ontario, including regulation of the largest stock exchange in the country (the Toronto Stock Exchange) and is one of the most active securities commissions. Hence, it is a logical candidate for evaluation.

Role and Authority of the OSC

The OSC is composed of from 9 to 14 members, appointed by the Ontario Lieutenant Governor in Council for terms not exceeding five years. Its mandate is to protect investors from unfair, improper, and fraudulent practices, to foster fair and efficient capital markets, and to maintain public confidence in their integrity.

Its authority derives from the Securities Act of Ontario. According to this Act, the OSC shall lay down:

- requirements for the timely, accurate, and efficient disclosure of information;

- restrictions on fraudulent and unfair market practices and procedures; and

- requirements for the maintenance of high standards of fitness and business conduct to ensure honest and responsible conduct by market participants.

Thus, the role of the OSC is to regulate securities trading in Ontario, including both the issuers of the securities themselves and the exchanges on which they are traded.

OSC's Relation to the CICA Handbook

According to the *Securities Act*, issuers of securities under the OSC's jurisdiction must file financial statements in accordance with GAAP. OSC National Policy Statement 27 (1992) states that GAAP "has the meaning ascribed to this term by the CICA Handbook."

Thus, the OSC effectively delegates financial statement accounting standards to the AcSB. However, the OSC issues standards itself where these do not directly affect the financial statements. For example, MD&A (Section 4.8.2) and requirements for disclosure of executive compensation (Section 10.7) are OSC standards.

13.3.3 THE FINANCIAL ACCOUNTING STANDARDS BOARD (FASB)

Establishment and Purpose of the FASB

The Financial Accounting Standards Board (FASB) in the United States was established in 1973. Its purpose is to establish and improve standards of financial accounting and reporting for the guidance and education of the public in the United States. To accomplish this, the FASB attempts to improve the usefulness of financial reporting by focusing on consistency and comparability, by updating standards (if necessary) for changes in the business and economic environment, and by improving the public understanding of the nature and purpose of information contained in financial reports.

In conducting its activities, the FASB is guided by certain perceptions. These include: objectivity in decision-making, consideration of the views of its constituents, promulgation of standards only when the expected benefits exceed the expected costs, implementation of changes in a manner that minimizes disruption to existing practice, and review and (if necessary) amendment of past decisions. It should be noted that, unlike the structure in Canada, the FASB is a body distinct from the American Institute of Certified Public Accountants (AICPA). While the AICPA is one of the sponsoring bodies and endorses FASB standards, it will be clear from the following that many other bodies are also involved in sponsoring the FASB.

Structure of the FASB

The FASB is the operational arm of a three-part organizational structure for financial accounting standard setting; the other two parts are the Financial Accounting Foundation (FAF) and the Financial Accounting Standards Advisory Council (FASAC).

The FAF consists of 16 trustees, of which 13 are elected from sponsoring organizations. These include four from practice (AICPA), one financial analyst, two from management, one academic, and five from various other sponsors. Of the remaining trustees, two are elected by the above trustees. One of these must be from the commercial banking industry and one from the business community in general. The sixteenth trustee is the senior elected AICPA official.

The FAF raises funds for all three groups in the structure, appoints FASB board members, reviews FASB performance, and appoints FASAC members.

The FASAC consists of a minimum of 20 (and usually 35 to 40) members appointed by the FAF. Although the breakdown of membership by profession is not specified as it is for the FAF, the membership should consist of individuals from diversified interests. FASAC acts as the liaison between FASB and the business and economic communities. It advises on project priorities and on the suitability of the FASB's preliminary positions on issues.

The FASB consists of seven board members, appointed by the FAF for a maximum of two five-year terms. Although background is taken into account when selecting board members, it is considered secondary to such qualifications as accounting knowledge, integrity, discipline, and judicial temperament. A majority of five of the seven members in favour is required to pass a new standard.

FASB board members are expected to be independent. They must sever all ties with previous employers, declare conflict of interest if necessary, and not accept fees or honoraria from any institution other than the FASB.

Standard Setting Process of the FASB

In setting and updating accounting and reporting standards, the FASB places heavy emphasis on **due process**. The process usually encompasses the following stages:

- **Preliminary evaluation of problems related to accounting and reporting standards**   This evaluation may be done by FASAC, the Emerging Issues Task Force (discussed below), FASB research staff, professional groups, or the SEC. Regardless of who identifies the problem, it is then brought to the attention of FASAC, which advises FASB on its importance and urgency.

- **Admission to the agenda of FASB**   To be admitted to the FASB agenda, an issue must be evaluated by FASAC and FASB to determine whether it meets criteria for admission. Specifically, the issue must be sufficiently significant, alternative solutions must be sufficiently different to be controversial, and there must be a high likelihood that the

FASB can resolve the issue to the satisfaction of the business and economic communities. If the problem is not immediately admitted to the agenda, it may still be assigned to FASB research staff for further study.

- **Early deliberations** This stage consists of more careful examination of the issue by the FASB. In addition to discussions by the FASB board members, early deliberations may involve creation of a special task force or advisory council to formalize contact with constituencies, or even (for major issues) conducting public hearings.

- **Tentative resolution** This involves a more formal description of the board members' views and of any consensus that may have developed. Once this consensus has been achieved, FASB publishes documentation of its proposed solution (an exposure draft, for example) to focus public interest on the issue.

- **Further deliberations** Once responses to an exposure draft are received, FASB deliberates further to analyze these responses. If the responses are sufficiently contradictory and controversial, this stage may also involve public hearings. Depending on the amount of response and the agreement between responses, there are three possibilities for this stage:
  - The project is terminated (if it is determined to be insignificant or unresolvable)
  - Another exposure draft is issued
  - A final pronouncement is issued

- **Final resolution** This stage consists of the issuance of a Final Pronouncement. The Final Pronouncement may be a Statement of Financial Accounting Standards, an Interpretation Statement, or a Technical Bulletin, depending on how significant the problem has finally been determined to be.

- **Subsequent review** After a Final Pronouncement has been issued, FASB periodically reviews its decision to determine whether further supplementation is needed.

13.3.4 THE SECURITIES AND EXCHANGE COMMISSION (SEC)

The SEC was founded in the United States in 1934, to regulate trading in the securities of firms whose securities are traded in more than one state and that meet certain size tests. As part of its mandate, the SEC has the responsibility to ensure that investors are supplied with adequate information. Consequently, like the OSC, it has the authority to issue accounting standards for firms under its jurisdiction. However, in ASR 150, the SEC delegated this responsibility to the FASB.

This is not to say that the SEC does not intervene in standard setting from time to time. For example, the SEC overrode SFAS 19, which required oil and gas companies to use successful-efforts accounting for exploration costs (recall our discussion in Section 8.5). This was done by means of ASR 253 (1978), which allowed use of either full-cost or successful-efforts accounting, and also proposed RRA, initially as supplementary information. As a result of this intervention, the FASB issued SFAS 25 in 1978, which amended SFAS 19 to allow both cost methods.

Nevertheless, it can be argued that instances such as these are "the exceptions that prove the rule," and that it is correct to say the SEC effectively delegates standard setting authority to the FASB.

13.4　*The International Accounting Standards Board (IASB)*

13.4.1　*ESTABLISHMENT AND OBJECTIVES OF THE IASB*

The International Accounting Standards Committee, (IASC)[1] the parent body of the **International Accounting Standards Board (IASB)**, was established in 1973 by agreement between accountancy bodies in Australia, Canada, France, Germany, Japan, Mexico, the Netherlands, the United Kingdom and Ireland, and the United States.

In 2001, the IASC reorganized, adopting a structure somewhat similar to that of the FASB in the United States. The objectives of the reorganized IASC are:

- to develop, in the public interest, a single set of high quality, understandable, and enforceable global accounting standards that require high quality, transparent, and comparable information in financial statements and other reporting to help participants in the world's capital markets and other users to make economic decisions;

- to promote the use and rigorous application of those standards; and

- to bring about convergence of national accounting standards and International Accounting Standards with high quality solutions.

The IASC is governed by a Board of 19 individuals, with geographic representation from North America, Europe, and Asia/Pacific.

The establishment of the IASC was part of the increased globalization and integration of economic activity that has taken place in recent years. In particular, this globalization includes securities markets, with many corporations listed on stock exchanges in two or more countries. Consequently, preparers of annual reports of large, multinational corporations are finding it necessary to prepare these reports to satisfy the securities legislation of more than one jurisdiction. For example, foreign firms that wish to trade their securities in the United States or Canada must satisfy the requirements of securities regulators in those countries. These include filing annual financial statements either in accordance with local GAAP or, if the statements are prepared under GAAP of some other jurisdiction, with a reconciliation of net income and balance sheet line items with local GAAP.

To the extent that international accounting standards become acceptable to securities regulators as a substitute for local GAAP, costs of multiple exchange listings will fall. This should lower firms' costs of capital as they are better able to tap more liquid sources of financing.

13.4.2 STRUCTURE OF THE IASB

The IASC trustees appoint the 14 members of the IASB, 12 of which are full-time positions. Funding is supplied by the IASC. There are no geographic requirements for Board members. However, different constituencies are represented. At least five members must have an auditing background, three a management background, and one academic. As is the case with the AcSB and FASB, there is supermajority voting for new standards (8 of 14).

13.4.3 AUTHORITY OF THE IASB

Unlike the AcSB and FASB, compliance with IASB standards is not mandatory. Compliance is up to the individual countries and firms involved. While legislation in many countries does require firms to conform to IASB standards, other countries have not gone this far. The European Union, for example, allows listed European firms it use IASB standards, their own national standards, or U.S. GAAP; although draft legislation is presently before the European Parliament which would require the use of IASB standards.

The International Organization of Securities Commissions (IOSCO) represents the world's securities regulators, including Canadian regulators and the SEC in the United States. It recommends to its members that they use IASB standards, although individual member countries may require reconciliation of IASB standards with their own GAAP.

Perhaps the main hurdle faced by the IASB is securing acceptance of its standards, without reconciliation, by the SEC. As mentioned, the SEC currently requires reconciliation with FASB standards if U.S.-listed firms' financial statements are prepared under IASB standards. At present, the SEC is deliberating whether to relax this requirement.

The SEC's willingness to accept IASB standards depends, of course, on the quality of those standards and their consistency with those of the FASB. The extent of consistency varies. For example, IAS 22 requires the purchase method of accounting for business combinations, consistent with SFAS 141. However, amortization of consolidated goodwill arising from acquisitions is required, unlike

SFAS 142 (see Section 7.5.2). IAS 39 requires that almost all derivative financial instruments be fair-valued, consistent in this regard with SFAS 133 (Section 7.4.3). Financial assets with a fixed maturity date and intended to be held to maturity are also to be fair-valued. From a measurement perspective, this latter requirement goes beyond SFAS 115 (Section 7.4.2), which retains historical cost accounting for such securities. Also unlike SFAS 115, IASB standards do not recognize Other Comprehensive Income (Section 7.4.2). Instead, unrealized gains and losses from fair valuing financial assets are included in a separate section of shareholders' equity.

Presumably, greater consistency will be needed before the SEC is willing to accept IASB GAAP without reconciliation. In this regard, it should be noted that the JWG Draft Standard (Section 7.4.5), which would require fair value accounting for all financial instruments, is a joint project of the IASB, FASB, AcSB, and several other standard-setting bodies. To the extent the draft standard is implemented, this will represent a major increase in international accounting standard consistency.

Another concern of the SEC is the *enforcement* of accounting standards. Lack of enforcement increases the exposure of the market to adverse selection and moral hazard problems, regardless of the quality of the underlying GAAP. In this regard, the IASB is in a different situation than the FASB. While IOSCO endorses the use of IASB standards, it does not have the SEC's enforcement authority. Enforcement is up to the authorities in the respective jurisdictions that adopt IASB standards. Even if IASB GAAP becomes acceptable, the SEC would have to be assured that enforcement is adequate before removing its requirement for reconciliation. Possibly, large international accounting firms could provide this assurance.

It is interesting to consider what might happen if the SEC did accept financial statements prepared under IASB standards. Specifically, suppose that the SEC allowed firms under its jurisdiction to report, without reconciliation, using either FASB or IASB standards. This proposal, which would introduce a measure of competition to the standard setting process, was discussed by Dye and Sunder (2001). One possible effect, they suggest, is a "race to the bottom," whereby each standard setter lowers its standards so as to attract firms and their managers away from the other. As a result, the potential for bad earnings management is increased. This outcome is analogous to the Nash equilibrium outcome of the game discussed in Example 9.1.

However, as Dye and Sunder discuss, there are forces to control such a tendency. For example, there would be investor reaction to a firm that chooses low quality accounting standards. As pointed out in Section 12.3.3, market forces reward managers who release full and timely information. Furthermore, a race to the bottom is inconsistent with the objectives of the IASC, which include high quality accounting standards and efforts to promote their convergence.

Indeed, a benefit of competition in standard setting derives from the impossibility of calculating the socially correct extent of regulation as concluded in Chapter 12. A monopolistic standard setter may attempt to maximize its influence by imposing more and more standards, as predicted by the interest group theory of regulation. As a result, the extent of regulation may go beyond its socially optimal level. Competition among standard setters would help to control this tendency since firms that did not like one set of standards could simply adopt the other, thereby causing the over-zealous standard setter to "lose customers." In addition, firms could signal their future potential by means of the set of standards they adopt.

Another result of competition is to reduce "network externalities." That is, investors would bear costs of having to learn more than one set of accounting standards. Lack of comparability does impose costs. However, Dye and Sunder suggest that these costs would be relatively low. For example, analysts and other experts could specialize in interpreting a particular set of standards. The results of their analyses would quickly be incorporated into share market values, thereby price-protecting ordinary investors. Indeed, as mentioned, the very fact that a firm chooses a particular set of accounting standards has information content.

While the question of competition between standard setters is complex, these arguments suggest that greater acceptance by national standard setters of IASB standards may have social benefits.

13.5 Relationship to Theories of Regulation

Our description of the standard setting process shows that it is characterized by due process. For example, in Canada, the United States, and internationally, major constituencies with an interest in financial reporting are represented on the standard-setting bodies. Also, there are provisions for public hearings, exposure drafts, and, generally, for openness, as well as requirements for super-majority votes in favour before new standards are issued.

This due process characteristic is consistent with conflict-based theories of constituency interaction. The sources of market failure in the production of information discussed in Chapter 12 imply that market forces cannot always be relied upon to generate the "right" accounting standards and procedures. Yet, the complexities arising from the diverse information needs and interests of investors and managers make it effectively impossible for standard setters to calculate the "right" accounting standards either. We simply do not know how to calculate the best tradeoff between the conflicting uses of information by investors and managers that is required by the public interest theory of regulation. This is why the choice of accounting standards is better regarded as a conflict between constituencies than as a process of calculation. The AcSB, the FASB, and the IASB are players in a complex game where affected constituencies choose strategies of lobbying for or against a proposed new standard.

If the players of the game are to accept the outcome (that is, the issuance or non-issuance of a new standard and, if issued, its specific reporting requirements) they must feel that the process was fair, and that their strategy at least had a chance of working. In terms of the game theoretic Example 9.1, the players must know the strategies available to the other parties. The willingness of players to accept a new standard is enhanced if they feel that their views were heard. This explains the attention to due process as a way of moderating the inherent constituency conflict in standard setting.

These considerations suggest that the interest group theory of regulation may be a better predictor of new standards than the public interest theory, since the interest group theory formally recognizes the existence of conflicting constituencies. To pursue this question further, we next consider some of the conflict leading up to a specific FASB standard.

13.6   *Conflict and Compromise*

13.6.1 *AN EXAMPLE OF CONSTITUENCY CONFLICT*

We described SFAS 115, "Accounting for Certain Investments in Debt and Equity Securities," in Section 7.4.2. However, we did not consider the process that led up to SFAS 115. Here, we consider aspects of this process, which provide an interesting and important example of the problems of developing a new standard. Exhibit 13.1 reproduces an article by Robin Goldwyn Blumenthal that appeared in *The Wall Street Journal*, September 11, 1992, following the release of an exposure draft by the FASB. The exposure draft specified that at least some securities held by firms be valued at fair value. Recall that this implies market value if reliably available. Otherwise, fair value can be determined by present value, use of models, or other appropriate techniques. The problems of gains trading, and of volatility of reported net income under the new proposed standard, were considered in Section 7.4.2. Here, our main interest is in the constituency conflicts leading up to SFAS 115.

EXHIBIT 13.1 FASB Moves Closer to Forcing Banks to Value Securities Near Market Prices

NEW YORK—The Financial Accounting Standards Board moved a step closer to implementing controversial rules that would require banks to value many of their securities closer to market prices.

In issuing its exposure draft, the FASB formally proposed rules on accounting for securities held as investments; the proposal is similar to a compromise approach outlined in July. Although there appears to be solid support for the proposal by six of the seven members on FASB's board, there is likely to be continuing strong opposition to the proposal during the comment period by banks, which in the past year have bought record amounts of securities.

"It's a huge change in accounting," said

Donna Fisher, manager of accounting policy at the American Bankers Association. In effect, the proposal would make it more difficult for banks to classify securities as long-term investments, and thus account for them at original cost rather than market value. Although the proposal would affect any company that invests in marketable equity securities and debt securities, it would have the greatest effect on financial institutions such as banks, whose investments in those securities represent about 30% of their total assets, Ms. Fisher said.

GAINS TRADING

The proposal, which is intended to standardize accounting methods on investments in securities for various industries, also attempts to address a practice by banks called gains trading, in which securities that have appreciated in value are sold to recognize gains while those that have fallen in value are held as long-term investments and thus recorded at original cost.

Under existing accounting rules, "there was a perception that people were inappropriately reporting something at cost when in fact they were not holding on to [the securities] for the long term," said Robert C. Wilkins, an FASB project manager.

The FASB, the chief rule-making body for accountants that is based in Norwalk, Conn., has been under pressure for several years from the Securities and Exchange Commission to hold investment securities at more up-to-date values, known as marking to market. SEC Chairman Richard Breeden began voicing his support for marking to market all investment securities two years ago.

Although the FASB had at one point considered eliminating the current three categories of investment securities and forcing companies to mark all of them to

market, it abandoned that approach because it couldn't figure out how to mark related liabilities to market, Mr. Wilkins said. In July, the FASB also eased its approach to declines in value of debt securities held as "available for sale." These would be booked to shareholders' equity on the balance sheet, rather than reducing profits on the income statement.

PLUSES AND MINUSES

Walter Schuetze, the SEC's chief accountant, said the proposal had pluses and minuses. "The plus is that more marketable securities will be accounted for at market in the balance sheet," Mr. Schuetze said. However, he pointed out that under this proposal, there is room for "so-called psychoanalytic accounting," which allows management to classify three different ways the same securities at the time they are purchased.

Mr. Schuetze also said the proposal didn't adequately address gains trading, and that it failed to give enough guidance on when to write down stocks and bonds when the decline in market price is deemed to be "other than temporary."

Banking representatives, however, had other views on the proposal. "They don't come out and say you must mark securities to market but the net effect we think will be very close," said Ms. Fisher of the American Bankers Association. She said that if the proposal is adopted, banks would need to try to reduce volatility in their capital accounts, possibly by investing in shorter-term securities.

Bankers say that for the most part they purchase intermediate-term securities with a maturity of two to five years. "Most of our securities are short term," said William J. Rossman, chief executive officer of Mid-State Bank in Altoona, Pa., and president of Robert Morris Associates, a trade group of commercial lenders. "You're not going to find too many banks taking short-term funds and investing in 30-year bonds."

The proposed rules must now go through a public comment period, in which the FASB undoubtedly will be hearing from opponents. The exposure draft could take effect as early as 1994 if it is approved.

Treasury Undersecretary Jerome Powell, in remarks to a mortgage bankers group, warned that market value accounting would make bank earnings very volatile and add to the credit crunch.

Diane Casey of the Independent Bankers Association of America, a group of 6,000 community banks, said the fight to soften the proposed rule is "far from over." The association contends that the proposal will hurt community banks and discourage many of them from purchasing local school district and sewer authority bonds, many of which aren't actively traded.

Before considering constituency conflicts, consider the effects of full marking-to-market, which Exhibit 13.1 mentions the FASB had considered at one point. Full marking-to-market would not only involve fair valuation of all of a firm's financial instruments, both assets and liabilities, but also involve including the unrealized gains and losses in reported net income, with consequent volatility. (This volatility would be reduced to the extent that it was hedged.) Note also that full marking-to-market would eliminate the ability of firms to engage in gains trading. If securities were valued at market, with gains and losses included in income as they occurred, management would not control the timing of these gains and losses. Also, there would be no effect on the bottom line upon sale, so that gains trading would be eliminated.

As might be expected, full marking-to-market would be objected to by banks' managers, since banks hold large amounts of financial assets and liabilities. Banks would see both the volatility of their earnings increase (to the extent this was not hedged) and their ability to engage in earnings management severely reduced. Exhibit 13.1 describes the objections of the American Bankers Association, Robert Morris Associates, and the Independent Bankers Association of America, all representing management.

In addition, the U.S. Treasury was concerned about economic consequences. It felt that marking-to-market would affect banks' operating and financial strategies, to the point where they would be unwilling to lend long-term, which would affect the availability of credit in the economy. This concern arises because as interest rates vary so does the market value of fixed-term securities. Since the longer the term the greater the market value variation in response to a given change in interest rates, banks would cut down on long-term lending in order to reduce volatility of earnings. Consequently, the Treasury strongly opposed the proposed standard.

Also, the original proposal for full marking-to-market accounting faced technical difficulties. Certain financial liabilities, such as banks' deposit liabilities, were difficult to value, because of core deposit intangibles. It appears that models to provide reliable values in the face of these difficulties were not available.

As suggested in the case of ESOs, (Section 8.3), if a standard has technical difficulties, it can be even more strongly attacked by its opponents. Here, inability to value core deposit intangibles was a major technical difficulty. To make matters worse, if financial liabilities were excused from the standard, then they could not hedge gains or losses on financial assets, thereby making concerns about volatility even greater.

However, Exhibit 13.1 also describes the support of another powerful constituency, the SEC, for full marking-to-market. This support is not hard to understand. As an agency whose role is to protect investors and encourage the proper operation of securities markets, the SEC would be expected to favour the conveying of fair values to investors. Also, the SEC favoured the recording of these fair values in the accounts (as opposed to footnote presentation), since, with such recording, gains trading would be eliminated.

Obviously, the FASB was in a difficult position as it tried to produce a standard that would be generally acceptable. Nevertheless, SFAS 115 passed in 1993, along the lines discussed in Section 7.4.2. The standard took effect for fiscal years beginning after December 15, 1993.

It is interesting to note again some of the compromises that were made in the standard, relative to the original goal of full mark-to-market accounting. First, liabilities are excluded, due to measurement difficulties. Second, to reduce volatility, some debt securities continue to be valued at cost under SFAS 115. Recall that these are securities for which the firm "has the positive intent and ability" to hold them to maturity. Marking-to-market is required for trading securities and for available-for-sale-securities. Third, to further reduce volatility, unrealized gains and losses on available-for-sale securities are excluded from reported net income and reported in other comprehensive income.

Presumably, the above compromises were made to reduce the objections of management. However, as a result, gains trading is not eliminated, and may even be encouraged since firms could realize gains merely by transferring securities from held-to-maturity to trading. However, by placing severe constraints on the ability both to classify securities as held-to-maturity in the first place and to reclassify, the FASB hoped to minimize the incidence of gains trading. Furthermore, expanded disclosure requirements under SFAS 115 would be more likely to reveal gains trading profits than before. In addition, if a firm were to sell part of its held-to-maturity securities before maturity, this would be inconsistent with intent to hold and would likely result in the remaining securities being reclassified to trading or available-for-sale.

These constraints on gains trading were apparently made to satisfy the SEC. Had the SEC decided not to go along, this would have put the FASB in a very difficult position It would have been caught between the demands of the SEC for more fair value accounting and the financial institutions for less.

13.6.2 COMPREHENSIVE INCOME

In 1997, SFAS 130, **Comprehensive Income**, was issued by the FASB. In the absence of a comparable Canadian standard, we discuss SFAS 130 here. Comprehensive income is defined as all changes in equity during the period except those resulting from investments by or distributions to owners. Thus, in addition to net income as calculated under GAAP, comprehensive income includes other items such as unrealized translation gains and losses resulting from consolidation of foreign subsidiaries under SFAS 52, unrealized gains and losses on marking-to-market available-for-sale securities under SFAS 115 (Section 7.4.2), and unrealized gains and losses on cash flow hedges of forecasted transactions under SFAS 133 (Section 7.4.4). In each of these cases, management objects to the inclusion of these items in net income, on the grounds that they are volatile, uncontrollable, and uninformative about their effort. Our study of contracting theory suggests reasons for management's concerns.

SFAS 130 requires that items such as these be included in a new statement, entitled **Other Comprehensive Income**, which can be presented either along with the income statement or in a separate statement of changes in shareholders' equity. In all cases, comprehensive income is shown as the sum of net income and other comprehensive income. To illustrate, we extend the heirarchy of earnings numbers given in Section 5.5 (again, ignoring income taxes) as follows:

Core earnings	xx
Unusual and non-recurring items	xx
Income from continuing operations	xx
Extraordinary items	xx
Net income	xx
Other comprehensive income	xx
Comprehensive income	xx

This dichotomization between realized (net income) and unrealized (other comprehensive income) earnings components emphasizes the dual role of financial reporting. Investors receive relevant balance sheet information about fair values of foreign subsidiaries and financial instruments, and can readily determine the nature and amounts of related unrealized gains and losses. However, management performance evaluation can exclude these items to the extent compensation committees use core earnings or net income as a harder measure of manager performance.

It is interesting that this approach to reporting has some potential to relieve the fundamental problem of financial accounting theory. The interests of managers and investors can be reconciled if net income is calculated so as to maximize correlation with manager effort, with other comprehensive income picking up other relevant gains and losses that are less informative about effort. Despite this potential, SFAS 130 ignores any mention of the role of net income in motivating manager performance. Nevertheless, this role seems implicit. For example, the standard states (paragraph 66) that other comprehensive income is not a measure of financial performance, implying that net income is. This interpretation is reinforced by the fact that, as mentioned, SFAS 130 allows other comprehensive income to be included in a statement of changes in shareholders' equity, that is, separate from the income statement. Thus, SFAS 130 seems to be an important compromise between investor and management interests in financial reporting.

The reporting of comprehensive income raises the question of whether it is decision useful for investors. This issue was investigated by Dhaliwal, Subramanyam, and Trezevant (1999). For a large sample of U.S. firms, they calculated the association between share returns and comprehensive income, and compared the result with the association between share and net income. They found no clear evidence that other comprehensive income is more highly correlated with share returns than net income, implying no additional decision usefulness. Skinner (1999) points out that this result is what we would expect given securities market efficiency. Much of the information about the components of other comprehensive income would have been available to the market from other sources, such as supplementary information in financial statement notes. Also, the components are of low persistence by definition.

Given a lack of decision usefulness, what is the purpose of SFAS 130? It seems that the standard represents a political compromise between investors' and managers' interests. Investors benefit from the decision usefulness of fair value accounting. Managers seem willing to accept fair value accounting providing that resulting unrealized gains and losses are excluded from net income.

13.6.3 CONCLUSIONS

There seems little doubt that a standard such as SFAS 115 is decision useful to investors—for example, recall our reference to the studies of Barth, Beaver and Landsman (1996), and Barth (1994) in Section 7.6.2 that found a securities market response to fair values of banks' loans and investments portfolios. Furthermore, the reduction in information asymmetry between management and investors that results from investors' enhanced knowledge of security values, and from reductions in gains trading, will improve the working of securities markets, with consequent social benefits. However, while these are valuable improvements, it should be clear that much more is required if a standard is to succeed. An acceptable compromise between the interests of affected constituencies is also essential. With respect to SFAS 130, the compromise is to exclude from net income unrealized gains and losses over which management has relatively little control and which are uninformative about manager effort. We will now consider the criteria for a successful standard in greater generality.

13.7   *Criteria for Standard Setting*

We have seen that there are a number of factors that affect the process of standard setting. Standards should be decision useful, but they should also be acceptable to other constituencies—in particular, management. This puts the standard setter in a conflict situation and it is difficult to predict what an acceptable resolution of this conflict will be. Nevertheless, we now suggest some criteria that should be kept in mind when trying to understand standard setting.

13.7.1 *DECISION USEFULNESS*

The criterion of decision usefulness underlies the information and measurement perspectives on financial reporting, and the empirical capital market studies. Recall that the more informative, that is, the less noisy, is an information system the stronger will be investor reaction to information produced by the system, other things equal. Thus, empirical evidence that security prices respond to accounting information suggests that investors find that information useful.

This suggests that a necessary condition for the success of a new standard is that it be decision useful. Of course, this can be hard to assess beforehand, since the market has not yet had a chance to respond to the standard. Nevertheless, the theory of rational investor decision-making can be used to predict decision usefulness. For example, Bandyopadhyay (Section 5.4.1) predicted that oil and gas companies' earnings reported under successful efforts were more informative than under full cost accounting, and provided evidence to this effect. Also, as argued in Chapter 6, the incorporation of fair values into financial reporting will increase investor decision usefulness to the extent that this tightens up the linkage between current and future performance.

However, while decision usefulness may be a necessary criterion for a successful standard, it is not sufficient to ensure success. We saw in Section 5.6 that, because of certain public good characteristics of accounting information, we cannot be sure that the standard that has the greatest decision usefulness is best for society. Since investors do not directly pay for accounting information, they may "overuse" it. Thus, a standard could appear to be decision useful, yet society would be worse off because the costs of producing the information were not taken into account. Furthermore, changes in standards can impose contracting costs on firms and their managers. In effect, as implied by the fundamental problem of financial accounting theory, standard setters must consider other criteria than decision usefulness.

13.7.2 *REDUCTION OF INFORMATION ASYMMETRY*

We saw in Section 12.3.3 that market forces operate to motivate management and investors to generate information. Standard setters should be aware of these forces and take advantage of them, to the extent possible, to reduce the need for standards. Unfortunately, market forces alone cannot ensure that the right amount of information is produced. As we saw in Section 12.4, one of the reasons for this is information asymmetry. Consequently, as suggested by Lev (1988), standard setters should use reduction of information asymmetry in capital and managerial labour markets as a criterion for new standards. Beyond any decision usefulness that such new standards possess, reduction of information asymmetry improves the operation of markets, since investors will perceive investing as more of a "level playing field." This will expand market liquidity, reduce the "lemons" phenomenon and generally produce social benefits from properly working markets.

Standard setters should also be aware of the informativeness of market price itself as a conveyor of information. As discussed in Section 4.4, the efficient market price of a firm's shares reflects, with noise, what is publicly known about that firm. Furthermore, more is publicly known about large firms than small firms to the extent they are in the public eye and have analyst and media following. Consequently, we would expect the extent of information asymmetry between managers and investors to be greater for small firms, suggesting that standard setters should require at least as high disclosure standards for small firms as for large firms. In this regard, it is interesting that while the *CICA Handbook* applies to all profit-oriented enterprises, certain disclosure exemptions for small firms are allowed, for example, with respect to earnings per share (paragraph 3500.06). Also, small firms are excused from MD&A (Section 4.8.2).

However, it should be noted that reduction of information asymmetry as a criterion is again a necessary condition for a successful standard but not a sufficient one. Just as decision useful information has a cost, so does reduction of information asymmetry. Consequently, it is hard to know when standards to reduce information asymmetry cease to be cost-effective.

13.7.3 ECONOMIC CONSEQUENCES OF NEW STANDARDS

As mentioned above, one of the costs of a new standard is the cost imposed on firms and managers to meet that standard. This goes beyond the out-of-pocket costs of producing the newly mandated information. Costs are also created by contract rigidities, as in an increased probability of violating debt covenants, and effects on the level and volatility of managers' future bonus streams. These costs can affect operating and financial policies. Furthermore, to the extent that new standards require the release of proprietary information, firms' future profitability can be unfavourably or favourably affected by the reduction of competitive advantage.

The reduction in managers' freedom to choose from different accounting policies that frequently results when a new standard is implemented is also a source of economic consequences. We argued in Section 12.3.5 that firms can signal inside information by accounting policy choice. Also, earnings management can reveal inside information, as discussed in Section 11.6. Obviously, if accounting policy choice is constrained, there is a reduction in the extent to which these private forces for information production can operate.

Finally, the Darrough and Stoughton model in Section 9.3 suggests that the greater the degree of competition in an industry the better the disclosure, other things equal. As a result, there may be less need for accounting standards in some industries than in others.

These considerations suggest that standard setters should weigh the possible economic consequences of new standards as an important source of cost that will affect both the need for the standard and the willingness of constituencies to accept it. Of course, it may be that the economic consequences of a new standard will be overstated during the debate leading to the standard. For example, would banks really stop long-term lending if their long-term investments have to be fully marked-to-market? Probably not, but the costs to banks of long-term lending would increase and, as a result, the charges to borrowers would likely rise.

13.7.4 THE POLITICAL ASPECTS OF STANDARD SETTING

Economic consequences leads directly to our last criterion, namely the political aspects of standard setting. Standard setters, in effect, must engineer a consensus sufficiently strong that even a constituency that does not like a new standard will nevertheless go along with it. This is the "delicate balancing" act that Zeff referred to (see Section 8.2). As should be apparent from Sections 13.3 and 13.4, the structure of standard setting bodies, both nationally and internationally, is designed to encourage such a consensus.

We conclude that the standard setting process seems most consistent with the interest group theory of regulation. Certainly, technical, and even theoretical, correctness is not sufficient to ensure the success of a standard. As we argued in Section 8.3, failure to record an expense for ESOs overstates net income and reduces the comparability of reported earnings across firms. Yet the FASB's exposure draft proposing fair value accounting for ESOs met with such resistance that it had to be withdrawn. While careful attention to due process may be time-consuming, such attention seems essential if costly and embarrassing retractions are to be minimized. Too many of these will threaten the existence of the standard setting body itself.

13.7.5 SUMMARY

Accounting standard setters can be guided by decision usefulness and reduction of information asymmetry. However, these criteria are not sufficient to ensure successful standard setting. The legitimate interests of management and other constituencies also need to be considered, as does careful attention to due process. Because of the fundamental problem of financial accounting theory, it seems that the actual process of standard setting is better described by the interest group theory of regulation than by the public interest theory.

13.8   *Conclusions*

In a sense, this whole book comes to a focus on standard setting. We saw, in Chapter 2, that under ideal conditions accounting and reporting standards are not needed, since there is only one way to account, on the basis of the present values of firms' future cash flows. Indeed, under ideal conditions one can question whether financial accounting is needed at all.

Fortunately, in view of our conclusion in Section 2.6 that accountants would not be needed under ideal conditions, such conditions do not exist. As a result, financial accounting becomes much more challenging. Information asymmetry is a major source of this challenge.

We have seen two major types of information asymmetry. The first is adverse selection. That is, managers and other insiders typically know more than outside investors about the state and prospects of the firm. Here, the accounting challenge is to convey information from inside to outside the firm, thereby improving investor decision-making, limiting the ability of insiders to exploit their information advantage, and enhancing the operation of capital markets.

The second type of information asymmetry is moral hazard. That is, the effort exerted by a manager is unobservable to shareholders and lenders in all but the smallest firms. Here, the accounting challenge is to provide a hard measure of managerial performance, that is, one that is highly correlated with manager effort. This enables incentive contracts to motivate manager performance, protect lenders, and inform the managerial labour market.

It is important to realize that the accounting system that best meets the first challenge is unlikely to best meet the second, so that actual financial reporting represents a compromise between the two. Specifically, investors need decision-relevant information to help them predict future firm performance. This implies not only a lot of information release, including extensive footnotes, MD&A, and even financial forecasts, but also fair value-based information. However, problems of volatility and possible subjectivity of fair values reduce the correlation of net income with manager performance. To the extent that historical cost accounting is less subject to these problems, it can be argued that it better meets the challenge of enabling efficient contracts.

It is this need for financial reporting to fulfill a dual role of meeting investors' information needs and the needs of efficient contracting that creates the fundamental problem of financial accounting theory. Investors, including securities commissions acting on their behalf, push for additional information, including fair value information. Management pushes the other way when they perceive that proposed standards will affect their flexibility under the contracts they have entered into, inhibit their ability to credibly communicate with the market through accounting policy choice, or reduce their ability to hide poor performance through "bad" earnings management. As mentioned, the standard setter must then seek a compromise between these conflicting interests. The structure of standard setting bodies is designed to facilitate such a compromise.

With the increasing globalization of commerce, including securities markets, the need for international accounting standards will expand. However, the difficulties of standard setting will also increase. In addition to investor-manager conflict, new constituencies will arise representing different levels of economic development, different business practices, and different cultures. Standard setting bodies will have to adapt to take these additional challenges into account.

Questions and Problems

1. Contrast the public interest and interest group theories of regulation with respect to:

    a. The role of the regulatory body.

    b. Their implications for the amount of the regulated commodity or service to be supplied.   (CGA-Canada)

2. Refer to the article "FASB Moves Closer to Forcing Banks to Value Securities Near Market Prices" (*The Wall Street Journal*, September 11, 1992), reproduced in Section 13.6.1.

    Required

    a. Describe how the structure of standard setting is designed to facilitate the resolution of constituency conflicts such as those described in the article.

    b. Explain why a more-than-majority vote by FASB members is required to pass a new standard.

3. The Joint Working Group draft standard, *Financial Instruments and Similar Items*, was outlined in Section 7.4.5. This draft standard proposes fair value accounting for all financial instruments.

    Required

    Describe and explain the objections that management is likely to raise with respect to the draft standard.

4. An article entitled "Bank Regulators Expected to Drop Plan Pegged to Market Value of Securities" appeared in *The Wall Street Journal* on November 9, 1994. It indicates that federal bank and thrift regulators will not require capital calculations for regulatory purposes to be made in accordance with SFAS 115. Rather, unrealized gains and losses arising from changes in the market value of "available

for sale" securities under SFAS 115 can be excluded in the calculation of regulatory capital. "Financial institutions are required to keep a minimum level of capital, based on a percentage of assets." According to the article, banks believe that unrealized gains and losses would have had a major impact on their reported capital if there were shifts in the market value of "available for sale" securities.

Kenneth Guenther, executive vice president of the Independent Bankers Association, is happy about the change in the rule. He states that "as interest rates rose this year, many banks witnessed big declines in the value of their 'available for sale' bonds." He believes that SFAS 115 would have made " 'perfectly healthy banks … [face] serious and unwarranted regulatory restrictions.' "

Required

a. Explain why excluding unrealized gains and losses from regulatory capital will reduce the concerns by bankers about SFAS 115.

b. According to Mr. Guenther of the Independent Bankers Association, SFAS 115 would have made "perfectly healthy banks" face "serious and unwarranted regulatory restrictions." Can a bank with a securities portfolio worth less than cost be perfectly healthy? Explain.

c. To what extent will this move by bank regulators compromise the objectives of SFAS 115? Explain.

5. The announcement reproduced here appeared in *Financial Accounting Series* (December 27, 1994). It reports that the FASB agreed not to require recognition of an expense for options granted to employees, including managers. This represents a backing off from a 1993 exposure draft that proposed that compensation expense be recorded equal to the fair value of options granted.

FASB AGREES NOT TO REQUIRE EXPENSE RECOGNITION FOR STOCK OPTIONS

The FASB has agreed to work toward improving disclosures about employee stock options and related arrangements in the notes to financial statements rather than requiring an expense charge for all options. The Board expects to encourage, rather than require, companies to adopt a new method that accounts for stock compensation awards based on their estimated fair value at the date they are granted. Companies would be permitted, however, to continue accounting under the present requirements, which do not require an expense charge for most options.

In June 1993, the FASB issued an

Exposure Draft on accounting for employee stock options, which would have required expense recognition for virtually all employee stock option plans. The Board has been redeliberating the issues for several months based on comment letters received, public hearing testimony, and much other information. The Board has been concentrating on ways to improve the method of estimating the value of options.

"The Board remains convinced that employee options have value and are compensation," said FASB Chairman Dennis R. Beresford. "However, in the final analysis, the Board decided that there simply isn't enough support for the basic notion of requiring expense recognition. Different constituents had different reasons for disagreeing with our conclusions on expense recognition, but most favored expanded note disclosures rather than changes to the current accounting requirements."

The approach that the FASB will now pursue would allow companies to continue following existing accounting rules, which result in zero compensation expense for most existing plans. However, those companies that do not recognize expense would have to disclose in a note to the financial statements the effect on net income had the company recognized expense for them based on FASB-specified guidelines.

According to Project Manager Diane W. Willis, "one of the important objectives of this project was to eliminate the bias against variable plans, such as option plans with terms that vary on company performance. Current rules require expense charges for many variable plans, while no expense is recognized for otherwise similar fixed plans. The new accounting method would eliminate this bias, so the Board decided to encourage companies to adopt it. The proposed disclosures for those who continue to follow existing accounting standards will permit users to compare companies that elect the new accounting with companies that do not."

Having reached this conclusion, the FASB needs to complete reconsideration of its 1993 Exposure Draft because its provisions will form the basis for the disclosures and elective accounting described above. The Board hasn't decided yet whether it will issue a final standard based on this conclusion or whether it will issue another Exposure Draft for public comment. That decision will be made when redeliberations are completed, probably in the second quarter of 1995. At this time, no decision has been made on an effective date for a new standard.

SOURCE: Permission to reprint portions of *Financial Accounting Series* of December 27, 1994, was obtained from the Financial Accounting Standards Board.

Required

a. With which theory of regulation is the 1993 exposure draft and subsequent change of policy most consistent? Explain.

b. To what extent will the new policy, which encourages expense recognition but allows an alternative note disclosure of the option cost, serve as a satisfactory substitute for mandatory expense recognition as originally proposed? Explain.

Note: The distinction in the announcement between fixed and variable plans is explained in Chapter 8, Note 1. The new standard referred to in the article is SFAS 123 (1995), discussed in Section 8.3.

6. The article here reproduced, from *The New York Times* (October 12, 1997), describes pressures to "kill" the FASB, and hand its duties over to the SEC. The reason for the pressure seems to be due to SFAS 133 (see Section 7.4.3), which requires firms to mark derivative instruments to market.

POLITICIANS THREATEN ACCOUNTING INTEGRITY

Sixty years ago, an intense battle was waged inside the young Securities and Exchange Commission. There was no consensus about how to fix what all agreed was the deplorable accounting that was showing up in corporate financial reports.

On one side was the commission's new chairman, William O. Douglas, who thought the commission should promulgate its own standards. On the other was the S.E.C.'s chief accountant, Carman C. Blough, who thought the Government could not do a good job and wanted it left to the private sector, with S.E.C. oversight. On a 3–2 vote of the commission in 1938, Douglas lost.

Blough then persuaded the American Institute of Certified Public Accountants that it needed to get moving. After hearing Blough give a harsh speech noting more than 30 questionable accounting practices that had been approved by accountants, the institute set up a Committee on Accounting Procedure to make rules. That body was replaced by the Accounting Principles Board in 1959 and by the Financial Accounting Standards Board in 1973, as the rule makers gained more power and independence.

The arrangements have sometimes been cumbersome and slow. It has been more than a decade since the board took up the question of accounting for derivatives, and only now is it poised to issue a rule. But the process has produced the best accounting anywhere and helped to make New York the financial capital of the world. It would be hard for the S.E.C. to match the detailed expertise of the F.A.S.B. and its staff.

Nonetheless, a campaign is on to kill the F.A.S.B. The banks are furious over the new derivatives rule, which would force users of derivatives to record the market value of those instruments in their financial reports. The banks say the rule will confuse investors and scare off some companies that would benefit from using derivatives. They have lobbied hard in Congress, and both the House and Senate have held hearings to bash the F.A.S.B. on the issue. Last week, John Reed, the chairman of Citicorp, called for abolishing the F.A.S.B. and transferring its duties to the S.E.C.

Mr. Reed's suggestion, as it happened, was published in a letter to the editor of the *Wall Street Journal* on the same day that the Senate killed campaign finance reform. The sad reality today is that injecting politics into accounting carries with it a real risk regarding accounting integrity. It is not hard to imagine a future S.E.C. budget being held up by a Congressman, or confirmation of a future S.E.C. chairman delayed by a senator, amid quiet negotiations regarding the need to change an accounting rule that threatens—quite unfairly, of course—to penalize the profits, and perhaps hurt investors and employees, of a company that has been a substantial supporter of the legislator.

The F.A.S.B.'s new derivatives rule is not perfect, but it is an improvement over current practice. If need be, it can be changed later. But the wisdom of that rule is much less important than the preservation of a process that has worked well without a hint of impropriety. If the politicians succeed in killing this rule, as they did with an earlier proposal to change accounting for employee stock options, it is hard to see how the F.A.S.B. will survive. And that would pose a real threat to continued investor confidence.

It is time for businesses, even those that don't like the derivatives proposal, to tell the politicians to leave accounting alone.

ALREADY THE OLDEST

Rule makers for American accounting:

Committee on Accounting Procedure
1938–1959   **21 years**

Accounting Principles Board
1959–1973   **14 years**

Financial Accounting Standard Board
1973–present   **24 years**

Required

a. Use the interest group theory of regulation to explain the reasons for the campaign to kill the FASB. Why would certain bank executives prefer accounting standards to be set by the SEC?

b. Use the public interest theory of regulation to evaluate the costs and benefits of moving financial accounting standard setting to the SEC. Include in your answer an evaluation of the structure of the FASB. Also consider the effects of such a move on investor confidence in capital markets.

7. On July 23, 1998, *The Globe and Mail*, in an article here reproduced, reported that the Office of the Superintendent of Financial Institutions (OSFI), a federal government agency, was planning to get into the financial accounting standard setting business. OSFI's concern was with Section 1580 of *CICA Handbook*, which laid down a size test that must be met if a business combination was to be accounted for as a pooling of interests (for details of the purchase versus pooling of interest accounting controversy, see Section 7.5.2 and, in particular, Example 7.1). The proposed OSFI standard would override Section 1580 of *CICA Handbook* to allow pooling criteria similar to more generous criteria in the United States.

OSFI DRAFTS ACCOUNTING RULE CHANGE FOR MERGERS

Could put Canada, U.S. banks on equal footing

Apowerful federal regulator is considering an unprecedented move that could greatly accelerate consolidation in the financial services industry.

The Office of the Superintendent of Financial Institutions is drafting policy aimed at putting Canadian and U.S. financial institutions on an equal footing on the merger front.

Canadian financial institutions have complained for years that the Canadian accounting system severely restricts their ability to snap up competitors on both sides of the border.

In a letter sent last week by OSFI deputy superintendent Nick Le Pan to several industry players and obtained by *The Globe and Mail*, the regulator agreed, saying "it has become clear that there is not a level playing field in accounting for mergers" and it has reopened its file on the issue.

"It looks to us like there are significant biases in who does mergers and those biases aren't, from a public policy point of view, the ones you would want to have," he said in an interview yesterday.

In his letter, Mr. Le Pan said industry discussions to resolve discrepancies between U.S. and Canadian accounting rules for financial deals failed to produce a solution. OSFI is drafting a policy that will come into effect Nov. 1, and could override Canadian generally accepted accounting principles (GAAP).

The new policy would only effect federally regulated financial institutions such as banks and trust and insurance companies, leaving other sectors to operate under existing Canadian Institute of Chartered Accountants (CICA) rules.

The OSFI guidelines will stay in place until CICA and its U.S. counterpart, the Financial Accounting Standards Board (FASB), agree on a Canada-U.S. standard, the letter said.

Current Canadian accounting standards set out by CICA allow for "pooling of interest" accounting on stock deals.

The key criterion is that one company can own no more than 55 per cent of the merged entity, with the other partner owning no less than 45 per cent, a policy that favours only mergers of equals, like the proposed deals between Royal Bank of Canada and Bank of Montreal, and Canadian Imperial Bank of Commerce and Toronto-Dominion Bank.

However, companies of vastly different sizes are hit with what is known as good will, the money paid for a company above its book value.

Good will must be amortized against earnings for years (in some cases up to 40 years) and as a result drags down a company's return on equity and marks up a company's book equity. Return on equity is often a leading indicator of a company's performance.

In the United States, pooling of interest guidelines don't take into account a company's size and as a result more transactions fall into the pooling category. For example, Merrill Lynch & Co. Inc. of New York was able to buy Canadian brokerage house Midland Walwyn Inc., a company roughly one-fortieth its size, using pooling of interest rules.

If, for example, Canada Trust or Bank of Nova Scotia had bought Midland, they would have taken after-tax good-will charges of $975-million or approximately $50-million a year, amortized over 20 years.

"The fact that Merrill didn't have to pay good will was its 100-per-cent advantage in that bidding process," said Mark Maxwell, banking analyst at CIBC Wood Gundy Securities Inc.

Sylvia Smith, CICA's director of accounting standards, called the OSFI's plan to override Canadian GAAP as a "serious move." While recognizing that changes have to be made, she said the U.S. model is also in need of an overhaul.

"We recognize there is a need to get a harmonized and better standard than everyone has right now. What is ironic is there is recognition that the FASB standard is deficient."

In the United States, companies hoping to use the pooling method must meet several criteria and because size is not one of them, it's easier to conform.

Part of the reason OSFI is acting now, Mr. Le Pan said, is because it could take years to change current accounting procedures. Ms. Smith said CICA and FASB hope to issue a policy paper for discussion in the first quarter of 1998. She said two years is an optimistic time frame for change.

In the meantime, she hopes OSFI will look at other alternatives.

For example, the OSFI said in its letter that one option is to have Canadian companies file separate financial statements in the United States that conform to U.S. GAAP rules.

Peter Currie, chief financial officer of Royal Bank, said it is easier for U.S. companies to apply pooling of interest guidelines to transactions and the bank welcomes the OSFI's move to reopen the file.

"This move by OSFI advantages us significantly vis-à-vis U.S. players as their industry consolidates," he said.

The proposed changes would leave other sectors, including unregulated financial companies, such as Toronto-based Newcourt Credit Group Inc., operating under the CICA guidelines. Newcourt, for example, has made 19 acquisitions in the past seven years and has equity-financed good will on its balance sheet of $1.8-billion.

SOURCE: Reprinted with permission from *The Globe and Mail*.

Required

a. Use efficient securities market theory to explain to managers of Canadian financial institutions that they need not be concerned about whether business combinations are accounted for as purchases or poolings of interest.

b. Despite efficient securities market theory, why are Canadian financial institutions and OSFI concerned that there is not a "level playing field" in accounting for business combinations?

c. Use the interest group theory of regulation to explain why OSFI is getting involved and why the CICA appears concerned about this possibility.

8. The article "Bean counters unite!" (*The Economist*, June 10, 1995) reports on efforts by the IASC (predecessor body to the IASB) to harmonize world accounting standards.

BEAN COUNTERS, UNITE!

Agreement on international accounting standards is closer than it has ever been. But can the present mood of goodwill last?

Not so many years ago, enthusiasts for international accounting standards seemed doomed to eternal frustration. Differences in the ways in which companies in different countries presented their financial results appeared so profound that no amount of compromise would result in meaningful international standards. Suddenly these differences appear smaller.

Helped by the globalisation of capital markets, the International Accounting Standards Committee (IASC) has won wide support for its efforts to harmonise accounting rules. If it can clear a few remaining hurdles, the IASC should be able to produce a workable framework by the end of the decade. The greater ease with which companies' disclosures could then be compared would benefit investors and issuers alike.

The IASC's task will not be easy, however. Political arguments about obscure accounting rules are surprisingly passionate. The most palpable tensions have been between America and Germany, two countries that epitomise very different approaches to financial reporting. America, led by its Securities and Exchange Commission (SEC) and Financial Accounting Standards Board (FASB), believes that the guiding principle should be for companies to give a "true and fair" view to shareholders. Germany,

in contrast, prefers that companies exercise "prudence" on behalf of stakeholders—which, in practice, thanks to Germany's weak equity culture, means on behalf of creditors and employees rather than shareholders. German accounts are largely driven by tax considerations.

All this came to a head in 1993 when Daimler-Benz, a top German car maker, broke ranks with other big German companies that were thinking of listing in America, and accepted some American accounting rules as a requirement for listing its shares. The American authorities took the view that the other German firms were trying to wriggle out of proper disclosure; the Germans accused the FASB and the SEC of trying needlessly to foist American standards on respectable international companies. The bitter quarrel suggested that accounting differences were too rooted in national corporate cultures to be overcome.

This impression was, however, misleading. For one thing, after nearly two decades of well-intentioned muddle, the IASC had begun to be more effective towards the end of the 1980s. A project to promote international harmonisation was beginning to yield tighter and more coherent standards.

At the same time, the continuing globalisation of capital markets has given firms a powerful incentive to abandon their resistance to change. Unless they can present their results in ways that foreign investors understand, companies may be unable to tap new sources of capital. They could, like Daimler-Benz, adopt the standards of the foreign market. But it would be much more convenient to agree on a single set of international rules that could be incorporated into, or sit alongside, the local ones. The greater the degree of incorporation, the closer firms would be to a single set of global accounts.

Momentum in this direction has never been so strong. The IASC has been working closely with the International Organisation of Securities Commissions (IOSCO), a club of securities-market regulators which includes America's SEC, in an effort to ensure that its standards are accepted by financial markets. When IOSCO holds its annual get-together next month, it is expected to announce a three-year programme with the IASC, to push standard-making along.

The two bodies' efforts have already yielded fruit. In April 1994 the SEC allowed foreign companies that wish to raise capital in America to use an international standard on cash-flow statements. Recently, two further international standards were given the nod. More approvals are expected. "Our desire is for high-standards," says Linda Quinn, head of the SEC's corporate-finance division. "That does not mean that they have to be identical with existing American standards."

SOFTENING

Compromise is in the air on the other side of the Atlantic too. Last year Bayer and Schering, two big German companies, adopted international standards for their 1994 accounts. Johannes Maret of Arthur Andersen, an accounting firm, thinks many more German firms will follow suit. Dozens of Swiss companies have already beaten them to it.

Perhaps most remarkably, German officialdom has recently indicated that it is prepared to make concessions. Last month Herbert Biener, a Justice Ministry official who represents Germany on an IOSCO accounting-standards working party, proposed that Germany should "tolerate" the use of international standards for consolidated accounts by companies seeking listings abroad. This would ease the reporting burden on Daimler-Benz and others that may choose to follow its lead. Instead of publishing two sets of group accounts to satisfy both German and American authorities, such firms could publish a single, internationally accepted set.

Even so, plenty could still go wrong. One potential interferer is the European Commission. European accounting laws are badly out of date and interpreted inconsistently. Officials in Brussels resent European firms' drift towards American standards. Although they have given up the dream of a set of European standards, the commission is still responsible for seeing that IASC standards conform with European law.

The prospect of any meddling appals nearly everyone, particularly if it becomes, in effect, a further layer of standards. Sir Bryan Carsberg, the IASC's recently appointed secretary-general, and a former head of Britain's Office of Fair Trading, would prefer to strengthen the commission's involvement with the IASC. Mr. Biener is blunter. He describes the commission's interest as "superfluous."

A second danger comes from the slow

pace of standard setting. The IASC must fill the remaining gaps in its armoury before it can claim to have a comprehensive set of standards. Sir Bryan accepts that the IASC is a "handful of years away from a complete set of standards." But he is optimistic that he can keep the body on course.

There are plenty of rocks on which it might founder. The body's attempt to introduce a comprehensive standard for the way firms should account for their use of hedging instruments such as derivatives was almost derailed last month by political in-fighting. As a result, America's FASB, which is expected to come out with such standards later this year, could beat Sir Bryan to it, thereby reopening tensions between the two camps. A proposed IASC standard on segment reporting (results by business or geography) will also highlight differences.

More generally, European firms remain suspicious about extending standards too far. They view American standards as excessively burdensome, pointing to over-zealous litigation as the cause of bloated and inflexible rulebooks. Europeans complain that in its recent tightening up of standards, the IASC has tilted too far towards America's rule-bound approach. The IASC will have to negotiate a fine line.

Still, for the moment, the winds are blowing in the IASC's favour. Next year the German government will start selling Deutsche Telekom, its telecoms monopoly, in a huge share offering that is bound to exceed the meagre appetite of local investors. The firm and its myriad advisers are already negotiating with the SEC on how it must report if it is to obtain a listing in America. Both sides are keen for a deal, which would in turn set a powerful precedent for other companies wishing to tap the American market. A happy outcome should make the IASC's task a little easier.

SOURCE: © 1995. The Economist Newspaper Group, Inc. Reprinted with permission. Further reproduction prohibited. www.economist.com

Required

a. What are the benefits of harmonized world accounting standards?

b. What constituencies are involved in setting world accounting standards that are not involved in Canadian standard setting? Do these additional constituencies make the setting of world accounting standards more difficult? Why?

c. Why does the SEC require that foreign firms that want to list their shares on United States stock exchanges in its jurisdiction meet United States accounting rules? Should the SEC agree to accept IASB standards in place of its own rules? Why?

9. Reproduced here is the Consolidated Statement of Changes in Shareholders' Equity from the 1998 annual report of Baldwin Technology Company Inc. Baldwin is a manufacturer of printing equipment, with head office in Norwalk, Connecticut and with shares traded on the American Stock Exchange. As can be seen, Baldwin has chosen to report comprehensive

BALDWIN TECHNOLOGY COMPANY, INC.
CONSOLIDATED STATEMENT OF CHANGES IN SHAREHOLDERS' EQUITY
(in thousands, except shares)

	Class A Common Stock		Class B Common Stock	
	Shares	Amount	Shares	Amount
Balance at June 30, 1995	16,011,586	$160	2,000,000	$20
Year ended June 30, 1996:				
Net income for the year				
Unrealized gain on available-for-sale securities, net of tax				
Translation adjustment				
Comprehensive income				
Stock issued in conjunction with the acquisition of Acrotec	350,000	4		
Stock options exercised	30,097			
Purchase of treasury stock				
Balance at June 30, 1996	16,391,683	164	2,000,000	20
Year ended June 30, 1997:				
Net loss for the year				
Unrealized loss on available for sale securities, net of tax				
Translation adjustment				
Comprehensive income				
Purchase of treasury stock				
Stock received in the settlement of an indemnification claim made under the Acrotec Stock Purchase Agreement				
Balance at June 30, 1997	16,391,683	164	2,000,000	20
Year ended June 30, 1998:				
Net income for the year				
Unrealized loss on available for sale securities, net of tax				
Translation adjustment				
Comprehensive income				
Stock options exercised	40,000			
Balance at June 30, 1998	16,431,683	$164	2,000,000	$20

1   Reflects the subdivision of common shares on a two-for-one basis on May 14, 1997.

Capital in Excess of Par Value	Retained Earnings	Cumulative Translation Adjustments	Unrealized Gain on Investments	Treasury Stock Shares	Amount	Comprehensive Income
$54,881	$41,631	$ 4,174		(338,373)	$(1,978)	
	2,518					$ 2,518
			$118			118
		(4,125)				(4,125)
						$ (1,489)
2,184						
120						
				(643,900)	(2,651)	
57,185	44,149	49	118	(982,273)	(4,629)	
	(37,997)					$(37,997)
			(5)			(5)
	489					489
						$(37,513)
				(156,400)	(481)	
				(128,246)	(800)	
57,185	6,152	538	113	(1,266,919)	(5,910)	
	9,016					$ 9,016
			(34)			(34)
		(3,961)				(3,961)
						$ 5,021
174						
$57,359	$15,168	$(3,423)	$ 79	(1,266,919)	$(5,910)	

income as part of a statement of changes in shareholders' equity rather than as part of the income statement.

Required

a. Describe and explain the source and nature of the unrealized loss on available for sale securities component of other comprehensive income shown on the June 30, 1998 comprehensive income statement.

b. If you were an investor or analyst, which measure of performance—net income or comprehensive income—would you use for the purpose of predicting the future performance of Baldwin? Explain.

c. If you were a member of the compensation committee of Baldwin's board of directors, which measure of performance would you use for manager bonus purposes? Explain.

d. A former member of the FASB stated that if unrealized gains and losses on available-for-sale securities had to be included in net income, rather than in comprehensive income, SFAS 115 would not be a viable financial reporting standard. Use the criteria for standard setting given in Section 13.7 to explain this statement.

10. El Paso Electric Company is a U.S. electric power generating company incorporated in the State of Texas. In its December 31, 2000 annual report, El Paso reported net income for the year of $58,392 (thousands). From this, it deducted an Other Comprehensive Loss of $1,277, being net unrealized losses for the year on marketable securities, reporting comprehensive income of $57,115 for the year.

Required

a. Explain why the $1,277 unrealized loss is not included in net income for the year.

b. As an investor, which earnings measure, net income or other comprehensive income, is most useful to you in deciding whether to buy, hold or sell El Paso shares? Explain.

c. As a member of the compensation committee of El Paso's Board of Directors, which performance measure, net income or other comprehensive income, is most useful to you in deciding on the amount of cash bonuses for senior officers for 2000? Explain.

d. El Paso is unusual in that it reports other comprehensive income as part of its income statement. Most firms report other comprehensive income as part of the statement of changes in shareholders' equity (see, for example, Problem 9 of this chapter). Why do most firms report other comprehensive income in this manner rather than as part of the income statement?

e. Canadian firms are not required to report other comprehensive income. Instead, fair value of financial instruments is reported as supplementary information in the Notes to the financial statements. Suppose that the AcSB proposes to adopt the JWG Draft Standard see (Section 7.4.5.), and that Canadian managers strongly object to this proposal. Would allowing unrealized gains and losses on financial instruments to be included in other comprehensive income, instead of in net income as under the JWG Draft Standard, further increase or reduce the objections of Canadian managers? Explain.

11. In its 1999 Annual Report, Scotiabank's auditors qualified their audit report. The problem was with the bank's provision for credit losses. During 1999, Scotiabank decided to increase its general provision for credit losses on loans receivable by $700 millions. This was in addition to a specific provision for loan losses on identified problem loans. The general provision applies to loans that have not as yet been specifically identified as in arrears.

Under GAAP, the $700 increase in the general provision should be charged as an expense of the year. However, Scotiabank obtained permission from the Superintendent of Financial Institutions Canada (OSFI) to charge $550 millions of this amount ($314 millions after tax) directly to retained earnings.

As a result, Scotiabank reported net income for 1999 of $1,551 millions. Net incomes for 1998 and 1997 were $1,394 millions and $1,514 millions, respectively.

This direct charge to retained earnings was criticized in the financial media. For example, Eric Reguly, in *The Globe and Mail*, December 7, 1999, called it "an accounting sleight-of-hand that has never been used by the Big Five Canadian banks." Reguly describes the objections of the OSC which, however, could do nothing because the federal Bank Act (administered by OSFI) overrides the Ontario Securities Act. OSFI permitted the direct charge, according to Reguly, because it wanted banks to have a "thicker safety cushion."

Required

a. Use the public interest theory of regulation to justify OSFI's permission for the direct charge to retained earnings.

b. Use the interest group theory of regulation to explain OSFI's permission for the direct charge.

c. Given that the treatment was fully disclosed in the Notes to Scotiabank's Annual Report, in the auditors' report, and in the media, how do you think the securities market would respond to this treatment?

Notes

1. Much of the material in this section is taken from the IASB's excellent Web site: <www.iasb.org.uk>

Bibliography

ABARBANELL, J.S. and B.J. BUSHEE, "Fundamental Analysis, Future Earnings, and Stock Prices," *Journal of Accounting Research* (Spring 1997), pp. 1-24.

ABARBANELL, J.S. and B.J. BUSHEE, "Abnormal Returns to a Fundamental Analysis Strategy," *The Accounting Review* (January 1998), pp. 19-45.

ABARBANELL, J.S., W.N. LANEN, and R.E. VERRECHIA, "Analysts' Forecasts as Proxies for Investor Beliefs in Empirical Research," *Journal of Accounting and Economics* (July 1995), pp. 31-60.

ABDEL-KHALIK, A.R., "The Effect of LIFO-Switching and Firm Ownership on Executive Pay," *Journal of Accounting Research* (Autumn 1985), pp. 427-447.

ABDEL-KHALIK, A.R. and J.C. MCKEOWN, "Understanding Accounting Changes in an Efficient Market: Evidence of Differential Reaction," *The Accounting Review* (October 1978), pp. 851-868.

ABOODY, D. and R. KRASZNIK, "CEO Stock Option Awards and the Timing of Corporate Voluntary Disclosures," *Journal of Accounting and Economics* (February 2000), pp. 73-100.

ACKERT, L.F., and B.F. SMITH, "Stock Price Volatility, Ordinary Dividends, and Other Cash Flows to Shareholders," *The Journal of Finance* (September 1993), pp. 1147-1160.

AKERLOF, G.A., "The Market for 'Lemons': Quality Uncertainty and the Market Mechanism," *Quarterly Journal of Economics* (August 1970), pp. 488-500.

ALCHIAN, A., "Uncertainty, Evolution and Economic Theory," *Journal of Political Economy* (June 1950), pp. 211-221.

AMERICAN ACCOUNTING ASSOCIATION COMMITTEE TO PREPARE A STATEMENT OF BASIC ACCOUNTING THEORY, *"A Statement of Basic Accounting Theory"* (American Accounting Association, 1966).

AMERICAN ACCOUNTING ASSOCIATION FINANCIAL ACCOUNTING STANDARDS COMMITTEE, "Equity Valuation Models and Measuring Goodwill Impairment" *Accounting Horizons* (June 2001), pp. 161-170.

AMERICAN INSTITUTE OF CERTIFIED PUBLIC ACCOUNTANTS STUDY GROUP ON THE OBJECTIVES OF FINANCIAL STATEMENTS, *"Objectives of Financial Statements,"* (New York, NY: AICPA, 1973).

AMIR, E., "The Market Valuation of Accounting Information: The Case of Postretirement Benefits other than Pensions," *The Accounting Review* (October 1993), pp. 703-724.

ANTLE, R. and A. SMITH, "An Empirical Examination of the Relative Performance Evaluation of Corporate Executives," *Journal of Accounting Research* (Spring 1986), pp. 1-39.

ARROW, K. J., *Social Choice and Individual Values*, Cowles Foundation Monograph (New York, NY: John Wiley, 1963).

ARYA, A., J. FELLINGHAM, and J. GLOVER, "Teams, Repeated Tasks and Implicit Incentives," *Journal of Accounting and Economics* (May 1997), pp. 7-30.

BABER, W.R., S. JANAKIRAMAN, and S-H. KANG, "Investment Opportunities and the Structure of Executive Compensation," *Journal of Accounting and Economics* (June 1996), pp. 297-318.

BABER, W.R., S-H. KANG, and K.R. KUMAR, "The Explanatory Power of Earnings Levels vs. Earnings Changes in the Context of Executive Compensation," *The Accounting Review* (October 1999), pp. 459-472.

BAIMAN, S and R. E. VERRECCHIA, "The Relation Among Capital Markets, Financial Disclosure, Production Efficiency, and Insider Trading," *Journal of Accounting Research* (Spring 1996), pp. 1-22.

BANKER, R.D. and S. DATAR, "Sensitivity, Precision, and Linear Aggregation of Signals for Performance Evaluation," *Journal of Accounting Research* (Spring 1989), pp. 21-39.

BALL, R. and E. BARTOV, "How Naive Is the Stock Market's Use of Earnings Information?" *Journal of Accounting and Economics* (June 1996), pp. 319-337.

BALL, R. and P. BROWN, "An Empirical Evaluation of Accounting Income Numbers," *Journal of Accounting Research* (Autumn 1968), pp. 159-178.

BALL, R. and S.P. KOTHARI, "Nonstationary Expected Returns: Implications for Tests of Market Efficiency and Serial Correlation in Returns," *Journal of Financial Economics* (1989), pp. 51-74.

BANDYOPADHYAY, S., "Market Reaction to Earnings Announcements of SE and FC Firms in the Oil and Gas Industry," *The Accounting Review* (October 1994), pp. 657-674.

BANZ, R.W., "The Relationship Between Return and Market Value of Common Stocks," *Journal of Financial Economics* (March 1981), pp. 3-18.

BARNEA, A., J. RONEN, and S. SADAN, "Classificatory Smoothing of Income with Extraordinary Items," *The Accounting Review* (January 1976), pp. 110-122.

BARTH, M.E., "Fair Value Accounting: Evidence from Investment Securities and the Market Value of Banks," *The Accounting Review* (January 1994), pp. 1-25.

BARTH, M.E., W.H. BEAVER, and W.R. LANDSMAN, "Value-Relevance of Banks' Fair Value Disclosures under SFAS 107," *The Accounting Review* (October 1996), pp. 513- 537.

BARTH, M.E., J.A.ELLIOTT, and M.W. FINN, "Market Rewards Associated with Patterns of Increasing Earnings," *Journal of Accounting Research* (Autumn 1999), pp. 387-413.

BARTON, J., "Does the Use of Financial Derivatives Affect Earnings Management Decisions?" *The Accounting Review* (January 2001), pp. 1-26.

BARTOV, E., S. RADHAKRISHNAN, and S. KRINSKY, "Investor Sophistication and Patterns in Stock Returns after Earnings Announcements," *The Accounting Review* (January 2000), pp. 43-63.

BCE INC., *1997 Annual Report* (Montreal, QC: BCE Inc., 1997).

BEAU CANADA EXPLORATION LTD., *1997 Annual Report* (Calgary, AB: Beau Canada Exploration Ltd., 1998).

BEAVER, W.H., "The Information Content of Annual Earnings Announcements," *Journal of Accounting Research* (Supplement, 1968), pp. 67-92.

BEAVER, W.H., "What Should be the FASB's Objectives?" *The Journal of Accountancy* (August 1973), pp. 49-56.

BEAVER, W.H., *Financial Reporting: An Accounting Revolution*, Second Edition (Englewood Cliffs, NJ: Prentice Hall, 1989).

BEAVER, W.H., R. CLARKE, and W.F. WRIGHT, "The Association Between Unsystematic Security Returns and the Magnitude of Earnings Forecast Errors," *Journal of Accounting Research* (Autumn 1979), pp. 316-340.

BEAVER, W.H. and J. DEMSKI, "The Nature of Income Measurement," *The Accounting Review* (January 1979), pp. 38-46.

BEAVER, W.H., P. KETTLER, and M. SCHOLES, "The Association Between Market-Determined and Accounting-Determined Risk Measures," *The Accounting Review* (October 1970), pp. 654-682.

BEAVER, W.H. and W.R. LANDSMAN, *The Incremental Information Content of FAS 33 Disclosures* (Stamford, CT: FASB, 1983).

BEGLEY, J., and G.A. FELTHAM, "The Relation Between Market Values, Earnings Forecasts, and Reported Earnings," *Contemporary Accounting Research* (Spring 2002), pp. 1-48.

BENSTON, G.J., "Required Disclosure and the Stock Market: An Evaluation of the Securities Exchange Act of 1934," *American Economic Review* (March 1973), pp. 132-155.

BERNARD, V.L., "Cross-Sectional Dependance and Problems in Inference in Market-Based Accounting Research," *Journal of Accounting Research* (Spring 1987), pp. 1-48.

BERNARD, V.L., "Capital Markets Research in Accounting During the 1980s: A Critical Review," working paper, University of Michigan, 1989.

BERNARD, V.L. and R.G. RULAND, "The Incremental Information Content of Historical Cost and Current Cost Income Numbers: Time Series Analysis for 1962–1980," *The Accounting Review* (October 1987), pp. 707-722.

BERNARD, V.L. and D.J. SKINNER, "What Motivates Managers' Choice of Discretionary Accruals?" *Journal of Accounting and Economics* (August-December 1996), pp. 313-325.

BERNARD, V.L. and J. THOMAS, "Post-Earnings Announcement Drift: Delayed Price Reaction or Risk Premium?" *Journal of Accounting Research* (Supplement, 1989), pp. 1-36.

BILLINGS, B.K., "Revisiting the Relation Between the Default Risk of Debt and the Earnings Response Coefficient," *The Accounting Review* (October 1999), pp. 509-522.

BLACK, F. and M. SCHOLES, "The Pricing of Options and Corporate Liabilities," *Journal of Political Economy* (May/June 1973), pp. 637-654.

BLAZENKO, G. and W.R. SCOTT, "A Model of Standard Setting in Auditing," *Contemporary Accounting Research* (Fall 1986), pp. 68-92.

BOLAND, L.A. and I.M. GORDON, "Criticizing Positive Accounting Theory," *Contemporary Accounting Research* (Fall 1992), pp. 147-170.

BOTOSAN, C.A., "Disclosure Level and the Cost of Equity Capital," *The Accounting Review* (July 1997), pp. 323-349.

BOTOSAN, C. A. and M. A. PLUMLEE, "Stock Option Expense: The Sword of Damocles Revealed," *The Accounting Review* (December 2001), pp. 311-327.

BOWEN, R.M., L. DuCHARME, and D. SHORES, "Stakeholders' Implicit Claims and Accounting Method Choice," *Journal of Accounting and Economics* (December 1995), pp. 255-295.

BOYLE, P. and P. BOYLE, *Derivatives: The Tools That Changed Finance* (London: Risk Books, 2001).

BROWN, L.D., R.L. HAGERMAN, P.A. GRIFFIN, and M. ZMIJEWSKI, "Security Analyst Superiority Relative to Univariate Time—Series Models in Forecasting Quarterly Earnings," *Journal of Accounting and Economics* (April 1987), pp. 61-87.

BROWN, R.G. and K.S. JOHNSTON, *Paciolo on Accounting* (New York, NY: McGraw-Hill, 1963).

BROWN, S., K. LO, and T. LYS, "Use of R^2 in Accounting Research: Measuring Changes in Value Relevance Over the Last Four Decades," *Journal of Accounting and Economics* (December 1999), pp.83-115.

BROWN, S.J. and J.B. WARNER, "Measuring Security Price Performance," *Journal of Financial Economics* (September 1980), pp. 205-258.

BROWN, L.D., and J.C.Y. HAN, "Do Stock Prices Fully Reflect the Implications of Current Earnings for Future Earnings for *ARI* Firms?" *Journal of Accounting Research* (Spring 2000), pp. 149-164.

BURGSTAHLER, D. and I. DICHEV, "Earnings Management to Avoid Earnings Decreases and Losses," *Journal of Accounting and Economics* (December 1997), pp. 99-126.

BUSHMAN, R.M. and R.J. INDJEJIKIAN, "Accounting Income, Stock Price and Managerial Compensation," *Journal of Accounting and Economics* (January/April/July 1993), pp. 3-23.

BUSHMAN, R.M., R.J. INDJEJIKIAN, and A. SMITH, "CEO Compensation: The Role of Individual Performance Evaluation," *Journal of Accounting and Economics* (April 1996), pp. 161-193.

CAHAN, S.F., "The Effect of Antitrust Investigations on Discretionary Accruals: A Refined Test of the Political-Cost Hypothesis," *The Accounting Review* (January 1992), pp. 77-95.

CANADIAN INSTITUTE OF CHARTERED ACCOUNTANTS, *CICA Handbook,* (Toronto, ON: CICA, 1998).

CHIEFTAIN INTERNATIONAL, INC., *2000 Annual Report* (Edmonton, AB: Chieftain International, Inc., 2001).

CHRISTENSEN, J., "Communication in Agencies," *The Bell Journal of Economics* (Autumn 1981), pp. 661-674.

CHRISTIE, A.A. and J. ZIMMERMAN, "Efficient and Opportunistic Choices of Accounting Procedures: Corporate Control Contests," *The Accounting Review* (October 1994), pp. 539-566.

CLARKSON, P., A. DONTOH, G.D. RICHARDSON, and S. SEFCIK, "The Voluntary Inclusion of Earnings Forecasts in IPO Prospectuses," *Contemporary Accounting Research* (Spring 1992), pp. 601-626.

COLLINS, D.W. and S.P. KOTHARI, "An Analysis of the Intertemporal and Cross-Sectional Determinants of Earnings Response Coefficients," *Journal of Accounting and Economics* (July 1989), pp. 143-181.

COLLINS, D.W., S.P. KOTHARI, J. SHANKEN, and R.G. SLOAN, "Lack of Timeliness versus Noise as Explanations for Low Contemporaneous Return-Earnings Association," *Journal of Accounting and Economics* (1994), pp. 289-324.

COURTEAU, L., J. KAO, and G.D. RICHARDSON, "Equity Valuation Employing the Ideal *versus* Ad Hoc Terminal Value Expression," *Contemporary Accounting Research* (forthcoming 2001).

CRANDALL, R.H., "Government Intervention—the PIP Grant Accounting Controversy," *Cost and Management* (September/October 1983), pp. 57-59.

CUSHING, B.E. and M.J. LECLERE, "Evidence on the Determinants of Inventory Accounting Policy Choice," *The Accounting Review* (April 1992), pp. 355-366.

DANIEL, K.D., D. HIRSHLEIFER, and A. SUBRAHMANYAM, "Investor Psychology and Security Market Investor Under- and Over-Reactions," *Journal of Finance* (December 1998), pp. 1839-1885.

DANIEL, K.D., D. HIRSHLEIFER, and A. SUBRAHMANYAM, "Covariance Risk, Mispricing, and the Cross Section of Security Returns, "*Journal of Finance* (forthcoming 2001).

DANIEL, K.D. and S. TITMAN, "Market Efficiency in an Irrational World," *Financial Analysts' Journal* (1999), pp. 28-40.

DARROUGH, M.N., "Disclosure Policy and Competition: Cournot vs. Bertrand," *The Accounting Review* (July 1993), pp. 534-561.

DARROUGH, M.N. and N.M. STOUGHTON, "Financial Disclosure Policy in an Entry Game," *Journal of Accounting and Economics* (January 1990), pp. 219-243.

DATAR, S.M., G.A. FELTHAM, and J.S. HUGHES, "The Role of Audits and Audit Quality in Valuing New Issues," *Journal of Accounting and Economics* (March 1991), pp. 3-49.

DE ANGELO, H., L.E. DE ANGELO, and D.J. SKINNER, "Accounting Choice in Troubled Companies," *Journal of Accounting and Economics* (January 1994), pp. 113-143.

DE ANGELO, L.E., "Auditor Size and Auditor Quality," *Journal of Accounting and Economics* (December 1981), pp. 183-199.

DECHOW, P.M., "Accounting Earnings and Cash Flows as Measures of Firm Performance: The Role of Accounting Accruals," *Journal of Accounting and Economics* (July 1994), pp. 3-42.

DECHOW, P.M., R.G. SLOAN, and A.P. SWEENEY, "Detecting Earnings Management," *The Accounting Review* (April 1995), pp. 193-225.

DECHOW, P.M., A.P. HUTTON, and R.G.SLOAN, "An Empirical Assessment of the Residual Income Valuation Model," *Journal of Accounting and Economics* (January 1999), pp. 1-34.

DECHOW, P.M., R.G. SLOAN, AND A.P. SWEENEY, "Causes and Consequences of Earnings Manipulation: An Analysis of Firms Subject to Enforcement Actions by the SEC," *Contemporary Accounting Research* (Spring 1996), pp. 1-36.

DEFOND, M.L. and J. JIAMBALVO, "Debt Covenant Violation and Manipulation of Accruals," *Journal of Accounting and Economics* (January 1994), pp. 145-176.

DEFOND, M.L. and C. W. PARK, "Smoothing Income in Anticipation of Future Earnings," *Journal of Accounting and Economics* (1997), pp. 115-139.

DeLONG, J.B., A. SUMMERS, and R.J. WALDMAN, "Positive Feedback Investment Strategies and Destabilizing Rational Speculation," *Journal of Finance* (June 1990), pp. 375-395.

DEMSKI, J., *Information Analysis* (Reading, MA: Addison-Wesley, 1972).

DEMSKI, J., "Positive Accounting Theory: A Review," *Accounting, Organizations and Society* (October 1988), pp. 623-629.

DEMSKI, J. and D.E.M. SAPPINGTON, "Delegated Expertise," *Journal of Accounting Research* (Spring 1987), pp. 68-89.

DEMSKI, J. and D.E.M. SAPPINGTON, "Fully Revealing Income Measurement," *The Accounting Review* (April 1990), pp. 363-383.

DHALIWAL, D.S., K.J. LEE, and N.L. FARGHER, "The Association Between Unexpected Earnings and Abnormal Security Returns in the Presence of Financial Leverage," *Contemporary Accounting Research* (Fall 1991), pp. 20-41.

DHALIWAL, D.S., K.R. SUBRAMANYAM, and R. TREZEVANT, "Is Comprehensive Income Superior to Net Income as a Measure of Firm Performance?" *Journal of Accounting and Economics* (January 1999), pp. 43-67.

DIAMOND, D.W. and R.E. VERRECCHIA, "Disclosure, Liquidity, and the Cost of Capital," *The Journal of Finance* (September 1991), pp. 1325-1359.

DOMTAR, *Annual Report 1996* (Montreal, QC: Domtar Inc., 1997).

DOPUCH, N. and M. PINCUS, "Evidence on the Choice of Inventory Accounting Methods: LIFO vs. FIFO," *Journal of Accounting Research* (Spring 1988), pp. 28-59.

DORAN, B.M., D.W. COLLINS, and D.S. DHALIWAL, "The Information Content of Historical Cost Earnings Relative to Supplemental Reserve-Based Accounting Data in the Extractive Petroleum Industry," *The Accounting Review* (July 1988), pp. 389-413.

DYCKMAN, T.R. and A.J. SMITH, "Financial Accounting and Reporting by Oil and Gas Producing Companies: A Study of Information Effects," *Journal of Accounting and Economics* (March 1979), pp. 45-76.

DYE, R.A., "Disclosure of Nonproprietary Information," *Journal of Accounting Research* (Spring 1985), pp. 123-145.

DYE, R.A., "Proprietary and Nonproprietary Disclosures," *Journal of Business* (April 1986), pp. 331-366.

DYE, R.A., "Earnings Management in an Overlapping Generations Model," *Journal of Accounting Research* (Autumn 1988), pp. 195-235.

DYE, R.A. and S. SUNDER, "Why Not Allow FASB and IASB Standards to Compete in the U.S.? *Accounting Horizons* (September 2001), pp. 257-271.

EASTON, P.D. and T.S. HARRIS, "Earnings as an Explanatory Variable for Returns," *Journal of Accounting Research* (Spring 1991), pp. 19-36.

EASTON, P.D., T.S. HARRIS, and J.A. OHLSON, "Aggregate Accounting Earnings Can Explain Most of Security Returns," *Journal of Accounting and Economics* (June/September 1992), pp. 119-142.

EASTON, P.D. and M.E. ZMIJEWSKI, "Cross-Sectional Variation in the Stock-Market Response to Accounting Earnings Announcements," *Journal of Accounting and Economics* (July 1989), pp. 117-141.

ECKERN, S. and R. WILSON, "On the Theory of the Firm in an Economy With Incomplete Markets," *The Bell Journal of Economics and Management Science* (Spring 1974), pp. 171-180.

ELLIOTT, J.A. and J.D. HANNA, "Repeated Accounting Write-Offs and the Information Content of Earnings," *Journal of Accounting Research* (Supplement 1996), pp. 135-169.

ELLIOTT, J.A., J.D. HANNA, and W.H. SHAW, "The Evaluation by the Financial Markets of Changes in Bank Loan Loss Reserve Levels," *The Accounting Review* (October 1991), pp. 847-861.

FAMA, E.F., "Efficient Capital Markets: A Review of Theory and Empirical Work," *Journal of Finance* (May 1970), pp. 383-417.

FAMA, E.F., "Agency Problems and the Theory of the Firm," *Journal of Political Economy* (April 1980), pp. 288-307.

FAMA, E.F., "Market Efficiency, Long-Term Returns and Behavioral Finance," *Journal of Financial Economics* (September 1998), pp. 283-306.

FELTHAM, G.A. and J.A. OHLSON, "Valuation and Clean Surplus Accounting for Operating and Financial Activities," *Contemporary Accounting Research* (Spring 1995), pp. 689-731.

FELTHAM, G.A. and J.A. OHLSON, "Uncertainty Resolution and the Theory of Depreciation Measurement," *Journal of Accounting Research* (Autumn 1996), pp. 209-234.

FELTHAM, G.A. and J. XIE, "Performance Measure Congruity and Diversity in Multi-Task Principal/Agent Relations," *The Accounting Review* (July 1994), pp. 429-453.

FINANCIAL ACCOUNTING STANDARDS BOARD, *Statement of Financial Accounting Concepts No. 1, Objectives of Financial Reporting by Business Enterprises* (Norwalk, CT: FASB, 1978).

FINANCIAL ACCOUNTING STANDARDS BOARD, *Statement of Financial Accounting Concepts No. 2, Qualitative Characteristics of Accounting Information* (Norwalk, CT: FASB, 1980).

FINANCIAL ACCOUNTING STANDARDS BOARD, *Statement of Financial Accounting Standards No. 2, Accounting for Research and Development Costs* (Norwalk, CT: FASB, 1974).

FINANCIAL ACCOUNTING STANDARDS BOARD, *Statement of Financial Accounting Standards No. 19, Financial Accounting and Reporting by Oil and Gas Producing Companies* (Norwalk, CT: FASB, 1977).

FINANCIAL ACCOUNTING STANDARDS BOARD, *Statement of Financial Accounting Standards No. 25, Suspension of Certain Accounting Requirements for Oil and Gas Producing Companies* (Norwalk, CT: FASB, 1979).

FINANCIAL ACCOUNTING STANDARDS BOARD, *Statement of Financial Accounting Standards No. 33, Financial Reporting and Changing Prices* (Norwalk, CT: FASB, 1979).

FINANCIAL ACCOUNTING STANDARDS BOARD, *Statement of Financial Accounting Standards No. 52, Foreign Currency Translation* (Norwalk, CT: FASB, 1981).

FINANCIAL ACCOUNTING STANDARDS BOARD, *Statement of Financial Accounting Standards No. 69, Disclosures about Oil and Gas Producing Activities* (Norwalk, CT: FASB, 1982).

FINANCIAL ACCOUNTING STANDARDS BOARD, *Statement of Financial Accounting Standards No. 87,*

Employers' Accounting for Pensions (Norwalk, CT: FASB, 1985).

FINANCIAL ACCOUNTING STANDARDS BOARD, *Statement of Financial Accounting Standards No. 106, Employers' Accounting for Postretirement Benefits Other Than Pensions* (Norwalk, CT: FASB, 1990).

FINANCIAL ACCOUNTING STANDARDS BOARD, *Statement of Financial Accounting Standards No. 107, Disclosures about Fair Value of Financial Instruments* (Norwalk, CT: FASB, 1991).

FINANCIAL ACCOUNTING STANDARDS BOARD, *Statement of Financial Accounting Standards No. 115, Accounting for Certain Investments in Debt and Equity Securities* (Norwalk, CT: FASB, 1993).

FINANCIAL ACCOUNTING STANDARDS BOARD, *Statement of Financial Accounting Standards No.123, Accounting for Stock-based Compensation* (Norwalk, CT: FASB, 1995).

FINANCIAL ACCOUNTING STANDARDS BOARD, *Statement of Financial Accounting Standards No. 130, Reporting Comprehensive Income* (Norwalk, CT: FASB, 1997).

FINANCIAL ACCOUNTING STANDARDS BOARD, *Statement of Financial Accounting Standards No. 133, Accounting for Derivative Instruments and Hedging Activities* (Norwalk, CT: FASB, 1998).

FINANCIAL ACCOUNTING STANDARDS BOARD, *Statement of Financial Accounting Standards No. 141, Business Combinations* (Norwalk, CT: FASB, 2001).

FINANCIAL ACOUNTING STANDARDS BOARD, *Statement of Financial Accounting Standards No. 142, Goodwill and Other Intangible Assets* (Norwalk, CT: FASB, 2001).

FINANCIAL INSTRUMENTS JOINT WORKING GROUP OF STANDARD SETTERS, *Financial Instruments and Similar Items, Draft Standard and Basis for Conclusion* (2001, JWG, Available on <www.cica.ca>).

FOSTER, G., C. OLSEN, and T. SHEVLIN, "Earnings Releases, Anomalies, and the Behavior of Security Returns," *The Accounting Review* (January 1977), pp. 574-603.

FRANKEL, R. and C.M.C. LEE, "Accounting Valuation, Market Expectation, and Cross-Sectional Stock Returns," *Journal of Accounting and Economics* (June 1998), pp. 283-319.

FRIEDLAN, J.M., "Accounting Choices of Issuers of Initial Public Offerings," *Contemporary Accounting Research* (Summer 1994), pp. 1-31.

GAVER, J.J. and K.M. GAVER, "The Relation Between Nonrecurring Accounting Transactions and CEO Cash Compensation," *The Accounting Review* (April 1998), pp. 235-253.

GHICAS, D. and V. PASTENA, "The Acquisition Value of Oil and Gas Firms: The Role of Historical Costs, Reserve Recognition Accounting, and Analysts' Appraisals," *Contemporary Accounting Research* (Fall 1989), pp. 125-142.

GJESDAL, F., "Accounting for Stewardship," *Journal of Accounting Research* (Spring 1981), pp. 208-231.

GONEDES, N. and N. DOPUCH, "Capital Market Equilibrium, Information Production, and Selected Accounting Techniques: Theoretical Framework and Review of Empirical Work," *Journal of Accounting Research* (Supplement, 1974), pp. 48-129.

GREIG, A.C., "Fundamental Analysis and Subsequent Stock Returns," *Journal of Accounting and Economics* (June/September 1992), pp. 373-411.

GROSSMAN, S., "On the Efficiency of Competitive Stock Markets Where Traders Have Diverse Information," *The Journal of Finance* (May 1976), pp. 573-585.

GROSSMAN, S., "The Informational Role of Warranties and Private Disclosure about Product Quality," *Journal of Law and Economics* (December 1981), pp. 461-484.

GUAY, W.R., "The Impact of Derivatives on Firm Risk: An Empirical Examination of New Derivatives Users," *Journal of Accounting and Economics* (January 1999), pp. 319-351.

HAMADA, R., "The Effect of the Firm's Capital Structure on the Systematic Risk of Common Stocks," *Journal of Finance* (May 1972), pp. 435-452.

HANNA, J.D., "Never Say Never," *CA Magazine* (August 1999), pp. 35-39.

HANNA, J.R., D.B. KENNEDY, and G.D. RICHARDSON, *Reporting the Effects of Changing Prices: A Review of the Experience with Section 4510* (Toronto, ON: CICA, 1990).

HARRIS, T.S. and J.A. OHLSON, "Accounting Disclosures and the Market's Evaluation of Oil and Gas Properties," *The Accounting Review* (October 1987), pp. 651-670.

HARRIS, T.S. and J.A. OHLSON, "Accounting Disclosures and the Market's Valuation of Oil and Gas Properties: Evaluation of Market Efficiency and Functional Fixation," *The Accounting Review* (October 1990), pp. 764-780.

HATFIELD, H.R., *Accounting* (New York, NY: Appleton-Century-Crofts, Inc., 1927).

HEALY, P.M., "The Effect of Bonus Schemes on Accounting Decisions," *Journal of Accounting and Economics* (April 1985), pp. 85-107.

HEALY, P.M., A.P. HUTTON, and K.G. PALEPU, "Stock Performance and Intermediation Changes Surrounding Sustained Increases in Disclosure," *Contemporary Accounting Research* (Fall 1999), pp. 485-520.

HEALY, P.M. and K.G. PALEPU, "The Effect of Firms' Financial Disclosure Strategies on Stock Prices," *Accounting Horizons* (March 1993), pp. 1-11.

HIRSHLEIFER, J., "The Private and Social Value of Information and the Reward to Inventive Activity," *American Economic Review* (September 1971), pp. 561-573.

HIRSHLEIFER, D., "Investor Psychology and Asset Pricing," *Journal of Finance* (August 2001), pp. 1533-1597.

HOLMSTRÖM, B., "Moral Hazard and Observability," *The Bell Journal of Economics* (Spring 1979), pp. 74-91.

HOLMSTRÖM, B., "Moral Hazard in Teams," *The Bell Journal of Economics* (Autumn 1982), pp. 324-340.

HOLTHAUSEN, R.W. and D.F. LARCKER, "The Prediction of Stock Returns using Financial Statement Information," *Journal of Accounting and*

Economics (June/September 1992), pp. 373-411.

HOLTHAUSEN, R.W., D.F. LARCKER, and R.G. SLOAN, "Annual Bonus Schemes and the Manipulation of Earnings," *Journal of Accounting and Economics* (February 1995), pp. 29-74.

HUDDART, S., "Employee Stock Options," *Journal of Accounting and Economics* (September 1994), pp. 207-231.

HUDDART, S. and M. LANG, "Employee Stock Option Exercises: An Empirical Analysis," *Journal of Accounting and Economics* (February 1996), pp. 5-43.

HUGHES, P.J., "Signalling by Direct Disclosure Under Asymmetric Information," *Journal of Accounting and Economics* (June 1986), pp. 119-142.

HUNT, H.G., "Potential Determinants of Corporate Inventory Accounting Decisions," *Journal of Accounting Research* (Autumn 1985), pp. 448-467.

IJIRI, Y., *Theory of Accounting Measurement*, Studies in Accounting Research, No. 10 (Sarasota, FL: American Accounting Association, 1975).

INTERNATIONAL ACCOUNTING STANDARDS BOARD, *International Accounting Standard IAS 22, Business Combinations (Revised 1998)* (London: IASB, 1998).

INTERNATIONAL ACCOUNTING STANDARDS BOARD, *International Accounting Standard IAS 39, Financial Instruments: Recognition and Measurement* (London: IASB, 1999).

ITTNER, C.D., D.F. LARCKER, and M.V. RAJAN, "The Choice of Performance Measures in Annual Bonus Contracts,"

The Accounting Review (April 1997), pp. 231-255.

JENSEN, M.C., "The Modern Industrial Revolution, Exit, and the Failure of Internal Control Systems," *The Journal of Finance* (July 1993), pp. 831-880.

JENSEN, M.C. and W.H. MECKLING, "Theory of the Firm: Managerial Behavior, Agency Costs and Ownership Structure," *Journal of Financial Economics* (October 1976), pp. 305-360.

JENSEN, M.C. and K.J. MURPHY, "CEO Incentives—It's Not How Much You Pay, But How," *Harvard Business Review* (May/June 1990), pp. 138-149.

JONES, J., "Earnings Management During Import Relief Investigations," *Journal of Accounting Research* (Autumn 1991), pp. 193-228.

KAHNEMAN, D. and A. TVERSKY, "Prospect Theory: An Analysis of Decision Under Risk," *Econometrica* (March 1979), pp. 263-291.

KAPLAN, R.S., "Comments on Paul Healy," *Journal of Accounting and Economics* (April 1985), pp. 109-113.

KIM, O. and Y. SUH, "Incentive Efficiency of Compensation Based on Accounting and Market Performance," *Journal of Accounting and Economics* (January/April/July 1993), pp. 25-53.

KIM, O. and R.E. VERRECCHIA, "Pre-announcement and Event-period Private Information," *Journal of Accounting and Economics* (1977), pp. 395-419.

KORMENDI, R.C. and R. LIPE, "Earnings Innovations, Earnings Persistence, and Stock Returns," *Journal of Business* (July 1987), pp. 323-346.

KOTHARI, S.P., "Capital Markets Research in Accounting," *Journal of Accounting and Economics* (September 2001), pp. 105-231.

KOTHARI, S.P., J. SHANKEN, and R. SLOAN, "Another Look at the Cross-Section of Expected Returns," *Journal of Finance* (March 1995), pp. 185-224.

KROSS, W., "Stock Returns and Oil and Gas Pronouncements: Replications and Extensions," *Journal of Accounting Research* (Autumn 1982), pp. 459-471.

KURZ, M., ed., *Endogenous Economic Fluctuations* (New York, NY: Springer-Verlag, 1997).

KURZ, M., "Endogenous Uncertainty: A Unified View of Market Volatility," working paper, Stanford University, September 1997.

LAFFONT, J.J., *The Economics of Uncertainty and Information* (Cambridge, MA: MIT Press, 1989).

LAMBERT, R.A. and D.F. LARCKER, "An Analysis of the Use of Accounting and Market Measures of Performance in Executive Compensation Contracts," *Journal of Accounting Research* (Supplement 1987), pp. 85-125.

LAMBERT, R.A. and D.F. LARCKER, "Firm Performance and the Compensation of Chief Executive Officers," working paper (January 1993).

LAMBERT, R.A., D.F. LARCKER, and R.E. VERRECCHIA, "Portfolio Considerations in Valuing Executive Compensation," *Journal of Accounting Research* (Spring 1991), pp. 129-149.

LANG, M.H. and R.J. LUNDHOLM, "Corporate Disclosure Policy and Analyst Behavior," *The Accounting Review* (October 1996), pp. 467-492.

LEE, C.M.C., "Measuring Wealth," *C.A. Magazine* (April 1996), pp. 32-37.

LEE, C.M.C., "Market Efficiency and Accounting Research: A Discussion of 'Capital Market Research in Accounting' by S.P. Kothari," *Journal of Accounting and Economics September 2001*), pp. 233-253.

LEE, C.M.C., B. MUCKLOW, and M.J. READY, "Spreads, Depths, and the Impact of Earnings Information: An Intraday Analysis," *The Review of Financial Studies* (1993), pp. 345-374.

LEE, C-W.J. and D.A. HSIEH, "Choice of Inventory Accounting Methods: Comparative Analysis of Alternative Hypotheses," *Journal of Accounting Research* (Autumn 1985), pp. 468-485.

LELAND, H.E. and D.H. PYLE, "Information Asymmetries, Financial Structure, and Financial Intermediation," *The Journal of Finance* (May 1977), pp. 371-387.

LEV, B., "On the Association Between Operating Leverage and Risk," *Journal of Financial and Quantitative Analysis* (September 1974), pp. 627-640.

LEV, B., "The Impact of Accounting Regulation on the Stock Market: The Case of Oil and Gas Companies," *The Accounting Review* (July 1979), pp. 485-503.

LEV, B., "Toward a Theory of Equitable and Efficient Accounting Policy," *The Accounting Review* (January 1988), pp. 1-22.

LEV, B., "On the Usefulness of Earnings: Lessons and Directions from Two Decades of Empirical Research," *Journal of Accounting Research* (Supplement, 1989), pp. 153-192.

LEV, B. and S.R. THIAGARAJAN, "Fundamental Information Analysis,"

Journal of Accounting Research (Autumn 1993), pp. 190-215.

LEV, B., and P. ZAROWIN, "The Boundaries of Financial Reporting and How to Extend Them," *Journal of Accounting Research* (Autumn 1999), pp. 353-385.

LINDAHL, F.W., "Dynamic Analysis of Inventory Accounting Choice," *Journal of Accounting Research* (Autumn 1989), pp. 201-226.

LINTNER, J., "The Valuation of Risky Assets and the Selection of Risky Investments in Stock Portfolios and Capital Budgets," *Review of Economics and Statistics* (February 1965), pp. 13-37.

LIU, C.C., S.G. RYAN, and J.M. WAHLEN, "Differential Valuation Implications of Loan Loss Provisions Across Banks and Fiscal Quarters," *The Accounting Review* (January 1997), pp. 133-146.

LYS, T., "Mandated Accounting Changes and Debt Covenants: The Case of Oil and Gas Companies," *Journal of Accounting and Economics* (April 1984), pp. 39-65.

MAGLIOLO, J., "Capital Market Analysis of Reserve Recognition Accounting," *Journal of Accounting Research* (Supplement, 1986), pp. 69-108.

MARK'S WORK WEARHOUSE LTD., *Annual Report, January 31, 2001* (Calgary, AB: Mark's Work Wearhouse Ltd., 2001).

McNICHOLS, M. and G.P. WILSON, "Evidence of Earnings Management from the Provision for Bad Debts," *Journal of Accounting Research* (Supplement, 1988), pp. 1-31.

MERINO, D.B. and M.D. NEIMARK, "Disclosure Regulation and Public Policy: A Sociohistorical Reappraisal," *Journal of*

Accounting and Public Policy (Fall 1982), pp. 33-57.

MERTON, R.C., "Theory of Rational Option Pricing," *Bell Journal of Economics and Management Science* (Spring 1973), pp. 141-183.

MERTON, R.C., "A Simple Model of Capital Market Equilibrium with Incomplete Markets," *The Journal of Finance* (July 1987), pp. 483-510.

MIAN, S.L. and C.W. SMITH, JR., "Incentives for Unconsolidated Financial Reporting," *Journal of Accounting and Economics* (January 1990), pp. 141-171.

MILGROM, P., "Good News and Bad News: Representation Theorems and Applications," *Bell Journal of Economics* (Autumn 1981), pp. 380-391.

MILLIGAN, J.W., "How the Government Railroaded Franklin Savings," *Institutional Investor* (January 1991), pp. 50-60.

MURPHY, K.J. and J.L. ZIMMERMAN, "Financial Performance Surrounding CEO Turnover," *Journal of Accounting and Economics* (January/April/July 1993), pp. 273-316.

MYERS, J.N., "Implementing Residual Income Valuation With Linear Information Dynamics," *The Accounting Review* (January 1999), pp. 1-28.

NEWMAN, P. and R. SANSING, "Disclosure Policies with Multiple Users," *Journal of Accounting Research* (Spring 1993), pp. 92-112.

O'BRIEN, P.C., "Analysts' Forecasts as Earnings Expectations," *Journal of Accounting and Economics* (January 1988), pp. 53-83.

ODEAN, T., "Volume, Volatility, Price and Profit When All Traders are Above Average," *Journal of Finance* (December 1998), pp. 1887-1934.

OHLSON, J.A., "On the Nature of Income Measurement: The Basic Results," *Contemporary Accounting Research* (Fall 1987), pp. 1-15.

ONTARIO SECURITIES COMMISSION, "Annual Information Form and Management's Discussion and Analysis of Financial Condition and Results of Operations – Policies," OSC Policy Statement No. 5.10, OSC *Bulletin* (November 10, 1989), pp. 4275-4299.

ONTARIO SECURITIES COMMISSION, "Statement of Executive Compensation," Form 40, Securities Act, Regulation 638/93, *The Ontario Gazette*, Vol. 126-39 (September 25, 1993), pp. 1203-1216.

ONTARIO SECURITIES COMMISSION, "OSC National Policy Statement No. 27," *OSC Bulletin* (December 18, 1992), pp. 6055-6144.

OU, J.A. and S.H. PENMAN, "Financial Statement Analysis and the Prediction of Stock Returns," *Journal of Accounting and Economics* (November 1989), pp. 295-329.

PATON, W.A. and A.C. LITTLETON, *An Introduction to Corporate Accounting Standards* (Ubana, IL: American Accounting Association, 1940).

PAVLIK, E.L., T.W. SCOTT, and P. TIESSEN, "Executive Compensation: Issues and Research," *Journal of Accounting Literature* (1993), pp. 131-189.

PELTZMAN, SAM, "Toward a More General Theory of Regulation," *The Journal of Law and Economics* (August 1976), pp. 21-240.

PENNO, M.C., "Information Quality and Voluntary Disclosure," *The Accounting Review* (April 1997), pp. 275-284.

POSNER, R.A., "Theories of Economic Regulation," *Bell Journal of Economics and Management Science* (Autumn 1974), pp. 335-358.

POURCIAU, S., "Earnings Management and Nonroutine Executive Changes," *Journal of Accounting and Economics* (January/April/July 1993), pp. 317-336.

PRATT, J.W., "Risk Aversion In the Small and In the Large," *Econometrica* (January-April 1964), pp. 122-136.

RAIFFA, H., *Decision Analysis: Introductory Lectures on Choices Under Uncertainty* (Reading, MA: Addison-Wesley, 1968).

RAMAKRISHNAN, R.T.S. and J.K. THOMAS, "Valuation of Permanent, Transitory and Price-Irrelevant Components of Reported Earnings," working paper, Columbia University Business School, July, 1991.

RYAN, S.G., "A Survey of Research Relating Accounting Numbers to Systematic Equity Risk, with Implications for Risk Disclosure Policy and Future Research," *Accounting Horizons* (June 1997), pp. 82-95.

SALY, P.J., "Repricing Executive Stock Options in a Down Market," *Journal of Accounting and Economics* (November 1994), pp. 325-356.

SAVAGE, L.J., *The Foundations of Statistics* (NY: Wiley, 1954).

SCHIPPER, K., "Commentary on Earnings Management," *Accounting Horizons* (December 1989), pp. 91-102.

SCHRAND, C.M., "The Association Between Stock-Price Interest Rate Sensitivity and Disclosures about Derivative Instruments," *The Accounting Review* (January 1997), pp. 87-109.

SCHRAND, C.M. AND B.R. WALTHER, "Strategic Benchmarks in Earnings Announcements: The Selective Disclosure of Prior-Period Earnings Components," *The Accounting Review* (April 2000), pp. 151-177.

SECURITIES ACT, *Revised Statutes of Ontario, 1990*, Vol. 11, Chapter 5.5 (Toronto, ON: Queen's Printer for Ontario, 1991).

SECURITIES AND EXCHANGE COMMISSION, *Accounting Series Release No. 150* (Washington, DC: SEC, 1973).

SECURITIES AND EXCHANGE COMMISSION, *Accounting Series Release No. 253* (Washington, DC: SEC, 1978).

SECURITIES AND EXCHANGE COMMISSION, *Disclosure of Accounting Policies for Derivative Financial Instruments and Derivative Commodity Instruments and Disclosure of Quantitative and Qualitative Information about Market Risk Inherent in Derivative Financial Instruments, Other Financial Instruments, and Derivative Commodity Instruments* (Washington, DC: SEC, 1997).

SENGUPTA, P., "Corporate Disclosure Quality and the Cost of Debt," *The Accounting Review* (October 1998), pp. 459-474.

SHARPE, W.F., "Capital Asset Prices: A Theory of Market Equilibrium Under Conditions of Risk," *The Journal of Finance* (September 1964), pp. 425-442.

SHEFRIN, H. and M. STATMAN, "The Disposition to Sell winners Too Early and Ride Losers Too Long," *Journal of Finance* (July 1985), pp. 777-790.

SHILLER, R.J., "Do Stock Prices Move Too Much to be Justified by Subsequent Changes in Dividends?" *The American Economic Review* (June 1981), pp. 421-436.

SHILLER, R.J., *Irrational Exuberance* (New York, NY: Broadway Books, 2000).

SKINNER, D.J., "How Well Does Net Income Measure Firm Performance? A Discussion of Two Studies," *Journal of Accounting and Economics* (January 1999), pp. 105-111.

SLOAN, R.G., "Accounting Earnings and Top Executive Compensation," *Journal of Accounting and Economics* (January/April/July 1993), pp. 55-100.

SLOAN, R.G., "Do Stock Prices Fully Reflect Information in Accruals and Cash Flows About Future Earnings?" *The Accounting Review* (July 1996), pp. 289-315.

SMITH, A., "Earnings and Management Incentives: Comments," *Journal of Accounting and Economics* (January/April/July 1993), pp. 337-347.

SPENCE, M., "Job Market Signalling," *Quarterly Journal of Economics* (August 1973), pp. 355-374.

STIGLER, G.J., "The Theory of Economic Regulation," *The Bell Journal of Economics and Management Science* (Spring 1971), pp. 3-21.

STOBER, T.L., "Summary Financial Statement Measures and Analysts' Forecasts of Earnings," *Journal of Accounting and Economics* (June/September 1992), pp. 347-372.

STOREY, R.K. and S. STOREY, *The Framework of Financial Accounting Concepts and Standards* (Norwalk, CT: Financial Accounting Standards Board, 1998).

STUDY GROUP ON THE OBJECTIVES OF FINANCIAL STATEMENTS, *Objectives of Financial Statements* (New York, NY: American Institute of Certified Public Accountants, 1973). (Also called the Trueblood committee report).

SUBRAMANYAM, K.R., "The Pricing of Discretionary Accruals," *Journal of Accounting and Economics* (August-December 1996), pp. 249-281.

SUNDER, S., "Relationship Between Accounting Changes and Stock Prices: Problems of Measurement and Some Empirical Evidence," *Journal of Accounting Research* (Supplement, 1973), pp. 1-45.

SWEENEY, A.P., "Debt-covenant Violations and Managers' Accounting Responses," *Journal of Accounting and Economics* (May 1994), pp. 281-308.

TITMAN, S. and B. TRUEMAN, "Information Quality and the Valuation of New Issues," *Journal of Accounting and Economics* (June 1986), pp. 159-172.

VERRECCHIA, R.E., "Discretionary Disclosure," *Journal of Accounting and Economics* (December 1983), pp. 179-194.

WARFIELD, T.D. and J.J. WILD, "Accounting Recognition and the Relevance of Earnings as an Explanatory Variable for Returns," *The Accounting Review* (October 1992), pp. 821-842.

WATTS, R.L. and J.L. ZIMMERMAN, *Positive Accounting Theory* (Englewood Cliffs, NJ: Prentice-Hall, 1986).

WATTS, R.L. and J.L. ZIMMERMAN, "Positive Accounting Theory: A Ten Year Perspective," *The Accounting Review* (January 1990), pp. 131-156.

WEIL, R.L., "Role of the Time Value of Money in Financial Reporting," *Accounting Horizons* (December 1990), pp. 47-67.

WELKER, M., "Disclosure Policy, Information Asymmetry, and Liquidity in Equity Markets," *Contemporary Accounting Research* (Spring 1995), pp. 801-827.

WOLFSON, M.A., "Empirical Evidence of Incentive Problems and their Mitigation in Oil and Gas Tax Shelter Programs," in J.W. Pratt and R.J. Zeckhauser, eds., *Principals and Agents: The Structure of Business* (Boston, MA: The President and Fellows of Harvard College, 1985), pp. 101-125.

WONG, M.H.F., "The Association between SFAS 119 Derivative Disclosures and the Foreign Exchange Risk Exposure of Manufacturing Firms," working paper, Haas School of Business, University of California at Berkeley, July 1998.

XIE, H., "The Mispricing of Abnormal Accruals," *The Accounting Review* (July 2001), pp. 357-373.

YERMACK, D., "Good Timing: CEO Stock Option Awards and Company News Announcements," *Journal of Finance* (1997), pp. 449-476.

ZEFF, S.A., "The Rise of Economic Consequences," *The Journal of Accountancy* (December 1978), pp. 56-63.

Index